the

Portable
Atheist

ESSENTIAL READINGS
FOR THE NONBELIEVER

selected and with introductions by

CHRISTOPHER HITCHENS

DA CAPO PRESS
A Member of the Perseus Books Group

List of credits/permissions can be found on page 481.

Every effort has been made to contact or trace all copyright holders. The publisher will be glad to make good any errors or omissions brought to our attention in future editions.

Introductions copyright © 2007 by Christopher Hitchens

Published by Da Capo Press,
A Member of the Perseus Books Group,
www.dacapopress.com

Da Capo Press books are available at special discounts for bulk purchases in the United States by corporations, institutions, and other organizations. For more information, please contact the Special Markets Department at the Perseus Books Group, 2300 Chestnut St., Suite 200, Philadelphia, PA 19103, or call (800) 810-4145, extension 5000, or email special.markets@perseusbooks.com.

Cataloging-in-Publication data for this book is available from the Library of Congress
ISBN-13: 978-0-306-81608-6

First Da Capo Press edition 2007

20 19 18

the
Portable
Atheist

ALSO BY CHRISTOPHER HITCHENS

Books

Hostage to History: Cyprus from the Ottomans to Kissinger
Blood, Class and Nostalgia: Anglo-American Ironies
Imperial Spoils: The Curious Case of the Elgin Marbles
Why Orwell Matters
No One Left to Lie To: The Triangulations of William Jefferson Clinton
Letters to a Young Contrarian
The Trial of Henry Kissinger
Thomas Jefferson: Author of America
Thomas Paine's "Rights of Man": A Biography
God Is Not Great: How Religion Poisons Everything

Pamphlets

Karl Marx and the Paris Commune
The Monarchy: A Critique of Britain's, Favorite Fetish
The Missionary Position: Mother Teresa in Theory and Practice
A Long Short War: The Postponed Liberation of Iraq

Collected Essays

Prepared for the Worst: Essays and Minority Reports
For the Sake of Argument
Unacknowledged Legislation: Writers in the Public Sphere
Love, Poverty and War: Journeys and Essays

Collaborations

James Callaghan: The Road to Number Ten (with Peter Kellner)
Blaming the Victims (edited with Edward Said)
When the Borders Bleed: The Struggle of the Kurds (photographs by Ed Kashi)
International Territory: The United Nations (photographs by Adam Bartos)
Vanity Fair's Hollywood (with Graydon Carter and David Friend)

Dedicated to the memory of Primo Levi (1919–1987) who had the moral fortitude to refuse false consolation even while enduring the "selection" process in Auschwitz:

"Silence slowly prevails and then, from my bunk on the top row, I see and hear old Kuhn praying aloud, with his beret on his head, swaying backwards and forwards violently. Kuhn is thanking God because he has not been chosen.

Kuhn is out of his senses. Does he not see Beppo the Greek in the bunk next to him, Beppo who is twenty years old and is going to the gas-chamber the day after tomorrow and knows it and lies there looking fixedly at the light without saying anything and without even thinking anymore? Can Kuhn fail to realize that next time it will be his turn? Does Kuhn not understand that what has happened today is an abomination, which no propitiatory prayer, no pardon, no expiation by the guilty, which nothing at all in the power of man can ever clean again?

If I was God, I would spit at Kuhn's prayer."

—From Primo Levi: *If This Is A Man* (1959)

"I too entered the Lager as a nonbeliever, and as a nonbeliever I was liberated and have lived to this day. Actually, the experience of the Lager with its frightful iniquity confirmed me in my nonbelief. It has prevented me, and still prevents me, from conceiving of any form of providence or transcendent justice . . . I must nevertheless admit that I experienced (and again only once) the temptation to yield, to seek refuge in prayer. This happened in October 1944, in the one moment in which I lucidly perceived the imminence of death . . . naked and compressed among my naked companions with my personal index card in hand, I was waiting to file past the 'commission' that with one glance would decide whether I should go immediately into the gas chamber or was instead strong enough to go on working. For one instance I felt the need to ask for help and asylum; then, despite my anguish, equanimity prevailed: one does not change the rules of the game at the end of the match, nor when you are losing. A prayer under these conditions would have been not only absurd (what rights could I claim? and from whom?) but blasphemous, obscene, laden with the greatest impiety of which a nonbeliever is capable. I rejected the temptation: I knew that otherwise were I to survive, I would have to be ashamed of it."

—From Primo Levi: *The Drowned and the Saved* (1986)

Contents

Acknowledgments

My warmest thanks are due to my agent, Steve Wasserman, and my publisher and editor, Ben Schafer, for the collaboration which initiated this volume. It's safe to say that without the devoted skill of Lori Hobkirk as copy editor and project editor and Cliff Corcoran as copyright and permissions editor, the scope and range of the collection would have been considerably less than it is.

When accused—probably correctly—of scientific plagiarism, Sir Isaac Newton was careful to say (again plagiarizing from an ancient acknowledgement) that he had "stood on the shoulders of giants." I am, in this effort as in all my other ones, immensely indebted to a small but growing group of devoted rationalists, who reject the absurd and wicked claims of the religious and who look for answers in the marvels and complexities of science, as well as in the higher and deeper reaches of literature. I am more proud than I can say that Salman Rushdie, Ian McEwan, and Ayaan Hirsi Ali contributed some hitherto unpublished work to this anthology. In the realm of the natural and physical sciences, the labors of Richard Dawkins, Daniel Dennett, Michael Shermer, Steven Weinberg, Anthony Grayling, and Sam Harris have been at once courageous, witty, and original, and it is my dearest hope that anybody picking up this book of excerpts will be impelled to read all these distinguished authors at their full length and full strength.

—*Christopher Hitchens*

Introduction

Christopher Hitchens

At the close of his imperishable novel *La Peste* ("The Plague"), Albert Camus gives us a picture of the thoughts of the good Dr. Rieux, as the town of Oran celebrates its recovery from—its survival of—a terrible visitation of disease. Rieux determines to remain lucid and to "complete this chronicle," in order that:

> He should not be one of those who held their peace but should bear witness in favor of those plague-stricken people; so that some memorial of the injustice and outrage done them might endure; and to state quite simply what we learn in a time of pestilence: that there are more things to admire in men than to despise.

afflicted by nightmares

This is part of the work, both of conscience and of memory. The pre-history of our species is hag-ridden with episodes of nightmarish ignorance and calamity, for which religion used to identify, not just the wrong explanation but the wrong culprit. Human sacrifices were made preeminently in times of epidemics, useless prayers were uttered, bogus "miracles" attested to, and scapegoats—such as Jews or heretics or witches—hunted down and burned. The few men of science and reason and medicine had all they could do to keep their libraries and laboratories intact, or their very lives safe from harm. Of course, when the evil had "passed over," there were equally idiotic ceremonies of hysterical thanksgiving, propitiating whatever local deities there might be . . .

win or regain the favor of a god/person by doing something that pleases them

And indeed, as he listened to the cries of joy rising from the town, Rieux remembered that such joy is always imperiled. He knew what those jubilant crowds did not know but could have learned from books: that the plague bacillus never dies or disappears for good; that it can lie dormant for years and years in furniture and linen-chests; that it bides its time in bedrooms, cellars, trunks and bookshelves; and that perhaps the day would come when, for the bane and the enlightening of men, it would rouse up its rats again and send them forth to die in a happy city.

something — typically a poison — that causes death; a cause of great distress

One is continually told, as an unbeliever, that it is old-fashioned to rail against the primitive stupidities and cruelties of religion because after all, in these enlightened times, the old superstitions have died away. Nine times out of ten, in debate with a cleric, one will be told not of some dogma of religious certitude but of some instance of charitable or humanitarian work undertaken by a religious person. Of course, this says nothing about the belief system involved: it may be true that Louis Farrakhan's Nation of Islam succeeds in weaning young black men off narcotics, but this would not alter the fact that the NoI is a racist crackpot organization. And has not Hamas—which publishes *The Protocols of the Learned Elders of Zion* on its Web site—won a reputation for its provision of social services? My own response has been to issue a challenge: name me an ethical statement made or an action performed by a believer that could not have been made or performed by a non-believer. As yet, I have had no takers. (Whereas, oddly enough, if you ask an audience to name a wicked statement or action directly attributable to religious faith, nobody has any difficulty in finding an example.)

No, the fact is that the bacilli are always lurking in the old texts and are latent in the theory and practice of religion. This anthology hopes to identify and isolate the bacilli more precisely, and also to vindicate Dr. Rieux by giving prominence to those who, then and now, have always counterposed enlightenment to the bane:

> The record of what had had to be done, and what assuredly would have
> to be done again in the never-ending fight against terror and its relentless
> onslaughts, despite their personal afflictions, by all who, while unable to
> be saints but refusing to bow down to pestilences, strive their utmost to
> be healers.

I am writing these words on July 4, 2007, the anniversary of the proclamation of the world's first secular republic. The men who wrote the Declaration were men of an Enlightenment temper, who quite understood that religion could be (in the words of William Blake) a "mind-forg'd manacle." As I scan the newspapers, I cannot help but notice that in one happy city—London—the rats have come vomiting from the sewers again. Car bombs have been planted outside nightclubs, in the hope of maiming and dismembering young women who have the nerve to be immodest in public. Blood-curdling yells, thirsty for the murder of Jews, Indians, and other riff-raff, issue from mosques and from tapes and films sold in their precincts. In one of the most secular and multicultural capitals in human history, the lives of everyone are being poisoned by hatred and violence. It then became clear that most of the principals in the bomb-plot were physicians, as if a special code of horror had just been disencrypted. The shock of this was considerable: men who took the Hippocratic oath were secretly committed to murder. Such naiveté. Dr. Rieux would have understood, as would Camus himself. "Medical men" have always been in attendance at torture sessions and executions, brought there by the clerics to lend extra tone and authority to the scene. The worst offenders in the Final Solution were doctors who saw a chance to conduct vile experiments. None was ever threatened by the Church with excommunication (they would have had to assist at a termination of an unwanted pregnancy in order to run such an awful risk). And today, those who award themselves permission to destroy the lives of others need only say that they have divine permission in order to read excuses for their actions from clerical authorities—excuses and euphemisms that are often published in respectable newspapers. An especially revolting example was provided by the murderous Dr. Baruch Goldstein and his apologists.

As it happened, on the same weekend as the discovery of the London and Glasgow bomb plot there came some devastating floods to the north of England, leaving thousands of people homeless. The Church of England was not slow to rush to the aid of the stricken. "This is a strong and definite judgment," announced the Bishop of Carlisle, "because the world has been arrogant in going its own way. We are reaping the consequences of our moral degradation." From a list of possible transgressions the Bishop (who has sources of information denied to the rest of us) selected recent legal moves to allow more rights to homosexuals. These, he said, placed us "in a situation where we are liable for God's judgment, which is intended to call us to repentance." Many of his senior colleagues, including one who has been spoken of as a future Archbishop of Canterbury, joined him in blaming the floods—which had only hit one geographical section of the country—on sexual preference. I have chosen this example because most people would agree that the Anglican/Episcopalian "communion" is among the most moderate and humane of modern religious institutions.

Yet who said this, and when, and while speaking of the likelihood of a nuclear holocaust? "The very worst it could do would be to sweep a vast number of people at one moment from this world into the other and more vital world, into which anyhow they must pass at one time." That was not Rafsanjani or Ahmadinejad, both of whom have gloatingly said that Islam could survive a nuclear exchange while the Jewish state could not. It was the mild, sheep-faced Archbishop of Canterbury, Geoffrey Fisher, who spoke not very many years ago. And, in a sense, and while we may laugh or jeer at the old fool, he would have been untrue to his faith if he had said otherwise. To admit that a thermonuclear catastrophe would be the end of civilization and of the biosphere would be, in religious terms, profane and defeatist. All religions must, at their core, *look forward* to the end of this world and to the longed-for moment when all will be revealed and when the sheep will be divided from the goats, or whatever other bucolic Bronze-Age desert analogy might seem apt. (In Papua New Guinea, where as in most tropical climes there are no sheep, the Christians use the most valued animal of the locals and refer to the congregation as "swine." Flock, herd: what difference does it make?)

Against this insane eschatology, with its death wish and its deep contempt for the life of the mind, atheists have always argued that this world is all that we have, and that our duty is to one another to make the very most and best of it. Theism cannot coexist with this unexceptionable conclusion. If we stay with animal analogies for a moment, owners of dogs will have noticed that, if you provide them with food and water and shelter and affection, they will think you are god. Whereas owners of cats are compelled to realize that, if you provide them with food and water and shelter and affection, they draw the conclusion that *they* are god. (Cats may sometimes share the cold entrails of a kill with you, but this is just what a god might do if he was in a good mood.) Religion, then, partakes of equal elements of the canine and the feline. It exacts maximum servility and abjection, requiring you to regard yourself as conceived and born in sin and owing a duty to a stern creator. But in return, it places you at the center of the universe and assures you that you are the personal object of a heavenly plan. Indeed, if you make the right propitiations you may even find that death has no sting, and that an exception to the rules of physical annihilation may be made in your own case. It cannot be said often enough that this preachment is immoral as well as irrational.

To be charitable, one may admit that the religious often seem unaware of how insulting their main proposition actually is. Exchange views with a believer even for a short time, and let us make the assumption that this is a mild and decent believer who does not open the bidding by telling you that your unbelief will endanger your soul and condemn you to hell. It will not be long until you are politely asked how you can possibly know right from wrong. Without holy awe, what is to prevent you from resorting to theft, murder, rape, and perjury? It will sometimes be conceded that non-believers have led ethical lives, and it will also be conceded (as it had better be) that many believers have been responsible for terrible crimes. Nonetheless, the working assumption is that we should have no moral compass if we were not somehow in thrall to an unalterable and unchallengeable celestial dictatorship. What a repulsive idea! As well as taking the axe to the root of everything that we have learned about evolutionary biology (societies that tolerate murder and theft and perjury will not last long, and those that violate the taboos on incest and cannibalism do in fact simply die out), it constitutes a radical attack on the very concept of human self-respect. It does so by suggesting that one could not do a right action or avoid a wrong one, except for the hope of a divine reward or the fear of divine retribution. Many of us, even the less unselfish, might hope to do better than that on our own. When I give blood, for example (something that several religions forbid), I do not lose a pint, but someone else gains one. There is something about this that appeals to me, and I derive other satisfactions as well from being of assistance to a fellow creature. Furthermore, I have a very rare blood type and I hope very much that when I am in need of a transfusion someone else will have thought and acted in precisely the same way that I have. Indeed, I can almost count on it. Nobody had to teach me any of this, let alone reinforce the teaching with sinister fairy-tales about appearances by the Archangel Gabriel. The so-called Golden Rule is innate in us, or is innate except in the sociopaths who do not care about others, and the psychopaths who take pleasure from cruelty. Evolution has no more weeded these out than it has succeeded in reducing the percentage of good people who are naturally homosexual. Religion invents a problem where none exists by describing the wicked as also made in the image of god and the sexually nonconformist as existing in a state of incurable mortal sin that can incidentally cause floods and earthquakes.

How did such evil nonsense ever come to be so influential? And why are we so continually locked in combat with its violent and intolerant votaries? Well, religion was the race's first (and worst) attempt to make sense of reality. It was the best the species could do at a time when we had no concept of physics, chemistry, biology or medicine. We did not know that we lived on a round planet, let alone that the said planet was in orbit in a minor and obscure solar system, which was also on the edge of an unimaginably vast cosmos that was exploding away from its original source of energy. We did not know that micro-organisms were so powerful and lived in our digestive systems in order to enable us to live, as well as mounting lethal attacks on us as parasites. We did not know of our close kinship with other animals. We believed that sprites, imps, demons, and djinns were hovering in the air about us. We imagined that thunder and lightning were portentous. It has taken us a long time to shrug off this heavy coat of ignorance and fear, and every time we do there are self-interested forces who want to compel us to put it back on again.

By all means let us agree that we are pattern-seeking mammals and that, owing to our restless intelligence and inquisitiveness, we will still prefer a conspiracy theory to no explanation at all. Religion was our first attempt at philosophy, just as alchemy was our first attempt at chemistry and astrology our first attempt to make sense of the movements of the heavens. I myself am a strong believer in the study of religion, first because culture and education involve a respect for tradition and for origins, and also because some of the early religious texts were among our first attempts at literature. But there is a reason why religions insist so much on strange events in the sky, as well as on less quantifiable phenomena such as dreams and visions. All of these things cater to our inborn stupidity, and our willingness to be persuaded against all the evidence that we are indeed the center of the universe and that everything is arranged with us in mind.

This pathetic solipsism can be noticed in all the arguments offered—with increasing desperation—against the interpretations of Darwin and Einstein. We now have better and simpler explanations of the origins of the species, and of the cosmos. ("Simpler" only because these explanations are more testable and consistent, not because they are not *very* much more complex.) But wait, pleads the believer. Let me grant you—finally!—the record of natural selection and the Hubble evidence for the big bang. Does this not show that the maker of all things was even more ingenious than we had thought? With the assistance of others who will be cited at proper length later in this book, let me try to put this poor argument out of its misery. Let us grant the assumption of the religious. Some one or some thing was indeed "present at the creation," and gave the order to let matter explode and then let the evolutionary process begin on this planet. Never mind that this assumption could never conceivably be proved. Make the assumption, anyway. After all, it cannot be decisively disproved, either, any more than any other random unsupported assumption.

The godly person still has all his work ahead of him. On what authority can he hope to show that the original flying-apart of matter was set in motion with the object of influencing life on a minute speck of a planet, billions of years later, at the very margins of the whirling nebulae and amid the extinction of innumerable other worlds? How is it to be demonstrated that the planner of this inconceivably vast enterprise had in mind the cretinous figure of the Bishop of Carlisle, wielding his shepherd's crook while connecting the sex-life of his parishioners to the weather?

Or again, and coming down in point of scale by several titanic orders of magnitude, and given that at least 98 percent of all species on this tiny speck of a planet made only a few hesitant steps "forward" before succumbing to extinction, on what warrant is it proposed that all this massive dying-out and occasional vast life-explosion (as in the Cambrian period) also had as its sole object the presence of ourselves? And isn't it odd that religion, which continually enjoins an almost masochistic modesty upon us in the face of god, should encourage such an extreme and impossible form of self-centeredness and self-regard? By trying to adjust to the findings that it once tried so viciously to ban and repress, religion has only succeeded in restating the same questions that undermined it in earlier epochs. What kind of designer or creator is so wasteful and capricious and approximate? What kind of designer or creator is so cruel and indifferent? And—most of all—what kind of designer or creator only chooses to "reveal" himself to semi-stupefied peasants in desert regions? I have met some highly intelligent believers, but history has no record of any human being who was remotely qualified to say that he knew or understood the mind of god. Yet this is precisely the qualification which the godly must claim—so modestly and so humbly—to possess. It is time to withdraw our "respect" from such fantastic claims, all of them aimed at the exertion of power over other humans in the real and material world.

There is no moral or intellectual equivalent between the different degrees of uncertainty here. The atheist generally says (though the bold Dr. Victor Stenger goes a bit further) that the existence of a deity cannot be *dis*-proved. It can only be found to be entirely lacking in evidence or proof. The theist can opt to be a mere deist, and to say that the magnificence of the natural order strongly implies an ordering force. (This was the view taken, at least in public, by opponents of religion such as Thomas Jefferson and Thomas Paine.) But the religious person *must* go further and say that this creative force is also an intervening one: one that cares for our human affairs and is interested in what we eat and with whom we have sexual relations, as well as in the outcomes of battles and wars. To assert this is quite simply to assert more than any human can possibly claim to know, and thus it falls, and should be discarded, and should have been discarded long ago.

Some things can be believed and some things simply cannot. I *might* choose to believe that Jesus of Nazareth was born of a virgin in Bethlehem, and that later he both did and did not die, since he was seen again by humans after the time of his apparent decease. Many have argued that the sheer unlikelihood of this story makes it fractionally more probable. Again, then, suppose that I grant the virgin birth and the resurrection. The religious still have all of their work ahead of them. These events, even if confirmed, would not prove that Jesus was the son of god. Nor would they prove the truth or morality of his teachings. Nor would they prove that there was an afterlife or a last judgment. His miracles, if verified, would likewise leave him one among many shamans and magicians, some of them mentioned in the Old Testament, who could apparently work wonders by sorcery. Many of the philosophers and logicians cited in this book take the view that miracles cannot and did not occur, and Albert Einstein took the view (which some stubbornly consider to be a deist one) that the miracle is that there *are* no miracles or other interruptions of a wondrous natural order. This is not a difference that can be split: either faith is sufficient or else miracles are required to reassure those—including the preachers—whose faith would otherwise not be strong enough. For me, witnessing an act of faith-healing or conjury would simply not be persuasive, even if I could credit it and even if I did not know people who could—and can and do—replicate such wonders on stage.

But here is something that is *impossible* for anyone to believe. The human species has been in existence as *Homo sapiens* for (let us not quarrel about the exact total) at least one hundred and fifty thousand years. An instant in evolutionary time, this is nonetheless a vast history when contemplated by primates with brains and imaginations of the dimensions that we can boast. In order to subscribe to monotheistic religion, one must believe that humans were born, struggled, and expired during this time, often dying in childbirth or for want of elementary nurture, and with a life-expectancy of perhaps three decades at most. Add to these factors the turf wars between discrepant groups and tribes, alarming outbreaks of disease, which had no germ theory to explain let alone palliate them, and associated natural disasters and human tragedies. And yet, for all these millennia, heaven watched with indifference and then—and only in the last six thousand years at the very least—decided that it was time to intervene as well as redeem. And heaven would only intervene and redeem in remote areas of the Middle East, thus ensuring that many more generations would expire before the news could begin to spread! Let me send a voice to Sinai and cement a pact with just one tribe of dogged and greedy yokels. Let me lend a son to be torn to pieces because he is misunderstood. . . . Let me tell the angel Gabriel to prompt an illiterate and uncultured merchant into rhetorical flights. At last the darkness that I have imposed will lift! The willingness even to entertain such elaborately mad ideas involves much more than the suspension of disbelief, or the dumb credulity that greets magic tricks.

It also involves ignoring or explaining away the many religious beliefs that antedated Moses. Our primeval ancestors were by no means atheistic: they raised temples and altars and offered the requisite terrified obsequies and sacrifices. Their religion was man-made, like all the others. There was a time when Greek thinkers denounced Christians and Zoroastrians denounced Muslims as "atheists" for their destruction of old sites and their prohibition of ancient rituals. The source of desecration and profanity is religious, as we can see from the way that today's believers violate the sanctity of each other's temples, from Bamiyan to Belfast to Baghdad. Richard Dawkins may have phrased it most pungently when he argued that everybody is an atheist in saying that there is a god—from Ra to Shiva—in which he does *not* believe. All that the serious and objective atheist does is to take the next step and to say that there is just one more god to disbelieve in. Human solipsism can generally be counted upon to become enraged and to maintain that this discountable god must not be the one in which the believer himself has invested so much credence. So it goes. But the man-made character of religion, from which monotheism swore to deliver us at least in its pagan form, persists in a terrifying shape in our own time, as believers fight each other over the correct interpretation and even kill members of their own faiths in battles over doctrine. Civilization has been immensely retarded by such arcane interfaith quarrels and could now be destroyed by their modern versions.

There is an argument within the community of those who reject all this fantasy about the utility of the word "atheist." For one thing, it is a pure negative: a statement of mere unbelief or disbelief. Dr. Jonathan Miller, for example, a distinguished physician and theater and opera director, is uneasy with the term for this reason: "I do not have," he once told me, "a special word for saying that I do not believe in the tooth fairy or in Santa Claus. I *presume* that my intelligent friends do not suppose that I believe such things." True enough—but we do not have to emerge from a past when tooth fairies and Father Christmas (both rather recent inventions) held sway. The fans of the tooth fairy do not bang on your door and try to convert you. They do not insist that their pseudo-science be taught in schools. They do not condemn believers in rival tooth fairies to death and damnation. They do not say that all morality comes from tooth fairy ceremonies, and that without the tooth fairy there would be fornication in the streets and the abolition of private property. They do not say that the tooth fairy made the world, and that all of us must therefore bow the knee to the Big Brother tooth fairy. They do not say that the tooth fairy will order you to kill your sister if she is seen in public with a man who is not her brother.

Thus it seems to me that there is what the poet Shelley once called the *necessity* of atheism. One cannot avoid taking a position. Either one attributes one's presence here to the laws of biology and physics, or one attributes it to a divine design. (You can tell a lot about friend or foe, depending on how he or she answers this inescapable question, and on how he or she faces its implications.) Yet, just like the believer, once we have made up our minds, we still have the bulk of our work lying ahead of us.

The rejection of the man-made concept of god is not a sufficient condition for intellectual or moral emancipation. Atheists have no right to go around looking superior. They have only fulfilled the *necessary* condition by throwing off the infancy of the species and disclaiming a special place in the natural scheme. They are now free, if they so choose, to become nihilists or sadists or solipsists on their own account. Some theories of the Superman derive from atheism, and a person who thought that heaven and hell were empty could conclude that he was free to do exactly as he wished. The fear that this might be the outcome—well-expressed by Fyodor Dostoyevsky—underlies many people's reluctance to abandon religious dogma. Yet many sadists and mass-murderers also claim to be hearing heavenly "voices" ordering them to commit their crimes, which would not in itself discredit religious faith. The argument about ethics and morality will have to go on in a post-religious society, just as it had to go on when religion was regnant and was often ordering good people to agree to evil things such as torture, slavery, or cruelty to children. The fact seems to be that there is a natural human revulsion from such things, whatever the super-ambient political or religious context may be.

There is also (and here I make a slightly different stress than does Dawkins) no special reason to credit "science" as the father or godfather of reason. As in the case of the doctors mentioned earlier, a commitment to experiment and find evidence is no guarantee of immunity to superstition and worse. Sir Isaac Newton was prey to the most idiotic opinions about alchemy. Joseph Priestley, the courageous Unitarian and skeptic who discovered oxygen, was a believer in the phlogiston theory. Alfred Russel Wallace, one of Darwin's greatest collaborators and progenitors, was a dedicated attender of spiritualist sessions where "ectoplasm" was produced by frauds to the applause of morons. Even today, there are important men of science—admittedly a minority—who maintain that their findings are compatible with belief in a creator. They may not be able to derive the one from the other, or even to claim to do so, but they testify to the extreme stubbornness with which intelligent people will cling to unsupported opinions.

xxii   *Introduction*

However, the original form of tyranny of man over man, and of man over the mind of man (sometimes called totalitarianism) was certainly theocratic, and no overcoming of the absolutist or of the arbitrary is complete unless it includes a clear-eyed rejection of any dictator whose rule is founded on the supernatural. I myself have tried to formulate a position I call "anti-theist." There are, after all, atheists who say that they wish the fable were true but are unable to suspend the requisite disbelief, or have relinquished belief only with regret. To this I reply: who wishes that there was a permanent, unalterable celestial despotism that subjected us to continual surveillance and could convict us of thought-crime, and who regarded us as its private property even after we died? How happy we ought to be, at the reflection that there exists not a shred of respectable evidence to support such a horrible hypothesis. And how grateful we should be to those of our predecessors who repudiated this utter negation of human freedom. There were many people long before Darwin or Einstein or even Galileo who saw through the claims of the rabbis and priests and imams. In earlier times, such repudiation often involved extraordinary courage. The ensuing pages will, I hope, introduce you to some of those who manifested this quality. Acquaintance with such minds will also, I think, help dissolve another objection to atheism.

It is sometimes argued that disbelief in a fearful and tempting heavenly despotism makes life into something arid and tedious and cynical: a mere existence without any consolation or any awareness of the numinous or the transcendent. What nonsense this is. In the first place, it commits an obvious error. It seems to say that we ought not to believe that we are an evolved animal species with faulty components and a short lifespan for ourselves and our globe, lest the consequences of the belief be unwelcome or discreditable to us. Could anything show more clearly the bad effects of wish-thinking? There can be no serious ethical position based on denial or a refusal to look the facts squarely in the face. But this does not mean that we must stare into the abyss all the time. (Only religion, oddly enough, has ever required that we obsessively do that.)

Believing then—as this religious objection implicitly concedes—that human life is actually worth living, one can combat one's natural pessimism by stoicism and the refusal of illusion, while embellishing the scene with any one of the following. There are the beauties of science and the extraordinary marvels of nature. There is the consolation and irony of philosophy. There are the infinite splendors of literature and poetry, not excluding the liturgical and devotional aspects of these, such as those found in John Donne or George Herbert. There is the grand resource of art and music and architecture, again not excluding those elements that aspire to the sublime. In all of these pursuits, any one of them enough to absorb a lifetime, there may be found a sense of awe and magnificence that does not depend at all on any invocation of the supernatural. Indeed, nobody armed by art and culture and literature and philosophy is likely to be anything but bored and sickened by ghost stories, UFO tales, spiritualist experiences, or babblings from the beyond. One can appreciate and treasure the symmetry and grandeur of the ancient Greek Parthenon, for example, without needing any share in the cults of Athena or Eleusis, or the imperatives of Athenian imperialism, just as one may listen to Mozart or admire Chartres and Durham without any nostalgia for feudalism, monarchism, and the sale of indulgences. The whole concept of culture, indeed, may partly consist in discriminating between these things. Religion asks us to do the opposite and to preserve the ancient dreads and prohibitions, even as we dwell amid modern architecture and modern weapons.

It is very often argued that religion must have some sort of potency and relevance, since it occurs so strongly at all times and in all places. None of the authors collected here would ever have denied that. Some of them would argue that religion is so much a part of our human or animal nature that it is actually ineradicable. This, for what it may be worth, is my own view. We are unlikely to cease making gods or inventing ceremonies to please them for as long as we are afraid of death, or of the dark, and for as long as we persist in self-centeredness. That could be a lengthy stretch of time. However, it is just as certain that we shall continue to cast a skeptical and ironic and even witty eye on what we have ourselves invented. If religion is innate in us, then so is our doubt of it and our contempt for our own weakness.

Some of the authors and writers and thinkers assembled in these pages are famous for other reasons than their intelligence and their moral courage on this point. Several of them are chiefly celebrated because they took on the most inflated reputation of all: the elevation into a godhead of all mankind's distilled fears and hatreds and stupidities. Some of them have had the experience of faith and the experience of losing it, while others were and are, in the words of Blaise Pascal, so made that they cannot believe.

Arguments for atheism can be divided into two main categories: those that dispute the existence of god and those that demonstrate the ill effects of religion. It might be better if I broadened this somewhat, and said those that dispute the existence of an *intervening* god. Religion is, after all, more than the belief in a supreme being. It is the cult of that supreme being and the belief that his or her wishes have been made known or can be determined. Defining matters in this way, I can allow myself to mention great critics such as Thomas Jefferson and Thomas Paine, who perhaps paradoxically regarded religion as an insult to god. And sooner or later, one must take a position on agnosticism. This word has not been with us for very long—it was coined by the great Thomas Huxley, one of Darwin's stalwart defenders in the original argument over natural selection. It is sometimes used as a half-way house by those who cannot make a profession of faith but are unwilling to repudiate either religion or god absolutely. Since, once again, I am defining as religious those who claim to know, I feel I can lay claim to some at least of those who do *not* claim to know. An agnostic does not believe in god, or disbelieve in him. Non-belief is not quite unbelief, but I shall press it into service and annex as many agnostics as I can for this collection.

Authors as diverse as Matthew Arnold and George Orwell have given thought to the serious question: what is to be done about morals and ethics now that religion has so much decayed? Arnold went almost as far as to propose that the study of literature replace the study of religion. I must say that I slightly dread the effect that this might have had on literary pursuit, but as a source of ethical reflection and as a mirror in which to see our human dilemmas reflected, the literary tradition is infinitely superior to the childish parables and morality tales, let alone the sanguinary and sectarian admonitions, of the "holy" books. So I have included what many serious novelists and poets have had to say on this most freighted of all subjects. And who, really, will turn away from George Eliot and James Joyce and Joseph Conrad in order to rescrutinize the bare and narrow and constipated and fearful world of Augustine, Aquinas, Luther, Calvin, and Osama bin Laden?

It is often unconsciously assumed that religious faith is somehow conservative and that atheism or "freethinking" are a part of the liberal tradition. This is for good and sufficient historical reason, having to do with the origins of the American and French revolutions. However, many honorable and intelligent conservatives have rejected "faith" on several grounds. These grounds may include sheer implausibility, or the apparent privilege given by religion to one of its main constituencies—that of the losers, the diseased, the inert, the mendicants, and the helpless. To many an upright poor person, it seems needless to invent a god who will wash the feet of beggars and exalt those who do not care to labor. What is this but a denial of thrift and a sickly obsession with the victim? The so-called common people are quite able to penetrate this ruse ("The good lord must indeed love the poor, since he made so many of them"). Many decent people are made uneasy by the constant injunction to give alms and to dwell among those who have lost their self-respect. They can also see the hook sticking out of the bait: abandon this useless life, leave your family, and follow the prophet who says that the world is soon to pass away. Such an injunction coupled with an implicit or explicit "or else" is repulsive to many conservatives who believe in self-reliance and personal integrity, and who distrust "charity," just as it was repulsive to the early socialists who did not think that poverty was an ideal or romantic or ennobled state.

Finally, I want to come to the question of sex. If anything proves that religion is not just man-made but masculine-made, it is the incessant repetition of rules and taboos governing the sexual life. The disease is pervasive, from the weird obsession with virginity and the one-way birth canal through which prophets are "delivered," through the horror of menstrual blood, all the way to the fascinated disgust with homosexuality and the pretended concern with children (who suffer worse at the hands of the faithful than any other group). Male and female genital mutilation; the terrifying of infants with hideous fictions about guilt and hell; the wild prohibition of masturbation: religion will never be able to live down the shame with which it has stained itself for generations in this regard, anymore than it can purge its own guilt for the ruining of formative periods of precious life.

A saving grace of the human condition (if I may phrase it like that) is a sense of humor. Many writers and witnesses, guessing the connection between sexual repression and religious fervor, have managed to rescue themselves and others from its deadly grip by the exercise of wit. And much of religion is so laughable on its face that writers from Voltaire to Bertrand Russell to Chapman Cohen have had great fun at its expense. In our own day, the humor of scientists such as Richard Dawkins and Carl Sagan has ridiculed the apparent inability of the creator to know, let alone to understand, what he has created. Gods seem not to know of any animals except the ones tended by their immediate worshippers and seem to be ignorant as well of microbes and the laws of physics. The self-evident man-madeness of religion, as well as its masculine-madeness in respect of religion's universal commitment to male domination, is one of the first things to strike the eye.

A terrible thing has now happened to religion. Except in the places where it can still enforce itself by fear superimposed on ignorance, it has become one opinion among many. It is forced to compete in the free market of ideas and, even when it strives to retain the old advantage of inculcating its teachings into children (for reasons that are too obvious to need underlining), it has to stand up in open debate and submit to free inquiry. In the summer of 2007, I was sitting in a studio in Dublin, debating with a lay spokesman of the Roman Catholic Church who turned out to be the only believing Christian on a discussion panel of five people. He was a perfectly nice and rather modest logic-chopping polemicist, happy enough to go for a glass of refreshment after the program, and I suddenly felt a piercing stab of pity for him. A generation ago in Ireland, the Church did not have to lower itself in this way. It raised its voice only slightly, and was instantly obeyed by the Parliament, the schools, and the media. It could and did forbid divorce, contraception, the publication of certain books, and the utterance of certain opinions. Now it is discredited and in decline. Its once-absolute doctrines appear ridiculous: only a few weeks before this radio show the Vatican had finally admitted that "Limbo" (traditional destination for the souls of unbaptised children) did not exist after all. There are also local reasons for the decline, the reverberations of the child-rape scandal being prominent among them, but the secularization of Ireland is a part of a wider enlightenment in which well-grounded unbelief has become a genuinely strong and rooted presence. The availability and accessibility of well-produced books, cassettes, and DVDs, emphasizing the triumphs of science and reason, is a large part of this success. And so, of course, is the increasingly clear realization, on the part of civilized people, that the main enemy we face is "faith-based."

Open the newspaper or turn on the television and see what the parties of god are doing to Iraq, in their attempt to reduce a once-advanced society to the level of Afghanistan or Somalia (the last two countries where the parties of god had things all their own way). Observe the menacing developments in neighboring Iran, where the believers in the imminent return of a tooth fairy known as the Twelfth Imam are reinforcing their apocalyptic talk by the acquisition of doomsday weaponry. Or shift your gaze to the western bank of the Jordan, where Messianic settlers hope, by stealing the land of others in accordance with biblical directives, to bring on Armageddon in their own way. The chief international backers of these religious colonists, the American evangelical fundamentalists, are simultaneously trying to teach stultifying pseudo-science in schools, criminalize homosexuality, forbid stem-cell research, and display Mosaic law in courtrooms. From Rome, the Holy Father proposes to remedy the situation by restoring the historically anti-Semitic "Tridentine" form of the Mass, preaching crusading rhetoric with one hand while capitulating to Islamism on the other and maintaining that condoms are worse than AIDS. In Europe and America, newspapers and theaters and universities quail at the demands of Muslim fundamentalists, sleepless in their search for things at which to take "offense."

So the enlightenment of which I was writing is by no means developing in a straight line. The alternative to it, however, is being delineated for us with extraordinary vividness. It is in the hope of strengthening and arming the resistance to the faith-based, and to faith itself, that this anthology of combat with humanity's oldest enemy is respectfully offered.

1

From *De Rerum Natura* (*On the Nature of Things*)

Translated by W. Hannaford Brown

LUCRETIUS

In January 1821, Thomas Jefferson wrote John Adams to "encourage a hope that the human mind will some day get back to the freedom it enjoyed 2000 years ago." This wish for a return to the era of philosophy would put Jefferson in the same period as Titus Lucretius Carus, thanks to whose six-volume poem *De Rerum Naturum* (*On the Nature of Things*) we have a distillation of the work of the first true materialists: Leucippus, Democritus, and Epicurus. These men concluded that the world was composed of atoms in perpetual motion, and Epicurus, in particular, went on to argue that the gods, if they existed, played no part in human affairs. It followed that events like thunderstorms were natural and not supernatural, that ceremonies of worship and propitiation were a waste of time, and that there was nothing to be feared in death.

Lucretius, addressing his friend Memmius and acting as his Virgil through this labyrinth of radical ideas, revived the "atomist" theory at a time of brute religious revival in Rome. He argued that religion was immoral as well as untrue: his reference to Iphianassa here is the Latin version of the Greek and Trojan story of Iphigenia, sacrificial victim to her own father in the House of Atreus.

Atomism was viciously persecuted as heresy throughout the early Christian era, and only one printed manuscript of *De Rerum Naturum* survived the flames. There are several translations; I have chosen the one translated by my fellow Devonian and Oxonian, W. Hannaford Brown. Brown's own manuscript was almost destroyed during the Nazi bombardment of England in 1943: if a religious book had survived so many vicissitudes we can easily imagine what the faithful would say. But Lucretius teaches us to live without such piffle.

From Book I
2

Now, for the rest, lend ears unstopped, and the intellect's keen edge;
Severed from cares, attend to a true philosophical system;
Lest it should hap that my gifts which I zealously set forth before you,
Scorned, you abandon untouched before they can be comprehended.
For 'tis high lore of heaven and of gods that I shall endeavour
Clearly to speak as I tell of the primary atoms of matter
Out of which Nature forms things: 'tis "things" she increases and fosters;
Then back to atoms again she resolves them and makes them to vanish.
"Things," for argument's sake, my wont is to speak of as "matter";
Also the "seeds" of those things to name the small parts which beget them:
Further, those infinitesimal parts, (an alternative figure)
Primary "atoms" to call, whereof matter was all first created.

3

When in full view on the earth man's life lay rotting and loathsome,
Crushed 'neath the ponderous load of Religion's cruel burdensome shackles,
Who out of heaven displayed her forehead of withering aspect,
Lowering over the heads of mortals with hideous menace,
Upraising mortal eyes 'twas a Greek who first, daring, defied her;
'Gainst man's relentless foe 'twas Man first framed to do battle.
Him could nor tales of the gods nor heaven's fierce thunderbolts' crashes
Curb; nay rather they inflamed his spirit's keen courage to covet.
His it should first be to shiver the close-bolted portals of Nature.
Therefore his soul's live energy triumphed, and far and wide compassed
World's walls' blazing lights, and the boundless Universe traversed
Thought-winged; from realms of space he comes back victorious and tells us
What we may, what we must not perceive; what law universal
Limits the ken of each, what deep-set boundary landmark:
Then how in turn underfoot Religion is hurled down and trampled,
Then how that victory lifts mankind to high level of heaven.

4

One apprehension assails me here, that haply you reckon
Godless the pathway you tread which leads to the Science of Nature
As to the highroad of sin. But rather how much more often
Has that same vaunted Religion brought forth deeds sinful and godless.
Thus the chosen Greek chiefs, the first of their heroes, at Aulis,
Trivia's altar befouled with the blood of Iphianassa.
For when the equal-trimmed ribbons, her virgin tresses encircling,
Unfurled from each fair cheek so bravely, so gallantly fluttered;

Soon as she saw her sorrowing sire in front of the altar
Standing, with serving-men near, their gleaming knives vainly concealing,
And, at the sight of her plight, her countrymen bitter tears shedding;
Dumb with fear, her knees giving way, to earth she fell sinking.
Nor in her woe could it be of avail to the hapless maiden
That it was she first gave to the king the title of father.
For, by men's hands upborne, she was, quivering, led to the altar;
Not, forsooth, to the end that, sacred rites duly completed,
With ringing clarion song of marriage she might be escorted;
But, pure maid foully slain in wedlock's appropriate season,
That she a victim might fall 'neath the slaughter stroke of her father,
So that a happy and lucky dispatch to the fleet might be granted!
Such are the darksome deeds brought to pass by Religion's fell promptings!

6

Now this terror and darkness of mind must surely be scattered,
Not by rays of the sun, nor by gleaming arrows of daylight,
But by the outward display and unseen workings of Nature.
And her first rule for us from this premiss shall take its beginning;
"Never did will of gods bring anything forth out of nothing."
For, in good sooth, it is thus that fear restraineth all mortals,
Since both in earth and sky they see that many things happen
Whereof they cannot by any known law determine the causes;
So their occurrence they ascribe to supernatural power.
Therefore when we have seen that naught can be made out of nothing,
Afterwards we shall more rightly discern the thing which we search for:—
Both out of what it is that everything can be created,
And in what way all came, without help of gods, into being.

7

If out of nothing things sprang into life, then every species
From all alike could be born, and none would need any seed-germ.
First, mature men might rise from the sea, and scale-bearing fishes
Out of the earth; or again, fledged birds burst full-grown from heaven.
Cattle and other beasts, and the whole tribe of wild herds, ungoverned
By any fixed law of birth, would of desert and tilth take possession.
Nor would each fruit be wont to remain to its own tree peculiar,
But all would change about, so that all could bear all kinds of produce.
How, if for each distinct kind there were no producing corpuscles,
Could any matrix for matter exist that is fixed and unchanging?
But, as it is, since all from definite seeds are created,
Therefore each is born and comes into regions of daylight

From out the place where dwells its substance, the primary atoms.
Thus each cannot spring from all in promiscuous fashion,
Since a peculiar power indwells each fixed kind of matter.
Secondly, why do we see spring flowers, see golden grain waving
Ripe in the sun, see grape clusters swell at the urge of the autumn,
If not because when, in their own time, the fixed seeds of matter
Have coalesced, then each creation comes forth into full view
When the recurrent seasons for each are propitious, and safely
Quickening Earth brings forth to the light her delicate offspring?
But if from nothing they came, then each would spring up unexpected
At undetermined times and in unfavouring seasons,
Seeing that there would then not be any primary atoms
Which from untimely creative conjunction could be kept asunder.
Nor, again, thirdly, would time be needed for growing of matter
When the seeds unite, if things can grow out of nothing;
For in a trice little children would reach the fulness of manhood:
Trees, again, would spring up by surprise, from earth sheer outleaping.
But 'tis apparent that none of this happens, since all things grow slowly,
As is but normal when each from a fixed seed in a fixed season
Grows, and growing, preserves its kind: thus telling us clearly
That from appropriate atoms each creature grows great and is nourished.

From Book II

5

But do not think that the gods condescend to consider such matters,
Or that they mark the careers of individual atoms
So as to study the laws of Nature whereunto they conform.
Nevertheless there are some, unaware of the fixed laws of matter,
Who think that Nature cannot, without supernatural power,
Thus nicely fit to manners of men the sequence of seasons,
Bringing forth corn, yea, all earth's fruits, which heavenly Pleasure,
Pilot of life, prompts men to approach, herself them escorting,
As by Venus' wiles she beguiles them their race to continue
So that humanity may not fail. When therefore they settle
That for the sake of man the gods designed all things, most widely
In all respects do they seem to have strayed from the path of true reason.
For even if I knew nothing concerning the nature of atoms,
Yet from heaven's very lore and legend's diversified story
I would make bold to aver and maintain that the order of Nature
Never by will of the gods for us mortals was ever created . . .

From Book III
15

Now then, in order that you may learn that the minds of live creatures
And their imponderable souls are to birth and death alike subject,
I will proceed to compose such verse as shall earn your attention,
By long study amassed, and devised by delightful endeavour.
Please comprise these natures twain 'neath one appellation:
When I pass on, for example, to speak of the soul, how 'tis mortal,
Know that I speak of the mind as well, inasmuch as together
Both one single entity form, one composite substance.
Firstly, then, since I have shewn that 'tis rare, and composed of small bodies;
Shaped from much smaller atoms than fashion a liquid like water,
Atoms far smaller than those which constitute mizzling and smoke-clouds—
For it is nimbler by far, and a far feebler blow sets it moving,
Stirred as it is by the films which mist and smoke shed around them,
As for example when steeped in sleep we seem to see altars
Breathing forth flames of fire, and exalting their smoke to the heavens;
Doubtless from objects like these such films as I speak of are gendered.
Since too, when vessels are shattered, you see how in every direction
Gushes the liquid flood, and the contents utterly vanish;
Since once again the mists and the smoke are dispersed by the breezes;
Know that the soul, too, is scattered abroad, and dies much more quickly,
And is the sooner resolved back into its primary atoms,
Once it has quitted the limbs of a man and abandoned his body.
For when the body, which forms its receptacle, cannot contain it,
Being from any cause crushed, or by issue of life-blood enfeebled,
How can you think that the soul can by fluid air be encompassed?
How can the air, than our body more rare, be able to hold it?

From Book V
39

Next, having gotten them huts and skins and fire; and when woman
Mated with man shared a man's abode; and when family duties
Therein were learnt; and as soon as they saw their own offspring arising;
Then 'twas that mankind first began to lose power of endurance.
Fire made their gelid frames less able to bear the cold weather
Out 'neath the open sky; their virility Venus exhausted:
Childrens' caresses too easily sapped the proud spirit of parents.
Neighbours in those days, too, began to form friendly agreements
Neither to inflict nor receive any hurt, and asked for indulgence

Towards their women and bairns, as with cries and gesticulations
And in their stammering speech they tried to explain to each other
That it is meet and right that all should pity the helpless.
And although harmony could not be won in every instance,
Yet did the greater part observe the conventions uprightly;
Else long since would the human race have been wholly abolished,
Nor could their seed till this present day have continued the species.

2

From
Rubáiyát of Omar Khayyám

A Paraphrase from Several Literal
Translations by Richard Le Gallienne

OMAR KHAYYÁM

Medieval Persia also produced a long and beautiful poem satirizing the claims and practices of religion. Though Omar Khayyám (1048–1131) is best remembered for his warm recommendations of wine, women, and song (preferences that would land him in trouble in today's Iran, as well) he was actually a very serious astronomer and mathematician who made many contributions to algebra, helped refine the calendar, and may have been an early proponent of the idea that the earth revolved around the sun.

Khayyám clearly doubted that god had revealed himself to some men and not to others, especially in light of the very obvious fact that those who claimed to interpret the revelation were fond of using their claim in order to acquire and wield power over others in this world. He was not the first to notice this aspect of religion, but he was among the wittiest.

The most celebrated translation of his immortal *Rubáiyát* into English was done by Edward Fitzgerald, but the verses as rendered by Richard Le Gallienne are sometimes better at conveying the pungency that underlies the ironic charm of these quatrains.

> The bird of life is singing on the bough
> His two eternal notes of "I and Thou"—
> O! hearken well, for soon the song sings through
> And, would we hear it, we must hear it now.
>
> The bird of life is singing in the sun,
> Short is his song, nor only just begun,—

A call, a trill, a rapture, then—so soon!—
A silence, and the song is done—is done.

Yea! what is man that deems himself divine?
Man is a flagon, and his soul the wine;
    Man is a reed, his soul the sound therein;
Man is a lantern, and his soul the shine.

Would you be happy! hearken, then, the way:
Heed not TO-MORROW, heed not YESTERDAY;
    The magic words of life are HERE and NOW—
O fools, that after some to-morrow stray!

Were I a Sultan, say what greater bliss
Were mine to summon to my side than this,—
    Dear gleaming face, far brighter than the moon!
O Love! and this immortalizing kiss.

To all of us the thought of heaven is dear—
Why not be sure of it and make it here?
    No doubt there is a heaven yonder too,
But 'tis so far away—and you are near.

Men talk of heaven,—there is no heaven but here;
Men talk of hell,—there is no hell but here;
    Men of hereafters talk, and future lives,—
O love, there is no other life—but here.

Gay little moon, that hath not understood!
She claps her hands, and calls the red wine good;
    O careless and beloved, if she knew
This wine she fancies is my true heart's blood.

Girl, have you any thought what your eyes mean?
You must have stolen them from some dead queen.
    O little empty laughing soul that sings
And dances, tell me—What do your eyes mean?

And all this body of ivory and myrrh,
O guard it with some little love and care;
    Know your own wonder, worship it with me,
See how I fall before it deep in prayer.

Nor idle I who speak it, nor profane,
This playful wisdom growing out of pain;
   How many midnights whitened into morn
Before the seeker knew he sought in vain.

You want to know the Secret—so did I,
Low in the dust I sought it, and on high
   Sought it in awful flight from star to star,
The Sultan's watchman of the starry sky.

Up, up, where Parwín's hoofs stamp heaven's floor,
My soul went knocking at each starry door,
   Till on the stilly top of heaven's stair,
Clear-eyed I looked—and laughed—and climbed no more.

Of all my seeking this is all my gain:
No agony of any mortal brain
   Shall wrest the secret of the life of man;
The Search has taught me that the Search is vain.

Yet sometimes on a sudden all seems clear—
Hush! hush! my soul, the Secret draweth near;
   Make silence ready for the speech divine—
If Heaven should speak, and there be none to hear!

Yea! sometimes on the instant all seems plain,
The simple sun could tell us, or the rain;
   The world, caught dreaming with a look of heaven,
Seems on a sudden tip-toe to explain.

Like to a maid who exquisitely turns
A promising face to him who, waiting, burns
   In hell to hear her answer—so the world
Tricks all, and hints what no man ever learns.

Look not above, there is no answer there;
Pray not, for no one listens to your prayer;
   NEAR is as near to God as any FAR,
And HERE is just the same deceit as THERE.

But here are wine and beautiful young girls,
Be wise and hide your sorrows in their curls,

Dive as you will in life's mysterious sea,
You shall not bring us any better pearls.

Allah, perchance, the secret word might spell;
If Allah be, He keeps His secret well;
   What He hath hidden, who shall hope to find?
Shall God His secret to a maggot tell?

So since with all my passion and my skill,
The world's mysterious meaning mocks me still,
   Shall I not piously believe that I
Am kept in darkness by the heavenly will?

How sad to be a woman—not to know
Aught of the glory of this breast of snow,
   All unconcerned to comb this mighty hair;
To be a woman and yet never know!

Were I a woman, I would all day long
Sing my own beauty in some holy song,
   Bend low before it, hushed and half afraid,
And say "I am a woman" all day long.

The Koran! well, come put me to the test—
Lovely old book in hideous error drest—
   Believe me, I can quote the Koran too,
The unbeliever knows his Koran best.

And do you think that unto such as you,
A maggot-minded, starved, fanatic crew,
   God gave the Secret, and denied it me?—
Well, well, what matters it! believe that too.

Old Khayyám, say you, is a debauchee;
If only you were half so good as he!
   He sins no sins but gentle drunkenness,
Great-hearted mirth, and kind adultery.

But yours the cold heart, and the murderous tongue,
The wintry soul that hates to hear a song,
   The close-shut fist, the mean and measuring eye,
And all the little poisoned ways of wrong.

So I be written in the Book of Love,
I have no care about that book above;
    Erase my name, or write it, as you please—
So I be written in the Book of Love.

What care I, love, for what the Sufis say?
The Sufis are but drunk another way;
    So you be drunk, it matters not the means,
So you be drunk—and glorify your clay.

Drunken myself, and with a merry mind,
An old man passed me, all in vine-leaves twined,
    I said, "Old man, hast thou forgotten God?"
"Go, drink yourself," he said, "for God is kind."

"Did God set grapes a-growing, do you think,
And at the same time make it sin to drink?
    Give thanks to HIM who foreordained it thus—
Surely HE loves to hear the glasses clink!"

From God's own hand this earthly vessel came,
He shaped it thus, be it for fame or shame;
    If it be fair—to God be all the praise,
If it be foul—to God alone the blame.

To me there is much comfort in the thought
That all our agonies can alter nought,
    Our lives are written to their latest word,
We but repeat a lesson HE hath taught.

Our wildest wrong is part of His great Right,
Our weakness is the shadow of His might,
    Our sins are His, forgiven long ago,
To make His mercy more exceeding bright.

When first the stars were made and planets seven,
Already was it told of me in Heaven
    That God had chosen me to sing His Vine,
And in my dust had thrown the vinous leaven.

3

Of Religion

From *Leviathan*

Thomas Hobbes

Atomist ideas began to revive in the seventeenth century. Sir Isaac Newton included ninety lines of *De Rerum Natura* in the early drafts of his *Principia*. Galileo's 1623 work, *Saggiatore*, was so infused with the atomic theory that its friends and critics both referred to it as an Epicurean book.

However, at no time was it other than extremely dangerous to profess any public doubt about religious orthodoxy. Galileo was to discover this to his cost. Thomas Hobbes (1588–1679), who had to live in exile and who was suspected of unsoundness by both sides in the English Civil War, took great care to make formal professions of loyalty to the established Church but found ways in his writing to throw doubt on faith. The heresy-hunters were probably shrewd, if literal-minded, to threaten him with a trial by Parliament on charges of atheism in 1666.

In Chapter XII of *Leviathan*, his massive essay on statecraft, Hobbes ridicules religion by supposedly defending true faith against paganism.

Seeing there are no signs, nor fruit of *religion,* but in man only; there is no cause to doubt, but that the seed of *religion,* is also only in man; and consisteth in some peculiar quality, or at least in some eminent degree thereof, not to be found in any other living creatures.

And first, it is peculiar to the nature of man, to be inquisitive into the causes of the events they see, some more, some less; but all men so much, as to be curious in the search of the causes of their own good and evil fortune.

Secondly, upon the sight of any thing that hath a beginning to think also it had a cause, which determined the same to begin, then when it did, rather than sooner or later.

Thirdly, whereas there is no other felicity of beasts, but the enjoying of their quotidian food, ease, and lusts; as having little or no foresight of the time to come, for want of observation, and memory of the order, consequence, and dependence of the things they see; man observeth how one event hath been produced by another; and remembereth in them antecedence and consequence; and when he cannot assure himself of the true causes of things (for the causes of good and evil fortune for the most part are invisible), he supposes causes of them, either such as his own fancy suggesteth; or trusteth the authority of other men, such as he thinks to be his friends, and wiser than himself.

The two first, make anxiety. For being assured that there be causes of all things that have arrived hitherto, or shall arrive hereafter; it is impossible for a man, who continually endeavoureth to secure himself against the evil he fears, and procure the good he desireth, not to be in a perpetual solicitude of the time to come; so that every man, especially those that are over provident, are in a state like to that of Prometheus. For as Prometheus, which interpreted, is, *the prudent man,* was bound to the hill Caucasus, a place of large prospect, where, an eagle feeding on his liver, devoured in the day, as much as was repaired in the night: so that man, which looks too far before him, in the care of future time, hath his heart all the day long, gnawed on by fear of death, poverty, or other calamity; and has no repose, nor pause of his anxiety, but in sleep.

This perpetual fear, always accompanying mankind in the ignorance of causes, as it were in the dark, must needs have for object something. And therefore when there is nothing to be seen, there is nothing to accuse, either of their good, or evil fortune, but some *power*, or agent *invisible:* in which sense perhaps it was, that some of the old poets said, that the gods were at first created by human fear: which spoken of the gods, that is to say, of the many gods of the Gentiles, is very true. But the acknowledging of one God, eternal, infinite, and omnipotent, may more easily be derived, from the desire men have to know the causes of natural bodies, and their several virtues, and operations; than from the fear of what was to befall them in time to come. For he that from any effect he seeth come to pass, should reason to the next and immediate cause thereof, and from thence to the cause of that cause, and plunge himself profoundly in the pursuit of causes; shall at last come to this, that there must be, as even the heathen philosophers confessed, one first mover; that is, a first, and an eternal cause of all things; which is that which men mean by the name of God: and all this without thought of their fortune; the solicitude whereof, both inclines to fear, and hinders them from the search of the causes of other things; and thereby gives occasion of feigning of as many gods, as there be men that feign them.

And for the matter, or substance of the invisible agents, so fancied; they could not by natural cogitation, fall upon any other conceit, but that it was the same with that of the soul of man; and that the soul of man, was of the same substance, with that which appeareth in a dream, to one that sleepeth; or in a looking-glass, to one that is awake; which, men not knowing that such apparitions are nothing else but creatures of the fancy, think to be real, and external substances; and therefore call them ghosts; as the Latins called them *imagines*, and *umbræ*; and thought them spirits, that is, thin aërial bodies; and those invisible agents, which they feared, to be like them; save that they appear, and vanish when they please. But the opinion that such spirits were incorporeal, or immaterial, could never enter into the mind of any man by nature; because, though men may put together words of contradictory signification, as *spirit*, and *incorporeal*; yet they can never have the imagination of any thing answering to them: and therefore, men that by their own meditation, arrive to the acknowledgment of one infinite, omnipotent, and eternal God, chose rather to confess he is incomprehensible, and above their understanding, than to define his nature by *spirit incorporeal*, and then confess their definition to be unintelligible: or if they give him such a title, it is not *dogmatically*, with intention to make the divine nature understood; but *piously*, to honour him with attributes, of significations, as remote as they can from the grossness of bodies visible.

Then, for the way by which they think these invisible agents wrought their effects; that is to say, what immediate causes they used, in bringing things to pass, men that know not what it is that we call *causing*, that is, almost all men, have no other rule to guess by, but by observing, and remembering what they have seen to precede the like effect at some other time, or times before, without seeing between the antecedent and subsequent event, any dependence or connexion at all: and therefore from the like things past, they expect the like things to come; and hope for good or evil luck, superstitiously, from things that have no part at all in the causing of it: as the Athenians did for their war at Lepanto, demand another Phormio; the Pompeian faction for their war in Africa, another Scipio; and others have done in diverse other occasions since. In like manner they attribute their fortune to a stander by, to a lucky or unlucky place, to words spoken, especially if the name of God be amongst them; as charming and conjuring, the liturgy of witches; insomuch as to believe, they have power to turn a stone into bread, bread into a man, or any thing into any thing.

Thirdly, for the worship which naturally men exhibit to powers invisible, it can be no other, but such expressions of their reverence, as they would use towards men; gifts, petitions, thanks, submission of body, considerate addresses, sober behavior, premeditated words, swearing, that is, assuring one another of their promises, by invoking them. Beyond that reason suggesteth nothing; but leaves them either to rest there; or for further ceremonies, to rely on those they believe to be wiser than themselves.

Lastly, concerning how these invisible powers declare to men the things which shall hereafter come to pass, especially concerning their good or evil fortune in general, or good or ill success in any particular undertaking, men are naturally at a stand: save that using to conjecture of the time to come, by the time past, they are very apt, not only to take casual things, after one or two encounters, for prognostics of the like encounter ever after, but also to believe the like prognostics from other men, of whom they have once conceived a good opinion.

And in these four things, opinion of ghosts, ignorance of second causes, devotion towards what men fear, and taking of things casual for prognostics, consisteth the natural seed of *religion*; which by reason of the different fancies, judgments, and passions of several men, hath grown up into ceremonies so different, that those which are used by one man, are for the most part ridiculous to another.

For these seeds have received culture from two sorts of men. One sort have been they, that have nourished, and ordered them, according to their own invention. The other have done it, by God's commandment, and direction: but both sorts have done it, with a purpose to make those men that relied on them, the more apt to obedience, laws, peace, charity, and civil society. So that the religion of the former sort, is a part of human politics, and teacheth part of the duty which earthly kings require of their subjects. And the religion of the latter sort is divine politics; and containeth precepts to those that have yielded themselves subjects in the kingdom of God. Of the former sort, were all the founders of commonwealths, and the lawgivers of the Gentiles: of the latter sort, were Abraham, Moses, and our blessed Saviour; by whom have been derived unto us the laws of the kingdom of God.

And for that part of religion, which consisteth in opinions concerning the nature of powers invisible, there is almost nothing that has a name, that has not been esteemed amongst the Gentiles, in one place or another, a god, or devil; or by their poets feigned to be inanimated, inhabited, or possessed by some spirit or other.

The unformed matter of the world, was a god, by the name of Chaos.

The heaven, the ocean, the planets, the fire, the earth, the winds, were so many gods.

Men, women, a bird, a crocodile, a calf, a dog, a snake, an onion, a leek, were deified. Besides that, they filled almost all places, with spirits called *demons:* the plains, with Pan, and Panises, or Satyrs; the woods, with Fawns, and Nymphs; the sea, with Tritons, and other Nymphs; every river, and fountain, with a ghost of his name, and with Nymphs; every house with its *Lares,* or familiars; every man with his *Genius*; hell with ghosts, and spiritual officers, as Charon, Cerberus, and the Furies; and in the night time, all places with *larvæ, lemures,* ghosts of men deceased, and a whole kingdom of fairies and bugbears. They have also ascribed divinity, and built temples to mere accidents, and qualities; such as are time, night, day, peace, concord, love, contention, virtue, honour, health, rust, fever, and the like; which when they prayed for, or against, they prayed to, as if there were ghosts of those names hanging over their heads, and letting fall, or withholding that good, or evil, for, or against which they prayed. They invoked also their own wit, by the name of Muses; their own ignorance, by the name of Fortune; their own lusts by the name of Cupid; their own rage, by the name of Furies; their own privy members, by the name of Priapus; and attributed their pollutions, to Incubi, and Succubæ: insomuch as there was nothing, which a poet could introduce as a person in his poem, which they did not make either a *god*, or a *devil*.

The same authors of the religion of the Gentiles, observing the second ground for religion, which is men's ignorance of causes; and thereby their aptness to attribute their fortune to causes, on which there was no dependence at all apparent, took occasion to obtrude on their ignorance, instead of second causes, a kind of second and ministerial gods; ascribing the cause of fecundity, to Venus; the cause of arts, to Apollo; of subtlety and craft, to Mercury; of tempests and storms, to Æolus; and of other effects, to other gods; insomuch as there was amongst the heathen almost as great variety of gods, as of business.

And to the worship, which naturally men conceived fit to be used towards their gods, namely, oblations, prayers, thanks, and the rest formerly named; the same legislators of the Gentiles have added their images, both in picture, and sculpture; that the more ignorant sort, that is to say, the most part or generality of the people, thinking the gods for whose representation they were made, were really included, and as it were housed within them, might so much the more stand in fear of them: and endowed them with lands, and houses, and officers, and revenues, set apart from all other human uses; that is, consecrated, and made holy to those their idols; as caverns, groves, woods, mountains, and whole islands; and have attributed to them, not only the shapes, some of men, some of beasts, some of monsters; but also the faculties, and passions of men and beasts: as sense, speech, sex, lust, generation, and this not only by mixing one with another, to propagate the kind of gods; but also by mixing with men, and women, to beget mongrel gods, and but inmates of heaven, as Bacchus, Hercules, and others; besides anger, revenge, and other passions of living creatures, and the actions proceeding from them, as fraud, theft, adultery, sodomy, and any vice that may be taken for an effect of power, or a cause of pleasure; and all such vices, as amongst men are taken to be against law, rather than against honour.

Lastly, to the prognostics of time to come; which are naturally, but conjectures upon experience of time past; and supernaturally, divine revelation; the same authors of the religion of the Gentiles, partly upon pretended experience, partly upon pretended revelation, have added innumerable other superstitious ways of divination; and made men believe they should find their fortunes, sometimes in the ambiguous or senseless answers of the priests at Delphi, Delos, Ammon, and other famous oracles; which answers, were made ambiguous by design, to own the event both ways; or absurd, by the intoxicating vapour of the place, which is very frequent in sulphurous caverns: sometimes in the leaves of the Sybils; of whose prophecies, like those perhaps of Nostradamus (for the fragments now extant seem to be the invention of later times), there were some books in reputation in the time of the Roman republic: sometimes in the insignificant speeches of madmen, supposed to be possessed with a divine spirit, which possession they called enthusiasm; and these kinds of foretelling events, were accounted theomancy, or prophecy: sometimes in the aspect of the stars at their nativity; which was called horoscopy, and esteemed a part of judiciary astrology: sometimes in their own hopes and fears, called thumomancy, or presage: sometimes in the prediction of witches, that pretended conference with the dead; which is called necromancy, conjuring, and witchcraft; and is but juggling and confederate knavery: sometimes in the casual flight, or feeding of birds; called augury: sometimes in the entrails of a sacrificed beast; which was *aruspicina*: sometimes in dreams: sometimes in croaking of ravens, or chattering of birds: sometimes in the lineaments of the face; which was called metoposcopy; or by palmistry in the lines of the hand; in casual words, called *omina*: sometimes in monsters, or unusual accidents; as eclipses, comets, rare meteors, earthquakes, inundations, uncouth births, and the like, which they called *portenta*, and *ostenta*, because they thought them to portend, or foreshow some great calamity to come; sometimes, in mere lottery, as cross and pile; counting holes in a sieve; dipping of verses in Homer, and Virgil; and innumerable other such vain conceits. So easy are men to be drawn to believe any thing, from such men as have gotten credit with them; and can with gentleness, and dexterity, take hold of their fear, and ignorance.

And therefore the first founders, and legislators of commonwealths among the Gentiles, whose ends were only to keep the people in obedience, and peace, have in all places taken care; first, to imprint in their minds a belief, that those precepts which they gave concerning religion, might not be thought to proceed from their own device, but from the dictates of some god, or other spirit; or else that they themselves were of a higher nature than mere mortals, that their laws might the more easily be received: so Numa Pompilius pretended to receive the ceremonies he instituted amongst the Romans, from the nymph Egeria: and the first king and founder of the kingdom of Peru, pretended himself and his wife to be the children of the Sun; and Mahomet, to set up his new religion, pretended to have conferences with the Holy Ghost, in form of a dove. Secondly, they have had a care, to make it believed, that the same things were displeasing to the gods, which were forbidden by the laws. Thirdly, to prescribe ceremonies, supplications, sacrifices, and festivals, by which they were to believe, the anger of the gods might be appeased; and that ill success in war, great contagions of sickness, earthquakes, and each man's private misery, came from the anger of the gods, and their anger from the neglect of their worship, or the forgetting, or mistaking some point of the ceremonies required. And though amongst the ancient Romans, men were not forbidden to deny, that which in the poets is written of the pains, and pleasures after this life: which divers of great authority, and gravity in that state have in their harangues openly derided; yet that belief was always more cherished, than the contrary.

And by these, and such other institutions, they obtained in order to their end, which was the peace of the commonwealth, that the common people in their misfortunes, laying the fault on neglect, or error in their ceremonies, or on their own disobedience to the laws, were the less apt to mutiny against their governors; and being entertained with the pomp, and pastime of festivals, and public games, made in honour of the gods, needed nothing else but bread to keep them from discontent, murmuring, and commotion against the state. And therefore the Romans, that had conquered the greatest part of the then known world, made no scruple of tolerating any religion whatsoever in the city of Rome itself; unless it had something in it, that could not consist with their civil government; nor do we read, that any religion was there forbidden, but that of the Jews; who, being the peculiar kingdom of God, thought it unlawful to acknowledge subjection to any mortal king or state whatsoever. And thus you see how the religion of the Gentiles was a part of their policy.

But where God himself, by supernatural revelation, planted religion; there he also made to himself a peculiar kingdom: and gave laws, not only of behaviour towards himself, but also towards one another; and thereby in the kingdom of God, the policy, and laws civil, are a part of religion; and therefore the distinc-tion of temporal, and spiritual domination, hath there no place. It is true, that God is king of all the earth: yet may he be king of a peculiar, and chosen nation. For there is no more incongruity therein, than that he that hath the general command of the whole army, should have withal a peculiar regiment, or com-pany of his own. God is king of all the earth by his power: but of his chosen people, he is king by covenant. But to speak more largely of the kingdom of God, both by nature, and covenant, I have in the following discourse assigned another place.

From the propagation of religion, it is not hard to understand the causes of the resolution of the same into its first seeds, or principles; which are only an opinion of a deity, and powers invisible, and supernatural; that can never be so abolished out of human nature, but that new religions may again be made to spring out of them, by the culture of such men, as for such purpose are in reputation.

For seeing all formed religion, is founded at first, upon the faith which a mul-titude hath in some one person, whom they believe not only to be a wise man, and to labour to procure their happiness, but also to be a holy man, to whom God himself vouchsafeth to declare his will supernaturally; it followeth neces-sarily, when they that have the government of religion, shall come to have either the wisdom of those men, their sincerity, or their love suspected; or when they shall be unable to show any probable token of divine revelation; that the reli-gion which they desire to uphold, must be suspected likewise; and, without the fear of the civil sword, contradicted and rejected.

That which taketh away the reputation of wisdom, in him that formeth a reli-gion, or addeth to it when it is already formed, is the enjoining of a belief of con-tradictories: for both parts of a contradiction cannot possibly be true: and therefore to enjoin the belief of them, is an argument of ignorance; which de-tects the author in that; and discredits him in all things else he shall propound as from revelation supernatural: which revelation a man may indeed have of many things above, but of nothing against natural reason.

That which taketh away the reputation of sincerity, is the doing or saying of such things, as appear to be signs, that what they require other men to believe, is not believed by themselves; all which doings, or sayings are therefore called scandalous, because they be stumbling blocks, that make men to fall in the way of religion; as injustice, cruelty, profaneness, avarice, and luxury. For who can believe, that he that doth ordinarily such actions as proceed from any of these roots, believeth there is any such invisible power to be feared, as he affrighteth other men withal, for lesser faults?

That which taketh away the reputation of love, is the being detected of private ends: as when the belief they require of others, conduceth or seemeth to conduce to the acquiring of dominion, riches, dignity, or secure pleasure, to themselves only, or specially. For that which men reap benefit by to themselves, they are thought to do for their own sakes, and not for love of others.

Lastly, the testimony that men can render of divine calling, can be no other, than the operation of miracles; or true prophecy, which also is a miracle; or extraordinary felicity. And therefore, to those points of religion, which have been received from them that did such miracles; those that are added by such, as approve not their calling by some miracle, obtain no greater belief, than what the custom and laws of the places, in which they be educated, have wrought into them. For as in natural things, men of judgment require natural signs, and arguments; so in supernatural things, they require signs supernatural, which are miracles, before they consent inwardly, and from their hearts.

All which causes of the weakening of men's faith, do manifestly appear in the examples following. First, we have the example of the children of Israel; who when Moses, that had approved his calling to them by miracles, and by the happy conduct of them out of Egypt, was absent but forty days, revolted from the worship of the true God, recommended to them by him; and setting up (*Exod.* xxxii. 1, 2) a golden calf for their god, relapsed into the idolatry of the Egyptians; from whom they had been so lately delivered. And again, after Moses, Aaron, Joshua, and that generation which had seen the great works of God in Israel (*Judges* ii. 11) were dead; another generation arose, and served Baal. So that miracles failing, faith also failed.

Again, when the sons of Samuel, (1 *Sam.* viii. 3) being constituted by their father judges in Bersabee, received bribes, and judged unjustly, the people of Israel refused any more to have God to be their king, in other manner than he was king of other people; and therefore cried out to Samuel, to choose them a king after the manner of the nations. So that justice failing, faith also failed; insomuch, as they deposed their God, from reigning over them.

And whereas in the planting of Christian religion, the oracles ceased in all parts of the Roman empire, and the number of Christians increased wonderfully every day, and in every place, by the preaching of the Apostles, and Evangelists; a great part of that success, may reasonably be attributed, to the contempt, into which the priests of the Gentiles of that time, had brought themselves, by their uncleanness, avarice, and juggling between princes. Also the religion of the church of Rome, was partly, for the same cause abolished in England, and many other parts of Christendom; insomuch, as the failing of virtue in the pastors, maketh faith fail in the people: and partly from bringing of the philosophy, and doctrine of Aristotle into religion, by the Schoolmen; from whence there arose so many contradictions, and absurdities, as brought the clergy into a reputation both of ignorance, and of fraudulent intention; and inclined people to revolt from them, either against the will of their own princes, as in France and Holland; or with their will, as in England.

Lastly, amongst the points by the church of Rome declared necessary for salvation, there be so many, manifestly to the advantage of the Pope, and of his spiritual subjects, residing in the territories of other Christian princes, that were it not for the mutual emulation of those princes, they might without war, or trouble, exclude all foreign authority, as easily as it has been excluded in England. For who is there that does not see, to whose benefit it conduceth, to have it believed, that a king hath not his authority from Christ, unless a bishop crown him ? That a king, if he be a priest, cannot marry? That whether a prince be born in lawful marriage, or not, must be judged by authority from Rome? That subjects may be freed from their allegiance, if by the court of Rome, the king be judged an heretic? That a king, as Childeric of France, may be deposed by a pope, as Pope Zachary, for no cause; and his kingdom given to one of his subjects? That the clergy and regulars, in what country soever, shall be exempt from the jurisdiction of their king in cases criminal? Or who does not see, to whose profit redound the fees of private masses, and vales of purgatory; with other signs of private interest, enough to mortify the most lively faith, if, as I said, the civil magistrate, and custom did not more sustain it, than any opinion they have of the sanctity, wisdom, or probity of their teachers? So that I may attribute all the changes of religion in the world, to one and the same cause; and that is, unpleasing priests; and those not only amongst Catholics, but even in that church that hath presumed most of reformation.

4

Theological-Political Treatise

BENEDICT DE SPINOZA

The seventeenth century saw The Netherlands emerge as a place of shelter for religious dissidents and dissidents from religion. Pierre Bayle and Rene Descartes both took advantage of its more tolerant atmosphere. However, there were limits to this latitude. Born Baruch de Spinoza in 1632—a year after the indictment of Galileo by the Inquisition—the young man followed the religious practice of the Spanish and Portuguese Jews who had moved to Amsterdam to escape Catholic persecution. But in 1656, Spinoza was anathematized and excommunicated by the elders of the synagogue for doubting the immortality of the soul and for recommending the separation of church and state. The Calvinist and Catholic authorities, ecumenical for once, heartily endorsed this condemnation. Changing his name to Benedict, Spinoza lived until 1677, supporting himself as a grinder of lenses and continuing to publish his philosophical meditations.

There are those who argue that he was not really an atheist because he never formally renounced the idea of a Supreme Being. However, once again the general climate of persecution makes it difficult to be certain of his innermost convictions. In his correspondence he would write the word *Caute!* (Latin for "take care") and place a little *sub rosa* drawing of a rose underneath. He gave a false name for the printer of this very work, and he left the author's page blank. Moreover, it can be doubted whether a pantheist is truly a theist, in that a god made manifest throughout Nature, who is part of what he "creates," is in some sense everywhere and nowhere. Certainly the idea of a personal or intervening god is made very much more difficult to defend as a result of Spinoza's intellectual exertions.

Men would never be superstitious, if they could govern all their circumstances by set rules, or if they were always favoured by fortune: but being frequently driven into straits where rules are useless, and being often kept fluctuating pitiably between hope and fear by the uncertainty of fortune's greedily coveted favours, they are consequently, for the most part, very prone to credulity. The human mind is readily swayed this way or that in times of doubt, especially when hope and fear are struggling for the mastery, though usually it is boastful, over-confident, and vain.

This as a general fact I suppose everyone knows, though few, I believe, know their own nature; no one can have lived in the world without observing that most people, when in prosperity, are so over-brimming with wisdom (however inexperienced they may be), that they take every offer of advice as a personal insult, whereas in adversity they know not where to turn, but beg and pray for counsel from every passer-by. No plan is then too futile, too absurd, or too fatuous for their adoption; the most frivolous causes will raise them to hope, or plunge them into despair—if anything happens during their fright which reminds them of some past good or ill, they think it portends a happy or unhappy issue, and therefore (though it may have proved abortive a hundred times before) style it a lucky or unlucky omen. Anything that excites their astonishment they believe to be a portent signifying the anger of the gods or of the Supreme Being, and, mistaking superstition for religion, account it impious not to avert the evil with prayer and sacrifice. Signs and wonders of this sort they conjure up perpetually, till one might think Nature as mad as themselves, they interpret her so fantastically.

Thus it is brought prominently before us, that superstition's chief victims are those persons who greedily covet temporal advantages; they it is, who (especially when they are in danger, and cannot help themselves) are wont with prayers and womanish tears to implore help from God: upbraiding Reason as blind, because she cannot show a sure path to the shadows they pursue, and rejecting human wisdom as vain; but believing the phantoms of imagination, dreams, and other childish absurdities, to be the very oracles of Heaven. As though God had turned away from the wise, and written His decrees, not in the mind of man but in the entrails of beasts, or left them to be proclaimed by the inspiration and instinct of fools, madmen, and birds. Such is the unreason to which terror can drive mankind!

Superstition, then, is engendered, preserved, and fostered by fear. If anyone desire an example, let him take Alexander, who only began superstitiously to seek guidance from seers, when he first learnt to fear fortune in the passes of Sysis (Curtius, v. 4); whereas after he had conquered Darius he consulted prophets no more, till a second time frightened by reverses. When the Scythians were provoking a battle, the Bactrians had deserted, and he himself was lying sick of his wounds, "he once more turned to superstition, the mockery of human wisdom, and bade Aristander, to whom he confided his credulity, inquire the issue of affairs with sacrificed victims." Very numerous examples of a like nature might be cited, clearly showing the fact, that only while under the dominion of fear do men fall a prey to superstition; that all the portents ever invested with the reverence of misguided religion are mere phantoms of dejected and fearful minds; and lastly, that prophets have most power among the people, and are most formidable to rulers, precisely at those times when the state is in most peril. I think this is sufficiently plain to all, and will therefore say no more on the subject.

The origin of superstition above given affords us a clear reason for the fact, that it comes to all men naturally, though some refer its rise to a dim notion of God, universal to mankind, and also tends to show, that it is no less inconsistent and variable than other mental hallucinations and emotional impulses, and further that it can only be maintained by hope, hatred, anger, and deceit; since it springs, not from reason, but solely from the more powerful phases of emotion. Furthermore, we may readily understand how difficult it is, to maintain in the same course men prone to every form of credulity. For, as the mass of mankind remains always at about the same pitch of misery, it never assents long to any one remedy, but is always best pleased by a novelty, which has not yet proved illusive.

This element of inconsistency has been the cause of many terrible wars and revolutions; for, as Curtius well says (lib. iv. chap. 10): "The mob has no ruler more potent than superstition," and is easily led, on the plea of religion, at one moment to adore its kings as gods, and anon to execrate and abjure them as humanity's common bane. Immense pains have therefore been taken to counteract this evil by investing religion, whether true or false, with such pomp and ceremony, that it may rise superior to every shock, and be always observed with studious reverence by the whole people—a system which has been brought to great perfection by the Turks, for they consider even controversy impious, and so clog men's minds with dogmatic formulas, that they leave no room for sound reason, not even enough to doubt with.

But if, in despotic statecraft, the supreme and essential mystery be to hoodwink the subjects, and to mask the fear, which keeps them down, with the specious garb of religion, so that men may fight as bravely for slavery as for safety, and count it not shame but highest honour to risk their blood and their lives for the vainglory of a tyrant; yet in a free state no more mischievous expedient could be planned or attempted. Wholly repugnant to the general freedom are such devices as enthralling men's minds with prejudices, forcing their judgment, or employing any of the weapons of quasi-religious sedition; indeed, such seditions only spring up, when law enters the domain of speculative thought, and opinions are put on trial and condemned on the same footing as crimes, while those who defend and follow them are sacrificed, not to public safety, but to their opponents' hatred and cruelty. If deeds only could be made the grounds of criminal charges, and words were always allowed to pass free, such seditions would be divested of every semblance of justification, and would be separated from mere controversies by a hard and fast line.

Now, seeing that we have the rare happiness of living in a republic, where everyone's judgment is free and unshackled, where each may worship God as his conscience dictates, and where freedom is esteemed before all things dear and precious, I have believed that I should be undertaking no ungrateful or unprofitable task, in demonstrating that not only can such freedom be granted without prejudice to the public peace, but also, that without such freedom, piety cannot flourish nor the public peace be secure.

Such is the chief conclusion I seek to establish in this treatise; but, in order to reach it, I must first point out the misconceptions which, like scars of our former bondage, still disfigure our notion of religion, and must expose the false views about the civil authority which many have most impudently advocated, endeavouring to turn the mind of the people, still prone to heathen superstition, away from its legitimate rulers, and so bring us again into slavery. As to the order of my treatise I will speak presently, but first I will recount the causes, which led me to write.

I have often wondered, that persons who make a boast of professing the Christian religion, namely, love, joy, peace, temperance, and charity to all men, should quarrel with such rancorous animosity, and display daily towards one another such bitter hatred, that this, rather than the virtues they claim, is the readiest criterion of their faith. Matters have long since come to such a pass, that one can only pronounce a man Christian, Turk, Jew, or Heathen, by his general appearance and attire, by his frequenting this or that place of worship, or employing the phraseology of a particular sect—as for manner of life, it is in all cases the same. Inquiry into the cause of this anomaly leads me unhesitatingly to ascribe it to the fact, that the ministries of the Church are regarded by the masses merely as dignities, her offices as posts of emolument—in short, popular religion may be summed up as respect for ecclesiastics. The spread of this misconception inflamed every worthless fellow with an intense desire to enter holy orders, and thus the love of diffusing God's religion degenerated into sordid avarice and ambition. Every church became a theatre, where orators, instead of church teachers, harangued, caring not to instruct the people, but striving to attract admiration, to bring opponents to public scorn, and to preach only novelties and paradoxes, such as would tickle the ears of their congregation. This state of things necessarily stirred up an amount of controversy, envy, and hatred, which no lapse of time could appease; so that we can scarcely wonder that of the old religion nothing survives but its outward forms (even these, in the mouth of the multitude, seem rather adulation than adoration of the Deity), and that faith has become a mere compound of credulity and prejudices—aye, prejudices too, which degrade man from rational being to beast, which completely stifle the power of judgment between true and false, which seem, in fact, carefully fostered for the purpose of extinguishing the last spark of reason! Piety, great God! and religion are become a tissue of ridiculous mysteries; men, who flatly despise reason, who reject and turn away from understanding as naturally corrupt, these, I say, these of all men, are thought, O lie most horrible! to possess light from on High. Verily, if they had but one spark of light from on

High, they would not insolently rave, but would learn to worship God more wisely, and would be as marked among their fellows for mercy as they now are for malice; if they were concerned for their opponents' souls, instead of for their own reputations, they would no longer fiercely persecute, but rather be filled with pity and compassion.

Furthermore, if any Divine light were in them, it would appear from their doctrine. I grant that they are never tired of professing their wonder at the profound mysteries of Holy Writ; still I cannot discover that they teach anything but speculations of Platonists and Aristotelians, to which (in order to save their credit for Christianity) they have made Holy Writ conform; not content to rave with the Greeks themselves, they want to make the prophets rave also; showing conclusively, that never even in sleep have they caught a glimpse of Scripture's Divine nature. The very vehemence of their admiration for the mysteries plainly attests, that their belief in the Bible is a formal assent rather than a living faith: and the fact is made still more apparent by their laying down beforehand, as a foundation for the study and true interpretation of Scripture, the principle that it is in every passage true and divine. Such a doctrine should be reached only after strict scrutiny and thorough comprehension of the Sacred Books (which would teach it much better, for they stand in need of no human fictions), and not be set up on the threshold, as it were, of inquiry.

As I pondered over the facts that the light of reason is not only despised, but by many even execrated as a source of impiety, that human commentaries are accepted as divine records, and that credulity is extolled as faith; as I marked the fierce controversies of philosophers raging in Church and State, the source of bitter hatred and dissension, the ready instruments of sedition and other ills innumerable, I determined to examine the Bible afresh in a careful, impartial, and unfettered spirit, making no assumptions concerning it, and attributing to it no doctrines, which I do not find clearly therein set down. With these precautions I constructed a method of Scriptural interpretation, and thus equipped proceeded to inquire—What is prophecy? in what sense did God reveal Himself to the prophets, and why were these particular men chosen by Him? Was it on account of the sublimity of their thoughts about the Deity and nature, or was it solely on account of their piety? These questions being answered, I was easily able to conclude, that the authority of the prophets has weight only in matters of morality, and that their speculative doctrines affect us little.

5

The Natural History of Religion

DAVID HUME

Of the many distinguished thinkers of the eighteenth century Enlightenment, I have chosen the brilliant Scottish philosopher David Hume (1711–1776). He was less flamboyant in his criticism of religion than Baron d'Holbach or Edward Gibbon, with both of whom he was in contact, but his dry understatement and rigor are in many ways more persuasive. After his treatment, it was no longer possible to discuss miracles or the argument from so-called "design" with quite the same confidence as before.

In the first passage here, Hume shows the man-made origins of faith and its reliance upon superstition. In the second, he subjects miraculous claims to a commonsense interrogation that reveals their spurious nature.

It was an axiom among the faithful (and still is in some quarters) that atheists on their deathbeds would recant and call for a priest. Many false and cynical rumors of this kind were spread by the godly, about Thomas Paine in particular. We are extremely fortunate in having a firsthand account by the greatest of English biographers of David Hume's last hours.

Impious Conceptions of the Divine Nature in Popular Religions of Both Kinds

The primary religion of mankind arises chiefly from an anxious fear of future events; and what ideas will naturally be entertained of invisible, unknown powers, while men lie under dismal apprehensions of any kind, may easily be conceived. Every image of vengeance, severity, cruelty, and malice must occur, and must augment the ghastliness and horror, which oppresses the amazed religionist. A panic having once seized the mind, the active fancy still farther multiplies the objects of terror; while that profound darkness, or, what is worse, that glimmering light, with which we are environed, represents the spectres of divinity under the most dreadful appearances imaginable. And no idea of perverse wickedness can be framed, which those terrified devotees do not readily, without scruple, apply to their deity.

This appears the natural state of religion, when surveyed in one light. But if we consider, on the other hand, that spirit of praise and eulogy, which necessarily has place in all religions, and which is the consequence of these very terrors, we must expect a quite contrary system of theology to prevail. Every virtue, every excellence, must be ascribed to the divinity, and no exaggeration will be deemed sufficient to reach those perfections, with which he is endowed. Whatever strains of panegyric can be invented, are immediately embraced, without consulting any arguments of phænomena: It is esteemed a sufficient confirmation of them, that they give us more magnificent ideas of the divine objects of our worship and adoration.

Here therefore is a kind of contradiction between the different principles of human nature, which enter into religion. Our natural terrors present the notion of a devilish and malicious deity: Our propensity to adulation leads us to acknowledge an excellent and divine. And the influence of these opposite principles are various, according to the different situation of the human understanding. . . .

But as men farther exalt their idea of their divinity, it is their notion of his power and knowledge only, not of his goodness, which is improved. On the contrary, in proportion to the supposed extent of his science and authority, their terrors naturally augment; while they believe, that no secrecy can conceal them from his scrutiny, and that even the inmost recesses of their breast lie open before him. They must then be careful not to form expressly any sentiment of blame and disapprobation. All must be applause, ravishment, extacy. And while their gloomy apprehensions make them ascribe to him measures of conduct, which, in human creatures, would be highly blamed, they must still affect to praise and admire that conduct in the object of their devotional addresses. Thus it may safely be affirmed, that popular religions are really, in the conception of their more vulgar votaries, a species of dæmonism; and the higher the deity is exalted in power and knowledge, the lower of course is he depressed in goodness and benevolence; whatever epithets of praise may be bestowed on him by his amazed adorers. Among idolaters, the words may be false, and belie the secret opinion: But among more exalted religionists, the opinion itself contracts a kind of falsehood, and belies the inward sentiment. The heart secretly detests such measures of cruel and implacable vengeance; but the judgment dares not but pronounce them perfect and adorable. And the additional misery of this inward struggle aggravates all the other terrors, by which these unhappy victims to superstition are forever haunted.

Lucian[1] observes that a young man, who reads the history of the gods in Homer or Hesiod, and finds their factions, wars, injustice, incest, adultery, and other immoralities so highly celebrated, is much surprised afterwards, when he comes into the world, to observe that punishments are by law inflicted on the same actions, which he had been taught to ascribe to superior beings. The contradiction is still perhaps stronger between the representations given us by some later religions and our natural ideas of generosity, lenity, impartiality, and justice; and in proportion to the multiplied terrors of these religions, the barbarous conceptions of the divinity are multiplied upon us. Nothing can preserve untainted the genuine principles of morals in our judgment of human conduct, but the absolute necessity of these principles to the existence of society. If common conception can indulge princes in a system of ethics, somewhat different from that which should regulate private persons; how much more those superior beings, whose attributes, views, and nature are so totally unknown to us? *Sunt superis sua jura.*[2] The gods have maxims of justice peculiar to themselves.

Bad Influence of Popular Religions on Morality

Here I cannot forbear observing a fact, which may be worth the attention of such as make human nature the object of their enquiry. It is certain, that, in every religion, however sublime the verbal definition which it gives of its divinity, many of the votaries, perhaps the greatest number, will still seek the divine favor, not by virtue and good morals, which alone can be acceptable to a perfect being, but either by frivolous observances, by intemperate zeal, by rapturous extasies, or by the belief of mysterious and absurd opinions. The least part of the *Sadder,* as well as of the *Pentateuch,*[3] consists in precepts of morality; and we may also be assured, that that part was always the least observed and regarded. When the old Romans were attacked with a pestilence, they never ascribed their sufferings to their vices, or dreamed of repentance and amendment. They never thought, that they were the general robbers of the world, whose ambition and avarice made desolate the earth, and reduced opulent nations to want and beggary. They only created a

---

1. *Necyomantia,* 3. Lucian of Samosata (120?–180?), Syrian-born Greek satirist. The work referred to by Hume is more commonly known as *Menippus* or *The Descent into Hades.*

2. "The gods have their own laws." Ovid, *Metamorphoses* 9.499.

3. *Sadder* refers to the *Seder Eliyyahu,* a Jewish book of homilies written between the third and thenth centuries C.E. The Pentateuch is the first five books of the Old Testament.

dictator, in order to drive a nail into a door; and by that means, they thought that they had sufficiently appeased their incensed deity.

In Ægina, one faction forming a conspiracy, barbarously and treacherously assassinated seven hundred of their fellow-citizens; and carried their fury so far, that, one miserable fugitive having fled to the temple, they cut off his hands, by which he clung to the gates, and carrying him out of holy ground, immediately murdered him. *By this impiety,* says Herodotus, (not by the other many cruel assassinations) *they offended the gods, and contracted an inexpiable guilt.*

Nay, if we should suppose, what never happens, that a popular religion were found, in which it was expressly declared, that nothing but morality could gain the divine favor; if an order of priests were instituted to inculcate this opinion, in daily sermons, and with all the arts of persuasion; yet so inveterate are the people's prejudices, that, for want of some other superstition, they would make the very attendance on these sermons the essentials of religion, rather than place them in virtue and good morals. The sublime prologue of Zaleucus's[4] laws inspired not the Locrians, as far as we can learn, with any sounder notions of the measures of acceptance with the deity, than were familiar to the other Greeks.

This observation, then, holds universally: But still one may be at some loss to account for it. It is not sufficient to observe, that the people, everywhere, degrade their deities into a similitude with themselves, and consider them merely as a species of human creatures, somewhat more potent and intelligent. This will not remove the difficulty. For there is no *man* so stupid, as that, judging by his natural reason, he would not esteem virtue and honesty the most valuable qualities, which any person could possess. Why not ascribe the same sentiment to his deity? Why not make all religion, or the chief part of it, to consist in these attainments?

Nor is it satisfactory to say, that the practice of morality is more difficult than that of superstition; and is therefore rejected. For, not to mention the excessive penances of the *Brachmans* and *Talapoins*[5]; it is certain, that the *Rhamadan*[6] of the Turks, during which the poor wretches, for many days, often in the hottest months of the year, and in some of the hottest climates of the world, remain without eating or drinking from the rising to the setting sun; this *Rhamadan,* I say, must be more severe than the practice of any moral duty, even to the most vicious and depraved of mankind. The four Lents of the Muscovites, and the austerities of some *Roman Catholics,* appear more disagreeable than meekness

---

4. Zaleucus (fl. 550 B.C.E.), lawgiver of the Locrians and disciple of Pythagoras.

5. Brahmans or Brahmins are the priestly caste among the Hindus. Talapoins are Buddhist monks.

6. The ninth month of the lunar calendar, during which Muslims are to abstain from eating and drinking between sunrise and sunset.

and benevolence. In short, all virtue, when men are reconciled to it by ever so little practice, is agreeable: All superstition is forever odious and burthensome.

Perhaps, the following account may be received as a true solution of the difficulty. The duties, which a man performs as a friend or parent, do not seem
merely owing to his benefactor or children; nor can he be wanting to these duties, without breaking through all the ties of nature and morality. A strong inclination may prompt him to the performance: A sentiment of order and moral
obligation joins its force to these natural ties: And the whole man, if truly virtuous, is drawn to his duty, without any effort or endeavour. Even with regard to
the virtues, which are more austere, and more founded on reflection, such as
public spirit, filial duty, temperance, or integrity; the moral obligation, in our
apprehension, removes all pretension to religious merit; and the virtuous conduct is deemed no more than what we owe to society and to ourselves. In all
this, a superstitious man finds nothing, which he has properly performed for
the sake of his deity, or which can peculiarly recommend him to the divine favor
and protection. He considers not, that the most genuine method of serving the
divinity is by promoting the happiness of his creatures. He still looks out for
some immediate service of the supreme Being, in order to allay those terrors,
with which he is haunted. And any practice, recommended to him, which either
serves to no purpose in life, or offers the strongest violence to his natural inclinations; that practice he will the more readily embrace, on account of those very
circumstances, which should make him absolutely reject it. It seems the more
purely religious, because it proceeds from no mixture of any other motive or
consideration. And if, for its sake, he sacrifices much of his ease and quiet, his
claim of merit appears still to rise upon him, in proportion to the zeal and devotion, which he discovers. In restoring a loan, or paying a debt, his divinity is no-
wise beholden to him; because these acts of justice are what he was bound to
perform, and what many would have performed, were there no god in the universe. But if he fast a day, or give himself a sound whipping; this has a direct reference, in his opinion, to the service of God. No other motive could engage him
to such austerities. By these distinguished marks of devotion, he has now acquired the divine favor; and may expect, in recompense, protection, and safety
in this world, and eternal happiness in the next.

Hence the greatest crimes have been found, in many instances, compatible
with a superstitious piety and devotion; Hence, it is justly regarded as unsafe to
draw any certain inference in favor of a man's morals, from the fervour or strict-
ness of his religious exercises, even though he himself believe them sincere. Nay,
it has been observed, that enormities of the blackest dye have been rather apt to
produce superstitious terrors, and increase the religious passion. Bomilcar, having formed a conspiracy for assassinating at once the whole senate of Carthage,
and invading the liberties of his country, lost the opportunity, from a continual
regard to omens and prophecies.[7] *Those who undertake the most criminal and most*

dangerous enterprises are commonly the most superstitious; as an ancient historian re-marks on this occasion. Their devotion and spiritual faith rise with their fears. Catiline was not contented with the established deities and received rites of the national religion: His anxious terrors made him seek new inventions of this kind; which he never probably had dreamed of, had he remained a good citizen, and obedient to the laws of his country.[8]

To which we may add, that, after the commission of crimes, there arise re-morses and secret horrors, which give no rest to the mind, but make it have re-course to religious rites and ceremonies, as expiations of its offences. Whatever weakens or disorders the internal frame promotes the interests of superstition: And nothing is more destructive to them than a manly, steady virtue, which ei-ther preserves us from disastrous, melancholy accidents, or teaches us to bear them. During such calm sunshine of the mind, these spectres of false divinity never make their appearance. On the other hand, while we abandon ourselves to the natural undisciplined suggestions of our timid and anxious hearts, every kind of barbarity is ascribed to the supreme Being, from the terrors with which we are agitated; and every kind of caprice, from the methods which we embrace in order to appease him. *Barbarity, caprice;* these qualities, however nominally disguised, we may universally observe, form the ruling character of the deity in popular religions. Even priests, instead of correcting these depraved ideas of mankind, have often been found ready to foster and encourage them. The more tremendous the divinity is represented, the more tame and submissive do men become his ministers: And the more unaccountable the measures of acceptance required by him, the more necessary does it become to abandon our natural rea-son, and yield to their ghostly guidance and direction. Thus it may be allowed, that the artifices of men aggravate our natural infirmities and follies of this kind, but never originally beget them. Their root strikes deeper into the mind, and springs from the essential and universal properties of human nature.

.   .   .

---

7. Bomilcar or Bormilcar was a Carthaginian general (fl. 310 B.C.E.) who unsuccess-fully sought to become tyrant in Carthage.

8. L. Sergius Catilina (108–62 B.C.E.), Roman patrician who attempted to lead a revolt against the government. Cicero delivered four celebrated orations condemning him.

Of Miracles

From *An Enquiry Concerning Human Understanding*

DAVID HUME

Part One

1   There is, in Dr. Tillotson's writings, an argument against the *real presence*, which is as concise, and elegant, and strong as any argument can possibly be supposed against a doctrine, so little worthy of a serious refutation. It is acknowledged on all hands, says that learned prelate, that the authority, either of the scripture or of tradition, is founded merely in the testimony of the Apostles, who were eyewitnesses to those miracles of our Saviour, by which he proved his divine mission. Our evidence, then, for the truth of the Christian religion is less than the evidence for the truth of our senses; because, even in the first authors of our religion, it was no greater; and it is evident it must diminish in passing from them to their disciples; nor can any one rest such confidence in their testimony, as in the immediate object of his senses. But a weaker evidence can never destroy a stronger; and therefore, were the doctrine of the real presence ever so clearly revealed in scripture, it were directly contrary to the rules of just reasoning to give our assent to it. It contradicts sense, though both the scripture and tradition, on which it is supposed to be built, carry not such evidence with them as sense; when they are considered merely as external evidences, and are not brought home to every one's breast, by the immediate operation of the Holy Spirit.

2   Nothing is so convenient as a decisive argument of this kind, which must at least *silence* the most arrogant bigotry and superstition, and free us from their impertinent solicitations. I flatter myself, that I have discovered an argument of a like nature, which, if just, will, with the wise and learned, be an everlasting check to all kinds of superstitious delusion, and consequently, will be useful as long as the world endures. For so long, I presume, will the accounts of miracles and prodigies be found in all history, sacred and profane.

3   Though experience be our only guide in reasoning concerning matters of fact; it must be acknowledged, that this guide is not altogether infallible, but in some cases is apt to lead us into errors. One, who in our climate, should expect better weather in any week of June than in one of December, would reason justly, and conformably to experience; but it is certain, that he may happen, in the event, to find himself mistaken. However, we may observe, that, in such a case, he would have no cause to complain of experience; because it commonly informs us beforehand of the uncertainty, by that contrariety of events, which we may learn from a diligent observation. All effects follow not with like certainty from their supposed causes. Some events are found, in all countries and all ages, to have been constantly conjoined together: Others are found to have been more variable, and sometimes to disappoint our expectations; so that, in our reasonings concerning matter of fact, there are all imaginable degrees of assurance, from the highest certainty to the lowest species of moral evidence.

4   A wise man, therefore, proportions his belief to the evidence. In such conclusions as are founded on an infallible experience, he expects the event with the last degree of assurance, and regards his past experience as a full *proof* of the future existence of that event. In other cases, he proceeds with more caution. He weighs the opposite experiments: He considers which side is supported by the greater number of experiments: To that side he inclines, with doubt and hesitation; and when at last he fixes his judgment, the evidence exceeds not what we properly call *probability*. All probability, then, supposes an opposition of experiments and observations, where the one side is found to overbalance the other, and to produce a degree of evidence, proportioned to the superiority. A hundred instances or experiments on one side, and fifty on another, afford a doubtful expectation of any event; though a hundred uniform experiments, with only one that is contradictory, reasonably beget a pretty strong degree of assurance. In all cases, we must balance the opposite experiments, where they are opposite, and deduct the smaller number from the greater, in order to know the exact force of the superior evidence.

5   To apply these principles to a particular instance; we may observe, that there is no species of reasoning more common, more useful, and even necessary to human life, than that which is derived from the testimony of men, and the reports of eyewitnesses and spectators. This species of reasoning, perhaps, one may deny to be founded on the relation of cause and effect. I shall not dispute about a word. It will be sufficient to observe that our assurance in any argument of this kind is derived from no other principle than our observation of the veracity of human testimony, and of the usual conformity of facts to the reports of witnesses. It being a general maxim, that no objects have any discoverable connexion together, and that all the inferences, which we can draw from one to another, are founded merely on our experience of their constant and regular conjunction; it is evident, that we ought not to make an exception to this maxim in favour of human testimony, whose connexion with any event seems, in itself, as little necessary as any other. Were not the memory tenacious to a certain degree; had not men commonly an inclination to truth and a principle of probity; were they not sensible to shame, when detected in a falsehood: Were not these, I say, discovered by *experience* to be qualities, inherent in human nature, we should never repose the least confidence in human

testimony. A man delirious, or noted for falsehood and villainy, has no manner of authority with us.

6   And as the evidence, derived from witnesses and human testimony, is founded on past experience, so it varies with the experience, and is regarded either as a *proof* or a *probability,* according as the conjunction between any particular kind of report and any kind of object has been found to be constant or variable. There are a number of circumstances to be taken into consideration in all judgments of this kind; and the ultimate standard, by which we determine all disputes, that may arise concerning them, is always derived from experience and observation. Where this experience is not entirely uniform on any side, it is attended with an unavoidable contrariety in our judgments, and with the same opposition and mutual destruction of argument as in every other kind of evidence. We frequently hesitate concerning the reports of others. We balance the opposite circumstances, which cause any doubt or uncertainty; and when we discover a superiority on any side, we incline to it; but still with a diminution of assurance, in proportion to the force of its antagonist.

7   This contrariety of evidence, in the present case, may be derived from several different causes; from the opposition of contrary testimony; from the character or number of the witnesses; from the manner of their delivering their testimony; or from the union of all these circumstances. We entertain a suspicion concerning any matter of fact, when the witnesses contradict each other; when they are but few, or of a doubtful character; when they have an interest in what they affirm; when they deliver their testimony with hesitation, or on the contrary, with too violent asseverations. There are many other particulars of the same kind, which may diminish or destroy the force of any argument, derived from human testimony.

8   Suppose, for instance, that the fact, which the testimony endeavours to establish, partakes of the extraordinary and the marvellous; in that case, the evidence, resulting from the testimony, admits of a diminution, greater or less, in proportion as the fact is more or less unusual. The reason why we place any credit in witnesses and historians, is not derived from any *connexion,* which we perceive *a priori,* between testimony and reality, but because we are accustomed to find a conformity between them. But when the fact attested is such a one as has seldom fallen under our observation, here is a contest of two opposite experiences; of which the one destroys the other, as far as its force goes, and the superior can only operate on the mind by the force, which remains. The very same principle of experience, which gives us a certain degree of assurance in the testimony of witnesses, gives us also, in this case, another degree of assurance against the fact, which they endeavour to establish; from which contradiction there necessarily arises a counterpoise, and mutual destruction of belief and authority.

9   *I should not believe such a story were it told me by Cato,* was a proverbial saving in Rome, even during the lifetime of that philosophical patriot. The incredibility of a fact, it was allowed, might invalidate so great an authority.

10   The Indian prince, who refused to believe the first relations concerning the effects of frost, reasoned justly; and it naturally required very strong testimony to engage his assent to facts, that arose from a state of nature, with which he was unacquainted, and which bore so little analogy to those events, of which he had had constant and uniform experience. Though they were not contrary to his experience, they were not conformable to it.

11   But in order to increase the probability against the testimony of witnesses, let us suppose, that the fact, which they affirm, instead of being only marvelous, is really miraculous; and suppose also, that the testimony considered apart and in itself, amounts to an entire proof; in that case, there is proof against proof, of which the strongest must prevail, but still with a diminution of its force in proportion to that of its antagonist.

12   A miracle is a violation of the laws of nature; and as a firm and unalterable experience has established these laws, the proof against a miracle, from the very nature of the fact, is as entire as any argument from experience can possibly be imagined. Why is it more than probable, that all men must die; that lead cannot, of itself, remain suspended in the air; that fire consumes wood, and is extinguished by water; unless it be, that these events are found agreeable to the laws of nature, and there is required a violation of these laws, or in other words, a miracle to prevent them? Nothing is esteemed a miracle, if it ever happen in the common course of nature. It is no miracle that a man, seemingly in good health, should die on a sudden; because such a kind of death, though more unusual than any other, has yet been frequently observed to happen. But it is a miracle, that a dead man should come to life; because that has never been observed in any age or country. There must, therefore, be a uniform experience against every miraculous event, otherwise the event would not merit that appellation. And as a uniform experience amounts to a proof, there is here a direct and full *proof*, from the nature of the fact, against the existence of any miracle; nor can such a proof be destroyed, or the miracle rendered credible, but by an opposite proof, which is superior.

13   The plain consequence is (and it is a general maxim worthy of our attention), "That no testimony is sufficient to establish a miracle, unless the testimony be of such a kind, that its falsehood would be more miraculous, than the fact, which it endeavours to establish: And even in that case there is a mutual destruction of arguments, and the superior only gives us an assurance suitable to that degree of force, which remains, after deducting the inferior." When anyone tells me, that he saw a dead man restored to life, I immediately consider with myself, whether it be more probable, that this person should either deceive or be deceived, or that the fact, which he relates, should really have happened. I weigh the one miracle against the other; and according to the superiority, which I discover, I pronounce my decision, and always reject the greater miracle. If the falsehood of his testimony would be more miraculous, than the event which he relates; then, and not till then, can he pretend to command my belief or opinion.

Part 2

14   In the foregoing reasoning we have supposed, that the testimony, upon which a miracle is founded, may possibly amount to an entire proof, and that the falsehood of that testimony would be a real prodigy: But it is easy to show, that we have been a great deal too liberal in our concession, and that there never was a miraculous event established on so full an evidence.

15   For *first*, there is not to be found, in all history, any miracle attested by a sufficient number of men, of such unquestioned good sense, education, and learning, as to secure us against all delusion in themselves; of such undoubted integrity, as to place them beyond all suspicion of any design to deceive others; of such credit and reputation in the eyes of mankind, as to have a great deal to lose in case of their being detected in any falsehood; and at the same time, attesting facts performed in such a public manner and in so celebrated a part of the world, as to render the detection unavoidable: All which circumstances are requisite to give us a full assurance in the testimony of men.

16   *Secondly*, we may observe in human nature a principle which, if strictly examined, will be found to diminish extremely the assurance, which we might, from human testimony, have in any kind of prodigy. The maxim, by which we commonly conduct ourselves in our reasonings, is, that the objects, of which we have no experience, resemble those, of which we have; that what we have found to be most usual is always most probable; and that where there is an opposition of arguments, we ought to give the preference to such as are founded on the greatest number of past observations. But though, in proceeding by this rule, we readily reject any fact which is unusual and incredible in an ordinary degree; yet in advancing farther, the mind observes not always the same rule; but when anything is affirmed utterly absurd and miraculous, it rather the more readily admits of such a fact, upon account of that very circumstance, which ought to destroy all its authority. The passion of *surprise* and *wonder*, arising from miracles, being an agreeable emotion, gives a sensible tendency towards the belief of those events, from which it is derived. And this goes so far, that even those who cannot enjoy this pleasure immediately, nor can believe those miraculous events, of which they are informed, yet love to partake of the satisfaction at secondhand or by rebound, and place a pride and delight in exciting the admiration of others.

17   With what greediness are the miraculous accounts of travelers received, their descriptions of sea and land monsters, their relations of wonderful adventures, strange men, and uncouth manners? But if the spirit of religion join itself to the love of wonder, there is an end of common sense; and human testimony, in these circumstances, loses all pretensions to authority. A religionist may be an enthusiast, and imagine he sees what has no reality: He may know his narrative to be false, and yet persevere in it, with the best intentions in the world, for the sake of promoting so holy a cause: Or even where this delusion has not place, vanity, excited by so strong a temptation, operates on him more powerfully than on the rest of mankind in any other circumstances; and self-interest with equal force. His auditors may not have, and commonly have not, sufficient judgment to canvass his evidence: What judgment they have, they renounce by principle, in these sublime and mysterious subjects: Or if they were ever so willing to employ it, passion and a heated imagination disturb the regularity of its operations. Their credulity increases his impudence: And his impudence overpowers their credulity.

18   Eloquence, when at its highest pitch, leaves little room for reason or reflection; but addressing itself entirely to the fancy or the affections, captivates the willing hearers, and subdues their understanding. Happily, this pitch it seldom attains. But what a Tully or a Demosthenes could scarcely effect over a Roman or Athenian audience, every Capuchin, every itinerant or stationary teacher can perform over the generality of mankind, and in a higher degree, by touching such gross and vulgar passions.

19   The many instances of forged miracles, and prophecies, and supernatural events, which, in all ages, have either been detected by contrary evidence, or which detect themselves by their absurdity, prove sufficiently the strong propensity of mankind to the extraordinary and the marvellous, and ought reasonably to beget a suspicion against all relations of this kind. This is our natural way of thinking, even with regard to the most common and most credible events. For instance: There is no kind of report which rises so easily, and spreads so quickly, especially in country places and provincial towns, as those concerning marriages; insomuch that two young persons of equal condition never see each other twice, but the whole neighbourhood immediately join them together. The pleasure of telling a piece of news so interesting, of propagating it, and of being the first reporters of it, spreads the intelligence. And this is so well known, that no man of sense gives attention to these reports, till he find them confirmed by some greater evidence. Do not the same passions, and others still stronger, incline the generality of mankind to believe and report, with the greatest vehemence and assurance, all religious miracles?

20   *Thirdly,* It forms a strong presumption against all supernatural and miraculous relations, that they are observed chiefly to abound among ignorant and barbarous nations; or if a civilized people has ever given admission to any of

them, that people will be found to have received them from ignorant and barbarous ancestors, who transmitted them with that inviolable sanction and authority, which always attend received opinions. When we peruse the first
histories of all nations, we are apt to imagine ourselves transported into some
new world; where the whole frame of nature is disjointed, and every element performs its operations in a different manner, from what it does at present. Battles,
revolutions, pestilence, famine and death, are never the effect of those natural
causes, which we experience. Prodigies, omens, oracles, judgments, quite obscure
the few natural events that are intermingled with them. But as the former grow
thinner every page, in proportion as we advance nearer the enlightened ages, we
soon learn, that there is nothing mysterious or supernatural in the case, but that
all proceeds from the usual propensity of mankind towards the marvelous, and
that, though this inclination may at intervals receive a check from sense and
learning, it can never be thoroughly extirpated from human nature.

21   *It is strange,* a judicious reader is apt to say, upon the perusal of these
wonderful historians, *that such prodigious events never happen in our days.* But it is
nothing strange, I hope, that men should lie in all ages. You must surely have
seen instances enough of that frailty. You have yourself heard many such marvellous relations started, which, being treated with scorn by all the wise and judicious, have at last been abandoned even by the vulgar. Be assured, that those
renowned lies, which have spread and flourished to such a monstrous height,
arose from like beginnings; but being sown in a more proper soil, shot up at last
into prodigies almost equal to those which they relate.

22   It was a wise policy in that false prophet, Alexander, who though
now forgotten, was once so famous, to lay the first scene of his impostures in
Paphlagonia, where, as Lucian tells us, the people were extremely ignorant and
stupid, and ready to swallow even the grossest delusion. People at a distance,
who are weak enough to think the matter at all worth enquiry, have no opportunity of receiving better information. The stories come magnified to them by
a hundred circumstances. Fools are industrious in propagating the imposture;
while the wise and learned are contented, in general, to deride its absurdity,
without informing themselves of the particular facts, by which it may be distinctly refuted. And thus the impostor above mentioned was enabled to proceed, from his ignorant Paphlagonians, to the enlisting of votaries, even among
the Grecian philosophers, and men of the most eminent rank and distinction
in Rome; nay, could engage the attention of that sage emperor Marcus Aurelius; so far as to make him trust the success of a military expedition to his delusive prophecies.

23   The advantages are so great, of starting an imposture among an ignorant people, that, even though the delusion should be too gross to impose on
the generality of them *(which, though seldom, is sometimes the case)* it has a much
better chance for succeeding in remote countries, than if the first scene had
been laid in a city renowned for arts and knowledge. The most ignorant and

barbarous of these barbarians carry the report abroad. None of their country-men have a large correspondence, or sufficient credit and authority to contra-dict and beat down the delusion. Men's inclination to the marvellous has full opportunity to display itself. And thus a story, which is universally exploded in the place where it was first started, shall pass for certain at a thousand miles dis-tance. But had Alexander fixed his residence at Athens, the philosophers of that renowned mart of learning had immediately spread, throughout the whole Ro-man empire, their sense of the matter; which, being supported by so great au-thority, and displayed by all the force of reason and eloquence, had entirely opened the eyes of mankind. It is true; Lucian, passing by chance through Pa-phlagonia, had an opportunity of performing this good office. But, though much to be wished, it does not always happen, that every Alexander meets with a Lucian, ready to expose and detect his impostures.

24   I may add as a *fourth* reason, which diminishes the authority of prodigies, that there is no testimony for any, even those which have not been ex-pressly detected, that is not opposed by an infinite number of witnesses; so that not only the miracle destroys the credit of testimony, but the testimony destroys itself. To make this the better understood, let us consider, that, in matters of re-ligion, whatever is different is contrary; and that it is impossible the religions of ancient Rome, of Turkey, of Siam, and of China should, all of them, be estab-lished on any solid foundation. Every miracle, therefore, pretended to have been wrought in any of these religions (and all of them abound in miracles), as its di-rect scope is to establish the particular system to which it is attributed; so has it the same force, though more indirectly, to overthrow every other system. In de-stroying a rival system, it likewise destroys the credit of those miracles, on which that system was established; so that all the prodigies of different religions are to be regarded as contrary facts, and the evidences of these prodigies, whether weak or strong, as opposite to each other. According to this method of reason-ing, when we believe any miracle of Mahomet or his successors, we have for our warrant the testimony of a few barbarous Arabians: And on the other hand, we are to regard the authority of Titus Livius, Plutarch, Tacitus, and, in short, of all the authors and witnesses, Grecian, Chinese, and Roman Catholic, who have re-lated any miracle in their particular religion; I say, we are to regard their testi-mony in the same light as if they had mentioned that Mahometan miracle, and had in express terms contradicted it, with the same certainty as they have for the miracle they relate. This argument may appear over subtle and refined; but is not in reality different from the reasoning of a judge, who supposes, that the credit of two witnesses, maintaining a crime against any one, is destroyed by the testimony of two others, who affirm him to have been two hundred leagues dis-tant, at the same instant when the crime is said to have been committed.

25   One of the best attested miracles in all profane history, is that which Tacitus reports of Vespasian, who cured a blind man in Alexandria, by means of his spittle, and a lame man by the mere touch of his foot; in obedience to a

vision of the god Serapis, who had enjoined them to have recourse to the Emperor, for these miraculous cures. The story may be seen in that fine historian where every circumstance seems to add weight to the testimony, and might be displayed at large with all the force of argument and eloquence, if any one were now concerned to enforce the evidence of that exploded and idolatrous superstition. The gravity, solidity, age, and probity of so great an emperor, who, through the whole course of his life, conversed in a familiar manner with his friends and courtiers, and never affected those extraordinary airs of divinity assumed by Alexander and Demetrius. The historian, a contemporary writer, noted for candour and veracity, and withal, the greatest and most penetrating genius, perhaps, of all antiquity; and so free from any tendency to credulity, that he even lies under the contrary imputation, of atheism and profaneness: The persons, from whose authority he related the miracle, of established character for judgment and veracity, as we may well presume; eyewitnesses of the fact, and confirming their testimony, after the Flavian family was despoiled of the empire, and could no longer give any reward, as the price of a lie. *Utrumque, qui interfuere, nunc quoque memorant, postquam nullum mendacio pretium.* To which if we add the public nature of the facts, as related, it will appear, that no evidence can well be supposed stronger for so gross and so palpable a falsehood.

26   There is also a memorable story related by Cardinal de Retz, which may well deserve our consideration. When that intriguing politician fled into Spain, to avoid the persecution of his enemies, he passed through Saragossa, the capital of Aragon, where he was shown, in the cathedral, a man, who had served seven years as a doorkeeper, and was well known to every body in town, that had ever paid his devotions at that church. He had been seen, for so long a time, wanting a leg; but recovered that limb by the rubbing of holy oil upon the stump; and the cardinal assures us that he saw him with two legs. This miracle was vouched by all the canons of the church; and the whole company in town were appealed to for a confirmation of the fact; that the cardinal found, by their zealous devotion, to be thorough believers of the miracle. Here the relater was also contemporary to the supposed prodigy, of an incredulous and libertine character, as well as of great genius; the miracle of so *singular* a nature as could scarcely admit of a counterfeit, and the witnesses very numerous, and all of them, in a manner, spectators of the fact, to which they gave their testimony. And what adds mightily to the force of the evidence, and may double our surprise on this occasion, is, that the cardinal himself, who relates the story, seems not to give any credit to it, and consequently cannot be suspected of any concurrence in the holy fraud. He considered justly, that it was not requisite, in order to reject a fact of this nature, to be able accurately to disprove the testimony, and to trace its falsehood, through all the circumstances of knavery and credulity which produced it. He knew, that, as this was commonly altogether impossible at any small distance of time and place; so was it extremely difficult, even where one was immediately present, by reason of the bigotry, ignorance,

cunning, and roguery of a great part of mankind. He therefore concluded, like a just reasoner, that such an evidence carried falsehood upon the very face of it, and that a miracle, supported by any human testimony, was more properly a subject of derision than of argument.

27   There surely never was a greater number of miracles ascribed to one person, than those, which were lately said to have been wrought in France upon the tomb of Abbé Paris, the famous Jansenist, with whose sanctity the people were so long deluded. The curing of the sick, giving hearing to the deaf, and sight to the blind, were everywhere talked of as the usual effects of that holy sepulchre. But what is more extraordinary; many of the miracles were immediately proved upon the spot, before judges of unquestioned integrity, attested by witnesses of credit and distinction, in a learned age, and on the most eminent theatre that is now in the world. Nor is this all: A relation of them was published and dispersed everywhere; nor were the Jesuits, though a learned body, supported by the civil magistrate, and determined enemies to those opinions, in whose favour the miracles were said to have been wrought, ever able distinctly to refute or detect them. Where shall we find such a number of circumstances, agreeing to the corroboration of one fact? And what have we to oppose to such a cloud of witnesses, but the absolute impossibility or miraculous nature of the events, which they relate? And this surely, in the eyes of all reasonable people, will alone be regarded as a sufficient refutation.

28   Is the consequence just, because some human testimony has the utmost force and authority in some cases, when it relates the battle of Philippi or Pharsalia for instance; that therefore all kinds of testimony must, in all cases, have equal force and authority? Suppose that the Caesarean and Pompeian factions had, each of them, claimed the victory in these battles, and that the historians of each party had uniformly ascribed the advantage to their own side; how could mankind, at this distance, have been able to determine between them? The contrariety is equally strong between the miracles related by Herodotus or Plutarch, and those delivered by Mariana, Bede, or any monkish historian.

29   The wise lend a very academic faith to every report which favours the passion of the reporter; whether it magnifies his country, his family, or himself, or in any other way strikes in with his natural inclinations and propensities. But what greater temptation than to appear a missionary, a prophet, an ambassador from heaven? Who would not encounter many dangers and difficulties, in order to attain so sublime a character? Or if, by the help of vanity and a heated imagination, a man has first made a convert of himself, and entered seriously into the delusion; who ever scruples to make use of pious frauds, in support of so holy and meritorious a cause?

30   The smallest spark may here kindle into the greatest flame; because the materials are always prepared for it. The *avidum genus auricularum*, the gazing populace, receive greedily, without examination, whatever sooths superstition, and promotes wonder.

31   How many stories of this nature have, in all ages, been detected and exploded in their infancy? How many more have been celebrated for a time, and have afterwards sunk into neglect and oblivion? Where such reports, therefore, fly about, the solution of the phenomenon is obvious; and we judge in conformity to regular experience and observation, when we account for it by the known and natural principles of credulity and delusion. And shall we, rather than have recourse to so natural a solution, allow of a miraculous violation of the most established laws of nature?

32   I need not mention the difficulty of detecting a falsehood in any private or even public history, at the place, where it is said to happen; much more when the scene is removed to ever so small a distance. Even a court of judicature, with all the authority, accuracy, and judgment, which they can employ, find themselves often at a loss to distinguish between truth and falsehood in the most recent actions. But the matter never comes to any issue, if trusted to the common method of altercations and debate and flying rumours; especially when men's passions have taken part on either side.

33   In the infancy of new religions, the wise and learned commonly esteem the matter too inconsiderable to deserve their attention or regard. And when afterwards they would willingly detect the cheat in order to undeceive the deluded multitude, the season is now past, and the records and witnesses, which might clear up the matter, have perished beyond recovery.

34   No means of detection remain, but those which must be drawn from the very testimony itself of the reporters: And these, though always sufficient with the judicious and knowing, are commonly too fine to fall under the comprehension of the vulgar.

35   Upon the whole, then, it appears, that no testimony for any kind of miracle has ever amounted to a probability, much less to a proof; and that, even supposing it amounted to a proof, it would be opposed by another proof; derived from the very nature of the fact, which it would endeavour to establish. It is experience only, which gives authority to human testimony; and it is the same experience, which assures us of the laws of nature. When, therefore, these two kinds of experience are contrary, we have nothing to do but subtract the one from the other, and embrace an opinion, either on one side, or the other, with that assurance which arises from the remainder. But according to the principle here explained, this subtraction, with regard to all popular religions, amounts to an entire annihilation; and therefore we may establish it as a maxim, that no human testimony can have such force as to prove a miracle, and make it a just foundation for any such system of religion.

36   I beg the limitations here made may be remarked, when I say, that a miracle can never be proved, so as to be the foundation of a system of religion. For I own, that otherwise, there may possibly be miracles, or violations of the usual course of nature, of such a kind as to admit of proof from human testimony; though, perhaps, it will be impossible to find any such in all the records

of history. Thus, suppose, all authors, in all languages, agree, that, from the first of January 1600, there was a total darkness over the whole earth for eight days: Suppose that the tradition of this extraordinary event is still strong and lively among the people: That all travelers, who return from foreign countries, bring us accounts of the same tradition, without the least variation or contradiction: It is evident that our present philosophers, instead of doubting the fact, ought to receive it as certain, and ought to search for the causes whence it might be derived. The decay, corruption, and dissolution of nature, is an event rendered probable by so many analogies, that any phenomenon, which seems to have a tendency towards that catastrophe, comes within the reach of human testimony, if that testimony be very extensive and uniform.

37   But suppose, that all the historians who treat of England, should agree, that, on the first of January 1600, Queen Elizabeth died; that both before and after her death she was seen by her physicians and the whole court, as is usual with persons of her rank; that her successor was acknowledged and proclaimed by the parliament; and that, after being interred a month, she again appeared, resumed the throne, and governed England for three years: I must confess that I should be surprised at the concurrence of so many odd circumstances, but should not have the least inclination to believe so miraculous an event. I should not doubt of her pretended death, and of those other public circumstances that followed it: I should only assert it to have been pretended, and that it neither was, nor possibly could be real. You would in vain object to me the difficulty, and almost impossibility of deceiving the world in an affair of such consequence; the wisdom and solid judgment of that renowned queen; with the little or no advantage which she could reap from so poor an artifice: All this might astonish me; but I would still reply, that the knavery and folly of men are such common phenomena, that I should rather believe the most extraordinary events to arise from their concurrence, than admit of so signal a violation of the laws of nature.

38   But should this miracle be ascribed to any new system of religion; men, in all ages, have been so much imposed on by ridiculous stories of that kind, that this very circumstance would be a full proof of a cheat, and sufficient, with all men of sense, not only to make them reject the fact, but even reject it without farther examination. Though the Being to whom the miracle is ascribed, be, in this case, Almighty, it does not, upon that account, become a whit more probable; since it is impossible for us to know the attributes or actions of such a Being, otherwise than from the experience which we have of his productions, in the usual course of nature. This still reduces us to past observation, and obliges us to compare the instances of the violation of truth in the testimony of men, with those of the violation of the laws of nature by miracles, in order to judge which of them is most likely and probable. As the violations of truth are more common in the testimony concerning religious miracles, than in that concerning any other matter of fact; this must diminish very much the

authority of the former testimony, and make us form a general resolution, never to lend any attention to it, with whatever specious pretence it may be covered.

39   Lord Bacon seems to have embraced the same principles of reasoning. "We ought," says he, "to make a collection or particular history of all monsters and prodigious births or productions, and in a word of every thing new, rare, and extraordinary in nature. But this must be done with the most severe scrutiny, lest we depart from truth. Above all, every relation must be considered as suspicious, which depends in any degree upon religion, as the prodigies of Livy: And no less so, everything that is to be found in the writers of natural magic or alchemy, or such authors, who seem, all of them, to have an unconquerable appetite for falsehood and fable."

40   I am the better pleased with the method of reasoning here delivered, as I think it may serve to confound those dangerous friends or disguised enemies to the Christian religion, who have undertaken to defend it by the principles of human reason. Our most holy religion is founded on *faith*, not on reason; and it is a sure method of exposing it to put it to such a trial, as it is, by no means, fitted to endure. To make this more evident, let us examine those miracles, related in scripture; and not to lose ourselves in too wide a field, let us confine ourselves to such as we find in the *Pentateuch*, which we shall examine, according to the principles of these pretended Christians, not as the word or testimony of God himself, but as the production of a mere human writer and historian. Here then we are first to consider a book, presented to us by a barbarous and ignorant people, written in an age when they were still more barbarous, and in all probability long after the facts which it relates, corroborated by no concurring testimony, and resembling those fabulous accounts, which every nation gives of its origin. Upon reading this book, we find it full of prodigies and miracles. It gives an account of a state of the world and of human nature entirely different from the present: Of our fall from that state: Of the age of man, extended to near a thousand years: Of the destruction of the world by a deluge: Of the arbitrary choice of one people, as the favourites of heaven; and that people the countrymen of the author: Of their deliverance from bondage by prodigies the most astonishing imaginable: I desire any one to lay his hand upon his heart, and after a serious consideration declare, whether he thinks that the falsehood of such a book, supported by such a testimony, would be more extraordinary and miraculous than all the miracles it relates; which is, however, necessary to make it be received, according to the measures of probability above established.

41   What we have said of miracles may be applied, without any variation, to prophecies; and indeed, all prophecies are real miracles, and as such only, can be admitted as proofs of any revelation. If it did not exceed the capacity of human nature to foretell future events, it would be absurd to employ any prophecy as an argument for a divine mission or authority from heaven. So that, upon the whole, we may conclude, that the Christian religion not only was at first attended with miracles, but even at this day cannot be believed by any reasonable person without one. Mere reason is insufficient to convince us of its veracity: And whoever is moved by *faith* to assent to it, is conscious of a continued miracle in his own person, which subverts all the principles of his understanding, and gives him a determination to believe what is most contrary to custom and experience.

6

An Account of
My Last Interview With
David Hume, Esq.

*[Partly recorded in my Journal,
partly enlarged from my memory, 3 March 1777.]*

JAMES BOSWELL

**James Boswell was reluctant to believe in Hume's stoicism, which is
what helps lend the account its authenticity. Hume died just as the
American Revolution—which he had foreseen and supported—was
breaking out. His own views had a marked effect on many of those
who signed the Declaration of Independence.**

On Sunday forenoon the 7 of July 1776, being too late for church, I went to see
Mr. David Hume, who was returned from London and Bath, just a-dying. I
found him alone, in a reclining posture in his drawing room. He was lean,
ghastly, and quite of an earthy appearance. He was dressed in a suit of grey cloth
with white metal buttons, and a kind of scratch wig. He was quite different
from the plump figure, which he used to present. He had before him Dr. Camp-
bell's *Philosophy of Rhetoric*. He seemed to be placid and even cheerful. He said he
was just approaching to his end. I think these were his words. I know not how I
contrived to get the subject of immortality introduced. He said he never had entertained any belief in religion since he began to read Locke and Clarke. I asked
him if he was not religious when he was young. He said he was, and he used to
read *The Whole Duty of Man*; that he made an abstract from the catalogue of vices
at the end of it, and examined himself by this, leaving out murder and theft and
such vices as he had no chance of committing, having no inclination to commit
them. This, he said, was strange work; for instance, to try if, notwithstanding
his excelling his schoolfellows, he had no pride or vanity. He smiled in ridicule
of this as absurd and contrary to fixed principles and necessary consequences,
not adverting that religious discipline does not mean to extinguish, but to moderate, the passions; and certainly an excess of pride or vanity is dangerous and

generally hurtful. He then said flatly that the morality of every religion was bad, and, I really thought, was not jocular when he said that when he heard a man was religious, he concluded he was a rascal, though he had known some instances of very good men being religious. This was just an extravagant reverse of the common remark as to infidels.

I had a strong curiosity to be satisfied if he persisted in disbelieving a future state even when he had death before his eyes. I was persuaded from what he now said, and from his manner of saying it, that he did persist. I asked him if it was not possible that there might be a future state. He answered it was possible that a piece of coal put upon the fire would not burn; and he added that it was a most unreasonable fancy that we should exist forever. That immortality, if it were at all, must be general; that a great proportion of the human race has hardly any intellectual qualities, that a great proportion dies in infancy before being possessed of reason; yet all these must be immortal; that a porter who gets drunk by ten o'clock with gin must be immortal; that the trash of every age must be preserved, and that new universes must be created to contain such infinite numbers. This appeared to me an unphilosophical objection, and I said, "Mr. Hume, you know spirit does not take up space."

I may illustrate what he last said by mentioning that in a former conversation with me on this subject he used pretty much the same mode of reasoning, and urged that Wilkes and his mob must be immortal. One night last May as I was coming up King Street, Westminster, I met Wilkes, who carried me into Parliament Street to see a curious procession pass: the funeral of a lamplighter attended by some hundreds of his fraternity with torches. Wilkes, who either is, or affects to be, an infidel, was rattling away, "I think there's an end of that fellow. I think he won't rise again." I very calmly said to him, "You bring into my mind the strongest argument that ever I heard against a future state"; and then told him David Hume's objection that Wilkes and his mob must be immortal. It seemed to make a proper impression, for he grinned abashment, as a Negro grows whiter when he blushes. But to return to my last interview with Mr. Hume.

I asked him if the thought of annihilation never gave him any uneasiness. He said not the least; no more than the thought that he had not been, as Lucretius observes. "Well," said I, "Mr. Hume, I hope to triumph over you when I meet you in a future state; and remember you are not to pretend that you was joking with all this infidelity." "No, no," said he. "But I shall have been so long there before you come that it will be nothing new." In this style of good humour and levity did I conduct the conversation. Perhaps it was wrong on so awful a subject. But as nobody was present, I thought it could have no bad effect. I however felt a degree of horror, mixed with a sort of wild, strange, hurrying recollection of my excellent mother's pious instructions, of Dr. Johnson's noble lessons, and of my religious sentiments and affections during the course of my life. I was like a man in sudden danger eagerly seeking his defensive arms; and I could not but be assailed by momentary doubts while I had actually before me a man of such strong abilities and extensive inquiry dying in the persuasion of being annihilated. But I maintained my faith. I told him that I believed the Christian religion as I believed history. Said he: "You do not believe it as you believe the Revolution." "Yes," said I, "but the difference is that I am not so much interested in the truth of the Revolution; otherwise I should have anxious doubts concerning it. A man who is in love has doubts of the affection of his mistress, without cause." I mentioned Soame Jenyns's little book in defense of Christianity, which was just published but which I had not yet read. Mr. Hume said, "I am told there is nothing of his usual spirit in it."

He had once said to me, on a forenoon while the sun was shining bright, that he did not wish to be immortal. This was a most wonderful thought. The reason he gave was that he was very well in this state of being, and that the chances were very much against his being so well in another state; and he would rather not be more than be worse. I answered that it was reasonable to hope he would be better; that there would be a progressive improvement. I tried him at this interview with that topic, saying that a future state was surely a pleasing idea. He said no, for that it was always seen through a gloomy medium; there was always a Phlegethon or a hell. "But," said I, "would it not be agreeable to have hopes of seeing our friends again?" and I mentioned three men lately deceased, for whom I knew he had a high value: Ambassador Keith, Lord Alemoor, and Baron Mure. He owned it would be agreeable, but added that none of them entertained such a notion. I believe he said, such a foolish, or such an absurd, notion; for he was indecently and impolitely positive in incredulity. "Yes," said I, "Lord Alemoor was a believer." David acknowledged that *he* had *some* belief.

I somehow or other brought Dr. Johnson's name into our conversation. I had often heard him speak of that great man in a very illiberal manner. He said upon this occasion, "Johnson should be pleased with my *History.*" Nettled by Hume's frequent attacks upon my revered friend in former conversations, I told him now that Dr. Johnson did not allow him much credit; for he said, "Sir, the fellow is a Tory by chance." I am sorry that I mentioned this at such a time. I was off my guard; for the truth is that Mr. Hume's pleasantry was such that there was no solemnity in the scene; and death for the time did not seem dismal. It surprised me to find him talking of different matters with a tranquility of mind and a clearness of head, which few men possess at any time. Two particulars I remember: Smith's *Wealth of Nations,* which he commended much, and Monboddo's *Origin of Language,* which he treated contemptuously. I said, "If I were you, I should regret annihilation. Had I written such an admirable history I should be sorry to leave it." He said, "I shall leave that history, of which you are pleased to speak so favourably, as perfect as I can." He said, too, that all the great abilities with which men had ever been endowed were relative to this world. He said he became a greater friend to the Stuart family as he advanced in studying for his history; and he hoped he had vindicated the two first of them so effectually that they would never again be attacked.

Mr. Lauder, his surgeon, came in for a little, and Mr. Mure, the Baron's son, for another small interval. He was, as far as I could judge, quite easy with both. He said he had no pain, but was wasting away. I left him with impressions that disturbed me for some time.

(Additions from memory, January 22, 1778.) Speaking of his singular notion that men of religion were generally bad men, he said, "One of the men" (or "The man"—I am not sure which) "of the greatest honour that I ever knew is my Lord Marischal, who is a downright atheist. I remember I once hinted something as if I believed in the being of a God, and he would not speak to me for a week." He said this with his usual grunting pleasantry, with that thick breath which fatness had rendered habitual to him, and that smile of simplicity, which his good humour constantly produced.

When he spoke against Monboddo, I told him that Monboddo said to me that he believed the abusive criticism upon his book in *The Edinburgh Magazine and Review* was written by Mr. Hume's direction. David seemed irritated, and said, "Does the *scoundrel*" (I am sure either *that* or "*rascal*") "say so?" He then told me that he had observed to one of the Faculty of Advocates that Monboddo was wrong in his observation that   and gave as a proof the line in Milton. When the review came out, he found this very remark in it, and said to that advocate, "Oho! I have discovered you"—reminding him of the circumstance.[1]

It was amazing to find him so keen in such a state. I must add one other circumstance, which is material, as it shows that he perhaps was not without some hope of a future state, and that his spirits were supported by a consciousness (or at least a notion) that his conduct had been virtuous. He said, "If there were a future state, Mr. Boswell, I think I could give as good an account of my life as most people."

---

1. Boswell never filled the blank.

7

A Refutation of Deism

PERCY BYSSHE SHELLEY

> It isn't so long since a test of Anglican orthodoxy was applied to
> anyone seeking to study or teach at Oxford and Cambridge univer-
> sities. One of the most celebrated victims of this theocratic policy
> was Shelley (1792–1811) who was expelled from University College,
> Oxford, for writing a pamphlet entitled *The Necessity of Atheism*. He
> and his poetry were much influenced by the climate of skepticism
> engendered by the French and Scottish enlightenments, and he
> himself was to marry the daughter of the freethinker William God-
> win. In this extract from *A Refutation of Deism*, Shelley sets about the
> propaganda of the creationists.

Design must be proved before a designer can be inferred. The matter in controversy is the existence of design in the Universe, and it is not permitted to assume
the contested premises and thence infer the matter in dispute. Insidiously to
employ the words contrivance, design, and adaptation before these circumstances are made apparent in the Universe, thence justly inferring a contriver is
a popular sophism against which it behooves us to be watchful.

To assert that motion is an attribute of mind, that matter is inert, that every
combination is the result of intelligence is also an assumption of the matter in
dispute.

Why do we admit design in any machine of human contrivance? Simply, because innumerable instances of machines having been contrived by human art
are present to our mind, because we are acquainted with persons who could
construct such machines; but if, having no previous knowledge of any artificial
contrivance, we had accidentally found a watch upon the ground, we should
have been justified in concluding that it was a thing of Nature, that it was a
combination of matter with whose cause we were unacquainted, and that any
attempt to account for the origin of its existence would be equally presumptuous and unsatisfactory.

The analogy, which you attempt to establish between the contrivances of human art and the various existences of the Universe, is inadmissible. We attribute
these effects to human intelligence, because we know before hand that human

intelligence is capable of producing them. Take away this knowledge, and the grounds of our reasoning will be destroyed. Our entire ignorance, therefore, of the Divine Nature leaves this analogy defective in its most essential point of comparison.

What consideration remains to be urged in support of the creation of the Universe by a supreme Being? Its admirable fitness for the production of certain effects, that wonderful consent of all its parts, that universal harmony by whose changeless laws innumerable systems of worlds perform their stated revolutions, and the blood is driven through the veins of the minutest animalcule that sports in the corruption of an insect's lymph: on this account did the Universe require an intelligent Creator, because it exists producing invariable effects, and inasmuch as it is admirably organized for the production of these effects, so the more did it require a creative intelligence.

Thus have we arrived at the substance of your assertion, "That whatever exists, producing certain effects, stands in need of a Creator, and the more conspicuous is its fitness for the production of these effects, the more certain will be our conclusion that it would not have existed from eternity, but must have derived its origin from an intelligent creator."

In what respect then do these arguments apply to the Universe, and not apply to God? From the fitness of the Universe to its end you infer the necessity of an intelligent Creator. But if the fitness of the Universe, to produce certain effects, be thus conspicuous and evident, how much more exquisite fitness to his end must exist in the Author of this Universe? If we find great difficulty from its admirable arrangement, in conceiving that the Universe has existed from all eternity, and to resolve this difficulty suppose a Creator, how much more clearly must we perceive the necessity of this very Creator's creation whose perfections comprehend an arrangement far more accurate and just.

The belief of an infinity of creative and created Gods, each more eminently requiring an intelligent author of his being than the foregoing, is a direct consequence of the premises, which you have stated. The assumption that the Universe is a design, leads to a conclusion that there are infinity of creative and created Gods, which is absurd. It is impossible indeed to prescribe limits to learned error, when Philosophy relinquishes experience and feeling for speculation.

Until it is clearly proved that the Universe was created, we may reasonably suppose that it has endured from all eternity. In a case where two propositions are diametrically opposite, the mind believes that which is less incomprehensible: it is easier to suppose that the Universe has existed from all eternity, than to conceive an eternal being capable of creating it. If the mind sinks beneath the weight of one, is it an alleviation to encrease the intolerability of the burthen?

A man knows, not only that he now is, but also that there was a time when he did not exist; consequently there must have been a cause. But we can only infer, from effects, causes exactly adequate to those effects. There certainly is a generative power which is effected by particular instruments; we cannot prove that it is inherent in these instruments, nor is the contrary hypothesis capable of demonstration. We admit that the generative power is incomprehensible, but to suppose that the same effects are produced by an eternal Omnipotent and Omniscient Being, leaves the cause in the same obscurity, but renders it more incomprehensible.

We can only infer from effects causes exactly adequate to those effects. An infinite number of effects demand an infinite number of causes, nor is the philosopher justified in supposing a greater connection or unity in the latter, than is perceptible in the former. The same energy cannot be at once the cause of the serpent and the sheep; of the blight by which the harvest is destroyed, and the sunshine by which it is matured; of the ferocious propensities by which man becomes a victim to himself, and of the accurate judgment by which his institutions are improved. The spirit of our accurate and exact philosophy is outraged by conclusions that contradict each other so glaringly.

The greatest, equally with the smallest motions of the Universe, are subjected to the rigid necessity of inevitable laws. These laws are the unknown causes of the known effects perceivable in the Universe. Their effects are the boundaries of our knowledge, their names the expressions of our ignorance. To suppose some existence beyond, or above them, is to invent a second and superfluous hypothesis to account for what has already been accounted for by the laws of motion and the properties of matter. I admit that the nature of these laws is incomprehensible, but the hypothesis of a Deity adds a gratuitous difficulty, which so far from alleviating those that it is adduced to explain, requires new hypotheses for the elucidation of its own inherent contradictions.

The laws of attraction and repulsion, desire and aversion, suffice to account for every phenomenon of the moral and physical world. A precise knowledge of the properties of any object is alone requisite to determine its manner of action. Let the mathematician be acquainted with the weight and volume of a cannonball, together with the degree of velocity and inclination with which it is impelled, and he will accurately delineate the course it must describe, and determine the force with which it will strike an object at a given distance. Let the influencing motive, present to the mind of any person be given, and the knowledge of his consequent conduct will result. Let the bulk and velocity of a comet be discovered, and the astronomer, by the accurate estimation of the equal and contrary actions of the centripetal and centrifugal forces, will justly predict the period of its return.

The anomalous motions of the heavenly bodies, their unequal velocities and frequent aberrations, are corrected by that gravitation by which they are caused. The illustrious Laplace has shewn, that the approach of the Moon to the Earth, and the Earth to the Sun, is only a secular equation of a very long period, which has its maximum and minimum. The system of the Universe then is upheld solely by physical powers. The necessity of matter is the ruler of the world. It is vain philosophy that supposes more causes than are exactly adequate to explain the phenomena of things. . . .

You assert that the construction of the animal machine, the fitness of certain animals to certain situations, the connexion between the organs of perception and that which is perceived; the relation between every thing which exists, and that which tends to preserve it in its existence, imply design. It is manifest that if the eye could not see, nor the stomach digest, the human frame could not preserve its present mode of existence. It is equally certain, however, that the elements of its composition, if they did not exist in one form, must exist in another; and that the combinations which they would form, must so long as they endured, derive support for their peculiar mode of being from their fitness to the circumstances of their situation.

It by no means follows, that because a being exists, performing certain functions, he was fitted by another being to the performance of these functions. So rash a conclusion would conduct, as I have before shewn, to an absurdity; and it becomes infinitely more unwarrantable from the consideration that the known laws of matter and motion, suffice to unravel, even in the present imperfect state of moral and physical science, the majority of those difficulties which the hypothesis of a Deity was invented to explain.

Doubtless no disposition of inert matter, or matter deprived of qualities, could ever have composed an animal, a tree, or even a stone. But matter deprived of qualities, is an abstraction, concerning which it is impossible to form an idea. Matter, such as we behold it, is not inert. It is infinitely active and subtile. Light, electricity and magnetism are fluids not surpassed by thought itself in tenuity and activity; like thought they are sometimes the cause and sometimes the effect of motion; and, distinct as they are from every other class of substances, with which we are acquainted, seem to possess equal claims with thought to the unmeaning distinction of immateriality.

The laws of motion and the properties of matter suffice to account for every phenomenon, or combination of phenomena exhibited in the Universe. That certain animals exist in certain climates, results from the consentaneity of their frames to the circumstances of their situation: let these circumstances be altered to a sufficient degree, and the elements of their composition must exist in some new combination no less resulting than the former from those inevitable laws by which the Universe is governed. . . .

What then is this harmony, this order that you maintain to have required for its establishment, what it needs not for its maintenance, the agency of a supernatural intelligence? Inasmuch as the order visible in the Universe requires one cause, so does the disorder whose operation is not less clearly apparent demand another. Order and disorder are no more than modifications of our own perceptions of the relations which subsist between ourselves and external objects, and if we are justified in inferring the operation of a benevolent power from the advantages attendant on the former, the evils of the latter bear equal testimony to the activity of a malignant principle, no less pertinacious in inducing evil out of good, than the other is unremitting in procuring good from evil.

If we permit our imagination to traverse the obscure regions of possibility, we may doubtless imagine, according to the complexion of our minds, that disorder may have a relative tendency to unmingled good, or order be relatively replete with exquisite and subtle evil. To neither of these conclusions, which are equally presumptuous and unfounded, will it become the philosopher to assent. Order and disorder are expressions denoting our perceptions of what is injurious or beneficial to ourselves, or to the beings in whose welfare we are compelled to sympathize by the similarity of their conformation to our own.

A beautiful antelope panting under the fangs of a tiger, a defenceless ox, groaning beneath the butcher's axe, is a spectacle, which instantly awakens compassion in a virtuous and unvitiated breast. Many there are, however, sufficiently hardened to the rebukes of justice and the precepts of humanity, as to regard the deliberate butchery of thousands of their species, as a theme of exultation and a source of honour, and to consider any failure in these remorseless enterprises as a defect in the system of things. The criteria of order and disorder are as various as those beings from whose opinions and feelings they result.

Populous cities are destroyed by earthquakes, and desolated by pestilence. Ambition is every where devoting its millions to incalculable calamity. Superstition, in a thousand shapes, is employed in brutalizing and degrading the human species, and fitting it to endure without a murmur the oppression of its innumerable tyrants. All this is abstractedly neither good nor evil because good and evil are words employed to designate that peculiar state of our own perceptions, resulting from the encounter of any object calculated to produce pleasure or pain. Exclude the idea of relation, and the words good and evil are deprived of import.

Earthquakes are injurious to the cities that they destroy, beneficial to those whose commerce was injured by their prosperity, and indifferent to others which are too remote to be affected by their influence. Famine is good to the corn-merchant, evil to the poor, and indifferent to those whose fortunes can at all times command a superfluity. Ambition is evil to the restless bosom it inhabits, to the innumerable victims who are dragged by its ruthless thirst for infamy, to expire in every variety of anguish, to the inhabitants of the country it depopulates, and to the human race whose improvement it retards; it is indifferent with regard to the system of the Universe, and is good only to the vultures and the jackals that track the conqueror's career, and to the worms who feast in security on the desolation of his progress. It is manifest that we cannot reason with respect to the universal system from that which only exists in relation to our own perceptions.

You allege some considerations in favor of a Deity from the universality of a belief in his existence.

The superstitions of the savage, and the religion of civilized Europe appear to you to conspire to prove a first cause. I maintain that it is from the evidence of revelation alone that this belief derives the slightest countenance.

That credulity should be gross in proportion to the ignorance of the mind that it enslaves, is in strict consistency with the principles of human nature. The idiot, the child and the savage, agree in attributing their own passions and propensities to the inanimate substances by which they are either benefited or injured. The former become Gods and the latter Demons; hence prayers and sacrifices, by the means of which the rude Theologian imagines that he may confirm the benevolence of the one, or mitigate the malignity of the other. He has averted the wrath of a powerful enemy by supplications and submission; he has secured the assistance of his neighbour by offerings; he has felt his own anger subside before the entreaties of a vanquished foe, and has cherished gratitude for the kindness of another. Therefore does he believe that the elements will listen to his vows. He is capable of love and hatred towards his fellow beings, and is variously impelled by those principles to benefit or injure them. The source of his error is sufficiently obvious. When the winds, the waves and the atmosphere act in such a manner as to thwart or forward his designs, he attributes to them the same propensities of whose existence within himself he is conscious when he is instigated by benefits to kindness, or by injuries to revenge. The bigot of the woods can form no conception of beings possessed of properties differing from his own: it requires, indeed, a mind considerably tinctured with science, and enlarged by cultivation to contemplate itself, not as the centre and model of the Universe, but as one of the infinitely various multitude of beings of which it is actually composed.

There is no attribute of God which is not either borrowed from the passions and powers of the human mind, or which is not a negation. Omniscience, Omnipotence, Omnipresence, Infinity, Immutability, Incomprehensibility, and Immateriality, are all words that designate properties and powers peculiar to organised beings, with the addition of negations, by which the idea of limitation is excluded.

That the frequency of a belief in God (for it is not Universal) should be any argument in its favor, none to whom the innumerable mistakes of men are familiar, will assert. It is among men of genius and science that Atheism alone is found, but among these alone is cherished an hostility to those errors, with which the illiterate and vulgar are infected.

How small is the proportion of whose who really believe in God, to the thousands who are prevented by their occupations from ever bestowing a serious thought upon the subject, and the millions who worship butterflies, bones, feathers, monkeys, calabashes and serpents. The word God, like other abstractions, signifies the agreement of certain propositions, rather than the presence of any idea. If we found our belief in the existence of God on the universal consent of mankind, we are duped by the most palpable of sophisms. The word

God cannot mean at the same time an ape, a snake, a bone, a calabash, a Trinity, and a Unity. Nor can that belief be accounted universal against which men of powerful intellect and spotless virtue have in every age protested. . . .

Intelligence is that attribute of the Deity, which you hold to be most apparent in the Universe. Intelligence is only known to us as a mode of animal being. We cannot conceive intelligence distinct from sensation and perception, which are attributes to organized bodies. To assert that God is intelligent, is to assert that he has ideas; and Locke has proved that ideas result from sensation. Sensation can exist only in an organized body, an organized body is necessarily limited both in extent and operation. The God of the rational Theosophist is a vast and wise animal. . . .

Thus, from the principles of that reason to which you so rashly appealed as the ultimate arbiter of our dispute, have I shewn that the popular arguments in favor of the being of God are totally destitute of colour. I have shewn the absurdity of attributing intelligence to the cause of those effects that we perceive in the Universe, and the fallacy that lurks in the argument from design. I have shewn that order is no more than a peculiar manner of contemplating the operation of necessary agents, that mind is the effect, not the cause of motion, that power is the attribute, not the origin of Being. I have proved that we can have no evidence of the existence of a God from the principles of reason.

8

Moral Influences in Early Youth: My Father's Character and Opinions

From *Autobiography*

JOHN STUART MILL

The son of another Scotsman, the philosopher James Mill, John Stuart Mill (1806–1873) is best remembered for the terrifying precocity of his education at the hands of his distinguished parent, and of other great contemporaries such as David Ricardo and Jeremy Bentham, whose theory of "the greatest happiness for the greatest number" he was to go on to refine. Mill's political career was distinguished by firm opposition to slavery and by advocacy of the rights of women. Even this great and brave Victorian was afraid to affirm his irreligious views in public: his three essays on the subject (including a brilliant critique of the notion of immortality) were not published until after his death. By a nice coincidence, he was a godfather to Bertrand Russell.

In my education, as in that of every one, the moral influences, which are so much more important than all others, are also the most complicated, and the most difficult to specify with any approach to completeness. Without attempting the hopeless task of detailing the circumstances by which, in this respect, my early character may have been shaped, I shall confine myself to a few leading points, which form an indispensable part of any true account of my education.

I was brought up from the first without any religious belief, in the ordinary acceptation of the term. My father, educated in the creed of Scotch presbyterianism, had by his own studies and reflexions been early led to reject not only the belief in revelation, also the foundations of what is commonly called Natural Religion. I have heard him say, that the turning point of his mind on the subject was reading Butler's *Analogy*. That work, of which he always continued to speak with respect, kept him, as he said, for some considerable time, a believer in the divine authority of Christianity; by proving to him, that whatever are the difficulties in believing that the Old and New Testaments proceed from, or record the acts of, a perfectly wise and good being, the same and still greater difficulties stand in the way of the belief, that a being of such a character can have been the Maker of the universe. He considered Butler's argument as conclusive against the only opponents for whom it was intended. Those who admit an omnipotent as well as perfectly just and benevolent maker and ruler of such a world as this, can say little against Christianity but what can, with at least equal force, be retorted against themselves. Finding, therefore, no halting place in Deism, he remained in a state of perplexity, until, doubtless after many struggles, he yielded to the conviction, that concerning the origin of things nothing whatever can be known. This is the only correct statement of his opinion; for dogmatic atheism he looked upon as absurd; as most of those, whom the world has considered atheists, have always done. These particulars are important, because they shew that my father's rejection of all that is called religious belief, was not, as many might suppose, primarily a matter of logic and evidence: the grounds of it were moral, still more than intellectual. He found it impossible to believe that a world so full of evil was the work of an Author combining infinite power with perfect goodness and righteousness. His intellect spurned the subtleties by which men attempt to blind themselves to this open contradiction. The Sabæan, or Manichæan theory of a Good and an Evil Principle, struggling against each other for the government of the universe, he would not have usually condemned; and I have heard him express surprise, that no one revived it in our time. He would have regarded it as a mere hypothesis; but he would have ascribed to it no depraving influence. As it was, his aversion to religion, in the sense usually attached to the term, was of same kind with that of Lucretius: he regarded it with the feelings due not to a mere mental delusion, but to a great moral evil. He looked upon it as the greatest enemy of morality: first, by setting up factitious excellencies,—belief in creeds, devotional feelings, and ceremonies, not connected with the good of human kind,—and causing these to be accepted as substitutes for genuine virtues: but above all, by radically vitiating the standard of morals; making it consist in doing the will of a being, on whom it lavishes indeed all the phrases of adulation, but whom in sober truth it depicts as eminently hateful. I have a hundred times heard him say, that all ages and nations have represented their gods as wicked, in a constantly increasing progression; that mankind have gone on adding trait after trait till they reached the most perfect conception of wickedness which the human mind could devise, and have called this God, and prostrated themselves before it. This *ne plus ultra* of wickedness he considered to be embodied in what is commonly presented to mankind as the creed of Christianity. Think (he used to say) of a being who would make a Hell—who would create the human race with the infallible foreknowledge, and therefore with the intention, that the great majority of them were to be consigned to horrible and everlasting torment. The time, I believe, is drawing near when this dreadful conception of an object of worship will be no longer identified with Christianity; and when all persons, with any sense of moral good and evil, will look upon it with the same indignation with which my father regarded it. My father was as well aware as any one that Christians do not, in general, undergo the demoralizing consequences which seem inherent in such a creed, in the manner or to the extent which might have been expected from it. The same slovenliness of thought, and subjection of the reason to fears, wishes, and affections, which enable them to accept a theory involving a contradiction in terms, prevents them from perceiving the logical consequences of the theory. Such is the facility with which mankind believe at one and the same time things inconsistent with one another, and so few are those who draw from what they receive as truths, any consequences but those recommended to them by their feelings, that multitudes have held the undoubting belief in an Omnipotent Author of Hell, and have nevertheless identified that being with the best conception they were able to form of perfect goodness. Their worship was not paid to the demon which such a Being as they imagined would really be, but to their own ideal of excellence. The evil is, that such a belief keeps the ideal wretchedly low; and opposes the most obstinate resistance to all thought which has a tendency to raise it higher. Believers shrink from every train of ideas that would lead the mind to a clear conception and an elevated standard of excellence, because they feel (even when they do not distinctly see) that such a standard would conflict with many of the dispensations of nature, and with much of what they are accustomed to consider as the Christian creed. And thus morality continues a matter of blind tradition, with no consistent principle, nor even any consistent feeling, to guide it.

It would have been wholly inconsistent with my father's ideas of duty, to allow me to acquire impressions contrary to his convictions and feelings respecting religion: and he impressed upon me from the first, that the manner in which the world came into existence was a subject on which nothing was known: that the question "Who made me?" cannot be answered, because we have no experience or authentic information from which to answer it; and that any answer only throws the difficulty a step further back, since the question immediately presents itself, Who made God? He, at the same time, took care that I should be acquainted with what had been thought by mankind on these impenetrable problems. I have mentioned at how early an age he made me a reader of ecclesiastical history; and he taught me to take the strongest interest in the Reformation, as the great and decisive contest against priestly tyranny for liberty of thought.

I am thus one of the very few examples, in this country, of one who has, not thrown off religious belief, but never had it: I grew up in a negative state with regard to it. I looked upon the modern exactly as I did upon the ancient religion, as something that in no way concerned me. It did not seem to me more strange that English people should believe what I did not, than that the men whom I read of in Herodotus should have done so. History had made the variety of opinions among mankind a fact familiar to me, and this was but a prolongation of that fact. This point in my early education had however incidentally one bad consequence deserving notice. In giving me an opinion contrary to that of the world, my father thought it necessary to give it as one which could not prudently be avowed to the world. This lesson of keeping my thoughts to myself, at that early age, was attended with some moral disadvantages; though my limited intercourse with strangers, especially such as were likely to speak to me on religion, prevented me from being placed in the alternative of avowal or hypocrisy. I remember two occasions in my boyhood, on which I felt myself in this alternative, and in both cases I avowed my disbelief and defended it. My opponents were boys, considerably older than myself: one of them I certainly staggered at the time, but the subject was never renewed between us: the other, who was surprised and somewhat shocked, did his best to convince me for some time, without effect.

The great advance in liberty of discussion, which is one of the most important differences between the present time and that of my childhood, has greatly altered the moralities of this question and I think that few men of my father's intellect and public spirit, holding with such intensity of moral conviction as he did, unpopular opinions on religion, or on any other of the great subjects of thought, would now either practise or inculcate the withholding of them from the world, unless in the cases, becoming fewer every day, in which frankness on these subjects would either risk the loss of means of subsistence, or would amount to exclusion from some sphere of usefulness peculiarly suitable to the capacities of the individual. On religion in particular the time appears to me to have come, when it is the duty of all who being qualified in point of knowledge, have on mature consideration satisfied themselves that the current opinions are not only false but hurtful, to make their dissent known; at least, if they are among those whose station, or reputation, gives their opinion a chance of being attended to. Such an avowal would put an end, at once and for ever, to the vulgar prejudice, that what is called, very improperly, unbelief, is connected with any bad qualities either of mind or heart. The world would be astonished if it knew how great a proportion of its brightest ornaments—of those most distinguished even in popular estimation for wisdom and virtue—are complete sceptics in religion; many of them refraining from avowal, less from personal considerations, than from a conscientious, though now in my opinion a most mistaken apprehension lest by speaking out what would tend to weaken existing beliefs, and by consequence (as they suppose) existing restraints, they should do harm instead of good.

Of unbelievers (so called) as well as of believers, there are many species, including almost every variety of moral type. But the best among them, as no one who has had opportunities of really knowing them will hesitate to affirm (believers rarely have that opportunity), are more genuinely religious, in the best sense of the word religion, than those who exclusively arrogate to themselves the title. The liberality of the age, or in other words the weakening of the obstinate prejudice, which makes men unable to see what is before their eyes because it is contrary to their expectations, has caused it to be very commonly admitted that a Deist may be truly religious: but if religion stands for any graces of character and not for mere dogma, the assertion may equally be made of many whose belief is far short of Deism. Though they may think the proof incomplete that the universe is a work of design, and though they assuredly disbelieve that it can have an Author and Governor who is absolute in power as well as perfect in goodness, they have that which constitutes the principal worth of all religions whatever, an ideal conception of a Perfect Being, to which they habitually refer as the guide of their conscience; and this ideal of Good is usually far nearer to perfection than the objective Deity of those, who think themselves obliged to find absolute goodness in the author of a world so crowded with suffering and so deformed by injustice as ours.

My father's moral convictions, wholly dissevered from religion, were very much of the character of those of the Greek philosophers; and were delivered with the force and decision which characterized all that came from him. Even at the very early age at which I read with him the *Memorabilia* of Xenophon, I imbibed from that work and from his comments a deep respect for the character of Socrates; who stood in my mind as a model of ideal excellence: and I well remember how my father at that time impressed upon me the lesson of the "Choice of Hercules." At a somewhat later period the lofty moral standard exhibited in the writings of Plato operated upon me with great force. My father's moral inculcations were at all times mainly those of the *Socratici viri*; justice, temperance (to which he gave a very extended application), veracity, perseverance, readiness to encounter pain and especially labour, regard for the public good; estimation of persons according to their merits, and of things according to their intrinsic usefulness; a life of exertion, in contradiction to one of self-indulgent sloth. These and other moralities he conveyed in brief sentences, uttered as occasion arose, of grave exhortation, or stern reprobation and contempt.

But though direct moral teaching does much, indirect does more; and the effect my father produced on my character, did not depend solely on what he said or did with that direct object, but also, and still more, on what manner of man he was.

In his views of life he partook of the character of the Stoic, the Epicurean, and the Cynic, not in the modern but the ancient sense of the word. In his personal qualities the Stoic predominated. His standard of morals was Epicurean, inasmuch as it was utilitarian, taking as the exclusive test of right and wrong, the tendency of actions to produce pleasure or pain. But he had (and this was the Cynic element) scarcely any belief in pleasure; at least in his later years, of which alone, on this point, I can speak confidently. He was not insensible to pleasures; but he deemed very few of them worth the price which, at least in the present state of society, must be paid for them. The greatest number of miscarriages in life, he considered to be attributable to the overvaluing of pleasures. Accordingly, temperance, in the large sense intended by the Greek philosophers—stopping short at the point of moderation in all indulgences—was with him, as with them, almost the central point of educational precept. His inculcations of this virtue fill a large place in my childish remembrances. He thought human life a poor thing at best, after the freshness of youth and of unsatisfied curiosity had gone by. This was a topic on which he did not often speak, especially, it may be supposed, in the presence of young persons: but when he did, it was with an air of settled and profound conviction. He would sometimes say, that if life were made what it might be, by good government and good education, it would be worth having: but he never spoke with anything like enthusiasm even of that possibility. He never varied in rating intellectual enjoyments above all others, even in value as pleasures, independently of their ulterior benefits. The pleasures of the benevolent affections he placed high in the scale; and used to say, that he had never known a happy old man, except those who were able to live over again in the pleasures of the young. For passionate emotions of all sorts, and for everything which has been said or written in exaltation of them, he professed the greatest contempt. He regarded them as a form of madness. "The intense" was with him a bye-word of scornful disapprobation. He regarded as an aberration of the moral standard of modern times, compared with that of the ancients, the great stress laid upon feeling. Feelings, as such, he considered to be no proper subjects of praise or blame. Right and wrong, good and bad, he regarded as qualities solely of conduct—of acts and omissions; there being no feeling which may not lead, and does not frequently lead, either to good or to bad actions: conscience itself, the very desire to act right, often leading people to act wrong. Consistently carrying out the doctrine, that the object of praise and blame should be the discouragement of wrong conduct and the encouragement of right, he refused to let his praise or blame be influenced by the motive of the agent. He blamed as severely what he thought a bad action, when the motive was a feeling of duty, as if the agents had been consciously evil doers. He would not have accepted as a plea in mitigation for inquisitors, that they sincerely believed burning heretics to be an obligation of conscience. But though he did not allow honesty of purpose to soften his disapprobation of actions, it had its full effect on his estimation of characters. No one prized conscientiousness and rectitude of intention more highly, or was more incapable of valuing any person in whom he did not feel assurance of it. But he disliked people quite as much for any other deficiency, provided he thought it equally likely to make them act ill. He disliked, for instance, a fanatic in any bad cause, as much or more than one who adopted the same cause from self-interest, because he thought him even more likely to be practically mischievous. And thus, his aversion to many intellectual errors, or what he regarded as such, partook, in a certain sense, of the character of a moral feeling. All this is merely saying that he, in a degree once common, but now very unusual, threw his feelings into his opinions; which truly it is difficult to understand how any one, who possesses much of both, can fail to do. None but those who do not care about opinions will confound it with intolerance. Those who, having opinions which they hold to be immensely important, and the contraries to be prodigiously hurtful, have any deep regard for the general good, will necessarily dislike, as a class and in the abstract, those who think wrong what they think right, and right what they think wrong: though they need not therefore be, nor was my father, insensible to good qualities in an opponent, nor governed in their estimation of individuals by one general presumption, instead of by the whole of their character. I grant that an earnest person, being no more infallible than other men, is liable to dislike people on account of opinions which do not merit dislike; but if he neither himself does them any ill office, nor connives at its being done by others, he is not intolerant: and the forbearance, which flows from a conscientious sense of the importance to mankind of the equal freedom of all opinions, is the only tolerance which is commendable, or, to the highest moral order of minds, possible.

9

Contribution to the Critique of Hegel's Philosophy of Right

Introduction

KARL MARX

The founder of the attempt to make socialism scientific rather than utopian was a man who had repudiated the Judaism of his ancestors, a man who hoped in vain to do for political economy what Charles Darwin had done for the natural sciences, and the author of perhaps the most widely quoted anti-religious remark ever made. In this discussion of Hegel, it can be seen that Marx was not as simplistic about the sources of belief as most people think. When read in context, the "opium" observation becomes more profound. Few now doubt that wars between different factions of religion (the subject of the rest of this essay) are the product of unresolved contradictions in the material world.

For Germany the *criticism of religion* is in the main complete, and criticism of religion is the premise of all criticism.

The *profane* existence of error is discredited after its *heavenly oratio pro aris et focis* has been rejected. Man, who looked for a superman in the fantastic reality of heaven and found nothing there but the *reflexion* of himself, will no longer be disposed to find but the *semblance* of himself, the non-human [*Unmensch*] where he seeks and must seek his true reality.

The basis of irreligious criticism is: *Man makes religion,* religion does not make man. In other words, religion is the self-consciousness and self-feeling of man who has either not yet found himself or has already lost himself again. But *man* is no abstract being squatting outside the world. Man is *the world of man,* the state, society. This state, this society, produce religion, *a reversed world-consciousness,* because they are *a reversed world.* Religion is the general theory of that world, its encyclopaedic compendium, its logic in a popular form, its spiritualistic *point d'honneur,* its enthusiasm, its moral sanction, its solemn completion, its universal ground for consolation and justification. It is *the fantastic realization* of the human essence because the *human essence* has no true reality. The struggle against religion is therefore mediately the fight against *the other world*, of which religion is the spiritual *aroma*.

Religious distress is at the same time the *expression* of real distress and the *protest* against real distress. Religion is the sigh of the oppressed creature, the heart of a heartless world, just as it is the spirit of a spiritless situation. It is the *opium* of the people.

The abolition of religion as the *illusory* happiness of the people is required for their *real* happiness. The demand to give up the illusions about its condition is the *demand to give up a condition which needs illusions*. The criticism of religion is therefore *in embryo the criticism of the vale of woe*, the *halo* of which is religion.

Criticism has plucked the imaginary flowers from the chain not so that man will wear the chain without any fantasy or consolation but so that he will shake off the chain and cull the living flower. The criticism of religion disillusions man to make him think and act and shape his reality like a man who has been disillusioned and has come to reason, so that he will revolve round himself and therefore round his true sun. Religion is only the illusory sun which revolves round man as long as he does not revolve round himself.

The task of history, therefore, once the *world beyond the truth* has disappeared, is to establish the *truth of this world*. The immediate *task of philosophy*, which is at the service of history, once the *saintly form* of human self-alienation has been unmasked, is to unmask self-alienation in its *unholy forms*. Thus the criticism of heaven turns into the criticism of the earth, the *criticism of religion* into the *criticism of right* and the *criticism of theology* into the *criticism of politics*.

The following exposition—a contribution to that work—bears immediately not on the original, but on a copy, the German *philosophy* of state and of right, for the single reason that it is written in *Germany*.

If one wanted to proceed from the *status quo* itself in Germany, even in the only appropriate way, i.e., negatively, the result would still be an *anachronism*. Even the negation of our political present is already covered with dust in the historical lumber-room of modern nations. If I negate the powdered pigtail, I still have an unpowdered pigtail. If I negate the German state of affairs in 1843, then, according to the French computation of time, I am hardly in the year 1789, and still less in the focus of the present.

Yes, German history flatters itself with a movement which no people in the heaven of history went through before it or will go through after it. For we shared the restorations of the modern nations although we had not shared their revolutions. We were restored, first because other nations dared to carry out a revolution and second because other nations suffered a counter-revolution, the first time because our rulers were afraid, and the second because our rulers were not afraid. Led by our shepherds, we never found ourselves in the company of freedom except once—on the *day of its burial*.

A school which legalizes the baseness of today by the baseness of yesterday, a school that declares rebellious every cry of the serf against the knout once that knout is a time-honoured, ancestral, historical one, a school to which history only shows its *a posteriori* as the God of Israel did to his servant Moses—the *historical school of right*—would hence have discovered German history had it not been a discovery of German history itself. Shylock, but Shylock the servant, it swears on its bond, its historical bond, its Christian-Germanic bond, to have every pound of flesh cut from the heart of the people.

Good-natured enthusiasts, Germanomaniacs by extraction and free-thinkers by reflexion, on the contrary, seek our history of freedom beyond our history in the ancient Teutonic forests. But what difference is there between the history of our freedom and the history of the boar's freedom if it can be found only in the forests? Besides, it is common knowledge that the forest echoes back what you shout into it. So peace to the ancient Teutonic forests!

War on the German state of affairs! By all means! They are *below the level of history,* they are *beneath any criticism,* but they are still an object of criticism like the criminal who is below the level of humanity but still an object for the *executioner.* In the struggle against that state of affairs criticism is no passion of the head, it is the head of passion. It is not a lancet, it is a weapon. Its object is its *enemy,* which it wants not to refute but to *exterminate.* For the spirit of that state of affairs is refuted. In itself it is no object *worthy of thought,* it is an *existence* which is as despicable as it is despised. Criticism does not need to make things clear to itself as regards this object, for it has already settled accounts with it. It no longer assumes the quality of an *end in itself,* but only of a *means.* Its essential pathos is *indignation,* its essential work is *denunciation.*

It is a case of describing the dull reciprocal pressure of all social spheres one on another, a general inactive ill humour, a limitedness which recognizes itself as much as it mistakes itself, within the frame of a government system which, living on the preservation of all wretchedness, is itself nothing but *wretchedness in office.*

What a sight! This infinitely proceeding division of society into the most manifold races opposed to one another by petty antipathies, uneasy consciences and brutal mediocrity, and which, precisely because of their reciprocal ambiguous and distrustful attitude, are all, without exception although with various formalities, treated by their *rulers* as *conceded existences.* And they must recognize and acknowledge as a *concession of heaven* the very fact that they are *mastered, ruled, possessed!* And on the other side are the rulers themselves, whose greatness is in inverse proportion to their number!

Criticism dealing with this content is criticism in a *hand-to-hand fight,* and in such a fight the point is not whether the opponent is a noble, equal, *interesting* opponent, the point is to *strike* him. The point is not to let the Germans have a minute for self-deception and resignation. The actual pressure must be made more pressing by adding to it consciousness of pressure, the shame must be made more shameful by publicizing it. Every sphere of German society must be shown as the *partie honteuse* of German society; these petrified relations must be forced to dance by singing their own tune to them! The people must be taught to be *terrified* at itself in order to give it *courage*. This will be fulfilling an impera-tive need of the German nation, and the needs of the nations are in themselves the ultimate reason for their satisfaction.

This struggle against the limited content of the German *status quo* cannot be without interest even for the *modern* nations, for the German *status quo* is the *open completion of the ancien régime,* and the *ancien régime* is the *concealed deficiency of the modern state.* The struggle against the German political present is the strug-gle against the past of the modern nations, and they are still burdened with re-minders of that past. It is instructive for them to see the *ancien régime,* which has been through its *tragedy* with them, playing its *comedy* as a German *revenant.* *Tragic* indeed was the history of the *ancien régime* so long as it was the pre-exist-ing power of the world, and freedom, on the other hand, was a personal notion; in short, as long as it believed and had to believe in its own justification. As long as the *ancien régime,* as an existing world order, struggled against a world that was only coming into being, there was on its side a historical error, not a per-sonal one. That is why its downfall was tragic.

On the other hand, the present German régime, an anachronism, a flagrant contradiction of generally recognized axioms, the nothingness of the *ancien régime* exhibited to the world, only imagines that it believes in itself and de-mands that the world should imagine the same thing. If it believed in its own *essence,* would it try to hide that essence under the *semblance* of an alien essence and seek refuge in hypocrisy and sophism? The modern *ancien régime* is rather only the *comedian* of a world order whose *true heroes* are dead. History is thor-ough and goes through many phases when carrying an old form to the grave. The last phase of a world-historical form is its *comedy.* The gods of Greece, al-ready tragically wounded to death in Aeschylus's *Prometheus Bound,* had to re-die a comic death in Lucian's *Dialogues.* Why this course of history? So that human-ity should part with its past *cheerfully.* This *cheerful* historical destiny is what we vindicate for the political authorities of Germany.

Meanwhile, once *modern* politico-social reality itself is subjected to criticism, once criticism rises to truly human problems, it finds itself outside the German *status quo* or else it would reach out for its object *below* its object. An example. The relation of industry, of the world of wealth generally, to the political world is one of the major problems of modern times. In what form is this problem be-ginning to engage the attention of the Germans? In the form of *protective duties,* of the *prohibitive system,* of *national economy.* Germanomania has passed out of man into matter, and thus one morning our cotton barons and iron heroes saw themselves turned into patriots. People are therefore beginning in Germany to acknowledge the sovereignty of monopoly on the inside through lending it *sov-ereignty on the outside.* People are therefore now about to begin in Germany with what people in France and England are about to end. The old corrupt condition against which these countries are revolting in theory and which they only bear as one bears chains is greeted in Germany as the dawn of a beautiful future which still hardly dares to pass from *crafty* theory to the most ruthless practice. Whereas the problem in France and England is: *Political economy* or *the rule of society over wealth,* in Germany it is: *National economy* or *the mastery of private property over nationality.* In France and England, then, it is a case of abolishing monopoly that has proceeded to its last consequences; in Germany it is a case of proceeding to the last consequences of monopoly. There it is a case of solution, here as yet a case of collision. This is an adequate example of the *German* form of modern problems, an example of how our history, like a clumsy recruit, still has to do extra drill on things that are old and hackneyed in history.

If therefore the *whole* German development did not exceed the German *political* development, a German could at the most have the share in the problems of the present that a *Russian* has. But, when the separate individual is not bound by the limitations of the nation, the nation as a whole is still less liberated by the liberation of one individual. The fact that Greece had a Scythian among its philosophers did not help the Scythians to make a single step towards Greek culture.

Luckily we Germans are not Scythians.

As the ancient peoples went through their pre-history in imagination, in *mythology,* so we Germans have gone through our post-history in thought, in *philosophy.* We are *philosophical* contemporaries of the present without being its *historical* contemporaries. German philosophy is the *ideal prolongation* of German history. If therefore, instead of the *œuvres incomplètes of* our real history, we criticize the *œuvres posthumes* of our ideal history, *philosophy,* our criticism is in the midst of the questions of which the present says: *that is the question.* What in progressive nations is a *practical* break with modern state conditions is in Germany, where even those conditions do not yet exist, at first a *critical* break with the philosophical reflexion of those conditions.

German philosophy of right and state is the only *German history* which is *al pari* with the *official* modern present. The German nation must therefore join this its dream-history to its present conditions and subject to criticism not only these existing conditions, but at the same time their abstract continuation. Its future cannot be *limited* either to the immediate negation of its real conditions of state and right or to the immediate implementation of its ideal state and right conditions, for it has the immediate negation of its real conditions in its ideal conditions, and it has almost *outlived* the immediate implementation of its ideal conditions in the contemplation of neighbouring nations. Hence it is with good reason that the *practical* political party in Germany demands the *negation of philosophy.* It is wrong, not in its demand, but in stopping at the demand, which it neither seriously implements nor can implement. It believes that it implements that negation by turning its back to philosophy and its head away from it and muttering a few trite and angry phrases about it. Owing to the limitation of its outlook it does not include philosophy in the circle of *German* reality or it even fancies it is *beneath* German practice and the theories that serve it. You demand that *real life embryos* be made the starting-point but you forget that the real life embryo of the German nation has grown so far only inside its *cranium*. In a word—*You cannot abolish philosophy without making it a reality.*

The same mistake, but with the factors *reversed*, was made by the *theoretical* party originating from philosophy.

In the present struggle it saw *only the critical struggle of philosophy against the German world*; it did not give a thought to the fact that *philosophy up to the present* itself belongs to this world and is its *completion*, although an ideal one. Critical towards its counterpart, it was uncritical towards itself when, proceeding from the *premises* of philosophy, it either stopped at the results given by philosophy or passed off demands and results from somewhere else as immediate demands and results of philosophy, although these, provided they are justified, can be obtained only by the *negation of philosophy up to the present*, of philosophy as such. We reserve ourselves the right to a more detailed description of this section. Its basic deficiency may be reduced to the following: *It thought it could make philosophy a reality without abolishing it.*

The criticism of *the German philosophy of state and right,* which attained its most consistent, richest and last formulation through *Hegel,* is both a critical analysis of the modern state and of the reality connected with it, and the resolute negation of the whole *manner of the German consciousness in politics and right* as practised hereto, the most distinguished, most universal expression of which, raised to the level of a *science*, is the *speculative philosophy of right* itself. If the speculative philosophy of right, that abstract extravagant *thinking* on the modern state, the reality of which remains a thing of the beyond, if only beyond the Rhine, was possible only in Germany, inversely the *German* thought-image of the modern state which makes abstraction of *real man* was possible only because and insofar as the modern state itself makes abstraction of *real man* or satisfies *the whole* of man only in imagination. In politics the Germans *thought* what other nations *did*. Germany was their *theoretical conscience*. The abstraction and presumption of its thought was always in step with the one-sidedness and lowliness of its reality. If therefore the *status quo* of *German statehood* expresses *the completion of the ancien régime,* the completion of the thorn in the flesh of the modern state, the *status quo of German state science* expresses the *incompletion of the modern state,* the defectiveness of its flesh itself.

Already as the resolute opponent of the previous form of *German* political consciousness the criticism of speculative philosophy of right strays, not into itself, but into *problems* which there is only one means of solving—*practice.*

It is asked: can Germany attain a practice *à la hauteur des principes,* i.e., a *revolution* which will raise it not only to the *official level* of the modern nations but to the *height of humanity* which will be the near future of those nations?

The weapon of criticism cannot, of course, replace criticism of the weapon, material force must be overthrown by material force; but theory also becomes a material force as soon as it has gripped the masses. Theory is capable of gripping the masses as soon as it demonstrates *ad hominem,* and it demonstrates *ad hominem* as soon as it becomes radical. To be radical is to grasp the root of the matter. But for man the root is man himself. The evident proof of the radicalism of German theory, and hence of its practical energy, is that it proceeds from a resolute *positive* abolition of religion. The criticism of religion ends with the teaching that *man is the highest essence for man,* hence with the *categoric imperative to overthrow all relations* in which man is a debased, enslaved, abandoned, despicable essence, relations which cannot be better described than by the cry of a Frenchman when it was planned to introduce a tax on dogs: Poor dogs! They want to treat you as human beings!

Even historically, theoretical emancipation has specific practical significance for Germany. For Germany's *revolutionary* past is theoretical, it is the *Reformation. As* the revolution then began in the brain of the *monk, so* now it begins in the brain of the *philosopher.*

Luther, we grant, overcame bondage out of *devotion* by replacing it by bondage out of *conviction.* He shattered faith in authority because he restored the authority of faith. He turned priests into laymen because he turned laymen into priests. He freed man from outer religiosity because he made religiosity the inner man. He freed the body from chains because he enchained the heart.

But if Protestantism was not the true solution of the problem it was at least the true setting of it. It was no longer a case of the layman's struggle against the *priest outside himself* but of his struggle against *his own priest inside himself,* his *priestly nature.* And if the Protestant transformation of the German laymen into priests emancipated the lay popes, the *princes,* with the whole of their priestly clique, the privileged and philistines, the philosophical transformation of priestly Germans into men will emancipate the *people.* But *secularization* will not stop at the *confiscation of church estates* set in motion mainly by hypocritical Prussia any more than emancipation stops at princes. The Peasant War, the most radical fact of German history, came to grief because of theology. Today, when theology itself has come to grief, the most unfree fact of German history, our *status quo,* will be shattered against philosophy. On the eve of the Reformation official Germany was the most unconditional slave of Rome. On the eve of its revolution it is the unconditional slave of less than Rome, of Prussia and Austria, of country junkers and philistines.

Meanwhile, a major difficulty seems to stand in the way of a *radical* German revolution.

For revolutions require a *passive* element, a *material* basis. Theory is fulfilled in a people only insofar as it is the fulfillment of the needs of that people. But will the monstrous discrepancy between the demands of German thought and the answers of German reality find a corresponding discrepancy between civil society and the state and between civil society and itself? Will the theoretical needs be immediate practical needs? It is not enough for thought to strive for realization, reality must itself strive towards thought.

But Germany did not rise to the intermediary stage of political emancipation at the same time as the modern nations. It has not yet reached in practice the stages which it has surpassed in theory. How can it do a *somersault*, not only over its own limitations, but also at the same time over the limitations of the modern nations, over limitations which it must in reality feel and strive for as for emancipation from its real limitations? Only a revolution of radical needs can be a radical revolution and it seems that precisely the preconditions and ground for such needs are lacking.

If Germany has accompanied the development of the modern nations only with the abstract activity of thought without taking an effective share in the real struggle of that development, it has, on the other hand, shared the *sufferings* of that development, without sharing in its enjoyment or its partial satisfaction. To the abstract activity on the one hand corresponds the abstract suffering on the other. That is why Germany will one day find itself on the level of European decadence before ever having been on the level of European emancipation. It will be comparable to a *fetish worshipper* pining away with the diseases of Christianity.

If we now consider the *German governments* we find that because of the circumstances of the time, because of Germany's condition, because of the standpoint of German education and finally under the impulse of its own fortunate instinct, they are driven to combine the *civilized shortcomings of the modern state world,* the advantages of which we do not enjoy, with the *barbaric deficiencies of the ancien régime,* which we enjoy in full; hence Germany must share more and more, if not in the reasonableness, at least in the unreasonableness of those state formations which are beyond the bounds of its *status quo.* Is there in the world, for example, a country which shares so naively in all the illusions of constitutional statehood without sharing in its realities as so-called constitutional Germany? And was it not perforce the notion of a German government to combine the tortures of censorship with the tortures of the French September laws which provide for freedom of the press? As you could find the *gods* of all nations in the Roman Pantheon, so you will find in the Germans' Holy Roman Empire all the *sins* of all state forms. That this eclecticism will reach a so far unprecedented height is guaranteed in particular by the *political-aesthetic gourmanderie* of a German king who intended to play all the roles of monarchy, whether feudal or bureaucratic, absolute or constitutional, autocratic or democratic, if not in the person of the people, at least in his own person, and if not for the people, at least for *himself. Germany, as the deficiency of the political present constituted as a world of its own,* will not be able to throw down the specific German limitations without throwing down the general limitation of the political present.

It is not the *radical* revolution, not the *general human* emancipation which is a utopian dream for Germany, but rather the partial, the *merely* political revolution, the revolution which leaves the pillars of the house standing. On what is a partial, a merely political revolution based? On *part of civil society emancipating* itself and attaining *general* domination; on a definite class, proceeding from its *particular situation,* undertaking the general emancipation of society. This class emancipates the whole of society but only provided the whole of society is in the same situation as this class, e.g., possesses money and education or can acquire them at will.

No class of civil society can play this role without arousing a moment of enthusiasm in itself and in the masses, a moment in which it fraternizes and merges with society in general, becomes confused with it and is perceived and acknowledged as its *general representative,* a moment in which its claims and rights are truly the claims and rights of society itself, a moment in which it is truly the social head and the social heart. Only in the name of the general rights of society can a particular class vindicate for itself general domination. For the storming of this emancipatory position, and hence for the political exploitation of all sections of society in the interests of its own section, revolutionary energy and spiritual self-feeling alone are not sufficient. For the *revolution of a nation* and the *emancipation of a particular class* of civil society to coincide, for *one* estate to be acknowledged as the estate of the whole society, all the defects of society must conversely be concentrated in another class, a particular estate must be the estate of the general stumbling-block, the incorporation of the general limitation, a particular social sphere must be recognized as the *notorious crime* of the whole of society, so that liberation from that sphere appears as general self-liberation. For *one* estate to be *par excellence* the estate of liberation, another estate must conversely be the obvious estate of oppression. The negative general significance of the French nobility and the French clergy determined the positive general significance of the nearest neighbouring and opposed class of the *bourgeoisie.*

But no particular class in Germany has the consistency, the penetration, the courage, or the ruthlessness that could mark it out as the negative representative of society. No more has any estate the breadth of soul that identifies itself, even for a moment, with the soul of the nation, the geniality that inspires material might to political violence, or that revolutionary daring which flings at the adversary the defiant words: *I am nothing but I must be everything.* The main stem of German morals and honesty, of the classes as well as of individuals, is rather that *modest egoism* which asserts its limitedness and allows it to be asserted against itself. The relation of the various sections of German society is therefore not dramatic but epic. Each of them begins to be aware of itself and begins to camp beside the others with all its particular claims not as soon as it is oppressed, but as soon as the circumstances of the time relations, without the section's own participation, create a social substratum on which it can in turn exert pressure. Even the *moral self-feeling of the German middle class* rests only on the consciousness that it is the common representative of the philistine mediocrity of all the other classes. It is therefore not only the German kings who accede to the throne *mal a propos,* it is every section of civil society which goes through a defeat before it celebrates victory and develops its own limitations before it overcomes the limitations facing it, asserts its narrow-hearted essence before it has been able to assert its magnanimous essence; thus the very opportunity of a great role has passed away before it is to hand, and every class, once it begins the struggle against the class opposed to it, is involved in the struggle against the class below it. Hence the higher nobility is struggling against the monarchy, the bureaucrat against the nobility, and the bourgeois against them all, while the proletariat is already beginning to find itself struggling against the bourgeoisie. The middle class hardly dares to grasp the thought of emancipation from its own standpoint when the development of the social conditions and the progress of political theory already declare that standpoint antiquated or at least problematic.

In France it is enough for somebody to be something for him to want to be everything; in Germany nobody can be anything if he is not prepared to renounce everything. In France partial emancipation is the basis of universal emancipation; in Germany universal emancipation is the *conditio sine qua non* of any partial emancipation. In France it is the reality of gradual liberation that must give birth to complete freedom, in Germany the impossibility of gradual liberation. In France every class of the nation is a *political idealist* and becomes aware of itself at first not as a particular class but as a representative of social requirements generally. The role of *emancipator* therefore passes in dramatic motion to the various classes of the French nation one after the other until it finally comes to the class which implements social freedom no longer with the provision of certain conditions lying outside man and yet created by human society, but rather organizes all conditions of human existence on the premises of social freedom. On the contrary, in Germany, where practical life is as spiritless as spiritual life is unpractical, no class in civil society has any need or capacity for general emancipation until it is forced by its *immediate* condition, by *material* necessity, by its *very chains.*

Where, then, is the *positive* possibility of a German emancipation?

Answer: In the formation of a class with *radical chains,* a class of civil society which is not a class of civil society, an estate which is the dissolution of all estates, a sphere which has a universal character by its universal suffering and claims no *particular right* because no *particular wrong* but *wrong generally is* perpetrated against it; which can invoke no *historical* but only its *human* title, which does not stand in any one-sided antithesis to the consequences but in all-round antithesis to the premises of German statehood; a sphere, finally, which cannot emancipate itself without emancipating itself from all other spheres of society and thereby emancipating all other spheres of society, which, in a word, is the *complete loss* of man and hence can win itself only through the *complete re-winning of man*. This dissolution of society as a particular estate is the *proletariat*.

The proletariat is beginning to appear in Germany as a result of the rising *industrial* movement. For it is not the *naturally arising* poor but the *artificially impoverished*, not the human masses mechanically oppressed by the gravity of society but the masses resulting from the *drastic dissolution* of society, mainly of the middle estate, that form the proletariat; although, as is easily understood, the naturally arising poor and the Christian-Germanic serfs gradually join its ranks.

By heralding the *dissolution of the hereto existing world order* the proletariat merely proclaims the *secret of its own existence*, for it is the *factual* dissolution of that world order. By demanding the *negation of private property*, the proletariat merely raises to the rank of a *principle of society* what society has raised to the rank of *its* principle, what is already incorporated in *it* as the negative result of society without its own participation. The proletarian then finds himself possessing the same right in regard to the world which is coming into being as the *German king* in regard to the world which has come into being when he calls the people *his* people as he calls the horse *his* horse. By declaring the people his private property the king merely proclaims that the private owner is king.

As philosophy finds its *material* weapon in the proletariat, so the proletariat finds its *spiritual* weapon in philosophy. And once the lightning of thought has squarely struck this ingenuous soil of the people the emancipation of the *Germans* into *men* will be accomplished.

Let us sum up the result:

The only *practically* possible liberation of Germany is liberation from the point of view of *the* theory which proclaims man to be the highest essence of man. In Germany emancipation from the *Middle Ages* is possible only as emancipation from the *partial* victories over the Middle Ages as well. In Germany *no* kind of bondage can be shattered without *every* kind of bondage being shattered. The *fundamental* Germany cannot revolutionize without revolutionizing *from the foundation*. *The emancipation of the German* is *the emancipation of man*. The *head* of this emancipation is *philosophy*, its *heart* is the *proletariat*. Philosophy cannot be made a reality without the abolition of the proletariat, the proletariat cannot be abolished without philosophy being made a reality.

When all inner requisites are fulfilled the *day of German resurrection* will be proclaimed by the *crowing of the cock of Gaul*.

10

Evangelical Teaching

George Eliot

Another student of Hegel (and Feuerbach and the other German idealists) was Mary Ann Evans (1819–1890) who wrote imperishable novels under the *nom de plume* of George Eliot. She translated David Friedrich Strauss's book *Das Leben Jesu,* with its subversive claim that the purported events of the New Testament were mythical. In defiance of Victorian morality, she set up a home with the married freethinker George Henry Lewes. George Eliot was one of the editors of the *Westminster Review* and in 1855 published an attack on a then well-known evangelical divine. I shall be surprised if this essay does not remind you of some more recent religious performers.

Given, a man with moderate intellect, a moral standard not higher than the average, some rhetorical affluence and great glibness of speech, what is the career in which, without the aid of birth or money, he may most easily attain power and reputation in English society? Where is that Goshen of mediocrity in which a smattering of science and learning will pass for profound instruction, where platitudes will be accepted as wisdom, bigoted narrowness as holy zeal, unctuous egoism as God-given piety? Let such a man become an evangelical preacher; he will then find it possible to reconcile small ability with great ambition, superficial knowledge with the prestige of erudition, a middling morale with a high reputation for sanctity. Let him shun practical extremes and be ultra only in what is purely theoretic: let him be stringent on predestination, but latitudinarian on fasting; unflinching in insisting on the eternity of punishment, but diffident of curtailing the substantial comforts of time; ardent and imaginative on the premillennial advent of Christ, but cold and cautious towards every other infringement of the *status quo.* Let him fish for souls not with the bait of inconvenient singularity, but with the dragnet of comfortable conformity. Let him be hard and literal in his interpretation only when he wants to hurl texts at the heads of unbelievers and adversaries, but when the letter of the Scriptures presses too closely on the genteel Christianity of the nineteenth century, let him use his spiritualizing alembic and disperse it into impalpable ether. Let him preach less of Christ than of Antichrist; let him be less definite in showing what sin is than in showing who is the Man of Sin, less expansive on the blessedness of faith than on the accursedness of infidelity. Above all, let him set up as an interpreter of prophecy, and rival Moore's Almanack in the prediction of political events, tickling the interest of hearers who are but moderately spiritual by showing how the Holy Spirit has dictated problems and charades for their benefit, and how, if they are ingenious enough to solve these, they may have their Christian graces nourished by learning precisely to whom they may point as the "horn that had eyes," "the lying prophet," and the "unclean spirits." In this way he will draw men to him by the strong cords of their passions, made reason-proof by being baptized with the name of piety. In this way he may gain a metropolitan pulpit; the avenues to his church will be as crowded as the passages to the opera; he has but to print his prophetic sermons and bind them in lilac and gold, and they will adorn the drawing-room table of all evangelical ladies, who will regard as a sort of pious "light reading" the demonstration that the prophecy of the locusts, whose sting is in their tail, is fulfilled in the fact of the Turkish commander's having taken a horse's tail for his standard, and that the French are the very frogs predicted in the Revelation.

Pleasant to the clerical flesh under such circumstances is the arrival of Sunday! Somewhat at a disadvantage during the week, in the presence of working-day interests and lay splendours, on Sunday the preacher becomes the cynosure of a thousand eyes, and predominates at once over the Amphitryon with whom he dines, and the most captious member of his church or vestry. He has an immense advantage over all other public speakers. The platform orator is subject to the criticism of hisses and groans. Counsel for the plaintiff expects the retort of counsel for the defendant. The honorable gentleman on one side of the House is liable to have his facts and figures shown up by his honourable friend on the opposite side. Even the scientific or literary lecturer, if he is dull or incompetent, may see the best part of his audience slip quietly out one by one. But the preacher is completely master of the situation: no one may hiss, no one may depart. Like the writer of imaginary conversations, he may put what imbecilities he pleases into the mouths of his antagonists, and swell with triumph when he has refuted them. He may riot in gratuitous assertions, confident that no man will contradict him; he may exercise perfect free-will in logic, and invent illustrative experience; he may give an evangelical edition of history with the inconvenient facts omitted;—all this he may do with impunity, certain that those of his hearers who are not sympathizing are not listening. For the Press has no band of critics who go the round of the churches and chapels, and are on the watch for a slip or defect in the preacher, to make a "feature" in their article: the clergy are practically the most irresponsible of all talkers. For this reason, at least, it is well that they do not always allow their discourses to be merely fugitive, but are often induced to fix them in that black and white in which they are open to the criticism of any man who has the courage and patience to treat them with thorough freedom of speech and pen.

It is because we think this criticism of clerical teaching desirable for the public good that we devote some pages to Dr. Cumming. He is, as every one knows, a preacher of immense popularity, and of the numerous publications in which he perpetuates his pulpit labours, all circulate widely, and some, according to their title-page, have reached the sixteenth thousand. Now our opinion of these publications is the very opposite of that given by a newspaper eulogist: we do *not* "believe that the repeated issues of Dr. Cumming's thoughts are having a beneficial effect on society," but the reverse; and hence, little inclined as we are to dwell on his pages, we think it worth while to do so, for the sake of pointing out in them what we believe to be profoundly mistaken and pernicious. Of Dr. Cumming personally we know absolutely nothing: our acquaintance with him is confined to a perusal of his works; our judgment of him is founded solely on the manner in which he has written himself down on his pages. We know neither how he looks nor how he lives. We are ignorant whether, like Saint Paul, he has a bodily presence that is weak and contemptible, or whether his person is as florid and as prone to amplification as his style. For aught we know, he may not only have the gift of prophecy but may bestow the profits of all his works to feed the poor, and be ready to give his own body to be burned with as much alacrity as he infers the everlasting burning of Roman Catholics and Puseyites. Out of the pulpit he may be a model of justice, truthfulness, and the love that thinketh no evil; but we are obliged to judge of his charity by the spirit we find in his sermons, and shall only be glad to learn that his practice is, in many respects, an amiable *non sequitur* from his teaching. . . .

One of the most striking characteristics of Dr. Cumming's writings is *unscrupulosity of statement*. His motto apparently is, *Christianitatem, quocunque modo, Christianitatem*; and the only system he includes under the term Christianity is Calvinistic Protestantism. Experience has so long shown that the human brain is a congenial nidus for inconsistent beliefs that we do not pause to inquire how Dr. Cumming, who attributes the conversion of the unbelieving to the Divine Spirit, can think it necessary to co-operate with that Spirit by argumentative white lies. Nor do we for a moment impugn the genuineness of his zeal for Christianity, or the sincerity of his conviction that the doctrines he preaches are necessary to salvation; on the contrary, we regard the flagrant unveracity found on his pages as an indirect result of that conviction—as a result, namely, of the intellectual and moral distortion of view which is inevitably produced by assigning to dogmas, based on a very complex structure of evidence, the place and authority of first truths. A distinct appreciation of the value of evidence—in other words, the intellectual perception of truth—is more closely allied to truthfulness of statement, or the moral quality of veracity, than is generally admitted. That highest moral habit, the constant preference of truth, both theoretically and practically, pre-eminently demands the co-operation of the intellect with the impulses—as is indicated by the fact that it is only found in anything like completeness in the highest class of minds. And it is commonly seen that, in proportion as religious sects believe themselves to be guided by direct inspiration rather than by a spontaneous exertion of their faculties, their sense of truthfulness is misty and confused. No one can have talked to the more enthusiastic Methodists and listened to their stories of miracles without perceiving that they require no other passport to a statement than that it accords with their wishes and their general conception of God's dealings; nay, they regard as a symptom of sinful skepticism an inquiry into the evidence for a story which they think unquestionably tends to the glory of God, and in retailing such stories, new particulars, further tending to His glory, are "borne in" upon their minds. Now, Dr. Cumming, as we have said, is no enthusiastic pietist: within a certain circle—within the mill of evangelical orthodoxy—his intellect is perpetually at work; but that principle of sophistication which our friends the Methodists derive from the predominance of their pietistic feelings is involved for him in the doctrine of verbal inspiration; what is for them a state of emotion submerging the intellect is with him a formula imprisoning the intellect, depriving it of its proper function—the free search for truth—and making it the mere servant-of-all-work to a foregone conclusion. Minds fettered by this doctrine no longer inquire concerning a proposition whether it is attested by sufficient evidence, but whether it accords with Scripture; they do not search for facts, as such, but for facts that will bear out their doctrine. They become accustomed to reject the more direct evidence in favour of the less direct, and where adverse evidence reaches demonstration they must resort to devices and expedients in order to explain away contradiction. It is easy to see that this mental habit blunts not only the perception of truth, but the sense of truthfulness, and that the man whose faith drives him into fallacies treads close upon the precipice of falsehood.

We have entered into this digression for the sake of mitigating the inference that is likely to be drawn from that characteristic of Dr. Cumming's works to which we have pointed. He is much in the same intellectual condition as that professor of Padua, who, in order to disprove Galileo's discovery of Jupiter's satellites, urged that as there were only seven metals there could not be more than seven planets—a mental condition scarcely compatible with candour. And we may well suppose that if the professor had held the belief in seven planets, and no more, to be a necessary condition of salvation, his mental vision would have been so dazed that even if he had consented to look through Galileo's telescope, his eyes would have reported in accordance with his inward alarms rather than with the external fact. So long as a belief in propositions is regarded as indispensable to salvation, the pursuit of truth *as such* is not possible, any more than it is possible for a man who is swimming for his life to make meteorological observations on the storm which threatens to overwhelm him. The sense of alarm and haste, the anxiety for personal safety, which Dr. Cumming insists upon as the proper religious attitude, unmans the nature, and allows no thorough, calm thinking, no truly noble, disinterested feeling. Hence, we by no means suspect that the unscrupulosity of statement with which we charge Dr. Cumming extends beyond the sphere of his theological prejudices: religion apart, he probably appreciates and practices veracity. . . .

In marshalling the evidences of Christianity, Dr. Cumming directs most of his arguments against opinions that are either totally imaginary, or that belong to the past rather than to the present; while he entirely fails to meet the difficulties actually felt and urged by those who are unable to accept Revelation. There can hardly be a stronger proof of misconception as to the character of free-thinking in the present day than the recommendation of Leland's *Short and Easy Method with the Deists,*—a method which is unquestionably short and easy for preachers disinclined to consider their stereotyped modes of thinking and arguing, but which has quite ceased to realize those epithets in the conversion of Deists. Yet Dr. Cumming not only recommends this book, but also takes the trouble himself to write a feebler version of its arguments. For example, on the question of the genuineness and authenticity of the New Testament writings, he says:

> If, therefore, at a period long subsequent to the death of Christ, a number of men had appeared in the world, drawn up a book which they christened by the name of Holy Scripture, and recorded these things which appear in it as facts when they were only the fancies of their own imagination, surely the *Jews* would have instantly reclaimed that no such events transpired, that no such person as Jesus Christ appeared in their capital, and that *their* crucifixion of Him, and their alleged evil treatment of His apostles, were mere fictions.

It is scarcely necessary to say that, in such argument as this, Dr. Cumming is beating the air. He is meeting a hypothesis which no one holds, and totally missing the real question. The only type of "infidel" whose existence Dr. Cumming recognizes is that fossil personage who "calls the Bible a lie and a forgery." He seems to be ignorant—or he chooses to ignore the fact—that there is a large body of eminently instructed and earnest men who regard the Hebrew and Christian Scriptures as a series of historical documents, to be dealt with according to the rules of historical criticism; and that an equally large number of men, who are not historical critics, find the dogmatic scheme built on the letter of the Scriptures opposed to their profoundest moral convictions. Dr. Cumming's infidel is a man who, because his life is vicious, tries to convince himself that there is no God, and that Christianity is an imposture, but who is all the while secretly conscious that he is opposing the truth, and cannot help "letting out" admissions "that the Bible is the Book of God." We are favoured with the following "Creed of the Infidel":

> I believe that there is no God, but that matter is God, and God is matter; and that it is no matter whether there is any God or not. I believe also that the world was not made, but that the world made itself, or that it had no

beginning, and that it will last for ever. I believe that man is a beast; that the soul is the body, and that the body is the soul; and that after death there is neither body nor soul. I believe that there is no religion, that *natural religion is the only religion, and all religion unnatural.* I believe not in Moses; I believe in the first philosophers. I believe not in the evangelists; I believe in Chubb, Collins, Toland, Tindal, and Hobbes. I believe in Lord Bolingbroke, and I believe not in Saint Paul. I believe not in revelation; I *believe in tradition; I believe in the Talmud; I believe in the Koran;* I believe not in the Bible. I believe in Socrates; I believe in Confucius; I believe in Mahomet; I believe not in Christ. And lastly, I *believe* in all unbelief.

The intellectual and moral monster whose creed is this complex web of contradictions is, moreover, according to Dr. Cumming, a being who unites much simplicity and imbecility with his Satanic hardihood,—much tenderness of conscience with his obdurate vice. Hear the "proof":

I once met with an acute and enlightened infidel, with whom I reasoned day after day, and for hours together; I submitted to him the internal, the external, and the experimental evidences, but made no impression on his scorn and unbelief. At length I entertained a suspicion that there was something morally, rather than intellectually wrong, and that the bias was not in the intellect, but in the heart; one day therefore I said to him—"I must now state my conviction, and you may call me uncharitable, but duty compels me: you are living in some known and gross sin." *The man's countenance became pale; he bowed and left me.*

Here we have the remarkable psychological phenomenon of an "acute and enlightened" man who, deliberately purposing to indulge in a favourite sin, and regarding the Gospel with scorn and unbelief, is nevertheless so much more scrupulous than the majority of Christians that he cannot "embrace sin and the Gospel simultaneously"; who is so alarmed at the Gospel in which he does not believe that he cannot be easy without trying to crush it; whose acuteness and enlightenment suggest to him, as a means of crushing the Gospel, to argue from day to day with Dr. Cumming; and who is withal so naive that he is taken by surprise when Dr. Cumming, failing in argument, resorts to accusation, and so tender in conscience that, at the mention of his sin, he turns pale and leaves the spot. If there be any human mind in existence capable of holding Dr. Cumming's "Creed of the Infidel," of at the same time believing in tradition and "believing in all unbelief," it must be the mind of the infidel just described, for whose existence we have Dr. Cumming's *ex officio* word as a theologian; and to theologians we may apply what Sancho Panza says of the bachelors of Salamanca, that they never tell lies—except when it suits their purpose.

The total absence from Dr. Cumming's theological mind of any demarcation between fact and rhetoric is exhibited in another passage, where he adopts the dramatic form:

Ask the peasant on the hills—*and I have asked amid the mountains of Braemar and Deeside*—"How do you know that this book is divine, and that the religion you profess is true? You never read Paley?" "No, I never heard of him." "You have never read Butler?" "No, I have never heard of him." "Nor Chalmers?" "No, I do not know him." "You have never read any books on evidence?" "No, I have read no such books. Then, how do you know this book is true?" "Know it! Tell me that the Dee, the Clunie, and the Garrawalt, the streams at my feet, do not run; that the winds do not sigh amid the gorges of these blue hills; that the sun does not kindle the peaks of Loch-na-Gar,—tell me my heart does not beat, and I will believe you; but do not tell me the Bible is not divine. I have found its truth illuminating my footsteps; its consolations sustaining my heart. May my tongue cleave to my mouth's roof, and my right hand forget its cunning, if I ever deny what is my deepest inner experience, that this blessed book is the Book of God."

Dr. Cumming is so slippery and lax in his mode of presentation that we find it impossible to gather whether he means to assert that this is what a peasant on the mountains of Braemar *did* say, or that it is what such a peasant *would* say: in the one case, the passage may be taken as a measure of his truthfulness; in the other, of his judgment.

His own faith, apparently, has not been altogether intuitive, like that of his rhetorical peasant, for he tells us that he has himself experienced what it is to have religious doubts. "I was tainted while at the University by this spirit of skepticism. I thought Christianity might not be true. The very possibility of its being true was the thought I felt I must meet and settle. Conscience could give me no peace till I had settled it. I read, and I have read from that day, for four-teen or fifteen years, till this, and now I am as convinced, upon the clearest evidence, that this book is the Book of God, as that I now address you." This experience, however, instead of impressing on him the fact that doubt may be the stamp of a truth-loving mind—that *sunt quibus non credidisse honor est, et fidei futurae pignus*—seems to have produced precisely the contrary effect. It has not enabled him even to conceive the condition of a mind "perplext in faith but pure in deed," craving light, yearning for a faith that will harmonize and cherish its highest powers and aspirations, but unable to find that faith in dogmatic Christianity. His own doubts apparently were of a different kind. Nowhere in his pages have we found a humble, candid, sympathetic attempt to meet the difficulties that may be felt by an ingenuous mind. Everywhere he supposes that the doubter is hardened, conceited, consciously shutting his eyes to the light—a fool who is to be answered according to his folly—that is, with ready replies made up of reckless assertions, of apocryphal anecdotes, and, where other resources fail, of vituperative imputations. As to the reading which he has prosecuted for fifteen years—*either* it has left him totally ignorant of the relation which his own religious creed bears to the criticism and philosophy of the nineteenth century, *or* he systematically blinks that criticism and that philosophy; and instead of honestly and seriously endeavouring to meet and solve what he knows to be the real difficulties, contents himself with setting up popinjays to shoot at, for the sake of confirming the ignorance and winning the cheap admiration of his evangelical hearers and readers. Like the Catholic preacher who, after throwing down his cap and apostrophizing it as Luther, turned to his audience and said, "You see this heretical fellow has not a word to say for himself," Dr. Cumming, having drawn his ugly portrait of the infidel, and put arguments of a convenient quality into his mouth, finds a "short and easy method" of confounding this "croaking frog."

In his treatment of infidels, we imagine he is guided by a mental process which may be expressed in the following syllogism: Whatever tends to the glory of God is true; it is for the glory of God that infidels should be as bad as possible; therefore, whatever tends to show that infidels are as bad as possible is true. All infidels, he tells us, have been men of "gross and licentious lives." Is there not some well-known unbeliever—David Hume, for example—of whom even Dr. Cumming's readers may have heard as an exception? No matter. Some one suspected that he was *not* an exception; and as that suspicion tends to the glory of God, it is one for a Christian to entertain. If we were unable to imagine this kind of self-sophistication, we should be obliged to suppose that, relying on the ignorance of his evangelical disciples, he fed them with direct and conscious falsehoods. "Voltaire," he informs them, "declares there is no God"; he was "an antitheist—that is, one who deliberately and avowedly opposed and hated God; who swore in his blasphemy that he would dethrone Him"; and "advocated the very depths of the lowest sensuality." With regard to many statements of a similar kind, equally at variance with truth, in Dr. Cumming's volumes, we presume that he has been misled by hearsay or by the second-hand character of his acquaintance with free-thinking literature. An evangelical preacher is not obliged to be well read. Here, however, is a case which the extremist supposition of educated ignorance will not reach. Even books of "evidences" quote from Voltaire the line—

Si Dieu n'existait pas, il faudrait l'inventer

even persons fed on the mere whey and buttermilk of literature must know that in philosophy Voltaire was nothing if not a theist—must know that he wrote not against God, but against Jehovah, the God of the Jews, whom he believed to be a false God—must know that to say Voltaire was an atheist on this ground is as absurd as to say that a Jacobite opposed hereditary monarchy because he declared the Brunswick family had no title to the throne. That Dr. Cumming should repeat the vulgar fables about Voltaire's death is merely what we might expect from the specimens we have seen of his illustrative stories.

A man whose accounts of his own experience are apocryphal is not likely to put borrowed narratives to any severe test.

The alliance between intellectual and moral perversion is strikingly typified by the way in which he alternates from the unveracious to the absurd, from misrepresentation to contradiction. Side by side with the adduction of "facts" such as those we have quoted, we find him arguing on one page that the doctrine of the Trinity was too grand to have been conceived by man, and was *therefore* Divine; and on another page, that the Incarnation *had* been preconceived by man, and is *therefore* to be accepted as Divine. But we are less concerned with the fallacy of his "ready replies" than with their falsity; and even of this we can only afford space for a very few specimens. Here is one: "There is a *thousand times* more proof that the Gospel of John was written by him than there is that the 'Anabasis' was written by Xenophon, or the 'Ars Poetica' by Horace." If Dr. Cumming had chosen Plato's Epistles or Anacreon's Poems, instead of the "Anabasis" or the "Ars Poetica," he would have reduced the extent of the falsehood, and would have furnished a ready reply, which would have been equally effective with his Sunday-school teachers and their disputants. Hence we conclude this prodigality of misstatement, this exuberance of mendacity, is an effervescence of zeal *in majorem gloriam Dei*. Elsewhere he tells us that "the idea of the author of the 'Vestiges' is that man is the development of a monkey, that the monkey is the embryo man; so that if you *keep a baboon long enough, it will develop itself into a man.*" How well Dr. Cumming has qualified himself to judge of the ideas in "that very unphilosophical book," as he pronounces it, may be inferred from the fact that he implies the author of the "Vestiges" to have *originated* the nebular hypothesis.

In the volume from which the last extract is taken, even the hardihood of assertion is surpassed by the suicidal character of the argument. It is called *The Church before the Flood,* and is devoted chiefly to the adjustment of the question between the Bible and Geology. Keeping within the limits we have prescribed to ourselves, we do not enter into the matter of this discussion; we merely pause a little over the volume in order to point out Dr. Cumming's mode of treating the question. He first tells us that "the Bible has not a single scientific error in it"; that *"its slightest intimations of scientific principles or natural phenomena have in every instance been demonstrated to be exactly and strictly true";* and he asks:

> How is it that Moses, with no greater education than the Hindoo or the ancient philosopher, has written his book, touching science at a thousand points, so accurately that scientific research has discovered no flaws in it; and yet in those investigations which have taken place in more recent centuries, it has not been shown that he has committed one single error, or made one solitary assertion which can be proved by the maturest science, or by the most eagle-eyed philosopher, to be incorrect, scientifically or historically?

According to this, the relation of the Bible to science should be one of the strong points of apologists for revelation: the scientific accuracy of Moses should stand at the head of their evidences; and they might urge with some cogency that, since Aristotle, who devoted himself to science, and lived many ages after Moses, does little else than err ingeniously, this fact, that the Jewish lawgiver, though touching science at a thousand points, has written nothing that has not been "demonstrated to be exactly and strictly true," is an irrefragable proof of his having derived his knowledge from a supernatural source. How does it happen, then, that Dr. Cumming forsakes this strong position? How is it that we find him, some pages further on, engaged in reconciling Genesis with the discoveries of science, by means of imaginative hypotheses and feats of "interpretation"? Surely that which has been demonstrated to be exactly and strictly true does not require hypothesis and critical argument, in order to show that it may *possibly* agree with those very discoveries by means of which its exact and strict truth has been demonstrated. And why should Dr. Cumming suppose, as we shall presently find him supposing, that men of science hesitate to accept the Bible because it appears to contradict their discoveries? By his own statement, that appearance of contradiction does not exist; on the contrary, it has been demonstrated that the Bible precisely agrees with their discoveries. Perhaps, however, in saying of the Bible that its "slightest intimations of scientific principles or natural phenomena have in every instance been demonstrated to be exactly and strictly true," Dr. Cumming merely means to imply that theologians have found out a way of explaining the Biblical text so that it no longer, in their opinion, appears to be in contradiction with the discoveries of science. One of two things, therefore: either, he uses language without the slightest appreciation of its real meaning; or, the assertions he makes on one page are directly contradicted by the arguments he urges on another.

Dr. Cumming's principles—or, we should rather say, confused notions—of Biblical interpretation, as exhibited in this volume, are particularly significant of his mental caliber. He says:

> Men of science, who are full of scientific investigation, and enamoured of scientific discovery, will hesitate before they accept a book which, they think, contradicts the plainest and the most unequivocal disclosures they have made in the bowels of the earth, or among the stars of the sky. To all these we answer, as we have already indicated, there is not the least dissonance between God's written book and the most mature discoveries of geological science. One thing, however, there may be: *there may be a contradiction between the discoveries of geology and our preconceived interpretations of the Bible.* But this is not because the Bible is wrong, but because our interpretation is wrong. (The italics in all cases are our own.)

Elsewhere he says:

It seems to me plainly evident that the record of Genesis, when read fairly, and not in the light of our prejudices,—*and mind you, the essence of Popery is to read the Bible in the light of our opinions, instead of viewing our opinions in the light of the Bible, in its plain and obvious sense,*—falls in perfectly with the assertion of geologists.

On comparing these two passages, we gather that when Dr. Cumming, under stress of geological discovery, assigns to the Biblical text a meaning entirely different from that which, on his own showing, was universally ascribed to it for more than three thousand years, he regards himself as "viewing his opinions in the light of the Bible in its plain and obvious sense"! Now he is reduced to one of two alternatives. either, he must hold that the "plain and obvious meaning" lies in the sum of knowledge possessed by each successive age—the Bible being an elastic garment for the growing thought of mankind; or, he must hold that some portions are amenable to this criterion, and others not so. In the former case, he accepts the principle of interpretation adopted by the early German rationalists; in the latter case, he has to show a further criterion by which we can judge what parts of the Bible are elastic and what rigid. If he says that the interpretation of the text is rigid wherever it treats of doctrines necessary to salvation, we answer, that for doctrines to be necessary to salvation they must first be true; and in order to be true, according to his own principle, they must be founded on a correct interpretation of the Biblical text. Thus he makes the necessity of doctrines to salvation the criterion of infallible interpretation, and infallible interpretation the criterion of doctrines being necessary to salvation. He is whirled round in a circle, having, by admitting the principle of novelty in interpretation, completely deprived himself of a basis. That he should seize the very moment in which he is most palpably betraying that he has no test of Biblical truth beyond his own opinion, as an appropriate occasion for flinging the rather novel reproach against Popery that its essence is to "read the Bible in the light of our opinions," would be an almost pathetic self-exposure, if it were not disgusting. Imbecility that is not even meek, ceases to be pitiable, and becomes simply odious.

Parenthetic lashes of this kind against Popery are very frequent with Dr. Cumming, and occur even in his more devout passages, where their introduction must surely disturb the spiritual exercises of his hearers. Indeed, Roman Catholics fare worse with him even than infidels. Infidels are the small vermin—the mice to be bagged *en passant.* The main object of his chase—the rats which are to be nailed up as trophies—are the Roman Catholics. Romanism is the masterpiece of Satan. But reassure yourselves! Dr. Cumming has been created. Antichrist is enthroned in the Vatican; but he is stoutly withstood by the Boanerges of Crown Court. The personality of Satan, as might be expected, is a very prominent tenet in Dr. Cumming's discourses; those who doubt it are, he thinks, "generally specimens of the victims of Satan as a triumphant seducer"; and it is through the medium of this doctrine that he habitually contemplates Roman Catholics. They are the puppets of which the Devil holds the strings. It is only exceptionally that he speaks of them as fellow men, acted on by the same desires, fears, and hopes as himself; his rule is to hold them up to his hearers as foredoomed instruments of Satan, and vessels of wrath. If he is obliged to admit that they are "no shams," that they are "thoroughly in earnest"—that is because they are inspired by hell, because they are under an "infranatural" influence. If their missionaries are found wherever Protestant missionaries go, this zeal in propagating their faith is not in them a consistent virtue, as it is in Protestants, but a "melancholy fact," affording additional evidence that they are instigated and assisted by the Devil. And Dr. Cumming is inclined to think that they work miracles, because that is no more than might be expected from the known ability of Satan who inspires them. He admits, indeed, that "there is a fragment of the Church of Christ in the very bosom of that awful apostasy," and that there are members of the Church of Rome in glory; but this admission is rare and episodical—is a declaration, *pro forma,* about as influential on the general disposition and habits as an aristocrat's profession of democracy.

This leads us to mention another conspicuous characteristic of Dr. Cumming's teaching—the *absence of genuine charity*. It is true that he makes large profession of tolerance and liberality within a certain circle; he exhorts Christians to Unity; he would have Churchmen fraternize with Dissenters, and exhorts these two branches of God's family to defer the settlement of their differences till the millennium. But the love thus taught is the love of the *clan,* which is the correlative of antagonism to the rest of mankind. It is not sympathy and helpfulness towards men as men, but towards men as Christians, and as Christians in the sense of a small minority. Dr. Cumming's religion may demand a tribute of love, but it gives a charter to hatred; it may enjoin charity, but it fosters all uncharitableness. If I believe that God tells me to love my enemies, but at the same time hates His own enemies and requires me to have one will with Him, which has the larger scope, love or hatred? And we refer to those pages of Dr. Cumming's in which he opposes Roman Catholics, Puseyites, and infidels—pages which form the larger proportion of what he has published—for proof that the idea of God which both the logic and spirit of his discourses keep present to his hearers is that of a God who hates His enemies, a God who teaches love by fierce denunciations of wrath—a God who encourages obedience to His precepts by elaborately revealing to us that His own government is in precise opposition to those precepts. We know the usual evasions on this subject. We know Dr. Cumming would say that even Roman Catholics are to be loved and succored as men; that he would help even that "unclean spirit," Cardinal Wiseman, out of a ditch. But who that is in the slightest degree acquainted with the action of the human mind will believe that any genuine and large charity can grow out of an exercise of love which is always to have an *arrière-pensée* of hatred? Of what quality would be the conjugal love of a husband who loved his spouse as a wife, but hated her as a woman? It is reserved for the regenerate mind, according to Dr. Cumming's conception of it, to be "wise, amazed, temperate and furious, loyal and neutral, in a moment." Precepts of charity uttered with faint breath at the end of a sermon are perfectly futile, when all the force of the lungs has been spent in keeping the hearer's mind fixed on the conception of his fellow men, not as fellow sinners and fellow sufferers, but as agents of hell, as automata through whom Satan plays his game upon earth,—not on objects which call forth their reverence, their love, their hope of good even in the most strayed and perverted, but on a minute identification of human things with such symbols as the scarlet whore, the beast out of the abyss, scorpions whose sting is in their tails, men who have the mark of the beast, and unclean spirits like frogs. You might as well attempt to educate a child's sense of beauty by hanging its nursery with the horrible and grotesque pictures in which the early painters represented the Last Judgment, as expect Christian graces to flourish on that prophetic interpretation which Dr. Cumming offers as the principal nutriment of his flock. Quite apart from the critical basis of that interpretation, quite apart from the degree of truth there may be in Dr. Cumming's prognostications—questions into which we do not choose to enter—his use of prophecy must be *a priori* condemned, in the judgment of right-minded persons, by its results as testified in the net moral effect of his sermons. The best minds that accept Christianity as a divinely inspired system believe that the great end of the Gospel is not merely the saving but the educating of men's souls, the creating within them of holy dispositions, the subduing of egoistical pretensions, and the perpetual enhancing of the desire that the will of God—a will synonymous with goodness and truth—may be done on earth. But what relation to all this has a system of interpretation which keeps the mind of the Christian in the position of a spectator at a gladiatorial show, of which Satan is the wild beast in the shape of the great red dragon, the two thirds of mankind the victims—the whole provided and got up by God for the edification of the saints? The demonstration that the Second Advent is at hand, if true, can have no really holy, spiritual effect; the highest state of mind inculcated by the Gospel is resignation to the disposal of God's providence—"Whether we live, we live unto the Lord; whether we die, we die unto the Lord"—not an eagerness to see a temporal manifestation which shall confound the enemies of God and give exaltation to the saints; it is to dwell in Christ by spiritual communion with His nature, not to fix the date when He shall appear in the sky. Dr. Cumming's delight in shadowing forth the downfall of the Man of Sin, in prognosticating the battle of Gog and Magog, and in advertising the premillennial Advent, is simply the transportation of political passions on to a so-called religious platform; it is the anticipation of the triumph of "our party," accomplished by our principal men being "sent for" into the clouds. Let us be understood to speak in all seriousness. If we were in search of amusement, we should not seek for it by examining Dr. Cumming's works in order to ridicule them. We are simply discharging a disagreeable duty in delivering our opinion that, judged by the highest standard even of orthodox Christianity, they are little calculated to produce

A closer walk with God, A calm and heavenly frame

but are more likely to nourish egoistic complacency and pretension, a hard and condemnatory spirit towards one's fellow men, and a busy occupation with the minutiae of events, instead of a reverent contemplation of great facts and a wise application of great principles. It would be idle to consider Dr. Cumming's theory of prophecy in any other light,—as a philosophy of history or a specimen of Biblical interpretation; it bears about the same relation to the extension of genuine knowledge as the astrological "house" in the heavens bears to the true structure and relations of the universe. . . .

One more characteristic of Dr. Cumming's writings, and we have done. This is the *perverted moral judgment* that everywhere reigns in them. Not that this perversion is peculiar to Dr. Cumming; it belongs to the dogmatic system which he shares with all evangelical believers. But the abstract tendencies of systems are represented in very different degrees, according to the different characters of those who embrace them; just as the same food tells differently on different constitutions: and there are certain qualities in Dr. Cumming that cause the perversion of which we speak to exhibit itself with peculiar prominence in his teaching. A single extract will enable us to explain what we mean:

The "thoughts" are evil. If it were possible for human eye to discern and to detect the thoughts that flutter round the heart of an unregenerate man—to mark their hue and their multitude—it would be found that they are indeed "evil." We speak not of the thief, and the murderer, and the adulterer, and such-like, whose crimes draw down the cognizance of earthly tribunals, and whose unenviable character it is to take the lead in the paths of sin; but we refer to the men who are marked out by their practice of many of the seemliest moralities of life—by the exercise of the kindliest affections, and the interchange of the sweetest reciprocities—and of these men, if unrenewed and unchanged, we pronounce that their thoughts are evil. To ascertain this, we must refer to the object around which our thoughts ought continually to circulate. The Scriptures assert that this object is *the glory of God;* that for this we ought to think, to act, and to speak; and that in thus thinking, acting, and speaking, there is involved the purest and most endearing bliss. Now it will be found true of the most amiable men that with all their good society and kindliness of heart, and all their strict and unbending integrity, they never or rarely think of the glory of God. The question never occurs to them—Will this redound to the glory of God? Will this make His name more known, His being more loved,

His praise more sung? And just inasmuch as their every thought comes short of this lofty aim, in so much does it come short of good, and entitle itself to the character of evil. If the glory of God is not the absorbing and the influential aim of their thoughts, then they are evil; but God's glory never enters into their minds. They are amiable, because it chances to be one of the constitutional tendencies of their individual character, left uneffaced by the Fall; and *they are just and upright, because they have perhaps no occasion to be otherwise, or find it subservient to their interests to maintain such a character.*

Again we read:

There are traits in the Christian character which the mere worldly man cannot understand. He can understand the outward morality, but he cannot understand the inner spring of it; he can understand Dorcas's liberality to the poor, but he cannot penetrate the ground of Dorcas's liberality. *Some men give to the poor because they are ostentatious, or because they think the poor will ultimately avenge their neglect; but the Christian gives to the poor, not only because he has sensibilities like other men,* but because inasmuch as ye did it to the least of these my brethren, ye did it unto me.

Before entering on the more general question involved in these quotations, we must point to the clauses we have marked with italics, where Dr. Cumming appears to express sentiments which, we are happy to think, are not shared by the majority of his brethren in the faith. Dr. Cumming, it seems, is unable to conceive that the natural man can have any other motive for being just and upright than that it is useless to be otherwise, or that a character for honesty is profitable; according to his experience, between the feelings of ostentation and selfish alarm and the feeling of love to Christ, there lie no sensibilities which can lead a man to relieve want. Granting, as we should prefer to think, that it is Dr. Cumming's exposition of his sentiments which is deficient rather than his sentiments themselves, still, the fact that the deficiency lies precisely here, and that he can overlook it not only in the haste of oral delivery but in the examination of proof-sheets is strongly significant of his mental bias—of the faint degree in which he sympathizes with the disinterested elements of human feeling, and of the fact, which we are about to dwell upon, that those feelings are totally absent from his religious theory. Now, Dr. Cumming invariably assumes that, in fulminating against those who differ from him, he is standing on a moral elevation to which they are compelled reluctantly to look up; that his theory of motives and conduct is in its loftiness and purity a perpetual rebuke to their low and vicious desires and practice. It is time he should be told that the reverse is the fact; that there are men who do not merely cast a superficial glance at his doctrine, and fail to see its beauty or justice, but who, after a close consideration of that doctrine, pronounce it to be subversive of true moral development, and therefore positively noxious. Dr. Cumming is fond of showing-up the teaching of Romanism, and accusing it of undermining true morality: it is time he should be told that there is a large body, both of thinkers and practical men, who hold precisely the same opinion of his own teaching—with this difference, that they do not regard it as the inspiration of Satan, but as the natural crop of a human mind where the soil is chiefly made up of egoistic passions and dogmatic beliefs.

Dr. Cumming's theory, as we have seen, is that actions are good or evil according as they are prompted or not prompted by an exclusive reference to the "glory of God." God, then, in Dr. Cumming's conception, is a Being who has no pleasure in the exercise of love and truthfulness and justice, considered as affecting the well-being of His creatures; He has satisfaction in us only in so far as we exhaust our motives and dispositions of all relation to our fellow beings, and replace sympathy with men by anxiety for the "glory of God." The deed of Grace Darling, when she took a boat in the storm to rescue drowning men and women, was not good if it was only compassion that nerved her arm and impelled her to brave death for the chance of saving others; it was only good if she asked herself—Will this redound to the glory of God? The man who endures tortures rather than betray a trust, the man who spends years in toil in order to discharge an obligation from which the law declares him free, must be animated not by the spirit of fidelity to his fellow man, but by a desire to make "the name of God more known." The sweet charities of domestic life—the ready hand and the soothing word in sickness, the forbearance towards frailties, the prompt helpfulness in all efforts and sympathy in all joys—are simply evil if they result from a "constitutional tendency," or from dispositions disciplined by the experience of suffering and the perception of moral loveliness. A wife is not to devote herself to her husband out of love to him and a sense of the duties implied by a close relation—she is to be a faithful wife for the glory of God; if she feels her natural affections welling up too strongly, she is to repress them; it would not do to act from natural affection—she must think of the glory of God. A man is to guide his affairs with energy and discretion, not from an honest desire to fulfill his responsibilities as a member of society and a father, but—that "God's praise may be sung." Dr. Cumming's Christian pays his debts for the glory of God: were it not for the coercion of that supreme motive, it would be evil to pay them. A man is not to be just from a feeling of justice; he is not to help his fellow men out of good will to his fellow men; he is not to be a tender husband and father out of affection; all his natural muscles and fibers are to be torn away and replaced by a patent steel-spring—anxiety for the "glory of God."

Happily, the constitution of human nature forbids the complete prevalence of such a theory. Fatally powerful as religious systems have been, human nature is stronger and wider than religious systems, and though dogmas may hamper, they cannot absolutely repress its growth: build walls round the living tree as you will, the bricks and mortar have by and by to give way before the slow and sure operation of the sap. But next to that hatred of the enemies of God which is the principle of persecution, there perhaps has been no perversion more obstructive of true moral development than this substitution of a reference to the glory of God for the direct promptings of the sympathetic feelings. Benevolence and justice are strong only in proportion as they are directly and inevitably called into activity by their proper objects: pity is strong only because we are strongly impressed by suffering; and only in proportion as it is compassion that speaks through the eyes when we soothe, and moves the arm when we succour, is a deed strictly benevolent. If the soothing or the succour be given because another being wishes or approves it, the deed ceases to be one of benevolence, and becomes one of deference, of obedience, of self-interest, or vanity. Accessory motives may aid in producing an *action*, but they presuppose the weakness of the direct motive; and conversely, when the direct motive is strong, the action of accessory motives will be excluded. If then, as Dr. Cumming inculcates, the glory of God is to be "the absorbing and the influential aim" in our thoughts and actions, this must tend to neutralize the human sympathies; the stream of feeling will be diverted from its natural current in order to feed an artificial canal. The idea of God is really moral in its influence—it really cherishes all that is best and loveliest in man—only when God is contemplated as sympathizing with the pure elements of human feeling, as possessing infinitely all those attributes which we recognize to be moral in humanity. In this light, the idea of God and the sense of His presence intensify all noble feeling, and encourage all noble effort, on the same principle that human sympathy is found a source of strength: the brave man feels braver when he knows that another stout heart is beating time with his; the devoted woman who is wearing out her years in patient effort to alleviate suffering or save vice from the last stages of degradation finds aid in the pressure of a friendly hand which tells her that there is one who understands her deeds, and in her place would do the like. The idea of a God who not only sympathizes with all we feel and endure for our fellow men, but who will pour new life into our too languid love, and give firmness to our vacillating purpose, is an extension and multiplication of the effects produced by human sympathy; and it has been intensified for the better spirits who have been under the influence of orthodox Christianity, by the contemplation of Jesus as "God manifest in the flesh." But Dr. Cumming's God is the very opposite of all this: He is a God who, instead of sharing and aiding our human sympathies, is directly in collision with them; who, instead of strengthening the bond between man and man, by encouraging the sense that they are both alike the objects of His love and care, thrusts Himself between them and forbids them to feel for each other except as they have relation to Him. He is a God who, instead of adding His solar force to swell the tide of those impulses that tend to give humanity a common life in which the good of one is the good of all, commands us to check those impulses, lest they should prevent us from thinking of His glory. It is in vain for Dr. Cumming to say that we are to love man for God's sake: with the conception of God which his teaching presents, the love of man for God's sake involves, as his writings abundantly show, a strong principle of hatred. We can only love one being for the sake of another when there is an habitual delight in associating the idea of those two beings—that is, when the object of our indirect love is a source of joy and honour to the object of our direct love. But, according to Dr. Cumming's theory, the majority of mankind—the majority of his neighbours—are in precisely the opposite relation to God. His soul has no pleasure in them: they belong more to Satan than to Him; and if they contribute to His glory, it is against their will. Dr. Cumming, then, can only love *some* men for God's sake; the rest he must in consistency *hate* for God's sake.

There must be many, even in the circle of Dr. Cumming's admirers, who would be revolted by the doctrine we have just exposed, if their natural good sense and healthy feeling were not early stifled by dogmatic beliefs, and their reverence misled by pious phrases. But as it is, many a rational question, many a generous instinct, is repelled as the suggestion of a supernatural enemy, or as the ebullition of human pride and corruption. This state of inward contradiction can be put an end to only by the conviction that the free and diligent exertion of the intellect, instead of being a sin, is a part of their responsibility—that Right and Reason are synonymous. The fundamental faith for man is faith in the result of a brave, honest, and steady use of all his faculties:

> Let knowledge grow from more to more,
>   But more of reverence in us dwell;
>   That mind and soul according well
> May make one music as before,
>   But vaster.

Before taking leave of Dr. Cumming, let us express a hope that we have in no case exaggerated the unfavourable character of the inferences to be drawn from his pages. His creed often obliges him to hope the worst of men, and to exert himself in proving that the worst is true; but thus far we are happier than he. We have no theory which requires us to attribute unworthy motives to Dr. Cumming, no opinions, religious or irreligious, which can make it a gratification to us to detect him in delinquencies. On the contrary, the better we are able to think of him as a man, while we are obliged to disapprove him as a theologian, the stronger will be the evidence for our conviction, that the tendency towards good in human nature has a force which no creed can utterly counteract, and which ensures the ultimate triumph of that tendency over all dogmatic perversions.

11

Autobiography

CHARLES DARWIN

The founder of modern biology (1809–188?) was another of those who did not abandon his religious views with a light heart. At Cambridge University he was proud to occupy the same rooms as had been lived in by William Paley, whose book *Theology* was the foundation text of the argument from design. Darwin even considered the priesthood as a young man, and embarked on his study of the natural world in the belief that it demonstrated the glory of God. Having voyaged to South America and the Galapagos Islands on board the good ship *Beagle*, however, he found himself confronting the evidence of evolution by natural selection. His *Origin of Species*, published in 1859, was very reluctant to accept its own implications and referred throughout to "creation" without mentioning "evolution." (The author himself feared that these very implications, if followed, would be like "confessing a murder.") By the time that he published *The Descent of Man* in 1871, Darwin felt able to be a little more explicit, but the religiosity of his wife, Emma, was a continued inhibition, and it was only in his *Autobiography*, from which this excerpt comes, and in a few letters to trusted friends, that he admitted that his work and his life had slowly abolished his faith.

During these two years [October 1836 to January 1839] I was led to think much about religion. Whilst on board the *Beagle* I was quite orthodox, and I remember being heartily laughed at by several of the officers (though themselves orthodox) for quoting the Bible as an unanswerable authority on some point of morality. I suppose it was the novelty of the argument that amused them. But I had gradually come by this time, i.e., 1836 to 1839, to see that the Old Testament was no more to be trusted than the sacred books of the Hindoos. The question then continually rose before my mind and would not be banished,—is it credible that if God were now to make a revelation to the Hindoos, he would permit it to be connected with the belief in Vishnu, Siva, &c., as Christianity is connected with the Old Testament? This appeared to me utterly incredible.

By further reflecting that the clearest evidence would be requisite to make any sane man believe in the miracles by which Christianity is supported,—and that the more we know of the fixed laws of nature the more incredible do miracles become,—that the men at that time were ignorant and credulous to a degree almost incomprehensible by us,—that the Gospels cannot be proved to have been written simultaneously with the events,—that they differ in many important details, far too important, as it seemed to me, to be admitted as the usual inaccuracies of eye-witnesses;—by such reflections as these, which I give not as having the least novelty or value, but as they influenced me, I gradually came to disbelieve in Christianity as a divine revelation. The fact that many false religions have spread over large portions of the earth like wild-fire had some weight with me.

But I was very unwilling to give up my belief; I feel sure of this, for I can well remember often and often inventing day-dreams of old letters between distinguished Romans, and manuscripts being discovered at Pompeii or elsewhere, which confirmed in the most striking manner all that was written in the Gospels. But I found it more and more difficult, with free scope given to my imagination, to invent evidence which would suffice to convince me. Thus disbelief crept over me at a very slow rate, but was at last complete. The rate was so slow that I felt no distress.

Although I did not think much about the existence of a personal God until a considerably later period of my life, I will here give the vague conclusions to which I have been driven. The old argument from design in Nature, as given by Paley, which formerly seemed to me so conclusive, fails, now that the law of natural selection has been discovered. We can no longer argue that, for instance, the beautiful hinge of a bivalve shell must have been made by an intelligent being, like the hinge of a door by man. There seems to be no more design in the variability of organic beings, and in the action of natural selection, than in the course which the wind blows. But I have discussed this subject at the end of my book on the *Variation of Domesticated Animals and Plants,* and the argument there given has never, as far as I can see, been answered.

But passing over the endless beautiful adaptations which we everywhere meet with, it may be asked how can the generally beneficent arrangement of the world be accounted for? Some writers indeed are so much impressed with the amount of suffering in the world, that they doubt, if we look to all sentient beings, whether there is more of misery or of happiness; whether the world as a whole is a good or bad one. According to my judgment happiness decidedly prevails, though this would be very difficult to prove. If the truth of this conclusion be granted, it harmonizes well with the effects which we might expect from natural selection. If all the individuals of any species were habitually to suffer to an extreme degree, they would neglect to propagate their kind; but we have no reason to believe that this has ever, or at least often occurred. Some other considerations, moreover, lead to the belief that all sentient beings have been formed so as to enjoy, as a general rule, happiness.

Every one who believes, as I do, that all the corporeal and mental organs (excepting those which are neither advantageous nor disadvantageous to the possessor) of all beings have been developed through natural selection, or the survival of the fittest, together with use or habit, will admit that these organs have been formed so that their possessors may compete successfully with other beings, and thus increase in number. Now an animal may be led to pursue that course of action which is most beneficial to the species by suffering, such as pain, hunger, thirst, and fear; or by pleasure, as in eating and drinking, and in the propagation of the species, &c.; or by both means combined, as in the search for food. But pain or suffering of any kind, if long continued, causes depression and lessens the power of action, yet is well adapted to make a creature guard itself against any great or sudden evil. Pleasurable sensations, on the other hand, may be long continued without any depressing effect; on the contrary, they stimulate the whole system to increased action. Hence it has come to pass that most or all sentient beings have been developed in such a manner, through natural selection, that pleasurable sensations serve as their habitual guides. We see this in the pleasure from exertion, even occasionally from great exertion of the body or mind,—in the pleasure of our daily meals, and especially in the pleasure derived from sociability, and from loving our families. The sum of such pleasures as these, which are habitual or frequently recurrent, give, as I can hardly doubt, to most sentient beings an excess of happiness over misery, although many occasionally suffer much. Such suffering is quite compatible with the belief in Natural Selection, which is not perfect in its action, but tends only to render each species as successful as possible in the battle for life with other species, in wonderfully complex and changing circumstances.

That there is much suffering in the world no one disputes. Some have attempted to explain this with reference to man by imagining that it serves for his moral improvement. But the number of men in the world is as nothing compared with that of all other sentient beings, and they often suffer greatly without any moral improvement. This very old argument from the existence of suffering against the existence of an intelligent First Cause seems to me a strong one; whereas, as just remarked, the presence of much suffering agrees well with the view that all organic beings have been developed through variation and natural selection.

At the present day the most usual argument for the existence of an intelligent God is drawn from the deep inward conviction and feelings which are experienced by most persons.

Formerly I was led by feelings such as those just referred to (although I do not think that the religious sentiment was ever strongly developed in me), to the firm conviction of the existence of God, and of the immortality of the soul. In my Journal I wrote that whilst standing in the midst of the grandeur of a Brazilian forest, "it is not possible to give an adequate idea of the higher feelings of wonder, admiration, and devotion, which fill and elevate the mind." I well remember my conviction that there is more in man than the mere breath of his body. But now the grandest scenes would not cause any such convictions and feelings to rise in my mind. It may be truly said that I am like a man who has become colour-blind, and the universal belief by men of the existence of redness makes my present loss of perception of not the least value as evidence. This argument would be a valid one if all men of all races had the same inward conviction of the existence of one God; but we know that this is very far from being the case. Therefore I cannot see that such inward convictions and feelings are of any weight as evidence of what really exists. The state of mind which grand scenes formerly excited in me, and which was intimately connected with a belief in God, did not essentially differ from that which is often called the sense of sublimity; and however difficult it may be to explain the genesis of this sense, it can hardly be advanced as an argument for the existence of God, any more than the powerful though vague and similar feelings excited by music.

With respect to immortality, nothing shows me [so clearly] how strong and almost instinctive a belief it is, as the consideration of the view now held by most physicists, namely, that the sun with all the planets will in time grow too cold for life, unless indeed some great body dashes into the sun, and thus gives it fresh life. Believing as I do that man in the distant future will be a far more perfect creature than he now is, it is an intolerable thought that he and all other sentient beings are doomed to complete annihilation after such long-continued slow progress. To those who fully admit the immortality of the human soul, the destruction of our world will not appear so dreadful.

Another source of conviction in the existence of God, connected with the reason, and not with the feelings, impresses me as having much more weight. This follows from the extreme difficulty or rather impossibility of conceiving this immense and wonderful universe, including man with his capacity of looking far backwards and far into futurity, as the result of blind chance or necessity. When thus reflecting I feel compelled to look to a First Cause having an intelligent mind in some degree analogous to that of man; and I deserve to be called a Theist. This conclusion was strong in my mind about the time, as far as I can remember, when I wrote the *Origin of Species;* and it is since that time that it has very gradually, with many fluctuations, become weaker. But then arises the doubt, can the mind of man, which has, as I fully believe, been developed from a mind as low as that possessed by the lowest animals, be trusted when it draws such grand conclusions?

I cannot pretend to throw the least light on such abstruse problems. The mystery of the beginning of all things is insoluble by us; and I for one must be content to remain an Agnostic.

12

An Agnostic's Apology

LESLIE STEPHEN

Another victim of Oxford and Cambridge theocracy, that other great Victorian Leslie Stephen (1832–1904) chafed at the idea that he had to become an ordained minister in order to teach at Trinity Hall. He accordingly resigned his post and became celebrated as the biographer of Thomas Hobbes, Samuel Johnson, and George Eliot. Best remembered in some circles as the founder of Britain's *Dictionary of National Biography*, Stephen earned himself another place in that volume as the father of Virginia Woolf. This essay is a defense of Thomas Huxley who, despite his rather crude "social Darwinist" principles, had routed Bishop Wilberforce in a historic debate on the theory of evolution that took place at Oxford shortly after the publication of Darwin's *Origin of Species*.

The name agnostic, originally coined by Professor Huxley about 1869, has gained general acceptance. It is sometimes used to indicate the philosophical theory which Mr. Herbert Spencer, as he tells us, developed from the doctrine of Hamilton and Mansel. Upon that theory I express no opinion. I take the word in a vaguer sense, and am glad to believe that its use indicates an advance in the courtesies of controversy. The old theological phrase for an intellectual opponent was Atheist—a name which still retains a certain flavour as of the stake in this world and hell-fire in the next, and which, moreover, implies an inaccuracy of some importance. Dogmatic Atheism—the doctrine that there is no God, whatever may be meant by God—is, to say the least, a rare phase of opinion. The word Agnosticism, on the other hand, seems to imply a fairly accurate appreciation of a form of creed already common and daily spreading. The Agnostic is one who asserts—what no one denies—that there are limits to the sphere of human intelligence. He asserts, further, what many theologians have expressly maintained, that those limits are such as to exclude at least what Lewes called "metempirical" knowledge. But he goes farther, and asserts, in opposition to theologians, that theology lies within this forbidden sphere. This last assertion raises the important issue; and, though I have no pretension to invent an opposition nickname, I may venture, for the purposes of this article, to describe the rival school as Gnostics.

The Gnostic holds that our reason can, in some sense, transcend the narrow limits of experience. He holds that we can attain truths not capable of verification, and not needing verification, by actual experiment or observation. He holds, further, that a knowledge of those truths is essential to the highest interests of mankind, and enables us in some sort to solve the dark riddle of the universe. A complete solution, as everyone admits, is beyond our power. But some answer may be given to the doubts which harass and perplex us when we try to frame any adequate conception of the vast order of which we form an insignificant portion. We cannot say why this or that arrangement is what it is; we can say, though obscurely, that some answer exists, and would be satisfactory, if we could only find it. Overpowered, as every honest and serious thinker is at times overpowered, by the sight of pain, folly, and helplessness, by the jarring discords which run through the vast harmony of the universe, we are yet enabled to hear at times a whisper that all is well, to trust to it as coming from the most authentic source, and that only the temporary bars of sense prevent us from recognizing with certainty that the harmony beneath the discords is a reality and not a dream. This knowledge is embodied in the central dogma of theology. God is the name of the harmony; and God is knowable. Who would not be happy in accepting this belief, if he could accept it honestly? Who would not be glad if he could say with confidence: "the evil is transitory, the good eternal: our doubts are due to limitations destined to be abolished, and the world is really an embodiment of love and wisdom, however dark it may appear to our faculties"? And yet, if the so-called knowledge be illusory, are we not bound by the most sacred obligations to recognise the facts? Our brief path is dark enough on any hypothesis. We cannot afford to turn aside after every *ignis fatuus* without asking whether it leads to sounder footing or to hopeless quagmires. Dreams may be pleasanter for the moment than realities; but happiness must be won by adapting our lives to the realities. And who, that has felt the burden of existence, and suffered under well-meant efforts at consolation, will deny that such consolations are the bitterest of mockeries? Pain is not an evil; death is not a separation; sickness is but a blessing in disguise. Have the gloomiest speculations of avowed pessimists ever tortured sufferers like those kindly platitudes? Is there a more cutting piece of satire in the language than the reference in our funeral service to the "sure and certain hope of a blessed resurrection"? To dispel genuine hopes might be painful, however salutary. To suppress these spasmodic efforts to fly in the face of facts would be some comfort, even in the distress which they are meant to alleviate.

Besides the important question whether the Gnostic can prove his dogmas, there is, therefore, the further question whether the dogmas, if granted, have any meaning. Do they answer our doubts, or mock us with the appearance of an answer? The Gnostics rejoice in their knowledge. Have they anything to tell us?

They rebuke what they call the "pride of reason" in the name of a still more exalted pride. The scientific reasoner is arrogant because he sets limits to the faculty in which he trusts, and denies the existence of any other faculty. They are humble because they dare to tread in the regions which he declares to be inaccessible. But without bandying such accusations, or asking which pride is the greatest, the Gnostics are at least bound to show some ostensible justification for their complacency. Have they discovered a firm resting place from which they are entitled to look down in compassion or contempt upon those who hold it to be a mere edifice of moonshine? If they have diminished by a scruple the weight of one passing doubt, we should be grateful: perhaps we should be converts. If not, why condemn Agnosticism?

I have said that our knowledge is in any case limited. I may add that, on any showing, there is a danger in failing to recognise the limits of possible knowledge. The word Gnostic has some awkward associations. It once described certain heretics who got into trouble from fancying that men could frame theories of the Divine mode of existence. The sects have been dead for many centuries. Their fundamental assumptions can hardly be quite extinct. Not long ago, at least, there appeared in the papers a string of propositions framed—so we were assured—by some of the most candid and most learned of living theologians. These propositions defined by the help of various languages the precise relations which exist between the persons of the Trinity. It is an odd, though far from an unprecedented, circumstance that the unbeliever cannot quote them for fear of profanity. If they were transplanted into the pages of the *Fortnightly Review*, it would be impossible to convince anyone that the intention was not to mock the simple-minded persons who, we must suppose, were not themselves intentionally irreverent. It is enough to say that they defined the nature of God Almighty with an accuracy from which modest naturalists would shrink in describing the genesis of a black-beetle. I know not whether these dogmas were put forward as articles of faith, as pious conjectures, or as tentative contributions to sound theory. At any rate, it was supposed that they were interesting to beings of flesh and blood. If so, one can only ask in wonder whether an utter want of reverence is most strongly implied in this mode of dealing with sacred mysteries; or an utter ignorance of the existing state of the world in the assumption that the question which really divides mankind is the double procession of the Holy Ghost; or an utter incapacity for speculation in the confusion of these dead exuviæ of long-past modes of thought with living intellectual tissue; or an utter want of imagination, or of even a rudimentary sense of humour, in the hypothesis that the promulgation of such dogmas could produce anything but the laughter of sceptics and the contempt of the healthy human intellect?

The sect which requires to be encountered in these days is not one which boggles over the *filioque*, but certain successors of those Ephesians who told Paul that they did not even know "whether there were any Holy Ghost." But it explains some modern phenomena when we find that the leaders of theology hope to reconcile faith and reason, and to show that the old symbols have still a right to the allegiance of our hearts and brains, by putting forth these portentous propositions. We are struggling with hard facts, and they would arm us with the forgotten tools of scholasticism. We wish for spiritual food, and are to be put off with these ancient mummeries of forgotten dogma. If Agnosticism is the frame of mind which summarily rejects these imbecilities, and would restrain the human intellect from wasting its powers on the attempt to galvanise into sham activity this *caput mortuum* of old theology, nobody need be afraid of the name. Argument against such adversaries would be itself a foolish waste of time. Let the dead bury their dead, and Old Catholics decide whether the Holy Ghost proceeds from the Father and the Son, or from the Father alone. Gentlemen, indeed, who still read the Athanasian Creed, and profess to attach some meaning to its statements, have no right to sneer at their brethren who persist in taking things seriously. But for men who long for facts instead of phrases, the only possible course is to allow such vagaries to take their own course to the limbo to which they are naturally destined, simply noting, by the way, that modern Gnosticism may lead to puerilities which one blushes even to notice.

It is not with such phenomena that we have seriously to deal. Nobody maintains that the unassisted human intellect can discover the true theory of the Trinity; and the charge of Agnosticism refers, of course, to the sphere of reason, not to the sphere of revelation. Yet those who attack the doctrine are chiefly believers in revelation; and as such they should condescend to answer one important question. Is not the denunciation of reason a commonplace with theologians? What could be easier than to form a catena of the most philosophical defenders of Christianity who have exhausted language in declaring the impotence of the unassisted intellect? Comte has not more explicitly enounced the incapacity of man to deal with the Absolute and the Infinite than a whole series of orthodox writers. Trust your reason, we have been told till we are tired of the phrase, and you will become Atheists or Agnostics. We take you at your word: we become Agnostics. What right have you to turn round and rate us for being a degree more logical than yourselves? Our right, you reply, is founded upon a Divine revelation to ourselves or our Church. Let us grant—it is a very liberal concession—that the right may conceivably be established; but still you are at one with us in philosophy, as we say, that the natural man can know nothing of the Divine nature. That is Agnosticism. Our fundamental principle is not only granted, but asserted. By what logical device you succeed in overleaping the barriers which you have declared to be insuperable is another question. At least you have no *prima facie* ground for attacking our assumption that the limits of the human intellect are what you declare them to be. This is no mere verbal retort. Half, or more than half, of our adversaries agree formally with our leading principle. They cannot attack us without upsetting the very ground upon which the ablest advocates of their own case rely. The last English writer who professed to defend Christianity with weapons drawn from wide and genuine philosophical knowledge was Dean Mansel. The whole substance of his argument was simply and solely the assertion of the first principles of Agnosticism. Mr. Herbert Spencer, the prophet of the Unknowable, the foremost representative of Agnosticism, professes in his programme to be carrying "a step further the doctrine put into shape by Hamilton and Mansel." Nobody, I suspect, would now deny, nobody except Dean Mansel himself, and the "religious" newspapers, ever denied very seriously, that the "further step" thus taken was the logical step. Opponents both from within and without the Church, Mr. Maurice and Mr. Mill, agreed that this affiliation was legitimate. The Old Testament represents Jehovah as human, as vindictive, as prescribing immoralities; therefore, Jehovah was not the true God; that was the contention of the infidel. We know nothing whatever about the true God was the reply; for God means the Absolute and the Infinite. Any special act may come from God, for it may be a moral miracle; any attribute may represent the character of God to man, for we know nothing whatever of His real attributes and cannot even conceive Him as endowed with attributes. The doctrine of the Atonement cannot be revolting, because it cannot have any meaning. Mr. Spencer hardly goes a step beyond his original, except, indeed, in candour.

Most believers repudiate Dean Mansel's arguments. They were an anachronism. They were fatal to the decaying creed of pure Theism, and powerless against the growing creed of Agnosticism. When theology had vital power enough to throw out fresh branches, the orthodox could venture to attack the Deist, and the Deist could assail the traditional beliefs. As the impulse grows fainter, it is seen that such a warfare is suicidal. The old rivals must make an alliance against the common enemy. The theologian must appeal for help to the metaphysician whom he reviled. Orthodoxy used to call Spinoza an Atheist; it is now glad to argue that even Spinoza is a witness on its own side. Yet the most genuine theology still avows its hatred of reason and distrusts sham alliances. Newman was not, like Dean Mansel, a profound metaphysician, but his admirable rhetoric expressed a far finer religious instinct. He felt more keenly, if he did not reason so systematically; and the force of one side of his case is undeniable. He holds that the unassisted reason cannot afford a sufficient support for a belief in God. He declares, as innumerable writers of less power have declared, that there is "no medium, in true philosophy, between Atheism and Catholicity, and that a perfectly consistent mind, under those circumstances in which it finds itself here below, must embrace either the one or the other." He looks in vain for any antagonist, except the Catholic Church, capable of baffling and withstanding "the fierce energy of passion, and the all-corroding, all-dissolving skepticism of the intellect in religious matters." Some such doctrine is in fact but a natural corollary from the doctrine of human corruption held by all genuine theologians. The very basis of orthodox theology is the actual separation of the creation from the Creator. In the *Grammar of Assent,* Newman tells us that we "can only glean from the surface of the world some faint and fragmentary views" of God. "I see," he proceeds, "only a choice of alternatives in view of so critical a fact; either there is no Creator, or He has disowned His creatures." The absence of God from His own world is the one prominent fact which startles and appalls him. Newman, of course, does not see or does not admit the obvious consequence. He asserts most emphatically that he believes in the existence of God as firmly as in his own existence; and he finds the ultimate proof of this doctrine—a proof not to be put into mood and figure—in the testimony of the conscience. But he apparently admits that Atheism is as logical, that is, as free from self-contradiction, as Catholicism. He certainly declares that though the ordinary arguments are conclusive, they are not in practice convincing. Sound reason would, of course, establish theology; but corrupt man does not and cannot reason soundly. Newman, however, goes further than this. His Theism can only be supported by help of his Catholicity. If, therefore, Newman had never heard of the Catholic Church—if, that is, he were in the position of the great majority of men now living, and of the overwhelming majority of the race which has lived since its first appearance, he would be driven to one of two alternatives. Either he would be an Atheist or he would be an Agnostic. His conscience might say, there is a God; his observation would say, there is no God. Moreover, the voice of conscience has been very differently interpreted. Newman's interpretation has no force for anyone who, like most men, does not share his intuitions. To such persons, therefore, there can be, on Newman's own showing, no refuge except the admittedly logical refuge of Atheism. Even if they shared his intuitions, they would be necessarily skeptics until the Catholic Church came to their aid, for their intuitions would be in hopeless conflict with their experience. I need hardly add that, to some minds, the proposed alliance with reason of a Church, which admits that its tenets are corroded and dissolved wherever free reason is allowed to play upon them, is rather suspicious. At any rate, Newman's arguments go to prove that man, as guided by reason, ought to be an Agnostic, and that, at the present moment, Agnosticism is the only reasonable faith for at least three-quarters of the race.

All, then, who think that men should not be dogmatic about matters beyond the sphere of reason or even conceivability, who hold that reason, however weak, is our sole guide, or who find that their conscience does not testify to the divinity of the Catholic God, but declares the moral doctrines of Catholicity to be demonstrably erroneous, are entitled to claim such orthodox writers as sharing their fundamental principles, though refusing to draw the legitimate inferences. The authority of Dean Mansel and Newman may of course be repudiated. In one sense, however, they are simply stating an undeniable fact. The race collectively is agnostic, whatever may be the case with individuals. Newton might be certain of the truth of his doctrines, whilst other thinkers were still convinced of their falsity. It could not be said that the doctrines were certainly true, so long as they were doubted in good faith by competent reasoners. Newman may be as much convinced of the truth of his theology as Professor Huxley of its error. But speaking of the race, and not of the individual, there is no plainer fact in history than the fact that hitherto no knowledge has been attained. There is not a single proof of natural theology of which the negative has not been maintained as vigorously as the affirmative.

You tell us to be ashamed of professing ignorance. Where is the shame of ignorance in matters still involved in endless and hopeless controversy? Is it not rather a duty? Why should a lad who has just run the gauntlet of examinations and escaped to a country parsonage be dogmatic, when his dogmas are denounced as erroneous by half the philosophers of the world? What theory of the universe am I to accept as demonstrably established? At the very earliest dawn of philosophy men were divided by earlier forms of the same problems which divide them now. Shall I be a Platonist or an Aristotelian? Shall I admit or deny the existence of innate ideas? Shall I believe in the possibility or in the impossibility of transcending experience? Go to the mediæval philosophy, says one controversialist. To which mediæval philosophy, pray? Shall I be a nominalist or a realist? And why should I believe you rather than the great thinkers of the seventeenth century, who agreed with one accord that the first condition of intellectual progress was the destruction of that philosophy? There would be no difficulty if it were a question of physical science. I might believe in Galileo and Newton and their successors down to Adams and Leverrier without hesitation, because they all substantially agree. But when men deal with the old problems there are still the old doubts. Shall I believe in Hobbes or in Descartes? Can I stop where Descartes stopped, or must I go on to Spinoza? Or shall I follow Locke's guidance, and end with Hume's skepticism? Or listen to Kant, and, if so, shall I decide that he is right in destroying theology, or in reconstructing it, or in both performances? Does Hegel hold the key of the secret, or is he a mere spinner of jargon? May not Feuerbach or Schopenhauer represent the true development of metaphysical inquiry? Shall I put faith in Hamilton and Mansel, and, if so, shall I read their conclusions by the help of Mr. Spencer, or shall I believe in Mill or in Green? State any one proposition in which all philosophers agree, and I will admit it to be true; or any one which has a manifest balance of authority, and I will agree that it is probable. But so long as every philosopher flatly contradicts the first principles of his predecessors, why affect certainty? The only agreement I can discover is, that there is no philosopher of whom his opponents have not said that his opinions lead logically either to Pantheism or to Atheism.

When all the witnesses thus contradict each other, the *prima facie* result is pure skepticism. There is no certainty. Who am I, if I were the ablest of modern thinkers, to say summarily that all the great men who differed from me are wrong, and so wrong that their difference should not even raise a doubt in my mind? From such skepticism there is indeed one, and, so far as I can see, but one, escape. The very hopelessness of the controversy shows that the reasoners have been transcending the limits of reason. They have reached a point where, as at the pole, the compass points indifferently to every quarter. Thus there is a chance that I may retain what is valuable in the chaos of speculation, and reject what is bewildering by confining the mind to its proper limits. But has any limit ever been suggested, except a limit which comes in substance to an exclusion of all ontology? In short, if I would avoid utter skepticism, must I not be an Agnostic?

Let us suppose, however, that this difficulty can be evaded. Suppose that, after calling witnesses from all schools and all ages, I can find ground for excluding all the witnesses who make against me. Let me say, for example, that the whole school which refuses to transcend experience errs from the wickedness of its heart and the consequent dullness of its intellect. Some people seem to think that a plausible and happy suggestion. Let the theologian have his necessary laws of thought, which enable him to evolve truth beyond all need of verification from experience. Where will the process end? The question answers itself. The path has been trodden again and again, till it is as familiar as the first rule of arithmetic. Admit that the mind can reason about the Absolute and the Infinite, and you will get to the position of Spinoza, or to a position substantially equivalent. In fact, the chain of reasoning is substantially too short and simple to be for a moment doubtful. Theology, if logical, leads straight to Pantheism. The Infinite God is everything. All things are bound together as cause and effect. God, the first cause, is the cause of all effects down to the most remote. In one form or other, that is the conclusion to which all theology approximates as it is pushed to its legitimate result.

Here, then, we have an apparent triumph over Agnosticism. But nobody can accept Spinoza without rejecting all the doctrines for which the Gnostics really contend. In the first place, revelation and the God of revelation disappear. The argument according to Spinoza against supernaturalism differs from the argument according to Hume in being more peremptory. Hume only denies that a past miracle can be proved by evidence: Spinoza denies that it could ever have happened. As a fact, miracles and a local revelation were first assailed by Deists more effectually than by skeptics. The old Theology was seen to be unworthy of the God of nature, before it was said that nature could not be regarded through the theological representation. And, in the next place, the orthodox assault upon the value of Pantheism is irresistible. Pantheism can give no ground for morality, for nature is as much the cause of vice as the cause of virtue; it can give no ground for an optimist view of the universe, for nature causes evil as much as it causes good. We no longer doubt, it is true, whether there be a God, for our God means all reality; but every doubt which we entertained about the universe is transferred to the God upon whom the universe is molded. The attempt to transfer to pure being or to the abstraction Nature the feelings with which we are taught to regard a person of transcendent wisdom and benevolence is, as theologians assert, hopeless. To deny the existence of God is in this sense the same as to deny the existence of no-God. We keep the old word; we have altered the whole of its contents. A Pantheist is, as a rule, one who looks upon the universe through his feelings instead of his reason, and who regards it with love because his habitual frame of mind is amiable. But he has no logical argument as against the Pessimist, who regards it with dread unqualified by love, or the Agnostic, who finds it impossible to regard it with any but a colourless emotion. . . .

There are two questions, in short, about the universe which must be answered to escape from Agnosticism. The great fact which puzzles the mind is the vast amount of evil. It may be answered that evil is an illusion, because God is benevolent; or it may be answered that evil is deserved, because God is just. In one case the doubt is removed by denying the existence of the difficulty, in the other it is made tolerable by satisfying our consciences. We have seen what natural reason can do towards justifying these answers. To escape from Agnosticism we become Pantheists; then the divine reality must be the counterpart of phenomenal nature, and all the difficulties recur. We escape from Pantheism by the illogical device of free-will. Then God is indeed good and wise, but God is no longer omnipotent. By His side we erect a fetish called free-will, which is potent enough to defeat all God's good purposes, and to make His absence from His own universe the most conspicuous fact given by observation; and which, at the same time, is by its own nature intrinsically arbitrary in its action. Your Gnosticism tells us that an almighty benevolence is watching over everything, and bringing good out of all evil. Whence, then, comes the evil? By free-will; that is, by chance! It is an exception, an exception which covers, say, half the phenomena, and includes all that puzzle us. Say boldly at once no explanation can be given, and then proceed to denounce Agnosticism. If, again, we take the moral problem, the Pantheist view shows desert as before God to be a contradiction in terms. We are what He has made us; nay, we are but manifestations of Himself—how can He complain? Escape from the dilemma by making us independent of God, and God, so far as the observed universe can tell us, becomes systematically unjust. He rewards the good and the bad, and gives equal reward to the free agent and the slave of fate. Where are we to turn for a solution?

Let us turn to revelation; that is the most obvious reply. By all means, though this is to admit that natural reason cannot help us; or, in other words, it directly produces more Agnosticism, though indirectly it makes an opening for revelation. There is, indeed, a difficulty here. Pure theism, as we have observed, is in reality as vitally opposed to historical revelation as simple skepticism. The word God is used by the metaphysician and the savage. It may mean anything, from "pure Being" down to the most degraded fetish. The "universal consent" is a consent to use the same phrase for antagonistic conceptions—for order and chaos, for absolute unity or utter heterogeneity, for a universe governed by a human will, or by a will of which man cannot form the slightest conception. This is, of course, a difficulty which runs off the orthodox disputant like water from a duck's back. He appeals to his conscience, and his conscience tells him just what he wants. It reveals a Being just at that point in the scale between the two extremes which is convenient for his purposes. I open, for example, a harmless little treatise by a divine who need not be named. He knows intuitively, so he says, that there is a God, who is benevolent and wise, and endowed with personality, that is to say, conceived anthropomorphically enough to be capable of acting upon the universe, and yet so far different from man as to be able to throw a decent veil of mystery over His more questionable actions. Well, I reply, my intuition tells me of no such Being. Then, says the divine, I can't prove my statements, but you would recognise their truth if your heart or your intellect were not corrupted: that is, you must be a knave or a fool. This is a kind of argument to which one is perfectly accustomed in theology. I am right, and you are wrong; and I am right because I am good and wise. By all means; and now let us see what your wisdom and goodness can tell us.

The Christian revelation makes statements which, if true, are undoubtedly of the very highest importance. God is angry with man. Unless we believe and repent we shall all be damned. It is impossible, indeed, for its advocates even to say this without instantly contradicting themselves. Their doctrine frightens them. They explain in various ways that a great many people will be saved without believing, and that eternal damnation is not eternal nor damnation. It is only the vulgar who hold such views, and who, of course, must not be disturbed in them; but they are not for the intelligent. God grants "uncovenanted mercies"—that is, He sometimes lets a sinner off, though He has not made a legal bargain about it—an explanation calculated to exalt our conceptions of the Deity! But let us pass over these endless shufflings from the horrible to the meaningless. Christianity tells us in various ways how the wrath of the Creator may be appeased and His goodwill ensured. The doctrine is manifestly important to believers; but does it give us a dearer or happier view of the universe? That is what is required for the confusion of Agnostics; and, if the mystery were in part solved, or the clouds thinned in the slightest degree, Christianity would triumph by its inherent merits. Let us, then, ask once more, Does Christianity exhibit the ruler of the universe as benevolent or as just?

If I were to assert that of every ten beings born into this world nine would be damned, that all who refused to believe what they did not hold to be proved, and all who sinned from overwhelming temptation, and all who had not had the good-fortune to be the subjects of a miraculous conversion or the recipients of a grace conveyed by a magical charm, would be tortured to all eternity, what would an orthodox theologian reply? He could not say, "That is false"; I might appeal to the highest authorities for my justification; nor, in fact, could he on his own showing deny the possibility. Hell, he says, exists; he does not know who will be damned; though he does know that all men are by nature corrupt and liable to be damned if not saved by supernatural grace. He might, and probably would, now say, "That is rash. You have no authority for saying how many will be lost and how many saved: you cannot even say what is meant by hell or heaven: you cannot tell how far God may be better than His word, though you may be sure that He won't be worse than His word." And what is all this but to say, We know nothing about it? In other words, to fall back on Agnosticism. The difficulty, as theologians truly say, is not so much that evil is eternal, as that evil exists. That is in substance a frank admission that, as nobody can explain evil, nobody can explain anything. Your revelation, which was to prove the benevolence of God, has proved only that God's benevolence may be consistent with the eternal and infinite misery of most of His creatures; you escape only by saying that it is also consistent with their not being eternally and infinitely miserable. That is, the revelation reveals nothing.

But the revelation shows God to be just. Now, if the free-will hypothesis be rejected—and it is rejected, not only by infidels, but by the most consistent theologians—this question cannot really arise at all. Jonathan Edwards will prove that there cannot be a question of justice as between man and God. The creature has no rights against his Creator. The question of justice merges in the question of benevolence; and Edwards will go on to say that most men are damned, and that the blessed will thank God for their tortures. That is logical, but not consoling. Passing this over, can revelation prove that God is just, assuming that justice is a word applicable to dealings between the potter and the pot?

And here we are sent to the "great argument of Butler." Like some other theological arguments already noticed, that great argument is to many minds—those of James Mill and of Dr. Martineau, for example—a direct assault upon Theism, or, in other words, an argument for Agnosticism. Briefly stated, it comes to this. The God of revelation cannot be the God of nature, said the Deists, because the God of revelation is unjust. The God of revelation, replied Butler, may be the God of nature, for the God of nature is unjust. Stripped of its various involutions, that is the sum and substance of this celebrated piece of reasoning. Butler, I must say in passing, deserves high credit for two things. The first is that he is the only theologian who has ever had the courage to admit that any difficulty existed when he was struggling most desperately to meet the difficulty; though even Butler could not admit that such a difficulty should affect a man's conduct. Secondly, Butler's argument really rests upon a moral theory, mistaken indeed in some senses, but possessing a stoical grandeur. To admit, however, that Butler was a noble and a comparatively candid thinker is not to admit that he ever faced the real difficulty. It need not be asked here by what means he evaded it. His position is in any case plain. Christianity tells us, as he thinks, that God damns men for being bad, whether they could help it or not; and that He lets them off, or lets some of them off, for the sufferings of others. He damns the helpless and punishes the innocent. Horrible! exclaims the infidel. Possibly, replies Butler, but nature is just as bad. All suffering is punishment. It strikes the good as well as the wicked. The father sins, and the son suffers. I drink too much, and my son has the gout. In another world we may suppose that the same system will be carried out more thoroughly. God will pardon some sinners because He punished Christ, and He will damn others everlastingly. That is His way. A certain degree of wrongdoing here leads to irremediable suffering, or rather to suffering remediable by death alone. In the next world there is no death; therefore, the suffering won't be remediable at all. The world is a scene of probation, destined to fit us for a better life. As a matter of fact, most men make it a discipline of vice instead of a discipline of virtue; and most men, therefore, will presumably be damned. We see the same thing in the waste of seeds and animal life, and may suppose, therefore, that it is part of the general scheme of Providence.

This is the Christian revelation according to Butler. Does it make the world better? Does it not, rather, add indefinitely to the terror produced by the sight of all its miseries, and justify James Mill for feeling that rather than such a God he would have no God? What escape can be suggested? The obvious one: it is all a mystery; and what is mystery but the theological phrase for Agnosticism? God has spoken, and endorsed all our most hideous doubts. He has said, let there be light, and there is no light—no light, but rather darkness visible, serving only to discover sights of woe.

The believers who desire to soften away the old dogmas—in other words, to take refuge from the unpleasant results of their doctrine with the Agnostics, and to retain the pleasant results with the Gnostics—have a different mode of escape. They know that God is good and just; that evil will somehow disappear and apparent injustice be somehow redressed. The practical objection to this amiable creed suggests a sad comment upon the whole controversy. We fly to religion to escape from our dark forebodings. But a religion which stifles these forebodings always fails to satisfy us. We long to hear that they are groundless. As soon as we are told that they are groundless we mistrust our authority. No poetry lives which reflects only the cheerful emotions. Our sweetest songs are those which tell of saddest thought. We can bring harmony out of melancholy; we cannot banish melancholy from the world. And the religious utterances, which are the highest form of poetry, are bound by the same law. There is a deep sadness in the world. Turn and twist the thought as you may, there is no escape. Optimism would be soothing if it were possible; in fact, it is impossible, and therefore a constant mockery; and of all dogmas that ever were invented, that which has least vitality is the dogma that whatever is, is right.

Let us, however, consider for a moment what is the net result of this pleasant creed. Its philosophical basis may be sought in pure reason or in experience; but, as a rule, its adherents are ready to admit that the pure reason requires the support of the emotions before such a doctrine can be established, and are therefore marked by a certain tinge of mysticism. They feel rather than know. The awe with which they regard the universe, the tender glow of reverence and love with which the bare sight of nature affects them, is to them the ultimate guarantee of their beliefs. Happy those who feel such emotions! Only, when they try to extract definite statements of fact from these impalpable sentiments, they should beware how far such statements are apt to come into terrible colli-sion with reality. And, meanwhile, those who have been disabused with Can-dide, who have felt the weariness and pain of all "this unintelligible world," and have not been able to escape into any mystic rapture, have as much to say for their own version of the facts. Is happiness a dream, or misery, or is it all a dream? Does not our answer vary with our health and with our condition? When, rapt in the security of a happy life, we cannot even conceive that our hap-piness will fail, we are practical optimists. When some random blow out of the dark crushes the pillars round which our life has been entwined as recklessly as a boy sweeps away a cobweb, when at a single step we plunge through the flimsy crust of happiness into the deep gulfs beneath, we are tempted to turn to Pes-simism. Who shall decide, and how? Of all questions that can be asked, the most important is surely this. Is the tangled web of this world composed chiefly of happiness or of misery? And of all questions that can be asked, it is surely the most unanswerable. For in no other problem is the difficulty of discarding the illusions arising from our own experience, of eliminating "the personal error" and gaining an outside standing-point, so hopeless.

In any case the real appeal must be to experience. Ontologists may manufac-ture libraries of jargon without touching the point. They have never made, or suggested the barest possibility of making, a bridge from the world of pure rea-son to the contingent world in which we live. To the thinker who tries to con-struct the universe out of pure reason, the actual existence of error in our minds and disorder in the outside world presents a difficulty as hopeless as that which the existence of vice and misery presents to the optimist who tries to construct the universe out of pure goodness. To say that misery does not exist is to contra-dict the primary testimony of consciousness; to argue on *à priori* grounds that misery or happiness predominates, is as hopeless a task as to deduce from the principle of the excluded middle the distance from St. Paul's to Westminster Abbey. Questions of fact can only be solved by examining facts. Perhaps such ev-idence would show—and if a guess were worth anything, I should add that I guess that it would show—that happiness predominates over misery in the com-position of the known world. I am, therefore, not prejudiced against the Gnos-tic's conclusion; but I add that the evidence is just as open to me as to him. The whole world in which we live may be an illusion—a veil to be withdrawn in some higher state of being. But be it what it may, it supplies all the evidence upon which we can rely. If evil predominates here, we have no reason to suppose that good predominates elsewhere. All the ingenuity of theologians can never shake our conviction that facts are what we feel them to be, nor invert the plain infer-ence from facts; and facts are just as open to one school of thought as to an-other.

What, then, is the net result? One insoluble doubt has haunted men's minds since thought began in the world. No answer has ever been suggested. One school of philosophers hands it to the next. It is denied in one form only to reappear in another. The question is not which system excludes the doubt, but how it expresses the doubt. Admit or deny the competence of reason in theory, we all agree that it fails in practice. Theologians revile reason as much as Agnostics; they then appeal to it, and it decides against them. They amend their plea by excluding certain questions from its jurisdiction, and those questions include the whole difficulty. They go to revelation, and revelation replies by calling doubt, mystery. They declare that their consciousness declares just what they want it to declare. Ours declares something else. Who is to decide? The only appeal is to experience, and to appeal to experience is to admit the fundamental dogma of Agnosticism.

Is it not, then, the very height of audacity, in face of a difficulty which meets us at every turn, which has perplexed all the ablest thinkers in proportion to their ability, which vanishes in one shape only to show itself in another, to declare roundly, not only that the difficulty can be solved, but that it does not exist? Why, when no honest man will deny in private that every ultimate problem is wrapped in the profoundest mystery, do honest men proclaim in pulpits that unhesitating certainty is the duty of the most foolish and ignorant? Is it not a spectacle to make the angels laugh? We are a company of ignorant beings, feeling our way through mists and darkness, learning only by incessantly repeated blunders, obtaining a glimmering of truth by falling into every conceivable error, dimly discerning light enough for our daily needs, but hopelessly differing whenever we attempt to describe the ultimate origin or end of our paths; and yet when one of us ventures to declare that we don't know the map of the universe as well as the map of our infinitesimal parish, he is hooted, reviled, and perhaps told that he will be damned to all eternity for his faithlessness. Amidst all the endless and hopeless controversies which have left nothing but bare husks of meaningless words, we have been able to discover certain reliable truths. They don't take us very far, and the condition of discovering them has been distrust of *a priori* guesses, and the systematic interrogation of experience. Let us, say some of us, follow at least this clue. Here we shall find sufficient guidance for the needs of life, though we renounce for ever the attempt to get behind the veil which no one has succeeded in raising; if, indeed, there be anything behind. You miserable Agnostics! is the retort throw aside such rubbish, and cling to the old husks. Stick to the words which profess to explain everything; call your doubts mysteries, and they won't disturb you any longer; and believe in those necessary truths of which no two philosophers have ever succeeded in giving the same version.

Gentlemen, we can only reply, wait till you have some show of agreement amongst yourselves. Wait till you can give some answer not palpably a verbal answer, to some one of the doubts which oppress us as they oppress you. Wait till you can point to some single truth, however trifling, which has been discovered by your method, and will stand the test of discussion and verification. Wait till you can appeal to reason without in the same breath vilifying reason. Wait till your Divine revelations have something more to reveal than the hope that the hideous doubts which they suggest may possibly be without foundation. Till then we shall be content to admit openly, what you whisper under your breath or hide in technical jargon, that the ancient secret is a secret still; that man knows nothing of the Infinite and Absolute; and that, knowing nothing, he had better not be dogmatic about his ignorance. And, meanwhile, we will endeavour to be as charitable as possible, and whilst you trumpet forth officially your contempt for our skepticism, we will at least try to believe that you are imposed upon by your own bluster.

13

Miracle

ANATOLE FRANCE

An enjoyable squib from Anatole France (1844–1924), winner of the 1921 Nobel Prize for Literature and lifelong foe of French clericalism, whose true name was Jacques-Anatole-François Thibault. It's nice to know that the title of the book from which this is taken was *Le Jardin d'Epicure*, or *The Garden of Epicurus*—a respectful nod to one of the Greek founders of skepticism.

We should not say: There are no miracles, because none has ever been proved. This always leaves it open to the Orthodox to appeal to a more complete state of knowledge. The truth is, no miracle can, from the nature of things, be stated as an established fact; to do so will always involve drawing a premature conclusion. A deeply rooted instinct tells us that whatever Nature embraces in her bosom is conformable to her laws, either known or occult. But, even supposing he could silence this presentiment of his, a man will never be in a position to say: "Such and such a fact is outside the limits of Nature." Our researches will never carry us as far as that. Moreover, if it is of the essence of miracle to elude scientific investigation, every dogma attesting it invokes an intangible witness that is bound to evade our grasp to the end of time.

This notion of miracles belongs to the infancy of the mind, and cannot continue when once the human intellect has begun to frame a systematic picture of the universe. The wise Greeks could not tolerate the idea. Hippocrates said, speaking of epilepsy: "This malady is called divine; but all diseases are divine, and all alike come from the gods." There he spoke as a natural philosopher. Human reason is less assured of itself nowadays. What annoys me above all is when people say: "We do not believe in miracles, because no miracle is proved."

Happening to be at Lourdes, in August, I paid a visit to the grotto where innumerable crutches were hung up in token of a cure. My companion pointed to these trophies of the sick-room and hospital ward, and whispered in my ear:

"One wooden leg would be more to the point." It was the word of a man of sense; but speaking philosophically, the wooden leg would be no whit more convincing than a crutch. If an observer of a genuinely scientific spirit were called upon to verify that a man's leg, after amputation, had suddenly grown again as before, whether in a miraculous pool or anywhere else, he would not cry: "Lo! a miracle." He would say this: "An observation, so far unique, points us to a presumption that under conditions still undetermined, the tissues of a human leg have the property of reorganizing themselves like a crab's or lobster's claws and a lizard's tail, but much more rapidly. Here we have a fact of nature in apparent contradiction with several other facts of the like sort. The contradiction arises from our ignorance, and clearly shows that the science of animal physiology must be reconstituted, or to speak more accurately, that it has never yet been properly constituted. It is little more than two hundred years since we first had any true conception of the circulation of the blood. It is barely a century since we learned what is implied in the act of breathing." I admit it would need some boldness to speak in this strain. But the man of science should be above surprise. At the same time, let us hasten to add, none of them have ever been put to such a proof, and nothing leads us to apprehend any such prodigy. Such miraculous cures as the doctors have been able to verify to their satisfaction are all quite in accordance with physiology. So far the tombs of the Saints, the magic springs and sacred grottoes, have never proved efficient except in the case of patients suffering from complaints either curable or susceptible of instantaneous relief. But were a dead man revived before our eyes, no miracle would be proved, unless we knew what life is and death is, and that we shall never know.

What is the definition of a miracle? We are told: a breach of the laws of nature. But we do not know the laws of nature; how, then, are we to know whether a particular fact is a breach of these laws or no?

"But surely we know some of these laws?"

"True, we have arrived at some idea of the correlation of things. But failing as we do to grasp all the natural laws, we can be sure of none, seeing they are mutually interdependent."

"Still, we might verify our miracle in those series of correlations we *have* arrived at."

"No, not with anything like philosophical certainty. Besides, it is precisely those series we regard as the most stable and best determined which suffer least interruption from the miraculous. Miracles never, for instance, try to interfere with the mechanism of the heavens. They never disturb the course of the celestial bodies, and never advance or retard the calculated date of an eclipse. On the contrary, their favourite field is the obscure domain of pathology as concerned with the internal organs, and above all nervous diseases. However, we must not confound a question of fact with one of principle. In principle the man of science is ill-qualified to verify a supernatural occurrence. Such verification presupposes a complete and final knowledge of nature, which he does not possess, and will never possess, and which no one ever did possess in this world. It is just

because I would not believe our most skilful oculists as to the miraculous healing of a blind man that *a fortiori* I do not believe Matthew or Mark either, who
were not oculists. A miracle is by definition unidentifiable and unknowable."

The savants cannot in any case certify that a fact is in contradiction with the
universal order that is with the unknown ordinance of the Divinity. Even God
could do this only by formulating a pettifogging distinction between the general manifestations and the particular manifestations of His activity, acknowledging that from time to time He gives little timid finishing touches to His
work and condescending to the humiliating admission that the cumbersome
machine He has set agoing needs every hour or so, to get it to jog along indifferently well, a push from its contriver's hand.

Science is well fitted, on the other hand, to bring back under the data of positive knowledge facts which seemed to be outside its limits. It often succeeds very
happily in accounting by physical causes for phenomena that had for centuries
been regarded as supernatural. Cures of spinal affections were confidently believed to have taken place at the tomb of the Deacon Paris at Saint-Médard and
in other holy places. These cures have ceased to surprise since it has become
known that hysteria occasionally simulates the symptoms associated with le-
sions of the spinal marrow.

The appearance of a new star to the mysterious personages whom the
Gospels call the "Wise Men of the East" (I assume the incident to be authentic
historically) was undoubtedly a miracle to the Astrologers of the Middle Ages,
who believed that the firmament, in which the stars were stuck like nails, was
subject to no change whatever. But, whether real or supposed, the star of the
Magi has lost its miraculous character for us, who know that the heavens are
incessantly perturbed by the birth and death of worlds, and who in 1866 saw a
star suddenly blaze forth in the Corona Borealis, shine for a month, and then
go out.

It did not proclaim the Messiah; all it announced was that, at an infinitely remote distance from our earth, an appalling conflagration was burning up a
world in a few days,—or rather had burnt it up long ago, for the ray that brought
us the news of this disaster in the heavens had been on the road for five hundred years and possibly longer.

The miracle of Bolsena is familiar to everybody, immortalized as it is in one of
Raphael's *Stanze* at the Vatican. A skeptical priest was celebrating Mass; the
host, when he broke it for Communion, appeared bespattered with blood. It is
only within the last ten years that the Academies of Science would not have
been sorely puzzled to explain so strange a phenomenon. Now no one thinks of
denying it, since the discovery of a microscopic fungus, the spores of which,
having germinated in the meal or dough, offer the appearance of clotted blood.
The naturalist who first found it, rightly thinking that here were the red

blotches on the wafer in the Bolsena miracle, named the fungus *micrococcus prodigiosus*.

There will always be a fungus, a star, or a disease that human science does not know of; and for this reason it must always behoove the philosopher, in the name of the undying ignorance of man, to deny every miracle and say of the most startling wonders,—the host of Bolsena, the star in the East, the cure of the paralytic and the like: Either it is not, or it is; and if it is, it is part of nature and therefore natural.

14

Thoughts of God

From *Fables of Man*

Mark Twain

Like Anatole France choosing a *nom de plume* less cumbersome than his given one, Samuel Langhorne Clemens became immortal as the author of *Tom Sawyer* and *Huckleberry Finn*. Beloved as an avuncular raconteur and as a humorous public speaker, Twain often had difficulty being taken seriously when he pronounced on graver topics. But those who have read his polemics against war and imperialism, and against the cruelties of religion, are aware that his wit could be mordant. As we keep finding in this story, the climate of bigotry often meant that these essays could not be published in Twain's lifetime.

How often we are moved to admit the intelligence exhibited in both the designing and the execution of some of His works. Take the fly, for instance. The planning of the fly was an application of pure intelligence, morals not being concerned. Not one of us could have planned the fly, not one of us could have constructed him; and no one would have considered it wise to try, except under an assumed name. It is believed by some that the fly was introduced to meet a long-felt want. In the course of ages, for some reason or other, there have been millions of these persons, but out of this vast multitude there has not been one who has been willing to explain what the want was. At least satisfactorily. A few have explained that there was need of a creature to remove disease-breeding garbage; but these being then asked to explain what long-felt want the disease-breeding garbage was introduced to supply, they have not been willing to undertake the contract.

There is much inconsistency concerning the fly. In all the ages he has not had a friend, there has never been a person in the earth who could have been persuaded to intervene between him and extermination; yet billions of persons have excused the Hand that made him—and this without a blush. Would they have excused a Man in the same circumstances, a man positively known to have invented the fly? On the contrary. For the credit of the race let us believe it

would have been all day with that man. Would persons consider it just to repro-
bate in a child, with its undeveloped morals, a scandal that they would overlook
in the Pope?

When we reflect that the fly was as not invented for pastime, but in the way of
business; that he was not flung off in a heedless moment and with no object in
view but to pass the time, but was the fruit of long and pains-taking labor and
calculation, and with a definite and far-reaching, purpose in view; that his character and conduct were planned out with cold deliberation, that his career was
foreseen and fore-ordered, and that there was no want which he could supply,
we are hopelessly puzzled, we cannot understand the moral lapse that was able
to render possible the conceiving and the consummation of this squalid and
malevolent creature.

Let us try to think the unthinkable: let us try to imagine a Man of a sort willing to invent the fly; that is to say, a man destitute of feeling; a man willing to
wantonly torture and harass and persecute myriads of creatures who had never
done him any harm and could not if they wanted to, and—the majority of
them—poor dumb things not even aware of his existence. In a word, let us try to
imagine a man with so singular and so lumbering a code of morals as this: that
it is fair and right to send afflictions upon the *just*—upon the unoffending as
well as upon the offending, without discrimination.

If we can imagine such a man, that is the man that could invent the fly, and
send him out on his mission and furnish him his orders: "Depart into the uttermost corners of the earth, and diligently do your appointed work. Persecute the
sick child; settle upon its eyes, its face, its hands, and gnaw and pester and sting;
worry and fret and madden the worn and tired mother who watches by the
child, and who humbly prays for mercy and relief with the pathetic faith of the
deceived and the unteachable. Settle upon the soldier's festering wounds in
field and hospital and drive him frantic while he also prays, and betweentimes
curses, with none to listen but you, Fly, who get all the petting and all the protection, without even praying for it. Harry and persecute the forlorn and forsaken wretch who is perishing of the plague, and in his terror and despair
praying; bite, sting, feed upon his ulcers, dabble your feet in his rotten blood,
gum them thick with plague-germs—feet cunningly designed and perfected for
this function ages ago in the beginning—carry this freight to a hundred tables,
among the just and the unjust, the high and the low, and walk over the food
and gaum it with filth and death. Visit all; allow no man peace till he get it in
the grave; visit and afflict the hard-worked and unoffending horse, mule, ox,
ass, pester the patient cow, and all the kindly animals that labor without fair reward here and perish without hope of it hereafter; spare no creature, wild or
tame; but wheresoever you find one, make his life a misery, treat him as the innocent deserve; and so please Me and increase My glory Who made the fly."

We hear much about His patience and forbearance and long-suffering; we
hear nothing about our own, which much exceeds it. We hear much about His

mercy and kindness and goodness—in words—the words of His Book and of His pulpit—and the meek multitude is content with this evidence, such as it is, seeking no further; but whoso searcheth after a concreted sample of it will in time acquire fatigue. There being no instances of it. For what are gilded as mercies are not in any recorded case more than mere common justices, and *due*—due without thanks or compliment. To rescue without personal risk a cripple from a burning house is not a mercy, it is a mere commonplace duty; anybody would do it that could. And not by proxy, either—delegating the work but confiscating the credit for it. If men neglected "God's poor" and "God's stricken and helpless ones" as He does, what would become of them? The answer is to be found in those dark lands where man follows His example and turns his indifferent back upon them: they get no help at all; they cry, and plead and pray in vain, they linger and suffer, and miserably die. If you will look at the matter rationally and without prejudice, the proper place to hunt for the facts of His mercy, is not where man does the mercies and He collects the praise, but in those regions where He has the field to Himself.

It is plain that there is one moral law for heaven and another for the earth. The pulpit assures us that wherever we see suffering and sorrow, which we can relieve and do not do it, we sin, heavily. *There was never yet a case of suffering or sorrow which God could not relieve.* Does He sin, then? If He is the Source of Morals He does—certainly nothing can be plainer than that, you will admit. Surely the Source of law cannot violate law and stand unsmirched; surely the judge upon the bench cannot forbid crime and then revel in it himself unreproached. Nevertheless we have this curious spectacle: daily the trained parrot in the pulpit gravely delivers himself of these ironies, which he has acquired at second-hand and adopted without examination, to a trained congregation which accepts them without examination, and neither the speaker nor the hearer laughs at himself. It does seem as if we ought to be humble when we are at a bench-show, and not put on airs of intellectual superiority there.

·   ·   ·

Bible Teaching
and Religious Practice

From *Europe and Elsewhere* and
A Pen Warmed Up In Hell

MARK TWAIN

Religion had its share in the changes of civilization and national character, of course. What share? The lion's In the history of the human race this has always been the case, will always be the case, to the end of time, no doubt; or at least until man by the slow processes of evolution shall develop into something really fine and high—some billions of years hence, say.

The Christian Bible is a drug store. Its contents remain the same; but the medical practice changes. For eighteen hundred years these changes were slight—scarcely noticeable. The practice was allopathic—allopathic in its rudest and crudest form. The dull and ignorant physician day and night, and all the days and all the nights, drenched his patient with vast and hideous doses of the most repulsive drugs to be found in the store's stock; he bled him, cupped him, purged him, puked him, salivated him, never gave his system a chance to rally, nor nature a chance to help. He kept him religion sick for eighteen centuries, and allowed him not a well day during all that time. The stock in the store was made up of about equal portions of baleful and debilitating poisons, and healing and comforting medicines; but the practice of the time confined the physician to the use of the former; by consequence, he could only damage his patient, and that is what he did.

Not until far within our century was any considerable change in the practice introduced; and then mainly, or in effect only, in Great Britain and the United States. In the other countries today, the patient either still takes the ancient treatment or does not call the physician at all. In the English-speaking countries the changes observable in our century were forced by that very thing just referred to—the revolt of the patient against the system; they were not projected by the physician. The patient fell to doctoring himself, and the physician's practice began to fall off. He modified his method to get back his trade. He did it gradually, reluctantly; and never yielded more at a time than the pressure compelled. At first he relinquished the daily dose of hell and damnation, and administered it every other day only; next he allowed another day to pass; then another and presently another; when he had restricted it at last to Sundays, and imagined that now there would surely be a truce, the homeopath arrived on the field and made him abandon hell and damnation altogether, and administered

119

Christ's love, and comfort, and charity and compassion in its stead. These had been in the drug store all the time, gold labeled and conspicuous among the long shelfloads of repulsive purges and vomits and poisons, and so the practice was to blame that they had remained unused, not the pharmacy. To the ecclesiastical physician of fifty years ago, his predecessor for eighteen centuries was a quack; to the ecclesiastical physician of today, his predecessor of fifty years ago was a quack. To the every-man-his-own-ecclesiastical-doctor of—when?—what will the ecclesiastical physician of today be? Unless evolution, which has been a truth ever since the globes, suns, and planets of the solar system were but wandering films of meteor dust, shall reach a limit and become a lie, there is but one fate in store for him.

The methods of the priest and the parson have been very curious; their history is very entertaining. In all the ages the Roman Church has owned slaves, bought and sold slaves, authorized and encouraged her children to trade in them. Long after some Christian peoples had freed their slaves the Church still held on to hers. If any could know, to absolute certainty, that all this was right, and according to God's will and desire, surely it was she, since she was God's specially appointed representative in the earth and sole authorized and infallible expounder of his Bible. There were the texts; there was no mistaking their meaning; she was right, she was doing in this thing what the Bible had mapped out for her to do. So unassailable was her position that in all the centuries she had no word to say against human slavery. Yet now at last, in our immediate day, we hear a Pope saying slave trading is wrong, and we see him sending an expedition to Africa to stop it. The texts remain: it is the practice that has changed. Why? Because the world has corrected the Bible. The Church never corrects it; and also never fails to drop in at the tail of the procession—and take the credit of the correction. As she will presently do in this instance.

Christian England supported slavery and encouraged it for two hundred and fifty years, and her church's consecrated ministers looked on, sometimes taking an active hand, the rest of the time indifferent. England's interest in the business may be called a Christian interest, a Christian industry. She had her full share in his revival after a long period of inactivity, and his revival was a Christian monopoly; that is to say, it was in the hands of Christian countries exclusively. English parliaments aided the slave traffic and protected it; two English kings held stock in slave-catching companies. The first regular English slave hunter—John Hawkins, of still revered memory—made such successful havoc, on his second voyage, in the matter of surprising and burning villages, and maiming, slaughtering, capturing, and selling their unoffending inhabitants, that his delighted queen conferred the chivalric honor of knighthood on him—a rank which had acquired its chief esteem and distinction in other and earlier fields of Christian effort. The new knight, with characteristic English frankness and brusque simplicity, chose as his device the figure of a Negro slave, kneeling and in chains. Sir John's work was the invention of Christians, was to remain a bloody and awful monopoly in the hands of Christians for a quarter of a millennium, was to destroy homes, separate families, enslave friendless men and women, and break a myriad of human hearts, to the end that Christian nations might be prosperous and comfortable, Christian churches be built, and the gospel of the meek and merciful Redeemer be spread abroad in the earth; and so in the name of his ship, unsuspected but eloquent and clear, lay hidden prophecy. She was called The Jesus.

But at last in England, an illegitimate Christian rose against slavery. It is curious that when a Christian rises against a rooted wrong at all, he is usually an illegitimate Christian, member of some despised and bastard sect. There was a bitter struggle, but in the end the slave trade had to go—and went. The Biblical authorization remained, but the practice changed.

Then—the usual thing happened; the visiting English critic among us began straightway to hold up his pious hands in horror at our slavery. His distress was unappeasable, his words full of bitterness and contempt. It is true we had not so many as fifteen hundred thousand slaves for him to worry about, while his England still owned twelve million, in her foreign possessions; but that fact did not modify his wail any, or stay his tears, or soften his censure. The fact that every time we had tried to get rid of our slavery in previous generations, but had always been obstructed, balked, and defeated by England, was a matter of no consequence to him; it was ancient history, and not worth the telling.

Our own conversion came at last. We began to stir against slavery. Hearts grew soft, here, there, and yonder. There was no place in the land where the seeker could not find some small budding sign of pity for the slave. No place in all the land but one—the pulpit. It yielded at last; it always does. It fought a strong and stubborn fight, and then did what it always does, joined the procession—at the tail end. Slavery fell. The slavery text remained; the practice changed, that was all.

During many ages there were witches. The Bible said so. The Bible commanded that they should not be allowed to live. Therefore the Church, after doing its duty in but a lazy and indolent way for eight hundred years, gathered up its halters, thumbscrews, and firebrands, and set about its holy work in earnest. She worked hard at it night and day during nine centuries and imprisoned, tortured, hanged, and burned whole hordes and armies of witches, and washed the Christian world clean with their foul blood.

Then it was discovered that there was no such thing as witches, and never had been. One does not know whether to laugh or to cry. Who discovered that there was no such thing as a witch—the priest, the parson? No, these never discover anything. At Salem, the parson clung pathetically to his witch text after the laity had abandoned it in remorse and tears for the crimes and cruelties it had persuaded them to do. The parson wanted more blood, more shame, more brutalities; it was the unconsecrated laity that stayed his hand. In Scotland the parson killed the witch after the magistrate had pronounced her innocent; and when the merciful legislature proposed to sweep the hideous laws against witches from the statute book, it was the parson who came imploring, with tears and imprecations, that they be suffered to stand.

There are no witches. The witch text remains; only the practice has changed. Hell fire is gone, but the text remains. Infant damnation is gone, but the text remains. More than two hundred death penalties are gone from the law books, but the texts that authorized them remain.

Is it not well worthy of note that of all the multitude of texts through which man has driven his annihilating pen he has never once made the mistake of obliterating a good and useful one? It does certainly seem to suggest that if man continues in the direction of enlightenment, his religious practice may, in the end, attain some semblance of human decency.

15

Author's Note to
The Shadow Line

JOSEPH CONRAD

A dislike or distrust of superstition and the supernatural need not mean there is a deafness to the marvelous and the mysterious. Here Joseph Conrad makes the distinction finely in his preface to one of his most powerful novels.

This story, which I admit to be in its brevity a fairly complex piece of work, was not intended to touch on the supernatural. Yet more than one critic has been inclined to take it in that way, seeing in it an attempt on my part to give the fullest scope to my imagination by taking it beyond the confines of the world of living, suffering humanity. But as a matter of fact my imagination is not made of stuff so elastic as all that. I believe that if I attempted to put the strain of the Supernatural on it, it would fail deplorably and exhibit an unlovely gap. But I could never have attempted such a thing, because all my moral and intellectual being is penetrated by an invincible conviction that whatever falls under the dominion of our senses must be in nature and, however exceptional, cannot differ in its essence from all the other effects of the visible and tangible world of which we are a self-conscious part. The world of the living contains enough marvels and mysteries as it is; marvels and mysteries acting upon our emotions and intelligence in ways so inexplicable that it would almost justify the conception of life as an enchanted state. No, I am too firm in my consciousness of the marvelous to be ever fascinated by the mere supernatural, which (take it any way you like) is but a manufactured article, the fabrication of minds insensitive to the intimate delicacies of our relation to the dead and to the living, in their countless multitudes; a desecration of our tenderest memories; an outrage on our dignity.

Whatever my native modesty may be it will never condescend so low as to seek help for my imagination within those vain imaginings common to all ages and that in themselves are enough to fill all lovers of mankind with unutterable sadness. As to the effect of a mental or moral shock on a common mind, it is quite a legitimate subject for study and description. Mr. Burns' moral being receives a severe shock in his relations with his late captain, and this in his diseased state turns into a mere superstitious fancy compounded of fear and animosity. This fact is one of the elements of the story, but there is nothing supernatural in it, nothing so to speak from beyond the confines of this world, which in all conscience holds enough mystery and terror in itself.

Perhaps if I had published this tale, which I have had for a long time in my mind, under the title of "First Command" no suggestion of the Supernatural would have been found in it by any impartial reader, critical or otherwise. I will not consider here the origins of the feeling in which its actual title, "The Shadow-Line," occurred to my mind. Primarily the aim of this piece of writing was the presentation of certain facts, which certainly were associated with the change from youth, carefree and fervent, to the more self-conscious and more poignant period of maturer life. Nobody can doubt that before the supreme trial of a whole generation I had an acute consciousness of the minute and insignificant character of my own obscure experience. There could be no question here of any parallelism. That notion never entered my bead. But there was a feeling of identity, though with an enormous difference of scale—as of one single drop measured against the bitter and stormy immensity of an ocean. And this was very natural too. For when we begin to meditate on the meaning of our own past it seems to fill all the world in its profundity and its magnitude. This book was written in the last three months of the year 1916. Of all the subjects of which a writer of tales is more or less conscious within himself this is the only one I found it possible to attempt at the time. The depth and the nature of the mood with which I approached it is best expressed perhaps in the dedication which strikes me now as a most disproportionate thing—as but another instance of the overwhelming greatness of our own emotion to ourselves.

This much having been said, I may pass on now to a few remarks about the mere material of the story. As to locality it belongs to that part of the Eastern Seas from which I have carried away into my writing life the greatest number of suggestions. From my statement that I thought of this story for a long time under the title of "First Command" the reader may guess that it is concerned with my personal experience. And as a matter of fact it is personal experience seen in perspective with the eye of the mind and coloured by that affection one can't help feeling for such events of one's life as one has no reason to be ashamed of. And that affection is as intense (I appeal here to universal experience) as the shame, and almost the anguish with which one remembers some unfortunate occurrences, down to mere mistakes in speech, that have been perpetrated by one in the past. The effect of perspective in memory is to make things loom large because the essentials stand out isolated from their surroundings of insignificant daily facts which have naturally faded out of one's mind. I remember that period of my sea-life with pleasure because begun inauspiciously it turned out in the end a success from a personal point of view, leaving a tangible proof in the terms of the letter the owners of the ship wrote to me two years afterwards when I resigned my command in order to come home. This resignation marked the beginning of another phase of my seaman's life, its terminal phase, if I may say so, which in its own way has coloured another portion of my writings. I didn't know then how near its end my sea-life was, and therefore I felt no sorrow except at parting with the ship. I was sorry also to break my connection with the firm who owned her and who were pleased to receive with friendly kindness and give their confidence to a man who had entered their service in an accidental manner and in very adverse circumstances. Without disparaging the earnestness of my purpose I suspect now that luck had no small part in the success of the trust reposed in me. And one cannot help remembering with pleasure the time when one's best efforts were seconded by a run of luck.

The words "Worthy of my undying regard" selected by me for the motto on the title page are quoted from the text of the book itself; and, though one of my critics surmised that they applied to the ship, it is evident from the place where they stand that they refer to the men of that ship's company: complete strangers to their new captain and who yet stood by him so well during those twenty days that seemed to have been passed on the brink of a slow and agonizing destruction. And *that* is the greatest memory of all! For surely it is a great thing to have commanded a handful of men worthy of one's undying regard.

16

God's Funeral

Thomas Hardy

For many people, as atheists are duly bound to recognize, the loss of faith is experienced not so much as a liberation as a bereavement. The great novelist Thomas Hardy strove to retain belief as long as he could, but when it fell away he felt it deserved a proper and moving poetic obsequy.

I

I saw a slowly-stepping train—
Lined on the brows, scoop-eyed and bent and hoar—
Following in files across a twilit plain
A strange and mystic form the foremost bore.

II

And by contagious throbs of thought
Or latent knowledge that within me lay
And had already stirred me, I was wrought
To consciousness of sorrow even as they.

III

The fore-borne shape, to my blurred eyes,
At first seemed man-like, and anon to change
To an amorphous cloud of marvellous size,
At times endowed with wings of glorious range.

IV

And this phantasmal variousness
Ever possessed it as they drew along:
Yet throughout all it symboled none the less
Potency vast and loving-kindness strong.

V

Almost before I knew I bent
Towards the moving columns without a word;

They, growing in bulk and numbers as they went,
Struck out sick thoughts that could be overheard:—

VI
"O man-projected Figure, of late
Imaged as we, thy knell who shall survive?
Whence came it we were tempted to create
One whom we can no longer keep alive?

VII
"Framing him jealous, fierce, at first,
We gave him justice as the ages rolled,
Will to bless those by circumstance accurst,
And long suffering, and mercies manifold.

VIII
"And, tricked by our own early dream
And need of solace, we grew self-deceived,
Our making soon our maker did we deem,
And what we had imagined we believed.

IX
"Till, in Time's stayless Stealthy swing,
Uncompromising rude reality
Mangled the Monarch of our fashioning,
Who quavered, sank; and now has ceased to be.

X
"So, toward our myth's oblivion,
Darkling, and languid-lipped, we creep and grope
Sadlier than those who wept in Babylon,
Whose Zion was a still abiding hope.

XI
"How sweet it was in years far hied
To scan the wheels of day with trustful prayer,
To lie down liegely at the eventide
And feel a blest assurance he was there!

XII
"And who or what shall fill his place?
Whither will wanderers turn distracted eyes

For some fixed star to stimulate their pace
Towards the goal of their enterprise?" . . .

XIII
Some in the background then I saw,
Sweet women, youths, men, all incredulous,
Who chimed: "This is a counterfeit of straw,
This requiem mockery! Still he lives to us!"

XIV
I could not buoy their faith: and yet
Many I had known: with all I sympathized;
And though struck speechless, I did not forget
That what was mourned for, I, too, long had prized.

XV
Still, how to bear such loss I deemed
The insistent question for each animate mind,
And gazing, to my growing sight there seemed
A pale yet positive gleam low down behind,

XVI
Whereof, to lift the general night,
A certain few who stood aloof had said,
"See you upon the horizon that small light—
Swelling somewhat?" Each mourner shook his head.

XVII
And they composed a crowd of whom
Some were right good, and many nigh the best . . .
Thus dazed and puzzled 'twixt the gleam and gloom
Mechanically I followed with the rest.

17

The Philosophy of Atheism

EMMA GOLDMAN

Not enough women contributors, I hear you say. Most religions
have directed their worst repression at impious females, burning
or stoning them according to taste, but those women who have resisted such tyranny are usually (see George Eliot above and Ayaan
Hirsi Ali below) worth more than their equivalent male weight.
Emma Goldman (1869–1940) was a Russian-born anarchist who
became a great champion of civil liberties and the rights of labor
in the United States. Deported by an unfeeling American administration to Bolshevik Russia in 1919 because of her opposition to
militarism and war, she was an early opponent of the Soviet "experiment" and in this essay groups religion with other man-made
systems of absolutism and unfreedom.

To give an adequate exposition of the philosophy of Atheism, it would be necessary to go into the historical changes of the belief in a Deity, from its earliest beginning to the present day. But that is not within the scope of the present paper.
However, it is not out of place to mention, in passing, that the concept God, Supernatural Power, Spirit, Deity, or in whatever other term the essence of Theism
may have found expression, has become more indefinite and obscure in the
course of time and progress. In other words, the God idea is growing more impersonal and nebulous in proportion as the human mind is learning to understand natural phenomena and in the degree that science progressively correlates
human and social events.

God, today, no longer represents the same forces as in the beginning of His
existence; neither does He direct human destiny with the same iron hand as of
yore. Rather does the God idea express a sort of spiritualistic stimulus to satisfy
the fads and fancies of every shade of human weakness. In the course of human
development the God idea has been forced to adapt itself to every phase of human affairs, which is perfectly consistent with the origin of the idea itself.

The conception of gods originated in fear and curiosity. Primitive man, unable to understand the phenomena of nature and harassed by them, saw in
every terrifying manifestation some sinister force expressly directed against

him; and as ignorance and fear are the parents of all superstition, the troubled fancy of primitive man wove the God idea.

Very aptly, the world-renowned atheist and anarchist, Michael Bakunin, says in his great work *God and the State:* "All religions, with their demi-gods, and their prophets, their messiahs and their saints, were created by the prejudiced fancy of men who had not attained the full development and full possession of their faculties. Consequently, the religious heaven is nothing but the mirage in which man, exalted by ignorance and faith, discovered his own image, but enlarged and reversed—that is, divinized. The history of religions, of the birth, grandeur, and the decline of the gods who had succeeded one another in human belief, is nothing, therefore, but the development of the collective intelligence and conscience of mankind. As fast as they discovered, in the course of their historically progressive advance, either in themselves or in external nature, a quality, or even any great defect whatever, they attributed them to their gods, after having exaggerated and enlarged them beyond measure, after the manner of children, by an act of their religious fancy. . . . With all due respect, then, to the metaphysicians and religious idealists, philosophers, politicians or poets: the idea of God implies the abdication of human reason and justice; it is the most decisive negation of human liberty, and necessarily ends in the enslavement of mankind, both in theory and practice."

Thus the God idea revived, readjusted, and enlarged or narrowed, according to the necessity of the time, has dominated humanity and will continue to do so until man will raise his head to the sunlit day, unafraid and with an awakened will to himself. In proportion as man learns to realize himself and mold his own destiny, theism becomes superfluous. How far man will be able to find his relation to his fellows will depend entirely upon how much he can outgrow his dependence upon God.

Already there are indications that theism, which is the theory of speculation, is being replaced by Atheism, the science of demonstration; the one hangs in the metaphysical clouds of the Beyond, while the other has its roots firmly in the soil. It is the earth, not heaven, which man must rescue if he is truly to be saved.

The decline of theism is a most interesting spectacle, especially as manifested in the anxiety of the theists, whatever their particular brand. They realize, much to their distress, that the masses are growing daily more atheistic, more anti-religious; that they are quite willing to leave the Great Beyond and its heavenly domain to the angels and sparrows; because more and more the masses are becoming engrossed in the problems of their immediate existence.

How to bring the masses back to the God idea, the spirit, the First Cause, etc.—that is the most pressing question to all theists. Metaphysical as all these questions seem to be, they yet have a very marked physical background. Inasmuch as religion, "Divine Truth," rewards and punishments are the trademarks of the largest, the most corrupt and pernicious, the most powerful and lucrative industry in the world, not excepting the industry of manufacturing guns and munitions. It is the industry of befogging the human mind and stifling the human heart. Necessity knows no law; hence the majority of theists are compelled to take up every subject, even if it has no bearing upon a deity or revelation or the Great Beyond. Perhaps they sense the fact that humanity is growing weary of the hundred and one brands of God.

How to raise this dead level of theistic belief is really a matter of life and death for all denominations. Therefore their tolerance; but it is a tolerance not of understanding, but of weakness. Perhaps that explains the efforts fostered in all religious publications to combine variegated religious philosophies and conflicting theistic theories into one denominational trust. More and more, the various concepts "of the only true God, the only pure spirit, the only true religion" are tolerantly glossed over in the frantic effort to establish a common ground to rescue the modern mass from the "pernicious" influence of atheistic ideas.

It is characteristic of theistic "tolerance" that no one really cares what the people believe in, just so they believe or pretend to believe. To accomplish this end, the crudest and vulgarest methods are being used. Religious endeavor meetings and revivals with Billy Sunday as their champion—methods which must outrage every refined sense, and which in their effect upon the ignorant and curious often tend to create a mild state of insanity not infrequently coupled with erotomania. All these frantic efforts find approval and support from the earthly powers; from the Russian despot to the American President; from Rockefeller and Wanamaker down to the pettiest businessman. They know that capital invested in Billy Sunday, the YMCA, Christian Science, and various other religious institutions will return enormous profits from the subdued, tamed, and dull masses.

Consciously or unconsciously, most theists see in gods and devils, heaven and hell, reward and punishment, a whip to lash the people into obedience, meekness and contentment. The truth is that theism would have lost its footing long before this but for the combined support of Mammon and power. How thoroughly bankrupt it really is, is being demonstrated in the trenches and battlefields of Europe today.

Have not all theists painted their Deity as the god of love and goodness? Yet after thousands of years of such preachments the gods remain deaf to the agony of the human race. Confucius cares not for the poverty, squalor and misery of the people of China. Buddha remains undisturbed in his philosophical indifference to the famine and starvation of the outraged Hindoos; Jahve continues deaf to the bitter cry of Israel; while Jesus refuses to rise from the dead against his Christians who are butchering each other.

The burden of all song and praise, "unto the Highest" has been that God stands for justice and mercy. Yet injustice among men is ever on the increase; the outrages committed against the masses in this country alone would seem enough to overflow the very heavens. But where are the gods to make an end to all these horrors, these wrongs, this inhumanity to man? No, not the gods, but MAN must rise in his mighty wrath. He, deceived by all the deities, betrayed by their emissaries, he, himself, must undertake to usher in justice upon the earth.

The philosophy of Atheism expresses the expansion and growth of the human mind. The philosophy of theism, if we can call it philosophy, is static and fixed. Even the mere attempt to pierce these mysteries represents, from the theistic point of view, non-belief in the all embracing omnipotence, and even a denial of the wisdom of the divine powers outside of man. Fortunately, however, the human mind never was, and never can be, bound by fixities. Hence it is forging ahead in its restless march towards knowledge and life. The human mind is realizing "that the universe is not the result of a creative fiat by some divine intelligence, out of nothing, producing a masterpiece in perfect operation," but that it is the product of chaotic forces operating through æons of time, of clashes and cataclysms, of repulsion and attraction crystallizing through the principle of selection into what the theists call "the universe guided into order and beauty." As Joseph McCabe well points out in his *Existence of God*: "a law of nature is not a formula drawn up by a legislator, but a mere summary of the observed facts—a 'bundle of facts.' Things do not act in a particular way because there is a law, but we state the 'law' because they act in that way."

The philosophy of Atheism represents a concept of life without any metaphysical Beyond or Divine Regulator. It is the concept of an actual, real world with its liberating, expanding and beautifying possibilities, as against an unreal world, which, with its spirits, oracles, and mean contentment, has kept humanity in helpless degradation.

It may seem a wild paradox, and yet it is pathetically true, that this real, visible world and our life should have been so long under the influence of metaphysical speculation, rather than of physical demonstrable forces. Under the lash of the theistic idea, this earth has served no other purpose than as a temporary station to test man's capacity for immolation to the will of God. But the moment man attempted to ascertain the nature of that will, he was told that it was utterly futile for "finite human intelligence" to get beyond the all-powerful infinite will. Under the terrific weight of this omnipotence, man has been bowed into the dust,—a will-less creature, broken and swarting in the dark. The triumph of the philosophy of Atheism is to free man from the nightmare of gods; it means the dissolution of the phantoms of the beyond. Again and again the light of reason has dispelled the theistic nightmare, but poverty, misery and fear have recreated the phantoms—though whether old or new, whatever their external form, they differed little in their essence. Atheism, on the other hand, in its philosophic aspect refuses allegiance not merely to a definite concept of God, but it refuses all servitude to the God idea, and opposes the theistic principle as such. Gods in their individual function are not half as pernicious as the principle of theism, which represents the belief in a supernatural, or even omnipotent, power to rule the earth and man upon it. It is the absolutism of theism, its pernicious influence upon humanity, its paralyzing effect upon thought and action, which Atheism is fighting with all its power.

The philosophy of Atheism has its root in the earth, in this life; its aim is the emancipation of the human race from all God-heads, be they Judaic, Christian, Mohammedan, Buddhistic, Brahministic, or what not. Mankind has been punished long and heavily for having created its gods; nothing but pain and persecution have been man's lot since gods began. There is but one way out of this blunder: Man must break his fetters which have chained him to the gates of heaven and hell, so that he can begin to fashion out of his reawakened and illumined consciousness a new world upon earth.

Only after the triumph of the Atheistic philosophy in the minds and hearts of man will freedom and beauty be realized. Beauty as a gift from heaven has proved useless. It will, however, become the essence and impetus of life when man learns to see in the earth the only heaven fit for man. Atheism is already helping to free man from his dependence upon punishment and reward as the heavenly bargain-counter for the poor in spirit.

Do not all theists insist that there can be no morality, no justice, honesty, or fidelity without the belief in a Divine Power? Based upon fear and hope, such morality has always been a vile product, imbued partly with self-righteousness, partly with hypocrisy. As to truth, justice, and fidelity, who have been their brave exponents and daring proclaimers? Nearly always the godless ones: the Atheists; they lived, fought, and died for them. They knew that justice, truth, and fidelity are not conditioned in heaven, but that they are related to and interwoven with the tremendous changes going on in the social and material life of the human race; not fixed and eternal, but fluctuating, even as life itself. To what heights the philosophy of Atheism may yet attain, no one can prophesy. But this much can already be predicted: only by its regenerating fire will human relations be purged from the horrors of the past.

Thoughtful people are beginning to realize that moral precepts, imposed upon humanity through religious terror, have become stereotyped and have therefore lost all vitality. A glance at life today, at its disintegrating character, its conflicting interests with their hatreds, crimes, and greed, suffices to prove the sterility of theistic morality.

Man must get back to himself before he can learn his relation to his fellows. Prometheus chained to the Rock of Ages is doomed to remain the prey of the vultures of darkness. Unbind Prometheus, and you dispel the night and its horrors.

Atheism in its negation of gods is at the same time the strongest affirmation of man, and through man, the eternal yea to life, purpose, and beauty.

18

A Letter on Religion

H. P. LOVECRAFT

Another master of the mysterious in fiction was Howard Phillips
Lovecraft (1890–1937) whose extraordinary work is, it seems, always
being "revived." However, as his letters demonstrate, he had no use
for religion. Here, he is writing to a friend named Maurice W. Moe
in 1918.

Your wonderment "What I have against religion" reminds me of your recent *Vagrant* essay—which I had the honour of perusing in manuscript some three years ago. To my mind, that essay *misses one point altogether.* Your "agnostic" has neglected to mention the very crux of all agnosticism—namely that the Judaeo-Christian mythology is NOT TRUE. I can see that in your philosophy *truth per se* has so small a place that you can scarcely realise what it is that Galpin and I are insisting upon. In your mind, MAN is the centre of everything, and his exact conformation to certain regulations of conduct HOWEVER EFFECTED, the only problem in the universe. Your world (if you will pardon my saying so) is *contracted.* All the mental vigour and erudition of the ages fail to disturb your complacent endorsement of empirical doctrines and purely pragmatic notions, because you voluntarily limit your horizon—*excluding certain facts, and certain undeniable mental tendencies of mankind.* In your eyes, man is torn between *only two* influences: the degrading instincts of the savage, and the temperate impulses of the philanthropist. To you, men are of but two classes—lovers of self and lovers of the race. To you, men have but two types of emotion—self-gratification, to be combated; and altruism, to be fostered. But you, consciously or unconsciously, are leaving out a vast and potent *tertium quid*—making an omission, which cannot but interfere with the validity of your philosophical conceptions. You are forgetting a human impulse that, despite its restriction to a relatively small number of men, has all through history proved itself as real and as vital as hunger—as potent as thirst or greed. I need not say that I refer to that simplest yet most exalted attribute of our species—the acute, persistent, unquenchable craving TO KNOW. Do you realise that to many men it makes a vast and profound difference whether or not the things about them are as they appear? . . .

I recognise a distinction between dream life and real life, between appearances and actualities. I confess to an overpowering desire to know whether I am asleep or awake—whether the environment and laws that affect me are external and permanent, or the transitory products of my own brain. I admit that I am very much interested in the relation I bear to the things about me—the time relation, the space relation, and the causative relation. I desire to know approximately what my life is in terms of history—human, terrestrial, solar, and cosmical; what my magnitude may be in terms of extension,—terrestrial, solar, and cosmical; and above all, what may be my manner of linkage to the general system—in what way, through what agency, and to what extent, the obvious guiding forces of creation act upon me and govern my existence. And if there be any less obvious forces, I desire to know them and their relation to me as well. Foolish, do I hear you say? Undoubtedly! I had better be a consistent pragmatist: get drunk and confine myself to a happy, swinish, contented little world— the gutter—till some policeman's No. 13 boot intrudes upon my philosophic repose. But I *cannot.* Why? Because some well-defined human impulse prompts me to discard the relative for the absolute. You would encourage me as far as the moral stage. You would agree with me that I had better see the world as it is than to forget my woes in the flowing bowl. But because I have a certain *momentum,* and am carried a step further from the merely relative, you frown upon me and declare me to be a queer, unaccountable creature, "immersed . . . in the VICIOUS abstractions of philosophy!"

Here, then, is the beginning of my religious or philosophical thought. I have not begun talking about morality yet, because I have not reached that point in the argument. *Entity* precedes morality. It is a prerequisite. What am I? What is the nature of the energy about me, and how does it affect me? So far I have seen nothing which could possibly give me the notion that cosmic force is the manifestation of a mind and will like my own infinitely magnified; a potent and purposeful consciousness which deals individually and directly with the miserable denizens of a wretched little flyspeck on the back door of a microscopic universe, and which singles this putrid excrescence out as the one spot whereto to send an onlie-begotten Son, whose mission is to redeem those accursed flyspeck-inhabiting lice which we call human beings—bah!! Pardon the "bah!" I feel several "bahs!," but out of courtesy I only say one. But it is all so very childish. I cannot help taking exception to a philosophy that would force this rubbish down my throat. "What have I against religion?" That is what I have against it! . . .

Now let us view *morality*—which despite your preconceived classification and identification has nothing to do with any particular form of religion. Morality is the adjustment of matter to its environment—the natural arrangement of molecules. More especially it may be considered as dealing with organic molecules. Conventionally it is the science of reconciling the animal *Homo* (more or less) *sapiens* to the forces and conditions with which he is surrounded. It is linked with religion only so far as the natural elements it deals with are deified and personified. Morality antedated the Christian religion, and has many times risen superior to coexistent religions. It has powerful support from very non-religious human impulses. Personally, I am intensely moral and intensely irreligious. My morality can be traced to two distinct sources, scientific and aesthetic. My love of truth is outraged by the flagrant disturbance of sociological relations involved in so-called wrong; whilst my aesthetic sense is outraged and disgusted with the violations of taste and harmony thereupon attendant. But to me the question presents no ground for connexion with the grovelling instinct of religion. However—you may exclude me from the argument, if you will. I *am* unduly secluded though unavoidably so. We will deal only with materials that may presumably lie within my feeble reach. Only one more touch of ego. I am *not* at all passive or indifferent in my zeal for a high morality. But I cannot consider morality the essence of religion, as you seem to. In discussing religion, the whole fabric must bear examination before the uses or purposes are considered. We must investigate the cause as well as alleged effects if we are to define the relation between the two, and the reality of the former. And more, granting that the phenomenon of faith is indeed the true cause of the observed moral effects; the absolute basis of that phenomenon remains to be examined. The issue between theists and atheists is certainly not, as you seem to think, the mere question of whether religion is useful or detrimental. In your intensely pragmatic mind, this question stands paramount—to such an extent that you presented no other subject of discussion in your very clever *Vagrant* article. But the "agnostic" of your essay must have been a very utilitarian agnostic (that such "utilitarian Agnostics" do exist, I will not deny. *Vide* any issue of *The Truth-seeker*! But are they typical?)! What the honest thinker wishes to know, has nothing to do with complex human conduct. He simply demands a scientific *explanation* of the things he sees. His only animus toward the church concerns its deliberate inculcation of demonstrable untruths in the community. This is human nature. No matter how white a lie may be—no matter how much good it may do—we are always more or less disgusted by its diffusion. The honest agnostic regards the church with respect for what it has done in the direction of virtue. He even supports it if he is magnanimous, and he certainly does nothing to impair whatever public usefulness it may possess. But in private, he would be more than a mere mortal if he were able to suppress a certain abstract resentment, or to curb the feeling of humour and so-called irreverence which inevitably arises from the contemplation of pious fraud, howsoever high-minded and benevolent.

The good effects of Christianity are neither to be denied, nor lightly esteemed, though candidly I will admit that I think them overrated. For example, the insignia of the Red Cross is practically the only religious thing about it. It is purely humanitarian and philanthropic, and has received just as much of its vitality from agnostic—or Jewish—sources, as from Christian sources. . . . These nominally Christian societies usurp the lion's share of social service merely because they are on the ground first. Free and rational thought is relatively new, and rationalists find it just as practicable to support these existing Christian charities as to organise new ones that might create a division of energy and therefore decrease the efficiency of organised charity as a whole. And by the way—was not Belgium relief work largely non-religious? I may be mistaken—but all this is aside from my main argument anyway. I am not protesting against the recognition of Christianity's accomplishments. This has nothing to do with absolute bases of faith.

19

Why I Am an Unbeliever

CARL VAN DOREN

There have always been those who, as Blaise Pascal phrased it, are "so made that they cannot believe." (And there are more of us than the faithful would like to think.) A conspicuous example was Carl Van Doren (1885–1950), a distinguished professor of English at Columbia University and biographer of Benjamin Franklin. Here, he confronts the tired, old argument that without faith there can be no foundation for ethics.

Let us be honest. There have always been men and women without the gift of faith. They lack it, do not desire it, and would not know what to do with it if they had it. They are apparently no less intelligent than the faithful, and apparently no less virtuous. How great the number of them is it would be difficult to say, but they exist in all communities and are most numerous where there is most enlightenment. As they have no organization and no creed, they can of course have no official spokesman. Nevertheless, any one of them who speaks out can be trusted to speak, in a way, for all of them. Like the mystics, the unbelievers, wherever found, are essentially of one spirit and one language. I cannot, however, pretend to represent more than a single complexion of unbelief.

The very terms that I am forced to use put me at the outset in a trying position. Belief, being first in the field, naturally took a positive term for itself and gave a negative term to unbelief. As an unbeliever, I am therefore obliged to seem merely to dissent from the believers no matter how much more I may do. Actually I do more. What they call unbelief, I call belief. Doubtless I was born to it, but I have tested it with reading and speculation, and I hold it firmly. What I have referred to as the gift of faith I do not, to be exact, regard as a gift. I regard it, rather, as a survival from an earlier stage of thinking and feeling: in short, as a form of superstition. It, and not the thing I am forced to name unbelief, seems to me negative. It denies the reason. It denies the evidences in the case, in the sense that it insists upon introducing elements that come not from the facts as shown but from the imaginations and wishes of mortals. Unbelief does not deny the reason and it sticks as closely as it can to the evidences.

I shall have to be more explicit. When I say I am an unbeliever, I do not mean merely that I am no Mormon or no Methodist, or even that I am no Christian or no Buddhist. These seem to me relatively unimportant divisions and subdivisions of belief. I mean that I do not believe in any god that has ever been devised, in any doctrine that has ever claimed to be revealed, in any scheme of immortality that has ever been expounded.

As to gods, they have been, I find, countless, but even the names, of most of them lie in the deep compost which is known as civilization, and the memories of few of them are green. There does not seem to me to be good reason for holding that some of them are false and some of them, or one of them, true. Each was created by the imaginations and wishes of men who could not account for the behavior of the universe in any other satisfactory way. But no god has satisfied his worshipers forever. Sooner or later they have realized that the attributes once ascribed to him, such as selfishness or lustfulness or vengefulness, are unworthy of the moral systems that men have evolved among themselves. Thereupon follows the gradual doom of the god, however long certain of the faithful may cling to his cult. In the case of the god who still survives in the loyalty of men after centuries of scrutiny, it can always be noted that little besides his name has endured. His attributes will have been so revised that he is really another god. Nor is this objection met by the argument that the concept of the god has been purified while the essence of him survived. In the concept alone can he be studied; the essence eludes the grasp of the human mind. I may prefer among the various gods that god who seems to me most thoroughly purged of what I regard as undivine elements, but I make my choice, obviously, upon principles that come from observation of the conduct of men. Whether a god has been created in the image of gross desires or of pure desires does not greatly matter. The difference proves merely that different men have desired gods and have furnished themselves with the gods they were able to conceive. Behind all their conceptions still lies the abyss of ignorance. There is no trustworthy evidence as to a god's absolute existence.

Nor does the thing called revelation, as I see it, carry the proof further. All the prophets swear that a god speaks through them, and yet they prophesy contradictions. Once more, men must choose in accordance with their own principles. That a revelation was announced long ago makes it difficult to examine, but does not otherwise attest its soundness. That some revealed doctrine has lasted for ages and has met the needs of many generations proves that it is the kind of doctrine that endures and satisfies, but not that it is divine. Secular doctrines that turned out to be perfectly false have also endured and satisfied. If belief in a god has to proceed from the assumption that he exists, belief in revelation has first to proceed from the assumption that a god exists and then to go further to the assumption that he communicates his will to certain men. But both are mere assumptions. Neither is, in the present state of knowledge, at all capable of proof. Suppose a god did exist, and suppose he did communicate his will to any of his creatures. What man among them could comprehend that language? What man could take that dictation? And what man could overwhelmingly persuade his fellows that he had been selected and that they must accept him as authentic? The best they could do would be to have faith in two assumptions and to test the revealed will by its correspondence to their imaginations and wishes. At this point it may be contended that revelation must be real because it arouses so much response in so many human bosoms. This does not follow without a leap of the reason into the realm of hypothesis. Nothing is proved by this general response except that men are everywhere very much alike. They have the same members, the same organs, the same glands, in varying degrees of activity. Being so much alike, they tend to agree upon a few primary desires. Fortunate the religion by which those desires appear to be gratified.

One desire by which the human mind is often teased is the desire to live after death. It is not difficult to explain. Men live so briefly that their plans far outrun their ability to execute them. They see themselves cut off before their will to live is exhausted. Naturally enough, they wish to survive, and, being men, believe in their chances for survival. But their wishes afford no possible proof. Life covers the earth with wishes, as it covers the earth with plants and animals. No wish, however, is evidence of anything beyond itself. Let millions hold it, and it is still only a wish. Let each separate race exhibit it, and it is still only a wish. Let the wisest hold it as strongly as the foolishest, and it is still only a wish. Whoever says he knows that immortality is a fact is merely hoping that it is. And whoever argues, as men often do, that life would be meaningless without immortality because it alone brings justice into human fate, must first argue, as no man has ever quite convincingly done, that life has an unmistakable meaning and that it is just. I, at least, am convinced on neither of these two points. Though I am, I believe, familiar with all the arguments, I do not find any of them notably better than the others. All I see is that the wish for immortality is widespread, that certain schemes of immortality imagined from it have here or there proved more agreeable than rival schemes and that they have been more generally accepted. The religions that provide these successful schemes I can credit with keener insight into human wishes than other religions have had, but I cannot credit them with greater authority as regards the truth. They are all guesswork.

That I think thus about gods, revelation, and immortality ought to be sufficient answer to the question why I am an unbeliever. It would be if the question were always reasonably asked, but it is not. There is also an emotional aspect to be considered. Many believers, I am told, have the same doubts, and yet have the knack of putting their doubts to sleep and entering ardently into the communion of the faithful. The process is incomprehensible to me. So far as I understand it, such believers are moved by their desires to the extent of letting them rule not only their conduct but also their thoughts. An unbeliever's desires have, apparently, less power over his reason. Perhaps this is only another way of saying that his strongest desire is to be as reasonable as he can. However the condition be interpreted, the consequence is the same. An honest unbeliever can no more make himself believe against his reason than he can make himself free of the pull of gravitation. For myself, I feel no obligation whatever to believe. I might once have felt it prudent to keep silence, for I perceive that the race of men, while sheep in credulity, are wolves for conformity; but just now, happily, in this breathing-spell of toleration, there are so many varieties of belief that even an unbeliever may speak out.

In so doing, I must answer certain secondary questions which unbelievers are often asked. Does it not persuade me, one question runs, to realize that many learned men have pondered upon supernatural matters and have been won over to belief? I answer, not in the least. With respect to the gods, revelation, and immortality no man is enough more learned than his fellows to have the right to insist that they follow him into the regions about which all men are ignorant. I am not a particle more impressed by some good old man's conviction that he is in the confidence of the gods than I am by any boy's conviction that there are fish in the horse-pond from which no fish has ever been taken. Does it not impress me to see some good old woman serene in the faith of a blessed immortality? No more than it impresses me to see a little girl full of trust in the universal munificence of a Christmas saint. Am I not moved by the spectacle of a great tradition of worship which has broadened out over continents and which brings all its worshipers punctually together in the observance of noble and dignified rites? Yes, but I am moved precisely by that as I am moved by the spectacle of men everywhere putting their seed seasonably in the ground, tending its increase, and patiently gathering in their harvests.

Finally, do I never suspect in myself some moral obliquity, or do I not at least regret the bleak outlook of unbelief? On these points I am, in my own mind, as secure as I know how to be. There is no moral obligation to believe what is unbelievable any more than there is a moral obligation to do what is undoable. Even in religion, honesty is a virtue. Obliquity, I should say, shows itself rather in prudent pretense or in voluntary self-delusion. Furthermore, the unbelievers have, as I read history, done less harm to the world than the believers. They have not filled it with savage wars or snarled casuistries, with crusades or persecutions, with complacency or ignorance. They have, instead, done what they could to fill it with knowledge and beauty, with temperance and justice, with manners and laughter. They have numbered among themselves some of the most distinguished specimens of mankind. And when they have been undistinguished, they have surely not been inferior to the believers in the fine art of minding their own affairs and so of enlarging the territories of peace.

Nor is the outlook of unbelief, to my way of thinking, a bleak one. It is merely rooted in courage and not in fear. Belief is still in the plight of those ancient races who out of a lack of knowledge peopled the forest with satyrs and the sea with ominous monsters and the ends of the earth with misshapen anthropophagi. So the pessimists among believers have peopled the void with witches and devils, and the optimists among them have peopled it with angels and gods. Both alike have been afraid to furnish the house of life simply. They have cluttered it with the furniture of faith. Much of this furniture, the most reasonable unbeliever would never think of denying, is very beautiful. There are breathing myths, there are comforting legends, there are consoling hopes. But they have, as the unbeliever sees them, no authority beyond that of poetry. That is, they may captivate if they can, but they have no right to insist upon conquering. Beliefs, like tastes, may differ. The unbeliever's taste and belief are austere. In the wilderness of worlds he does not yield to the temptation to belittle the others by magnifying his own. Among the dangers of chance he does not look for safety to any watchful providence whose special concern he imagines he is. Though he knows that knowledge is imperfect, he trusts it alone. If he takes, therefore, the less delight in metaphysics, he takes the more in physics. Each discovery of a new truth brings him a vivid joy. He builds himself up, so far as he can, upon truth, and barricades himself with it. Thus doing, he never sags into superstition, but grows steadily more robust and blithe in his courage. However many fears he may prove unable to escape, he does not multiply them in his imagination and then combat them with his wishes. Austerity may be simplicity and not bleakness.

Does the unbeliever lack certain of the gentler virtues of the believer, the quiet confidence, the unquestioning obedience? He may, yet it must always be remembered that the greatest believers are the greatest tyrants. If the freedom rather than the tyranny of faith is to better the world, then the betterment lies in the hands, I think, of the unbelievers. At any rate, I take my stand with them.

20

Memorial Service

H. L. MENCKEN

It can't be said of Henry Louis Mencken (1880–1956) that he bid adieu to faith with any reluctance. He seems to have been born with a contempt for it, which was vividly expressed in his early work on Friedrich Nietzsche. Tempted too much by eugenics and "social Darwinism" again, Mencken nonetheless did invaluable work against the biblical fundamentalists and other fanatics who tried to ban both alcohol and the teaching of evolution, and his accounts of the famous Scopes "monkey trial" in Tennessee in 1925 have deservedly become classics of reporting. Here he trains his lynx-like eye on ancient gods and delivers a funeral oration much less regretful than Thomas Hardy's.

Where is the graveyard of dead gods? What lingering mourner waters their mounds? There was a day when Jupiter was the king of the gods, and any man who doubted his puissance was *ipso facto* a barbarian and an ignoramus. But where in all the world is there a man who worships Jupiter today? And what of Huitzilopochtli? In one year—and it is no more than five hundred years ago—fifty thousand youths and maidens were slain in sacrifice to him. Today, if he is remembered at all, it is only by some vagrant savage in the depths of the Mexican forest. Huitzilopochtli, like many other gods, had no human father; his mother was a virtuous widow; he was born of an apparently innocent flirtation that she carried on with the sun. When he frowned, his father, the sun, stood still. When he roared with rage, earthquakes engulfed whole cities. When he thirsted he was watered with ten thousand gallons of human blood. But today Huitzilopochtli is as magnificently forgotten as Alien G. Thurman. Once the peer of Allah, Buddha and Wotan, he is now the peer of General Coxey, Richmond P. Hobson, Nan Patterson, Alton B. Parker, Adelina Patti, General Weyler, and Tom Sharkey.

Speaking of Huitzilopochtli recalls his brother, Tezcatilpoca. Tezcatilpoca was almost as powerful: he consumed twenty-five thousand virgins a year. Lead me to his tomb: I would weep, and hang a *couronne des perles*. But who knows where it is? Or where the grave of Quetzalcoatl is? Or Tialoc?

Or Chalchihuitlicue? Or Xiehtecutli? Or Centeotl, that sweet one? Or Tla-zolteotl, the goddess of love? Or Mictlan? Or Ixtlilton? Or Omacatl? Or Ya-catecutli? Or Mixcoatl? Or Xipe? Or all the host of Tzitzimitles? Where are their bones? Where is the willow on which they hung their harps? In what for-lorn and unheard-of hell do they await the resurrection morn? Who enjoys their residuary estates? Or that of Dis, whom Cæsar found to be the chief god of the Celts? Or that of Tarves, the bull? Or that of Moccos, the pig? Or that of Epona, the mare? Or that of Mullo, the celestial jack-ass? There was a time when the Irish revered all these gods as violently as they now hate the English. But today even the drunkest Irishman laughs at them.

But they have company in oblivion: the hell of dead gods is as crowded as the Presbyterian hell for babies. Damona is there, and Esus, and Drunemeton, and Silvana, and Dervones, and Adsalluta, and Deva, and Belisama, and Axona, and Vintios, and Taranuous, and Sulis, and Cocidius, and Adsmerius, and Dumiatis, and Caletos, and Moccus, and Ollovidius, and Albiorix, and Leucitius, and Vitu-cadrus, and Ogmios, and Uxellimus, and Borvo, and Grannos, and Mogons. All mighty gods in their day, worshiped by millions, full of demands and imposi-tions, able to bind and loose—all gods of the first class, not dilettanti. Men la-bored for generations to build vast temples to them—temples with stones as large as hay-wagons. The business of interpreting their whims occupied thou-sands of priests, wizards, archdeacons, evangelists, haruspices, bishops, arch-bishops. To doubt them was to die, usually at the stake. Armies took to the field to defend them against infidels: villages were burned, women and children were butchered, cattle were driven off. Yet in the end they all withered and died, and today there is none so poor to do them reverence. Worse, the very tombs in which they lie are lost, and so even a respectful stranger is debarred from paying them the slightest and politest homage.

What has become of Sutekh, once the high god of the whole Nile valley? What has become of:

Resheph	Baal
Anath	Astarte
Ashtoreth	Hadad
El	Addu
Nergal	Shalem
Nebo	Dagon
Ninib	Sharrab
Melek	Yau
Ahijah	Amon-Re
Isis	Osiris
Ptah	Sebek
Anubis	Molech?

All these were once gods of the highest eminence. Many of them are mentioned with fear and trembling in the Old Testament. They ranked, five or six thousand years ago, with Jahveh himself; the worst of them stood far higher than Thor. Yet they have all gone down the chute, and with them the following:

Bilé	Gwydion
Lêr	Manawyddan
Arianrod	Nuada Argetlam
Morrigu	Tagd
Govannon	Goibniu
Gunfled	Odin
Sokk-mimi	Llaw Gyffes
Momctona	Lleu
Dagda	Ogma
Kerridwen	Mider
Pwyll	Rigantona
Ogyrvan	Marzin
Dea Dia	Mars
Ceros	Jupiter
Vaticanus	Cunina
Edulia	Potina
Adeona	Statilinus
Iuno Lucina	Diana of Ephesus
Saturn	Robigus
Furrina	Pluto
Vediovis	Ops
Consus	Meditrina
Cronos	Vesta
Enki	Tilmun
Engurra	Zer-panitu
Belus	Merodach
Dimmer	U-ki
Mu-ul-lil	Dauke
Ubargisi	Gasan-abzu
Ubilulu	Elum
Gasan-lil	U-Tin-dir ki
U-dimmer-an-kia	Marduk
Enurestu	Nin-lil-la
U-sab-sib	Nin
U-Mersi	Persephone
Tammuz	Istar
Venus	Lagas

Bau	U-urugal
Mulu-hursang	Sirtumu
Anu	Ea
Beltis	Nirig
Nusku	Nebo
Ni-zu	Samas
Sahi	Ma-banba-anna
Aa	En-Mersi
Allatu	Amurru
Sin	Assur
AbilAddu	Aku
Apsu	Beltu
Dagan	Dumu-zi-abzu
Elali	Kuski-banda
Isum	Kaawanu
Mami	Nin-azu
Nin-man	Lugal-Amarada
Zaraqu	Qarradu
Suqamunu	Ura-gala
Zagaga	Ueras

You may think I spoof. That I invent the names. I do not. Ask the rector to lend you any good treatise on comparative religion: you will find them all listed. They were gods of the highest standing and dignity—gods of civilized peoples— worshipped and believed in by millions. All were theoretically omnipotent, omniscient, and immortal. And all are dead.

21

From
The Future of an Illusion

Translated and edited by James Strachey

SIGMUND FREUD

Richard Wollheim once described Sigmund Freud's work as an essay "in the deafness of the mind" and, whatever we may now think about the father of modern psychology, it is impossible not to regard his insights into the unconscious as seminal and revolutionary. Fascinated by totem and taboo and by the manacles that the mind forges for itself, Freud here subjects religious belief to a calm and even quite sympathetic—if pitying—diagnosis.

VI

I think we have prepared the way sufficiently for an answer to both these questions. It will be found if we turn our attention to the psychical origin of religious ideas. These which are given out as teachings are not precipitates of experience or end-results of thinking: they are illusions, fulfillments of the oldest, strongest, and most urgent wishes of mankind. The secret of their strength lies in the strength of those wishes. As we already know, the terrifying impression of helplessness in childhood aroused the need for protection—for protection through love—which was provided by the father; and the recognition that this helplessness lasts throughout life made it necessary to cling to the existence of a father, but this time a more powerful one. Thus the benevolent rule of a divine Providence allays our fear of the dangers of life; the establishment of a moral world-order ensures the fulfillment of the demands of justice, which have so often remained unfulfilled in human civilization; and the prolongation of earthly existence in a future life provides the local and temporal framework in which these wish-fulfillments shall take place. Answers to the riddles that tempt the curiosity of man, such as how the universe began or what the relation is between body and mind, are developed in conformity with the underlying assumptions of this system. It is an enormous relief to the individual psyche if the conflicts of its childhood arising from the father-complex—conflicts which it has never wholly overcome—are removed from it and brought to a solution which is universally accepted.

When I say that these things are all illusions, I must define the meaning of the word. An illusion is not the same thing as an error; nor is it necessarily an error. Aristotle's belief that vermin are developed out of dung (a belief to which ignorant people still cling) was an error; so was the belief of a former generation of doctors that *tabes dorsalis* is the result of sexual excess. It would be incorrect to call these errors illusions. On the other hand, it was an illusion of Columbus's that he had discovered a new sea-route to the Indies. The part played by his wish in this error is very clear. One may describe as an illusion the assertion made by certain nationalists that the Indo-Germanic race is the only one capable of civilization; or the belief, which was only destroyed by psycho-analysis, that children are creatures without sexuality. What is characteristic of illusions is that they are derived from human wishes. In this respect they come near to psychiatric delusions. But they differ from them, too, apart from the more complicated structure of delusions. In the case of delusions, we emphasize as essential their being in contradiction with reality. Illusions need not necessarily be false—that is to say unrealizable or in contradiction to reality. For instance, a middle-class girl may have the illusion that a prince will come and marry her. This is possible; and a few such cases have occurred. That the Messiah will come and found a golden age is much less likely. Whether one classifies this belief as an illusion or as something analogous to a delusion will depend on one's personal attitude. Examples of illusions which have proved true are not easy to find, but the illusion of the alchemists that all metals can be turned into gold might be one of them. The wish to have a great deal of gold, as much gold as possible, has, it is true, been a good deal damped by our present-day knowledge of the determinants of wealth, but chemistry no longer regards the transmutation of metals into gold as impossible. Thus we call a belief an illusion when a wish-fulfillment is a prominent factor in its motivation, and in doing so we disregard its relations to reality, just as the illusion itself sets no store by verification.

Having thus taken our bearings, let us return once more to the question of religious doctrines. We can now repeat that all of them are illusions and insusceptible of proof. No one can be compelled to think them true, to believe in them. Some of them are so improbable, so incompatible with everything we have laboriously discovered about the reality of the world, that we may compare them—if we pay proper regard to the psychological differences—to delusions. Of the reality value of most of them we cannot judge; just as they cannot be proved, so they cannot be refuted. We still know too little to make a critical approach to them. The riddles of the universe reveal themselves only slowly to our investigation; there are many questions to which science today can give no answer. But scientific work is the only road which can lead us to a knowledge of reality outside ourselves. It is once again merely an illusion to expect anything from intuition and introspection; they can give us nothing but particulars about our own mental life, which are hard to interpret, never any information about the questions which religious doctrine finds it so easy to answer. It would be insolent to let one's own arbitrary will step into the breach and, according to one's personal estimate, declare this or that part of the religious system to be less or more acceptable. Such questions are too momentous for that; they might be called too sacred.

At this point one must expect to meet with an objection. "Well then, if even obdurate skeptics admit that the assertions of religion cannot be refuted by reason, why should I not believe in them, since they have so much on their side—tradition, the agreement of mankind, and all the consolations they offer?" Why not, indeed? Just as no one can be forced to believe, so no one can be forced to disbelieve. But do not let us be satisfied with deceiving ourselves that arguments like these take us along the road of correct thinking. If ever there was a case of a lame excuse we have it here. Ignorance is ignorance; no right to believe anything can be derived from it. In other matters no sensible person will behave so irresponsibly or rest content with such feeble grounds for his opinions and for the line he takes. It is only in the highest and most sacred things that he allows himself to do so. In reality these are only attempts at pretending to oneself or to other people that one is still firmly attached to religion, when one has long since cut oneself loose from it. Where questions of religion are concerned, people are guilty of every possible sort of dishonesty and intellectual misdemeanour. Philosophers stretch the meaning of words until they retain scarcely anything of their original sense. They give the name of "God" to some vague abstraction which they have created for themselves; having done so they can pose before all the world as deists, as believers in God, and they can even boast that they have recognized a higher, purer concept of God, notwithstanding that their God is now nothing more than an insubstantial shadow and no longer the mighty personality of religious doctrines. Critics persist in describing as "deeply religious" anyone who admits to a sense of man's insignificance or impotence in the face of the universe, although what constitutes the essence of the religious attitude is not this feeling but only the next step after it, the reaction to it which seeks a remedy for it. The man who goes no further, but humbly acquiesces in the small part which human beings play in the great world—such a man is, on the contrary, irreligious in the truest sense of the word.

To assess the truth-value of religious doctrines does not lie within the scope of the present enquiry. It is enough for us that we have recognized them as being, in their psychological nature, illusions. But we do not have to conceal the fact that this discovery also strongly influences our attitude to the question which must appear to many to be the most important of all. We know approximately at what periods and by what kind of men religious doctrines were created. If in addition we discover the motives which led to this, our attitude to the problem of religion will undergo a marked displacement. We shall tell ourselves that it would be very nice if there were a God who created the world and was a

benevolent Providence, and if there were a moral order in the universe and an after-life; but it is a very striking fact that all this is exactly as we are bound to wish
it to be. And it would be more remarkable still if our wretched, ignorant, and
downtrodden ancestors had succeeded in solving all these difficult riddles of
the universe.

VII

Having recognized religious doctrines as illusions, we are at once faced by a further question: may not other cultural assets of which we hold a high opinion
and by which we let our lives be ruled be of a similar nature? Must not the assumptions that determine our political regulations be called illusions as well?
And is it not the case that in our civilization the relations between the sexes are
disturbed by an erotic illusion or a number of such illusions? And once our suspicion has been aroused, we shall not shrink from asking too whether our conviction that we can learn something about external reality through the use of
observation and reasoning in scientific work—whether this conviction has any
better foundation. Nothing ought to keep us from directing our observation to
our own selves or from applying our thought to criticism of itself. In this field a
number of investigations open out before us, whose results could not but be decisive for the construction of a *Weltanschauung*. We surmise, moreover, that such
an effort would not be wasted and that it would at least in part justify our suspicion. But the author does not dispose of the means for undertaking so comprehensive a task; he needs must confine his work to following out one only of
these illusions—that, namely, of religion.

But now the loud voice of our opponent brings us to a halt. We are called to
account for our wrong-doing:

> Archaeological interests are no doubt most praiseworthy, but no one under-
> takes an excavation if by doing so he is going to undermine the habitations
> of the living so that they collapse and bury people under their ruins. The doc-
> trines of religion are not a subject one can quibble about like any other. Our
> civilization is built up on them, and the maintenance of human society is
> based on the majority of men's believing in the truth of those doctrines. If
> men are taught that there is no almighty and all-just God, no divine world-
> order and no future life, they will feel exempt from all obligation to obey the
> precepts of civilization. Everyone will, without inhibition or fear, follow his
> asocial, egoistic instincts and seek to exercise his power; Chaos, which we
> have banished through many thousands of years of the work of civilization,
> will come again. Even if we knew, and could prove, that religion was not in
> possession of the truth, we ought to conceal the fact and behave in the way
> prescribed by the philosophy of "As if"—and this in the interest of the preser-
> vation of us all. And apart from the danger of the undertaking, it would be a
> purposeless cruelty. Countless people find their one consolation in religious

doctrines, and can only bear life with their help. You would rob them of their support, without having anything better to give them in exchange. It is admitted that so far science has not achieved much, but even if it had advanced much further it would not suffice for man. Man has imperative needs of another sort, which can never be satisfied by cold science; and it is very strange—indeed, it is the height of inconsistency—that a psychologist who has always insisted on what a minor part is played in human affairs by the intelligence as compared with the life of the instincts—that such a psychologist should now try to rob mankind of a precious wish-fulfillment and should propose to compensate them for it with intellectual nourishment.

What a lot of accusations all at once! Nevertheless I am ready with rebuttals for them all; and, what is more, I shall assert the view that civilization runs a greater risk if we maintain our present attitude to religion than if we give it up.

But I hardly know where to begin my reply. Perhaps with the assurance that I myself regard my undertaking as completely harmless and free of risk. It is not I who am overvaluing the intellect this time. If people are as my opponents describe them—and I should not like to contradict them—then there is no danger of a devout believer's being overcome by my arguments and deprived of his faith. Besides, I have said nothing which other and better men have not said before me in a much more complete, forcible, and impressive manner. Their names are well known, and I shall not cite them, for I should not like to give an impression that I am seeking to rank myself as one of them. All I have done—and this is the only thing that is new in my exposition—is to add some psychological foundation to the criticisms of my great predecessors. It is hardly to be expected that precisely this addition will produce the effect which was denied to those earlier efforts. No doubt I might be asked here what is the point of writing these things if I am certain that they will be ineffective. But I shall come back to that later.

The one person this publication may injure is myself. I shall have to listen to the most disagreeable reproaches for my shallowness, narrow-mindedness, and lack of idealism or of understanding for the highest interests of mankind. But on the one hand, such remonstrances are not new to me; and on the other, if a man has already learnt in his youth to rise superior to the disapproval of his contemporaries, what can it matter to him in his old age when he is certain soon to be beyond the reach of all favour or disfavour? In former times it was different. Then utterances such as mine brought with them a sure curtailment of one's earthly existence and an effective speeding-up of the opportunity for gaining a personal experience of the after-life. But, I repeat, those times are past and today writings such as this bring no more danger to their author than to their readers. The most that can happen is that the translation and distribution of his book will be forbidden in one country or another—and precisely, of course, in a country that is convinced of the high standard of its culture. But if one puts in any plea at all for the renunciation of wishes and for acquiescence in Fate, one must be able to tolerate this kind of injury too.

The further question occurred to me whether the publication of this work might not after all do harm. Not to a person, however, but to a cause—the cause of psycho-analysis. For it cannot be denied that psycho-analysis is my creation, and it has met with plenty of mistrust and ill-will. If I now come forward with such displeasing pronouncements, people will be only too ready to make a displacement from my person to psycho-analysis. "Now we see," they will say, "where psycho-analysis leads to. The mask has fallen; it leads to a denial of God and of a moral ideal, as we always suspected. To keep us from this discovery we have been deluded into thinking that psycho-analysis has no *Weltanschauung* and never can construct one."

An outcry of this kind will really be disagreeable to me on account of my many fellow-workers, some of whom do not by any means share my attitude to the problems of religion. But psycho-analysis has already weathered many storms and now it must brave this fresh one. In point of fact psycho-analysis is a method of research, an impartial instrument, like the infinitesimal calculus, as it were. If a physicist were to discover with the latter's help that after a certain time the earth would be destroyed, we would nevertheless hesitate to attribute destructive tendencies to the calculus itself and therefore to proscribe it. Nothing that I have said here against the truth-value of religions needed the support of psycho-analysis; it had been said by others long before analysis came into existence. If the application of the psycho-analytic method makes it possible to find a new argument against the truths of religion, *tant pis* for religion; but defenders of religion will by the same right make use of psycho-analysis in order to give full value to the affective significance of religious doctrines.

And now to proceed with our defence. Religion has clearly performed great services for human civilization. It has contributed much towards the taming of the asocial instincts. But not enough. It has ruled human society for many thousands of years and has had time to show what it can achieve. If it had succeeded in making the majority of mankind happy, in comforting them, in reconciling them to life and in making them into vehicles of civilization, no one would dream of attempting to alter the existing conditions. But what do we see instead? We see that an appallingly large number of people are dissatisfied with civilization and unhappy in it, and feel it as a yoke which must be shaken off; and that these people either do everything in their power to change that civilization, or else go so far in their hostility to it that they will have nothing to do with civilization or with a restriction of instinct. At this point it will be objected against us that this state of affairs is due to the very fact that religion has lost a part of its influence over human masses precisely because of the deplorable effect of the advances of science. We will note this admission and the reason given for it, and we shall make use of it later for our own purposes; but the objection itself has no force.

It is doubtful whether men were in general happier at a time when religious doctrines held unrestricted sway; more moral they certainly were not. They have always known how to externalize the precepts of religion and thus to nullify their intentions. The priests, whose duty it was to ensure obedience to religion, met them half-way in this. God's kindness must lay a restraining hand on His justice. One sinned, and then one made a sacrifice or did penance and then one was free to sin once more. Russian introspectiveness has reached the pitch of concluding that sin is indispensable for the enjoyment of all the blessings of divine grace, so that, at bottom, sin is pleasing to God. It is no secret that the priests could only keep the masses submissive to religion by making such large concessions as these to the instinctual nature of man. Thus it was agreed: God alone is strong and good, man is weak and sinful. In every age immorality has found no less support in religion than morality has. If the achievements of religion in respect to man's happiness, susceptibility to culture and moral control are no better than this, the question cannot but arise whether we are not over-rating its necessity for mankind, and whether we do wisely in basing our cultural demands upon it.

Let us consider the unmistakable situation as it is today. We have heard the admission that religion no longer has the same influence on people that it used to. (We are here concerned with European Christian civilization.) And this is not because its promises have grown less but because people find them less credible. Let us admit that the reason—though perhaps not the only reason—for this change is the increase of the scientific spirit in the higher strata of human society. Criticism has whittled away the evidential value of religious documents, natural science has shown up the errors in them, and comparative research has been struck by the fatal resemblance between the religious ideas which we revere and the mental products of primitive peoples and times.

The scientific spirit brings about a particular attitude towards worldly matters; before religious matters it pauses for a little, hesitates, and finally there too crosses the threshold. In this process there is no stopping; the greater the number of men to whom the treasures of knowledge become accessible, the more widespread is the falling-away from religious belief—at first only from its obsolete and objectionable trappings, but later from its fundamental postulates as well. The Americans who instituted the "monkey trial" at Dayton have alone shown themselves consistent. Elsewhere the inevitable transition is accomplished by way of half-measures and insincerities.

Civilization has little to fear from educated people and brain-workers. In them the replacement of religious motives for civilized behaviour by other, secular motives would proceed unobtrusively; moreover, such people are to a large extent themselves vehicles of civilization. But it is another matter with the great mass of the uneducated and oppressed, who have every reason for being enemies of civilization. So long as they do not discover that people no longer believe in God, all is well. But they will discover it, infallibly, even if this piece of

writing of mine is not published. And they are ready to accept the results of scientific thinking, but without the change having taken place in them which scientific thinking brings about in people. Is there not a danger here that the
hostility of these masses to civilization will throw itself against the weak spot
that they have found in their task-mistress? If the sole reason why you must
not kill your neighbour is because God has forbidden it and will severely punish you for it in this or the next life—then, when you learn that there is no God
and that you need not fear His punishment, you will certainly kill your neighbour without hesitation, and you can only be prevented from doing so by mundane force. Thus either these dangerous masses must be held down most
severely and kept most carefully away from any chance of intellectual awakening, or else the relationship between civilization and religion must undergo a
fundamental revision.

22

Selected Writings on Religion

ALBERT EINSTEIN
Compiled by Miguel Chavez

Another master of the modern world, to whom we owe an enormously expanded idea of the nature of the universe, Albert Einstein (1879–1955) was a great humanist and humanitarian. His opinion on religious matters was eagerly sought because it seemed, to many people, that his own intelligence was almost godlike. Declining such idolatry, Einstein always insisted that the miraculous thing about the natural order was that there *were* no miracles, and that it operated according to astonishing regularities. This placed him firmly in the tradition of Spinoza in repudiating the notion of a god who took an interest in human affairs. The following excerpts from his frequent commentary on religious matters should suffice to answer those (most notably his most recent biographer Walter Isaacson) who attempt to conscript him posthumously into the camp of belief.

"It was, of course, a lie what you read about my religious convictions, a lie which is being systematically repeated. I do not believe in a personal God and I have never denied this but have expressed it clearly. If something is in me which can be called religious then it is the unbounded admiration for the structure of the world so far as our science can reveal it."

—Albert Einstein, in a letter March 24, 1954; from *Albert Einstein, the Human Side*, Helen Dukas and Banesh Hoffman, eds., Princeton, New Jersey: Princeton University Press, 1981, p. 43.

"When I was a fairly precocious young man I became thoroughly impressed with the futility of the hopes and strivings that chase most men restlessly through life. Moreover, I soon discovered the cruelty of that chase, which in those years was much more carefully covered up by hypocrisy and glittering words than is the case today. By the mere existence of his stomach everyone was condemned to participate in that chase. The stomach might well be satisfied by such participation, but not man insofar as he is a thinking and feeling being.

"As the first way out there was religion, which is implanted into every child by way of the traditional education-machine. Thus I came—though the child of entirely irreligious (Jewish) parents—to a deep religiousness, which, however, reached an abrupt end at the age of twelve. Through the reading of popular scientific books I soon reached the conviction that much in the stories of the Bible could not be true. The consequence was a positively fanatic orgy of freethinking coupled with the impression that youth is intentionally being deceived by the state through lies; it was a crushing impression. Mistrust of every kind of authority grew out of this experience, a skeptical attitude toward the convictions that were alive in any specific social environment—an attitude that has never again left me, even though, later on, it has been tempered by a better insight into the causal connections. It is quite clear to me that the religious paradise of youth, which was thus lost, was a first attempt to free myself from the chains of the 'merely personal,' from an existence dominated by wishes, hopes, and primitive feelings. Out yonder there was this huge world, which exists independently of us human beings and which stands before us like a great, eternal riddle, at least partially accessible to our inspection and thinking. The contemplation of this world beckoned as a liberation, and I soon noticed that many a man whom I had learned to esteem and to admire had found inner freedom and security in its pursuit. The mental grasp of this extra-personal world within the frame of our capabilities presented itself to my mind, half consciously, half unconsciously, as a supreme goal. Similarly motivated men of the present and of the past, as well as the insights they had achieved, were the friends who could not be lost. The road to this paradise was not as comfortable and alluring as the road to the religious paradise; but it has shown itself reliable, and I have never regretted having chosen it."

— Albert Einstein, *Autobiographical Notes*, Chicago, Illinois: Open Court
Publishing Company, 1979, pp. 3–5.

"My position concerning God is that of an agnostic. I am convinced that a vivid consciousness of the primary importance of moral principles for the betterment and ennoblement of life does not need the idea of a law-giver, especially a law-giver who works on the basis of reward and punishment."

— Albert Einstein in a letter to M. Berkowitz, October 25, 1950; Einstein
Archive 59–215; from Alice Calaprice, ed., *The Expanded Quotable Einstein*,
Princeton, New Jersey: Princeton University Press, 2000, p. 216.

"The fairest thing we can experience is the mysterious. It is the fundamental emotion which stands at the cradle of true art and true science. He who knows it not and can no longer wonder, no longer feel amazement, is as good as dead, a snuffed-out candle. It was the experience of mystery—even if mixed with fear—that engendered religion. A knowledge of the existence of something we cannot penetrate, of the manifestations of the profoundest reason and the most radiant beauty, which are only accessible to our reason in their most elementary forms—it is this knowledge and this emotion that constitute the truly religious attitude; in this sense, and in this alone, I am a deeply religious man. I cannot conceive of a God who rewards and punishes his creatures, or has a will of the type of which we are conscious in ourselves. An individual who should survive his physical death is also beyond my comprehension, nor do I wish it otherwise; such notions are for the fears or absurd egoism of feeble souls. Enough for me the mystery of the eternity of life, and the inkling of the marvelous structure of reality, together with the single-hearted endeavour to comprehend a portion, be it never so tiny, of the reason that manifests itself in nature."

—Albert Einstein, *The World as I See It*, Secaucus, New Jersey: The Citadel Press, 1999, p. 5.

"The idea of a personal God is quite alien to me and seems even naïve."

—Albert Einstein in a letter to Beatrice Frohlich, December 17, 1952; Einstein Archive 59 797; from *The Expanded Quotable Einstein*, p. 217.

"It seems to me that the idea of a personal God is an anthropological concept which I cannot take seriously. I feel also not able to imagine some will or goal outside the human sphere. My views are near those of Spinoza: admiration for the beauty of and belief in the logical simplicity of the order which we can grasp humbly and only imperfectly. I believe that we have to content ourselves with our imperfect knowledge and understanding and treat values and moral obligations as a purely human problem—the most important of all human problems."

—Albert Einstein, 1947; from Banesh Hoffmann, *Albert Einstein: Creator and Rebel*, New York: New American Library, 1972, p. 95.

"I am a deeply religious nonbeliever. . . . This is a somewhat new kind of religion."

—Albert Einstein, in a letter to Hans Muehsam, March 30, 1954; Einstein Archive 38–434; from *The Expanded Quotable Einstein*, p. 218.

"I believe in Spinoza's God who reveals himself in the orderly harmony of what exists, not in a God who concerns himself with fates and actions of human beings."

—Albert Einstein, upon being asked if he believed in God by Rabbi Herbert Goldstein of the Institutional Synagogue, New York, April 24, 1921, published in *The New York Times,* April 25, 1929; from *Einstein: The Life and Times*, Ronald W. Clark, New York: World Publishing Co., 1971, p. 413; also cited as a telegram to a Jewish newspaper, 1929, Einstein Archive 33–272, from *The Expanded Quotable Einstein*, p. 204.

"I do not believe in immortality of the individual, and I consider ethics to be an exclusively human concern with no superhuman authority behind it."
       —Albert Einstein, letter to a Baptist pastor in 1953; from *Albert Einstein the Human Side*, p. 39.

"Why do you write to me 'God should punish the English'? I have no close connection to either one or the other. I see only with deep regret that God punishes so many of His children for their numerous stupidities, for which only He Himself can be held responsible; in my opinion, only His nonexistence could excuse Him."
       —Albert Einstein, letter to Edgar Meyer, a Swiss colleague, January 2, 1915; from *The Expanded Quotable Einstein*, p. 201.

"It is quite possible that we can do greater things than Jesus, for what is written in the Bible about him is poetically embellished."
       —Albert Einstein, quoted in W. I. Hermanns, "A Talk with Einstein," October 1943, Einstein Archive 55-285; from *The Expanded Quotable Einstein*, p. 215.

"I cannot imagine a God who rewards and punishes the objects of his creation, whose purposes are modeled after our own—a God, in short, who is but a reflection of human frailty. Neither can I believe that the individual survives the death of his body, although feeble souls harbor such thoughts through fear or ridiculous egotisms."
       —Albert Einstein, quoted in *The New York Times* obituary, April 19, 1955; from George Seldes, ed., *The Great Thoughts*, New York: Ballantine Books, 1996, p. 134.

"The most important human endeavor is the striving for morality in our actions. Our inner balance and even our very existence depend on it. Only morality in our actions can give beauty and dignity to life. To make this a living force and bring it to clear consciousness is perhaps the foremost task of education. The foundation of morality should not be made dependent on myth nor tied to any authority lest doubt about the myth or about the legitimacy of the authority imperil the foundation of sound judgment and action."
       —Albert Einstein, letter to a minister November 20, 1950; from *Albert Einstein, the Human Side*, p. 95.

"A God who rewards and punishes is inconceivable to him for the simple reason that a man's actions are determined by necessity, external and internal, so that in God's eyes he cannot be responsible, any more than an inanimate object is responsible for the motions it undergoes. Science has therefore been charged with undermining morality, but the charge is unjust. A man's ethical behavior should be based effectually on sympathy, education, and social ties and needs; no religious basis is necessary. Man would indeed be in a poor way if he had to be restrained by fear of punishment and hopes of reward after death. It is therefore easy to see why the churches have always fought science and persecuted its devotees."

—Albert Einstein, "Religion and Science," in *The New York Times Magazine*, November 9, 1930, pp. 3–4; from *The Expanded Quotable Einstein*, pp. 205–206.

"The religious feeling engendered by experiencing the logical comprehensibility of profound interrelations is of a somewhat different sort from the feeling that one usually calls religious. It is more a feeling of awe at the scheme that is manifested in the material universe. It does not lead us to take the step of fashioning a god-like being in our own image—a personage who makes demands of us and who takes an interest in us as individuals. There is in this neither a will nor a goal, nor a must, but only sheer being. For this reason, people of our type see in morality a purely human matter, albeit the most important in the human sphere."

—Albert Einstein, letter to a Rabbi in Chicago; from *Albert Einstein, the Human Side*, pp. 69–70.

"I have never imputed to Nature a purpose or a goal, or anything that could be understood as anthropomorphic. What I see in Nature is a magnificent structure that we can comprehend only very imperfectly, and that must fill a thinking person with a feeling of humility. This is a genuinely religious feeling that has nothing to do with mysticism."

—Albert Einstein, replying to a letter in 1954 or 1955; from *Albert Einstein, the Human Side*, p. 39.

"I do not believe that a man should be restrained in his daily actions by being afraid of punishment after death or that he should do things only because in this way he will be rewarded after he dies. This does not make sense. The proper guidance during the life of a man should be the weight that he puts upon ethics and the amount of consideration that he has for others."

—Albert Einstein; from Peter A. Bucky, *The Private Albert Einstein*, Kansas City: Andrews & McMeel, 1992, p. 86.

"Scientific research is based on the idea that everything that takes place is determined by laws of nature, and therefore this holds for the action of people. For this reason, a research scientist will hardly be inclined to believe that events could be influenced by a prayer, i.e. by a wish addressed to a supernatural Being."

—Albert Einstein in response to a child who had written him in 1936 and asked if scientists pray; from *Albert Einstein, the Human Side*, p. 32.

"I cannot conceive of a personal God who would directly influence the actions of individuals, or would directly sit in judgment on creatures of his own creation. I cannot do this in spite of the fact that mechanistic causality has, to a certain extent, been placed in doubt by modern science. [He was speaking of Quantum Mechanics and the breaking down of determinism.] My religiosity consists in a humble admiration of the infinitely superior spirit that reveals itself in the little that we, with our weak and transitory understanding, can comprehend of reality. Morality is of the highest importance—but for us, not for God."

   —Albert Einstein; from *Albert Einstein, the Human Side*, p. 66.

"The finest emotion of which we are capable is the mystic emotion. Herein lies the germ of all art and all true science. Anyone to whom this feeling is alien, who is no longer capable of wonderment and lives in a state of fear is a dead man. To know that what is impenetrable for us really exists and manifests itself as the highest wisdom and the most radiant beauty, whose gross forms alone are intelligible to our poor faculties—this knowledge, this feeling . . . that is the core of the true religious sentiment. In this sense, and in this sense alone, I rank myself among profoundly religious men."

   "The idea of a personal God is an anthropological concept which I am unable to take seriously."

   —Albert Einstein, letter to Hoffman and Dukas, 1946; from *Albert Einstein, the Human Side*.

"The further the spiritual evolution of mankind advances, the more certain it seems to me that the path to genuine religiosity does not lie through the fear of life, and the fear of death, and blind faith, but through striving after rational knowledge."

   —Albert Einstein, *Science, Philosophy, and Religion*, a 1934 symposium
   published by the Conference on Science, Philosophy, and Religion in
   Their Relation to the Democratic Way of Life, Inc., New York, 1941; from
   Einstein's *Out of My Later Years*, Westport, Connecticut: Greenwood Press,
   1970, pp. 29–30.

"I cannot believe that God plays dice with the cosmos."

   —Albert Einstein on quantum mechanics, published in the *London Observer*,
   April 5, 1964; also quoted as "God does not play dice with the world," in
   Einstein: The Life and Times, Ronald W. Clark, New York: World Publishing
   Co., 1971, p. 19.

"I cannot accept any concept of God based on the fear of life or the fear of death or blind faith. I cannot prove to you that there is no personal God, but if I were to speak of him I would be a liar."

   —Albert Einstein; from *Einstein: The Life and Times*, p. 622.

"During the youthful period of mankind's spiritual evolution human fantasy created gods in man's own image, who, by the operations of their will were supposed to determine, or at any rate to influence, the phenomenal world. Man sought to alter the disposition of these gods in his own favor by means of magic and prayer. The idea of God in the religions taught at present is a sublimation of that old concept of the gods. Its anthropomorphic character is shown, for instance, by the fact that men appeal to the Divine Being in prayers and plead for the fulfillment of their wishes.

"Nobody, certainly, will deny that the idea of the existence of an omnipotent, just, and omnibeneficent personal God is able to accord man solace, help, and guidance; also, by virtue of its simplicity it is accessible to the most undeveloped mind. But, on the other hand, there are decisive weaknesses attached to this idea in itself, which have been painfully felt since the beginning of history. That is, if this being is omnipotent, then every occurrence, including every human action, every human thought, and every human feeling and aspiration is also His work; how is it possible to think of holding men responsible for their deeds and thoughts before such an almighty Being? In giving out punishment and rewards He would to a certain extent be passing judgment on Himself. How can this be combined with the goodness and righteousness ascribed to Him?

"The main source of the present-day conflicts between the spheres of religion and of science lies in this concept of a personal God. It is the aim of science to establish general rules which determine the reciprocal connection of objects and events in time and space. For these rules, or laws of nature, absolutely general validity is required—not proven. It is mainly a program, and faith in the possibility of its accomplishment in principle is only founded on partial successes. But hardly anyone could be found who would deny these partial successes and ascribe them to human self-deception. The fact that on the basis of such laws we are able to predict the temporal behavior of phenomena in certain domains with great precision and certainty is deeply embedded in the consciousness of the modern man, even though he may have grasped very little of the contents of those laws. He need only consider that planetary courses within the solar system may be calculated in advance with great exactitude on the basis of a limited number of simple laws. In a similar way, though not with the same precision, it is possible to calculate in advance the mode of operation of an electric motor, a transmission system, or of a wireless apparatus, even when dealing with a novel development.

"To be sure, when the number of factors coming into play in a phenomenological complex is too large, scientific method in most cases fails us. One need only think of the weather, in which case prediction even for a few days ahead is impossible. Nevertheless no one doubts that we are confronted with a causal connection whose causal components are in the main known to us. Occurrences in this domain are beyond the reach of exact prediction because of the variety of factors in operation, not because of any lack of order in nature.

"We have penetrated far less deeply into the regularities obtaining within the realm of living things, but deeply enough nevertheless to sense at least the rule of fixed necessity. One need only think of the systematic order in heredity, and in the effect of poisons, as for instance alcohol, on the behavior of organic beings. What is still lacking here is a grasp of connections of profound generality, but not a knowledge of order in itself.

"The more a man is imbued with the ordered regularity of all events the firmer becomes his conviction that there is no room left by the side of this ordered regularity for causes of a different nature. For him neither the rule of human nor the rule of divine will exists as an independent cause of natural events. To be sure, the doctrine of a personal God interfering with natural events could never be refuted, in the real sense, by science, for this doctrine can always take refuge in those domains in which scientific knowledge has not yet been able to set foot.

"But I am persuaded that such behavior on the part of the representatives of religion would not only be unworthy but also fatal. For a doctrine which is able to maintain itself not in clear light but only in the dark, will of necessity lose its effect on mankind, with incalculable harm to human progress. In their struggle for the ethical good, teachers of religion must have the stature to give up the doctrine of a personal God, that is, give up that source of fear and hope which in the past placed such vast power in the hands of priests. In their labors they will have to avail themselves of those forces which are capable of cultivating the Good, the True, and the Beautiful in humanity itself. This is, to be sure, a more difficult but an incomparably more worthy task."

—Albert Einstein, *Science, Philosophy, and Religion*; from Einstein's *Out of My Later Years*, pp. 26–29.

"I cannot then believe in this concept of an anthropomorphic God who has the powers of interfering with these natural laws. As I said before, the most beautiful and most profound religious emotion that we can experience is the sensation of the mystical. And this mysticality is the power of all true science."

—Albert Einstein; from Peter A. Bucky, *The Private Albert Einstein*, Kansas City: Andrews & McMeel, 1992, p. 86.

"The mystical trend of our time, which shows itself particularly in the rampant growth of the so-called Theosophy and Spiritualism, is for me no more than a symptom of weakness and confusion. Since our inner experiences consist of reproductions, and combinations of sensory impressions, the concept of a soul without a body seems to me to be empty and devoid of meaning."

—Albert Einstein, in a letter February 5, 1921; from *Albert Einstein, the Human Side*, p. 40.

"Mere unbelief in a personal God is no philosophy at all."
   —Albert Einstein, letter to V. T. Aaltonen, May 7, 1952, Einstein Archive
   59–059; from *The Expanded Quotable Einstein*, p. 216.

"I have repeatedly said that in my opinion the idea of a personal God is a child-like one. You may call me an agnostic, but I do not share the crusading spirit of the professional atheist whose fervor is mostly due to a painful act of liberation from the fetters of religious indoctrination received in youth. I prefer an atti-tude of humility corresponding to the weakness of our intellectual understand-ing of nature and of our own being."
   —Albert Einstein, to Guy H. Raner, Jr., September 28, 1949; from Michael R.
   Gilmore, "Einstein's God: Just What Did Einstein Believe About God?,"
   Skeptic, 1997, 5(2): 64.

"For science can only ascertain what *is*, but not what *should be*, and outside of its domain value judgments of all kinds remain necessary. Religion, on the other hand, deals only with evaluations of human thought and action: it cannot justi-fiably speak of facts and relationships between facts."
   —Albert Einstein, *Out of My Later Years*, p. 25.

"In view of such harmony in the cosmos which I, with my limited human mind, am able to recognize, there are yet people who say there is no God. But what really makes me angry is that they quote me for the support of such views."
   —Albert Einstein, according to the testimony of Prince Hubertus of
   Lowenstein; as quoted by Ronald W. Clark, *Einstein: The Life and Times*,
   p. 425.

"I received your letter of June 10th. I have never talked to a Jesuit priest in my life and I am astonished by the audacity to tell such lies about me. From the viewpoint of a Jesuit priest I am, of course, and have always been an atheist. Your counter-arguments seem to me very correct and could hardly be better for-mulated. It is always misleading to use anthropomorphical concepts in dealing with things outside the human sphere—childish analogies. We have to admire in humility the beautiful harmony of the structure of this world as far as we can grasp it. And that is all."
   —Albert Einstein, to Guy H. Raner, Jr., July 2, 1945, responding to a rumor
   that a Jesuit priest had caused Einstein to convert from atheism; from
   Michael R. Gilmore, "Einstein's God: Just What Did Einstein Believe About
   God?," *Skeptic*, 1997, 5(2): 62.

"I am convinced that some political and social activities and practices of the Catholic organizations are detrimental and even dangerous for the community as a whole, here and everywhere. I mention here only the fight against birth control at a time when overpopulation in various countries has become a serious threat to the health of people and a grave obstacle to any attempt to organize peace on this planet."

—Albert Einstein in a letter, 1954; from Paul Blanshard, *American Freedom and Catholic Power*, New Jersey: Greenwood Publishing, 1984, p. 10.

"His [Einstein] was not a life of prayer and worship. Yet he lived by a deep faith—a faith not capable of rational foundation—that there are laws of Nature to be discovered. His lifelong pursuit was to discover them. His realism and his optimism are illuminated by his remark: 'Subtle is the Lord, but malicious He is not' (*Raffiniert ist der Herrgott aber böshaft ist er nicht*). When asked by a colleague what he meant by that, he replied: 'Nature hides her secret because of her essential loftiness, but not by means of ruse' (*Die Natur verbirgt ihr Geheimnis durch die Erhabenheit ihres Wesens, aber nicht durch List*)."

—Abraham Pais, *Subtle Is the Lord: The Science and the Life of Albert Einstein*, Oxford University Press, New York, 1982.

"However, Einstein's God was not the God of most other men. When he wrote of religion, as he often did in middle and later life, he tended to adopt the belief of Alice's Red Queen that 'words mean what you want them to mean,' and to clothe with different names what to more ordinary mortals—and to most Jews—looked like a variant of simple agnosticism. Replying in 1929 to a cabled inquiry from Rabbi Goldstein of New York, he said that he believed 'in Spinoza's God who reveals himself in the harmony of all that exists, not in a God who concerns himself with the fate and actions of men.' And it is claimed that years later, asked by Ben-Gurion whether he believed in God, 'even he, with his great formula about energy and mass, agreed that there must be something behind the energy.' No doubt. But much of Einstein's writing gives the impression of belief in a God even more intangible and impersonal than a celestial machine minder, running the universe with indisputable authority and expert touch. Instead, Einstein's God appears as the physical world itself, with its infinitely marvelous structure operating at atomic level with the beauty of a craftsman's wristwatch, and at stellar level with the majesty of a massive cyclotron. This was belief enough. It grew early and rooted deep. Only later was it dignified by the title of cosmic religion, a phrase which gave plausible respectability to the views of a man who did not believe in a life after death and who felt that if virtue paid off in the earthly one, then this was the result of cause and effect rather than celestial reward. Einstein's God thus stood for an orderly system obeying rules which could be discovered by those who had the courage, imagination, and persistence to go on searching for them. It was to this past which he began to turn his mind soon after the age of twelve. The rest of his life everything else was to seem almost trivial by comparison."

—Ronald W. Clark, *Einstein: The Life and Times*, New York: World Publishing, 1971, pp. 19–20.

"That a man can take pleasure in marching in formation to the strains of a band is enough to make me despise him. He has only been given his big brain by mistake; a backbone was all he needed. This plague-spot of civilization ought to be abolished with all possible speed."

"A hundred times every day I remind myself that my inner and outer life depend on the labors of other men, living and dead, and that I must exert myself in order to give in the measure as I have received and am still receiving."

—Albert Einstein

23

From *A Clergyman's Daughter*

George Orwell

Kierkegaard's famous "leap of faith" suffers from the huge moral and practical disadvantage that it cannot be made only once, but has to be performed again and again. George Orwell (1903–1950) believed that the decline of religion, and especially the decline of the belief in personal immortality, required us to evolve a post-theistic basis for morality. Here, in his first novel, *A Clergyman's Daughter*, we see his protagonist Dorothy, her lonely mind upon a knife-edge as she discovers that the "leap" suffers from acutely diminishing returns.

Kneeling, with head bent and hands clasped against her knees, she set herself swiftly to pray for forgiveness before her father should reach her with the wafer. But the current of her thoughts had been broken. Suddenly it was quite useless attempting to pray; her lips moved, but there was neither heart nor meaning in her prayers. She could hear Proggett's boots shuffling and her father's clear low voice murmuring "Take and eat," she could see the worn strip of red carpet beneath her knees, she could smell dust and eau-de-Cologne and mothballs; but of the Body and Blood of Christ, of the purpose for which she had come here, she was as though deprived of the power to think. A deadly blankness had descended upon her mind. It seemed to her that actually she *could* not pray. She struggled, collected her thoughts, uttered mechanically the opening phrases of a prayer; but they were useless, meaningless—nothing but the dead shells of words. Her father was holding the wafer before her in his shapely, aged hand. He held it between finger and thumb, fastidiously, somehow distastefully, as though it had been a spoon of medicine. His eye was upon Miss Mayfill, who was doubling herself up like a geometrid caterpillar, with many creakings, and crossing herself so elaborately that one might have imagined that she was sketching a series of braid frogs on the front of her coat. For several seconds Dorothy hesitated and did not take the wafer. She dared not take it. Better, far better to step down from the altar than to accept the sacrament with such chaos in her heart!

Then it happened that she glanced sidelong, through the open south door. A momentary spear of sunlight had pierced the clouds. It struck downwards through the leaves of the limes, and a spray of leaves in the doorway gleamed with a transient, matchless green, greener than jade or emerald or Atlantic waters. It was as though some jewel of unimaginable splendour had flashed for an instant, filling the doorway with green light, and then faded. A flood of joy ran through Dorothy's heart. The flash of living colour had brought back to her, by a process deeper than reason, her peace of mind, her love of God, her power of worship. Somehow, because of the greenness of the leaves, it was again possible to pray. O all ye green things upon the earth, praise ye the Lord! She began to pray, ardently, joyfully, thankfully. The wafer melted upon her tongue.

24

In Westminster Abbey

JOHN BETJEMAN

If the Church of England ever had a national bard after George Herbert, that bard was certainly John Betjeman, whose love of architecture and liturgy was expressed in numerous (and humorous) works of near-devotion. However, he was not blind to the absurdity and self-centeredness of personal prayer, as this gentle but biting little satire, written in 1940, will show.

Let me take this other glove off
   As the vox humana swells,
And the beauteous fields of Eden
Bask beneath the Abbey bells.
   Here, where England's statesmen lie,
Listen to a lady's cry.

Gracious Lord, oh bomb the Germans.
   Spare their women for Thy Sake,
And if that is not too easy
   We will pardon Thy Mistake.
But, gracious Lord, whate'er shall be,
Don't let anyone bomb me.

Keep our Empire undismembered
   Guide our Forces by Thy Hand,
Gallant blacks from far Jamaica,
   Honduras and Togoland;
Protect them Lord in all their fights,
And, even more, protect the whites.

Think of what our Nation stands for,
   Books from Boots and country lanes,
Free speech, free passes, class distinction,

Democracy and proper drains.
Lord, put beneath Thy special care
One-eighty-nine Cadogan Square.

Although dear Lord I am a sinner,
   I have done no major crime;
Now I'll come to Evening Service
   Whensoever I have the time.
So, Lord, reserve for me a crown.
And do not let my shares go down.

I will labour for Thy Kingdom,
   Help our lads to win the war,
Send white feathers to the cowards
   Join the Women's Army Corps,
Then wash the Steps around Thy Throne
In the Eternal Safety Zone.

Now I feel a little better,
   What a treat to hear Thy word,
Where the bones of leading statesmen,
   Have so often been interr'd.
And now, dear Lord, I cannot wait
Because I have a luncheon date.

25

Monism and Religion

Chapman Cohen

I must include one of my personal favorites: a little-known champion of the Freethought movement. Born in 1868 and self-educated, Chapman Cohen (1868–1954) became the third president of the National Secular Society in Britain: the organization founded after Charles Bradlaugh had been denied his seat in Parliament for refusing to swear a religious oath of allegiance. Cohen kept his private life close, and little is known about him apart from his refusal to join a separate secular movement for Jews. His monument is "Essays In Freethinking," from which this selection is drawn.

It was a sound instinct that led the religious world to brand the Pantheism of Spinoza as Atheism. Equally sound was the judgment of Charles Bradlaugh in resting his Atheism upon a Monistic interpretation of nature. Every intelligible Theism involves a dualism or a pluralism, while every non-theism is as inevitably driven, sooner or later, to a monism. With an instinct sharpened by perpetual conflict, the Churches saw that, no matter the terminology in which the monism is disguised, its final outcome is Atheism. For the essence of the Atheistic position is not the establishment of any particular theory of matter, or force, or volition, but that, given a first principle as a starting-point, all else follows as a matter of the most rigid necessity. It thus dispenses with interference, or, to use a favourite mystifying expression of Sir Oliver Lodge, guidance, at any step of the cosmic process. To call the monism advocated a spiritual monism does not alter the fact; it only disguises it from superficial observers and shallow thinkers. Spiritual and material are mere words, and words, as we have been told, are the counters of wise men and the money of fools. It is the thing, the conception, that matters, and the mechanical conception of cosmic evolution is Atheism, under whatever form it may be disguised.

Monism—too much emphasis cannot be placed upon this truth—admits of no breaks, allows for no interference, no guidance, no special providence. From star mist to planet, on through protoplasm to man, it asserts the existence of an unbroken sequence. If there are any gaps they are in our knowledge, not in things themselves. The promise and potency of all subsequent phenomena is, for Monism, contained in the primitive substance, whatever its nature may be. Every advance in scientific research is based, tacitly or avowedly, upon an acceptance of this belief.

What place does the individual hold in such a conception of things? Clearly he can be no exception to the general principle of causation. The same principle that accounts for the development of the species as a biological phenomenon must also explain the individual as a sociological or psychological product. Either the individual is the necessary product of his antecedents or he is not. If he is, we have merely another phase of a general problem, only in a highly complex form. If he is not, then we have an absolute creation of something, a reintroduction of a disguised supernaturalism, and our scientific principle breaks down. The greatest genius, the most striking individual the world has ever seen, forms no exception to this universal principle of causation. Indeed, when the believer throws at the head of the Atheist the names of Shakespeare or Beethoven, and asks how can natural processes explain their existence, he is needlessly confusing the issue. First, because the problem of explaining the existence of the genius is no greater, fundamentally, than explaining the existence of the fool. Show me how to explain the complex processes that result in the existence of a penny-a-liner, and I will explain the existence of the author of *Hamlet*. The problem is substantially the same whichever we take. And, secondly, to take either the genius or the fool as a finished project, and study him in isolation, is emphatically not the way to set to work. We could not explain a man, or an animal, or a plant by such a method. Evolution ought to at least have taught us that the explanation of a thing is to be sought in its history. Behind the greatest musician and behind the greatest poet there lies that long history of the race leading to the rude rhythmical howlings and gutteral ejaculations of the primitive savage, without which, as a starting-point, neither poet nor musician would have existed. The greatest and the least of men are links in a chain of being, and can neither separate themselves from all that has gone before nor from that which will come after them.

I have put the claims of a Monistic conception of nature as strongly and as plainly as possible, in order to meet fairly a challenge raised by a prominent clergyman, in a recent issue of a religious weekly. We are told that the issue today lies between Monism and Christianity, and Monism is ruled out of court on account of its supposed depreciation of the individual. Even were this depreciation of the individual admitted it might still be argued that the real value of any theory depends ultimately upon its truth. The argument from consequences is only valid if it can be shown that these are in obvious conflict with facts. In that case, we should have to admit that our first principles were faulty, and revise them accordingly. Facts are facts, and sooner or later we are compelled to deal with them. Theories may ignore them, but the consequences follow just the same. It is not merely our duty to face the facts, it is to our interest to do so. All life is an adaptation of organism to environment, and all healthy mental life is the expression of a harmony between our ideas of facts and the facts themselves. And without posing as a philosophical Gradgrind, one may confidently assert that the man or the philosophy that ignores facts will sooner or later come to grief.

The article in question is headed, "Is the Individual Doomed?" and the answer is that he is if Monism prevails. With Christianity, we are told, the individual is everything; with Monism the individual is nothing. The Christian view of the individual acts as a powerful incentive to progress; the Monistic view "is utterly devoid of the dynamic which can generate any great social reform." While the conception of humanity as an organic structure in which the individual is ultimately merged is brushed aside in the following:

> The smallest and forlornest actual slum baby appeals to our sympathy immeasurably more than a vast, dim, aggregate of indistinguishable items called the Race, for we have actually met the slum baby, and we have never met—and what is more, we never shall meet—the Race. . . . No matter by how many times we multiply nothing, the result is still—nothing. . . . If we wish to be social reformers in earnest, we must take care of the individual and the race will take care of itself.

That the concrete example of a suffering slum baby appeals to us more than an abstract proposition about the race is true; but instead of this proving the case, it is, as will be seen later, dependent upon the fact of race, and is only an illustration of its influence. And to say that we must take care of the individual if we wish to take care of the race is a mere *ipse dixit*, since the question at issue is whether or not we are best promoting the interests of the individual when we keep our mind steadily on the question of race welfare. Finally, when we are told that the conception of man as a mere cell in the social tissue, an item in the long story of human progress is "devoid of the dynamic which can generate any social reform," the reply is that no other factor has shown itself of such inspiring force with social reformers. One need go no further back than the French Revolution of 1789—one of the most "dynamic" events of modern history—to prove this. The schools of St. Simon, Owen, Fourier, with the modern development of Socialism on its higher side, are all permeated by a conception of human development that we are told is fatal to social progress. In fact it is next to impossible to point to a great social movement that has not been inspired by the conception of humanity as a slowly developing organism from which the individual springs, and in which the individual is ultimately merged.

Our preacher may be correct in saying that with Christianity the individual is everything; he is quite wrong in saying that with Monism the individual is nothing. The question is ultimately one of the nature and function of the individual, and to assume that unless we assert that he is independent of the social structure we are destroying him is quite beside the point. We do not annihilate the earth by showing its place in the solar system; we do not annihilate the cell by showing its place in the organism; nor do we destroy the individual by showing him to be a cell in the social tissue. On the contrary, it is only when man is thought of in this sense that we really begin to form a genuine conception of individuality.

One of the errors of Christianity has been to make constant appeals to the individual without considering those conditions of which individual life is the expression. It has preached purity of thought and deed while leaving untouched conditions that make purity of life an impossibility. It has taught morality without realizing that morality is not something that is grafted on life, but something that springs from social life and is conditioned in its expression by the prevailing social conditions. All the ethical failures and extravagances of moral teaching that dog the history of Christianity are attributable to this initial error. It may be quite correct to say the Christian teaching is that we must look to the individual and leave the race to attend to itself; but it is none the less a mistaken teaching. For you can only permanently affect the individual through a modification of those conditions that are summed up in the phrase "social environment." I do not mean here an environment that covers only the material conditions of existence, but include all those mental forces that play so large a part in moulding the life of each of us. If man is to be morally, mentally, and physically healthy, he must live in an environment which permits health in all these directions. Otherwise we may appeal to the individual as long as *we* choose; our appeal even in the most favourable of circumstances, will only be in the nature of a stimulant, and like all such will be of a temporary nature only. Doctors, scientists, sociologists, all shades of real thinkers, are fast realizing that it is the race problem that is the vital one, and this, not in the interests of an abstract entity called the Race, but in the best interests of the individual himself.

In thus contrasting the Monistic and the Christian view of the function of the individual, there is raised the old question of the relations of the individual to society. And although the limited influence of social conditions is admitted, the main position is that of a species of sociological atomism. Our preacher would agree with those writers who argue that society is a mere aggregate of individual human beings. On the other hand, one may submit that, while society is an aggregate of individuals, it is yet something more than is given in any number of individuals merely added together. The strength of an army is not the mere sum total of the strengths of the individual members composing it; it is that plus the addition of what results from combination. The product of a chemical compound is not to be discovered by adding together the properties or qualities of its constituents. Some quality is given in the combination not to be found in its constituent parts. And in the same way no amount of adding together of individuals can give us all that we find in a social structure. We cannot, try how we may, derive society from the individual. We can, as will be seen, derive the individual from society.

I am not claiming the existence of some mysterious social ego presiding over society, as theologians conceived a soul dominating the organism. My point is that just as *I* am made up of the various parts of my organism plus the combination of these parts, and that just as the relations between the parts are as real as the parts themselves, so there develops a social force which expresses the relations existing between all individuals, and which is as real as the individuals themselves. And this is strictly analogous to all that we know, scientifically, of other forces. The law of gravitation, the laws of heat, light, and sound are the expressions of a relation, and have no existence apart from the relations between atoms of matter. And it would be as absurd to deny the existence of gravitation, because it cannot be shown apart from matter, as it is to deny the existence of this social force, because we cannot separate it from the individuals that comprise society.

It is perfectly true that, apart from individuals, society has no existence, but it is equally true that, apart from society, the individual ceases to be. Society is no more an abstraction than is the individual. When we speak of society it is true that we are expressing the totality of individual actions, but it is also true that when we speak of the individual we are expressing the result of a whole complex of social forces. Take from the individual all that society gives him in the shape of language, beliefs, clothing, institutions, take away the relations existing between him and his fellows, and the individual, as we know him, has ceased to exist. One view of the case is certainly as true as the other; and when such opposing conclusions can be logically reached, it is highly probable that the truth lies between the two, or in a combination of both. The truth is that either aspect alone represents a one-sided view of the subject. Neither individual nor society can, or ought to be, considered separately. Both are aspects of the same fact. The individual is a concrete expression of social forces; society is an organism precisely because, like all organisms, one cannot understand aright any one of the parts without considering its relation to the whole, and because one cannot appreciate the whole without understanding the nature and function of each of the parts.

One may reach the same conclusion by another method. Much is often made of the statement that the end of social action is the production of strong individuals. This is true; but individuation is the product, biologically, of a differentiation, and this, instead of making the part less dependent on the whole, really involves a greater coherence and a more profound interdependence of parts. In the animal organism the taking on of specific functions by certain groups of cells involves the performance of other functions by other groups; and thus, while in view of a specific function a particular cell group may be said to acquire a greater individuality, from another point of view its individuality is an expression of the organized cell life of the entire organism. With equal truth this generalisation holds good of the individual in relation to society. Social action necessarily results, not in the production of individuals who are above social forces and who control them, but in the production of individualities that express the highly elaborated social forces behind and around them. There is positively no other source for their existence. An individual cannot create new forces; he can only utilize those already existing. And unless he is the exact equivalent of all the forces that preceded him, neither more nor less, we have in the individual something that is impossible of explanation, and which cuts the ground from under all scientific and all coherent thinking. The very feeling of the individual that he is controlling social forces is a trick of the imagination, which ultimately expresses the deeper truth I have indicated.

The most striking apparent exceptions will be seen to enforce this truth. Probably in thinking of strong, almost lawless individualities, many would light upon these "money kings" whose actions seem to be fettered by no consideration of social service. And yet, putting on one side that we are here dealing with the old predatory instincts modified to meet new conditions, the fact remains that the most lawless of the group are as dependent upon social forces as any others. For these men hold the wealth they have, and pursue the methods they employ, wholly in virtue of the social discipline—respect for private property, for freedom of action, habits of obedience, which the people have been subjected to, and to the laws—expressions of the same social discipline—which protects them from assault. So that, paradoxical as it may sound, the very people who imagine themselves free from the control of the social forces, are those who are most dependent upon their existence and operation.

We can, now, I think, see more clearly the futility of the remark that "the smallest and forlornest actual slum baby appeals to our sympathy immeasurably more than a vast dim aggregate of indistinguishable items called the Race." Naturally, because we have here a concrete illustration of a universal fact, without which the general fact would not be appreciated. But the very sympathy which is excited is race-born, is an expression of that race solidarity which is thought of so little value. And sympathy, while immediately directed towards the individual, is ultimately directed towards race-welfare. The love of the mother for her child is nature's method of securing race preservation; and the sympathy of one person with another is nature's method of securing that social cooperation and efficiency without which human life would cease to exist. It is always good not to lose the particular in the general, but it is also good not to lose sight of the fact that the particular is only what it is because of its relation to the general.

If what has been said be correct, what, it may be asked, becomes of the individual? Well, the individual is as much there as ever; we simply realize his true worth and function in the social organism. The individual is no more doomed than an analysis of the laws of light destroys the beauty of a sunset. We are as able as ever to appreciate the individual, but it is an intelligent appreciation that comes from a perception of his true nature and of his relations to humanity as a whole, in place of the unreasoning and helpless wonder of a disguised supernaturalism. The individual stands, not as the chance product of incomprehensible powers, but as the necessary result and expression of social forces always in operation.

That this conception robs us of the incentive to progress I do not for a moment believe. In the first place, progress itself is not such a chance thing as to be dependent upon the voluntary cooperation of any one person or of any group of persons. Those who study carefully the history of ideas of progress in general will see the truth of Spencer's statement that human progress is all of a piece with the unfolding of a flower and the development of a planet, a complex illustration of the laws of causation. All ideas are born of the past operating upon the present; and although ideas cannot run without feet, they must find a particular human vehicle for their expression, yet it is much nearer the truth to say that these find their vent in individuals than that individuals create the ideas themselves. Flattering to self-esteem as is the notion that ideas depend for their existence upon this or that individual, it is one that is quite devoid of scientific foundation.

Secondly, it is largely a question of how we are to set to work. If the individual originates social forces, our efforts must be concentrated on individuals, or, as it is said, "We must take care of the individual and leave the race to take care of itself." If, however, the individual is the expression of countless social actions and reactions, then the line of effort must be in the direction of modifying social conditions so as to make for a more desirable manhood. And if we are to be guided by experience, one need have no hesitation in declaring for the latter method. For all experience testifies to the futility of our expecting ideas and beliefs to flourish in an unsuitable environment. Moral teaching is equally futile unless the general environment is such as gives it countenance. To do Christianity justice, one must admit that there has never been with it any lack of mere moral instruction; but there has been a fatal neglect of the conditions that would give the moral instruction force. A people is always what its environment makes it; only we must be careful to count in the environment the biological and psychological forces along with the purely material ones.

Finally, there is the question of inspiration. This is ultimately a question of imagination. Our preacher thinks the slum baby more effective than anything else. Others there are who find little inspiration in particular individuals, who may be quite unattractive objects. To them the story of human progress appeals far more powerfully. They feel that, unlovely and undesirable as certain individuals may be, their unloveliness and undesirability are atoned for by the worthiness of humanity as a whole. It is not that they multiply nothing to get something, or that they hope by a multiplication of ugliness to get beauty, but the conception of a slowly developing humanity compensates for the partial failures and for the marred beauty of isolated instances. And surely there is in this human story, from cave man to poet, philosopher, and scientist, enough inspiration to fire the most sluggish imagination. There is enough to make one feel that, whatever our failures may be, they are neither eternal nor irremediable; that the course of evolution has loaded the dice in our favour; and that even though as individuals we are mere links in the chain of beings, as links we still play our parts, and so serve to provide a finer metal out of which may be forged the links that follow.

Spiritual Vision

In one of his writings Mr. G. K. Chesterton says that the real question at issue between the Christian and the Freethinker is, "Are there or are there not certain powers and experiences possible to the human mind which really occur when the mind is suitably disposed? Is the religious history of mankind a chronicle of accidental lies, delusions, and coincidences, or is it a chronicle of real things which we happen not to be able to do, and real visions which we happen not to be able to see?" As is not unusual with Mr. Chesterton, he succeeds here in saying nothing in particular, while apparently expressing a deal in a small compass. For, far from meeting the case of the scientific Freethinker, it shows no real appreciation of it. Mr. Chesterton's case is that the Christian saint or mystic is, by the exercise of certain spiritual expriences, brought into another world of being. The Freethinker does not deny the experiences—without the qualifying "spiritual"—but he submits there is another and more rational explanation at hand.

Let us take a few examples. The [Roman] Catholic Church will produce clouds of testimony from men and women to the effect that certain visions were seen under certain circumstances. These circumstances are usually long vigils, fasting, praying, a more or less solitary life, and constant meditation upon mystical matters. These witnesses will dilate upon the feeling of exaltation that accompanied and preceded such visions, and will describe the subjective experiences with all the detail that one might use in describing a fit of indigestion, or an attack of the toothache. Now, no Freethinker who understands his case would say these witnesses were all liars. Nor would he say that they were *all* insane in the general sense of the word. Neither would he deny that under the same conditions he himself would in all probability experience the same kind of visions and feelings. What he would say, and what he does say, is that all this religious testimony can be explained on pathological grounds as due to an unwholesome nervous strain. If any modern cares to try the experiment, and sit, like some Hindoo fakir, for so many hours per day contemplating his stomach, and repeating the sacred word "Om," we do not hesitate in saying that he, too, will see visions; and in that case he need not cite a "cloud of witnesses"—he can cite himself.

.　　.　　.

An Old Story

CHAPMAN COHEN

"Now the birth of Jesus Christ was in this wise. When his mother, Mary, was espoused to Joseph, before they came together she was found with child of the Holy Ghost." Now the birth of the Greek demi-god, Perseus, was in this wise. When Acristus, King of Argon, was warned that he would be killed by the son of his daughter Danae, he built a tower of brass, in which she was imprisoned, and so hoped to frustrate the oracle. But the God Jupiter visited the maiden in a shower of gold, and thus was Perseus born. And the birth of the Aztec God, Huitzilopochtli, was in this wise. When Catlicus, the serpent-skirted, was in the open air, a little ball of feathers floated down from the heavens. She caught it and hid it in her bosom. And of this was the god born. The birth of the God Attis was in this wise. From the blood of the murdered Agdestris sprang a pomegranate tree, and some of the fruit thereof the virgin Nana gathered and laid it in her bosom, and thus was the god born. Also the founder of the Manchu dynasty of China was born in this wise. A heavenly maiden was bathing one day when she found on the skirt of her raiment a certain red fruit. She ate, and was delivered of a son. Likewise was Fo-Hi born of a virgin. And the virgin daughter of a king of the Mongols awakened one night and found herself embraced by a great light and gave birth to three boys, one of whom was the famous Genghis Khan. In Korea, the daughter of the river Ho was fertilized by the rays of the sun, and gave birth to a wonderful boy. Likewise was Chrishna [sic] born of the virgin Devaka; Horus was born of the virgin Isis; Mercury was born of the virgin Maia; and Romulus was born of the virgin Rhea Sylvia. Many other stories might be related, but of all these there is none true but the first. Millions of Christians say so. For it is in the New Testament, and none of the others are. And to the eye of faith the distinction is of profound importance.

What is the meaning of it all? Why were all these gods and demi-gods born in this manner? Well, thereby hangs a tale, and its complete unravelment would carry us back a very long way in the history of human nature. The first point to be grasped is that most of the things that to us are commonplace, are really discoveries that are made only after the passing of many generations. Nothing seems to us, for example, more certain and more natural than death. Yet there exists ample proof that death, as a natural fact, is as much of a discovery as is the nature of the moon's phases. Primitive mankind treats death as the result of being bewitched by an enemy, or killed by one of the tribal spirits. Only slowly is the true nature of death recognized. And the same principle holds good of birth. Nothing seems more certain than that birth is the result of the union of two people—a man and a woman. But this, too, is a discovery that mankind has to make, and although the discovery has now been made practically all over the world, there are some exceptions, and the prevalence of certain customs and superstitions is enough to prove that they resemble, in the intellectual world, those rudimentary organs which man carries about with him in his physical structure. They are the surviving indications of a lower state of culture from which the higher and truer has been derived. And a comprehension of the process enables us to understand why "the birth of Jesus Christ was in this wise." Nothing else can.

In his *Legend of Perseus* and in his *Primitive Paternity*, Mr. E. S. Hartland has brought forward a mass of illustrations to prove two things. First, the widespread belief in the supernatural birth of gods and national heroes; and, second, the equally widespread vogue of superstitious and magical practices to obtain children, and which are a practical ignoring of the biological laws governing their production. Thus, a tribe of natives in Northwestern Australia believe that birth is quite independent of sexual intercourse. The North Queenslanders believe that babies are brought to women by Nature spirits, the function of the husband being apparently to invoke the spirits to do their work. On the Proserpine River, a supernatural being named Kunya inserts the baby in a woman while she is bathing. Some places are held to be the favourite ground for these unincarnated spirits, and women who have no desire for children will, when passing these spots, ape the walk and appearance of extreme age, in order to deceive the waiting spirit. On the Slave Coast of West Africa, it is believed that the child is derived from the ancestral spirits. Other parts of the world furnish similar examples. And as a product of beliefs such as these we have world-wide magical practices in order to obtain children. For these there is no need to travel far. They exist all over Europe, and almost any comprehensive work on comparative mythology will give illustrations of the practices current among Christian peoples who believe that by them fecundity is secured. And the whole point to the once almost universal belief that the child is not the physiological consequence of the union of the sexes, but is in sober truth a supernatural product.

Now, what has been said is well known to all writers on comparative mythology and anthropology. But these works have an aggravating knack of stopping short at just the point where they begin to be of real importance. For the value, perhaps the whole value, of a comprehension of the religious beliefs of the lower races lies in their relation to the religious beliefs of the races that are more advanced. But, owing to the widespread fear of vested interests, this is very seldom done. The origin of the savage gods is clearly indicated in scores of authoritative works; but there are few, if any, of our first-class men that have the courage to point to the further truth that our modern ideas of god are descended from these primitive and clearly mistaken beliefs, and rest on no other and no better foundations. The consequence is that, when one tries to trace the development of the Christian belief in the Virgin Birth from such savage and primitive beliefs as have been above indicated one finds oneself almost on virgin soil. But, starting from the fact that the nature of procreation and birth is a genuine discovery that is made by man in the course of his intellectual development, one may dimly see how the belief in the supernatural birth of the scores of gods that have ruled over the minds of men came to be established. At any rate, its persistence only serves to drive home the lesson that all religion, no matter how refined, has its roots in the delusions that have their sway over the mind of mankind in its most primitive stages.

To our mind it is quite clear that in the Christian story of the Virgin Birth, as in the other classical versions of the same legend that have been quoted, we have a survival of the primitive belief that all birth is supernatural. And it is not difficult to conceive that as a better knowledge of procreation—at least of the fact, if not of the process—gained ground, the interference of the spiritual world in the matter of birth would be restricted to the appearance of striking personalities. In this we are only following the ordinary course of the history of the supernatural, where from everything being thought of as being due to the gods, we get their interference only on special occasions—occasions that become more and more rare as human knowledge becomes more and more precise. Thus, in course of time, it is not every man who is born of the tribal spirits and gods, but only the specially favoured individual. Sexual intercourse between human beings and the gods, such as appears in plain form in some of the legends, and in a veiled form in others, thus carries us back far beyond the period of the classical mythologies to the most primitive form of human thought. The mythologies are themselves late survivals, and their ready acceptance may be partly accounted for by the fact that, as popular folk-lore shows, there are still active in all parts of the world beliefs and practices which associate birth with supernatural intervention. Into the course of the development that derived the Gospel story from the belief of the primitive savage we have now neither the time nor the space to enter, but that the one is derived from the other there cannot be reasonable doubt. Later there gathers round the sexual act all sorts of mystical interpretation, but here, as in other cases, it is the savage that provides the true starting-point. And to the informed the truth of religion is no longer a question of historical or philosophical enquiry, it is the psychology of religion that is of consequence. Not whether men are justified in their belief, but how they came to believe these things to be true is the pertinent enquiry. Anthropology holds within it the secret of divinity. When the missionary sets forth to convert the savage, he is attacking the parent of his religion. For the savage alone can tell him why "the birth of Jesus was in this wise."

26

An Outline of
Intellectual Rubbish

BERTRAND RUSSELL

The godson of John Stuart Mill had several careers as philosopher, mathematician, and opponent of injustice. His rather disordered private life also helped furnish the material for a notable autobiography. At different times, his stubborn views on sexual freedom and the dangers of war and empire caused him to be banned from teaching in the United States and imprisoned in the United Kingdom. A single pamphlet, *Why I Am Not A Christian*, became a classic from which the Christian churches have yet to recover. I chose this essay, written in the very dark year of 1943, because it expresses a certain stoical optimism and because it connects the nonsense of religious belief to the prevalence of other popular superstitions. In his extraordinarily prescient *Practice and Theory of Bolshevism*, written just after the Russian revolution, Russell distinguished himself by being one of the first to notice the connection between modern totalitarian thought and the religious impulse toward subjection.

Man is a rational animal—so at least I have been told. Throughout a long life, I have looked diligently for evidence in favor of this statement, but so far I have not had the good fortune to come across it, though I have searched in many countries spread over three continents. On the contrary, I have seen the world plunging continually further into madness. I have seen great nations, formerly leaders of civilization, led astray by preachers of bombastic nonsense. I have seen cruelty, persecution, and superstition increasing by leaps and bounds, until we have almost reached the point where praise of rationality is held to mark a man as an old fogey regrettably surviving from a bygone age. All this is depressing, but gloom is a useless emotion. In order to escape from it, I have been driven to study the past with more attention than I had formerly given to it, and have found, as Erasmus found, that folly is perennial and yet the human race has survived. The follies of our own times are easier to bear when they are seen against the background of past follies. In what follows I shall mix the sillinesses of our day with those of former centuries. Perhaps the result may help in seeing our own times in perspective, and as not much worse than other ages that our ancestors lived through without ultimate disaster.

Aristotle, so far as I know, was the first man to proclaim explicitly that man is a rational animal. His reason for this view was one which does not now seem very impressive; it was, that some people can do sums. He thought that there are three kinds of soul: the vegetable soul, possessed by all living things, both plants and animals, and concerned only with nourishment and growth; the animal soul, concerned with locomotion, and shared by man with the lower animals; and finally the rational soul, or intellect, which is the Divine mind, but in which men participate to a greater or less degree in proportion to their wisdom. It is in virtue of the intellect that man is a rational animal. The intellect is shown in various ways, but most emphatically by mastery of arithmetic. The Greek system of numerals was very bad, so that the multiplication table was quite difficult, and complicated calculations could only be made by very clever people. Now-a-days, however, calculating machines do sums better than even the cleverest people, yet no one contends that these useful instruments are immortal, or work by divine inspiration. As arithmetic has grown easier, it has come to be less respected. The consequence is that, though many philosophers continue to tell us what fine fellows we are, it is no longer on account of our arithmetical skill that they praise us.

Since the fashion of the age no longer allows us to point to calculating boys as evidence that man is rational and the soul, at least in part, immortal, let us look elsewhere. Where shall we look first? Shall we look among eminent statesmen, who have so triumphantly guided the world into its present condition? Or shall we choose the men of letters? Or the philosophers? All these have their claims, but I think we should begin with those whom all right-thinking people acknowledge to be the wisest as well as the best of men, namely the clergy. If *they* fail to be rational, what hope is there for us lesser mortals? And alas—though I say it with all due respect—there have been times when their wisdom has not been very obvious, and, strange to say, these were especially the times when the power of the clergy was greatest.

The Ages of Faith, which are praised by our neo-scholastics, were the time when the clergy had things all their own way. Daily life was full of miracles wrought by saints and wizardry perpetrated by devils and necromancers. Many thousands of witches were burnt at the stake. Men's sins were punished by pestilence and famine, by earthquake, flood, and fire. And yet, strange to say, they were even more sinful than they are now-a-days. Very little was known scientifically about the world. A few learned men remembered Greek proofs that the earth is round, but most people made fun of the notion that there are antipodes. To suppose that there are human beings at the antipodes was heresy. It was generally held (though modern Catholics take a milder view) that the immense majority of mankind are damned. Dangers were held to lurk at every turn. Devils would settle on the food that monks were about to eat, and would take possession of the bodies of incautious feeders who omitted to make the sign of the Cross before each mouthful. Old-fashioned people still say "bless you" when one sneezes, but they have forgotten the reason for the custom. The reason was that people were thought to sneeze out their souls, and before their souls could get back lurking demons were apt to enter the unsouled body; but if any one said "God bless you," the demons were frightened off.

Throughout the last 400 years, during which the growth of science had gradually shown men how to acquire knowledge of the ways of nature and mastery over natural forces, the clergy have fought a losing battle against science, in astronomy and geology, in anatomy and physiology, in biology and psychology and sociology. Ousted from one position, they have taken up another. After being worsted in astronomy, they did their best to prevent the rise of geology; they fought against Darwin in biology, and at the present time they fight against scientific theories of psychology and education. At each stage, they try to make the public forget their earlier obscurantism, in order that their present obscurantism may not be recognized for what it is. Let us note a few instances of irrationality among the clergy since the rise of science, and then inquire whether the rest of mankind are any better.

When Benjamin Franklin invented the lightning rod, the clergy, both in England and America, with the enthusiastic support of George III, condemned it as an impious attempt to defeat the will of God. For, as all right-thinking people were aware, lightning is sent by God to punish impiety or some other grave sin— the virtuous are never struck by lightning. Therefore if God wants to strike any one, Benjamin Franklin ought not to defeat His design; indeed, to do so is helping criminals to escape. But God was equal to the occasion, if we are to believe the eminent Dr. Price, one of the leading divines of Boston. Lightning having been rendered ineffectual by the "iron points invented by the sagacious Dr. Franklin," Massachusetts was shaken by earthquakes, which Dr. Price perceived to be due to God's wrath at the "iron points." In a sermon on the subject he said, "In Boston are more erected than elsewhere in New England, and Boston seems to be more dreadfully shaken. Oh! there is no getting out of the mighty hand of God." Apparently, however, Providence gave up all hope of curing Boston of its wickedness, for, though lightning rods became more and more common, earthquakes in Massachusetts have remained rare. Nevertheless, Dr. Price's point of view, or something very like it, is still held by one of the most influential of living men. When, at one time, there were several bad earthquakes in India, Mahatma Gandhi solemnly warned his compatriots that these disasters had been sent as a punishment for their sins.

Even in my own native island this point of view still exists. During the last war, the British Government did much to stimulate the production of food at home. In 1916, when things were not going well, a Scottish clergyman wrote to the newspapers to say that military failure was due to the fact that, with government sanction, potatoes had been planted on the Sabbath. However, disaster was averted, owing to the fact that the Germans disobeyed *all* the Ten Commandments, and not only one of them.

Sometimes, if pious men are to be believed, God's mercies are curiously selective. Toplady, the author of "Rock of Ages," moved from one vicarage to another; a week after the move, the vicarage he had formerly occupied burnt down, with great loss to the new vicar. Thereupon Toplady thanked God; but what the new vicar did is not known. Borrow, in his "Bible in Spain," records how without mishap he crossed a mountain pass infested by bandits. The next party to cross, however, were set upon, robbed, and some of them murdered; when Borrow heard of this, he, like Toplady, thanked God.

Although we are taught the Copernican astronomy in our textbooks, it has not yet penetrated to our religion or our morals, and has not even succeeded in destroying belief in astrology. People still think that the Divine Plan has special reference to human beings, and that a special Providence not only looks after the good, but also punishes the wicked. I am sometimes shocked by the blasphemies of those who think themselves pious—for instance, the nuns who never take a bath without wearing a bathrobe all the time. When asked why, since no man can see them, they reply: "Oh, but you forget the good God." Apparently they conceive of the Deity as a Peeping Tom, whose omnipotence enables Him to see through bathroom walls, but who is foiled by bathrobes. This view strikes me as curious.

The whole conception of "Sin" is one which I find very puzzling, doubtless owing to my sinful nature. If "Sin" consisted in causing needless suffering, I could understand; but on the contrary, sin often consists in avoiding needless suffering. Some years ago, in the English House of Lords, a bill was introduced to legalize euthanasia in cases of painful and incurable disease. The patient's consent was to be necessary, as well as several medical certificates. To me, in my simplicity, it would seem natural to require the patient's consent, but the late Archbishop of Canterbury, the English official expert on Sin, explained the erroneousness of such a view. The patient's consent turns euthanasia into suicide, and suicide is sin. Their Lordships listened to the voice of authority, and rejected the bill. Consequently, to please the Archbishop—and his God, if he reports truly—victims of cancer still have to endure months of wholly useless agony, unless their doctors or nurses are sufficiently humane to risk a charge of murder. I find difficulty in the conception of a God who gets pleasure from contemplating such tortures; and if there were a God capable of such wanton cruelty, I should certainly not think Him worthy of worship. But that only proves how sunk I am in moral depravity.

I am equally puzzled by the things that are sin and by the things that are not. When the Society for the Prevention of Cruelty to Animals asked the pope for his support, he refused it, on the ground that human beings owe no duty to the lower animals, and that ill-treating animals is not sinful. This is because animals have no souls. On the other hand, it is wicked to marry your deceased wife's sister—so at least the Church teaches—however much you and she may wish to marry. This is not because of any unhappiness that might result, but because of certain texts in the Bible.

The resurrection of the body, which is an article of the Apostles' Creed, is a dogma which has various curious consequences. There was an author not very many years ago, who had an ingenious method of calculating the date of the end of the world. He argued that there must be enough of the necessary ingredients of a human body to provide everybody with the requisites at the Last Day. By carefully calculating the available raw material, he decided that it would all have been used up by a certain date. When that date comes, the world must end, since otherwise the resurrection of the body would become impossible. Unfortunately I have forgotten what the date was, but I believe it is not very distant.

St. Thomas Aquinas, the official philosopher of the Catholic Church, discussed lengthily and seriously a very grave problem, which, I fear, modern theologians unduly neglect. He imagines a cannibal who has never eaten anything but human flesh, and whose father and mother before him had like propensities. Every particle of his body belongs rightfully to someone else. We cannot suppose that those who have been eaten by cannibals are to go short through all eternity. But, if not, what is left for the cannibal? How is he to be properly roasted in hell, if all his body is restored to its original owners? This is a puzzling question, as the Saint rightly perceives.

In this connection the orthodox have a curious objection to cremation, which seems to show an insufficient realization of God's omnipotence. It is thought that a body which has been burnt will be more difficult for Him to collect together again than one which has been put underground and transformed into worms. No doubt collecting the particles from the air and undoing the chemical work of combustion would be somewhat laborious, but it is surely blasphemous to suppose such a work impossible for the Deity. I conclude that the objection to cremation implies grave heresy. But I doubt whether my opinion will carry much weight with the orthodox.

It was only very slowly and reluctantly that the Church sanctioned the dissection of corpses in connection with the study of medicine. The pioneer in dissection was Vesalius, who was Court physician to the Emperor Charles V. His medical skill led the emperor to protect him, but after the emperor was dead he got into trouble. A corpse which he was dissecting was said to have shown signs of life under the knife, and he was accused of murder. The Inquisition was induced by King Phillip II to take a lenient view, and only sentenced him to a pilgrimage to the Holy Land. On the way home he was shipwrecked and died of exhaustion. For centuries after this time, medical students at the Papal University in Rome were only allowed to operate on lay figures, from which the sexual parts were omitted.

The sacredness of corpses is a widespread belief. It was carried furthest by the Egyptians, among whom it led to the practice of mummification. It still exists in full force in China. A French surgeon, who was employed by the Chinese to teach Western medicine, relates that his demand for corpses to dissect was received with horror, but he was assured that he could have instead an unlimited supply of live criminals. His objection to this alternative was totally unintelligible to his Chinese employers.

Although there are many kinds of sin, seven of which are deadly, the most fruitful field for Satan's wiles is sex. The orthodox Catholic doctrine on this subject is to be found in St. Paul, St. Augustine, and St. Thomas Aquinas. It is best to be celibate, but those who have not the gift of continence may marry. Intercourse in marriage is not sin, provided it is motivated by desire for offspring. All intercourse outside marriage is sin, and so is intercourse within marriage if any measures are adopted to prevent conception. Interruption of pregnancy is sin, even if, in medical opinion, it is the only way of saving the mother's life; for medical opinion is fallible, and God can always save a life by miracle if He sees fit. (This view is embodied in the law of Connecticut.) Venereal disease is God's punishment for sin. It is true that, through a guilty husband, this punishment may fall on an innocent woman and her children, but this is a mysterious dispensation of Providence, which it would be impious to question. We must also not inquire why venereal disease was not divinely instituted until the time of Columbus. Since it is the appointed penalty for sin, all measures for its avoidance are also sin—except, of course, a virtuous life. Marriage is nominally indissoluble, but many people who seem to be married are not. In the case of influential Catholics, some ground for nullity can often be found, but for the poor there is no such outlet, except perhaps in cases of impotence. Persons who divorce and remarry are guilty of adultery in the sight of God.

The phrase "in the sight of God" puzzles me. One would suppose that God sees everything, but apparently this is a mistake. He does not see Reno, for you cannot be divorced in the sight of God. Registry offices are a doubtful point. I notice that respectable people, who would not call on anybody who lives in open sin, are quite willing to call on people who have had only a civil marriage; so apparently God does see registry offices.

Some eminent men think even the doctrine of the Catholic Church deplorably lax where sex is concerned. Tolstoy and Mahatma Gandhi, in their old age, laid it down that *all* sexual intercourse is wicked, even in marriage and with a view to offspring. The Manicheans thought likewise, relying upon men's native sinfulness to supply them with a continually fresh crop of disciples. This doctrine, however, is heretical, though it is equally heretical to maintain that marriage is as praiseworthy as celibacy. Tolstoy thinks tobacco almost as bad as sex; in one of his novels, a man who is contemplating murder smokes a cigarette first in order to generate the necessary homicidal fury. Tobacco, however, is not prohibited in the Scriptures, though, as Samuel Butler points out, St. Paul would no doubt have denounced it if he had known of it.

It is odd that neither the Church nor modern public opinion condemns petting, provided it stops short at a certain point. At what point sin begins is a matter as to which casuists differ. One eminently orthodox Catholic divine laid it down that a confessor may fondle a nun's breasts, provided he does it without evil intent. But I doubt whether modern authorities would agree with him on this point.

Modern morals are a mixture of two elements: on the one hand, rational precepts as to how to live together peaceably in a society, and on the other hand traditional taboos derived originally from some ancient superstition, but proximately from sacred books, Christian, Mohammedan, Hindu, or Buddhist. To some extent the two agree; the prohibition of murder and theft, for instance, is supported both by human reason and by Divine command. But the prohibition of pork or beef has only scriptural authority, and that only in certain religions. It is odd that modern men, who are aware of what science has done in the way of bringing new knowledge and altering the conditions of social life, should still be willing to accept the authority of texts embodying the outlook of very ancient and very ignorant pastoral or agricultural tribes. It is discouraging that many of the precepts whose sacred character is thus uncritically acknowledged should be such as to inflict much wholly unnecessary misery. If men's kindly impulses were stronger, they would find some way of explaining that these precepts are not to be taken literally, any more than the command to "sell all that thou hast and give to the poor."

There are logical difficulties in the notion of sin. We are told that sin consists in disobedience to God's commands, but we are also told that God is omnipotent. If He is, nothing contrary to His will can occur; therefore when the sinner disobeys His commands, He must have intended this to happen. St. Augustine boldly accepts this view, and asserts that men are led to sin by a blindness with which God afflicts them. But most theologians, in modern times, have felt that, if God causes men to sin, it is not fair to send them to hell for what they cannot help. We are told that sin consists in acting contrary to God's will. This, however, does not get rid of the difficulty. Those who, like Spinoza, take God's omnipotence seriously, deduce that there can be no such thing as sin. This leads to frightful results. What! said Spinoza's contemporaries, was it not wicked of Nero to murder his mother? Was it not wicked of Adam to eat the apple? Is one action just as good as another? Spinoza wriggles, but does not find any satisfactory answer. *If* everything happens in accordance with God's will, God must have wanted Nero to murder his mother; therefore, since God is good, the murder must have been a good thing. From this argument there is no escape.

On the other hand, those who are in earnest in thinking that sin is disobedience to God are compelled to say that God is not omnipotent. This gets out of all the logical puzzles, and is the view adopted by a certain school of liberal theologians. It has, however, its own difficulties. How are we to know what really is God's will? If the forces of evil have a certain share of power, they may deceive us into accepting as Scripture what is really their work. This was the view of the Gnostics, who thought that the Old Testament was the work of an evil spirit.

As soon as we abandon our own reason, and are content to rely upon authority, there is no end to our troubles. Whose authority? The Old Testament? The New Testament? The Koran? In practice, people choose the book considered sacred by the community in which they are born, and out of that book they choose the parts they like, ignoring the others. At one time, the most influential text in the Bible was: "Thou shalt not suffer a witch to live." Now-a-days, people pass over this text, in silence if possible; if not, with an apology. And so, even when we have a sacred book, we still choose as truth whatever suits our own prejudices. No Catholic, for instance, takes seriously the text which says that a bishop should be the husband of one wife.

People's beliefs have various causes. One is that there is some evidence for the belief in question. We apply this to matters of fact, such as "what is so-and-so's telephone number?" or "who won the World Series?" But as soon as it comes to anything more debatable, the causes of belief become less defensible. We believe, first and foremost, what makes us feel that we are fine fellows. Mr. Homo, if he has a good digestion and a sound income, thinks to himself how much more sensible he is than his neighbor so-and-so, who married a flighty wife and is always losing money. He thinks how superior his city is to the one 50 miles away: it has a bigger Chamber of Commerce and a more enterprising Rotary Club, and its mayor has never been in prison. He thinks how immeasurably his country surpasses all others. If he is an Englishman, he thinks of Shakespeare and Milton, or of Newton and Darwin, or of Nelson and Wellington, according to his temperament. If he is a Frenchman, he congratulates himself on the fact that for centuries France has led the world in culture, fashions, and cookery. If he is a Russian, he reflects that he belongs to the only nation which is truly international. If he is a Yugoslav, he boasts of his nation's pigs; if a native of the Principality of Monaco, he boasts of leading the world in the matter of gambling.

But these are not the only matters on which he has to congratulate himself. For is he not an individual of the species *homo sapiens*? Alone among animals he has an immortal soul, and is rational; he knows the difference between good and evil, and has learnt the multiplication table. Did not God make him in His own image? And was not everything created for man's convenience? The sun was made to light the day, and the moon to light the night—though the moon, by some oversight, only shines during half the nocturnal hours. The raw fruits of the earth were made for human sustenance. Even the white tails of rabbits, according to some theologians, have a purpose, namely to make it easier for sportsmen to shoot them. There are, it is true, some inconveniences: lions and tigers are too fierce, the summer is too hot, and the winter too cold. But these things only began after Adam ate the apple; before that, all animals were vegetarians, and the season was always spring. If only Adam had been content with peaches and nectarines, grapes and pears and pineapples, these blessings would still be ours.

Self-importance, individual or generic, is the source of most of our religious beliefs. Even sin is a conception derived from self-importance. Borrow relates how he met a Welsh preacher who was always melancholy. By sympathetic questioning he was brought to confess the source of his sorrow: that at the age of seven he had committed the sin against the Holy Ghost. "My dear fellow," said Borrow, "don't let that trouble you; I know dozens of people in like case. Do not imagine yourself cut off from the rest of mankind by this occurrence; if you inquire, you will find multitudes who suffer from the same misfortune." From that moment, the man was cured. He had enjoyed feeling singular, but there was no pleasure in being one of a herd of sinners. Most sinners are rather less egotistical; but theologians undoubtedly enjoy the feeling that Man is the special object of God's wrath, as well as of His love. After the Fall—so Milton assures us—

> The Sun
> Had first his precept so to move, so shine,
> As might affect the Earth with cold and heat
> Scarce tolerable, and from the North to call
> Decrepit Winter, from the South to bring
> Solstitial summer's heat.

However disagreeable the results may have been, Adam could hardly help feeling flattered that such vast astronomical phenomena should be brought about to teach him a lesson. The whole of theology, in regard to hell no less than to heaven, takes it for granted that Man is what is of most importance in the Universe of created beings. Since all theologians are men, this postulate has met with little opposition.

Since evolution became fashionable, the glorification of Man has taken a new form. We are told that evolution has been guided by one great Purpose: through the millions of years when there were only slime, or trilobites, throughout the ages of dinosaurs and giant ferns, of bees and wild flowers, God was preparing the Great Climax. At last, in the fullness of time, He produced Man, including such specimens as Nero and Caligula, Hitler and Mussolini, whose transcendent glory justified the long painful process. For my part, I find even eternal damnation less incredible, and certainly less ridiculous, than this lame and impotent conclusion which we are asked to admire as the supreme effort of Omnipotence. And if God is indeed omnipotent, why could He not have produced the glorious result without such a long and tedious prologue?

Apart from the question whether Man is really so glorious as the theologians of evolution say he is, there is the further difficulty that life on this planet is almost certainly temporary. The earth will grow cold, or the atmosphere will gradually fly off, or there will be an insufficiency of water, or, as Sir James Jeans genially prophesies, the sun will burst and all the planets will be turned into gas. Which of those will happen first, no one knows; but in any case the human race will ultimately die out. Of course, such an event is of little importance from the point of view of orthodox theology, since men are immortal, and will continue to exist in heaven and hell when none are left on earth. But in that case why bother about terrestrial developments? Those who lay stress on the gradual progress from the primitive slime to Man attach an importance to this mundane sphere which should make them shrink from the conclusion that all life on earth is only a brief interlude between the nebula and the eternal frost, or perhaps between one nebula and another. The importance of Man, which is the one indispensable dogma of the theologians, receives no support from a scientific view of the future of the solar system.

There are many other sources of false belief besides self-importance. One of these is love of the marvelous. I knew at one time a scientifically minded conjuror, who used to perform his tricks before a small audience, and then get them, each separately, to write down what they had seen happen. Almost always they wrote down something much more astonishing than the reality, and usually something which no conjuror could have achieved; yet they all thought they were reporting truly what they had seen with their own eyes. This sort of falsification is still more true of rumors. A tells B that last night he saw Mr.—, the eminent prohibitionist, slightly the worse for liquor; B tells C that A saw the good man reeling drunk, C tells D that he was picked up unconscious in the ditch, D tells E that he is well known to pass out every evening. Here, it is true, another motive comes in, namely malice. We like to think ill of our neighbors, and are prepared to believe the worst on very little evidence. But even where there is no such motive, what is marvelous is readily believed unless it goes against some strong prejudice. All history until the eighteenth century is full of prodigies and wonders which modern historians ignore, not because they are less well attested than facts which the historians accept, but because modern taste among the learned prefers what science regards as probable. Shakespeare relates how on the night before Caesar was killed,

> A common slave—you know him well by sight—
> Held up his left hand, which did flame and burn
> Like twenty torches join'd; and yet his hand,
> Not sensible of fire, remain'd unscorch'd.
> Besides—I have not since put up my sword—
> Against the Capitol I met a lion,
> Who glar'd upon me, and went surly by,

> Without annoying me; and there were drawn
> Upon a heap a hundred ghastly women,
> Transformed with their fear, who swore they saw
> Men all in fire walk up and down the streets.

Shakespeare did not invent these marvels; he found them in reputable historians, who are among those upon whom we depend for our knowledge concerning Julius Caesar. This sort of thing always used to happen at the death of a great man or the beginning of an important war. Even so recently as 1914 the "angels of Mons" encouraged the British troops. The evidence for such events is very seldom first-hand, and modern historians refuse to accept it—except, of course, where the event is one that has religious importance.

Every powerful emotion has its own myth-making tendency. When the emotion is peculiar to an individual, he is considered more or less mad if he gives credence to such myths as he has invented. But when an emotion is collective, as in war, there is no one to correct the myths that naturally arise. Consequently in all times of great collective excitement unfounded rumors obtain wide credence. In September, 1914, almost everybody in England believed that Russian troops had passed through England on the way to the Western Front. Everybody knew someone who had seen them, though no one had seen them himself.

This myth-making faculty is often allied with cruelty. Ever since the middle ages, the Jews have been accused of practicing ritual murder. There is not an iota of evidence for this accusation, and no sane person who has examined it believes it. Nevertheless it persists. I have met white Russians who were convinced of its truth, and among many Nazis it is accepted without question. Such myths give an excuse for the infliction of torture, and the unfounded belief in them is evidence of the unconscious desire to find some victim to persecute.

There was, until the end of the eighteenth century, a theory that insanity is due to possession by devils. It was inferred that any pain suffered by the patient is also suffered by the devils, so that the best cure is to make the patient suffer so much that the devils will decide to abandon him. The insane, in accordance with this theory, were savagely beaten. This treatment was tried on King George III when he was mad, but without success. It is a curious and painful fact that almost all the completely futile treatments that have been believed in during the long history of medical folly have been such as caused acute suffering to the patient. When anaesthetics were discovered, pious people considered them an attempt to evade the will of God. It was pointed out, however, that when God extracted Adam's rib He put him into a deep sleep. This proved that anaesthetics are all right for *men*; women, however, ought to suffer, because of the curse of Eve. In the West votes for women proved this doctrine mistaken, but in Japan, to this day, women in childbirth are not allowed any alleviation through anaesthetics. As the Japanese do not believe in Genesis, this piece of sadism must have some other justification.

The fallacies about "race" and "blood," which have always been popular, and which the Nazis have embodied in their official creed, have no objective justification; they are believed solely because they minister to self-esteem and to the impulse toward cruelty. In one form or another, these beliefs are as old as civilization; their forms change, but their essence remains. Herodotus tells how Cyrus was brought up by peasants, in complete ignorance of his royal blood; at the age of twelve his kingly bearing toward other peasant boys revealed the truth. This is a variant of an old story which is found in all Indo-European countries. Even quite modern people say that "blood will tell." It is no use for scientific physiologists to assure the world that there is no difference between the blood of a Negro and the blood of a white man. The American Red Cross, in obedience to popular prejudice, at first, when America became involved in the present war, decreed that no Negro blood should be used for blood transfusion. As a result of an agitation, it was conceded that Negro blood might be used, but only for Negro patients. Similarly, in Germany, the Aryan soldier who needs blood transfusion is carefully protected from the contamination of Jewish blood.

In the matter of race, there are different beliefs in different societies. Where monarchy is firmly established, kings are of a higher race than their subjects. Until very recently, it was universally believed that men are congenitally more intelligent than women; even so enlightened a man as Spinoza decides against votes for women on this ground. Among white men, it is held that white men are by nature superior to men of other colors, and especially to black men; in Japan, on the contrary, it is thought that yellow is the best color. In Haiti, when they make statues of Christ and Satan, they make Christ black and Satan white. Aristotle and Plato considered Greeks so innately superior to barbarians that slavery is justified so long as the master is Greek and the slave barbarian. The Nazis and the American legislators who made the immigration laws consider the Nordics superior to Slavs or Latins or any other white men. But the Nazis, under the stress of war, have been led to the conclusion that there are hardly any true Nordics outside Germany; the Norwegians, except Quisling and his few followers, have been corrupted by intermixture with Finns and Laps and such. Thus politics are a clue to descent. The biologically pure Nordic loves Hitler, and if you do not love Hitler, that is proof of tainted blood.

All this is, of course, pure nonsense, known to be such by everyone who has studied the subject. In schools in America, children of the most diverse origins are subjected to the same educational system, and those whose business it is to measure intelligence quotients and otherwise estimate the native ability of students are unable to make any such racial distinctions as are postulated by the theorists of race. In every national or racial group there are clever children and stupid children. It is not likely that, in the United States, colored children will develop as successfully as white children, because of the stigma of social inferiority; but in so far as congenital ability can be detached from environmental influence, there is no clear distinction among different groups. The whole conception of superior races is merely a myth generated by the overweening self-esteem of the holders of power. It may be that, some day, better evidence will be forthcoming; perhaps, in time, educators will be able to prove (say) that Jews are on the average more intelligent than gentiles. But as yet no such evidence exists, and all talk of superior races must be dismissed as nonsense.

There is a special absurdity in applying racial theories to the various populations of Europe. There is not in Europe any such thing as a pure race. Russians have an admixture of Tartar blood, Germans are largely Slavonic, France is a mixture of Celts, Germans, and people of Mediterranean race, Italy the same with the addition of the descendants of slaves imported by the Romans. The English are perhaps the most mixed of all. There is no evidence that there is any advantage in belonging to a pure race. The purest races now in existence are the Pygmies, the Hottentots, and the Australian aborigines; the Tasmanians, who were probably even purer, are extinct. They were not the bearers of a brilliant culture. The ancient Greeks, on the other hand, emerged from an amalgamation of northern barbarians and an indigenous population; the Athenians and Ionians, who were the most civilized, were also the most mixed. The supposed merits of racial purity are, it would seem, wholly imaginary.

Superstitions about blood have many forms that have nothing to do with race. The objection to homicide seems to have been, originally, based on the ritual pollution caused by the blood of the victim. God said to Cain: "The voice of thy brother's blood crieth unto me from the ground." According to some anthropologists, the mark of Cain was a disguise to prevent Abel's blood from finding him; this appears also to be the original reason for wearing mourning. In many ancient communities no difference was made between murder and accidental homicide; in either case equally ritual ablution was necessary. The feeling that blood defiles still lingers, for example in the Churching of Women and in taboos connected with menstruation. The idea that a child is of his father's "blood" has the same superstitious origin. So far as actual blood is concerned, the mother's enters into the child, but not the father's. If blood were as important as is supposed, matriarchy would be the only proper way of tracing descent.

In Russia, where, under the influence of Karl Marx, people since the revolution have been classified by their economic origin, difficulties have arisen not unlike those of German race theorists over the Scandinavian Nordics. There were two theories that had to be reconciled: on the one hand, proletarians were good and other people were bad; on the other hand, communists were good and other people were bad. The only way of effecting a reconciliation was to alter the meaning of words. A "proletarian" came to mean a supporter of the government; Lenin, though born a Prince, was reckoned a member of the proletariat. On the other hand, the word "kulak," which was supposed to mean a rich peasant, came to mean any peasant who opposed collectivization. This sort of absurdity always arises when one group of human beings is supposed to be inherently better than another. In America, the highest praise that can be bestowed on an eminent colored man after he is safely dead is to say, "he was *a white* man." A courageous woman is called "masculine": Macbeth, praising his wife's courage, says:

> Bring forth men children only,
> For thy undaunted mettle should compose
> Nothing but males.

All these ways of speaking come of unwillingness to abandon foolish generalizations.

In the economic sphere there are many widespread superstitions. Why do people value gold and precious stones? Not simply because of their rarity: there are a number of elements called "rare earths" which are much rarer than gold, but no one will give a penny for them except a few men of science. There is a theory, for which there is much to be said, that gold and gems were valued originally on account of their supposed magical properties. The mistakes of governments in modern times seem to show that this belief still exists among the sort of men who are called "practical." At the end of the last war, it was agreed that Germany should pay vast sums to England and France, and they in turn should pay vast sums to the United States. Every one wanted to be paid in money rather than goods; the "practical" men failed to notice that there is not that amount of money in the world. They also failed to notice that money is no use unless it is used to buy goods. As they would not use it in this way, it did no good to anyone. There was supposed to be some mystic virtue about gold that made it worth while to dig it up in the Transvaal and put it underground again in bank vaults in America. In the end, of course, the debtor countries had no more money, and, since they were not allowed to pay in goods, they went bankrupt. The Great Depression was the direct result of the surviving belief in the magical properties of gold. It is to be feared that some similar superstition will cause equally bad results after the end of the present war.

Politics is largely governed by sententious platitudes which are devoid of truth.

One of the most widespread popular maxims is, "human nature cannot be changed." No one can say whether this is true or not without first defining "human nature." But as used it is certainly false. When Mr. A utters the maxim, with an air of portentous and conclusive wisdom, what he means is that all men everywhere will always continue to behave as they do in his own home town. A little anthropology will dispel this belief. Among the Tibetans, one wife has many husbands, because men are too poor to support a whole wife; yet family life, according to travellers, is no more unhappy than elsewhere. The practice of lending one's wife to a guest is very common among uncivilized tribes. The Australian aborigines, at puberty, undergo a very painful operation which, throughout the rest of their lives, greatly diminishes sexual potency. Infanticide, which might seem contrary to human nature, was almost universal before the rise of Christianity, and is recommended by Plato to prevent over-population. Private property is not recognized among some savage tribes. Even among highly civilized people, economic considerations will override what is called "human nature." In Moscow, where there is an acute housing shortage, when an unmarried woman is pregnant, it often happens that a number of men contend for the legal right to be considered the father of the prospective child, because whoever is judged to be the father acquires the right to share the woman's room, and half a room is better than no room.

In fact, adult "human nature" is extremely variable, according to the circumstances of education. Food and sex are very general requirements, but the hermits of the Thebaid eschewed sex altogether and reduced food to the lowest point compatible with survival. By diet and training, people can be made ferocious or meek, masterful or slavish, as may suit the educator. There is no nonsense so arrant that it cannot be made the creed of the vast majority by adequate governmental action. Plato intended his Republic to be founded on a myth which he admitted to be absurd, but he was rightly confident that the populace could be induced to believe it. Hobbes, who thought it important that people should reverence the government however unworthy it might be, meets the argument that it might be difficult to obtain general assent to anything so irrational by pointing out that people have been brought to believe in the Christian religion, and, in particular, in the dogma of transubstantiation. If he had been alive now, he would have found ample confirmation in the devotion of German youth to the Nazis.

The power of governments over men's beliefs has been very great ever since the rise of large States. The great majority of Romans became Christian after the Roman emperors had been converted. In the parts of the Roman Empire that were conquered by the Arabs, most people abandoned Christianity for Islam. The division of Western Europe into Protestant and Catholic regions was determined by the attitude of governments in the sixteenth century. But the power of governments over belief in the present day is vastly greater than at any earlier time. A belief, however untrue, is important when it dominates the actions of large masses of men. In this sense, the beliefs inculcated by the Japanese, Russian, and German governments are important. Since they are completely divergent, they cannot all be true, though they may well all be false. Unfortunately they are such as to inspire men with an ardent desire to kill one another, even to the point of almost completely inhibiting the impulse of self-preservation. No one can deny, in face of the evidence, that it is easy, given military power, to produce a population of fanatical lunatics. It would be equally easy to produce a population of sane and reasonable people, but many governments do not wish to do so, since such people would fail to admire the politicians who are at the head of these governments.

There is one peculiarly pernicious application of the doctrine that human nature cannot be changed. This is the dogmatic assertion that there will always be wars, because we are so constituted that we feel a need of them. What is true is that a man who has had the kind of diet and education that most men have will wish to fight when provoked. But he will not actually fight unless he has a chance of victory. It is very annoying to be stopped by a speed cop, but we do not fight him because we know that he has the overwhelming forces of the State at his back. People who have no occasion for war do not make any impression of being psychologically thwarted. Sweden has had no war since 1814, but the Swedes were, a few years ago, one of the happiest and most contented nations in the world. I doubt whether they are so still, but that is because, though neutral, they are unable to escape many of the evils of war. If political organization were such as to make war obviously unprofitable, there is nothing in human nature that would compel its occurrence, or make average people unhappy because of its not occurring. Exactly the same arguments that are now used about the impossibility of preventing war were formerly used in defense of dueling, yet few of us feel thwarted because we are not allowed to fight duels.

I am persuaded that there is absolutely no limit to the absurdities that can, by government action, come to be generally believed. Give me an adequate army, with power to provide it with more pay and better food than falls to the lot of the average man, and I will undertake, within thirty years, to make the majority of the population believe that two and two are three, that water freezes when it gets hot and boils when it gets cold, or any other nonsense that might seem to serve the interest of the State. Of course, even when these beliefs had been generated, people would not put the kettle in the ice-box when they wanted it to boil. That cold makes water boil would be a Sunday truth, sacred and mystical, to be professed in awed tones, but not to be acted on in daily life. What would happen would be that any verbal denial of the mystic doctrine would be made illegal, and obstinate heretics would be "frozen" at the stake. No person who did not enthusiastically accept the official doctrine would be allowed to teach or to have any position of power. Only the very highest officials, in their cups, would whisper to each other what rubbish it all is; then they would laugh and drink again. This is hardly a caricature of what happens under some modern governments.

The discovery that man can be scientifically manipulated, and that governments can turn large masses this way or that as they choose, is one of the causes of our misfortunes. There is as much difference between a collection of mentally free citizens and a community molded by modern methods of propaganda as there is between a heap of raw materials and a battleship. Education, which was at first made universal in order that all might be able to read and write, has been found capable of serving quite other purposes. By instilling nonsense it unifies populations and generates collective enthusiasm. If all governments taught the same nonsense, the harm would not be so great. Unfortunately each has its own brand, and the diversity serves to produce hostility between the devotees of different creeds. If there is ever to be peace in the world, governments will have to agree either to inculcate no dogmas, or all to inculcate the same. The former, I fear, is a Utopian ideal, but perhaps they could agree to teach collectively that all public men, everywhere, are completely virtuous and perfectly wise. Perhaps, when the war is over, the surviving politicians may find it prudent to combine on some such programme.

But if conformity has its dangers, so has nonconformity.

Some "advanced thinkers" are of the opinion that any one who differs from the conventional opinion must be in the right. This is a delusion; if it were not, truth would be easier to come by than it is. There are infinite possibilities of error, and more cranks take up unfashionable errors than unfashionable truths. I met once an electrical engineer whose first words to me were: "How do you do? There are two methods of faith-healing, the one practised by Christ and the one practised by most Christian Scientists. I practice the method practiced by Christ." Shortly afterwards, he was sent to prison for making out fraudulent balance-sheets. The law does not look kindly on the intrusion of faith into this region. I knew also an eminent lunacy doctor who took to philosophy, and taught a new logic which, as he frankly confessed, he had learnt from his lunatics. When he died he left a will founding a professorship for the teaching of his new scientific methods, but unfortunately he left no assets. Arithmetic proved recalcitrant to lunatic logic. On one occasion a man came to ask me to recommend some of my books, as he was interested in philosophy. I did so, but he returned next day saying that he had been reading one of them, and had found only one statement he could understand, and that one seemed to him false. I asked him what it was, and he said it was the statement that Julius Caesar is dead. When I asked him why he did not agree, he drew himself up and said: "Because I am Julius Caesar." These examples may suffice to show that you cannot make sure of being right by being eccentric.

Science, which has always had to fight its way against popular beliefs, now has one of its most difficult battles in the sphere of psychology.

People who think they know all about human nature are always hopelessly at sea when they have to do with any abnormality. Some boys never learn to be what, in animals, is called "house trained." The sort of person who won't stand any nonsense deals with such cases by punishment; the boy is beaten, and when he repeats the offense he is beaten worse. All medical men who have studied the matter know that punishment only aggravates the trouble. Sometimes the cause is physical, but usually it is psychological, and only curable by removing some deep-seated and probably unconscious grievance. But most people enjoy punishing anyone who irritates them, and so the medical view is rejected as fancy nonsense. The same sort of thing applies to men who are exhibitionists; they are sent to prison over and over again, but as soon as they come out they repeat the offense. A medical man who specialized in such ailments assured me that the exhibitionist can be cured by the simple device of having trousers that button up the back instead of the front. But this method is not tried because it does not satisfy people's vindictive impulses.

Broadly speaking, punishment is likely to prevent crimes that are sane in origin, but not those that spring from some psychological abnormality. This is now partially recognized; we distinguish between plain theft, which springs from what may be called rational self-interest, and kleptomania, which is a mark of something queer. And homicidal maniacs are not treated like ordinary murderers. But sexual aberrations rouse so much disgust that it is still impossible to have them treated medically rather than punitively. Indignation, though on the whole a useful social force, becomes harmful when it is directed against the victims of maladies that only medical skill can cure.

The same sort of thing happens as regards whole nations. During the last war, very naturally, people's vindictive feelings were aroused against the Germans, who were severely punished after their defeat. Now many people are arguing that the Versailles Treaty was ridiculously mild, since it failed to teach a lesson; this time, we are told, there must be *real* severity. To my mind, we shall be more likely to prevent a repetition of German aggression if we regard the rank and file of the Nazis as we regard lunatics than if we think of them as merely and simply criminals. Lunatics, of course, have to be restrained; we do not allow them to carry firearms. Similarly the German nation will have to be disarmed. But lunatics are restrained from prudence, not as a punishment, and so far as prudence permits we try to make them happy. Everybody recognizes that a homicidal maniac will only become more homicidal if he is made miserable. In Germany at the present day, there are, of course, many men among the Nazis who are plain criminals, but there must also be many who are more or less mad. Leaving the leaders out of account (I do not urge leniency toward them), the bulk of the German nation is much more likely to learn cooperation with the rest of the world if it is subjected to a kind but firm curative treatment than if it is regarded as an outcast among the nations. Those who are being punished seldom learn to feel kindly toward the men who punish them. And so long as the Germans hate the rest of mankind peace will be precarious.

When one reads of the beliefs of savages, or of the ancient Babylonians and Egyptians, they seem surprising by their capricious absurdity. But beliefs that are just as absurd are still entertained by the uneducated even in the most modern and civilized societies. I have been gravely assured, in America, that people born in March are unlucky and people born in May are peculiarly liable to corns. I do not know the history of these superstitions, but probably they are derived from Babylonian or Egyptian priestly lore. Beliefs begin in the higher social strata, and then, like mud in a river, sink gradually downward in the educational scale; they may take 3,000 or 4,000 years to sink all the way. You may find your colored help making some remark that comes straight out of Plato—not the parts of Plato that scholars quote, but the parts where he utters obvious nonsense, such as that men who do not pursue wisdom in this life will be born again as women. Commentators on great philosophers always politely ignore their silly remarks.

Aristotle, in spite of his reputation, is full of absurdities. He says that children should be conceived in the Winter, when the wind is in the North, and that if people marry too young the children will be female. He tells us that the blood of females is blacker then that of males; that the pig is the only animal liable to measles; that an elephant suffering from insomnia should have its shoulders rubbed with salt, olive oil, and warm water; that women have fewer teeth than men, and so on. Nevertheless, he is considered by the great majority of philosophers a paragon of wisdom.

Superstitions about lucky and unlucky days are almost universal. In ancient times they governed the actions of generals. Among ourselves the prejudice against Friday and the number thirteen is very active; sailors do not like to sail on Friday, and many hotels have no thirteenth floor. The superstitions about Friday and thirteen were once believed by those reputed wise; now such men regard them as harmless follies. But probably 2,000 years hence many beliefs of the wise of our day will have come to seem equally foolish. Man is a credulous animal, and must believe *something*; in the absence of good grounds for belief, he will be satisfied with bad ones.

Belief in "nature" and what is "natural" is a source of many errors. It used to be, and to some extent still is, powerfully operative in medicine. The human body, left to itself, has a certain power of curing itself; small cuts usually heal, colds pass off, and even serious diseases sometimes disappear without medical treatment. But aids to nature are very desirable, even in these cases. Cuts may turn septic if not disinfected, colds may turn to pneumonia, and serious diseases are only left without treatment by explorers and travellers in remote regions, who have no option. Many practices which have come to seem "natural" were originally "unnatural," for instance clothing and washing. Before men adopted clothing they must have found it impossible to live in cold climates. Where there is not a modicum of cleanliness, populations suffer from various diseases, such as typhus, from which Western nations have become exempt. Vaccination was (and by some still is) objected to as "unnatural." But there is no consistency in such objections, for no one supposes that a broken bone can be mended by "natural" behavior. Eating cooked food is "unnatural"; so is heating our houses. The Chinese philosopher Lao-tse, whose traditional date is about 600 B.C., objected to roads and bridges and boats as "unnatural," and in his disgust at such mechanistic devices left China and went to live among the Western barbarians. Every advance in civilization has been denounced as unnatural while it was recent.

The commonest objection to birth control is that it is against "nature." (For some reason we are not allowed to say that celibacy is against nature; the only reason I can think of is that it is not new.) Malthus saw only three ways of keeping down the population; moral restraint, vice, and misery. Moral restraint, he admitted, was not likely to be practised on a large scale. "Vice," i.e., birth control, he, as a clergyman, viewed with abhorrence. There remained misery. In his comfortable parsonage, he contemplated the misery of the great majority of mankind with equanimity, and pointed out the fallacies of reformers who hoped to alleviate it. Modern theological opponents of birth control are less honest. They pretend to think that God will provide, however many mouths there may be to feed. They ignore the fact that He has never done so hitherto, but has left mankind exposed to periodical famines in which millions died of hunger. They must be deemed to hold—if they are saying what they believe—that from this moment onward God will work a continual miracle of loaves and fishes which He has hitherto thought unnecessary. Or perhaps they will say that suffering here below is of no importance; what matters is the hereafter. By their own theology, most of the children whom their opposition to birth control will cause to exist will go to hell. We must suppose, therefore, that they oppose the amelioration of life on earth because they think it a good thing that many millions should suffer eternal torment. By comparison with them, Malthus appears merciful.

Women, as the object of our strongest love and aversion, rouse complex emotions which are embodied in proverbial "wisdom."

Almost everybody allows himself or herself some entirely unjustifiable generalization on the subject of woman. Married men, when they generalize on that subject, judge by their wives; women judge by themselves. It would be amusing to write a history of men's views on women. In antiquity, when male supremacy was unquestioned and Christian ethics were still unknown, women were harmless but rather silly, and a man who took them seriously was somewhat despised. Plato thinks it a grave objection to the drama that the playwright has to imitate women in creating his female roles. With the coming of Christianity woman took on a new part, that of the temptress; but at the same time she was also found capable of being a saint. In Victorian days the saint was much more emphasized than the temptress; Victorian men could not admit themselves susceptible to temptation. The superior virtue of women was made a reason for keeping them out of politics, where, it was held, a lofty virtue is impossible. But the early feminists turned the argument round, and contended that the participation of women would ennoble politics. Since this has turned out to be an illusion, there has been less talk of women's superior virtue, but there are still a number of men who adhere to the monkish view of woman as the temptress. Women themselves, for the most part, think of themselves as the sensible sex, whose business it is to undo the harm that comes of men's impetuous follies. For my part I distrust *all* generalizations about women, favorable and unfavorable, masculine and feminine, ancient and modern; all alike, I should say, result from paucity of experience.

The deeply irrational attitude of each sex toward women may be seen in novels, particularly in bad novels. In bad novels by men, there is the woman with whom the author is in love, who usually possesses every charm, but is somewhat helpless, and requires male protection; sometimes, however, like Shakespeare's Cleopatra, she is an object of exasperated hatred, and is thought to be deeply and desperately wicked. In portraying the heroine, the male author does not write from observation, but merely objectifies his own emotions. In regard to his other female characters, he is more objective, and may even depend upon his notebook; but when he is in love, his passion makes a mist between him and the object of his devotion. Women novelists, also, have two kinds of women in their books. One is themselves, glamorous and kind, and object of lust to the wicked and of love to the good, sensitive, high-souled, and constantly misjudged. The other kind is represented by all other women, and is usually portrayed as petty, spiteful, cruel, and deceitful. It would seem that to judge women without bias is not easy either for men or for women.

Generalizations about national characteristics are just as common and just as unwarranted as generalizations about women. Until 1870, the Germans were thought of as a nation of spectacled professors, evolving everything out of their inner consciousness, and scarcely aware of the outer world, but since 1870 this conception has had to be very sharply revised. Frenchmen seem to be thought of by most Americans as perpetually engaged in amorous intrigue; Walt Whitman, in one of his catalogues, speaks of "the adulterous French couple on the sly settee." Americans who go to live in France are astonished, and perhaps disappointed, by the intensity of family life. Before the Russian Revolution, the Russians were credited with a mystical Slav soul, which, while it incapacitated them for ordinary sensible behavior, gave them a kind of deep wisdom to which more practical nations could not hope to attain. Suddenly everything was changed: mysticism was taboo, and only the most earthly ideals were tolerated. The truth is that what appears to one nation as the national character of another depends upon a few prominent individuals, or upon the class that happens to have power. For this reason, all generalizations on this subject are liable to be completely upset by any important political change.

To avoid the various foolish opinions to which mankind are prone, no super-human genius is required. A few simple rules will keep you, not from *all* error, but from silly error.

If the matter is one that can be settled by observation, make the observation yourself. Aristotle could have avoided the mistake of thinking that women have fewer teeth than men, by the simple device of asking Mrs. Aristotle to keep her mouth open while he counted. He did not do so because he thought he knew. Thinking that you know when in fact you don't is a fatal mistake, to which we are all prone. I believe myself that hedgehogs eat black beetles, because I have been told that they do; but if I were writing a book on the habits of hedgehogs, I should not commit myself until I had seen one enjoying this unappetizing diet. Aristotle, however, was less cautious. Ancient and medieval authors knew all about unicorns and salamanders; not one of them thought it necessary to avoid dogmatic statements about them because he had never seen one of them.

Many matters, however, are less easily brought to the test of experience. If, like most of mankind, you have passionate convictions on many such matters, there are ways in which you can make yourself aware of your own bias. If an opinion contrary to your own makes you angry, that is a sign that you are subconsciously aware of having no good reason for thinking as you do. If some one maintains that two and two are five, or that Iceland is on the equator, you feel pity rather than anger, unless you know so little of arithmetic or geography that his opinion shakes your own contrary conviction. The most savage controversies are those about matters as to which there is no good evidence either way. Persecution is used in theology, not in arithmetic, because in arithmetic there is knowledge, but in theology there is only opinion. So whenever you find yourself getting angry about a difference of opinion, be on your guard; you will probably find, on examination, that your belief is going beyond what the evidence warrants.

A good way of ridding yourself of certain kinds of dogmatism is to become aware of opinions held in social circles different from your own. When I was young, I lived much outside my own country in France, Germany, Italy, and the United States. I found this very profitable in diminishing the intensity of insular prejudice. If you cannot travel, seek out people with whom you disagree, and read a newspaper belonging to a party that is not yours. If the people and the newspaper seem mad, perverse, and wicked, remind yourself that you seem so to them. In this opinion both parties may be right, but they cannot both be wrong. This reflection should generate a certain caution.

Becoming aware of foreign customs, however, does not always have a beneficial effect. In the seventeenth century, when the Manchus conquered China, it was the custom among the Chinese for the women to have small feet, and among the Manchus for the men to wear pigtails. Instead of each dropping their own foolish custom, they each adopted the foolish custom of the other, and the Chinese continued to wear pigtails until they shook off the dominion of the Manchus in the revolution of 1911.

For those who have enough psychological imagination, it is a good plan to imagine an argument with a person having a different bias. This has one advantage, and only one, as compared with actual conversation with opponents; this one advantage is that the method is not subject to the same limitations of time or space. Mahatma Gandhi deplores railways and steamboats and machinery; he would like to undo the whole of the industrial revolution. You may never have an opportunity of actually meeting any one who holds this opinion, because in Western countries most people take the advantage of modern technique for granted. But if you want to make sure that you are right in agreeing with the prevailing opinion, you will find it a good plan to test the arguments that occur to you by considering what Gandhi might say in refutation of them.

I have sometimes been led actually to change my mind as a result of this kind of imaginary dialogue, and, short of this, I have frequently found myself growing less dogmatic and cocksure through realizing the possible reasonableness of a hypothetical opponent.

Be very wary of opinions that flatter your self-esteem. Both men and women, nine times out of ten, are firmly convinced of the superior excellence of their own sex. There is abundant evidence on both sides. If you are a man, you can point out that most poets and men of science are male; if you are a woman, you can retort that so are most criminals. The question is inherently insoluble, but self-esteem conceals this from most people. We are all, whatever part of the world we come from, persuaded that our own nation is superior to all others. Seeing that each nation has its characteristic merits and demerits, we adjust our standard of values so as to make out that the merits possessed by our nation are the really important ones, while its demerits are comparatively trivial. Here, again, the rational man will admit that the question is one to which there is no demonstrably right answer. It is more difficult to deal with the self-esteem of man as man, because we cannot argue out the matter with some nonhuman mind. The only way I know of dealing with this general human conceit is to remind ourselves that man is a brief episode in the life of a small planet in a little corner of the universe, and that, for aught we know, other parts of the cosmos may contain beings as superior to ourselves as we are to jellyfish.

Other passions besides self-esteem are common sources of error; of these perhaps the most important is fear. Fear sometimes operates directly, by inventing rumors of disaster in war-time, or by imagining objects of terror, such as ghosts; sometimes it operates indirectly, by creating belief in something comforting, such as the elixir of life, or heaven for ourselves and hell for our enemies. Fear has many forms—fear of death, fear of the dark, fear of the unknown, fear of the herd, and that vague generalized fear that comes to those who conceal from themselves their more specific terrors. Until you have admitted your own fears to yourself, and have guarded yourself by a difficult effort of will against their mythmaking power, you cannot hope to think truly about many matters of great importance, especially those with which religious beliefs are concerned. Fear is the main source of superstition and one of the main sources of cruelty. To conquer fear is the beginning of wisdom, in the pursuit of truth as in the endeavor after a worthy manner of life.

There are two ways of avoiding fear: one is by persuading ourselves that we are immune from disaster, and the other is by the practice of sheer courage. The latter is difficult, and to everybody becomes impossible at a certain point. The former has therefore always been more popular. Primitive magic has the purpose of securing safety, either by injuring enemies, or by protecting oneself by talismans, spells, or incantations. Without any essential change, belief in such ways of avoiding danger survived throughout the many centuries of Babylonian civilization, spread from Babylon throughout the empire of Alexander, and was acquired by the Romans in the course of their absorption of Hellenistic culture. From the Romans it descended to medieval Christendom and Islam. Science has now lessened the belief in magic, but many people place more faith in mascots than they are willing to avow, and sorcery, while condemned by the Church, is still officially a *possible* sin.

Magic, however, was a crude way of avoiding terrors, and, moreover, not a very effective way, for wicked magicians might always prove stronger than good ones. In the fifteenth, sixteenth, and seventeenth centuries, dread of witches and sorcerers led to the burning of hundreds of thousands convicted of these crimes. But newer beliefs, particularly as to the future life, sought more effective ways of combating fear. Socrates on the day of his death (if Plato is to be believed) expressed the conviction that in the next world he would live in the company of the gods and heroes, and surrounded by just spirits who would never object to his endless argumentation. Plato, in his "Republic," laid it down that cheerful views of the next world must be enforced by the State, not because they were true, but to make soldiers more willing to die in battle. He would have none of the traditional myths about Hades, because they represented the spirits of the dead as unhappy.

Orthodox Christianity, in the Ages of Faith, laid down very definite rules for salvation. First, you must be baptized; then, you must avoid all theological error; last, you must, before dying, repent of your sins and receive absolution. All this would not save you from purgatory, but it would insure your ultimate arrival in heaven. It was not necessary to *know* theology. An eminent cardinal stated authoritatively that the requirements of orthodoxy would be satisfied if you murmured on your death-bed: "I believe all that the Church believes; the Church believes all that I believe." These very definite directions ought to have made Catholics sure of finding the way to heaven. Nevertheless, the dread of hell persisted, and has caused, in recent times, a great softening of the dogmas as to who will be damned. The doctrine, professed by many modern Christians, that everybody will go to heaven, ought to do away with the fear of death, but in fact this fear is too instinctive to be easily vanquished. F. W. H. Myers, whom spiritualism had converted to belief in a future life, questioned a woman who had lately lost her daughter as to what she supposed had become of her soul. The mother replied: "Oh, well, I suppose she is enjoying eternal bliss, but I wish you wouldn't talk about such unpleasant subjects." In spite of all that theology can do, heaven remains, to most people, an "unpleasant subject."

The most refined religions, such as those of Marcus Aurelius and Spinoza, are still concerned with the conquest of fear. The Stoic doctrine was simple: it maintained that the only true good is virtue, of which no enemy can deprive me; consequently, there is no need to fear enemies. The difficulty was that no one could really believe virtue to be the only good, not even Marcus Aurelius, who, as emperor, sought not only to make his subjects virtuous, but to protect them against barbarians, pestilences, and famines. Spinoza taught a somewhat similar doctrine. According to him, our true good consists in indifference to our mundane fortunes. Both these men sought to escape from fear by pretending that such things as physical suffering are not really evil. This is a noble way of escaping from fear, but is still based upon false belief. And if genuinely accepted, it would have the bad effect of making men indifferent, not only to their own sufferings, but also to those of others.

Under the influence of great fear, almost everybody becomes superstitious. The sailors who threw Jonah overboard imagined his presence to be the cause of the storm which threatened to wreck their ship. In a similar spirit the Japanese, at the time of the Tokyo earthquake took to massacring Koreans and Liberals. When the Romans won victories in the Punic wars, the Carthaginians became persuaded that their misfortunes were due to a certain laxity which had crept into the worship of Moloch. Moloch liked having children sacrificed to him, and preferred them aristocratic; but the noble families of Carthage had adopted the practice of surreptitiously substituting plebeian children for their own offspring. This, it was thought, had displeased the god, and at the worst moments even the most aristocratic children were duly consumed in the fire. Strange to say, the Romans were victorious in spite of this democratic reform on the part of their enemies.

Collective fear stimulates herd instinct, and tends to produce ferocity toward those who are not regarded as members of the herd. So it was in the French Revolution, when dread of foreign armies produced the reign of terror. And it is to be feared that the Nazis, as defeat draws nearer, will increase the intensity of their campaign for exterminating Jews. Fear generates impulses of cruelty, and therefore promotes such superstitious beliefs as seem to justify cruelty. Neither a man nor a crowd nor a nation can be trusted to act humanely or to think sanely under the influence of a great fear. And for this reason poltroons are more prone to cruelty than brave men, and are also more prone to superstition. When I say this, I am thinking of men who are brave in all respects, not only in facing death. Many a man will have the courage to die gallantly, but will not have the courage to say, or even to think, that the cause for which he is asked to die is an unworthy one. Obloquy is, to most men, more painful than death; that is one reason why, in times of collective excitement, so few men venture to dissent from the prevailing opinion. No Carthaginian denied Moloch, because to do so would have required more courage than was required to face death in battle.

But we have been getting too solemn. Superstitions are not always dark and cruel; often they add to the gaiety of life. I received once a communication from the god Osiris, giving me his telephone number; he lived, at that time, in a suburb of Boston. Although I did not enroll myself among his worshipers, his letter gave me pleasure. I have frequently received letters from men announcing themselves as the Messiah, and urging me not to omit to mention this important fact in my lectures. During prohibition, there was a sect which maintained that the communion service ought to be celebrated in whiskey, not in wine; this tenet gave them a legal right to a supply of hard liquor, and the sect grew rapidly. There is in England a sect which maintains that the English are the lost ten tribes; there is a stricter sect, which maintains that they are only the tribes of Ephraim and Manasseh. Whenever I encounter a member of either of these sects, I profess myself an adherent of the other, and much pleasant argumentation results. I like also the men who study the Great Pyramid, with a view to deciphering its mystical lore. Many great books have been written on this subject, some of which have been presented to me by their authors. It is a singular fact that the Great Pyramid always predicts the history of the world accurately up to the date of publication of the book in question, but after that date it becomes less reliable. Generally the author expects, very soon, wars in Egypt, followed by Armageddon and the coming of Antichrist, but by this time so many people have been recognized as Antichrist that the reader is reluctantly driven to skepticism.

I admire especially a certain prophetess who lived beside a lake in Northern New York State about the year 1820. She announced to her numerous followers that she possessed the power of walking on water, and that she proposed to do so at 11 o'clock on a certain morning. At the stated time, the faithful assembled in their thousands beside the lake. She spoke to them, saying: "Are you all entirely persuaded that I can walk on water?" With one voice they replied: "We are." "In that case," she announced, "there is not need for me to do so." And they all went home much edified.

Perhaps the world would lose some of its interest and variety if such beliefs were wholly replaced by cold science. Perhaps we may allow ourselves to be glad of the Abecedarians, who were so-called because, having rejected all profane learning, they thought it wicked to learn the ABC. And we may enjoy the perplexity of the South American Jesuit who wondered how the sloth could have traveled, since the Flood, all the way from Mount Ararat to Peru—a journey which its extreme tardiness of locomotion rendered almost incredible. A wise man will enjoy the goods of which there is a plentiful supply, and of intellectual rubbish he will find an abundant diet, in our own age as in every other.

27

Aubade

PHILIP LARKIN

Cherished and even revered by many people who did and do not share his pessimistic reactionary opinions, Philip Larkin has a fair claim to be the exemplary English poet of the late twentieth century. Wedded as he was to a traditional and even hierarchic view of society, Larkin could not make himself believe in the Anglican orthodoxy that was the moral keystone of that mentality. An *aubade* is a poem about lovers parting at dawn; in this instance, Larkin's love is life itself, accompanied by the grim but honest realization that it does not extend beyond the grave and that we delude ourselves by imagining otherwise.

Of *Church Going* I would simply want to say that—not unlike Thomas Hardy's verses—it combines the maximum of respect with the minimum of credulity.

> I work all day, and get half drunk at night.
> Waking at four to soundless dark, I stare.
> In time the curtain edges will grow light.
> Till then I see what's really always there:
> Unresting death, a whole day nearer now,
> Making all thought impossible but how
> And where and when I shall myself die.
> Arid interrogation: yet the dread
> Of dying, and being dead,
> Flashes afresh to hold and horrify.
>
> The mind blanks at the glare. Not in remorse
> —The good not used, the love not given, time
> Torn off unused—nor wretchedly because
> An only life can take so long to climb
> Clear of its wrong beginnings, and may never:
> But at the total emptiness forever,

The sure extinction that we travel to
And shall be lost in always. Not to be here,
Not to be anywhere,
And soon; nothing more terrible, nothing more true.

This is a special way of being afraid
No trick dispels. Religion used to try,
That vast moth-eaten musical brocade
Created to pretend we never die
And specious stuff that says no rational being
Can fear a thing it cannot feel, not seeing
that this is what we fear—no sight, no sound,
No touch or taste or smell, nothing to think with,
Nothing to love or link with,
The anaesthetic from which none come round.

And so it stays just on the edge of vision,
A small unfocused blur, a standing chill
That slows each impulse down to indecision
Most things may never happen: this one will,
And realisation of it rages out
In furnace fear when we are caught without
People or drink. Courage is no good:
It means not scaring others. Being brave
Lets no-one off the grave.
Death is no different whined at than withstood.

Slowly light strengthens, and the room takes shape.
It stands plain as a wardrobe, what we know,
Have always known, know that we can't escape
Yet can't accept. One side will have to go.
Meanwhile telephones crouch, getting ready to ring
In locked-up offices, and all the uncaring
Intricate rented world begins to rouse.
The sky is white as clay, with no sun.
Work has to be done.
Postmen like doctors go from house to house.

Church Going

PHILIP LARKIN

Once I am sure there's nothing going on
I step inside, letting the door thud shut.
Another church: matting, seats, and stone,
And little books; sprawlings of flowers, cut
For Sunday, brownish now; some brass and stuff
Up at the holy end; the small neat organ;
And a tense, musty, unignorable silence,
Brewed God knows how long. Hatless, I take off
My cycle-clips in awkward reverence,
Move forward, run my hand around the font.
From where I stand, the roof looks almost new—
Cleaned or restored? Someone would know: I don't.
Mounting the lectern, I peruse a few
Hectoring large-scale verses, and pronounce
"Here endeth" much more loudly than I'd meant.
The echoes snigger briefly. Back at the door
I sign the book, donate an Irish sixpence,
Reflect the place was not worth stopping for.

Yet stop I did: in fact I often do,
And always end much at a loss like this,
Wondering what to look for; wondering, too,
When churches fall completely out of use
What we shall turn them into, if we shall keep
A few cathedrals chronically on show,
Their parchment, plate, and pyx in locked cases,
And let the rest rent-free to rain and sheep.
Shall we avoid them as unlucky places?

Or, after dark, will dubious women come
To make their children touch a particular stone;
Pick simples for a cancer; or on some
Advised night see walking a dead one?
Power of some sort or other will go on
In games, in riddles, seemingly at random;

But superstition, like belief, must die,
And what remains when disbelief has gone?
Grass, weedy pavement, brambles, buttress, sky,

A shape less recognizable each week,
A purpose more obscure. I wonder who
Will be the last, the very last, to seek
This place for what it was; one of the crew
That tap and jot and know what rood-lofts were?
Some ruin-bibber, randy for antique,
Or Christmas-addict, counting on a whiff
Of gown-and-bands and organ-pipes and myrrh?
Or will he be my representative,

Bored, uninformed, knowing the ghostly silt
Dispersed, yet tending to this cross of ground
Through suburb scrub because it held unspilt
So long and equably what since is found
Only in separation? marriage, and birth,
And death, and thoughts of these? for whom was built
This special shell? For, though I've no idea
What this accoutred frowsty barn is worth,
It pleases me to stand in silence here;

A serious house on serious earth it is,
In whose blent air all our compulsions meet,
Are recognised, and robed as destinies.
And that much never can be obsolete,
Since someone will forever be surprising
A hunger in himself to be more serious,
And gravitating with it to this ground,
Which, he once heard, was proper to grow wise in,
If only that so many dead lie round

28

The Wandering Jew
and the Second Coming

MARTIN GARDNER

All "scriptural" pseudo-scholarship is a strenuous attempt to make things come out right and to square a circle. Here, a serious mind trains itself on one such attempt, and shows that stupid ideas have stupid consequences—and nasty consequences as well.

The legend of a wandering Jew, unable to die until the Second Coming, is surely the strangest of all myths intended to combat the notion that Jesus was mistaken when he said he would return within the lifetime of someone then living. I have summarized its sad, colorful history in an essay that appeared in Free Inquiry *(Summer 1995).*

As the year 2000 approaches, it would not surprise me to see a picture of the Wandering Jew on the front page of one of the supermarket tabloids. Some intrepid photographer will spot him trudging a dusty road, with his sturdy walking stick and long white beard, and perhaps obtain an interview about his sufferings over the past two millennia.

> For the son of man shall come in the glory of his Father, with his angels, and then he shall reward every man according to his works. Verily I say unto you. There be some standing here, which shall not taste of death till they see the Son of man coming in his kingdom.
>
> —Matthew 16; 27, 28

The statement of Jesus quoted above from Matthew, and repeated in similar words by Mark (8.38, 9:1) and Luke (9:26,27) is for Bible fundamentalists one of the most troublesome of all New Testament passages.

It is possible, of course, that Jesus never spoke those sentences, but all scholars agree that the first-century Christians expected the Second Coming in their lifetimes. In Matthew 24, after describing dramatic signs of his imminent return, such as the falling of stars and the darkening of the moon and sun, Jesus added: Verily I say unto you. This generation shall not pass until all these things be fulfilled."

Until about 1933 Seventh-Day Adventists had a clever way of rationalizing this prophecy. They argued that a spectacular meteor shower of 1833 was the falling of the stars, and that there was a mysterious darkening of sun and moon in the United States in 1870. Jesus meant that a future generation witnessing these celestial events would be the one to experience his Second Coming.

For almost a hundred years Adventist preachers and writers of books assured the world that Jesus would return within the lifetimes of some who had seen the great meteor shower of 1833. After 1933 passed, the church gradually abandoned this interpretation of Christ's words. Few of today's faithful are even aware that their church once trumpeted such a view. Although Adventists still believe Jesus will return very soon, they no longer set conditions for an approximate date.

How do they explain the statements of Jesus quoted in the epigraph? Following the lead of Saint Augustine and other early Christian commentators, they take the promise to refer to Christ's Transfiguration. Ellen White, the prophetess who with her husband founded Seventh-day Adventism, said it this way in her life of Christ, *The Desire of Ages:* "The Savior's promise to the disciples was now fulfilled. Upon the mount the future kingdom of glory was represented in miniature. . . ."

Hundreds of adventist sects since the time of Jesus, starting with the Montanists of the second century, have all interpreted Christ's prophetic statements about his return to refer to *their* generation. Apocalyptic excitement surged as the year 1000 approached. Similar excitement is now gathering momentum as the year 2000 draws near. Expectation of the Second Coming is not confined to adventist sects. Fundamentalists in mainstream Protestant denominations are increasingly stressing the imminence of Jesus' return. Baptist Billy Graham, for example, regularly warns of the approaching battle of Armageddon and the appearance of the Anti-Christ. He likes to emphasize the Bible's assertion that the Second Coming will occur after the gospel is preached to all nations. This could not take place, Graham insists, until the rise of radio and television.

Preacher Jerry Falwell is so convinced that he will soon be raptured—caught up in the air to meet the return of Jesus—that he once said he has no plans for a burial plot. Austin Miles, who once worked for Pat Robertson, reveals in his book *Don't Call Me Brother* (1989) that Pat once seriously considered plans to televise the Lord's appearance in the skies! Today's top native drumbeater for a soon Second Coming is Hal Lindsey. His many books on the topic, starting with *The Late Great Planet Earth*, have sold by the millions.

For the past two thousand years individuals and sects have been setting dates for the Second Coming. When the Lord fails to show, there is often no recognition of total failure. Instead, errors are found in the calculations and new dates set. In New Harmony, Indiana, an adventist sect called the Rappites was established by George Rapp. When he became ill he said that were he not absolutely certain the Lord intended him and his flock to witness the return of Jesus, he would think this was his last hour. So saying, he died.

The Catholic Church, following Augustine, long ago moved the Second Coming far into the future at some unspecified date. Liberal Protestants have tended to take the Second Coming as little more than a metaphor for the gradual establishment of peace and justice on earth. Julia Ward Howe, a Unitarian minister, had this interpretation in mind when she began her famous *Battle Hymn of the Republic* with "Mine eyes have seen the glory of the coming of the Lord. . . ." Protestant fundamentalists, on the other hand, believe that Jesus described actual historical events that would precede his literal return to earth to banish Satan and judge the quick and the dead. They also find it unthinkable that the Lord could have blundered about the time of his Second Coming.

The difficulty in interpreting Christ's statement about some of his listeners not tasting of death until he returned is that he described the event in exactly the same phrases he used in Matthew 24. He clearly was not there referring to his transfiguration, or perhaps (as another "out" has it) to the fact that his kingdom would soon be established by the formation of the early church. Assuming that Jesus meant exactly what he said, and that he was not mistaken, how can his promise be unambiguously justified?

During the Middle Ages several wonderful legends arose to preserve the accuracy of Christ's prophecies. Some were based on John 21. When Jesus said to Peter "Follow me," Peter noticed John walking behind him and asked, "Lord, what shall this man do?" The Lord's enigmatic answer was, "If I will that he tarry till I come, what is that to thee?"

We are told that this led to a rumor that John would not die. However, the writer of the fourth gospel adds: "Yet Jesus said not unto him, He shall not die; but if I will that he tarry till I come, what is that to thee?" Theologians in the Middle Ages speculated that perhaps John did not die. He was either wandering about the earth, or perhaps he ascended bodily into heaven. A more popular legend was that John had been buried in a state of suspended animation, his heart faintly throbbing, to remain in an unknown grave until Jesus returns.

These speculations about John rapidly faded as a new and more powerful legend slowly took shape. Perhaps Jesus was not referring to John when he said he could ask someone to tarry, but to someone else. This would also explain the remarks quoted in the epigraph. Someone not mentioned in the gospels, alive in Jesus's day, was somehow cursed to remain alive for centuries until judgment day, wandering over the earth and longing for death.

Who was this Wandering Jew? Some said it was Malchus, whose ear Peter sliced off. Others thought it might be the impenitent thief who was crucified beside Jesus. Maybe it was Pilate, or one of Pilate's servants. The version that became dominant identified the Wandering Jew as a shopkeeper—his name varied—who watched Jesus go by his doorstep, staggering under the weight of the cross he carried. Seeing how slowly and painfully the Lord walked, the man struck Jesus on the back, urging him to go faster. "I go," Jesus replied, "but you will tarry until I return."

As punishment for his rudeness, the shopkeeper's doom is to wander the earth, longing desperately to die but unable to do so. In some versions of the legend, he stays the same age. In others, he repeatedly reaches old age only to be restored over and over again to his youth. The legend seems to have first been recorded in England in the thirteenth century before it rapidly spread throughout Europe. It received an enormous boost in the early seventeenth century when a pamphlet appeared in Germany about a Jewish shoemaker named Ahasuerus who claimed to be the Wanderer. The pamphlet was endlessly reprinted in Germany and translated into other languages. The result was a mania comparable to today's obsessions with UFOs, Abominable Snowmen, and Elvis Presley. Scores of persons claiming to be the Wandering Jew turned up in cities all over England and Europe during the next two centuries. In the U.S. as late as 1868 a Wandering Jew popped up in Salt Lake City, home of the Mormon adventist sect. It is impossible now to decide in individual cases whether these were rumors, hoaxes by imposters, or cases of self-deceived psychotics.

The Wandering Jew became a favorite topic for hundreds of poems, novels, and plays, especially in Germany where such works continue to proliferate to this day. Even Goethe intended to write an epic about the Wanderer, but only finished a few fragments. It is not hard to understand how anti-Semites in Germany and elsewhere would see the cobbler as representing all of Israel, its people under God's condemnation for having rejected his Son as their Messiah.

Gustave Doré produced twelve remarkable woodcuts depicting episodes in the Wanderer's life. They were first published in Paris in 1856 to accompany a poem by Pierre Dupont. English editions followed with translations of the verse.

By far the best known novel about the Wanderer is Eugene Sue's French work *Le Juif Errant* (The Wandering Jew), first serialized in Paris in 1844–1845 and published in ten volumes. George Croly's three-volume *Salathiel* (1827), later retitled *Tarry Thou Till I Come*, was an enormously popular earlier novel. (In *Don Juan*, Canto 11, Stanza 57, Byron calls the author Reverend Roley-Poley.) In Lew Wallace's *Prince of India* (1893), the Wanderer is a wealthy Oriental potentate.

George Macdonald's *Thomas Wingfold, Curate* (1876) introduces the Wandering Jew as an Anglican minister. Having witnessed the Crucifixion, and in constant agony over his sin, Wingfold is powerless to overcome a strange compulsion. Whenever he passes a roadside cross, or even a cross on top of a church, he has an irresistible impulse to climb on the cross, wrap his arms and legs around it, and cling there until he drops to the ground unconscious! He falls in love, but realizing that his beloved will age and die while he remains young, he tries to kill himself by walking into an active volcano. His beloved follows, and is incinerated by the molten lava. There is a surprisingly happy ending. Jesus appears, forgives the Wanderer, and leads him off to Paradise to reunite with the woman who died for him. The novel is not among the best of this Scottish writer's many admired fantasies.

My First Two Thousand Years, by George Sylvester Viereck and Paul Eldridge (1928) purports to be the erotic autobiography of the Wandering Jew. The same two authors, in 1930, wrote *Salome, the Wandering Jewess,* an equally erotic novel covering her two thousand years of lovemaking. The most recent novel about the Wanderer is by German ex-Communist Stefan Heym, a pseudonym for Hellmuth Flieg. In his *The Wandering Jew,* published in West Germany in 1981 and in a U.S. edition three years later, the Wanderer is a hunchback who tramps the roads with Lucifer as his companion. The fantasy ends with the Second Coming, Armageddon, and the Wanderer's forgiveness.

Sue's famous novel is worth a quick further comment. The Wanderer is Ahasuerus, a cobbler. His sister Herodias, the wife of King Herod, becomes the Wandering Jewess. The siblings are minor characters in a complex plot. Ahasuerus is tall, with a single black eyebrow stretching over both eyes like a Mark of Cain. Seven nails on the soles of his iron boots produce crosses when he walks across snow. Wherever he goes an outbreak of cholera follows. Eventually the two siblings are pardoned and allowed "the happiness of eternal sleep." Sue was a French socialist. His Wanderer is a symbol of exploited labor, Herodias a symbol of exploited women. Indeed, the novel is an angry blast at Catholicism, capitalism, and greed.

The Wandering Jew appears in several recent science fiction novels, notably Walter Miller's *A Canticle for Leibowitz* (1960), and Wilson Tucker's *The Planet King* (1959) where he becomes the last man alive on earth. At least two movies have dealt with the legend, the most recent a 1948 Italian film starring Vittorio Gassman.

Rafts of poems by British and U.S. authors have retold the legend. The American John Saxe, best known for his verse about the blind men and the elephant, wrote a seventeen-stanza poem about the Wanderer. British poet Caroline Elizabeth Sarah Norton's forgettable "Undying One" runs to more than a hundred pages. Oliver Herford, an American writer of light verse, in "Overheard in a Garden" turns the Wanderer into a traveling salesman peddling a book about himself. "The Wandering Jew" (1920) by Edwin Arlington Robinson, is surely the best of such poems by an American writer.

Charles Timothy Brooks (1813–1883) was a New England Unitarian minister as well as a prolific versifier and translator of Goethe and other German poets. His "Wandering Jew," based on a German poem whose author I do not know, was reprinted in dozens of pre–1900 American anthologies.

The Wandering Jew once said to me,
  I passed through a city in the cool of the year;
A man in the garden plucked fruit from a tree.
  I asked, "How long has the city been here?"
And he answered me, as he plucked away—
  "It has always stood where it stands to-day,
And here it will stand forever and aye."
  Five hundred years rolled by, and then
  I traveled the self-same road again.

No trace of the city there I found:
  A shepherd sat blowing his pipe alone;
His flock went quietly nibbling round.
  I asked, "How long has the city been gone?"
And he answered me, and he piped away—
  "The new ones bloom and the old decay,
This is my pasture ground for aye."
  Five hundred years rolled by, and then
  I traveled the self-same road again.

And I came to the sea, and the waves did roar,
  And a fisherman threw his net out clear,
And when heavy laden he dragged it ashore.
  I asked, "How long has the sea been here?"
And he laughed, and he said, and he laughed away—
  "As long as yon billows have tossed their spray
They've fished and they've fished in this self-same bay."
  Five hundred years rolled by, and then
  I traveled the self-same road again.

And I came to a forest, vast and free.
  And a woodman stood in the thicket near—
His axe he laid at the foot of a tree.
  I asked., "How long have the woods been here?"
And he answered. "These woods are a covert for aye;
  My ancestors dwelt here alway,
And trees have been here since creation's day."
  Five hundred years rolled by, and then
  I traveled the self-same road again.

And I found there a city, and far and near
  Resounded the hum of toil and glee,

> *And I asked, "How long has the city been here?*
> > *And where is the pipe, and the wood, and the sea?"*
> *And they answered me, as they went their way.*
> > *"Things always have stood as they stand to-day.*
> *And so they will stand forever and aye."*
> > *I'll wait five hundred years, and then*
> > *I'll travel the selfsame road again.*

In England, Shelley was the most famous poet to become fascinated by the legend. In his lengthy poem "The Wandering Jew," written or partly written when he was seventeen, the Wanderer is called Paulo. A fiery cross on his forehead is kept concealed under a cloth band. In the third Canto, after sixteen centuries of wandering, Paulo recounts the origin of his suffering to Rosa, a woman he loves:

> *How can I paint that dreadful day,*
> *That time of terror and dismay,*
> *When, for our sins, a Saviour died,*
> *And the meek Lamb was crucified!*
> As dread that day, when, borne along
> To slaughter by the insulting throng,
> Infuriate for Deicide.
> I mocked our Saviour, and I cried,
> "Go, go," "Ah! I will go," said he,
> "Where scenes of endless bliss invite;
> To the blest regions of the light
> I go, but thou shall here remain—
> Thou diest not till I come again."

The Wandering Jew is also featured in Shelley's short poem "The Wandering Jew's Soliloquy," and in two much longer works, "Hellas" and "Queen Mab." In "Queen Mab," as a ghost whose body casts no shadow, Ahasuerus bitterly denounces God as an evil tyrant. In a lengthy note about this Shelley quotes from a fragment of a German work "whose title I have vainly endeavored to discover. I picked it up, dirty and torn, some years ago. . . ."

In this fragment the Wanderer describes his endless efforts to kill himself. He tries vainly to drown. He leaps into an erupting Mount Etna where he suffers intense heat for ten months before the volcano belches him out. Forest fires fail to consume him. He tries to get killed in wars but arrows, spears, clubs, swords, bullets, mines, and trampling elephants have no effect on him.

29

The Demon-Haunted World

CARL SAGAN

A tremendous number of people owe their portion of scientific education to the elegant and witty Carl Sagan (1934–1996). His academic work in astronomy and his gift for clear exposition took him from the pinnacles of Harvard and Cornell to the more demotic arena of television and film and fiction, where his novel *Contact* won him widespread renown. Not unlike Bertrand Russell, Sagan had the faculty of connecting ancient superstitions to modern ones: in *The Demon-Haunted World* he calmly showed how religion drew on primitive fears and helped to reinforce them, and in his Gifford lectures at the University of Glasgow he connected the slavish belief in gods to the idiotic cult of UFOs and other post-modern delusions.

> *There are demon-haunted worlds, regions of utter darkness.*
> —*THE ISA UPANISHAD* (INDIA, CA. 600 B.C.)

> *Fear of things invisible is the natural seed of that which every one in himself calleth religion.*
> —THOMAS HOBBES, *LEVIATHAN* (1651)

The gods watch over us and guide our destinies, many human cultures teach; other entities, more malevolent, are responsible for the existence of evil. Both classes of beings, whether considered natural or supernatural, real or imaginary, serve human needs. Even if they're wholly fanciful, people feel better believing in them. So in an age when traditional religions have been under withering fire from science, is it not natural to wrap up the old gods and demons in scientific raiment and call them aliens?

.   .   .

Belief in demons was widespread in the ancient world. They were thought of as natural rather than supernatural beings. Hesiod casually mentions them.

Socrates described his philosophical inspiration as the work of a personal, benign demon. His teacher, Diotima of Mantineia, tells him (in Plato's *Symposium*) that "Everything demonic is intermediate between God and mortal. God has no contact with man," she continues; "only through the demonic is there intercourse and conversation between man and gods, whether in the waking state or during sleep."

Plato, Socrates' most celebrated student, assigned a high role to demons: "No human nature invested with supreme power is able to order human affairs," he said, "and not overflow with insolence and wrong. . . ."

> We do not appoint oxen to be the lords of oxen, or goats of goats, but we ourselves are a superior race and rule over them. In like manner God, in his love of mankind, placed over us the demons, who are a superior race, and they with great ease and pleasure to themselves, and no less to us, taking care of us and giving us peace and reverence and order and justice never failing, made the tribes of men happy and united.

He stoutly denied that demons were a source of evil, and represented Eros, the keeper of sexual passions, as a demon, not a god, "neither mortal nor immortal, neither good nor bad." But all later Platonists, including the Neo-Platonists who powerfully influenced Christian philosophy, held that some demons were good and others evil. The pendulum was swinging. Aristotle, Plato's famous student, seriously considered the contention that dreams are scripted by demons. Plutarch and Porphyry proposed that the demons, who filled the upper air, came from the Moon.

The early Church Fathers, despite having imbibed Neo-Platonism from the culture they swam in, were anxious to separate themselves from "pagan" belief-systems. They taught that all of pagan religion consisted of the worship of demons and men, both misconstrued as gods. When St. Paul complained (Ephesians 6:14) about wickedness in high places, he was referring not to government corruption, but to demons, who lived in high places:

> For we wrestle not against flesh and blood, but against principalities, against powers, against the rulers of the darkness of this world, against spiritual wickedness in high places.

From the beginning, much more was intended than demons as a mere poetic metaphor for evil in the hearts of men.

St. Augustine was much vexed with demons. He quotes the pagan thinking prevalent in his time: "The gods occupy the loftiest regions, men the lowest, the demons the middle region. . . . They have immortality of body, but passions of the mind in common with men." In Book VIII of *The City of God* (begun in 413), Augustine assimilates this ancient tradition, replaces gods by God, and demonizes the demons—arguing that they are, without exception, malign. They have no redeeming virtues. They are the fount of all spiritual and material evil. He calls them "aerial animals . . . most eager to inflict harm, utterly alien from righteousness, swollen with pride, pale with envy, subtle in deceit." They may profess to carry messages between God and man, disguising themselves as angels of the Lord, but this pose is a snare to lure us to our destruction. They can assume any form, and know many things—"demon" *means* "knowledge" in Greek—especially about the material world. However intelligent, they are deficient in charity. They prey on "the captive and outwitted minds of men," wrote Tertullian. "They have their abode in the air, the stars are their neighbors, their commerce is with the clouds."

In the eleventh century, the influential Byzantine theologian, philosopher, and shady politician, Michael Psellus, described demons in these words:

These animals exist in our own life, which is full of passions, for they are present abundantly in the passions, and their dwelling-place is that of matter, as is their rank and degree. For this reason they are also subject to passions and fettered to them.

One Richalmus, abbot of Schönthal, around 1270 penned an entire treatise on demons, rich in first-hand experience: He sees (but only when his eyes are shut) countless malevolent demons, like motes of dust, buzzing around his head—and everyone else's. Despite successive waves of rationalist, Persian, Jewish, Christian, and Moslem world views, despite revolutionary social, political, and philosophical ferment, the existence, much of the character, and even the name of demons remained unchanged from Hesiod through the Crusades.

Demons, the "powers of the air," come down from the skies and have unlawful sexual congress with women. Augustine believed that witches were the offspring of these forbidden unions. In the Middle Ages, as in classical antiquity, nearly everyone believed such stories. The demons were also called devils, or fallen angels. The demonic seducers of women were labeled incubi; of men, succubi. There are cases in which nuns reported, in some befuddlement, a striking resemblance between the incubus and the priest-confessor, or the bishop, and awoke the next morning, as one fifteenth-century chronicler put it, to "find themselves polluted just as if they had commingled with a man." There are similar accounts, but in harems not convents, in ancient China. So many women reported incubi, argued the Presbyterian religious writer Richard Baxter (in his *Certainty of the World of Spirits,* 1691), "that 'tis impudence to deny it."

As they seduced, the incubi and succubi were perceived as a weight bearing down on the chest of the dreamer. *Mare,* despite its Latin meaning, is the Old English word for incubus, and *nightmare* meant originally the demon that sits on the chests of sleepers, tormenting them with dreams. In Athanasius' *Life of St. Anthony* (written around 360) demons are described as coming and going at will in locked rooms; 1400 years later, in his work *De Daemonialitate,* the Franciscan scholar Ludovico Sinistrari assures us that demons pass through walls.

The external reality of demons was almost entirely unquestioned from antiquity through late medieval times. Maimonides denied their reality, but the overwhelming majority of rabbis believed in *dybbuks.* One of the few cases I can find where it is even hinted that demons might be *internal,* generated in our minds, is when Abba Poemen—one of the desert fathers of the early Church—was asked, "How do the demons fight against me?"

"The demons fight against you?" Father Poemen asked in turn. "Our own wills become the demons, and it is these which attack us."

The medieval attitudes on incubi and succubi were influenced by Macrobius' fourth-century *Commentary on the Dream of Scipio,* which went through dozens of editions before the European Enlightenment. Macrobius described phantoms (*phantasmata*) seen "in the moment between wakefulness and slumber." The dreamer "imagines" the phantoms as predatory. Macrobius had a skeptical side which his medieval readers tended to ignore.

Obsession with demons began to reach a crescendo when, in his famous Bull of 1484, Pope Innocent VIII declared,

> It has come to Our ears that members of both sexes do not avoid to have intercourse with evil angels, incubi, and succubi, and that by their sorceries, and by their incantations, charms, and conjurations, they suffocate, extinguish, and cause to perish the births of women

as well as generate numerous other calamities. With this Bull, Innocent initiated the systematic accusation, torture, and execution of countless "witches" all over Europe. They were guilty of what Augustine had described as "a criminal tampering with the unseen world." Despite the evenhanded "members of both sexes" in the language of the Bull, unsurprisingly it was mainly girls and women who were so persecuted.

Many leading Protestants of the following centuries, their differences with the Catholic Church notwithstanding, adopted nearly identical views. Even humanists such as Desiderius Erasmus and Thomas More believed in witches. "The giving up of witchcraft," said John Wesley, the founder of Methodism, "is in effect the giving up of the Bible." William Blackstone, the celebrated jurist, in his *Commentaries on the Laws of England* (1765), asserted:

> To deny the possibility, nay, actual existence of witchcraft and sorcery is at once flatly to contradict the revealed word of God in various passages of both the Old and New Testament.

Innocent commended "Our dear sons Henry Kramer and James Sprenger," who "have been by Letters Apostolic delegated as Inquisitors of these heretical [de]pravities." If "the abominations and enormities in question remain unpunished," the souls of multitudes face eternal damnation.

The pope appointed Kramer and Sprenger to write a comprehensive analysis, using the full academic armory of the late fifteenth century. With exhaustive citations of Scripture and of ancient and modern scholars, they produced the *Malleus Maleficarum,* the "Hammer of Witches"—aptly described as one of the most terrifying documents in human history. Thomas Ady, in *A Candle in the Dark,* condemned it as "villainous Doctrines & Inventions," "horrible lyes and impossibilities," serving to hide "their unparalleled cruelty from the ears of the world." What the *Malleus* comes down to, pretty much, is that if you're accused of witchcraft, you're a witch. Torture is an unfailing means to demonstrate the validity of the accusation. There are no rights of the defendant. There is no opportunity to confront the accusers. Little attention is given to the possibility that accusations might be made for impious purposes—jealousy, say, or revenge, or the greed of the inquisitors who routinely confiscated for their own private benefit the property of the accused. This technical manual for torturers also includes methods of punishment tailored to release demons from the victim's body before the process kills her. The *Malleus* in hand, the Pope's encouragement guaranteed, inquisitors began springing up all over Europe.

It quickly became an expense account scam. All costs of investigation, trial, and execution were borne by the accused or her relatives—down to per diems for the private detectives hired to spy on her, wine for her guards, banquets for her judges, the travel expenses of a messenger sent to fetch a more experienced torturer from another city, and the faggots, tar and hangman's rope. Then there was a bonus to the members of the tribunal for each witch burned. The convicted witch's remaining property, if any, was divided between Church and State. As this legally and morally sanctioned mass murder and theft became institutionalized, as a vast bureaucracy arose to serve it, attention was turned from poor hags and crones to the middle class and well-to-do of both sexes.

The more who, under torture, confessed to witchcraft, the harder it was to maintain that the whole business was mere fantasy. Since each "witch" was made to implicate others, the numbers grew exponentially. These constituted "frightful proofs that the Devil is still alive," as it was later put in America in the Salem witch trials. In a credulous age, the most fantastic testimony was soberly accepted—that tens of thousands of witches had gathered for a Sabbath in public squares in France, or that 12,000 of them darkened the skies as they flew to Newfoundland. The Bible had counseled, "Thou shalt not suffer a witch to live." Legions of women were burnt to death. And the most horrendous tortures were routinely applied to every defendant, young or old, after the instruments of torture were first blessed by the priests. Innocent himself died in 1492, following unsuccessful attempts to keep him alive by transfusion (which resulted in the deaths of three boys) and by suckling at the breast of a nursing mother. He was mourned by his mistress and their children.

In Britain witch-finders, also called "prickers," were employed, receiving a handsome bounty for each girl or woman they turned over for execution. They had no incentive to be cautious in their accusations. Typically they looked for "devil's marks"—scars or birthmarks or nevi—that when pricked with a pin neither hurt nor bled. A simple sleight of hand often gave the appearance that the pin penetrated deep into the witch's flesh. When no visible marks were apparent, "invisible marks" sufficed. Upon the gallows, one mid-seventeenth-century pricker "confessed he had been the death of above 220 women in England and Scotland, for the gain of twenty shillings apiece."

In the witch trials, mitigating evidence or defense witnesses were inadmissible. In any case, it was nearly impossible to provide compelling alibis for accused witches: The rules of evidence had a special character. For example, in more than one case a husband attested that his wife was asleep in his arms at the very moment she was accused of frolicking with the devil at a witch's Sabbath; but the archbishop patiently explained that a demon had taken the place of the wife. The husbands were not to imagine that their powers of perception could exceed Satan's powers of deception. The beautiful young women were perforce consigned to the flames.

There were strong erotic and misogynistic elements—as might be expected in a sexually repressed, male-dominated society with inquisitors drawn from the class of nominally celibate priests. The trials paid close attention to the quality and quantity of orgasm in the supposed copulations of defendants with demons or the Devil (although Augustine had been certain "we cannot call the Devil a fornicator"), and to the nature of the Devil's "member" (cold, by all reports). "Devil's marks" were found "generally on the breasts or private parts" according to Ludovico Sinistrari's 1700 book. As a result pubic hair was shaved, and the genitalia were carefully inspected by the exclusively male inquisitors. In the immolation of the 20-year-old Joan of Arc, after her dress had caught fire the Hangman of Rouen slaked the flames so onlookers could view "all the secrets which can or should be in a woman."

The chronicle of those who were consumed by fire in the single German city of Würzburg in the single year 1598 penetrates the statistics and lets us confront a little of the human reality:

> The steward of the senate named Gering; old Mrs. Kanzler; the tailor's fat wife; the woman cook of Mr. Mengerdorf; a stranger; a strange woman; Baunach, a senator, the fattest citizen in Würtzburg; the old smith of the court; an old woman; a little girl, nine or ten years old; a younger girl, her little sister; the mother of the two little aforementioned girls; Liebler's daughter; Goebel's

child, the most beautiful girl in Würtzburg; a student who knew many languages; two boys from the Minster, each twelve years old; Stepper's little daughter; the woman who kept the bridge gate; an old woman; the little son of the town council bailiff; the wife of Knertz, the butcher; the infant daughter of Dr. Schultz; a little girl; Schwartz, canon at Hach. . . .

On and on it goes. Some were given special humane attention: "The little daughter of Valkenberger was privately executed and burnt." There were 28 public immolations, each with 4 to 6 victims on average, in that small city in a single year. This was a microcosm of what was happening all across Europe. No one knows how many were killed altogether—perhaps hundreds of thousands, perhaps millions. Those responsible for prosecuting, torturing, judging, burning, and justifying were selfless. Just ask them.

They could not be mistaken. The confessions of witchcraft could not be based on hallucinations, say, or desperate attempts to satisfy the inquisitors and stop the torture. In such a case, explained the witch judge Pierre de Lancre (in his 1612 book, *Description of the Inconstancy of Evil Angels),* the Catholic Church would be committing a great crime by burning witches. Those who raise such possibilities are thus attacking the Church and *ipso facto* committing a mortal sin. Critics of witch-burning were punished and, in some cases, themselves burnt. The inquisitors and torturers were doing God's work. They were saving souls. They were foiling demons.

Witchcraft of course was not the only offense that merited torture and burning at the stake. Heresy was a still more serious crime, and both Catholics and Protestants punished it ruthlessly. In the sixteenth century the scholar William Tyndale had the temerity to contemplate translating the New Testament into English. But if people could actually read the Bible in their own language instead of arcane Latin, they could form their own, independent religious views. They might conceive of their own private unintermediated line to God. This was a challenge to the job security of Roman Catholic priests. When Tyndale tried to publish his translation, he was hounded and pursued all over Europe. Eventually he was captured, garroted, and then, for good measure, burned at the stake. His copies of the New Testament (which a century later became the basis of the exquisite King James translation) were then hunted down house-to-house by armed posses—Christians piously defending Christianity by preventing other Christians from knowing the words of Christ. Such a cast of mind, such a climate of absolute confidence that knowledge should be rewarded by torture and death were unlikely to help those accused of witchcraft.

Burning witches is a feature of Western civilization that has, with occasional political exceptions, declined since the sixteenth century. In the last judicial execution of witches in England a woman and her nine-year-old daughter were hanged. Their crime was raising a rainstorm by taking their stockings off. In our time, witches and djinns are found as regular fare in children's entertainment, exorcism of demons is still practiced by the Roman Catholic and other churches, and the proponents of one cult still denounce as sorcery the cultic practices of another. We still use the word "pandemonium" (literally, all demons). A crazed and violent person is still said to be demonic. (Not until the eighteenth century was mental illness no longer generally ascribed to supernatural causes; even insomnia had been considered a punishment inflicted by demons.) More than half of Americans tell pollsters they "believe" in the Devil's existence, and 10 percent have communicated with him, as Martin Luther reported he did regularly. In a 1992 "spiritual warfare manual" called *Prepare for War,* Rebecca Brown informs us that abortion and sex outside of marriage "will almost always result in demonic infestation"; that meditation, yoga and martial arts are designed so unsuspecting Christians will be seduced into worshiping demons; and that "rock music didn't 'just happen,' it was a carefully masterminded plan by none other than Satan himself." Sometimes "your loved ones are demonically bound and blinded." Demonology is today still part and parcel of many earnest faiths.

And what is it that demons do? In the *Malleus,* Kramer and Sprenger reveal that "devils . . . busy themselves by interfering with the process of normal copulation and conception, by obtaining human semen, and themselves transferring it." Demonic artificial insemination in the Middle Ages goes back at least to St. Thomas Aquinas, who tells us in *On the Trinity* that "demons can transfer the semen which they have collected and inject it into the bodies of others." His contemporary, St. Bonaventura, spells it out in a little more detail: Succubi "yield to males and receive their semen; by cunning skill, the demons preserve its potency, and afterwards, with the permission of God, they become incubi and pour it out into female repositories." The products of these demon-mediated unions are also, when they grow up, visited by demons. A multi-generational transspecies sexual bond is forged. And these creatures, we recall, are well known to fly; indeed they inhabit the upper air.

There is no spaceship in these stories. But most of the central elements of the alien abduction account are present, including sexually obsessive non-humans who live in the sky, walk through walls, communicate telepathically, and perform breeding experiments on the human species. Unless *we* believe that demons really exist, how can we understand so strange a belief system, embraced by the whole Western world (including those considered the wisest among us), reinforced by personal experience in every generation, and taught by Church and State? Is there any real alternative besides a shared delusion based on common brain wiring and chemistry?

The God Hypothesis

CARL SAGAN

The Gifford Lectures are supposed to be on the topic of natural theology. Natural theology has long been understood to mean theological knowledge that can be established by reason and experience and experiment alone. Not by revelation, not by mystical experience, but by reason. And this is, in the long, historical sweep of the human species, a reasonably novel view. For example, we might look at the following sentence written by Leonardo da Vinci. In his notebooks he says, "Whoever in discussion adduces authority uses not intellect but rather memory."

This was an extremely heterodox remark for the early sixteenth century, when most knowledge was derived from authority. Leonardo himself had many clashes of this sort. During a trip to an Apennine mountaintop, he had discovered the fossilized remains of shellfish that ordinarily lived on the ocean floor. How did this come about? The conventional theological wisdom was that the Great Flood of Noah had inundated the mountaintops and carried the clams and oysters with it. Leonardo, remembering that the Bible says that the flood lasted only forty days, attempted to calculate whether this would be sufficient time to carry the shellfish with them, even if the mountaintops were inundated. During what state in the life cycle of the shellfish had they been deposited?— and so on. He came to the conclusion this didn't work, and proposed a quite daring alternative; namely, that over immense vistas of geological time the mountaintops had pushed up through the oceans. And that posed all sorts of theological difficulties. But it is the correct answer, as I think it's fair to say it has been definitively established in our time.

If we are to discuss the idea of God and be restricted to rational arguments, then it is probably useful to know what we are talking about when we say "God." This turns out not to be easy. The Romans called the Christians atheists. Why? Well, the Christians had a god of sorts, but it wasn't a real god. They didn't believe in the divinity of apotheosized emperors or Olympian gods. They had a peculiar, different kind of god. So it was very easy to call people who believed in a different kind of god atheists. And that general sense that an atheist is anybody who doesn't believe exactly as I do prevails in our own time.

Now, there is a constellation of properties that we generally think of when we in the West, or more generally in the Judeo-Christian-Islamic tradition, think of

God. The fundamental differences among Judaism, Christianity, and Islam are trivial compared to their similarities. We think of some being who is omnipotent, omniscient, compassionate, who created the universe, is responsive to prayer, intervenes in human affairs, and so on.

But suppose there were definitive proof of some being who had some but not all of these properties. Suppose somehow it were demonstrated that there was a being who originated the universe but is indifferent to prayer. . . . Or, worse, a god who was oblivious to the existence of humans. That's very much like Aristotle's god. Would that be God or not? Suppose it were someone who was omnipotent but not omniscient, or vice versa. Suppose this god understood all the consequences of his actions but there were many things he was unable to do, so he was condemned to a universe in which his desired ends could not be accomplished. These alternative kinds of gods are hardly ever thought about or discussed. A priori there is no reason they should not be as likely as the more conventional sorts of gods.

And the subject is further confused by the fact that prominent theologians such as Paul Tillich, for example, who gave the Gifford Lectures many years ago, explicitly denied God's existence, at least as a supernatural power. Well, if an esteemed theologian (and he's by no means the only one) denies that God is a supernatural being, the subject seems to me to be somewhat confused. The range of hypotheses that are seriously covered under the rubric "God" is immense. A naive Western view of God is an outsize, light-skinned male with a long white beard, who sits on a very large throne in the sky and tallies the fall of every sparrow.

Contrast this with a quite different vision of God, one proposed by Baruch Spinoza and by Albert Einstein. And this second kind of god they called God in a very straightforward way. Einstein was constantly interpreting the world in terms of what God would or wouldn't do. But by God they meant something not very different from the sum total of the physical laws of the universe; that is, gravitation plus quantum mechanics plus grand unified field theories plus a few other things equaled God. And by that all they meant was that here were a set of exquisitely powerful physical principles that seemed to explain a great deal that was otherwise inexplicable about the universe. Laws of nature, as I have said earlier, that apply not just locally, not just in Glasgow, but far beyond: Edinburgh, Moscow, Peking, Mars, Alpha Centauri, the center of the Milky Way, and out by the most distant quasars known. That the same laws of physics apply everywhere is quite remarkable. Certainly that represents a power greater than any of us. It represents an unexpected regularity to the universe. It need not have been. It could have been that every province of the cosmos had its own laws of nature. It's not apparent from the start that the same laws have to apply everywhere.

Now, it would be wholly foolish to deny the existence of laws of nature. And if that is what we are talking about when we say God, then no one can possibly be an atheist, or at least anyone who would profess atheism would have to give a coherent argument about why the laws of nature are inapplicable.

I think he or she would be hard-pressed. So with this latter definition of God, we all believe in God. The former definition of God is much more dubious. And there is a wide range of other sorts of gods. And in every case we have to ask, "What kind of god are you talking about, and what is the evidence that this god exists?"

Certainly if we are restricted to natural theology, it is insufficient to say, "I believe in that sort of god, because that's what I was told when I was young," because other people are told different things about quite different religions that contradict those of my parents. So they can't all be right. And in fact they all may be wrong. It is certainly true that many different religions are mutually inconsistent. It's not that they just aren't perfect simulacrums of each other but rather that they grossly contradict each other.

I'll give you a simple example; there are many. In the Judeo-Christian-Islamic tradition, the world is a finite number of years old. By counting up the begats in the Old Testament, you can come to the conclusion that the world is a good deal less than ten thousand years old. In the seventeenth century, the archbishop of Armagh, James Ussher, made a courageous but fundamentally flawed effort to count them up precisely. He came to a specific date on which God created the world. It was October 23 in 4004 B.C., a Sunday.

Now, think again of all the possibilities: worlds without gods; gods without worlds; gods that are made by preexisting gods; gods that were always here; gods that never die; gods that do die; gods that die more than once; different degrees of divine intervention in human affairs; zero, one, or many prophets; zero, one, or many saviors; zero, one, or many resurrections; zero, one, or many gods. And related questions about sacrament, religious mutilation, and scarification, baptism, monastic orders, ascetic expectations, the presence or absence of an afterlife, days to eat fish, days not to eat at all, how many afterlives you have coming to you, justice in this world or the next world or no world at all, reincarnation, human sacrifice, temple prostitution, jihads, and so forth. It's a vast array of things that people believe. Different religions believe different things. There's a grab bag of religious alternatives. And there are clearly more combinations of alternatives than there are religions, even though there are something like a few thousand religions on the planet today. In the history of the world, there probably were many tens, maybe hundreds of thousands, if you think back to our hunter-gatherer ancestors when the typical human community was a hundred or so people. Back then there were as many religions as there were hunter-gatherer bands, although the differences between them were probably not all that great. But nobody knows, since, unfortunately, we have virtually no knowledge left of what our ancestors for the greatest part of the tenure of humans on this planet believed, because word-of-mouth tradition is inadequate and writing had not been invented.

So, considering this range of alternatives, one thing that comes to my mind is how striking it is that when someone has a religious-conversion experience, it is almost always to the religion or one of the religions that are mainly believed in his or her community. Because there are so many other possibilities. For example, it's very rare in the West that someone has a religious-conversion experience in which the principal deity has the head of an elephant and is painted blue. That is quite rare. But in India there is a blue, elephant-headed god that has many devotees. And seeing depictions of this god there is not so rare. How is it that the apparition of elephant gods is restricted to Indians and doesn't happen except in places where there is a strong Indian tradition? How is that apparitions of the Virgin Mary are common in the West but rarely occur in places in the East where there isn't a strong Christian tradition? Why don't the details of the religious belief cross over the cultural barriers? It is hard to explain unless the details are entirely determined by the local culture and have nothing to do with something that is externally valid.

Put another way, any preexisting predisposition to religious belief can be powerfully influenced by the indigenous culture, wherever you happen to grow up. And especially if the children are exposed early to a particular set of doctrine and music and art and ritual, then it is as natural as breathing, which is why religions make such a large effort to attract the very young.

Or let's take another possibility. Suppose a new prophet arises who claims a revelation from God, and that revelation contravenes the revelations of all previous religions. How is the average person, someone not so fortunate as to have received this revelation personally, to decide whether this new revelation is valid or not? The only dependable way is through natural theology. You have to ask, "What is the evidence?" And it's insufficient to say, "Well, there is this extremely charismatic person who said that he had a conversion experience." Not enough. There are lots of charismatic people who have all sorts of mutually exclusive conversion experiences. They can't all be right. Some of them have to be wrong. Many of them have to be wrong. It's even possible that all of them are wrong. We cannot depend entirely on what people say. We have to look at what the evidence is.

I would like now to turn to the issue of alleged evidence or, as they're called, proofs of the existence of God. And I will mainly spend my time on the Western proofs. But to show an ecumenical spirit, let me begin with some Hindu proofs, which in many ways are as sophisticated and certainly more ancient than the Western arguments.

Udayana, an eleventh-century logician, had a set of seven proofs of the existence of God, and I won't mention all of them; I'll just try to convey a sense of it. And, by the way, the kind of god that Udayana is talking about is not exactly the same, as you might imagine, as the Judeo-Christian-Islamic god. His god is all-knowing and imperishable but not necessarily omnipotent and compassionate.

First, Udayana reasons that all things must have a cause. The world is full of things. Something must have made those things. And this is very similar to a Western argument that we'll come to shortly.

Secondly, an argument not heard in the West is the argument from atomic combinations. It is quite sophisticated. It says at the beginning of Creation, atoms had to be bonded with each other to make bigger things. And such a bonding of atoms always requires the activity of a conscious agent. Well, now we know that's false. Or we know, at least, that there are laws of atomic interaction that determine how atoms bind together. It's a subject called chemistry. And you might say that this is due to the intervention of a deity but it does not require the direct intervention of a deity. All the deity has to do is establish the laws of chemistry and retire.

Third is an argument from the suspension of the world. The world isn't falling, as is clear by just looking out. We're not hurtling through space, apparently, and therefore something is holding the world up, and that something is God. Well, this is a quite natural view of things. It's connected with the idea that we are stationary and at the center of the universe, a misapprehension that all peoples all over the world have had. In fact we are falling at a terrific rate of speed in orbit around the Sun. And every year we go 2 pi times the radius of the Earth orbit. If you work that out, you'll find it's extremely fast.

Fourth is an argument from the existence of human skills. And this is very close to the von Daniken argument that if someone didn't show us how to do things, we wouldn't know how to do it. I think there's plentiful argument against that.

Then there is the existence of authoritative knowledge separate from human skills. How would we know things that are in, for example, the Vedas, the Hindu holy books, unless God had written them? The idea that humans were able to write the Vedas was difficult for Udayana to accept.

Well, this gives a sense of these arguments and shows that there is a pervasive human wish to give a rational explanation for the existence of a God or gods, and also, I maintain, it demonstrates that these arguments are not always highly successful. Let me now go to some of the Western arguments, which may be entirely familiar to everyone, in which case I apologize.

First of all, there is the cosmological argument, which is not very different from the argument we just heard. The cosmological argument in the West essentially has to do with causality. There are things all around us; those things were caused by something else. And so, after a while, you find yourself back to remote times and causes. Well, it can't go on forever, an infinite regress of causes, as Aristotle and later Thomas Aquinas argued, and therefore you need to come to an uncaused first cause. Something that started everything going that was not itself caused; that is, that was always there. And this is defined as God.

There are two conflicting hypotheses here, two alternative hypotheses. One is that the universe was always here, and the other is that God was always here.

Why is it immediately obvious that one of these is more likely than the other? Or, put another way, if we say that God made the universe, it is reasonable to then ask, "And who made God?"

Virtually every child asks that question and is usually shushed by the parents and told not to ask embarrassing questions. But how does saying that God made the universe, and never mind asking where God came from, how is that more satisfying than to say the universe was always here?

In modern astrophysics there are two contending views. First of all, there is no doubt in my mind, and I think almost all astrophysicists agree, that the evidence from the expansion of the universe, the mutual recession of the galaxies and from what is called the three-degree black-body background radiation, suggests that something like 13 or 15 billion years ago all the matter in the universe was compressed into an extremely small volume, and that something that can surely be called an explosion happened at that time, and that the subsequent expansion of the universe and the condensation of matter led to galaxies, stars, planets, living beings, and all the rest of the details of the universe we see around us.

Now, what happened before that? There are two views. One is "Don't ask that question," which is very close to saying that God did it. And the other is that we live in an oscillating universe in which there is an infinite number of expansions and contractions.[1]

We happen to be roughly 15,000 million years out from the last expansion. And some, let's say, 80,000 million years from now, the expansion will stop, to be replaced by a compression, and all the matter will fly together to a very small volume and then expand again with no information trickling through the cusps in the expansion process.

The former of these views happens, by chance, to be close to the Judeo-Christian-Islamic view, the latter close to the standard Hindu views. And so, if you like, you can think of the varying contentions of these two major religious views being fought out on the field of contemporary satellite astronomy. Because that's where the answer to this question will very likely be decided. Is there enough matter in the universe to prevent the expansion from continuing forever, so that the self-gravity will make the expansion stop and be followed by a contraction? Or is there not enough matter in the universe to stop the expansion, so everything keeps expanding forever? This is an experimental question. And it is very likely that in our lifetime we will have the answer to it. And I stress that this is very different from the usual theological approach, where there is never an experiment that can be performed to test out any contentious issue.

---

1. In 1998, two international teams of astronomers independently reported unexpected evidence that the expansion of the universe is accelerating. These findings suggest that the universe is not oscillating but will continue to expand forever.

Here there is one. So we don't have to make judgments now. All we have to do is maintain some tolerance for ambiguity until the data are in, which may happen in a decade or less. It is possible that the Hubble Space Telescope, scheduled for launch next summer, will provide the answer to this question. It's not guaranteed, but it is possible.[2]

Now, by the way, on this issue of who's older, God or the universe, there's actually a three-by-three matrix: God can have always existed but will not exist for all future time. That is to say God might have no beginning but might have an end. God might have a beginning but no end. God might have no beginning and no end. Likewise for the universe. The universe might be infinitely old, but it will end. The universe might have begun a finite time ago but will go on forever, or it might have always existed and will never end. Those are just the logical possibilities. And it's curious that human myth has some of those possibilities but not others. I think in the West it's quite clear that there is a human or animal life-cycle model that has been imposed on the cosmos. It's a natural thing to think about, but after a while its limitations, I think, become clear.

Also, I should say something about the Second Law of Thermodynamics. An argument that is sometimes used to justify a belief in God is that the Second Law of Thermodynamics says that the universe as a whole runs down, that is, the net amount of order in the universe must decline. Chaos must increase as time goes on; that is, in the entire universe. It doesn't say that in a given locale, such as the Earth, the amount of order can't increase, and clearly it has. Living things are much more complex, have much more order in them, than the raw materials from which life formed some 4,000 million years ago. But this increase in order on the Earth is done, it is easy enough to calculate, at the expense of a decrease in order on the Sun, which is the source of the energy that drives terrestrial biology. It's by no means clear, by the way, that the Second Law of Thermodynamics applies to the universe as a whole, because it is an experimental law, and we don't have experience with the universe as a whole. But it's always struck me as curious that those who wish to apply the Second Law to theological issues do not ask whether God is subject to the Second Law. Because if God were subject to the Second Law of Thermodynamics, then God could have only a finite lifetime. And again, there is an asymmetric use of the principles of physics when theology confronts thermodynamics.

Also, by the way, if there were an uncaused first cause, that by no means says anything about omnipotence or omniscience, or compassion, or even monotheism. And Aristotle, in fact, deduced several dozen first causes in his theology.

The second standard Western argument using reason for God is the so-called argument from design, which we have already talked about, both in its biologi-

───────────

2. Earth-based telescopes provided the answer in 1998. See previous note.

cal context and in the recent astrophysical incarnation called the anthropic principle. It is at best an argument from analogy; that is, that some things were made by humans and now here is something more complex that wasn't made by us, so maybe it was made by an intelligent being smarter than us. Well, maybe, but that is not a compelling argument. I tried to stress earlier the extent to which misunderstandings, failure of the imagination, and especially the lack of awareness of new underlying principles may lead us into error with the argument from design. The extraordinary insights of Charles Darwin on the biological end of the argument of design provide clear warning that there may be principles that we do not yet divine (if I may use that word) underlying apparent order.

There is certainly a lot of order in the universe, but there is also a lot of chaos. The centers of galaxies routinely explode, and if there are inhabited worlds and civilizations there, they are destroyed by the millions, with each explosion of the galactic nucleus or a quasar. That does not sound very much like a god who knows what he, she, or it is doing. It sounds more like an apprentice god in over his head. Maybe they start them out at the centers of galaxies and then after a while, when they get some experience, move them on to more important assignments.

Then there is the moral argument for the existence of God generally attributed to Immanuel Kant, who was very good at showing the deficiencies of some of the other arguments. Kant's argument is very simple. It's just that we are moral beings; therefore God exists. That is, how else would we know to be moral?

Well, first of all you might argue that the premise is dubious. The degree to which humans can be said to be moral beings without the existence of some police force is open at least to debate. But let's put that aside for the moment. Many animals have codes of behavior. Altruism, incest taboos, compassion for the young, you find in all sorts of animals. Nile crocodiles carry their eggs in their mouths for enormous distances to protect the young. They could make an omelette out of it, but they choose not to do so. Why not? Because those crocodiles who enjoy eating the eggs of their young leave no offspring. And after a while all you have is crocodiles who know how to take care of the young. It's very easy to see. And yet we have a sense of thinking of that as being somehow ethical behavior. I'm not against taking care of children; I'm strongly for it. All I'm saying is, it does not follow if we are powerfully motivated to take care of our young or the young of everybody on the planet, that God made us do it. Natural selection can make us do it, and almost surely has. What's more, once humans reach the point of awareness of their surroundings, we can figure things out, and we can see what's good for our own survival as a community or a nation or a species and take steps to ensure our survival. It's not hopelessly beyond our ability. It's not clear to me that this requires the existence of God to explain the limited but definite degree of moral and ethical behavior that is apparent in human society.

Then there is the curious argument, unique to the West, called the "ontological argument," which is generally associated with [St.] Anselm, who died in 1109. His argument can be very simply stated: God is perfect. Existence is an essential attribute of perfection. Therefore, God exists. Got it? I'll say it again. God is perfect. Existence is an essential attribute of perfection. You can't be perfect if you don't exist, Anselm says. Therefore God exists. While this argument has for brief moments captured very significant thinkers (Bertrand Russell describes how it suddenly hit him that Anselm might be right—for about fifteen minutes), this is not considered a successful argument. The twentieth-century logician Ernest Nagel described it as "confounding grammar with logic."

What does it mean, "God is perfect"? You need a separate description of what constitutes perfection. It's not enough to say "perfect" and do not ask what "perfect" means. And how do you know God is perfect? Maybe that's not the god that exists, the perfect one. Maybe it's only imperfect ones that exist. And then why is it that existence is an essential attribute of perfection? Why isn't nonexistence an essential attribute of perfection? We are talking words. In fact, there is the remark that is sometimes made about Buddhism, I think in a kindly light, that their god is so great he doesn't even have to exist. And that is the perfect counterpoise to the ontological argument. In any case, I do not think that the ontological argument is compelling.

Then there's the argument from consciousness. I think, therefore, God exists; that is, how could consciousness come into being? And, indeed, we do not know the details in any but the very broadest brush about the evolution of consciousness. That is on the agenda of future neurological science. But we do know, for example, that an earthworm introduced into a Y-shaped glass tube with, let's say, an electric shock on the right-hand fork and food in the left-hand fork, rapidly learns to take the left fork. Does an earthworm have consciousness if it is able after a certain number of trials invariably to know where the food is and the shock isn't? And if an earthworm has consciousness, could a protozoan have consciousness? Many phototropic microorganisms know to go to the light. They have some kind of internal perception of where the light is, and nobody taught them that it's good to go to the light. They had that information in their hereditary material. It's encoded into their genes and chromosomes. Well, did God put that information there, or might it have evolved through natural selection?

It is clearly good for the survival of microorganisms to know where the light is, especially the ones that photosynthesize. It is certainly good for earthworms to know where the food is. Those earthworms that can't figure out where the food is leave few offspring. After a while the ones that survive know where the food is. Those phototropic or phototactic offspring have encoded into their genetic material how to find the light. It is not apparent that God has entered into the process. Maybe, but it's not a compelling argument. And the general view of many, not all, neurobiologists is that consciousness is a function of the number and complexity of neuronal linkages of the architecture of the brain. Human consciousness is what happens when you get to something like 10^{11} neurons and 10^{14} synapses. This raises all sorts of other questions: What is consciousness like when you have 10^{20} synapses or 10^{30}? What would such a being have to say to us any more than we would have to say to the ants? So at least it does not seem to me that the argument from consciousness, a continuum of consciousness running through the animal and plant kingdoms, proves the existence of God. We have an alternative explanation that seems to work pretty well. We don't know the details, although work on artificial intelligence may help to clarify that. But we don't know the details of the alternative hypothesis either. So it could hardly be said that this is compelling.

Then there's the argument from experience. People have religious experiences. No question about it. They have them worldwide, and there are some interesting similarities in the religious experiences that are had worldwide. They are powerful, emotionally extremely convincing, and they often lead to people reforming their lives and doing good works, although the opposite also happens. Now, what about this? Well, I do not mean in any way to object to or deride religious experiences. But the question is, can any such experience provide other than anecdotal evidence of the existence of God or gods? One million UFO cases since 1947. And yet, as far as we can tell, they do not correspond—any of them—to visitations to the Earth by spacecraft from elsewhere. Large numbers of people can have experiences that can be profound and moving and still not correspond to anything like an exact sense of external reality. And the same can be said not just about UFOs but also about extrasensory perception and ghosts and leprechauns and so on. Every culture has things of this sort. That doesn't mean that they all exist; it doesn't mean that any of them exist.

I also note that religious experiences can be brought on by specific molecules. There are many cultures that consciously imbibe or ingest those molecules in order to bring on a religious experience. The peyote cult of some Native Americans is exactly that, as is the use of wine as a sacrament in many Western religions. It's a very long list of materials that are taken by humans in order to produce a religious experience. This suggests that there is some molecular basis for the religious experience and that it need not correspond to some external reality. I think it's a fairly central point—that religious experiences, personal religious experiences, not the natural theological evidence for God, if any, can be brought on by molecules of finite complexity.

So if I then run through these arguments—the cosmological argument, the argument from design, the moral argument, the ontological argument, the argument from consciousness, and the argument from experience—I must say that the net result is not very impressive. It is very much as if we are seeking a rational justification for something that we otherwise hope will be true.

And then there are certain classical problems with the existence of God. Let me mention a few of them. One is the famous problem of evil. This basically goes as follows: Grant for a moment that evil exists in the world and that unjust actions sometimes go unpunished. And grant also that there is a God that is benevolent toward human beings, omniscient, and omnipotent. This God loves justice, this God observes all human actions, and this God is capable of intervening decisively in human affairs. Well, it was understood by the pre-Socratic philosophers that all four of these propositions cannot simultaneously be true. At least one has to be false. Let me say again what they are. That evil exists, that God is benevolent, that God is omniscient, that God is omnipotent. Let's just see about each of them.

First of all, you might say, "Well, evil doesn't exist in the world. We can't see the big picture, that a little pool of evil here is awash in a great sea of good that it makes possible." Or, as medieval theologians used to say, "God uses the Devil for his own purposes." This is clearly the three-monkey argument about "hear no evil . . ." and has been described by a leading contemporary theologian as a gratuitous insult to mankind, a symptom of insensitivity and indifference to human suffering. To be assured that all the miseries and agonies men and women experience are only illusory. Pretty strong.

This is clearly hoping that the disquieting facts go away if you merely call them something else. It is argued that some pain is necessary for a greater good. But why, exactly? If God is omnipotent, why can't He arrange it so there is no pain? It seems to me a very telling point.

The other alternatives are that God is not benevolent or compassionate. Epicurus held that God was okay but that humans were the least of His worries. There are a number of Eastern religions that have something like that same flavor. Or God isn't omniscient; He doesn't know everything; He has business elsewhere and so doesn't know that humans are in trouble. One way to think about it is there are several times 10^{11} worlds in every galaxy and several times 10^{11} galaxies, and God's busy.

The other possibility is that God isn't omnipotent. He can't do everything. He could maybe start the Earth off or create life, intervene occasionally in human history, but can't be bothered day in and day out to set things right here on Earth. Now, I don't claim to know which of these four possibilities is right, but it's clear that there is a fundamental contradiction at the heart of the Western theological view produced by the problem of evil. And I've read an account of a recent theological conference devoted to this problem, and it clearly was an embarrassment to the assembled theologians.

This raises an additional question—a related question—and that has to do with microintervention. Why in any case is it necessary for God to intervene in human history, in human affairs, as almost every religion assumes happens? That God or the gods come down and tell humans, "No, don't do that, do this, don't forget this, don't pray in this way, don't worship anybody else, mutilate your children as follows." Why is there such a long list of things that God tells people to do? Why didn't God do it right in the first place? You start out the universe, you can do anything. You can see all future consequences of your present action. You want a certain desired end. Why don't you arrange it in the beginning? The intervention of God in human affairs speaks of incompetence. I don't say incompetence on a human scale. Clearly all of the views of God are much more competent than the most competent human. But it does not speak of omnicompetence. It says there are limitations.

I therefore conclude that the alleged natural theological arguments for the existence of God, the sort we're talking about, simply are not very compelling. They are trotting after the emotions, hoping to keep up. But they do not provide any satisfactory argument on their own. And yet it is perfectly possible to imagine that God, not an omnipotent or an omniscient god, just a reasonably competent god, could have made absolutely clear-cut evidence of His existence. Let me give a few examples.

Imagine that there is a set of holy books in all cultures in which there are a few enigmatic phrases that God or the gods tell our ancestors are to be passed on to the future with no change. Very important to get it exactly right. Now, so far that's not very different from the actual circumstances of alleged holy books. But suppose that the phrases in question were phrases that we would recognize today that could not have been recognized then. Simple example: The Sun is a star. Now, nobody knew that, let's say, in the sixth century B.C., when the Jews were in the Babylonian exile and picked up the Babylonian cosmology from the principal astronomers of the time. Ancient Babylonian science is the cosmology that is still enshrined in the book of Genesis. Suppose instead the story was "Don't forget, the Sun is a star." Or "Don't forget, Mars is a rusty place with volcanoes. Mars, you know, that red star? That's a world. It has volcanoes, it's rusty, there are clouds, there used to be rivers. There aren't anymore. You'll understand this later. Trust me. Right now, don't forget."

Or, "A body in motion tends to remain in motion. Don't think that bodies have to be moved to keep going. It's just the opposite, really. So later on you'll understand that if you didn't have friction, a moving object would just keep moving." Now, we can imagine the patriarchs scratching their heads in bewilderment, but after all it's God telling them. So they would copy it down dutifully, and this would be one of the many mysteries in holy books that would then go on to the future until we could recognize the truth, realize that no one back then could possibly have figured it out, and therefore deduce the existence of God.

There are many cases that you can imagine like this. How about "Thou shalt not travel faster than light"? Okay, you might argue that nobody was at imminent risk of breaking that commandment. It would have been a curiosity: "We don't understand what that one's about, but all the others we abide by." Or "There are no privileged frames of reference." Or how about some equations?

Maxwell's laws in Egyptian hieroglyphics or ancient Chinese characters or ancient Hebrew. And all the terms are defined: "This is the electric field, this is the magnetic field." We don't know what those are, but we'll just copy them down, and then later, sure enough, it's Maxwell's laws or the Schrodinger equation. Anything like that would have been possible had God existed and had God wanted us to have evidence of His existence. Or in biology. How about, "Two strands entwined is the secret of life"? You may say that the Greeks were onto that because of the caduceus. You know, in the American army all the physicians wore the caduceus on their lapels, and various medical insurance schemes also use it. And it is connected with, if not the existence of life, at least saving it. But there are very few people who use this to say that the correct religion is the religion of the ancient Greeks, because they had the one symbol that survives critical scrutiny later on.

This business of proofs of God, had God wished to give us some, need not be restricted to this somewhat questionable method of making enigmatic statements to ancient sages and hoping they would survive. God could have engraved the Ten Commandments on the Moon. Large. Ten kilometers across per commandment. And nobody could see it from the Earth but then one day large telescopes would be invented or spacecraft would approach the Moon, and there it would be, engraved on the lunar surface. People would say, "How could that have gotten there?" And then there would be various hypotheses, most of which would be extremely interesting.

Or why not a hundred-kilometer crucifix in Earth orbit? God could certainly do that. Right? Certainly, create the universe? A simple thing like putting a crucifix in Earth orbit? Perfectly possible. Why didn't God do things of that sort? Or, put another way, why should God be so clear in the Bible and so obscure in the world?

I think this is a serious issue. If we believe, as most of the great theologians hold, that religious truth occurs only when there is a convergence between our knowledge of the natural world and revelation, why is it that this convergence is so feeble when it could easily have been so robust?

So, to conclude, I would like to quote from Protagoras in the fifth century B.C., the opening lines of his *Essay on the Gods*:

About the gods I have no means of knowing either that they exist or that they do not exist or what they are to look at. Many things prevent my knowing. Among others, the fact that they are never seen.

30

From *Roger's Version*

JOHN UPDIKE

This great American writer is as far as I know not an atheist, but he has the novelist's ability to put an admirable argument into the mouth of an unsympathetic character. Here, Kriegman deals with a frequently heard cocktail-party argument about the supposedly marvelous contingencies that make our existence possible in the first place. (We shall be returning to this point in less literary and less vernacular forms.)

"You go, sweetheart. O.K., young fella, hit me with those theories of yours."

To Dale at the moment these theories are as hatefully irrelevant and obscure as the exact words being exchanged in the cheerful cacophony of these many rooms of mine, where the word "Bitburg" keeps sounding like a bird chirp. Esther's closeness, and the ambiguity of their conversation, have tantalized him; his renewed glimpse and scent of the woman-lover, that radiant animal who waits crouching at the head of the stairs, at the end of all these crooked, noisy, obstructed social corridors, have left him dazed. His mind aches like an overexercised body. Yet he politely offers, as on the other side of the world priests peddle candles in the clamor of the weary holy places, the cosmic arguments: the hugely long odds against the big bang's having worked out so well, the horizon, smoothness, and flatness problems, the incredible necessary precision of the weak- and strong-force constants, not to mention that of the gravitational-coupling constant and the neutron mass, were any of which different by even a few ten-thousandths the universe would have been too explosive or diffuse, too short-lived or too utterly homogenous to contain galaxies, stars, planets, life, and Man.

Kriegman hears all this out with bursts of rapid nodding that bounce his chins on the knot of his necktie and wag the blossoms of the azalea garland he still wears. As if better to understand, he has put on large squarish horn-rims, trifocals; behind their lenses, between sips from his flexible plastic glass of white wine (Almaden Mountain Rhine, $8.87 per three-liter jug at Boulevard Bottle), his small eyes jump and change size as they jiggle among the three levels of focal length. "Well," he says at last, smiling like a man who even as he talks is listening to a background music with sentimental associations, "no-body denies the big bang has a few wrinkles we don't comprehend yet, we may never comprehend for that matter; for example, I was reading the other day that even the oldest star clusters show traces of the heavy elements, which is strange because there's no older generation of stars to have cooked them up and as you know the particle mechanics of the big bang could only have sup-plied helium and hydrogen, right?"

Dale wonders if he's supposed to say, "Right." He foresees that he will not have to say very much.

"Listen, there's always going to be wrinkles," Kriegman is telling him with a fatherly gruffness. "This primal fireball et cetera, and all this field theory in those first fractions of a second, we're talking about virtually incomprehensible events, ridiculously long ago. These astrophysicists are just whistling 'Dixie' three-quarters of the time."

"Right," Dale says. "That's what I say."

"Yeah, but no need to go all obscurantist either. Let me give you a homework assignment. Want a homework assignment?"

Dale nods, feeling weak, with a child's grateful weakness when he is told he is sick and must be put to bed.

"Look up in *Sky and Telescope,* one of last summer's issues I think it was, a hel-luva funny piece in this connection they reprinted from some book in which a bunch of rotifers—you know what rotifers are, don't you?—microscopic aquatic doohickeys with an anterior retractile disc of cilia that makes them look like their heads are spinning—of course they aren't really, any more than owls can turn their heads clear around, it just gives that impression—*anyway,* a bunch of these rotifers are imagined in learned conversation concerning why their puddle had to be exactly the way it was—temperature, alkalinity, mud at the bottom sheltering methane-producing bacteria, all the rest of it—it was clever as hell like I said—and from the fact that if any of these things were even a little bit differ-ent—if the heat necessary to vaporize water was any lower, for example, or the freezing temperature of water any higher—this Little Puddlian Philosophical Society, I think it was called, but you can check that when you look it up, de-duced that the whole operation was providential and obviously the universe ex-isted to produce their little puddle and *them!* That's more or less what you're trying to tell me, young fella, except you ain't no rotifer!"

Kriegman's constant benign smile widens into an audible chuckle. His lips are curious in being the exact same shade of swarthiness as his face, like muscles in a sepia anatomy print. As he raises his glass to these exemplary lips Dale in-tervenes with "I think, sir—"

"Fuck the 'sir' stuff. Name's Myron. Not Ron, mind you. *Myron.*"

"I think it's a little more than that, what I'm trying to say; the puddle analogy is as if the anthropic principle were being argued from the Earth as opposed to the other planets, which of course we can now see, if we ever doubted it, aren't suitable for life. In that sense, yes, we're here because we're here. But in the case of the universe, where you have only one, why should, say, the observed recessional velocity so exactly equal the necessary escape velocity?"

"How do you know there's only one universe? There might be zillions. There's no logical reason to say the universe we can observe is the only one."

"I know there's no logical reason—"

"Are we talking logic or not? Don't start getting all intuitive and subjective on me, my pal, because I'm pretty much a pragmatist myself on some scores. If it helps you through the night to believe the moon is green cheese—"

"I don't—"

"Don't believe it is? Good for you. I don't either. Those rocks they brought back didn't test out as green cheese. But my daughter Florence does; some zonked-out punk with purple hair tells her it is when she's as stoned as he is. She thinks she's a Tibetan Buddhist, except on weekends. Her sister Miriam talks about joining some Sufi commune over in New York State. I don't let it get to me, it's their lives. But you, if I size you up right, young fella, you're pulling my leg."

"I—"

"You really give a damn about cosmology, I'll tell you where the interesting work is being done right now: it's the explanation of how things popped up out of nothing. The picture's filling in from a number of directions, as clear as the hand in front of your face." He tipped his head back to see Dale better and his eyes seemed to multiply in the trifocals. "As you know," he said, "inside the Planck length and the Planck duration you have this space-time foam where the quantum fluctuations from matter to non-matter really have very little meaning, mathematically speaking. You have a Higgs field tunneling in a quantum fluctuation through the energy barrier in a false-vacuum state, and you get this bubble of broken symmetry that by negative pressure expands exponentially, and in a couple of microseconds you can have something go from next to nothing to the size and mass of the observable present universe. How about a drink? You look pretty dry, standing there."

Kriegman takes another plastic glass of white wine from the tray one of the Irish girls is reluctantly passing, and Dale shakes his head, refusing. His stomach has been nervous all this spring. Pastrami and milk don't mix.

My dear friend and neighbor Myron Kriegman takes a lusty swallow, licks his smiling lips, and continues in his rapid rasping voice. "O.K.; still, you say, you have to begin with *something* before you have a Higgs field; how do you get to almost nothing from *absolutely* nothing? Well, the answer turns out to be good old simple geometry. You're a mathematician, you'll dig this. What do we know about the simplest structures yet, the quarks? We know—come on, fella, *think.*"

Dale gropes. The party noise has increased, a corner high in his stomach hurts, Esther is laughing on the other side of the living room, beneath the knob-and-spindle header of the archway, exhaling smoke in a plume, her little face tipped back jauntily. "They come in colors and flavors," he says, "and carry positive or negative charges in increments of a third—"

Kriegman pounces: "You've got it! They invariably occur in threes, and cannot be pried apart. Now what does that suggest to you? Think. Three things, inseparable."

Father, Son, and Holy Ghost floats across Dale's field of inner vision but does not make it to his lips. Nor does Id, Ego, and Superego. Nor Kriegman's three daughters.

"The three dimensions of space!" Kriegman proclaims. "They can't be pried apart, either. Now, let's ask ourselves, what's so hot about three dimensions? Why don't we live in two, or four, or twenty-four?"

Odd that the man would mention those almost-magic, almost-revelatory numbers that Dale used to circle painstakingly in red; he now sees them to have been illusions, ripples in nothingness such as Kriegman is rhapsodizing about.

"You're not thinking. Because," the answer gleefully runs, "you need no more or less than three dimensions to make a *knot*, a knot that tightens on itself and won't pull apart, and that's what the ultimate particles are—knots in space-time. You can't make a knot in two dimensions because there's no over or under, and—here's the fascinating thing, see if you can picture it—you can make a ravelling in four dimensions but it isn't a knot, it won't hold, it will just pull apart, it won't per*sist*. Hey, you're going to ask me—I can see it in your face— what's this concept, persistence? For persistence you need time, right? And that's the key right there: without time you don't have anything, and if time was two-dimensional instead of one, you wouldn't have anything either, since you could turn around in it and there wouldn't be any causality. Without causality, there wouldn't be a universe, it would keep reversing itself. I know this stuff must be pretty elementary to you, I can see from the way you keep looking over my shoulder."

"No, I just—"

"If you've changed your mind about wanting a drink, it's not Esther's going to get it for you, you should ask one of the girls."

Dale blushes, and tries to focus on this tireless exposition, though he feels like a knot in four dimensions, unravelling. "I beg your pardon," he says, "how did you say we get from nothing to something?"

Kriegman lightly pats himself on the top of his head to make sure the garland is still in place. "O.K. Good question. I was just filling in the geometry so you can see the necessity behind space-time as it is and don't go getting all teleological on me. A lesser number of spatial dimensions, it just so happens, couldn't provide enough juxtapositions to get molecules of any complexity, let alone, say, brain cells. More than four, which is what you have with space-time, the complexity increases but not significantly: four is plenty, sufficient. O.K.?"

Dale nods, thinking of Esther and myself, himself and Verna. Juxtapositions.

"So," says Kriegman. "Imagine nothing, a total vacuum. But wait! There's something in it! Points, potential geometry. A kind of dust of structureless points. Or, if that's too woolly for you, try 'a Borel set of points not yet assembled into a manifold of any particular dimensionality.' Think of this dust as swirling; since there's no dimension yet, no nearness or farness, it's not exactly swirling as you and I know swirling but, anyway, some of them blow into straight lines and then vanish, because there's nothing to hold the structure. Same thing if they happen, by chance—all this is chance, blind chance it has to be, Jesus"—Kriegman is shrinking, growing stooped; his chins are melting more solidly into his chest; he bobs like a man being given repeated blows on the back of his head—"if they configure into two dimensions, into three, even into four where the fourth isn't time; they all vanish, just accidents in this dust of points, nothing could be said to exist, until even the word 'until' is deceptive, implying duration, which doesn't exist yet—until bingo! Space-time. Three spatial dimensions, plus time. It knots. It freezes. The seed of the universe has come into being. Out of nothing. Out of nothing and brute geometry, laws that can't be otherwise, nobody handed them to Moses, nobody had to. Once you've got that seed, that little itty-bitty mustard seed—ka-*boom*! Big Bang is right around the corner."

"But—" Dale is awed not so much by what this man says as by his fervor, the light of faith in his little tripartite spectacles, the tan monotone of his face and its cascading folds, his receding springy hair, his thick eyebrows thrust outward and up like tiny rhinoceros horns. This man is living, he is on top of his life, life is no burden to him. Dale feels crushed beneath his beady, shuttling, joyful, and unembarrassed gaze. "But," he weakly argues, " 'dust of points,' 'freezes,' 'seed'—this is all metaphor."

"What isn't?" Kriegman says. "Like Plato says, shadows at the back of the cave. Still, you can't quit on reason; next thing you'll get somebody like Hitler or Bonzo's pal running things. Look. You know computers. Think binary. When matter meets antimatter, both vanish, into pure energy. But both existed; I mean, there was a condition we'll call 'existence.' Think of one and minus one. Together they add up to zero, nothing, *nada, niente,* right? Picture them together, then picture them *separating*—peeling apart." He hands Dale his drink and demonstrates separating with his thick hairy hands palm to palm, then gliding upward and apart. "Get it?" He makes two fists at the level of his shoulders. "Now you have something, you have *two* somethings, where once you had nothing."

"But in the binary system," Dale points out, handing back the squeezable glass, "the alternative to one isn't minus one, it's zero. That's the beauty of it, mechanically."

"O.K. Gotcha. You're asking me, What's this minus one? I'll tell you. It's a *plus one moving backward in time.* This is all in the space-time foam, inside the Planck duration, don't forget. The dust of points gives birth to time, and time gives birth to the dust of points. Elegant, huh? It *has* to be. It's blind chance, plus pure math. They're proving it, every day. Astronomy, particle physics, it's all coming together. Relax into it, young fella. It feels great. Space-time foam.'"

Kriegman is joking; Dale prefers him zealous, evangelical on behalf of nonbelief. Esther has vanished from the archway. New guests keep arriving: Noreen Davis, the black receptionist who so smilingly gave him those forms seven months ago, with her bald co-worker in the Divinity School front office, and somebody who looks like Amy Eubank but can't be, his recognition apparatus must be out of whack. He masochistically asks Kriegman, "How about the origin of life? Those odds are pretty impossible, too. I mean, to get a self-replicating organism with its own energy system."

Kriegman snorts; he twists his face downward as if suddenly very shy; his whole body beneath its garland, in its dirty corduroy jacket with patched elbows and loose buttons, appears to melt and then to straighten again into a bearing almost military. "Now that just happens to be right up my alley," he tells Dale. "That other stuff was just glorified bullshit, way out of my field, I don't know what the hell a Borel set of points are. But I happen to know *exactly* how life arose; it's brand-new news, at least to the average layman like yourself. Clay. Clay is the answer. Crystal formation in fine clays provided the template, the scaffolding, for the organic compounds and the primitive forms of life. All life did, you see, was take over the phenotype that crystalline clays had evolved on their own, the genetic pass-down factor being entirely controlled by the crystal growth and epitaxy, and the mutation factor deriving from crystal defects, which supply, you don't need me to tell you, the stable alternative configurations you need for information storage. So, you're going to ask, where's the evolution? Picture the pore space of a sandstone, young fella. Every rainstorm, all sorts of mineral solutions are percolating through. Various types of replicating crystals are present, each reproducing its characteristic defects. Some fit together so tightly they form an impervious plug: this is no good. Others are so loose they're washed away when the rains come: this is no good either. But a third type both hangs in there and lets the geochemical solutions, let's even call them nutrients, wash through: this is good. This type of crystal multiplies and grows. It *grows*. Now in that sandstone pore you have a sticky, permeable paste that replicates itself. You have a prototype of life." Kriegman takes a long swallow of my Almaden and smacks his lips. A half-empty glass sits abandoned on the walnut end table beside the red settee, and my beloved neighbor deftly swaps it with his own, emptied glass.

"But—" Dale says, expecting to be interrupted. "But, you're going to say, how about us? How were the organic molecules introduced? And why? Well, not to get too technical, some of the amino acids, di- and tricarboxylic acids, make some metal ions, like aluminum, more soluble. This gives us a proto-enzyme. Others, like the polyphosphates, are especially adhesive, which, like I say, has survival value in this prezoic world we're trying to picture. Heterocyclic bases like adenine have a tendency to stick *between* the layers of clay; pretty soon, relatively speaking, you're going to get some RNA-like polymer, with its negatively charged backbone, interacting with the edges of clay particles, which tend to bear a positive charge. *Then*—listen, I know I'm boring the pants off you, I can see from your eyes you're dying to mix it up with somebody over my shoulder, maybe one of my girls. Miriam's the one you might take a shine to, if you don't mind a little Sufi propaganda; it's the no-alcohol part of it that I couldn't hack. Then, as I was saying, once you've got something like RNA in *not* the primordial soup this time—nobody in the know ever was too comfortable with that crackbrained theory: too—what's the word?—soupy—but a nice crisp paste of clay genes, organic replication is right around the corner, first as a subsystem, a kind of optional extra parallel with the crystal growth, and then taking over with that gene swap I mentioned earlier, and the clay genes falling away, since the organic molecules, mostly carbon, can do the job better, once they're established. Believe me, pal, it fills a lot of theoretical holes. Nothing to matter, dead matter to life, smooth as silk. God? Forget the old bluffer."

31

Conclusions and Implications

From *The Miracle of Theism: Arguments for and Against the Existence of God*

J. L. MACKIE

For some reason, many of the arguments about Church and State, and about divine will versus natural selection, have taken place at Oxford University. If Shelley or Huxley had known that J. L. Mackie (of Shelley's own college) would be intervening in this old dispute in the late twentieth century, they could have relaxed in the knowledge that a brilliant philosopher had laid waste to the enemy camp.

(a) The Challenge of Nihilism

We may approach our conclusion by considering Hans Küng's massive work, *Does God Exist?*[1] Subtitled "An Answer for Today," this book not only brings together many lines of thought that bear upon this question, but also sets out to interpret our whole present moral and intellectual situation. It displays a fantastic wealth of learning; it is also extremely diffuse. Time and again after raising an issue Küng will slightly change the subject, and often when we need an argument he gives us a quotation, a report of the views of yet another thinker, or even a fragment of biography. I think he is also unduly concerned with contemporary relevance, and is liable to tell us that some statement or argument is out of date, when all that matters is whether

---

1. H. Küng, *Does God Exist?* (Collins, London, 1980; first published in German as *Existiert Gott?* by Piper-Verlag, Munich, 1978).

it is true or false, sound or unsound. Nevertheless, as we shall find, there is a main connecting thread of argument, and his final answer, at least, is explicit (p. 702):

> After the difficult passage through the history of the modern age from the time of Descartes and Pascal, Kant and Hegel, considering in detail the objections raised in the critique of religion by Feuerbach, Marx and Freud, seriously confronting Nietzsche's nihilism, seeking the reason for our fundamental trust and the answer in trust in God, in comparing finally the alternatives of the Eastern religions, entering also into the question "Who is God?" and of the God of Israel and of Jesus Christ: after all this, it will be understood why the question "Does God exist?" can now be answered by a clear, convinced Yes, justifiable at the bar of critical reason.

However, the substance of his discussion is far less satisfactory. One crucial question is whether his final "Yes" is to the god of traditional theism or to some "replacement for God"; but the answer to this question is far from clear. For example, in his *Interim Results II: Theses on secularity and historicity of God* we find this (pp. 185–186):

> God is not a supramundane being above the clouds, in the physical heaven. The naive, anthropomorphic idea is obsolete . . . For man's being and action, this means that God is not an almighty, absolute ruler exercising unlimited power just as he chooses over world and man.
>
> God is not an extramundane being, beyond the stars, in the metaphysical heaven. The rationalistic-deistic idea is obsolete . . . For man's being and action, this means that God is not now—so to speak—a constitutionally reigning monarch who is bound, for his part, by a constitution based on natural and moral law and who has largely retired from the concrete life of the world and man.
>
> God is in this world, and this world is in God. There must be a uniform understanding of reality. God is not only a (supreme) finite . . . alongside finite things. He is in fact the infinite in the finite, transcendence in immanence, the absolute in the relative. It is precisely as the absolute that God can enter into a relationship with the world of man . . . God is therefore the absolute who includes and creates relativity, who, precisely as free, makes possible and actualizes relationship: God as the absolute-relative, here-hereafter, transcendent-immanent, all-embracing and all-permeating most real reality in the heart of things, in man, in the history of mankind, in the world . . . For man's being and action, this means that God is the close-distant, secular-nonsecular God, who precisely as sustaining, upholding us in all life and movement, failure and falling, is also always present and encompassing us.

And, after rejecting both the "Greek-metaphysical" and the "medieval-meta-physical" concepts of God, he adds (p. 188):

God is the living God, always the selfsame, dynamically actual and continu-ally active in history. Precisely as the eternally perfect, he is free to seize the "possibility" of becoming historical. . . . For man's being and action, this means that God is the living God who in all his indisposability and freedom knows and loves man, acts, moves, and attracts in man's history.

Later, for comparison with Eastern religions, he reports and seems to endorse "the Western tradition of a negative theology from Pseudo-Dionysius to Hei-degger": (pp. 601–602):

God cannot be grasped in any concept, cannot be fully expressed in any state-ment, cannot be defined in any definition: he is the incomprehensible, inex-pressible, indefinable.
    Neither does the concept of being embrace him . . . he is not an existent: he transcends everything . . . but . . . he is not outside all that is; inherent in the world and man, he determines their being from within . . .
    In God therefore transcendence and immanence coincide . . . Before God, all talk emerges from listening silence and leads to speaking silence.

Later again, in discussing "the God of the Bible," he says (p. 632):

God is not a person as man is a person. The all-embracing and all-penetrating is never an object that man can view from a distance in order to make state-ments about it. The primal ground, primal support and primal goal of all real-ity . . . is not an individual person among other persons, is not a superman or superego.

But also (p. 633):

A God who founds personality cannot himself be nonpersonal . . . God is not neuter, not an "it," but a God of men . . . He is spirit in creative freedom, the primordial identity of justice and love, one who faces me as founding and em-bracing all interhuman personality. . . . It will be better to call the most real re-ality not personal or impersonal but . . . transpersonal or suprapersonal.

But, despite all this, Küng also accepts in some sense the God of the Bible who, he says, is wholly and entirely essentially a "*God with a human face*" (p. 666). It is "overhasty" to dissociate the God of the philosophers from the God of the Bible, but also "superficial" simply to harmonize them. Rather, we should "*see the rela-tionship in a truly dialectical way. In the God of the Bible, the God of the philosophers is the best, threefold sense of the Hegelian term* "sublated" (aufgehoben)—at one and the same time affirmed, negated, and transcended." What is more, he "venture[s] without hesitation to declare: *Credo in Jesum Christum, filium Dei unigenitum*" (I believe in Jesus Christ, the only-begotten son of God) and "can confidently say even now: *Credo in Spiritum Sanctum*" (I believe in the Holy Spirit) (pp. 688, 699). That is, for all the contrary appearances, he affirms his own orthodoxy.

Küng is obviously fond of having it all ways at once. This is further illustrated by his remarks about miracles (pp. 650–651). Miracles recorded in the Bible "cannot be proved historically to be violations of the laws of nature"; a miracle is merely "everything that arouses man's wonder," not necessarily a divine intervention violating natural law. The miracle stories are "lighthearted popular narratives intended to provoke admiring faith." (If so, we may comment, they have no tendency to support any kind of supernaturalism or theism.) Yet "no one who links belief in God with miracles is to be disturbed in his religious feelings. The sole aim here is to provide a helpful answer to modern man for whom miracles are a hindrance to his belief in God." That is, if your belief in God is supported by miracles, Küng will endorse them for you; but if you find them an obstacle to belief, he will explain them away! Similarly he quotes with approval Bultmann's remark: "By faith I can understand an idea or a decision as a divine inspiration, without detaching the idea or decision from its link with its psychological justification" (p. 653).

One main strand in Küng's thinking brings him close to Hume's Demea, who stands for an infinite and incomprehensible god against the anthropomorphism of Cleanthes. But then we should recall how Hume uses Demea's view to prepare the way for Philo's skepticism. A god as indescribable and indeterminate as the one Küng seems to offer provides no purchase for reasoning, nothing of which argument can take hold in order to support the thesis that such a god exists.

Nevertheless, Küng claims to have given an argument. As we saw, he says that his "Yes" is "justifiable at the bar of critical reason." Against such writers as Norman Malcolm and D. Z. Phillips, he says firmly that "the question of truth cannot be avoided. And this truth can be tested by experience, as we shall see, by indirect verification through the experience of reality" (p. 505). And again (p. 528):

> No, theology cannot evade the demands for confirmation of belief in God: *Not a blind, but a* justifiable belief: *a person should not be abused, but convinced by arguments, so that he can make a responsible decision of faith. Not a belief devoid of reality, but a belief related to reality.*

Part of his case consists of his replies to the various arguments for atheism, essentially various proposed natural histories of religion. As we saw there, despite the weaknesses of some oversimplified theories, a satisfactory natural history of religion can be outlined. Küng's criticisms come in the end to no more than what we have conceded and stressed, that such an explanation of religious beliefs is not a primary argument against their truth. He still needs a positive argument for theism; and indeed he tries to give one.

He concedes (p. 533) that "There is no direct experience of God." Equally he explicitly rejects (though for inadequately stated reasons) the cosmological, teleological, and ontological proofs (pp. 534–535). But he says that though "the *probative character of the proofs of God is finished* today," yet their "non-demonstrable content" remains important. For the ontological proof, he offers only the (deplorable) suggestion that it should be "understood less as a proof than as an expression of trusting faith"; but, as we shall see, he really uses the cosmological and teleological arguments in an altered form—indeed, in a form that has some resemblance to Swinburne's, in that he proposes that "belief in God is to be verified but not proved" (p. 536). Küng, however, combines this with echoes both of the moral proofs and of the will to believe: "*an inductive lead does not seem impossible, attempting to throw light on the experience of uncertain reality, which is accessible to each and everyone, in order thus—as it were, by way of 'practical reason,' of the 'ought,' or (better) of the 'whole man'—to confront man as thinking and acting with a rationally justifiable decision that goes beyond pure reason and demands the whole person.*" Since his argument thus brings together several different strands, we may be able to use discussion of it to introduce the fulfillment of the undertaking . . . not merely to examine separately the various arguments for the existence of a god, but also to consider their combined effect, and to weigh them together against the various arguments on the other side, before reaching our final conclusion. This conclusion will be reached in section (b) below.

For Küng the question is not whether we can or cannot advance from an already established knowledge of the natural world, or of consciousness, or of morality, to further, specifically theistic, hypotheses or conclusions. His strategy is rather to argue that in present day thought rationality, both speculative and practical, is threatened along with theism by a pervasive tendency to nihilism. This nihilism, of which he finds the most powerful exponent in Nietzsche, is summed up as the denial of the three classical transcendentals: there is no unity, no truth, no goodness. Man deludes himself in thinking he has found any totality, system, or organization in events; he has sought a meaning in events that is not there; there is no absolute nature of things nor a "thing-in-itself"; the world is valueless and purposeless. Nihilism presents itself "as insight into the nothingness, contradictoriness, meaninglessness, worthlessness, of reality" (p. 421).

Küng insists that "*The thoroughgoing uncertainty of reality itself makes nihilism possible, whether in practical life . . . or in philosophical or unphilosophical reflection.*" Moreover, it is irrefutable: "*There is no rationally conclusive argument against the possibility of nihilism. It is indeed at least possible that this human life, in the last resort, is meaningless, that chance, blind fate, chaos, absurdity and illusion rule the world*"

(p. 423). On the other hand, nihilism is not provable. It is not *a priori* impossible that *"in the last resort, everything is nevertheless identical, meaningful, valuable, real"* (p. 424). Consequently the basic question is, "Can nihilism be overcome, and, if so, how?" (p. 425).

The fundamental alternative, Küng says, is between trust and mistrust, "in which I stake myself without security or guarantee . . . either I regard reality . . . as trustworthy and reliable—or not"—a choice which he explicitly compares with Pascal's wager (p. 438). Fundamental trust, he adds, is natural to man, it makes us "open to reality," and *The Yes can be consistently maintained in practice,"* whereas the opposite of each of these holds for fundamental distrust (pp. 443–446). There is a *"way of critical rationality"* which is '*a middle way between an irrational 'uncritical dogmatism' and a 'critical rationalism' that also, in the last resort, rests on irrational foundations"*; it is a *"completely reasonable risk, which, however, always remains a risk"* (p. 450).

So far so good, though Küng has rather exaggerated the threat. That there is *some* reality is beyond doubt. The extreme of nihilism would be to deny that reality is discoverable or understandable; but there is no serious case for this denial. Küng differentiates the critical rationality which he defends from the "critical rationalism" which he rejects (and which he finds, perhaps mistakenly, in Karl Popper and Hans Albert), on the ground that the latter dispenses, as the former does not, with any critical examination of the foundations of our knowledge and so involves an irrational faith in reason. We can agree that nothing is to be exempt from criticism, not even the critical method itself, though of course not everything can be criticized at once: while we are examining any one issue, we must take various other things for granted. This precludes the attainment of certainty, and it should exclude the search for certainty. But there is no great mystery about this, nor any great modernity. Some of the essential points . . . were made by William James in defence of a fallibilist, experimental, but optimistic and risk-taking empiricism. As James says, a risk which gives us our only chance of discovering the truth, or even approaching it, is indeed a reasonable risk.

Further, the assumption that there is some order, some regularity, to be found in the world—not necessarily strict causal determinism—both is a regulative principle which we can and do use in developing and testing other hypotheses and also is itself a hypothesis of a very broad kind, which in turn is open to testing and confirmation.[2] This seems to be the main thing that Küng means by "unity," so this too is covered by "critical rationality," that is, by a fallibilistic but optimistic empiricism. Such an approach, whatever name we give it, can thus be

---

2. See the Appendix to *The Cement of the Universe* (see n. 2 to Chapter 1, p. 20, above) and "A Defence of Induction" (see n. 9 to Chapter 8, p. 148, above).

seen to be reasonable in itself, and not in need of any further justification or support.

The reply to nihilism about unity and truth is therefore straightforward, and we can agree with the substance of what Küng says about this. His reply to nihilism about goodness or value is trickier and more controversial. He quotes with approval the view of H. Sachsse that there is a present and pressing need for the development of "relevant and practical norms" (p. 466). He concedes that *Today less than ever can we call down from heaven ready-made solutions,* or deduce them theologically from an immutable universal essential nature of man." He concedes, too, that "There is in fact what Nietzsche called a 'genealogy of morals'"—that is, that concrete existing ethical systems have been developed by a socio-historical process—and that today we have to *work out 'on earth' discriminating solutions* for all the difficult problems. We are responsible for our morality" (p. 469). All this is strikingly similar to the main theme of my *Ethics: Inventing Right and Wrong*[3]—and, what is more important, it is in itself an adequate *reply* to nihilism about value. But then Küng seems to slide to a very different thesis (p. 470):

> *Any acceptance of meaning, truth and rationality, of values and ideals . . . presupposes a* fundamental trust *in uncertain reality: by contrast with nihilism, an assent in principle to its fundamental identity, meaningfulness and value . . . Only if the reality of the world and man, as accepted in fundamental trust, is characterized by an ultimate identity, meaningfulness and value, can individual norms of genuinely human behavior and action be deduced in an appropriate way from this reality and—decisively—from the essential human needs, pressures and necessities . . .*

This is radically different. Now Küng is suggesting that we must after all postulate an *objective* value from which (along with the empirical facts of human needs, and so on) we might *deduce* specific norms. But this is an error, and in contrast with it we must hold fast to the thesis that value itself is a human and social product. This is not to deny, however, that there is an ethical variety of "fundamental trust" which is needed at the basis of our moral systems. We require, perhaps, a confident hope that we can find principles of co-operation in the midst of competition. This would be a generalization of the practical "precursive faith" of which William James speaks: only if people trust one another before each can be sure that the others are trustworthy will they have a chance of establishing effective cooperation.

There is, then, a reply to nihilism about goodness or value, which again can be seen to be reasonable in itself, and not in need of any further justification or

---

3. See n. 7 to Chapter 6, p. 115, above.

support. But it is significantly different from the reply that Küng gives. Or rather, he both suggests this reply and slides to a different one.

But where, we may ask, does God come into all this? With comic condescension, Küng allows that *"On the basis of fundamental trust, even an atheist can lead a genuinely human, that is, humane, and in this sense moral, life,"* and that *"Even atheists and agnostics are not necessarily nihilists, but can be humanists and moralists"* (p. 472). Nevertheless, he now makes the crucial step in the direction of theism: "It must now be obvious that the fundamental trust in the identity, meaningfulness and value of reality, which is the presupposition of human science and autonomous ethics, is justified in the last resort only if reality itself—of which man is also a part—is not groundless, unsupported and aimless" (p. 476).

No. This is not obvious at all. Indeed it is false, and Küng's own argument shows it to be false. The kind of fundamental trust that counters nihilism about truth and "unity," the "critical rationality" of which he speaks, is reasonable *in its own right* for the reasons he has given. And the same is true of the motives for the invention of value. There is no need to look for or postulate any "ground, support, or goal" for reality. The broad hypothesis that there is some order in the world is one which it is reasonable to adopt tentatively, but also to test; and it has been strongly confirmed by the inquiries which have (implicitly) tested it. Likewise, though the inventing of moral values has gone on mainly spontaneously, it is reasonable in the sense that it is only by having the attitudes which that invention expresses that we are able to live together without destroying one another. Each of these is defensible on its own: neither needs any further support.

But it is upon this utterly unwarranted step that Küng bases his further case for a god. He is seeking not, indeed, a demonstrative proof, but an "indirect verification," of God as the supposedly required primal ground, primal support, and primal goal of all reality.

He first asserts that *"If God exists, then the grounding reality is not ultimately groundless . . . the supporting reality is not ultimately unsupported . . . evolving reality is not ultimately without aim . . . and reality suspended between being and not being is not ultimately under suspicion of being a void."* He adds that while this hypothesis opposes nihilism, it can also explain the *appearance of* nihilism: reality appears to be ultimately groundless, unsupported, and aimless "Because uncertain reality is itself *not God."* Similarly, the hypothesis that God exists can give ultimate meaning and hope to one's own life; but it can also explain the *appearance* of meaninglessness and emptiness here "Because man *is not God"* (pp. 566–568).

By contrast, he thinks, atheism would imply an ultimately unjustified fundamental trust in reality, and therefore the danger of "the possible disunion, meaninglessness, worthlessness, hollowness of reality as a whole" (p. 571).

Küng concludes that *"Affirmation of God implies an* ultimately justified *fundamental trust in reality. If someone affirms God, he knows why he can trust reality."* Hence "there is no stalemate between belief in God and atheism" (p. 572). Though this affirmation "rests, in the last resort, on a *decision"* (p. 569), because there is no conclusive argument either for or against it, yet "trust in God is by no means ir-rational. . . I know . . . *by the very fact* of doing this, that I am doing the right thing . . . what cannot be proved *in advance* I experience *in the accomplishment,"* and this provides *"a fundamental certainty."* Thus understood, *"Belief in God . . . is a matter not only of human reason but of the whole concrete, living man"* (pp. 573–574).

I have summarized Küng's argument as far as possible in his own words, be-cause a paraphrase would not only detract from its eloquence but also risk dis-torting a view that contains so many complexities and contrasts. My criticisms must, and can, be briefer.

Küng's final step seems to claim that the very act of believing in God is self-verifying; but he gives no reason at all for this claim. The act may carry with it a conviction of certainty: the relief of ceasing to doubt is pleasantly reassuring. But this is purely subjective: to rely on this would be merely another form of the assumption that there is a kind of experience which guarantees the objective va-lidity of its content or intentional object which Küng himself has rightly dis-missed (p. 533). Alternatively, the suggestion may be that in postulating a god one is postulating *that which grounds both itself and everything else.* But to claim that the very content of this postulation gives it objective certainty is to employ yet again the ontological argument, and Küng has rightly dismissed this too (pp. 533, 535).

If we delete this unsound final step, Küng's argument turns essentially upon the confirming of a hypothesis, and in particular upon the relative confirma-tion of the god-hypothesis as against that of an objective natural world (in-cluding human beings) which has no further ground or support or goal. As for the explanation of the *appearance of* nihilism, the god-hypothesis is in exactly the same position as its naturalistic rival. The one says that though there is a god, this god is not obvious, and "uncertain reality" is not this god, that is, is not its own primal ground, support, or goal; the other says simply that there is no such primal ground, support, or goal. In either case the lack of any obvious primal ground leaves room for nihilism. The two rival hypotheses are equal also in their explanations of the *appearance* of meaninglessness in human life. But though they are equally able to explain the appearance of nihilism, the god-hypothesis is the less economical. Its merits, if any, must be due to the other aspect, to its allegedly providing reality with a ground, support, and goal, and man with an objectively valid aim. But Küng has said nothing to explain *how* the god-hypothesis is supposed to do this. Indeed, the Demea-like indeter-minacy of his account of God would make it hard for him to do so. But what he hints at is, in fact, a set of suggestions which we have already explicitly stated and examined, especially in Swinburne's inductive versions of the cos-mological and design arguments, in Leslie's extreme axiarchism. To avoid as-suming "the groundlessness and instability of reality as a whole," Küng suggests that it may be reasonable to assume "a cause of all causes"; and to avoid assuming the meaninglessness and aimlessness of reality as a whole it may be reasonable to assume "an end of ends" (pp. 534–535), or again "*a God who will bring to perfection the world and man*" (p. 657). "Believing in God as Finisher of the world means coolly and realistically—and even more, without succumbing to the violent benefactors of the people—to work for a better future, a better society, in peace, freedom and justice, and at the same time to know without illusions that this can always only be sought but never completely realized by man" (p. 659).

But the explanations at which Küng hints are completely undermined by the criticisms we have given of the specific arguments in Chapters 5, 6, 7, 8, and 13. As I have said, we have no empirical basis, in a knowledge of direct, unmediated, fulfilments of will, from which we might extrapolate to anything like Swinburne's personal explanation as a way of using a god to explain the world or its details. Nor, correspondingly, do we have any empirical basis for the axiarchist's suggestion that value as such may be intrinsically creative. Nor, again, could we find any ultimately plausible account of how moral values might rest upon or be created or sustained by a god. Still less do we need anything like a god to counter the supposed threat of aimlessness. Men are themselves purposive beings. In their own nature they unavoidably pursue aims and goals; they do not need these to be given them from outside. To be sure, their purposes are limited, specific, and above all conflicting: diverse strivings do not automatically resolve themselves into any grand harmonious everlasting Purpose. That is why there is a real and continuing task of inventing norms and principles through which we can achieve some rough approximation to harmony or at least contain within tolerable limits the inescapable conflicts of purpose.[4] We can welcome Küng's realistic appreciation of this task and his readiness to take part in it. But neither participation in this task, nor the generalization of William James's "precursive faith" which we may need to bring to it, depends in any way on a belief in "God as Finisher"; rather, their reasonability arises directly out of a human appreciation of the human situation, as Küng's own argument shows. Nor are the difficult details of this task made any easier by postulating any sort of god.

If the specific suggestions of personal explanation, creative value, and the various forms of the moral argument fail, we are left with the postulation of a god as merely *that which* somehow supplies a ground, support, or goal for reality. But to postulate an entity as *that which* does something gives us no real additional explanation. If we say, for example, that reality is supported because there is something that supports it, the alleged explanation merely repeats what was to be explained; at best, we have a place-holder for a real explanation. Moreover, even if this god-hypothesis did somehow explain the world or moral values or

---

4. Cf. Chapter 6 of *Hume's Moral Theory* (see no. 2 to Chapter 6, p. 106, above), and my "Cooperation, Competition, and Moral Philosophy," in *Cooperation and Competition in Animals and Man*, edited by A. Colman (Van Nostrand, London, forthcoming).

human purposes, we should face again the familiar objection: Why is this (un-certain) god not as much in need of further explanation or support as "uncer-tain reality"? To say that God is introduced by definition as that which explains itself, that which terminates the regress of explanation, is again empty and use-less; but any attempt to explain and justify the claim that he has such a special status leads us, as we have seen, to the concept which underlies the ontological proof....

Küng's strategy, as we have seen, is to incorporate the question of the exis-tence of a god within the wider question of how modern man is to meet the challenge of nihilism, and to suggest that the latter can be solved only by a deci-sion in favour of an affirmative answer to the former. But this is wrong. Ironi-cally, he has himself supplied all the materials for showing that the challenge of both intellectual and moral or practical nihilism can be met in purely human terms, by what Küng calls a "fundamental trust" which is reasonable in its own right—that is, equivalently, by a fallibilist empiricism on the intellectual side and on the practical side by the invention of value. The further postulation of a god, even as indeterminate and mysterious a god as Küng's, is a gratuitous addi-tion to this solution, an attempted underpinning which is as needless as it is incomprehensible.

(b) The Balance of Probabilities

We can now bring together the many different arguments for theism which we have discussed, and consider their combined effect. But some of them cannot be combined with one another. The thesis that there is a Berkeleian god is so dif-ferent from any view that adds a god, either immanent or transcendent (or both immanent and transcendent, like Küng's), to the ordinary material or spatio-temporal world, that arguments for the one cannot assist those for the other. There is a similar discrepancy between Swinburne's (or Cleanthes') explicitly personal god and the creative value proposed by extreme axiarchism, though Küng's god is perhaps so medially placed between these that he could share some arguments with each of them. Moreover, the ontological argument, in all its forms, has been shown to be simply unsound; it can contribute no weight at all to the case for theism. On the contrary, its failure does, as Kant said, though not exactly in the way that Kant thought, undermine the various forms of cos-mological argument: even if the concept of a being whose essence includes exis-tence is admissible, such a being would *not* exist in all logically possible worlds, and its existence in the actual world would not be *a priori* certain or self-explana-tory; it would not terminate the regress of explanation. But there is at least one interesting and important possibility of consilience, namely that which would bring together (1) reported miracles, (2) inductive versions of the design and consciousness arguments, picking out as "marks of design" both the fact that there are causal regularities at all and the fact that the fundamental natural laws and physical constants are such as to make possible the development of life and consciousness, (3) an inductive version of the cosmological argument, seeking an answer to the question "Why is there any world at all?" (4) the suggestion that there are objective moral values whose occurrence likewise calls for further explanation, and (5) the suggestion that some kinds of religious experience can be best understood as direct awareness of something supernatural. These various considerations might be held jointly to support the hypothesis that there is a personal or quasi-personal god.

In evaluating this possibility, we must note how in principle a hypothesis can be supported by the consilience of different considerations, each of which, on its own, leaves the balance of probabilities against that hypothesis. Suppose that there are several pieces of evidence, e_1, e_2 and e_3 each of which would fit in with a hypothesis h, but each of which, on its own, is explained with less initial improbability on some other grounds, say by g_1, g_2, and g_3 respectively. Yet if the improbability involved in postulating h is less than the *sum* of the improbabilities involved in the rival explanations g_1, g_2, and g_3, though it is greater than each of these improbabilities separately, the balance of probabilities when we take e_1, e_2 and e_3 together will favour the hypothesis h. It is important that it is just the one initial improbability of h that is weighed in turn against the improbabilities of g_1, g_2, g_3, and then against the sum of these.

But the supposed consilience of theistic arguments does not satisfy the requirements of this formal pattern. As we have seen, the first and fifth of these considerations are extremely weak: all the evidence that they can muster is easily explained in natural terms, without any improbabilities worth taking into account. Consciousness and the actual phenomena of morality and valuing as a human activity are explained without further improbabilities, given that the natural world is such as to allow life to evolve, so the only improbabilities to be scored against the naturalistic kind of explanation are whatever may be involved in there being causal regularities, the fundamental laws and physical constants being as they are, and there being any world at all. Against the rival theistic hypothesis we should have to score the (significant) improbability that if there were a god he (or it) would create a world with causal laws, and one with our specific causal laws and constants, but also the great improbability of there being a process of the unmediated fulfilment of will, and, besides, the basic improbability of there being a god at all. For while the naturalist had admittedly no reply to Leibniz's question "Why is there a world at all?" the theist, once deprived of the illusory support of the ontological argument, is equally embarrassed by the question "Why is there a god at all?" Whatever initial improbability there may be in the unexplained brute fact that there is a world, there is a far greater initial improbability in what the theist has to assert as the unexplained brute fact that there is a god capable of creating a world.

In the end, therefore, we can agree with what Laplace said about God: we have no need of that hypothesis. This conclusion can be reached by an examination precisely of the arguments advanced in favour of theism, without even bringing into play what have been regarded as the strongest considerations on the other side, the problem of evil and the various natural histories of religion. When these are thrown into the scales, the balance tilts still further against theism. Although we could not (in Chapter 9) rule out the possibility that some acceptable modification of traditional theism might enable it to accommodate the occurrence of evils, we saw that no sound solution of this sort has yet been offered; the extreme difficulty that theism has in reconciling *its own* doctrines with one another in this respect must tell heavily against it. Also, although the clear possibility of developing an adequate natural explanation of the origin, evolution, and persistence of religious belief is not a primary argument against theism, and could be brushed aside if there were any cogent positive case for the existence of a god, yet, since there is no such case, it helps to make the negative case still more conclusive. It removes the vague but obstinate feeling that where so many people have believed so firmly—and sometimes fervently—and where religious thought and organization have been so tenacious and so resilient "there must be something in it." We do not need to invoke the "higher causes" by which Machiavelli (with his tongue in his cheek) said that ecclesiastical principalities are upheld.[5] The occurrence, even the continuing occurrence, of theism is not, in Hume's phrase, a continued miracle which subverts all the principles of our understanding.

The balance of probabilities, therefore, comes out strongly against the existence of a god. Chapter 11 has shown that we cannot escape the implications of this result by making a voluntary faith intellectually respectable. The most that we could allow was James's experimental approach, and, as we saw, it would be very hard for this to yield a favourable result. In Chapter 12 we saw the failure of some popular attempts to free religion from the need to defend its traditional factual beliefs; and in Chapter 13 we considered, but rejected, some replacements for a god of the traditional sort. There is at any rate no easy way of defending religion once it is admitted that the literal, factual claim that there is a god cannot be rationally sustained.

(c) The Moral Consequences of Atheism

But some readers, I know, even some thoughtful and fairminded readers, will not be satisfied. I suspect that the most lasting obstacle to the acceptance of atheism is a lingering notion that such acceptance would be morally and practically disastrous. It may, therefore, be relevant to end with a brief survey of the moral consequences of atheism.

---

5. N. Machiavelli, *The Prince* (many editions), Chapter 11.

There are four main kinds of view about the general nature and status of morality. The first of these sees moral rules and principles, whatever other functions they may serve, as being essentially the commands or requirements of a god (or gods), backed up by the promise of rewards and the threat of penalties either in this life or in an afterlife. The second (Kantian, rationalist, or intuitionist) sees moral principles as objectively valid prescriptions, formulated or discovered by human reason or intellect, and autonomously authoritative, independently of any god; if someone who holds this view also believes that there is a god, he will see the goodness of this god as consisting in his exemplifying these independent principles. A third view is that which we considered at the end of Chapter 6, according to which there *are* objectively valid principles as the second view maintains, but they are in some way created and sustained in existence by a god. The fourth (Humean, sentimentalist, subjectivist, or naturalistic) view is that morality is essentially a human, social product, that moral concepts, principles, and practices have developed by some process of biological and social evolution. Their origin and persistence are due somehow to the fact that they enable human beings, whose natural situation includes a mixture of competitive and co operative forces, and a need for co-operation, to survive and nourish better, by limiting the competition and facilitating the co-operation. But morality is not, on this view, necessarily understood in this light by those who adhere to it: it is possible that its adherents should hold one of the other three views, and yet that a correct description, from the outside, of their thinking and conduct should be given by this naturalistic account.

Now if some adherent to a morality has held either the first or the third of these views, so that *he* has seen morality as essentially dependent upon some god, then it is indeed possible that if he then ceases to believe in that god his adherence to that morality will be undermined: the immediate moral consequences of *his* atheism may be deplorable. This is a good reason for not tying morality to religious teaching at a time when religious belief is itself fragile. The point is well made by Richard Robinson's story of a priest saying to a pair of well-behaved atheists, "I can't understand you boys; if I didn't believe in God I should be having a high old time."[6] But if either our second view (of an autonomous objective ethics) or our fourth (naturalist or sentimentalist) view is correct, there is no reason to suppose that such undermining will be either a lasting or a general effect of the decay of religious belief. Indeed, it is hardly even necessary that either of these views should be *correct*: it is enough that they are available to the atheist. But in particular if, as I have argued elsewhere, the

---

6. R. Robinson, *An Atheist's Values* (Oxford University Press, 1964; paperback Basil Blackwell, Oxford, 1975), p. 137. The story is no doubt apocryphal. This book as a whole gives a very full answer to the question of the moral consequences of atheism. References in the text to Robinson are to pages in this work.

fourth view is correct, then morality has a genuine causal source of its own.[7] It is basically a matter of feelings and attitudes, partly instinctive, developed by biological evolution, and partly acquired, developed by socio-historical evolution and passed on from generation to generation less by deliberate education than by the automatic transmission of cultural traits. Since it has such a source, quite independent of religion, it is certain to survive when religion decays.

However, this may seem to be too abstract, too *a priori*, an argument. Is there any better, more empirical, evidence about the contrasting moral consequences of theism and of atheism? The only simple answer to this question is that there is no simple answer. Neither theists nor atheists have any monopoly of either the vices or the virtues. Nor is any statistical survey likely to establish a clear causal tendency for religious belief, or the lack of it, to encourage either virtue or vice. This is partly because the determination of what is to count as virtue or as vice, or of the relative importance of particular virtues and vices, is itself relevantly controversial; this is one of the issues on which believers and non-believers are divided. Another reason is that there are indefinitely many degrees of belief and disbelief. But even if we confined our survey to an agreed core of virtues on the one hand and of vices on the other, and to unequivocal samples of theists and atheists, any statistical results would still be indecisive. For if there were, as I suspect there would then be, some positive correlation between atheism and virtue, this would still not establish a causal tendency for atheism as such to promote virtue. It could be too easily explained away by the fact that, other things being equal, there is likely to be a higher incidence of disbelief among the "wise and learned," for the reason hinted at by Hume in his essay on miracles.[8]

Since there is little prospect of reliable direct empirical evidence, we must fall back on some general considerations. What differences would it make to morality if there were, or if there were not, a god, and again if people associated, or did not associate, their morality with religious belief?

The unsatisfactory character of the first, divine command, view of morality was pointed out by Plato, whose objections have been echoed many times.[9] If moral values were constituted *wholly* by divine commands, so that goodness *consisted* in conformity to God's will, we could make no sense of the theist's own claims that God is good and that he seeks the good of his creation. However, it would be possible to hold coherently that while the goodness of some states of affairs—for example, of one sort of human life as contrasted with others—is independent of God's will, it is only his commands that supply the

---

7. See the works referred to in nn. 3 and 4 (pp. 246 and 250) above.

8. *Enquiry concerning Human Understanding*, Section 10; cf. Chapter 1 above.

9. Plato, *Euthyphro*. The exact force of "the Euthyphro dilemma" is considered in Chapter 10 of my *Ethics: Inventing Right and Wrong*.

prescriptive element in morality. Or they could be seen as supplying an additional prescriptive element. A religious morality might then be seen as imposing stronger obligations.

Both these variants, however, as Kant pointed out, tend to corrupt morality, replacing the characteristically moral motives—whether these are construed as a rational sense of duty and fairness, or as specific virtuous dispositions, or as generous, co-operative, and sympathetic feelings—by a purely selfish concern for the agent's own happiness, the desire to avoid divine punishments and to enjoy the rewards of God's favour, in this life or in an afterlife. This divine command view can also lead people to accept, as moral, requirements that have no discoverable connection—indeed, no connection at all—with human purposes or well-being, or with the well-being of any sentient creatures. That is, it can foster a tyrannical, irrational morality. Of course, if there were not only a benevolent god but also a reliable revelation of his will, then we might be able to get from it expert moral advice about difficult issues, where we could not discover for ourselves what are the best policies. But there is no such reliable revelation. Even a theist must see that the purported revelations, such as the Bible and the Koran, condemn themselves by enshrining rules which we must reject as narrow, out-dated, or barbarous. As Küng says, "We are responsible for our morality." More generally, tying morality to religious belief is liable to devalue it, not only by undermining it, temporarily, if the belief decays, but also by subordinating it to other concerns while the belief persists.

There is, indeed, a strain in religion that positively welcomes sin as a precondition for salvation. Jesus himself is reported as saying "I am not come to call the righteous, but sinners to repentance." Luther says that "God is the god of the humble, the miserable, the oppressed, and the desperate," and that "that pernicious and pestilent opinion of man's own righteousness . . . suffereth not God to come to his own natural and proper work." And William James reports (at second hand) an orthodox minister who said that Dr. Channing (the eminent Unitarian) "is excluded from the highest form of religious life by the extraordinary rectitude of his character."[10]

It is widely supposed that Christian morality is particularly admirable. Here it is important to distinguish between the original moral teachings of Jesus, so far as we can determine them, and later developments in the Christian tradition. Richard Robinson has examined the synoptic gospels (Matthew, Mark, and Luke) as the best evidence for Jesus's own teaching, and he finds in them five major precepts: "love God, believe in me, love man, be pure in heart, be humble." The reasons given for these precepts are "a plain matter of promises and

---

10. Matthew 9:13. The passage from Luther is quoted by James on pp. 244–245 of *The Varieties of Religious Experience* (see n. 1 to Chapter 10, p. 178, above) and the story about Dr. Channing in no. 1 on p. 466 of the same work.

threats": they are "that the kingdom of heaven is at hand," and that "those who obey these precepts will be rewarded in heaven, while those who disobey will have weeping and gnashing of teeth." Robinson notes that "Certain ideals that are prominent elsewhere are rather conspicuously absent from the synoptic gospels." These include beauty, truth, knowledge, and reason:

> As Jesus never recommends knowledge, so he never recommends the virtue that seeks and leads to knowledge, namely reason. On the contrary, he regards certain beliefs as in themselves sinful . . . whereas it is an essential part of the ideal of reason to hold that no belief can be morally wrong if reached in the attempt to believe truly. Jesus again and again demands faith; and by faith he means believing certain very improbable things without considering evidence or estimating probabilities; and that is contrary to reason. (p. 149)

Robinson adds:

> Jesus says nothing on any social question except divorce, and all ascriptions of any political doctrine to him are false. He does not pronounce about war, capital punishment, gambling, justice, the administration of law, the distribution of goods, socialism, equality of income, equality of sex, equality of colour, equality of opportunity, tyranny, freedom, slavery, self-determination, or contraception. There is nothing Christian about being for any of these things, nor about being against them, if we mean by "Christian" what Jesus taught according to the synoptic gospels.
>
>   The Jesus of the synoptic gospels says little on the subject of sex. He is against divorce. He speaks of adultery as a vice, and perhaps includes in adultery all extramarital intercourse. The story of the woman taken in adultery, which is of a synoptic character though it appears in texts of John, preaches a humane and forgiving attitude towards sexual errors. Jesus shows no trace of that dreadful hatred of sex as such which has disfigured the subsequent history of the Christian churches . . . (p. 149)

Robinson goes on to comment on the morality of the Bible:

> Newman said that when non-Christians read the Christian Bible "they are much struck with the high tone of its precepts" (Sermon on John xiii. 17). That is contrary to my experience. I shall never forget the first time I read the Old Testament after I had acquired the habit of independent judgment. I was horrified at its barbarity, and bewildered that it had been widely held up as a store of ideals. It seemed to describe a savage people, fierce and brutal, no more admirable than the worse of the savage cultures that anthropologists describe to us today, and a great deal less admirable than the gentler cultures they report.

Nor will Newman's words fit the impression made by the synoptic gospels. They are a beautiful and fascinating piece of literature; and they preach the great precept "love thy neighbour." But this precept is overshadowed in them both by the harsh unloving behaviour of the preacher, and by its absolute subordination to the unreasonable commands to love God and believe in Jesus. (pp. 150–151)

Robinson urges us to reject these commands and the associated values of piety, faith, and improvidence. He reminds us that "many of man's most terrible actions have been done out of piety, and that piety is responsible for our shameful wars of religion." He also characterizes the view that belief, or disbelief, can be sinful as a "blasphemy against reason." He says that we should accept the precept to love our neighbours, "extended as Jesus perhaps extended it to love of all humanity, and still further to love of all life, as he certainly did not extend it" (p. 152), and such consequential attitudes as generosity, gentleness, mercy, and the observance of the golden rule. However, we might well query (though Robinson does not) the precise command to love your neighbour *as yourself*. This seems unrealistically to prescribe a degree of altruism that is in general not humanly possible, and so to make of morality a fantasy rather than something that people can seriously try to practise and can ask of one another. Robinson does query the injunction to be pure in heart, and also the call for humility: it is better to make true estimates both of oneself and of others, and not lie about them, though in public "the right choice will usually be to refrain from drawing attention either to our superiorities or to our inferiorities" (pp. 153–154).

The later tradition of Christian ethics has tended to add to Jesus's teaching some deplorable elements, such as hostility to sex, and many more admirable ones, such as concern with justice and the other requirements for the nourishing of human life in society, and ideals of beauty, truth, knowledge, and (up to a point) reason. But it has in general retained the concern with salvation and an afterlife, and the view that disbelief, or even doubt, or criticism of belief, is sinful, with the resulting tendencies to the persecution of opponents—including, of course, the adherents of rival Christian sects and rival religions— the discouragement of discussion, hostility (even now in some places) to the teaching of well-confirmed scientific truths, like the theory of evolution, and the propagation of contrary errors, and the intellectual dishonesty of trying to suppress one's own well-founded doubts. Many people are shocked at the way in which the Unification Church ('the Moonies') entraps converts and enslaves their minds and emotions; but the same methods have been and are used by many more orthodox sects. Religion has, indeed, a remarkable ability to give vices the air of virtues, providing a sanctified outlet for some of the nastiest human motives. It is fashionable to ascribe the horrors of Nazism to an atheistic nationalism; but in fact the attitudes to the Jews which it expressed had long been established within the Christian tradition in Germany and elsewhere (sanctioned, for example, by Luther's writing[11]), and the Old Testament itself reports many atrocities as having been not merely approved but positively demanded by God and his spokesmen.[12] And while, following Robinson, I have spoken here particularly of Christian ethics, it is only too obvious that Islamic fundamentalism displays today, more clearly than Christianity has done recently, the worst aspects of religious morality. We do not need to go back in history to illustrate the dictum of Lucretius: *Tantum religio potuit suadere malorum* (So great are the evils that religion could prompt!)[13] By contrast, there is a long tradition of an essentially humanist morality, from Epicurus to John Stuart Mill and modern writers, including Richard Robinson himself, centred on the conditions for the flourishing of human life and stressing intellectual honesty, tolerance, free inquiry, and individual rights.

There are, then, some marked dangers in a distinctively religious morality. But they are dangers only, not inevitable consequences of associating morality with religion. We can echo, in reverse, Küng's concession: it is possible—for even a religious believer "to lead a genuinely human, that is humane, and in this sense moral life"; even theists are not necessarily narrow-minded dogmatists, intolerant persecutors, or propagators of timid credulity and a crudely calculating selfish version of morality itself. Even within Islam there have been thinkers who have tried to develop its humane and liberal tendencies, and to tone down its cruelty, intolerance, and its unfairness between the sexes, though at present their influence is in decline.

But are there no corresponding dangers in a distinctively non-religious morality? Admittedly, there are. As Robinson says, the Roman Catholic church is only "The second most intolerant and active body in the world today" (p. 216). Communist parties are expressly anti-religious, and profess an overriding concern with human welfare, but they are also intolerant, ruthless, and, once in power, they too make virtues of tyranny and persecution. And one must recognize that the Catholic church, despite its own illiberal tendencies, sometimes contributes significantly to the resistance to tyrannical states, whether communist or not. More generally, humanist moral thinking is prone either to illusions about necessary progress or to an over-optimistic voluntarism—that is, to assuming that "we" (whoever that may be) can make or remake the world as we would wish it to be, forgetting that the interplay of many different purposes is liable to result in the fulfillment of none of them.

---

11. E.g., *On the Jews and their Lies*, in Vol. 47 of Luther's *Works*, edited by H. T. Lehman (Fortress Press, Philadelphia, 1971), pp. 121–306, recommends the burning of synagogues and of the Jews' houses, confiscation of their books, forbidding of worship and teaching, or alternatively expulsion of the Jews from the country.

12. E.g. Joshua 8, 10, and 11; 1 Samuel 15.

13. *De Rerum Natura*, Book I, line 101.

An alleged weakness, not of non-religious moralities in general, but specifically of moralities explained and understood in the naturalistic way outlined above, is that different groups of people can develop different moral views, which will produce conflict when these groups are in contact with one another, and that there is, on this basis, no clear way of resolving such conflicts. This is true. But it is not a *distinctive* weakness of the naturalistic approach. Absolutist and objectivist moralities, including ones with religious attachments, also differ from one another, and there is no clear way of resolving their conflicts either. That each party *believes* that some one morality is objectively right is no guarantee that they will be able to agree on what it is. Indeed, conflicts between rival absolutists are likely to be less resolvable than conflicts between those who understand morality in a naturalistic way, for the latter can more easily appreciate the merits of compromise and adjustment, or of finding, for the areas of contact, a *ius gentium,* a common core of principles on which they can agree.

Another supposed weakness is this: it may be thought particularly difficult to derive any respect for non-human life, any valuing of nature in general, from a purely secular, human approach. But it is worth noting that Robinson, for example, specifically includes among his "atheist's values" a "love of all life" (p. 152; see also pp. 186-187). In fact there is no question of *deriving* a morality from the facts of the human situation. What we can do is to *understand* how moral thinking can develop and what functions it serves; and we can also understand how it naturally extends itself beyond a quasi-contractual system by the operation of what Hume called "sympathy."[14]

In contrast with any such real or supposed weaknesses in non-religious morality, we should note its distinctive merits, in particular its cultivation of a courageous realism in the face of the less palatable facts of life—and of death. But we need not dwell on this merit, since, as we have seen, it is dramatically recognized in Phillips's attempt to take over, in the name of religion, the traditional non-believers' attitude to the loss of one's friends, the attitude of coming to terms with such loss without either denying it or suppressing it. The non-believer comes to terms with the inevitability of his own death in a similar way. Küng has likewise tried to take over in the name of religion the traditional non-believers' view of morality itself: "We are responsible for our morality." Robinson says that "The main irrationality of religion is preferring comfort to truth" (p. 117). Phillips and Küng are implicitly recognizing this traditional weakness in religion, and are proposing that religion should follow atheism in doing without it.

In Phillips, the moral take-over bid is linked with a strong tendency to disguise atheism on the theoretical side, and Küng's concept of God is so complex

---

14. See pp. 193–195 of *Ethics: Inventing Right and Wrong,* and the article mentioned in no. 4 above.

and so indeterminate that his position, too, may not be really so far removed from atheism. Should we then object to such take-overs? So long as the position adopted is, in substance, atheistic, what does it matter if it is *called* religion? After all, Epicurus was willing to postulate happy and immortal gods safely isolated from all contact with human affairs; Spinoza was willing to speak of *Deus sive natura,* identifying nature with God; and even Hume proposed a compromise:

> The theist allows, that the original intelligence is very different from human reason: The atheist allows, that the original principle of order bears some remote analogy to it. Will you quarrel, Gentlemen, about the degrees, and enter into a controversy, which admits not of any precise meaning, nor consequently of any determination.[15]

Today, however, it is more honest and less misleading to reject such compromises and evasions, which can too easily serve as a cover for the reintroduction of characteristically theistic views both on the intellectual and on the moral side.

Alternatively, is there any merit in Braithwaite's approach, in retaining the religious "stories" as a psychological support for a morality, while explicitly rejecting any suggestion that they are factually true? This we might allow, provided that the morality they support is not of the kind we have been criticizing as distinctively religious. Apart from their other faults, such moralities have a tendency to be dangerously over-optimistic. Particularly in the field of international affairs, leaders who have too strong or too fundamentalist a faith may pursue policies which they know to be reckless, in the expectation that God will prevent the worst—and, for humanity, final-disasters. Such reliance would be quite different from the "fundamental trust" which Küng has reasonably advocated on purely human grounds. There are inevitable uncertainties in human affairs. Machiavelli speculated that "fortune is the ruler of one half of our actions, but . . . she allows the other half, or a little less, to be governed by us."[16] Damon Runyon put it more briefly: "Nothing human is better than two to one." If so, the only reasonable plan is to do the best we can, taking all possible precautions against the worst disasters, but *then* to meet the uncertainties with cheerful confidence. "Trust in God and keep your powder dry," understood as Braithwaite might understand it, may be good practical advice. But to trust God to keep your powder dry for you is the height of folly.

---

15. *Dialogues concerning Natural Religion*, Part XII.
16. *The Prince*, Chapter 25.

32

Genesis Revisted

A Scientific Creation Story

MICHAEL SHERMER

It was a black day for fundamentalist Christianity when Dr. Michael
Shermer stopped trying to believe in the impossible and became a
convert to reason and objective investigation. His elegant contributions to the magazine *Skeptical Magazine* have attracted a wide audience and his book *Why Darwin Matters* became an instant classic of
scientific explanation.

Originally published in *Darwin: A Norton Critical Edition*, selected and edited by
Philip Appleman (New York: W. W. Norton, 2001), 625–626.

To convey the logical absurdity of trying to squeeze the round peg of science
into the square hole of religion, I penned the following scientific revision of
the Genesis creation story. It is not intended as a sacrilege of the poetic beauty
of Genesis; rather, it is a mere extension of what the creationists have already
done to Genesis in their insistence that it be read not as mythic saga but as scientific prose. If Genesis were written in the language of modern science, it
would read something like this.

In the beginning—specifically on October 23, 4004 B.C., at noon—out of quantum foam fluctuation God created the Big Bang, followed by cosmological inflation and an expanding universe. And darkness was upon the face of the deep,
so He commanded hydrogen atoms (which He created from Quarks) to fuse
and become helium atoms and in the process release energy in the form of light.
And the light maker he called the sun, and the process He called fusion. And He
saw the light was good because now He could see what he was doing, so he created Earth. And the evening and the morning were the first day.
  And God said, Let there be lots of fusion light makers in the sky. Some of
these fusion makers He grouped into collections He called galaxies, and these

appeared to be millions and even billions of light years from Earth, which would mean that they were created before the first creation in 4004 B.C. This was confusing, so God created tired light, and the creation story was preserved. And created He many wondrous splendors such as Red Giants, White Dwarfs, Quasars, Pulsars, Supernova, Worm Holes, and even Black Holes out of which nothing can escape. But since God cannot be constrained by nothing, He created Hawking radiation through which information can escape from Black Holes. This made God even more tired than tired light, and the evening and the morning were the second day.

And God said, Let the waters under the heavens be gathered together unto one place, and let the continents drift apart by plate tectonics. He decreed sea floor spreading would create zones of emergence, and He caused subduction zones to build mountains and cause earthquakes. In weak points in the crust God created volcanic islands, where the next day He would place organisms that were similar to but different from their relatives on the continents, so that still later created creatures called humans would mistake them for evolved descendants created by adaptive radiation. And the evening and the morning were the third day.

And God saw that the land was barren, so He created animals bearing their own kind, declaring Thou shalt not evolve into new species, and thy equilibrium shall not be punctuated. And God placed into the rocks, fossils that appeared older than 4004 B.C. that were similar to but different from living creatures. And the sequence resembled descent with modification. And the evening and morning were the fourth day.

And God said, Let the waters bring forth abundantly the moving creatures that hath life, the fishes. And God created great whales whose skeletal structure and physiology were homologous with the land mammals he would create later that day. God then brought forth abundantly all creatures, great and small, declaring that microevolution was permitted, but not macroevolution. And God said, *Natura non facit saltum*—Nature shall not make leaps. And the evening and morning were the fifth day.

And God created the pongidids and hominids with 98 percent genetic similarity, naming two of them Adam and Eve. In the book in which God explained how He did all this, in one chapter He said he created Adam and Eve together out of the dust at the same time, but in another chapter He said He created Adam first, then later created Eve out of one of Adam's ribs. This caused confusion in the valley of the shadow of doubt, so God created theologians to sort it out.

And in the ground placed He in abundance teeth, jaws, skulls, and pelvises of transitional fossils from pre-Adamite creatures. One chosen as his special creation He named Lucy, who could walk upright like a human but had a small brain like an ape. And God realized this too was confusing, so he created pale-oanthropologists to figure it out.

Just as He was finishing up the loose ends of the creation God realized that Adam's immediate descendants would not understand inflationary cosmology, global general relativity, quantum mechanics, astrophysics, biochemistry, pale-ontology, and evolutionary biology, so he created creation myths. But there were so many creation stories throughout the world God realized this too was confusing, so created He anthropologists and mythologists.

By now the valley of the shadow of doubt was overrunneth with skepticism, so God became angry, so angry that God lost His temper and cursed the first humans, telling them to go forth and multiply themselves (but not in those words). But the humans took God literally and now there are six billion of them. And the evening and morning were the sixth day.

By now God was tired, so He proclaimed, "Thank me it's Friday," and He made the weekend. It was a good idea.

33

That Undiscovered Country

A. J. AYER

Please forgive another Oxonian. Sir Alfred Ayer, the author of *Language Truth and Logic* and one of the importers of the ideas of the Vienna Circle to the English-speaking world, was a splendid teacher of philosophy and a tireless defender of free expression. In an episode of the kind that will become more familiar to us as medicine advances, he appeared to "die" at least once before his actual death. Here is his response to those who—like the slanderers of Thomas Paine and the ghouls who haunted David Hume—misunderstood what he had meant to say.

My first attack of pneumonia occurred in the United States. I was in hospital for ten days in New York, after which the doctors said that I was well enough to leave. A final X-ray, however, which I underwent on the last morning, revealed that one of my lungs was not yet free from infection. This caused the most sympathetic of my doctors to suggest that it would be good for me to spend a few more days in hospital. I respected his opinion but since I was already dressed and psychologically disposed to put my illness behind me, I decided to take the risk. I spent the next few days in my stepdaughter's apartment, and then made arrangements to fly back to England.

When I arrived I believed myself to be cured and incontinently plunged into an even more hectic social round than that to which I had become habituated before I went to America. Retribution struck me on Sunday, May 30. I had gone out to lunch, had a great deal to eat and drink, and chattered incessantly. That evening I had a relapse. I could eat almost none of the food that a friend had brought to cook in my house.

On the next day, which was a bank holiday, I had a long-standing engagement to lunch at the Savoy with a friend who was very eager for me to meet her son. I would have put them off if I could, but my friend lives in Exeter and I had no idea how to reach her in London. So I took a taxi to the Savoy and just managed to stagger into the lobby. I could eat hardly any of the delicious grilled sole that I ordered but forced myself to keep up my end of the conversation. I left early and took a taxi home.

That evening I felt still worse. Once more I could eat almost none of the dinner another friend had brought me. Indeed, she was so alarmed by my weakness that she stayed overnight. When I was no better the next morning, she telephoned to my general practitioner and to my elder son, Julian. The doctor did little more than promise to try to get in touch with the specialist, but Julian, who is unobtrusively very efficient, immediately rang for an ambulance. The ambulance came quickly with two strong attendants, and yet another friend, who had called opportunely to pick up a key, accompanied it and me to University College Hospital.

I remember very little of what happened from then on. I was taken to a room in the private wing, which had been reserved for me by the specialist, who had a consulting room on the same floor. After being X-rayed and subjected to a number of tests, which proved beyond question that I was suffering gravely from pneumonia, I was moved into intensive care in the main wing of the hospital.

Fortunately for me, the young doctor who was primarily responsible for me had been an undergraduate at New College, Oxford, while I was a Fellow. This made him extremely anxious to see that I recovered; almost too much so, in fact, for he was so much in awe of me that he forbade me to be disturbed at night, even when the experienced sister and nurse believed it to be necessary.

Under his care and theirs I made such good progress that I expected to be moved out of intensive care and back into the private wing within a week. My disappointment was my own fault. I did not attempt to eat the hospital food. My family and friends supplied all the food I needed. I am particularly fond of smoked salmon, and one evening I carelessly tossed a slice of it into my throat. It went down the wrong way and almost immediately the graph recording my heartbeats plummeted. The ward sister rushed to the rescue, but she was unable to prevent my heart from stopping. She and the doctor subsequently told me that I died in this sense for four minutes, and I have had no reason to disbelieve them.

The doctor alarmed my son Nicholas, who had flown from New York to be by my bedside, by saying that it was not probable that I should recover, and moreover, that if I did recover physically it was not probable that my mental powers would be restored. The nurses were more optimistic, and Nicholas sensibly chose to believe them.

I have no recollection of anything that was done to me at that time. Friends have told me that I was festooned with tubes, but I have never learned how many of them there were or, with one exception, what purposes they served. I do not remember having a tube inserted in my throat to bring up the quantity of phlegm which had lodged in my lungs. I was not even aware of my numerous visitors, so many of them, in fact, that the sister had to set a quota. I know that the doctors and nurses were surprised by the speed of my recovery and that when I started speaking, the specialist expressed astonishment that anyone with so little oxygen in his lungs should be so lucid.

My first recorded utterance, which convinced those who heard it that I had not lost my wits, was the exclamation: "You are all mad." I am not sure how this should be interpreted. It is possible that I took my audience to be Christians and was telling them that I had not discovered anything "on the other side." It is also possible that I took them to be skeptics and was implying that I had discovered something. I think the former is more probable, as in the latter case I should more properly have exclaimed, "We are all mad." All the same, I cannot be sure.

The earliest remarks of which I have any cognizance, apart from my first exclamation, were made several hours after my return to life. They were addressed to a Frenchwoman with whom I had been friends for over 15 years. I woke to find her seated by my bedside and started talking to her in French as soon as I recognized her. My French is fluent and I spoke rapidly, approximately as follows: "Did you know that I was dead? The first time that I tried to cross the river I was frustrated, but my second attempt succeeded. It was most extraordinary. My thoughts became persons."

The content of those remarks suggests that I have not wholly put my classical education behind me. In Greek mythology the souls of the dead, now only shadowly embodied, were obliged to cross the river Styx in order to reach Hades, after paying an obol to the ferryman, Charon. I may also have been reminded of my favorite philosopher, David Hume, who, during his last illness, "a disorder of the bowels," imagined that Charon, growing impatient, was calling him "a lazy loitering rogue." With his usual politeness, Hume replied that he saw without regret his death approaching and that he was making no effort to postpone it. This is one of the rare occasions on which I have failed to follow Hume. Clearly I had made an effort to prolong my life.

The only memory that I have of an experience, closely encompassing my death, is very vivid. I was confronted by a red light, exceedingly bright, and also very painful even when I turned away from it. I was aware that this light was responsible for the government of the universe. Among its ministers were two creatures who had been put in charge of space. These ministers periodically inspected space and had recently carried out such an inspection. They had, however, failed to do their work properly, with the result that space, like a badly fitting jigsaw puzzle, was slightly out of joint.

A further consequence was that the laws of nature had ceased to function as they should. I felt that it was up to me to put things right. I also had the motive of finding a way to extinguish the painful light. I assumed that it was signaling that space was awry and that it would switch itself off when order was restored. Unfortunately, I had no idea where the guardians of space had gone and feared that even if I found them I should not be able to communicate with them. It then occurred to me that whereas, until the present century, physicists accepted the Newtonian severance of space and time, it had become customary, since the vindication of Einstein's general theory of relativity, to treat space-time as a single whole. Accordingly, I thought that I could cure space by operating upon time.

I was vaguely aware that the ministers who had been given charge of time were in my neighborhood and I proceeded to hail them. I was again frustrated. Either they did not hear me, or they chose to ignore me, or they did not understand me. I then hit upon the expedient of walking up and down, waving my watch, in the hope of drawing their attention not to my watch itself but to the time which it measured. This elicited no response. I became more and more desperate, until the experience suddenly came to an end.

This experience could well have been delusive. A slight indication that it might have been veridical has been supplied by my French friend, or rather by her mother, who also underwent a heart arrest many years ago. When her daughter asked her what it had been like, she replied that all that she remembered was that she must stay close to the red light.

On the face of it, these experiences, on the assumption that the last one was veridical, are rather strong evidence that death does not put an end to consciousness. Does it follow that there is a future life? Not necessarily. The trouble is that there are different criteria for being dead, which are indeed logically compatible but may not always be satisfied together.

In this instance, I am given to understand that the arrest of the heart does not entail, either logically or causally, the arrest of the brain. In view of the very strong evidence in favor of the dependence of thoughts upon the brain, the most probable hypothesis is that my brain continued to function although my heart had stopped.

If I had acquired good reason to believe in a future life, it would have applied not only to myself. Admittedly, the philosophical problem of justifying one's confident belief in the existence and contents of other minds has not yet been satisfactorily solved. Even so, with the possible exception of Fichte, who proclaimed that the world was his idea but may not have meant it literally, no philosopher has acquiesced in solipsism. No philosopher has seriously asserted that of all the objects in the universe, he alone was conscious. Moreover it is commonly taken for granted, not only by philosophers, that the minds of others bear a sufficiently close analogy to one's own. Consequently, if I had been vouchsafed a reasonable expectation of a future life, other human beings could expect one too.

Let us grant, for the sake of argument, that we could have future lives. What form could they take? The easiest answer is that they would consist in the prolongation of our experiences, without any physical attachment. This is the theory that should appeal to radical empiricists. It is, indeed, consistent with the concept of personal identity which was adopted both by Hume and by William James, according to which one's identity consists, not in the possession of an enduring soul, but in the sequence of one's experiences, guaranteed by memory.

They did not apply their theory to a future life, in which Hume at any rate disbelieved.

For those who are attracted by this theory, as I am, the main problem, which Hume admitted that he was unable to solve, is to discover the relation, or relations, which have to hold between experiences for them to belong to one and the same self.

William James thought that he had found the answers with his relations of the felt togetherness and continuity of our thoughts and sensations, coupled with memory, in order to unite experiences that are separated in time. But while memory is undoubtedly necessary, it can be shown that it is not wholly sufficient.

I myself carried out a thorough examination and development of the theory in my book *The Origins of Pragmatism*. I was reluctantly forced to conclude that I could not account for personal identity without falling back on the identity, through time, of one or more bodies that the person might successively occupy. Even then, I was unable to give a satisfactory account of the way in which a series of experiences is tied to a particular body at any given time.

The admission that personal identity through time requires the identity of a body is a surprising feature of Christianity. I call it surprising because it seems to me that Christians are apt to forget that the resurrection of the body is an element in their creed. The question of how bodily identity is sustained over intervals of time is not so difficult. The answer might consist in postulating a reunion of the same atoms, perhaps in there being no more than a strong physical resemblance, possibly fortified by a similarity of behavior.

A prevalent fallacy is the assumption that a proof of an afterlife would also be a proof of the existence of a deity. This is far from being the case. If, as I hold, there is no good reason to believe that a god either created or presides over this world, there is equally no good reason to believe that a god created or presides over the next world, on the unlikely supposition that such a thing exists.

It is conceivable that one's experiences in the next world, if there are any, will supply evidence of a god's existence, but we have no right to presume on such evidence, when we have not had the relevant experiences.

It is worth remarking, in this connection, that the two important Cambridge philosophers in this century, J. E. McTaggart and C. D. Broad, who have believed—in McTaggart's case that he would certainly survive his death, in Broad's that there was about a 50 percent probability that he would—were both of them atheists. McTaggart derived his certainty from his metaphysics, which implied that what we confusedly perceive as material objects, in some cases housing minds, are really souls, eternally viewing one another with something of the order of love.

The less fanciful Broad was impressed by the findings of psychical research. He was certainly too intelligent to think that the superior performances of a few persons in the game of guessing unseen cards, which he painstakingly proved to be statistically significant, had any bearing upon the likelihood of a future life. He must therefore have been persuaded by the testimony of mediums. He was surely aware that most mediums have been shown to be frauds, but he was convinced that some have not been.

Not that this made him optimistic. He took the view that this world was very nasty and that there was a fair chance that the next world, if it existed, was even nastier. Consequently, he had no compelling desire to survive. He just thought that there was an even chance of his doing so. One of his better epigrams was that if one went by the reports of mediums, life in the next world was like a perpetual bump supper at a Welsh university.

If Broad was an atheist, my friend Dr. Alfred Ewing was not. Ewing, who considered Broad to be a better philosopher than Wittgenstein, was naive, unworldly even by academic standards, intellectually shrewd, unswervingly honest, and a devout Christian. Once, to tease him, I said: "Tell me, Alfred, what do you most look forward to in the next world?" He replied immediately: "God will tell me whether there are *a priori* propositions." It is a wry comment on the strange character of our subject that this answer should be so funny.

My excuse for repeating this story is that such philosophical problems as the question whether the propositions of logic and pure mathematics are deductively analytic or factually synthetic, and, if they are analytic, whether they are true by convention, are not to be solved by acquiring more information. What is needed is that we succeed in obtaining a clearer view of what the problems involve. One might hope to achieve this in a future life, but really we have no good reason to believe that our intellects will be any sharper in the next world, if there is one, than they are in this. A god, if one exists, might make them so, but this is not something that even the most enthusiastic deist can count on.

The only philosophical problem that our finding ourselves landed on a future life might clarify would be that of the relation between mind and body, if our future lives consisted, not in the resurrection of our bodies, but in the prolongation of the series of our present experiences. We should then be witnessing the triumph of dualism, though not the dualism which Descartes thought that he had established. If our lives consisted in an extended series of experiences, we should still have no good reason to regard ourselves as spiritual substances.

So there it is. My recent experiences have slightly weakened my conviction that my genuine death, which is due fairly soon, will be the end of me, though I continue to hope that it will be. They have not weakened my conviction that there is no god. I trust that my remaining an atheist will allay the anxieties of my fellow supporters of the British Humanist Association, the Rationalist Press Association and the South Place Ethical Society.

Later Developments

Ayer's article was published in the United States by the National Review *on October 14, 1988. It was featured on the cover as "A. J. Ayer's Intimations of Immortality." Its subtitle—"What Happens When the World's Most Eminent Atheist Dies"—was no more misleading than the title chosen by the* Sunday Telegraph. *Scientists interviewed by the* Manchester Guardian *were skeptical about any "intimations of immortality." According to Colin Blakemore, professor of physiology at Cambridge, "What happened to Freddie Ayer was that lack of oxygen disordered the interpretative methods of his cortex, which led to hallucinations." Sir Herman Bondi, a distinguished physicist who is master of Churchill College, Cambridge, and president of the Rationalist Press Association, is quoted as "totally unimpressed," adding that "it is difficult enough to be wise when one is well." Ayer himself published what amounted to a retraction in the* Spectator *of October 15, 1988, entitled "Postscript to a Postmortem." He now asserted that his experience had not weakened and "never did weaken" his conviction that death means annihilation. "I said in my article," he went on, "that the most probable explanation of my experiences was that my brain had not ceased to function during the four minutes of my heart arrest. I have since been told, rightly or wrongly, that it would not have functioned on its own for any longer period without being damaged. I thought it so obvious that the persistence of my brain was the most probable explanation that I did not bother to stress it. I stress it now. No other hypothesis comes anywhere near to superseding it."*

34

Thank Goodness!

Daniel C. Dennett

The great Daniel Dennet, professor of philosophy and director of the Center of Cognitive Studies at Tufts University, adds his own contribution to the literature of the "near-death experience." With this number of humorous and courageous and thoughtful witnesses, we have a fighting chance of destroying the whole perverted myth of the unbeliever's last-minute wonderment and abjection.

There are no atheists in foxholes, according to an old but dubious saying, and there is at least a little anecdotal evidence in favor of it in the notorious cases of famous atheists who have emerged from near-death experiences to announce to the world that they have changed their minds. The British philosopher Sir A. J. Ayer, who died in 1989, is a fairly recent example. Here is another anecdote to ponder.

Two weeks ago, I was rushed by ambulance to a hospital where it was determined by c-t scan that I had a "dissection of the aorta"—the lining of the main output vessel carrying blood from my heart had been torn up, creating a two-channel pipe where there should only be one. Fortunately for me, the fact that I'd had a coronary artery bypass graft seven years ago probably saved my life, since the tangle of scar tissue that had grown like ivy around my heart in the intervening years reinforced the aorta, preventing catastrophic leakage from the tear in the aorta itself. After a nine-hour surgery, in which my heart was stopped entirely and my body and brain were chilled down to about 45 degrees to prevent brain damage from lack of oxygen until they could get the heart-lung machine pumping, I am now the proud possessor of a new aorta and aortic arch, made of strong Dacron fabric tubing sewn into shape on the spot by the surgeon, attached to my heart by a carbon-fiber valve that makes a reassuring little click every time my heart beats.

As I now enter a gentle period of recuperation, I have much to reflect on, about the harrowing experience itself and even more about the flood of supporting messages I've received since word got out about my latest adventure. Friends were anxious to learn if I had had a near-death experience, and if so, what effect it had had on my longstanding public atheism. Had I had an epiphany? Was I going to follow in the footsteps of Ayer (who recovered his aplomb and insisted a few days later "what I should have said is that my experiences have weakened, not my belief that there is no life after death, but my inflexible attitude towards that belief"), or was my atheism still intact and unchanged?

Yes, I did have an epiphany. I saw with greater clarity than ever before in my life that when I say "Thank goodness!" this is not merely a euphemism for "Thank God!" (We atheists don't believe that there is any God to thank.) I really do mean *thank goodness*! There is a lot of goodness in this world, and more goodness every day, and this fantastic human-made fabric of excellence is genuinely responsible for the fact that I am alive today. It is a worthy recipient of the gratitude I feel today, and I want to celebrate that fact here and now.

To whom, then, do I owe a debt of gratitude? To the cardiologist who has kept me alive and ticking for years, and who swiftly and confidently rejected the original diagnosis of nothing worse than pneumonia. To the surgeons, neurologists, anesthesiologists, and the perfusionist, who kept my systems going for many hours under daunting circumstances. To the dozen or so physician assistants, and to nurses and physical therapists and X-ray technicians and a small army of phlebotomists so deft that you hardly know they are drawing your blood, and the people who brought the meals, kept my room clean, did the mountains of laundry generated by such a messy case, wheel-chaired me to X-ray, and so forth. These people came from Uganda, Kenya, Liberia, Haiti, the Philippines, Croatia, Russia, China, Korea, India—and the United States, of course—and I have never seen more impressive mutual respect, as they helped each other out and checked each other's work. But for all their teamwork, this local gang could not have done their jobs without the huge background of contributions from others. I remember with gratitude my late friend and Tufts colleague, physicist Allan Cormack, who shared the Nobel Prize for his invention of the c-t scanner. Allan—you have posthumously saved yet another life, but who's counting? The world is better for the work you did. Thank goodness. Then there is the whole system of medicine, both the science and the technology, without which the best-intentioned efforts of individuals would be roughly useless. So I am grateful to the editorial boards and referees, past and present, of *Science, Nature, Journal of the American Medical Association, Lancet*, and all the other institutions of science and medicine that keep churning out improvements, detecting and correcting flaws.

Do I *worship* modern medicine? Is science my *religion*? Not at all; there is no aspect of modern medicine or science that I would exempt from the most rigorous scrutiny, and I can readily identify a host of serious problems that still need to be fixed. That's easy to do, of course, because the worlds of medicine and science are already engaged in the most obsessive, intensive, and humble self-assessments yet known to human institutions, and they regularly make public the results of their self-examinations. Moreover, this open-ended rational criticism, imperfect as it is, is the secret of the astounding success of these human enterprises. There are measurable improvements every day. Had I had my blasted aorta a decade ago, there would have been no prayer of saving me. It's hardly routine today, but the odds of my survival were actually not so bad (these days, roughly 33 percent of aortic dissection patients die in the first twenty-four hours after onset without treatment, and the odds get worse by the hour thereafter).

One thing in particular struck me when I compared the medical world on which my life now depended with the religious institutions I have been studying so intensively in recent years. One of the gentler, more supportive themes to be found in every religion (so far as I know) is the idea that what really matters is what is in your heart: if you have good intentions, and are trying to do what (God says) is right, that is all anyone can ask. Not so in medicine! If you are wrong—especially if you should have known better—your good intentions count for almost nothing. And whereas taking a leap of faith and acting without further scrutiny of one's options is often celebrated by religions, it is considered a grave sin in medicine. A doctor whose devout faith in his personal revelations about how to treat aortic aneurysm led him to engage in untested trials with human patients would be severely reprimanded if not driven out of medicine altogether. There are exceptions, of course. A few swashbuckling, risk-taking pioneers are tolerated and (if they prove to be right) eventually honored, but they can exist only as rare exceptions to the ideal of the methodical investigator who scrupulously rules out alternative theories before putting his own into practice. Good intentions and inspiration are simply not enough.

In other words, whereas religions may serve a benign purpose by letting many people feel comfortable with the level of morality they themselves can attain, no religion holds its members to the high standards of moral responsibility that the secular world of science and medicine does! And I'm not just talking about the standards "at the top"—among the surgeons and doctors who make life or death decisions every day. I'm talking about the standards of conscientiousness endorsed by the lab technicians and meal preparers, too. This tradition puts its faith in the *unlimited* application of reason and empirical inquiry, checking and re-checking, and getting in the habit of asking "What if I'm wrong?" Appeals to faith or membership are never tolerated. Imagine the reception a scientist would get if he tried to suggest that others couldn't replicate his results because they just didn't share the faith of the people in his lab! And, to return to my main point, it is the goodness of this tradition of reason and open inquiry that I thank for my being alive today.

What, though, do I say to those of my religious friends (and yes, I have quite a few religious friends) who have had the courage and honesty to tell me that they have been praying for me? I have gladly forgiven them, for there are few circumstances more frustrating than not being able to help a loved one in any more direct way. I confess to regretting that I could not pray (sincerely) for my friends and family in time of need, so I appreciate the urge, however clearly I recognize its futility. I translate my religious friends' remarks readily enough into one version or another of what my fellow brights have been telling me: "I've been thinking about you, and wishing with all my heart [another ineffective but irresistible self-indulgence] that you come through this OK." The fact that these dear friends *have* been thinking of me in this way, and have taken an effort to let me know, is in itself, without any need for a supernatural supplement, a wonderful tonic. These messages from my family and from friends around the world have been literally heart-warming in my case, and I am grateful for the boost in morale (to truly manic heights, I fear!) that it has produced in me. But I am not joking when I say that I have had to forgive my friends who said that they were *praying* for me. I have resisted the temptation to respond "Thanks, I appreciate it, but did you also sacrifice a goat?" I feel about this the same way I would feel if one of them said "I just paid a voodoo doctor to cast a spell for your health." What a gullible waste of money that could have been spent on more important projects! Don't expect me to be grateful, or even indifferent. I do appreciate the affection and generosity of spirit that motivated you, but wish you had found a more reasonable way of expressing it.

But isn't this awfully harsh? Surely it does the world no harm if those who can honestly do so pray for me! No, I'm not at all sure about that. For one thing, if they *really* wanted to do something useful, they could devote their prayer time and energy to some pressing project that they can do something about. For another, we now have quite solid grounds (e.g., the recently released Benson study at Harvard) for believing that intercessory prayer simply doesn't work. Anybody whose practice shrugs off that research is subtly undermining respect for the very goodness I am thanking. If you insist on keeping the myth of the effectiveness of prayer alive, you owe the rest of us a justification in the face of the evidence. Pending such a justification, I will excuse you for indulging in your tradition; I know how comforting tradition can be. But I want you to recognize that what you are doing is morally problematic at best. If you would even *consider* filing a malpractice suit against a doctor who made a mistake in treating you, or suing a pharmaceutical company that didn't conduct all the proper control tests before selling you a drug that harmed you, you must acknowledge your tacit appreciation of the high standards of rational inquiry to which the medical world holds itself, and yet you continue to indulge in a practice for which there is no known rational justification at all, and take yourself to be actually making a contribution. (Try to imagine your outrage if a pharmaceutical company responded to your suit by blithely replying "But we prayed good and hard for the success of the drug! What more do you want?")

The best thing about saying *thank goodness* in place of *thank God* is that there really are lots of ways of repaying your debt to goodness—by setting out to create more of it, for the benefit of those to come. Goodness comes in many forms, not just medicine and science. Thank goodness for the music of, say, Randy

Newman, which could not exist without all those wonderful pianos and recording studios, to say nothing of the musical contributions of every great composer from Bach through Wagner to Scott Joplin and the Beatles. Thank goodness for fresh drinking water in the tap, and food on our table. Thank goodness for fair elections and truthful journalism. If you want to express your gratitude to goodness, you can plant a tree, feed an orphan, buy books for schoolgirls in the Islamic world, or contribute in thousands of other ways to the manifest improvement of life on this planet now and in the near future.

Or you can thank God—but the very idea of repaying God is ludicrous. What could an omniscient, omnipotent Being (the Man Who has Everything?) do with any paltry repayments from you? (And besides, according to the Christian tradition God has already redeemed the debt for all time, by sacrificing his own son. Try to repay *that* loan!) Yes, I know, those themes are not to be understood *literally*; they are symbolic. I grant it, but then the idea that by thanking God you are actually doing some good has got to be understood to be just symbolic, too. I prefer real good to symbolic good.

Still, I excuse those who pray for me. I see them as like tenacious scientists who resist the evidence for theories they don't like long after a graceful concession would have been the appropriate response. I applaud you for your loyalty to your own position—but remember: loyalty to tradition is not enough. You've got to keep asking yourself: What if I'm wrong? In the long run, I think religious people can be asked to live up to the same moral standards as secular people in science and medicine.

35

A Personal Word

From *A Farewell to God*

CHARLES TEMPLETON

The road to Damascus was not and is not a one-way street. For many years, Charles Templeton (1915–2001) was the second string to the boring racist charlatan Billy Graham: addressing massive crowds in sports stadiums and allegedly bringing thousands of the credulous to Christ, there came a time when he found he could not participate in the racket any longer. His de-conversion is a testament from an honest if simple man, and also contains a close-up of the mediocre demagogue who has served as spiritual counselor to successive American presidents.

Early that summer, I flew to Montreat, North Carolina, to spend a day with Billy and Ruth Graham. Billy and I had become close friends, although our backgrounds were radically different. Billy was a country boy, raised in a deeply religious household on a farm in the American South. He had graduated from Bob Jones College in Tennessee and Wheaton College in Illinois—both Christian fundamentalist schools—and had a B.A. in anthropology.

We talked long and earnestly about my decision. Both of us sensed that, for all our avowed intentions to maintain our friendship, our feet were now set on divergent paths.

Later that summer, just before I enrolled at Princeton, we met again in New York City. On this occasion we spent the better part of two days closeted in a room in the Taft Hotel. All our differences came to a head in a discussion, which better than anything I know explains Billy Graham and his phenomenal success as an evangelist.

In the course of our conversation I said, "But, Billy, it's simply not possible any longer to believe, for instance, the biblical account of creation. The world wasn't created over a period of days a few thousand years ago; it has evolved over millions of years. It's not a matter of speculation; it's demonstrable fact."

"I don't accept that," Billy said. "And there are reputable scholars who don't."

"Who are these scholars?" I said. "Men in conservative Christian colleges?"

"Most of them, yes," he said. "But that's not the point. I believe the Genesis account of creation because it's in the Bible. I've discovered something in my ministry: when I take the Bible literally, when I proclaim it as the Word of God, my preaching has power. When I stand on the platform and say, 'God says,' or 'the Bible says,' the Holy Spirit uses me. There are results. Wiser men than you and I have been arguing questions like this for centuries. I don't have the time or the intellect to examine all sides of each theological dispute, so I've decided, once and for all, to stop questioning and accept the Bible as God's Word."

"But, Billy," I protested, "you can't do that. You don't dare stop thinking about the most important question in life. Do it and you begin to die. It's intellectual suicide."

"I don't know about anybody else," he said, "but I've decided that that's the path for me."

We talked about my going to Princeton and I pressed him to go with me. "Bill," I said, "face it. We've been successful in large part because of our abilities on the platform. Part of that stems from our energy, our convictions, our youth. But we won't always be young. We need to grow, to develop some intellectual sinew. Come with me to Princeton."

"I can't go to a university here in the States," he said. "I'm president of a Bible college, for goodness' sake!" He was—Northwestern Bible College, a fundamentalist school in Minneapolis.

"Resign," I said. "That's not what you're best fitted for; you're an evangelist. Come with me to Princeton."

There was an extended silence. Then, suddenly, he got up and came toward me. "Chuck," he said, "I can't go to a college here in the States. But I can and will do this: if we can get accepted by a university outside the country, maybe in England—Oxford, for instance—I'll go with you."

He stood in front of me, his hand outstretched. I know Billy well enough to know that, had I taken his hand, he would have kept his word. But I couldn't do it. I had resigned my church. I had been accepted at Princeton. The fall term was only weeks away. It was too late.

.   .   .

Not many months later, Billy travelled to Los Angeles to begin the campaign that would catapult him overnight to international prominence. I have sometimes wondered what would have happened had I taken his hand that day. I am certain of this: he would not be the Billy Graham he has become, and the history of mass-evangelism would be quite different.

As was inevitable, Billy and I drifted apart. We often talked on the telephone and got together on occasion but, with the years, the occasions became fewer. One afternoon in the early 1970s he telephoned to say that he was in Toronto and suggested that he have dinner at my home. He wanted to meet my wife and children and to spend a long evening talking.

The evening ended earlier than planned; we simply ran out of subjects of mutual interest. As I drove him to his hotel in downtown Toronto, the conversation became desultory. On the drive home I felt a profound sense of sorrow. Marshall Frady in his book, *Billy Graham,* quotes Billy as saying to him:

> "I love Chuck to this very day. He's one of the few men I have ever loved in my life. He and I had been so close. But then, all of a sudden, our paths were parting. He began to be a little cool to me then. I think . . ." He pauses and then offers with a faint little smile, "I think that Chuck felt sorry for me."

It will sound unforgivably condescending, but I do. He has given up the life of unrestricted thought. I occasionally watch Billy in his televised campaigns. Forty years after our working together he is saying the same things, using the same phrases, following the same pattern. When he gives the invitation to come forward, the sequence, even the words, are the same. I turn off the set and am sometimes overtaken by sadness.

I think Billy is what he has to be. I disagree with him at almost every point in his views on God and Christianity and think that much of what he says in the pulpit is puerile, archaic nonsense. But there is no feigning in Billy Graham: he believes what he believes with an invincible innocence. He is the only mass-evangelist I would trust.

And I miss him.

.   .   .

Questions to Ask Yourself

CHARLES TEMPLETON

Is it not foolish to close one's eyes to the reality that much of the Christian faith is simply impossible to accept as fact? And is it not a fundamental error to base one's life on theological concepts formulated centuries ago by relatively primitive men who believed that the world was flat, that Heaven was "up there" somewhere, and that the universe had been created and was controlled by a jingoistic and intemperate deity who would punish you forever if you did not behave exactly as instructed?

Listed below is a repetition of some of the questions raised in the preceding pages [of *A Farewell to God*]. Put them to yourself.

· Is it not likely that had you been born in Cairo you would be a Muslim and, as 840 million people do, would believe that "there is no God but God and Muhammad is his prophet"?
· If you have been born in Calcutta would you not in all probability be a Hindu and, as 650 million people do, accept the Vedas and the Upanishads as sacred scriptures and hope sometime in the future to dwell in Nirvana?
· Is it not probable that, had you been born in Jerusalem, you would be a Jew and, as some 13 million people do, believe that Yahweh is God and that the Torah is God's Word?
· Is it not likely that had you been born in Peking, you would be one of the millions who accept the teachings of the Buddha or Confucius or Lao-Tse and strive to follow their teachings and example?
· Is it not likely that you, the reader, are a Christian because your parents were before you?
· If there is a loving God, why does he permit—much less create—earthquakes, droughts, floods, tornadoes, and other natural disasters which kill thousands of innocent men, women, and children every year?
· How can a loving, omnipotent God permit—much less create—encephalitis, cerebral palsy, brain cancer, leprosy, Alzheimer's, and other incurable illnesses to afflict millions of men, women, and children, most of whom are decent people?
· How could a loving Heavenly Father create an endless Hell and, over the centuries, consign millions of people to it because they do not or cannot or will not accept certain religious beliefs? And, having done so, how could he torment them *forever*?

· Why are there literally hundreds of Christian denominations and
  independent congregations, all of them basing their beliefs on the Bible,
  and most of them convinced that all the others are, in some ways,
  wrong?

· If all Christians worship the same God, why can they not put aside their
  theological differences and co-operate actively with one another?

· If God is a loving Father, why does he so seldom answer his needy
  children's prayers?

· How can one believe the biblical account of the creation of the world in
  six days when every eminent physicist agrees that all living species have
  evolved over millions of years from primitive beginnings?

· Is it possible for an intelligent man or woman to believe that God
  fashioned the first male human being from a handful of dust and the
  first woman from one of the man's ribs?

· Is it possible to believe that the Creator of the universe would personally
  impregnate a Palestinian virgin in order to facilitate getting his Son into
  the world as a man?

· The Bible says that "the Lord thy God is a jealous God." But if you are
  omnipotent, omniscient, omnipresent, eternal, and the creator of all
  that exists, of whom could you possibly be jealous?

· Why, in a world filled with suffering and starvation, do Christians
  spend millions on cathedrals and sanctuaries and relatively little on aid
  to the poor and the needy?

· Why does the omnipotent God, knowing that there are tens of
  thousands of men, women, and children starving to death in a parched
  land, simply let them waste away and die when all that is needed is rain?

· Why would the Father of *all* mankind have a Chosen People and favor
  them over the other nations on earth?

· Why would a God who is "no respecter of persons" prohibit adultery
  and then bless, honour, and allow to prosper a king who had seven
  hundred wives and three hundred concubines?

· Why is the largest Christian church controlled entirely by men, with no
  woman—no matter how pious or gifted—permitted to become a priest, a
  monsignor, a bishop, an archbishop, a cardinal, or pope?

· Jesus's last words to his followers were "Go ye into all the world and
  preach the Gospel to every creature. And, lo, I am with you always." But,
  despite this and to this date—some two thousand years later—billions of
  men and women have never so much as heard the Christian Gospel. Why?

36

Why There Almost Certainly Is No God

From *The God Delusion*

RICHARD DAWKINS

All right, one more Oxonian. In a time of expanding and indeed ex ploding knowledge of biology, Richard Dawkins has educated a generation of people in the intricacies and wonders (far more impressive than anything supernatural) of our species and of others. It will be a long time before his books—*The Selfish Gene, The Blind Watchmaker*, and *Climbing Mount Improbable* among many others—are superseded as works of explication and indeed innovation in their field. Professor Dawkins reminds us that evolution by natural selection is indeed "only a theory": the most successful and the most testable theory in human history. He further reminds us that there are competing explanations for how this theory operates in practice. This is as it should be. There are some believers in scientific method who hold that evolution does not contradict or even overlap with the weird world of theology. Dawkins is impatient with such a fuzzy view of the matter and here gives a hint or two about the ultimate incompatibility of the scientific outlook with the religious one. Had he not chosen to abandon his religion for the materialist worldview, he might have earned a living as a satirist, as the ensuing two *feuilletons* demonstrate.

> *The priests of the different religions sects . . . dread the advance of science as witches do the approach of daylight, and scowl on the fatal harbinger announcing the subdivision of the duperies on which they live.*
>
> —THOMAS JEFFERSON

The Ultimate Boeing 747

The argument from improbability is the big one. In the traditional guise of the argument from design, it is easily today's most popular argument offered in favor of the existence of God and it is seen, by an amazingly large number of theists, as completely and utterly convincing. It is indeed a very strong and, I suspect, unanswerable argument—but in precisely the opposite direction from the theist's intention. The argument from improbability, properly deployed, comes close to proving that God does *not* exist. My name for the statistical demonstration that God almost certainly does not exist is the Ultimate Boeing 747 gambit.

The name comes from Fred Hoyle's amusing image of the Boeing 747 and the scrapyard. I am not sure whether Hoyle ever wrote it down himself, but it was attributed to him by his close colleague Chandra Wickramasinghe and is presumably authentic. Hoyle said that the probability of life originating on Earth is no greater than the chance that a hurricane, sweeping through a scrapyard, would have the luck to assemble a Boeing 747. Others have borrowed the metaphor to refer to the later evolution of complex living bodies, where it has a spurious plausibility. The odds against assembling a fully functioning horse, beetle, or ostrich by randomly shuffling its parts are up there in 747 territory. This, in a nutshell, is the creationist's favourite argument—an argument that could be made only by somebody who doesn't understand the first thing about natural selection: somebody who thinks natural selection is a theory of chance whereas—in the relevant sense of chance—it is the opposite.

The creationist misappropriation of the argument from improbability always takes the same general form, and it doesn't make any difference if the creationist chooses to masquerade in the politically expedient fancy dress of "intelligent design" (ID).[1] Some observed phenomenon—often a living creature or one of its more complex organs, but it could be anything from a molecule up to the universe itself—is correctly extolled as statistically improbable. Sometimes the language of information theory is used: the Darwinian is challenged to explain the source of all the information in living matter, in the technical sense of information content as a measure of improbability or "surprise value." Or the argument may invoke the economist's hackneyed motto: there's no such thing as a free lunch—and Darwinism is accused of trying to get something for nothing. In fact, as I shall show in this chapter, Darwinian natural selection is the only known solution to the otherwise unanswerable riddle of where the information comes from. It turns out to be the God Hypothesis that tries to get something for nothing. God tries to have his free lunch and be it too. However statistically improbable the entity you seek to

---

1. Intelligent design has been unkindly described as creationism in a cheap tuxedo.

explain by invoking a designer, the designer himself has got to be at least as improbable. God is the Ultimate Boeing 747.

The argument for improbability states that complex things could not have come about by chance. But many people *define* "come about by chance" as "a synonym for come about in the absence of deliberate design." Not surprisingly, therefore, they think improbability is evidence of design. Darwinian natural selection shows how wrong this is with respect to biological improbability. And although Darwinism may not be directly relevant to the inanimate world—cosmology, for example—it raises our consciousness in areas outside its original territory of biology.

A deep understanding of Darwinism teaches us to be wary of the easy assumption that design is the only alternative to chance, and teaches us to seek out graded ramps of slowly increasing complexity. Before Darwin, philosophers such as Hume understood that the improbability of life did not mean it had to be designed, but they couldn't imagine the alternative. After Darwin, we all should feel, deep in our bones, suspicious of the very idea of design. The illusion of design is a trap that has caught us before, and Darwin should have immunized us by raising our consciousness. Would that he had succeeded with all of us.

Natural Selection as a Consciousness-Raiser

In a science-fiction starship, the astronauts were homesick: "Just to think that it's springtime back on Earth!" You may not immediately see what's wrong with this, so deeply ingrained is the unconscious northern hemisphere chauvinism in those of us who live there, and even some who don't. "Unconscious" is exactly right. That is where consciousness-raising comes in. It is for a deeper reason than gimmicky fun that, in Australia and New Zealand, you can buy maps of the world with the South Pole on top. What splendid consciousness-raisers those maps would be, pinned to the walls of our northern hemisphere classrooms. Day after day, the children would be reminded that "north" is an arbitrary polarity which has no monopoly on "up." The map would intrigue them as well as raise their consciousness. They'd go home and tell their parents—and, by the way, giving children something with which to surprise their parents is one of the greatest gifts a teacher can bestow.

It was the feminists who raised my consciousness of the power of consciousness-raising. "Herstory" is obviously ridiculous, if only because the "his" in "history" has no etymological connection with the masculine pronoun. It is as etymologically silly as the sacking, in 1999, of a Washington official whose use of "niggardly" was held to give racial offence. But even daft examples like "niggardly" or "herstory" succeed in raising consciousness. Once we have smoothed our philological hackles and stopped laughing, herstory shows us history from a different point of view. Gendered pronouns notoriously are the front line of such consciousness-raising. He or she must ask himself or herself whether his or her sense of style could ever allow himself or herself to write like this. But if we can just get over the clunking infelicity of the language, it raises our consciousness to the sensitivities of half the human race. Man, mankind, the Rights of Man, all men are created equal, one man one vote—English too often seems to exclude woman.[2] When I was young, it never occurred to me that women might feel slighted by a phrase like "the future of man." During the intervening decades, we have all had our consciousness raised. Even those who still use "man" instead of "human" do so with an air of self-conscious apology—or truculence, taking a stand for traditional language, even deliberately to rile feminists. All participants in the *Zeitgeist* have had their consciousness raised, even those who choose to respond negatively by digging in their heels and redoubling the offence.

Feminism shows us the power of consciousness-raising, and I want to borrow the technique for natural selection. Natural selection not only explains the whole of life; it also raises our consciousness to the power of science to explain how organized complexity can emerge from simple beginnings without any deliberate guidance. A full understanding of natural selection encourages us to move boldly into other fields. It arouses our suspicion, in those other fields, of the kind of false alternatives that once, in pre-Darwinian days, beguiled biology. Who, before Darwin, could have guessed that something so apparently *designed* as a dragonfly's wing or an eagle's eye was really the end product of a long sequence of non-random but purely natural causes?

Douglas Adams's moving and funny account of his own conversion to radical atheism—he insisted on the "radical" in case anybody should mistake him for an agnostic—is testimony to the power of Darwinism as a consciousness-raiser. I hope I shall be forgiven the self-indulgence that will become apparent in the following quotation. My excuse is that Douglas's conversion by my earlier books—which did not set out to convert anyone—inspired me to dedicate to his memory this book—which does! In an interview, reprinted posthumously in *The Salmon of Doubt*, he was asked by a journalist how he became an atheist. He began his reply by explaining how he became an agnostic, and then proceeded:

And I thought and thought and thought. But I just didn't have enough to go on, so I didn't really come to any resolution. I was extremely doubtful about the idea of god, but I just didn't know enough about anything to have a good working model of any other explanation for, well, life, the universe, and every-

_____

2. Classical Latin and Greek were better equipped. Latin *Homo* (Greek *anthropo-*) means human, as opposed to *vir* (*andro-*) which means man, and *femina* (*gyne-*) which means woman. Thus anthropology pertains to all humanity, where andrology and gynecology are sexually exclusive branches of medicine.

thing to put in its place. But I kept at it, and I kept reading and I kept thinking. Sometime around my early thirties I stumbled upon evolutionary biology, particularly in the form of Richard Dawkins's books *The Selfish Gene* and then *The Blind Watchmaker,* and suddenly (on, I think the second reading of *The Selfish Gene)* it all fell into place. It was a concept of such stunning simplicity, but it gave rise, naturally, to all of the infinite and baffling complexity of life. The awe it inspired in me made the awe that people talk about in respect of religious experience seem, frankly, silly beside it. I'd take the awe of understanding over the awe of ignorance any day.

The concept of stunning simplicity that he was talking about was, of course, nothing to do with me. It was Darwin's theory of evolution by natural selection—the ultimate scientific consciousness-raiser. Douglas, I miss you. You are my cleverest, funniest, most open-minded, wittiest, tallest, and possibly only convert. I hope this book might have made you laugh—though not as much as you made me.

That scientifically savvy philosopher Daniel Dennett pointed out that evolution counters one of the oldest ideas we have: "the idea that it takes a big fancy smart thing to make a lesser thing. I call that the trickle-down theory of creation. You'll never see a spear making a spear maker. You'll never see a horse shoe making a blacksmith. You'll never see a pot making a potter." Darwin's discovery of a workable process that does that very counterintuitive thing is what makes his contribution to human thought so revolutionary, and so loaded with the power to raise consciousness.

It is surprising how necessary such consciousness-raising is, even in the minds of excellent scientists in fields other than biology. Fred Hoyle was a brilliant physicist and cosmologist, but his Boeing 747 misunderstanding, and other mistakes in biology such as his attempt to dismiss the fossil *Archaeopteryx* as a hoax, suggest that he needed to have his consciousness raised by some good exposure to the world of natural selection. At an intellectual level, I suppose he understood natural selection. But perhaps you need to be steeped in natural selection, immersed in it, swim about in it, before you can truly appreciate its power.

Other sciences raise our consciousness in different ways. Fred Hoyle's own science of astronomy puts us in our place, metaphorically as well as literally, scaling down our vanity to fit the tiny stage on which we play out our lives— our speck of debris from the cosmic explosion. Geology reminds us of our brief existence both as individuals and as a species. It raised John Ruskin's consciousness and provoked his memorable heart cry of 1851: "If only the Geologists would let me alone, I could do very well, but those dreadful hammers! I hear the clink of them at the end of every cadence of the Bible verses." Evolution does the same thing for our sense of time—not surprisingly, since it works on the geological timescale. But Darwinian evolution, specifically natural selection, does something more. It shatters the illusion of design within the domain of biology, and teaches us to be suspicious of any kind of design hypothesis in physics and cosmology as well. I think the physicist Leonard Susskind had this in mind when he wrote, "I'm not an historian but I'll venture an opinion: Modern cosmology really began with Darwin and Wallace. Unlike anyone before them, they provided explanations of our existence that completely rejected supernatural agents . . . Darwin and Wallace set a standard not only for the life sciences but for cosmology as well." Other physical scientists who are far above needing any such consciousness-raising are Victor Stenger, whose book *Has Science Found God?* (the answer is no) I strongly recommend, and Peter Atkins, whose *Creation Revisited* is my favourite work of scientific prose poetry.

I am continually astonished by those theists who, far from having their consciousness raised in the way that I propose, seem to rejoice in natural selection as "God's way of achieving his creation." They note that evolution by natural selection would be a very easy and neat way to achieve a world full of life. God wouldn't need to do anything at all! Peter Atkins, in the book just mentioned, takes this line of thought to a sensibly godless conclusion when he postulates a hypothetically lazy God who tries to get away with as little as possible in order to make a universe containing life. Atkins's lazy God is even lazier than the deist God of the eighteenth-century Enlightenment: *deus otiosus*—literally God at leisure, unoccupied, unemployed, superfluous, useless. Step by step, Atkins succeeds in reducing the amount of work the lazy God has to do until he finally ends up doing nothing at all: he might as well not bother to exist. My memory vividly hears Woody Allen's perceptive whine: "If it turns out that there is a God, I don't think that he's evil. But the worst that you can say about him is that basically he's an under-achiever."

Irreducible Complexity

It is impossible to exaggerate the magnitude of the problem that Darwin and Wallace solved. I could mention the anatomy, cellular structure, biochemistry, and behaviour of literally any living organism by example. But the most striking feats of apparent design are those picked out—for obvious reasons—by creationist authors, and it is with gentle irony that I derive mine from a creationist book. *Life—How Did It Get Here?*, with no named author but published by the Watchtower Bible and Tract Society in sixteen languages and eleven million copies, is obviously a firm favourite because no fewer than six of those eleven million copies have been sent to me as unsolicited gifts by well-wishers from around the world.

Picking a page at random from this anonymous and lavishly distributed work, we find the sponge known as Venus' Flower Basket *(Euplectella)*, accompanied by a quotation from Sir David Attenborough, no less: "When you look at a complex sponge skeleton such as that made of silica spicules which is known as Venus' Flower Basket, the imagination is baffled. How could quasi-independent microscopic cells collaborate to secrete a million glassy splinters and construct such an intricate and beautiful lattice? We do not know." The Watchtower authors lose no time in adding their own punchline: "But one thing we do know: Chance is not the likely designer." No indeed, chance is not the likely designer. That is one thing on which we can all agree. The statistical improbability of phenomena such as *Euplectella*'s skeleton is the central problem that any theory of life must solve. The greater the statistical improbability, the less plausible is chance as a solution: that is what improbable means. But the candidate solutions to the riddle of improbability are not, as is falsely implied, design and chance. They are design and natural selection. Chance is not a solution, given the high levels of improbability we see in living organisms, and no sane biologist ever suggested that it was. Design is not a real solution either, as we shall see later; but for the moment I want to continue demonstrating the problem that any theory of life must solve: the problem of how to escape from chance.

Turning Watchtower's page, we find the wonderful plant known as Dutchman's Pipe (*Aristolochia trilobata*), all of whose parts seem elegantly designed to trap insects, cover them with pollen and send them on their way to another Dutchman's Pipe. The intricate elegance of the flower moves Watchtower to ask: "Did all of this happen by chance? Or did it happen by intelligent design?" Once again, no of *course* it didn't happen by chance. Once again, intelligent design is not the proper alternative to chance. Natural selection is not only a parsimonious, plausible, and elegant solution; it is the only workable alternative to chance that has ever been suggested. Intelligent design suffers from exactly the same objection as chance. It is simply not a plausible solution to the riddle of statistical improbability. And the higher the improbability, the more implausible intelligent design becomes. Seen clearly, intelligent design will turn out to be a redoubling of the problem. Once again, this is because the designer himself (/herself/itself) immediately raises the bigger problem of his own origin. Any entity capable of intelligently designing something as improbable as a Dutchman's Pipe (or a universe) would have to be even more improbable than a Dutchman's Pipe. Far from terminating the vicious regress, God aggravates it with a vengeance.

Turn another Watchtower page for an eloquent account of the giant redwood (*Sequoiadendron giganteum*), a tree for which I have a special affection because I have one in my garden—a mere baby, scarcely more than a century old, but still the tallest tree in the neighbourhood. "A puny man, standing at a sequoia's base, can only gaze upward in silent awe at its massive grandeur. Does it make sense to believe that the shaping of this majestic giant and of the tiny seed that packages it was not by design?" Yet again, if you think the only alternative to design is chance then, no, it does not make sense. But again the authors omit all mention of the real alternative, natural selection, either because they genuinely don't understand it or because they don't want to.

The process by which plants, whether tiny pimpernels or massive wellingtonias, acquire the energy to build themselves is photosynthesis. Watchtower again: "'There are about seventy separate chemical reactions involved in photosynthesis,' one biologist said. 'It is truly a miraculous event.' Green plants have been called nature's 'factories'—beautiful, quiet, nonpolluting, producing oxygen, recycling water and feeding the world. Did they just happen by chance? Is that truly believable?" No, it is not believable; but the repetition of example after example gets us nowhere. Creationist "logic" is always the same. Some natural phenomenon is too statistically improbable, too complex, too beautiful, too awe-inspiring to have come into existence by chance. Design is the only alternative to chance that the authors can imagine. Therefore a designer must have done it. And science's answer to this faulty logic is also always the same. Design is not the only alternative to chance. Natural selection is a better alternative. Indeed, design is not a real alternative at all because it raises an even bigger problem than it solves: who designed the designer? Chance and design both fail as solutions to the problem of statistical improbability, because one of them is the problem, and the other one regresses to it. Natural selection is a real solution. It is the only workable solution that has ever been suggested. And it is not only a workable solution, it is a solution of stunning elegance and power.

What is it that makes natural selection succeed as a solution to the problem of improbability, where chance and design both fail at the starting gate? The answer is that natural selection is a cumulative process, which breaks the problem of improbability up into small pieces. Each of the small pieces is slightly improbable, but not prohibitively so. When large numbers of these slightly improbable events are stacked up in series, the end product of the accumulation is very very improbable indeed, improbable enough to be far beyond the reach of chance. It is these end products that form the subjects of the creationist's wearisomely recycled argument. The creationist completely misses the point, because he (women should for once not mind being excluded by the pronoun) insists on treating the genesis of statistical improbability as a single, one-off event. He doesn't understand the power of *accumulation*.

In *Climbing Mount Improbable*, I expressed the point in a parable. One side of the mountain is a sheer cliff, impossible to climb, but on the other side is a gentle slope to the summit. On the summit sits a complex device such as an eye or a bacterial flagellar motor. The absurd notion that such complexity could spontaneously self-assemble is symbolized by leaping from the foot of the cliff to the top in one bound. Evolution, by contrast, goes around the back of the mountain and creeps up the gentle slope to the summit: easy! The principle of climbing the gentle slope as opposed to leaping up the precipice is so simple, one is tempted to marvel that it took so long for a Darwin to arrive on the scene and discover it. By the time he did, nearly three centuries had elapsed since Newton's *annus mirabilis,* although his achievement seems, on the face of it, harder than Darwin's.

Another favourite metaphor for extreme improbability is the combination lock on a bank vault. Theoretically, a bank robber could get lucky and hit upon the right combination of numbers by chance. In practice, the bank's combination lock is designed with enough improbability to make this tantamount to impossible—almost as unlikely as Fred Hoyle's Boeing 747. But imagine a badly designed combination lock that gave out little hints progressively—the equivalent of the "getting warmer" of children playing Hunt the Slipper. Suppose that when each one of the dials approaches its correct setting, the vault door opens another chink, and a dribble of money trickles out. The burglar would home in on the jackpot in no time.

Creationists who attempt to deploy the argument from improbability in their favour always assume that biological adaptation is a question of the jackpot or nothing. Another name for the "jackpot or nothing" fallacy is "irreducible complexity" (IC). Either the eye sees or it doesn't. Either the wing flies or it doesn't. There are assumed to be no useful intermediates. But this is simply wrong. Such intermediates abound in practice—which is exactly what we should expect in theory. The combination lock of life is a "getting warmer, getting cooler, getting warmer" Hunt the Slipper device. Real life seeks the gentle slopes at the back of Mount Improbable, while Creationists are blind to all but the daunting precipice at the front.

Darwin devoted an entire chapter of the *Origin of Species* to "Difficulties on the theory of descent with modification," and it is fair to say that this brief chapter anticipated and disposed of every single one of the alleged difficulties that have since been proposed, right up to the present day. The most formidable difficulties are Darwin's "organs of extreme perfection and complication," sometimes erroneously described as "irreducibly complex." Darwin singled out the eye as posing a particularly challenging problem: "To suppose that the eye with all its inimitable contrivances for adjusting the focus to different distances, for admitting different amounts of light, and for the correction of spherical and chromatic aberration, could have been formed by natural selection, seems, I freely confess, absurd in the highest degree." Creationists gleefully quote this sentence again and again. Needless to say, they never quote what follows. Darwin's fulsomely free confession turned out to be a rhetorical device. He was drawing his opponents towards him so that his punch, when it came, struck the harder. The punch, of course, was Darwin's effortless explanation of exactly how the eye evolved by gradual degrees. Darwin may not have used the phrase "irreducible complexity," or "the smooth gradient up Mount Improbable," but he clearly understood the principle of both.

"What is the use of half an eye?" and "What is the use of half a wing?" are both instances of the argument from "irreducible complexity." A functioning unit is said to be irreducibly complex if the removal of one of its parts causes the whole to cease functioning. This has been assumed to be self-evident for both eyes and wings. But as soon as we give these assumptions a moment's thought, we immediately see the fallacy. A cataract patient with the lens of her eye surgically removed can't see clear images without glasses, but can see enough not to bump into a tree or fall over a cliff. Half a wing is indeed not as good as a whole wing, but it is certainly better than no wing at all. Half a wing could save your life by easing your fall from a tree of a certain height. And 51 percent of a wing could save you if you fall from a slightly taller tree. Whatever fraction of a wing you have, there is a fall from which it will save your life where a slightly smaller winglet would not. The thought experiment of trees of different height, from which one might fall, is just one way to see, in theory, that there must be a smooth gradient of advantage all the way from 1 per cent of a wing to 100 percent. The forests are replete with gliding or parachuting animals illustrating, in practice, every step of the way up that particular slope of Mount Improbable.

By analogy with the trees of different height, it is easy to imagine situations in which half an eye would save the life of an animal where 49 percent of an eye would not. Smooth gradients are provided by variations in lighting conditions, variations in the distance at which you catch sight of your prey—or your predators. And, as with wings and flight surfaces, plausible intermediates are not only easy to imagine: they are abundant all around the animal kingdom. A flatworm has an eye that, by any sensible measure, is less than half a human eye. *Nautilus* (and perhaps its extinct ammonite cousins who dominated Paleozoic and Mesozoic seas) has an eye that is intermediate in quality between flatworm and human. Unlike the flatworm eye, which can detect light and shade but see no image, the *Nautilus* '"pinhole camera" eye makes a real image; but it is a blurred and dim image compared to ours. It would be spurious precision to put numbers on the improvement, but nobody could sanely deny that these invertebrate eyes, and many others, are all better than no eye at all, and all lie on a continuous and shallow slope up Mount Improbable, with our eyes near a peak—not the highest peak but a high one. In *Climbing Mount Improbable,* I devoted a whole chapter each to the eye and the wing, demonstrating how easy it was for them to evolve by slow (or even, maybe, not all that slow) gradual degrees, and I will leave the subject here.

So, we have seen that eyes and wings are certainly not irreducibly complex; but what is more interesting than these particular examples is the general lesson we should draw. The fact that so many people have been dead wrong over these obvious cases should serve to warn us of other examples that are less obvious, such as the cellular and biochemical cases now being touted by those creationists who shelter under the politically expedient euphemism of "intelligent design theorists."

We have a cautionary tale here, and it is telling us this: do not just declare things to be irreducibly complex; the chances are that you haven't looked carefully enough at the details, or thought carefully enough about them. On the other hand, we on the science side must not be too dogmatically confident. Maybe there is something out there in nature that really does preclude, by its *genuinely* irreducible complexity, the smooth gradient of Mount Improbable. The creationists are right that, if genuinely irreducible complexity could be properly demonstrated, it would wreck Darwin's theory. Darwin himself said as much: "If it could be demonstrated that any complex organ existed which could not possibly have been formed by numerous, successive, slight modifications, my theory would absolutely break down. But I can find no such case." Darwin could find no such case, and nor has anybody since Darwin's time, despite strenuous, indeed desperate, efforts. Many candidates for this holy grail of creationism have been proposed. None has stood up to analysis.

In any case, even though genuinely irreducible complexity would wreck Darwin's theory if it were ever found, who is to say that it wouldn't wreck the intelligent design theory as well? Indeed, it already *has* wrecked the intelligent design theory, for, as I keep saying and will say again, however little we know about God, the one thing we can be sure of is that he would have to be very very complex and presumably irreducibly so!

The Worship of Gaps

Searching for particular examples of irreducible complexity is a fundamentally unscientific way to proceed: a special case of arguing from present ignorance. It appeals to the same faulty logic as "the God of the Gaps" strategy condemned by the theologian Dietrich Bonhoeffer. Creationists eagerly seek a gap in present-day knowledge or understanding. If an apparent gap is found, it is *assumed* that God, by default, must fill it. What worries thoughtful theologians such as Bonhoeffer is that gaps shrink as science advances, and God is threatened with eventually having nothing to do and nowhere to hide. What worries scientists is something else. It is an essential part of the scientific enterprise to admit ignorance, even to exult in ignorance as a challenge to future conquests. As my friend Matt Ridley has written, "Most scientists are bored by what they have already discovered. It is ignorance that drives them on." Mystics exult in mystery and want it to stay mysterious. Scientists exult in mystery for a different reason: it gives them something to do. More generally, as I shall repeat in Chapter 8, one of the truly bad effects of religion is that it teaches us that it is a virtue to be satisfied with not understanding.

Admissions of ignorance and temporary mystification are vital to good science. It is therefore unfortunate, to say the least, that the main strategy of creation propagandists is the negative one of seeking out gaps in scientific knowledge and claiming to fill them with "intelligent design" by default. The following is hypothetical but entirely typical. A creationist speaking: "The elbow joint of the lesser spotted weasel frog is irreducibly complex. No part of it would do any good at all until the whole was assembled. Bet you can't think of a way in which the weasel frog's elbow could have evolved by slow gradual degrees." If the scientist fails to give an immediate and comprehensive answer, the creationist draws a *default* conclusion: "Right then, the alternative theory, 'intelligent design,' wins by default." Notice the biased logic: if theory A fails in some particular, theory B must be right. Needless to say, the argument is not applied the other way around. We are encouraged to leap to the default theory without even looking to see whether it fails in the very same particular as the theory it is alleged to replace. Intelligent design—ID—is granted a Get Out Of Jail Free card, a charmed immunity to the rigorous demands made of evolution.

But my present point is that the creationist ploy undermines the scientist's natural—indeed necessary—rejoicing in (temporary) uncertainty. For purely political reasons, today's scientist might hesitate before saying: "Hm, interesting point. I wonder how the weasel frog's ancestors *did* evolve their elbow joint. I'm not a specialist in weasel frogs, I'll have to go to the University Library and take a look. Might make an interesting project for a graduate student." The moment a scientist said something like that—and long before the student began the project—the default conclusion would become a headline in a creationist pamphlet: "Weasel frog could only have been designed by God."

There is, then, an unfortunate hook-up between science's methodological need to seek out areas of ignorance in order to target research, and ID's need to seek out areas of ignorance in order to claim victory by default. It is precisely the fact that ID has no evidence of its own, but thrives like a weed in gaps left by scientific knowledge, that sits uneasily with science's need to identify and proclaim the very same gaps as a prelude to researching them. In this respect, science finds itself in alliance with sophisticated theologians like Bonhoeffer, united against the common enemies of naive, populist theology and the gap theology of intelligent design.

The creationists' love affair with "gaps" in the fossil record symbolizes their whole gap theology. I once introduced a chapter on the so-called Cambrian Explosion with the sentence, "It is as though the fossils were planted there without any evolutionary history." Again, this was a rhetorical overture, intended to whet the reader's appetite for the full explanation that was to follow. Sad hindsight tells me now how predictable it was that my patient explanation would be excised and my overture itself gleefully quoted out of context. Creationists adore "gaps" in the fossil record, just as they adore gaps generally.

Many evolutionary transitions are elegantly documented by more or less continuous series of gradually changing intermediate fossils. Some are not, and these are the famous "gaps." Michael Shermer has wittily pointed out that if a new fossil discovery neatly bisects a "gap," the creationist will declare that there are now twice as many gaps! But in any case, note yet again the unwarranted use of a default. If there are no fossils to document a postulated evolutionary transition, the default assumption is that there was no evolutionary transition, therefore God must have intervened.

It is utterly illogical to demand complete documentation of every step of any narrative, whether in evolution or any other science. You might as well demand, before convicting somebody of murder, a complete cinematic record of the murderer's every step leading up to the crime, with no missing frames. Only a tiny fraction of corpses fossilize, and we are lucky to have as many intermediate fossils as we do. We could easily have had no fossils at all, and still the evidence for evolution from other sources, such as molecular genetics and geographical distribution, would be overwhelmingly strong. On the other hand, evolution makes the strong prediction that if a *single* fossil turned up in the *wrong* geological stratum, the theory would be blown out of the water. When challenged by a zealous Popperian to say how evolution could ever be falsified, J. B. S. Haldane famously growled: "Fossil rabbits in the Precambrian." No such anachronistic fossils have ever been authentically found, despite discredited creationist legends of human skulls in the Coal Measures and human footprints interspersed with dinosaurs'.

Gaps, by default in the mind of the creationist, are filled by God. The same applies to all apparent precipices on the massif of Mount Improbable, where the graded slope is not immediately obvious or is otherwise overlooked. Areas where there is a lack of data, or a lack of understanding, are automatically assumed to belong, by default, to God. The speedy resort to a dramatic proclamation of "irreducible complexity" represents a failure of the imagination. Some biological organ, if not an eye then a bacterial flagellar motor or a biochemical pathway, is *decreed* without further argument to be irreducibly complex. No attempt is made to *demonstrate* irreducible complexity. Notwithstanding the cautionary tales of eyes, wings, and many other things, each new candidate for the dubious accolade is assumed to be transparently, self-evidently irreducibly complex, its status asserted by fiat. But think about it. Since irreducible complexity is being deployed as an argument for design, it should no more be asserted by fiat than design itself. You might as well simply assert that the weasel frog (bombardier beetle, etc.) demonstrates design, without further argument or justification. That is no way to do science.

The logic turns out to be no more convincing than this: "I [insert own name] am personally unable to think of any way in which [insert biological phenomenon] could have been built up step by step. Therefore it is irreducibly complex. That means it is designed." Put it like that, and you immediately see that it is vulnerable to some scientist coming along and finding an intermediate; or at least imagining a plausible intermediate. Even if no scientists do come up with an explanation, it is plain bad logic to assume that "design" will fare any better. The reasoning that underlies "intelligent design" theory is lazy and defeatist—classic "God of the Gaps" reasoning. I have previously dubbed it the Argument from Personal Incredulity.

Imagine that you are watching a really great magic trick. The celebrated conjuring duo Penn and Teller have a routine in which they simultaneously appear to shoot each other with pistols, and each appears to catch the bullet in his teeth. Elaborate precautions are taken to scratch identifying marks on the bullets before they are put in the guns, the whole procedure is witnessed at close range by volunteers from the audience who have experience of firearms, and apparently all possibilities for trickery are eliminated. Teller's marked bullet ends up in Penn's mouth and Penn's marked bullet ends up in Teller's. I [Richard Dawkins] am utterly unable to think of any way in which this could be a trick. The Argument from Personal Incredulity screams from the depths of my prescientific brain centres, and almost compels me to say, "It must be a miracle. There is no scientific explanation. It's got to be supernatural." But the still small voice of scientific education speaks a different message. Penn and Teller are world-class illusionists. There is a perfectly good explanation. It is just that I am too naive, or too unobservant, or too unimaginative, to think of it. That is the proper response to a conjuring trick. It is also the proper response to a biological phenomenon that appears to be irreducibly complex. Those people who leap from personal bafflement at a natural phenomenon straight to a hasty invocation of the supernatural are no better than the fools who see a conjuror bending a spoon and leap to the conclusion that it is "paranormal."

In his book *Seven Clues to the Origin of Life,* the Scottish chemist A. G. Cairns-Smith makes an additional point, using the analogy of an arch. A free-standing arch of rough-hewn stones and no mortar can be a stable structure, but it is irreducibly complex: it collapses if any one stone is removed. How, then, was it built in the first place? One way is to pile a solid heap of stones, then carefully remove stones one by one. More generally, there are many structures that are irreducible in the sense that they cannot survive the subtraction of any part, but which were built with the aid of scaffolding that was subsequently subtracted and is no longer visible. Once the structure is completed, the scaffolding can be removed safely and the structure remains standing. In evolution, too, the organ or structure you are looking at may have had scaffolding in an ancestor which has since been removed.

"Irreducible complexity" is not a new idea, but the phrase itself was invented by the creationist Michael Behe in 1996. He is credited (if credited is the word) with moving creationism into a new area of biology: biochemistry and cell biology, which he saw as perhaps a happier hunting ground for gaps than eyes or wings. His best approach to a good example (still a bad one) was the bacterial flagellar motor.

The flagellar motor of bacteria is a prodigy of nature. It drives the only known example, outside human technology, of a freely rotating axle. Wheels for big animals would, I suspect, be genuine examples of irreducible complexity, and this is probably why they don't exist. How would the nerves and blood vessels get across the bearing?[3] The flagellum is a thread-like propeller, with which the bacterium burrows its way through the water. I say "burrows" rather than "swims" because, on the bacterial scale of existence, a liquid such as water would not feel as a liquid feels to us. It would feel more like treacle, or jelly, or even sand, and the bacterium would seem to burrow or screw its way through the water rather than swim. Unlike the so-called flagellum of larger organisms like protozoans, the bacterial flagellum doesn't just wave about like a whip, or row like an oar. It has a true, freely rotating axle which turns continuously inside a bearing, driven by a remarkable little molecular motor. At the molecular level, the motor uses essentially the same principle as muscle, but in free rotation rather than in intermittent contraction.[4] It has been happily described as a tiny outboard motor (although by engineering standards—and unusually for a biological mechanism—it is a spectacularly inefficient one).

Without a word of justification, explanation or amplification, Behe simply *proclaims* the bacterial flagellar motor to be irreducibly complex. Since he offers no argument in favour of his assertion, we may begin by suspecting a failure of his imagination. He further alleges that specialist biological literature has ignored the problem. The falsehood of this allegation was massively and (to Behe) embarrassingly documented in the court of Judge John E. Jones in Pennsylvania in 2005, where Behe was testifying as an expert witness on behalf of a group of creationists who had tried to impose "intelligent design" creationism on the science curriculum of a local public school—a move of "breathtaking inanity," to quote Judge Jones (phrase and man surely destined for lasting fame). This wasn't the only embarrassment Behe suffered at the hearing, as we shall see.

The key to demonstrating irreducible complexity is to show that none of the parts could have been useful on its own. They all needed to be in place before

---

3. There is an example in fiction. The children's writer Philip Pullman, in *His Dark Materials*, imagines a species of animals, the "mulefa," that co-exist with trees that produce perfectly round seedpods with a hole in the centre. These pods the mulefa adopt as wheels. The wheels, not being part of the body, have no nerves or blood vessels to get twisted around the "axle" (a strong claw of horn or bone). Pullman perceptively notes an additional point: the system works only because the planet is paved with natural basalt ribbons, which serve as "roads." Wheels are no good over rough country.

4. Fascinatingly, the muscle principle is deployed in yet a third mode in some insects such as flies, bees, and bugs, in which the flight muscle is intrinsically oscillatory, like a reciprocating engine. Whereas other insects such as locusts send nervous instructions for each wing stroke (as a bird does), bees send an instruction to switch on (or switch off) the oscillatory motor. Bacteria have a mechanism which is neither a simple contractor (like a bird's flight muscle) nor a reciprocator (like a bee's flight muscle), but a true rotator: in that respect it is like an electric motor or a Wankel engine.

any of them could do any good (Behe's favourite analogy is a mousetrap). In fact, molecular biologists have no difficulty in finding parts functioning outside the whole, both for the flagellar motor and for Behe's other alleged examples of irreducible complexity. The point is well put by Kenneth Miller of Brown University, for my money the most persuasive nemesis of "intelligent design," not least because he is a devout Christian. I frequently recommend Miller's book, *Finding Darwin's God,* to religious people who write to me having been bamboozled by Behe.

In the case of the bacterial rotary engine, Miller calls our attention to a mechanism called the Type Three Secretory System or TTSS. The TTSS is not used for rotatory movement. It is one of several systems used by parasitic bacteria for pumping toxic substances through their cell walls to poison their host organism. On our human scale, we might think of pouring or squirting a liquid through a hole; but, once again, on the bacterial scale things look different. Each molecule of secreted substance is a large protein with a definite, three-dimensional structure on the same scale as the TTSS's own: more like a solid sculpture than a liquid. Each molecule is individually propelled through a carefully shaped mechanism, like an automated slot machine dispensing, say, toys or bottles, rather than a simple hole through which a substance might "flow." The goods-dispenser itself is made of a rather small number of protein molecules, each one comparable in size and complexity to the molecules being dispensed through it. Interestingly, these bacterial slot machines are often similar across bacteria that are not closely related. The genes for making them have probably been "copied and pasted" from other bacteria: something that bacteria are remarkably adept at doing, and a fascinating topic in its own right, but I must press on.

The protein molecules that form the structure of the TTSS are very similar to components of the flagellar motor. To the evolutionist it is clear that TTSS components were commandeered for a new, but not wholly unrelated, function when the flagellar motor evolved. Given that the TTSS is tugging molecules through itself, it is not surprising that it uses a rudimentary version of the principle used by the flagellar motor, which tugs the molecules of the axle round and round. Evidently, crucial components of the flagellar motor were already in place and working before the flagellar motor evolved. Commandeering existing mechanisms is an obvious way in which an apparently irreducibly complex piece of apparatus could climb Mount Improbable.

A lot more work needs to be done, of course, and I'm sure it will be. Such work would never be done if scientists were satisfied with a lazy default such as "intelligent design theory" would encourage. Here is the message that an imaginary "intelligent design theorist" might broadcast to scientists: "If you don't understand how something works, never mind: just give up and say God did it. You don't know how the nerve impulse works? Good! You don't understand how memories are laid down in the brain? Excellent! Is photosynthesis a bafflingly complex process? Wonderful! Please don't go to work on the problem, just give up, and appeal to God. Dear scientist, don't *work* on your mysteries. Bring us your mysteries, for we can use them. Don't squander precious ignorance by researching it away. We need those glorious gaps as a last refuge for God." St. Augustine said it quite openly: "There is another form of temptation, even more fraught with danger. This is the disease of curiosity. It is this which drives us to try and discover the secrets of nature, those secrets which are beyond our understanding, which can avail us nothing and which man should not wish to learn" (quoted in Freeman 2002).

Another of Behe's favourite alleged examples of "irreducible complexity" is the immune system. Let Judge Jones himself take up the story:

> In fact, on cross-examination, Professor Behe was questioned concerning his 1996 claim that science would never find an evolutionary explanation for the immune system. He was presented with fifty-eight peer-reviewed publications, nine books, and several immunology textbook chapters about the evolution of the immune system; however, he simply insisted that this was still not sufficient evidence of evolution, and that it was not "good enough."

Behe, under cross-examination, by Eric Rothschild, chief counsel for the plaintiffs, was forced to admit that he hadn't read most of those fifty-eight peer-reviewed papers. Hardly surprising, for immunology is hard work. Less forgivable is that Behe dismissed such research as "unfruitful." It certainly is unfruitful if your aim is to make propaganda among gullible laypeople and politicians, rather than to discover important truths about the real world. After listening to Behe, Rothschild eloquently summed up what every honest person in that courtroom must have felt:

> Thankfully, there are scientists who do search for answers to the question of the origin of the immune system . . . It's our defense against debilitating and fatal diseases. The scientists who wrote those books and articles toil in obscurity, without book royalties or speaking engagements. Their efforts help us combat and cure serious medical conditions. By contrast, Professor Behe and the entire intelligent design movement are doing nothing to advance scientific or medical knowledge and are telling future generations of scientists, don't bother.

As the American geneticist Jerry Coyne put it in his review of Behe's book: "If the history of science shows us anything, it is that we get nowhere by labelling our ignorance 'God.'" Or, in the words of an eloquent blogger, commenting on an article on intelligent design in the *Guardian* by Coyne and me,

Why is God considered an explanation for anything? It's not—it's a failure to explain, a shrug of the shoulders, an "I dunno" dressed up in spirituality and ritual. If someone credits something to God, generally what it means is that they haven't a clue, so they're attributing it to an unreachable, unknowable sky-fairy. Ask for an explanation of where that bloke came from, and odds are you'll get a vague, pseudo-philosophical reply about having always existed, or being outside nature. Which, of course, explains nothing.

Darwinism raises our consciousness in other ways. Evolved organs, elegant and efficient as they often are, also demonstrate revealing flaws—exactly as you'd expect if they have an evolutionary history, and exactly as you would not expect if they were designed. I have discussed examples in other books: the recurrent laryngeal nerve, for one, which betrays its evolutionary history in a massive and wasteful detour on its way to its destination. Many of our human ailments, from lower back pain to hernias, prolapsed uteruses and our susceptibility to sinus infections, result directly from the fact that we now walk upright with a body that was shaped over hundreds of millions of years to walk on all fours. Our consciousness is also raised by the cruelty and wastefulness of natural selection. Predators seem beautifully "designed" to catch prey animals, while the prey animals seem equally beautifully "designed" to escape them. Whose side is God on?

Gerin Oil

RICHARD DAWKINS

Gerin Oil (or Geriniol to give it its scientific name) is a powerful drug which acts directly on the central nervous system to produce a range of symptoms, often of an anti-social or self-damaging nature. It can permanently modify the child brain to produce adult disorders, including dangerous delusions, which are hard to treat. The four doomed flights of September 11, 2001, were Gerin Oil trips: all nineteen of the hijackers were high on the drug at the time. Historically, Gerinoilism was responsible for atrocities such as the Salem witch hunts and the massacres of Native South Americans by conquistadors. Gerin Oil fuelled most of the wars of the European Middle Ages and, in more recent times, the carnage that attended the partitioning of the Indian subcontinent and of Ireland.

Gerin Oil intoxication can drive previously sane individuals to run away from a normally fulfilled human life and retreat to closed communities of confirmed addicts. These communities are usually limited to one sex only, and they vigorously, often obsessively, forbid sexual activity. Indeed, a tendency towards agonized sexual prohibition emerges as a drably recurring theme amid all the colorful variations of Gerin Oil symptomatology. Gerin Oil does not seem to reduce the libido per se, but it frequently leads to a preoccupation with reducing the sexual pleasure of others. A current example is the prurience with which many habitual "Oilers" condemn homosexuality.

As with other drugs, refined Gerin Oil in low doses is largely harmless, and can serve as a lubricant on social occasions such as marriages, funerals, and state ceremonies. Experts differ over whether such social tripping, though harmless in itself, is a risk factor for upgrading to harder and more addictive forms of the drug.

Medium doses of Gerin Oil, though not in themselves dangerous, can distort perceptions of reality. Beliefs that have no basis in fact are immunized, by the drug's direct effects on the nervous system, against evidence from the real world. Oil-heads can be heard talking to thin air or muttering to themselves, apparently in the belief that private wishes so expressed will come true, even at the cost of other people's welfare and mild violation of the laws of physics. This autolocutory disorder is often accompanied by weird tics and hand gestures, manic stereotypes such as rhythmic head-nodding toward a wall, or obsessive compulsive orientation syndrome (OCOS: facing towards the east five times a day).

Gerin Oil in strong doses is hallucinogenic. Hardcore mainliners may hear voices in the head, or experience visual illusions which seem to the sufferers so real that they often succeed in persuading others of their reality. An individual who convincingly reports high-grade hallucinations may be venerated, and even followed as some kind of leader, by others who regard themselves as less fortunate. Such follower-pathology can long post-date the original leader's death, and may expand into bizarre psychedelia such as the cannibalistic fantasy of "drinking the blood and eating the flesh" of the leader.

Chronic abuse of Geriniol can lead to "bad trips," in which the user suffers terrifying delusions, including fears of being tortured, not in the real world but in a postmortem fantasy world. Bad trips of this kind are bound up with a morbid punishment-lore, which is as characteristic of this drug as the obsessive fear of sexuality already noted. The punishment-culture fostered by Gerin Oil ranges from "smack" through "lash" to getting "stoned" (especially adulteresses and rape victims), and "demanifestation" (amputation of one hand), up to the sinister fantasy of allo-punishment or "cross-topping," the execution of one individual for the sins of others.

You might think that such a potentially dangerous and addictive drug would head the list of proscribed intoxicants, with exemplary sentences handed out for pushing it. But no, it is readily obtainable anywhere in the world and you don't even need a prescription. Professional traffickers are numerous, and organized in hierarchical cartels, openly trading on street corners and in purpose-made buildings. Some of these cartels are adept at fleecing poor people desperate to feed their habit. "Godfathers" occupy influential positions in high places, and they have the ear of royalty, of presidents and prime ministers. Governments don't just turn a blind eye to the trade, they grant it tax-exempt status. Worse, they subsidize schools founded with the specific intention of getting children hooked.

I was prompted to write this article by the smiling face of a happy man in Bali. He was ecstatically greeting his death sentence for the brutal murder of large numbers of innocent holidaymakers whom he had never met, and against whom he bore no personal grudge. Some people in the court were shocked at his lack of remorse. Far from remorse, his response was one of obvious exhilaration. He punched the air, delirious with joy that he was to be "martyred," to use the jargon of his group of abusers. Make no mistake about it, that beatific smile, looking forward with unalloyed pleasure to the firing squad, is the smile of a junkie. Here we have the archetypal mainliner, doped up with hard, unrefined, unadulterated, high-octane Gerin Oil.

Whatever your view of the vengeance and deterrence theories of capital punishment, it should be obvious that this case is special. Martyrdom is a strange revenge against those who crave it, and, far from deterring, it always recruits more martyrs than it kills. The important point is that the problem would not arise in the first place if children were protected from getting hooked on a drug with such a bad prognosis for their adult minds.

Atheists for Jesus

RICHARD DAWKINS

The argument, like a good recipe, needs to be built up gradually, with the ingredients mustered in advance. First, the apparently oxymoronic title. In a society where the majority of theists are at least nominally Christian, the two words are treated as near synonyms. Bertrand Russell's famous advocacy of atheism was called *Why I Am Not a Christian* rather than, as it probably should have been, *Why I Am Not a Theist*. All Christians are theists, it seems to go without saying.

Of course Jesus was a theist, but that is the least interesting thing about him. He was a theist because, in his time, everybody was. Atheism was not an option, even for so radical a thinker as Jesus. What was interesting and remarkable about Jesus was not the obvious fact that he believed in the God of his Jewish religion, but that he rebelled against many aspects of Yahweh's vengeful nastiness. At least in the teachings that are attributed to him, he publicly advocated niceness and was one of the first to do so. To those steeped in the Sharia-like cruelties of Leviticus and Deuteronomy, to those brought up to fear the vindictive, Ayatollah-like God of Abraham and Isaac, a charismatic young preacher who advocated generous forgiveness must have seemed radical to the point of subversion. No wonder they nailed him.

> Ye have heard that it hath been said, An eye for an eye, and a tooth for a tooth: But I say unto you, That ye resist not evil: but whosoever shall smite thee on thy right cheek, turn to him the other also. And if any man will sue thee at the law, and take away thy coat, let him have thy cloke also. And whosoever shall compel thee to go a mile, go with him twain. Give to him that asketh thee, and from him that would borrow of thee turn not thou away. Ye have heard that it hath been said, Thou shalt love thy neighbour, and hate thine enemy. But I say unto you, Love your enemies, bless them that curse you, do good to them that hate you, and pray for them which despitefully use you, and persecute you.

My second ingredient is another paradox, which begins in my own field of Darwinism. Natural selection is a deeply nasty process. Darwin himself remarked,

> What a book a devil's chaplain might write on the clumsy, wasteful, blundering low and horridly cruel works of nature.

It was not just the facts of nature, among which he singled out the larvae of Ichneumon wasps and their habit of feeding within the bodies of live caterpillars.

The theory of natural selection itself seems calculated to foster selfishness at the expense of public good, violence, callous indifference to suffering, short term greed at the expense of long term foresight. If scientific theories could vote, evolution would surely vote Republican. My paradox comes from the *un*-Darwinian fact, which any of us can observe in our own circle of acquaintances, that so many individual people are kind, generous, helpful, compassionate, nice: the sort of people of whom we say, "She's a real saint." Or, "He's a true Good Samaritan."

We all know people (is it significant that the ones I can think of are mostly women?) to whom we can sincerely say: "If only everybody were like you, the world's troubles would melt away." The milk of human kindness is only a metaphor but, naive as it sounds, I contemplate some of my friends and I feel like trying to *bottle* whatever it is that makes them so kind, so selfless, so apparently un-Darwinian.

Darwinians can come up with explanations for human niceness: generalisations of the well-established models of kin selection and reciprocal altruism, the stocks-in-trade of the 'selfish gene' theory, which sets out to explain how altruism and cooperation among individual animals can stem from self-interest at the genetic level. But the sort of super niceness I am talking about in humans goes too far. It is a misfiring, even a perversion of the Darwinian take on niceness. Well, if that's a perversion, it's the kind of perversion we need to encourage and spread.

Human super niceness is a perversion of Darwinism because, in a wild population, it would be removed by natural selection. It is also, although I haven't the space to go into detail about this third ingredient of my recipe, an apparent perversion of the sort of rational choice theory by which economists explain human behaviour as calculated to maximize self-interest.

Let's put it even more bluntly. From a rational choice point of view, or from a Darwinian point of view, human super niceness is just plain dumb. And yes, it is the kind of dumb that should be encouraged—which is the purpose of my article. How can we do it? How shall we take the minority of super nice humans that we all know, and increase their number, perhaps until they even become a majority in the population? Could super niceness be induced to spread like an epidemic? Could super niceness be packaged in such a form that it passes down the generations in swelling traditions of longitudinal propagation?

Well, do we know of any comparable examples, where stupid ideas have been known to spread like an epidemic? Yes, by God! Religion. Religious beliefs are irrational. Religious beliefs are dumb and dumber: super dumb. Religion drives otherwise sensible people into celibate monasteries, or crashing into New York skyscrapers. Religion motivates people to whip their own backs, to set fire to themselves or their daughters, to denounce their own grandmothers as witches, or, in less extreme cases, simply to stand or kneel, week after week, through ceremonies of stupefying boredom. If people can be infected with such self-harming stupidity, infecting them with niceness should be child's play.

Religious beliefs most certainly spread in epidemics and, even more obviously, they pass down the generations to form longitudinal traditions and promote enclaves of locally peculiar irrationality. We may not understand why humans behave in the weird ways we label religious, but it is a manifest fact that they do. The existence of religion is evidence that humans eagerly adopt irrational beliefs and spread them, both longitudinally in traditions and horizontally in epidemics of evangelism. Could this susceptibility, this palpable vulnerability to infections of irrationality be put to genuinely good use?

Humans undoubtedly have a strong tendency to learn from and copy admired role models. Under propitious circumstances, the epidemiological consequences can be dramatic. The hairstyle of a footballer, the dress sense of a singer, the speech mannerisms of a game show host, such trivial idiosyncrasies can spread through a susceptible age cohort like a virus. The advertising industry is professionally dedicated to the science—or it may be an art—of launching memetic epidemics and nurturing their spread. Christianity itself was spread by the equivalents of such techniques, originally by St. Paul and later by priests and missionaries who systematically set out to increase the numbers of converts in what turned out to be exponential growth. Could we achieve exponential amplification of the numbers of super nice people?

This week I had a public conversation in Edinburgh with Richard Holloway, former bishop of that beautiful city. Bishop Holloway has evidently outgrown the supernaturalism which most Christians still identify with their religion (he describes himself as post-Christian and as a "recovering Christian"). He retains a reverence for the poetry of religious myth, which is enough to keep him going to church. And in the course of our Edinburgh discussion he made a suggestion which went straight to my core. Borrowing a poetic myth from the worlds of mathematics and cosmology, he described humanity as a "singularity" in evolution. He meant exactly what I have been talking about in this essay, although he expressed it differently. The advent of human super niceness is something unprecedented in four billion years of evolutionary history. It seems likely that, after the *Homo sapiens* singularity, evolution may never be the same again.

Be under no illusions, for Bishop Holloway was not. The singularity is a product of blind evolution itself, not the creation of any unevolved intelligence. It resulted from the natural evolution of the human brain which, under the blind forces of natural selection, expanded to the point where, all unforeseen, it overreached itself and started to behave insanely from the selfish gene's point of view. The most transparently un-Darwinian misfiring is contraception, which divorces sexual pleasure from its natural function of gene-propagation. More subtle over-reachings include intellectual and artistic pursuits which squander, by the selfish genes' lights, time and energy that should be devoted to surviving and reproducing. The big brain achieved the evolutionarily unprecedented feat of genuine foresight: became capable of calculating long-term consequences beyond short-term selfish gain. And, at least in some individuals, the brain

over-reached itself to the extent of indulging in that super niceness whose singular existence is the central paradox of my thesis. Big brains can take the driving, goal-seeking mechanisms that were originally favoured for selfish gene
reasons, and divert (subvert? pervert?) them away from their Darwinian goals
and into other paths.

I am no memetic engineer, and I have very little idea how to increase the numbers of the super nice and spread their memes through the meme pool. The best
I can offer is what I hope may be a catchy slogan. "Atheists for Jesus" would
grace a T-shirt. There is no strong reason to choose Jesus as icon, rather than
some other role model from the ranks of the super nice such as Mahatma
Gandhi (not the odiously self-righteous Mother Teresa, heavens no). I think we
owe Jesus the honour of separating his genuinely original and radical ethics
from the supernatural nonsense which he inevitably espoused as a man of his
time. And perhaps the oxymoronic impact of "Atheists for Jesus" might be just
what is needed to kick start the meme of super niceness in a post-Christian society. If we play our cards right—could we lead society away from the nether regions of its Darwinian origins into kinder and more compassionate uplands of
post-singularity enlightenment?

I think a reborn Jesus would wear the T-shirt. It has become a commonplace
belief that, were he to return today, he would be appalled at what is being done
in his name, by Christians ranging from the Catholic Church to the fundamentalist Religious Right. Less obviously but still plausibly, in the light of modern
scientific knowledge I think he would see through supernaturalist obscurantism. But of course, modesty would compel him to turn his T-shirt around:
"Jesus for Atheists."

37

Cosmic Evidence

From *God: The Failed Hypothesis*

Victor Stenger

The majority view of the atheist school is that the existence of god can neither be proved nor disproved, and that therefore the theistic position must collapse because its adherents must claim to know more than anyone can possibly know (not just about the existence of a creator, but about his thoughts on sex, diet, war, and other matters). Greatly daring, Professor Victor Stenger advances the argument that we now know enough to discard the god hypothesis altogether.

> *The only laws of matter are those which our minds must fabricate, and the only laws of mind are fabricated for it by matter.*
>
> —James Clerk Maxwell

Miracles

Let us now move from Earth to the cosmos in our search for evidence of the creator God of Judaism, Christianity, and Islam. From a modern scientific perspective, what are the empirical and theoretical implications of the hypothesis of a supernatural creation? We need to seek evidence that the universe (1) had an origin and (2) that origin cannot have happened naturally. One sign of a supernatural creation would be a direct empirical confirmation that a miracle was necessary in order to bring the universe into existence. That is, cosmological data should either show evidence for one or more violations of well-established laws of nature or the models developed to describe those data should require some causal ingredient that cannot be understood—and be probably not understandable—in purely material or natural terms.

Now, as philosopher David Hume pointed out centuries ago, many problems exist with the whole notion of miracles. Three types of possible miracles can be identified: (1) violations of established laws of nature, (2) inexplicable events, and (3) highly unlikely coincidences. The latter two can be subsumed into the first since they also would imply a disagreement with current knowledge.

In previous chapters I have given examples of observations that would confirm the reality of supernatural powers of the human mind. We can easily imagine cosmic phenomena that would forever defy material expectations. Suppose a new planet were to suddenly appear in the solar system. Such an observation would violate energy conservation and reasonably be classified as a supernatural event.

Scientists will make every effort to find a natural mechanism for any unusual event, and the layperson is likely to agree that such a mechanism might be possible since "science does not know everything."

However, science knows a lot more than most people realize. Despite the talk of "scientific revolutions" and "paradigm shifts," the basic laws of physics are essentially the same today as they were at the time of Newton. Of course they have been expanded and revised, especially with the twentieth-century developments of relativity and quantum mechanics. But anyone familiar with modern physics will have to agree that certain fundamentals, in particular the great conservation principles of energy and momentum, have not changed in four hundred years.[1] The conservation principles and Newton's laws of motion still appear in relativity and quantum mechanics. Newton's law of gravity is still used to calculate the orbits of spacecraft.

Conservation of energy and other basic laws hold true in the most distant observed galaxy and in the cosmic microwave background, implying that these laws have been valid for over thirteen billion years. Surely any observation of their violation during the puny human life span would be reasonably termed a miracle.

Theologian Richard Swinburne suggests that we define a miracle as a nonrepeatable exception to a law of nature.[2] Of course, we can always redefine the law to include the exception, but that would be somewhat arbitrary. Laws are meant to describe repeatable events. So, we will seek evidence for violations of well-established laws that do not repeat themselves in any lawful pattern.

No doubt God, if he exists, is capable of repeating miracles if he so desires. However, repeatable events provide more information that may lead to an eventual natural description, while a mysterious, unrepeated event is likely to remain mysterious. Let us give the God hypothesis every benefit of the doubt and keep open the possibility of a miraculous origin for inexplicable events and unlikely coincidences, examining any such occurrences on an individual basis. If

---

1. Conservation of energy was not immediately recognized but was already implicit in Newton's laws of mechanics.

2. Richard Swinburne, *The Existence of God* (Oxford: Clarendon Press, 1979), p. 229.

even with the loosest definition of a miracle none is observed to occur, then we will have obtained strong support for the case against the existence of a God who directs miraculous events.

Let us proceed to look for evidence of a miraculous creation in our observations of the cosmos.

Creating Matter

Until early in the twentieth century, there were strong indications that one or more miracles were required to create the universe. The universe currently contains a large amount of matter that is characterized by the physical quantity we define as mass. Prior to the twentieth century, it was believed that matter could neither be created nor destroyed, just changed from one type to another. So the very existence of matter seemed to be a miracle, a violation of the assumed law of conservation of mass that occurred just once—at the creation.

However, in his special theory of relativity published in 1905, Albert Einstein showed that matter can be created out of energy and can disappear into energy What all science writers call "Einstein's famous equation," $E = mc^2$, relates the mass m of a body to an equivalent rest energy, E, where c is a universal constant, the speed of light in a vacuum. That is, a body at rest still contains energy.

When a body is moving, it carries an additional energy of motion called *kinetic energy*. In chemical and nuclear interactions, kinetic energy can be converted into rest energy, which is equivalent to generating mass.[3] Also, the reverse happens; mass or rest energy can be converted into kinetic energy. In that way, chemical and nuclear interactions can generate kinetic energy, which then can be used to run engines or blow things up.

So, the existence of mass in the universe violates no law of nature. Mass can come from energy. But, then, where does the energy come from? The law of conservation of energy, also known as the *first law of thermodynamics,* requires that energy come from somewhere. In principle, the creation hypothesis could be confirmed by the direct observation or theoretical requirement that conservation of energy was violated 13.7 billion years ago at the start of the big bang.

However, neither observations nor theory indicates this to have been the case. The first law allows energy to convert from one type to another as long as the total for a closed system remains fixed. Remarkably, the total energy of the universe appears to be zero. As famed cosmologist Stephen Hawking said in his 1988 best seller, *A Brief History of Time,* "In the case of a universe that is approximately uniform in space, one can show that the negative gravitational energy

---

3. It is commonly thought that only nuclear reactions convert between rest and kinetic energy. This also happens in chemical reactions. However, the changes in the masses of the reactants in that case are too small to be generally noticed.

exactly cancels the positive energy represented by the matter. So the total energy of the universe is zero.[4] Specifically, within small measurement errors, the
mean energy density of the universe is exactly what it should be for a universe
that appeared from an initial state of zero energy, within a small quantum
uncertainty.[5]

A close balance between positive and negative energy is predicted by the modern extension of the big bang theory called the *inflationary big bang*, according to
which the universe underwent a period of rapid, exponential inflation during a
tiny fraction of its first second.[6] The inflationary theory has recently undergone
a number of stringent observational tests that would have been sufficient to
prove it false. So far, it has successfully passed all these tests.

In short, the existence of matter and energy in the universe did not require
the violation of energy conservation at the assumed creation. In fact, the data
strongly support the hypothesis that no such miracle occurred. If we regard
such a miracle as predicted by the creator hypothesis, then that prediction is not
confirmed.

This example also serves to once more refute the assertion that science has
nothing to say about God. Suppose our measurement of the mass density of the
universe had *not* turned out to be exactly the value required for a universe to
have begun from a state of zero energy. Then we would have had a legitimate,
scientific reason to conclude that a miracle, namely, a violation of energy conservation, was needed to bring the universe into being. While this might not
conclusively prove the existence of a creator to everyone's satisfaction, it would
certainly be a strong mark in his favor.

Creating Order

Another prediction of the creator hypothesis also fails to be confirmed by the
data. If the universe were created, then it should have possessed some degree of
order at the creation—the design that was inserted at that point by the Grand
Designer. This expectation of order is usually expressed in terms of the *second*

---

4. Stephen W. Hawking, *A Brief History of Time: From the Big Bang to Black Holes* (New
York: Bantam, 1988), p. 129.

5. Technically, the total energy of the universe cannot be defined for all possible situations in general relativity. However, in V. Faraoni and F. I. Cooperstock, "On the Total
Energy of Open Friedmann-Robertson-Walker Universes," *Astrophysical Journal* 587
(2003): 483–486, it is shown that the total energy of the universe can be defined for the
most common types of cosmologies and is zero in these cases. This included the case
where the density is critical.

6. Alan Guth, *The Inflationary Universe* (New York: Addison-Wesley, 1997).

law of thermodynamics, which states that the total *entropy* or *disorder* of a closed system must remain constant or increase with time. It would seem to follow that if the universe today is a closed system, it could not always have been so. At some point in the past, order must have been imparted from the outside.

Prior to 1929, this was a strong argument for a miraculous creation. However, in that year astronomer Edwin Hubble reported that the galaxies are moving away from one another at speeds approximately proportional to their distance, indicating that the universe is expanding. This provided the earliest evidence for the big bang. For our purposes, an expanding universe could have started in total chaos and still formed localized order consistent with the second law.

The simplest way to see this is with a (literally) homey example. Suppose that whenever you clean your house, you empty the collected rubbish by tossing it out the window into your yard. Eventually the yard would be filled with rubbish. However, you can continue doing this with a simple expedient. Just keep buying up the land around your house and you will always have more room to toss the rubbish. You are able to maintain localized order—in your house—at the expense of increased disorder in the rest of the universe.

Similarly, parts of the universe can become more orderly as the rubbish, or entropy, produced during the ordering process (think of it as disorder being removed from the system being ordered) is tossed out into the larger, ever-expanding surrounding space. The total entropy of the universe increases as the universe expands, as required by the second law.[7] However, the maximum possible entropy increases even faster, leaving increasingly more room for order to form. The reason for this is that the maximum entropy of a sphere of a certain radius (we are thinking of the universe as a sphere) is that of a black hole of that radius. The expanding universe is not a black hole and so has less than maximum entropy. Thus, while becoming more disorderly on the whole as time goes by, our expanding universe is not maximally disordered. But, once it was.

Suppose we extrapolate the expansion back 13.7 billion years to the earliest definable moment, the *Planck time*, 6.4×10^{-44} second when the universe was confined to the smallest possible region of space that can be operationally defined, a *Planck sphere* that has a radius equal to the *Planck length*, 1.6×10^{-35} meter. As expected from the second law, the universe at that time had lower entropy than it has now. However, that entropy was also as high as it possibly could have been for an object that small, because a sphere of Planck dimensions is equivalent to a black hole.

---

7. The mathematical derivation of the curves on this plot is given in Appendix C of Victor J. Stenger, *Has Science Found God? The Latest Results in the Search for Purpose in the Universe* (Amherst, NY: Prometheus Books, 2003), pp. 356–357.

This requires further elaboration. I seem to be saying that the entropy of the universe was maximal when the universe began, yet it has been increasing ever since. Indeed, that's exactly what I am saying. When the universe began, its entropy was as high as it could be for an object of that size because the universe was equivalent to a black hole from which no information can be extracted. Currently the entropy is higher but not maximal, that is, not as high as it could be for an object of the universe's current size. The universe is no longer a black hole.

I also need to respond here to an objection that has been raised by physicists who have heard me make this statement. They point out, correctly, that we currently do not have a theory of quantum gravity that we can apply to describe physics earlier than the Planck time. I have adopted Einstein's operational definition of time as what you read on a clock. In order to measure a time interval smaller than the Planck time, you would need to make that measurement in a region smaller than the Planck length, which equals the Planck time multiplied by the speed of light. According to the Heisenberg uncertainty principle of quantum mechanics, such a region would be a black hole, from which no information can escape. This implies that no time interval can be defined that is smaller than the Planck time.[8]

Consider the present time. Clearly we do not have any qualms about applying established physics "now" and for short times earlier or later, as long as we do not try to do so for time intervals shorter than the Planck time. Basically, by definition time is counted off as an integral number of units where one unit equals the Planck time. We can get away with treating time as a continuous variable in our mathematical physics, such as we do when we use calculus, because the units are so small compared to anything we measure in practice. We essentially extrapolate our equations through the Planck intervals within which time is unmeasurable and thus indefinable. If we can do this "now," we can do it at the end of the earliest Planck interval where we must begin our description of the beginning of the big bang.

At that time, our extrapolation from later times tells us that the entropy was maximal. In that case, the disorder was complete and no structure could have been present. Thus, the universe began with no structure. It has structure today consistent with the fact that its entropy is no longer maximal.

In short, according to our best current cosmological understanding, our universe began with no structure or organization, designed or otherwise. It was a state of chaos.

We are thus forced to conclude that the complex order we now observe could *not* have been the result of any initial design built into the universe at the so-

---

8. The mathematical proof of this is given in Appendix A, Stenger, *Has Science Found God?* pp. 351–353.

called creation. The universe preserves no record of what went on before the big bang. The Creator, if he existed, left no imprint. Thus he might as well have been nonexistent.

Once again we have a result that might have turned out otherwise and provided strong scientific evidence for a creator. If the universe were not expanding but a firmament, as described in the Bible, then the second law would have required that the entropy of the universe was lower than its maximum allowed value in the past. Thus, if the universe had a beginning, it would have begun in a state of high order necessarily imposed from the outside. Even if the universe extended into the infinite past, it would be increasingly orderly in that direction, and the source of that order would defy natural description.

The empirical fact of the big bang has led some theists to argue that this, in itself, demonstrates the existence of a creator. In 1951 Pope Pius XII told the Pontifical Academy, "Creation took place in time, therefore there is a Creator, therefore God exists."[9] The astronomer/priest Georges-Henri Lemaitre, who first proposed the idea of a big bang, wisely advised the pope not make this statement "infallible."

Christian apologist William Lane Craig has made a number of sophisticated arguments that he claims show that the universe must have had a beginning and that beginning implies a personal creator.[10] One such argument is based on *general relativity,* the modern theory of gravity that was published by Einstein in 1916 and that has, since then, passed many stringent empirical tests."[11]

In 1970 cosmologist Stephen Hawking and mathematician Roger Penrose, using a theorem derived earlier by Penrose, "proved" that a *singularity* exists at the beginning of the big bang.[12] Extrapolating general relativity back to zero time, the universe gets smaller and smaller while the density of the universe and the gravitational field increases. As the size of the universe goes to zero, the density and gravitational field, at least according to the mathematics of general relativity, become infinite. At that point, Craig claims, time must stop and, therefore, no prior time can exist.

9. Pope Pius XII, "The Proofs for Existence of God in the Light of Modern Natural Science," Address by Pope Pius XII to the Pontifical Academy of Sciences, November 22, 1951, reprinted as "Modern Science and the Existence of God," *Catholic Mind* 49 (1972): 182–192.

10. William Lane Craig and Quentin Smith, *Theism, Atheism, and Big Bang Cosmology* (Oxford: Clarendon Press, 1997).

11. Clifford M. Will, *Was Einstein Right? Putting General Relativity to the Test* (New York: Basic Books, 1986).

12. Stephen W. Hawking and Roger Penrose, "The Singularities of Gravitational Collapse and Cosmology," *Proceedings of the Royal Society of London*, series A, 314 (1970): 529–548.

However, Hawking has repudiated his own earlier proof. In his best seller *A Brief History of Time,* he avers, "There was in fact no singularity at the beginning of the universe."[13] This revised conclusion, concurred with by Penrose, follows from quantum mechanics, the theory of atomic processes that was developed in the years following the introduction of Einstein's theories of relativity. Quantum mechanics, which also is now confirmed to great precision, tells us that general relativity, at least as currently formulated, must break down at times less than the Planck time and at distances smaller than the Planck length, mentioned earlier. It follows that general relativity cannot be used to imply that a singularity occurred prior to the Planck time and that Craig's use of the singularity theorem for a beginning of time is invalid.

Craig and other theists also make another, related argument that the universe had to have had a beginning at some point, because if it were infinitely old, it would have taken an infinite time to reach the present. However, as philosopher Keith Parsons has pointed out, "To say the universe is infinitely old is to say that it had no beginning—not a beginning that was infinitely long ago."[14]

Infinity is an abstract mathematical concept that was precisely formulated in the work of mathematician Georg Cantor in the late nineteenth century. However, the symbol for infinity, " ∞ ," is used in physics simply as a shorthand for "a very big number." Physics is counting. In physics, time is simply the count of ticks on a clock. You can count backward as well as forward. Counting forward you can get a very big but never mathematically infinite positive number and time "never ends." Counting backward you can get a very big but never mathematically infinite negative number and time "never begins." Just as we never reach positive infinity, we never reach negative infinity. Even if the universe does not have a mathematically infinite number of events in the future, it still need not have an end. Similarly, even if the universe does not have a mathematically infinite number of events in the past, it still need not have a beginning. We can always have one event follow another, and we can always have one event precede another.

Craig claims that if it can be shown that the universe had a beginning, this is sufficient to demonstrate the existence of a personal creator. He casts this in terms of the *kalâm cosmological argument,* which is drawn from Islamic theology.[15] The argument is posed as a syllogism:

---

13. Hawking, *A Brief History of Time*, p. 50.

14. Keith Parsons, "Is There a Case for Christian Theism?" In *Does God Exist? The Debate Between Theists & Atheists*, J. P. Moreland and Kai Nielsen (Amherst, NY: Prometheus Books, 1993), p. 177. See also Wes Morriston, "Creation *Ex Nihilo* and the Big Bang," *Philo* 5, no. 1 (2002): 23–33.

15. William Lane Craig, *The Kalâm Cosmological Argument*, Library of Philosophy and Religion (London: Macmillan, 1979); *The Cosmological Argument from Plato to Leibniz*, Library of Philosophy and Religion (London: Macmillan, 1980).

1. Whatever begins to exist has a cause.
2. The universe began to exist.
3. Therefore, the universe has a cause.

The *kalâm* argument has been severely challenged by philosophers on logical grounds,[16] which need not be repeated here since we are focusing on the science.

In his writings, Craig takes the first premise to be self-evident, with no justification other than common, everyday experience. That's the type of experience that tells us the world is flat. In fact, physical events at the atomic and subatomic level are observed to have no evident cause. For example, when an atom in an excited energy level drops to a lower level and emits a photon, a particle of light, we find no cause of that event. Similarly, no cause is evident in the decay of a radioactive nucleus.

Craig has retorted that quantum events are still "caused," just caused in a nonpredetermined manner—what he calls "probabilistic causality." In effect, Craig is thereby admitting that the "cause" in his first premise could be an accidental one, something spontaneous—something not predetermined. By allowing probabilistic cause, he destroys his own case for a predetermined creation.

We have a highly successful theory of probabilistic causes—quantum mechanics. It does not predict when a given event will occur and, indeed, assumes that individual events are not predetermined. The one exception occurs in the interpretation of quantum mechanics given by David Bohm.[17] This assumes the existence of yet-undetected subquantum forces. While this interpretation has some supporters, it is not generally accepted because it requires superluminal connections that violate the principles of special relativity.[18] More important, no evidence for subquantum forces has been found.

Instead of predicting individual events, quantum mechanics is used to predict the statistical distribution of outcomes of ensembles of similar events. This it can do with high precision. For example, a quantum calculation will tell you how many nuclei in a large sample will have decayed after a given time. Or you

---

16. Smith in *Theism, Atheism, and Big Bang Cosmology*, by Craig and Smith; Graham Oppy, "Arguing about the Kalâm Cosmological Argument," *Philo* 5, no. 1 (Spring/Summer 2002): 34–61, and references therein; Arnold Guminski, "The Kalâm Cosmological Argument: The Questions of the Metaphysical Possibility of an Infinite Set of Real Entities," *Philo* 5, no. 2 (Fall/Winter 2002): 196–215; Nicholas Everitt, *The Non-Existence of God* (London, New York: Routledge, 2004), pp. 68–72.

17. David Bohm and B. J. Hiley, *The Undivided Universe: An Ontological Interpretation of Quantum Mechanics* (London: Routledge, 1993).

18. I discuss this in detail in Victor J. Stenger, *The Unconscious Quantum: Metaphysics in Modern Physics and Cosmology* (Amherst, NY: Prometheus Books, 1995).

can predict the intensity of light from a group of excited atoms, which is a measure of the total number of photons emitted. But neither quantum mechanics nor any other existing theory—including Bohm's—can say anything about the behavior of an individual nucleus or atom. The photons emitted in atomic transitions come into existence spontaneously, as do the particles emitted in nuclear radiation. By so appearing, without predetermination, they contradict the first premise.

In the case of radioactivity, the decays are observed to follow an exponential decay "law." However, this statistical law is exactly what you expect if the probability for decay in a given small time interval is the same for all time intervals of the same duration. In other words, the decay curve itself is evidence for each individual event occurring unpredictably and, by inference, without being predetermined.

Quantum mechanics and classical (Newtonian) mechanics are not as separate and distinct from one another as is generally thought. Indeed, quantum mechanics changes smoothly into classical mechanics when the parameters of the system, such as masses, distances, and speeds, approach the classical regime.[19] When that happens, quantum probabilities collapse to either zero or 100 percent, which then gives us certainty at that level. However, we have many examples where the probabilities are not zero or 100 percent. The quantum probability calculations agree precisely with the observations made on ensembles of similar events.

Note that even if the *kalâm* conclusion were sound and the universe had a cause, why could that cause itself not be natural? As it is, the *kalâm* argument fails both empirically and theoretically without ever having to bring up the second premise about the universe having a beginning.

The Origin

Nevertheless, another nail in the coffin of the *kalâm* argument is provided by the fact that the second premise also fails. As we saw above, the claim that the universe began with the big bang has no basis in current physical and cosmological knowledge.

The observations confirming the big bang do not rule out the possibility of a prior universe. Theoretical models have been published suggesting mechanisms by which our current universe appeared from a preexisting one, for example, by

---

19. Quantum mechanics becomes classical mechanics when Planck's constant h is set equal to zero.

a process called quantum tunneling or so-called quantum fluctuations.[20] The equations of cosmology that describe the early universe apply equally for the other side of the time axis, so we have no reason to assume that the universe began with the big bang.

In *The Comprehensible Cosmos*, I presented a specific scenario for the purely natural origin of the universe, worked out mathematically at a level accessible to anyone with an undergraduate mathematics or physics background.[21] This was based on the *no boundary model* of James Hartle and Stephen Hawking.[22] In that model, the universe has no beginning or end in space or time. In the scenario I presented, our universe is described as having "tunneled" through the chaos at the Planck time from a prior universe that existed for all previous time.

While he avoided technical details in *A Brief History of Time*, the no boundary model was the basis of Hawking's oft-quoted statement. "So long as the universe had a beginning, we could suppose it had a creator. But if the universe is really completely self-contained, having no boundary or edge, it would have neither beginning nor end; it would simply be. What place then, for a creator?"[23]

Prominent physicists and cosmologists have published, in reputable scientific journals, a number of other scenarios by which the universe could have come about "from nothing" naturally.[24] None can be "proved" at this time to represent the exact way the universe appeared, but they serve to illustrate that any argument for the existence of God based on this gap in scientific knowledge fails, since plausible natural mechanisms can be given within the framework of existing knowledge.

---

20. David Atkatz and Heinz Pagels, "Origin of the Universe as Quantum Tunneling Event," *Physical Review* D25 (1982): 2065–2067; Alexander Vilenkin, "Birth of Inflationary Universes," *Physical Review* D27 (1983): 2848–2855; David Atkatz, "Quantum Cosmology for Pedestrians," *American Journal of Physics* 62 (1994): 619–627.

21. Victor J. Stenger, *The Comprehensible Cosmos: Where Do the Laws of Physics Come From?* (Amherst, NY: Prometheus Books, 2006), supplement H.

22. J. B. Hartle and S. W. Hawking, "Wave Function of the Universe," *Physical Review* D28 (1983): 2960–2975.

23. Hawking, *A Brief History of Time*, pp. 140–141.

24. E. P. Tryon, "Is the Universe a Quantum Fluctuation?" *Nature* 246 (1973): 396–397; Atkatz and Pagels, "Origin of the Universe as Quantum Tunneling Event"; Alexander Vilenkin, "Quantum Creation of Universes," *Physical Review* D30 (1984): 509; Andre Linde, "Quantum Creation of the Inflationary Universe," *Lettere Al Nuovo Cimento* 39 (1984): 401–405; T. R. Mongan, "Simple Quantum Cosmology: Vacuum Energy and Initial State," *General Relativity and Gravitation* 37 (2005): 967–970.

As I have emphasized, the God of the gaps argument for God fails when a plausible scientific account for a gap in current knowledge can be given. I do not dispute that the exact nature of the origin of the universe remains a gap in scientific knowledge.

But I deny that we are bereft of any conceivable way to account for that origin scientifically.

In short, empirical data and the theories that successfully describe those data indicate that the universe did not come about by a purposeful creation. Based on our best current scientific knowledge, it follows that no creator exists who left a cosmological imprint of a purposeful creation.

Intervening in the Cosmos

This still leaves open the possibility that a god exists who may have created the universe in such a way that did not require any miracles and did not leave any imprint of his intentions. Of course, this is no longer the traditional Judeo-Christian-Islamic God, whose imprint is supposedly everywhere. But, perhaps those religions can modify their theologies and posit a god who steps in later, after the Planck time, to ensure that his purposes are still served despite whatever plans he had of creation being wiped out by the chaos at the Planck time.

In that case, we can again expect to find, in observations or well-established theories, some evidence of places where this god has intervened in the history of the cosmos. In previous chapters we sought such evidence on Earth, in the phenomena of life and mind. Here we move to the vast space beyond Earth.

History gives us many examples of unexpected events in the heavens that at first appeared miraculous. In 585 BCE a total eclipse of the sun over Asia Minor ended a battle between the Medes and the Lydians, with both sides fleeing in terror. In probably the first known case of a scientific prediction, Thales of Miletus had predicted the eclipse based on Babylonian records.

Eclipses are sufficiently rare that they are not so regular a part of normal human experience as are the rising and setting of the sun and the phases of the moon. However, they do repeat and behave lawfully, as do these more familiar phenomena. That's why today we can give the exact date (on our current calendar) of Thales's eclipse: May 28, 585 BCE. This demonstrates the remarkable power of science to both predict the future and postdict the past. About that time, Nebuchadnezzar II destroyed Jerusalem and carried the Judeans off into exile in Babylonia (where they would pick up their creation myth). The Buddha is said to have attained enlightenment at almost exactly the same time. Confucius would be born a few decades later.

Comets are a similar example of spectacular astronomical phenomena that ancient people commonly regarded as supernatural omens but science has since described in natural terms, that is, with purely material models. In the seventeenth century, Edmund Halley (d. 1742) used the mechanical theories developed by his friend Isaac Newton (d. 1727) to predict that a comet seen in 1682 would return in 1759. Indeed it did, after Halley's death, and has done so every seventy-six years since. Most comets appear unexpectedly, having such extended orbits that they have spent human history outside our view. However, records indicate that Halley's comet has appeared perhaps twenty-nine times in history.

In more recent times, other astronomical phenomena have occurred unexpectedly and could not be immediately understood. These include pulsars, supernovas, quasars, and gamma-ray bursts. But, as with other examples, these phenomena eventually repeated in one way or another, in time or in space. This allowed us to learn enough to eventually understand their nature in purely physical terms.

At no time and at no place in the sky have we run across an event above the noise that did not repeat sometime or someplace and could not be accounted for in terms of established natural science. We have yet to encounter an observable astronomical phenomenon that requires a supernatural element to be added to a model in order to describe the event. In fact, we have no cosmic phenomenon that meets the Swinburne criterion for a miracle. A God who plays a sufficiently active role to produce miraculous events in the cosmos has not been even glimpsed at by our best astronomical instruments to date. Observations in cosmology look just as they can be expected to look if there is no God.

Where Do the Laws of Physics Come From?

We have seen that the origin and the operation of the universe do not require any violations of laws of physics. This probably will come as a surprise to the layperson who may have heard otherwise from the pulpit or the media. However, the scientifically savvy believer might concede this point for the sake of argument and then retort, "Okay, then where did the laws of physics come from?" The common belief is that they had to come from somewhere outside the universe. But that is not a demonstrable fact. There is no reason why the laws of physics cannot have come from within the universe itself.

Physicists invent mathematical models to describe their observations of the world. These models contain certain general principles that have been traditionally called "laws" because of the common belief that these are rules that actually govern the universe the way civil laws govern nations. However, as I showed in my previous book, *The Comprehensible Cosmos,* the most fundamental laws of physics are not restrictions on the behavior of matter. Rather they are restrictions on the way physicists may describe that behavior.[25]

---

25. Stenger, *The Comprehensible Cosmos.*

In order for any principle of nature we write down to be objective and universal, it must be formulated in such a way that it does not depend on the point of view of any particular observer. The principle must be true for all points of view, from every "frame of reference." And so, for example, no objective law can depend on a special moment in time or a position in space that may be singled out by some preferred observer.

Suppose I were to formulate a law that said that all objects move naturally toward me. That would not be very objective. But this was precisely what people once thought—that Earth was the center of the universe and the natural motion of bodies was toward Earth. The Copernican revolution showed this was wrong and was the first step in the gradual realization of scientists that their laws must not depend on frame of reference.

In 1918 mathematician Emmy Noether proved that the most important physical laws of all—conservation of energy, linear momentum, and angular momentum—will automatically appear in any model that does not single out a special moment in time, position in space, and direction in space.[26] Later it was realized that Einstein's special theory of relativity follows if we do not single out any special direction in four-dimensional space-time.

These properties of space-time are called *symmetries*. For example, the rotational symmetry of a sphere is a result of the sphere singling out no particular direction in space. The four space-time symmetries described above are just the natural symmetries of a universe with no matter, that is, a void. They are just what they should be if the universe appeared from an initial state in which there was no matter—from nothing.

Other laws of physics, such as conservation of electric charge and the various force laws, arise from the generalization of space-time symmetries to the abstract spaces physicists use in their mathematic models. This generalization is called *gauge invariance*, which is likened to a principle I more descriptively refer to as *point-of-view invariance*.

The mathematical formulations of these models (which are provided in *The Comprehensible Cosmos*) must reflect this requirement if they are to be objective and universal. Surprisingly, when this is done, most of the familiar laws of physics appear naturally. Those that are not immediately obvious can be seen to plausibly arise by a process, known as *spontaneous symmetry breaking*.

---

26. E. Noether, "Invarianten beliebiger Differentialausdrücke," *Nachr. d. König. Gesellsch. d. Wiss. zu Göttingen, Math-phys.* Klasse (1918): 37–44; Nina Byers, "E. Noether's Discovery of the Deep Connection between Symmetries and Conservation Laws," *Israel Mathematical Conference Proceedings* 12 (1999), http://www.physics.ucla.edu/~cwp/articles/ noether.asg/noether.html (accessed July 1, 2006). This contains links to Noether's original paper including an English translation.

So where did the laws of physics come from? They came from nothing! Most are statements composed by humans that follow from the symmetries of the void out of which the universe spontaneously arose. Rather than being handed down from above, like the Ten Commandments, they look exactly as they should look if they were not handed down from anywhere. And this is why, for example, a violation of energy conservation at the beginning of the big bang would be evidence for some external creator. Even though they invented it, physicists could not simply change the "law." It would imply a miracle or, more explicitly, some external agency that acted to break the time symmetry that leads to conservation of energy. But, as we have seen, no such miracle is required by the data.

Thus we are justified in applying the conservation laws to the beginning of the big bang at the Planck time. At that time, as we saw earlier in this chapter, the universe had no structure. That meant that it had no distinguishable place, direction, or time. In such a situation, the conservation laws apply.

Now, this is certainly not a commonly understood view. Normally we think of laws of physics as part of the structure of the universe. But here I am arguing that the three great conservation laws are not part of any structure. Rather they follow from the very lack of structure at the earliest moment.

No doubt this concept is difficult to grasp. My views on this particular issue are not recognized by a consensus of physicists, although I insist that the science I have used is well established and conventional. I am proposing no new physics or cosmology but merely providing an interpretation of established knowledge in those fields as it bears on the question of the origin of physical law, a question few physicists ever ponder.

I must emphasize another important point, which has been frequently misunderstood. I am not suggesting that the laws of physics can be anything we want them to be, that they are merely "cultural narratives," as has been suggested by authors associated with the movement called postmodernism.[27] They are what they are because they agree with the data.

Whether or not you will buy into my account of the origin of physical law, I hope you will allow that I have at minimum provided a plausible natural scenario for a gap in scientific knowledge, that gap being a clear consensus on the origin of physical law. Once again, I do not have the burden of proving this scenario. The believer who wishes to argue that God is the source of physical law has the burden of proving (1) that my account is wrong, (2) that no other natural account is possible, and (3) that God did it.

---

27. Walter Truett Anderson, *The Truth About the Truth* (New York: Jeremy P. Tarcher/Putnam, 1996).

Why Is There Something
Rather Than Nothing?

If the laws of physics follow naturally from empty space-time, then where did
that empty space-time come from? Why is there something rather than nothing? This question is often the last recourse of the theist who seeks to argue for
the existence of God from physics and cosmology and finds that all his other arguments fail. Philosopher Bede Rundle calls it "philosophy's central, and most
perplexing, question." His simple (but book-length) answer: "There has to be
something."[28]

Clearly many conceptual problems are associated with this question. How do
we define "nothing"? What are its properties? If it has properties, doesn't that
make it something? The theist claims that God is the answer. But, then, why is
there God rather than nothing? Assuming we can define "nothing," why should
nothing be a more natural state of affairs than something? In fact, we can give a
plausible scientific reason based on our best current knowledge of physics and
cosmology that something is more natural than nothing!

In Chapter 2 we saw how nature is capable of building complex structures by
processes of self-organization, how simplicity begets complexity. Consider the
example of the snowflake, the beautiful six-pointed pattern of ice crystals that
results from the direct freezing of water vapor in the atmosphere. Our experience tells us that a snowflake is very ephemeral, melting quickly into drops of
liquid water that exhibit far less structure. But that is only because we live in a
relatively high-temperature environment, where heat reduces the fragile
arrangement of crystals to a simpler liquid. Energy is required to break the symmetry of a snowflake.

In an environment where the ambient temperature is well below the melting
point of ice, as it is in most of the universe far from the highly localized effects
of stellar heating, any water vapor would readily crystallize into complex, asymmetric structures. Snowflakes would be eternal, or at least would remain intact
until cosmic rays tore them apart.

This example illustrates that many simple systems of particles are unstable,
that is, have limited lifetimes as they undergo spontaneous phase transitions to
more complex structures of lower energy. Since "nothing" is as simple as it gets,
we cannot expect it to be very stable. It would likely undergo a spontaneous
phase transition to something more complicated, like a universe containing
matter. The transition of nothing-to-something is a natural one, not requiring
any agent. As Nobel laureate physicist Frank Wilczek has put it, "The answer to

---

28. Bede Rundle, *Why There Is Something Rather Than Nothing* (Oxford: Clarendon Press,
2004).

the ancient question 'Why is there something rather than nothing?' would then be that 'nothing' is unstable."[29]

In the nonboundary scenario for the natural origin of the universe I mentioned earlier, the probability for there being something rather than nothing actually can be calculated; it is over 60 percent.[30]

In short, the natural state of affairs is something rather than nothing. An empty universe requires supernatural intervention—not a full one. Only by the constant action of an agent outside the universe, such as God, could a state of nothingness be maintained. The fact that we have something is just what we would expect if there is no God.

---

29. Frank Wilczek, "The Cosmic Asymmetry Between Matter and Antimatter," *Scientific American* 243, no. 6 (1980): 82–90.

30. Stenger, *The Comprehensible Cosmos*, supplement H.

38

A Working
Definition of Religion

From "Breaking Which Spell?"

Daniel C. Dennett

Any atheist in any argument with the religious will soon find that many, if not most, "believers" are choosing *á la carte* from an infinite menu of possible affirmations. We wish them luck, even as we wish that they could make their incoherent beliefs consistent. With great generosity, Daniel Dennett suggests that "belief in belief" is at the root of all this, and that people really would rather assert some vague faith than none at all. He even concedes that this may sometimes have been helpful. However, he inquires politely whether people who talk in this fashion can possibly mean what they appear to say.

> *Philosophers stretch the meaning of words until they retain scarcely anything of their original sense; by calling "God" some vague abstraction which they have created for themselves, they pose as deists, as believers, before the world; they may even pride themselves on having attained a higher and purer idea of God, although their God is nothing but an insubstantial shadow and no longer the mighty personality of religious doctrine.*
>
> —Sigmund Freud, *The Future of an Illusion*

How do I define religion? It doesn't matter *just* how I define it, since I plan to examine and discuss the neighboring phenomena that (probably) aren't religions—spirituality, commitment to secular organizations, fanatical devotion to ethnic groups (or sports teams), superstition. . . . So, wherever I "draw the line," I'll be going over the line in any case. As you will see, what we usually call religions are composed of a variety of quite different phenomena, arising from different circumstances and having different implications, forming a loose family of phenomena, not a "natural kind" like a chemical element or a species.

328

What is the essence of religion? This question should be considered askance. Even if there is a deep and important affinity between many or even most of the world's religions, there are sure to be variants that share some typical features while lacking one or another "essential" feature. As evolutionary biology advanced during the last century, we gradually came to appreciate the deep reasons for grouping living things the way we do—sponges are animals, and birds are more closely related to dinosaurs than frogs are—and new surprises are still being discovered every year. So we should expect— and tolerate—some difficulty in arriving at a counterexample-proof definition of something as diverse and complex as religion. Sharks and dolphins look very much alike and behave in many similar ways, but they are not the same sort of thing at all. *Perhaps,* once we understand the whole field better, we will see that Buddhism and Islam, for all their similarities, deserve to be considered two entirely different species of cultural phenomenon. We can start with common sense and tradition and consider them both to be religions, but we shouldn't blind ourselves to the prospect that our initial sorting may have to be adjusted as we learn more. Why is *suckling one's young* more fundamental than *living in the ocean*? Why is *having a backbone* more fundamental than *having wings*? It may be obvious now, but it wasn't obvious at the dawn of biology.

In the United Kingdom, the law regarding cruelty to animals draws an important moral line at whether the animal is a vertebrate: as far as the law is concerned, you may do what you like to a live worm or fly or shrimp, but not to a live bird or frog or mouse. It's a pretty good place to draw the line, but laws can be amended, and this one was. Cephalopods—octopus, squid, cuttlefish—were recently made *honorary vertebrates,* in effect, because they, unlike their close mollusc cousins the clams and oysters, have such strikingly sophisticated nervous systems. This seems to me a wise political adjustment, since the similarities that mattered to the law and morality didn't line up perfectly with the deep principles of biology.

We may find that drawing a boundary between *religion* and its nearest neighbors among cultural phenomena is beset with similar, but more vexing, problems. For instance, since the law (in the United States, at least) singles out religions for special status, declaring something that has been regarded as a religion to be really something else is bound to be of more than academic interest to those involved. Wicca (witchcraft) and other New Age phenomena have been championed as religions by their adherents precisely in order to elevate them to the legal and social status that religions have traditionally enjoyed. And, coming from the other direction, there are those who have claimed that evolutionary biology is really "just another religion," and hence its doctrines have no place in the public-school curriculum. Legal protection, honor, prestige, and a *traditional exemption from certain sorts of analysis and criticism*—a great deal hinges on how we define religion. How should I handle this delicate issue?

Tentatively, I propose to define religions as *social systems whose participants avow belief in a supernatural agent or agents whose approval is to be sought.* This is, of course, a circuitous way of articulating the idea that a religion without *God* or *gods* is like a vertebrate without a backbone. Some of the reasons for this roundabout language are fairly obvious; others will emerge over time—and the definition is subject to revision, a place to start, not something carved in stone to be defended to the death. According to this definition, a devout Elvis Presley fan club is not a religion, because, although the members may, in a fairly obvious sense, *worship* Elvis, he is not deemed by them to be literally supernatural, but just to have been a particularly superb human being. (And if some fan clubs decide that Elvis is truly immortal and divine, then they are indeed on the way to starting a new religion.) A supernatural agent need not be very *anthropomorphic.* The Old Testament Jehovah is definitely a sort of divine man (not a woman), who sees with eyes and hears with ears—and talks and acts in real time. (God *waited* to *see* what Job would do, and *then* he *spoke* to him.) Many contemporary Christians, Jews, and Muslims insist that God, or Allah, being omniscient, has no need for anything like sense organs, and, being eternal, does not act in real time. This is puzzling, since many of them continue to pray to God, to hope that God *will* answer their prayers tomorrow, to express gratitude to God for *creating* the universe, and to use such locutions as "what God intends us to do" and "God have mercy," acts that *seem* to be in flat contradiction to their insistence that their God is not at all anthropomorphic. According to a long-standing tradition, this tension between God as agent and God as eternal and immutable Being is one of those things that are simply beyond human comprehension, and it would be foolish and arrogant to try to understand it. That is as it may be, and this topic will be carefully treated later in the book, but we cannot proceed with my definition of religion (or any other definition, really) until we (tentatively, pending further illumination) get a *little* clearer about the spectrum of views that are discernible through this pious fog of modest incomprehension. We need to seek further interpretation before we can decide how to classify the doctrines these people espouse.

For some people, prayer is not literally *talking to God* but, rather, a "symbolic" activity, a way of talking to *oneself* about one's deepest concerns, expressed metaphorically. It is rather like beginning a diary entry with "Dear Diary." If what they call God is really not an agent in their eyes, a being that can *answer* prayers, *approve* and *disapprove, receive* sacrifices, and *mete out* punishment or forgiveness, then, although they may call this Being God, and stand in awe of it (not *Him),* their creed, whatever it is, is not really a religion according to my definition. It is, perhaps, a wonderful (or terrible) surrogate for religion, or a *former* religion, an offspring of a genuine religion that bears many family resemblances to religion, but it is another species altogether. In order to get clear about what religions *are,* we will have to allow that some religions may have turned into things that aren't religions anymore. This has certainly happened to particular practices and traditions that used to be parts of genuine religions. The rituals of Halloween are no longer religious rituals, at least in America. The people who go to great effort and expense to participate in them are not, thereby, practicing religion, even though their activities can be placed in a clear line of descent from religious practices. Belief in Santa Claus has also lost its status as a religious belief.

For others, prayer really is talking to God, who (not *which*) really does listen, and forgive. Their creed is a religion, according to my definition, provided that they are part of a larger social system or community, not a congregation of one. In this regard, my definition is profoundly at odds with that of William James, who defined religion as "the feelings, acts, and experiences of individual men in their solitude, so far as they apprehend themselves to stand in relation to whatever they may consider the divine" (1902, p. 31). He would have no difficulty identifying a lone believer as a person with a religion; he himself was apparently such a one. This concentration on individual, private religious *experience* was a tactical choice for James; he thought that the creeds, rituals, trappings, and political hierarchies of "organized" religion were a distraction from the root phenomenon, and his tactical path bore wonderful fruit, but he could hardly deny that those social and cultural factors hugely affect the content and structure of the individual's experience. Today, there are reasons for trading in James's psychological microscope for a wide-angle biological and social telescope, looking at the factors, over large expanses of both space and time, that shape the experiences and actions of individual religious people.

But just as James could hardly deny the social and cultural factors, I could hardly deny the existence of individuals who very sincerely and devoutly take themselves to be the lone communicants of what we might call private religions. Typically these people have had considerable experience with one or more world religions and have chosen not to be joiners. Not wanting to ignore them, but needing to distinguish them from the much, much more typical religious people who identify themselves with a particular creed or church that has many other members, I shall call them *spiritual* people, but not *religious*. They are, if you like, honorary vertebrates.

There are many other variants to be considered in due course—for instance, people who pray, and believe in the efficacy of prayer, but don't believe that this efficacy is channeled through an agent God who literally hears the prayer. I want to postpone consideration of all these issues until we have a clearer sense of where these doctrines sprang from. The core phenomenon of religion, I am proposing, invokes gods who are effective agents in real time, and who play a central role in the way participants think about what they ought to do. I use the evasive word "invokes" here because, as we shall see in a later chapter, the standard word "belief" tends to distort and camouflage some of the most interesting features of religion. To put it provocatively, religious belief isn't always *belief*. And why is the approval of the supernatural agent or agents to be sought? That clause is included to distinguish religion from "black magic" of various sorts.

There are people—very few, actually, although juicy urban legends about "satanic cults" would have us think otherwise—who take themselves to be able to command demons with whom they form some sort of unholy alliance. These (barely existent) social systems are on the boundary with religion, but I think it is appropriate to leave them out, since our intuitions recoil at the idea that people who engage in this kind of tripe deserve the special status of the devout. What apparently grounds the widespread respect in which religions of all kinds are held is the sense that those who are religious are well-intentioned, trying to lead morally good lives, earnest in their desire not to do evil, and to make amends for their transgressions. Somebody who is both so selfish and so gullible as to try to make a pact with evil supernatural agents in order to get his way in the world lives in a comic-book world of superstition and deserves no such respect.

If God Is Dead,
Is Everything Permitted?

ELIZABETH ANDERSON

How could we stop ourselves from indulging in murder, rape, theft, perjury, and genocide if we believed the heavens were empty? The question is posed upside-down and inside out and wrong-way round, as this elegant and tough-minded essay confirms.

At the Institute for Creation Research Museum in Santee, California, visitors begin their tour by viewing a plaque displaying the "tree of evolutionism," which, it is said (following Matt. 7:18), "bears only corrupt fruits." The "evil tree" of evolution is a stock metaphor among proponents of the literal truth of the biblical story of creation. In different versions, it represents evolutionary theory as leading to abortion, suicide, homosexuality, the drug culture, hard rock, alcohol, "dirty books," sex education, alcoholism, crime, government regulation, inflation, racism, Nazism, communism, terrorism, socialism, moral relativism, secularism, feminism, and humanism, among other phenomena regarded as evil. The roots of the evil tree grow in the soil of "unbelief," which nourishes the tree with "sin." The base of its trunk represents "no God"—that is, atheism.

The evil tree vividly displays two important ideas. First, the fundamental religious objection to the theory of evolution is not scientific but moral. Evolutionary theory must be opposed because it leads to rampant immorality, on both the personal and political scales. Second, the basic cause of this immorality is atheism. Evolutionary theory bears corrupt fruit because it is rooted in denial of the existence of God.

Most forms of theism today are reconciled to the truth of evolutionary theory. But the idea of the evil tree still accurately depicts a core objection to atheism. Few people of religious faith object to atheism because they think the evidence for the existence of God is compelling to any rational inquirer. Most of the faithful haven't considered the evidence for the existence of God in a spirit of rational inquiry—that is, with openness to the possibility that the evidence goes against their faith. Rather, I believe that people object to atheism because they think that without God, morality is impossible. In the famous words (mis)attributed to Dostoyevsky, "If God is dead, then everything is permitted." Or, in the less-famous words of Senator Joe Lieberman, we must not suppose "that morality can be maintained without religion."

Why think that religion is necessary for morality? It might be thought that people wouldn't *know* the difference between right and wrong if God did not reveal it to them. But that can't be right. Every society, whether or not it was founded on theism, has acknowledged the basic principles of morality, excluding religious observance, which are laid down in the Ten Commandments. Every stable society punishes murder, theft, and bearing false witness; teaches children to honor their parents; and condemns envy of one's neighbor's possessions, at least when such envy leads one to treat one's neighbors badly. People figured out these rules long before they were exposed to any of the major monotheistic religions. This fact suggests that moral knowledge springs not from revelation but from people's experiences in living together, in which they have learned that they must adjust their own conduct in light of others' claims.

Perhaps, then, the idea that religion is necessary for morality means that people wouldn't *care* about the difference between right and wrong if God did not promise salvation for good behavior and threaten damnation for bad behavior. On this view, people must be goaded into behaving morally through divine sanction. But this can't be right, either. People have many motives, such as love, a sense of honor, and respect for others, that motivate moral behavior. Pagan societies have not been noticeably more immoral than theistic ones. In any event, most theistic doctrines repudiate the divine sanction theory of the motive to be moral. Judaism places little emphasis on hell. Christianity today is dominated by two rival doctrines of salvation. One says that the belief that Jesus is one's savior is the one thing necessary for salvation. The other says that salvation is a free gift from God that cannot be earned by anything a person may do or believe. Both doctrines are inconsistent with the use of heaven and hell as incentives to morality.

A better interpretation of the claim that religion is necessary for morality is that *there wouldn't be a difference between right and wrong* if God did not make it so. Nothing would really be morally required or prohibited, so everything would be permitted. William Lane Craig, one of the leading popular defenders of Christianity, advances this view. Think of it in terms of the authority of moral rules. Suppose a person or group proposes a moral rule—say, against murder. What would give this rule authority over those who disagree with it? Craig argues that, in the absence of God, nothing would. Without God, moral disputes reduce to mere disputes over subjective preferences. There would be no right or wrong answer. Since no individual has any inherent authority over another, each would be free to act on his or her own taste. To get authoritative moral rules, we need an authoritative commander. Only God fills that role. So, the moral rules get their authority, their capacity to obligate us, from the fact that God commands them.

Sophisticates will tell you that this moralistic reasoning against atheism is illogical. They say that whether God exists depends wholly on the factual evidence, not on the moral implications of God's existence. Do not believe them. We know the basic moral rules—that it is wrong to engage in murder, plunder, rape, and torture, to brutally punish people for the wrongs of others or for blameless error, to enslave others, to engage in ethnic cleansing and genocide—with greater confidence than we know any conclusions drawn from elaborate factual or logical reasoning. If you find a train of reasoning that leads to the conclusion that everything, or even just these things, is permitted, this *is* a good reason for you to reject it. Call this "the moralistic argument." So, if it is true that atheism entails that everything is permitted, this is a strong reason to reject atheism.

While I accept the general form of the moralistic argument, I think it applies more forcefully to theism than to atheism. This objection is as old as philosophy. Plato, the first systematic philosopher, raised it against divine command theories of morality in the fifth century BCE. He asked divine-command moralists: are actions right because God commands them, or does God command them because they are right? If the latter is true, then actions are right independent of whether God commands them, and God is not needed to underwrite the authority of morality. But if the former is true, then God could make any action right simply by willing it or by ordering others to do it. This establishes that, if the authority of morality depends on God's will, then, *in principle,* anything is permitted.

This argument is not decisive against theism, considered as a purely philosophical idea. Theists reply that because God is necessarily good, He would never do anything morally reprehensible Himself, nor command us to perform heinous acts. The argument is better applied to the purported *evidence* for theism. I shall argue that if we take the evidence for theism with *utmost seriousness,* we will find ourselves committed to the proposition that the most heinous acts are permitted. Since we know that these acts are not morally permitted, we must therefore doubt the evidence for theism.

Now "theism" is a pretty big idea, and the lines of evidence taken to support one or another form of it are various. So I need to say more about theism and the evidence for it. By "theism" I mean belief in the God of Scripture. This is the God of the Old and New Testaments and the Koran—the God of Judaism, Christianity, and Islam. It is also the God of any other religion that accepts one or more of these texts as containing divine revelation, such as the Mormon Church, the Unification Church, and Jehovah's Witnesses. God, as represented in Scripture, has plans for human beings and intervenes in history to realize those plans. God has a moral relationship to human beings and tells humans how to live. By focusing on theism in the Scriptural sense, I narrow my focus in two ways. First, my argument doesn't immediately address polytheism or paganism, as is found, for example, in the religions of Zeus and Baal, Hinduism, Wicca. (I'll argue later that, since the evidence for polytheism is on a par with the evidence for theism, any argument that undermines the latter undermines the former.) Second, my argument doesn't immediately address deism, the philosophical idea of God as a first cause of the universe, who lays down the laws of nature and then lets them run like clockwork, indifferent to the fate of the people subject to them.

What, then, is the evidence for theism? It is Scripture, plus any historical or contemporary evidence of the same kind as presented in Scripture: testimonies of miracles, revelations in dreams, or what people take to be direct encounters with God: experiences of divine presence, and prophecies that have been subject to test. Call these things "extraordinary evidence," for short. Other arguments for the existence of God offer cold comfort to theists. Purely theoretical arguments, such as for the necessity of a first cause of the universe, can at most support deism. They do nothing to show that the deity in question cares about human beings or has any moral significance. I would say the same about attempts to trace some intelligent design in the evolution of life. Let us suppose, contrary to the scientific evidence, that life is the product of design. Then the prevalence of predation, parasitism, disease, and imperfect human organs strongly supports the view that the designer is indifferent to us.

The core evidence for theism, then, is Scripture. What if we accept Scripture as offering evidence of a God who has a moral character and plans for human beings, who intervenes in history and tells us how to live? What conclusions should we draw from Scripture about God's moral character and about how we ought to behave? Let us begin with the position of the fundamentalist, of one who takes Scripture with utmost seriousness, as the inerrant source of knowledge about God and morality. It we accept biblical inerrancy, I'll argue, we must conclude that much of what we take to be morally evil is in fact morally permissible and even required.

Consider first God's moral character, as revealed in the Bible. He routinely punishes people for the sins of others. He punishes all mothers by condemning them to painful childbirth, for Eve's sin. He punishes all human beings by condemning them to labor, for Adam's sin (Gen. 3:16–18). He regrets His creation, and in a fit of pique, commits genocide and ecocide by flooding the earth (Gen. 6:7). He hardens Pharaoh's heart against freeing the Israelites (Ex. 7:3), so as to provide the occasion for visiting plagues upon the Egyptians, who, as helpless subjects of a tyrant, had no part in Pharaoh's decision. (So much for respecting free will, the standard justification for the existence of evil in the world.) He kills all the firstborn sons, even of slave girls who had no part in oppressing the Israelites (Ex. 11:5). He punishes the children, grandchildren, great-grandchildren, and great great-grandchildren of those who worship any other god (Ex. 20:3–5). He sets a plague upon the Israelites, killing twenty-four thousand, because some of them had sex with the Baal-worshiping Midianites (Num. 25:1–9). He lays a three-year famine on David's people for *Saul's* slaughter of the Gibeonites (2 Sam. 21:1). He orders David to take a census of his men, and then sends a plague on Israel, killing seventy thousand for David's sin in taking the census (2 Sam. 24:10–15). He sends two bears out of the woods to tear forty-two children to pieces, because they called the prophet Elisha a bald head (2 Kings 2:23–24). He condemns the Samarians, telling them that their *children* will be "dashed to the ground, their pregnant women ripped open" (Hosea 13:16). This is but a sample of the evils celebrated in the Bible.

Can all this cruelty and injustice be excused on the ground that God may do what humans may not? Look, then, at what God commands humans to do. He commands us to put to death adulterers (Lev. 20.10), homosexuals (Lev. 20:13), and people who work on the Sabbath (Ex. 35:2). He commands us to cast into exile people who eat blood (Lev. 7:27), who have skin diseases (Lev. 13:46), and who have sex with their wives while they are menstruating (Lev. 20:18). Blasphemers must be stoned (Lev. 24:16), and prostitutes whose fathers are priests must be burned to death (Lev. 21:9). That's just the tip of the iceberg. God repeatedly directs the Israelites to commit ethnic cleansing (Ex. 34:11–14, Lev. 26:7–9) and genocide against numerous cities and tribes: the city of Hormah (Num. 21:2–3), the land of Bashan (Num. 21:33–35), the land of Heshbon (Deut. 2:26–35), the Canaanites, Hittites, Hivites, Perizzites, Girgashites, Amorites, and Jebusites (Josh. 1–12). He commands them to show their victims "no mercy" (Deut. 7:2), to "not leave alive anything that breathes" (Deut. 20:16). In order to ensure their complete extermination, he thwarts the free will of the victims by hardening their hearts (Deut. 2:30, Josh. 11:20) so that they do not sue for peace. These genocides are, of course, instrumental to the wholesale theft of their land (Josh. 1:1–6) and the rest of their property (Deut. 20:14, Josh. 11:14). He tells eleven tribes of Israel to nearly exterminate the twelfth tribe, the Benjamites, because a few of them raped and killed a Levite's concubine. The resulting bloodbath takes the lives of 40,000 Israelites and 25,100 Benjamites (Judg. 20:21, 25, 35). He helps Abijiah kill half a million Israelites (2 Chron. 13:15–20) and helps Asa kill a million Cushites, so his men can plunder all their property (2 Chron. 14:8–13).

Consider also what the Bible *permits.* Slavery is allowed (Lev. 25:44–46, Eph. 6:5, Col. 3:22). Fathers may sell their daughters into slavery (Ex. 21:7). Slaves may be beaten, as long as they survive for two days after (Ex. 21:20–21, Luke 12:45–48). Female captives from a foreign war may be raped or seized as wives (Deut. 21:10–14). Disobedient children should be beaten with rods (Prov. 13:24, 23:13). In the Old Testament, men may take as many wives and concubines as they like because adultery for men consists only in having sex with a woman who is married (Lev. 18:20) or engaged to someone else (Deut. 22:23). Prisoners of war may be tossed off a cliff (2 Chron. 24:12). Children may be sacrificed to God in return for His aid in battle (2 Kings 3:26–27, Judges 11), or to persuade Him to end a famine (2 Sam. 21).

Christian apologists would observe that most of these transgressions occur in the Old Testament. Isn't the Old Testament God a stern and angry God, while Jesus of the New Testament is all-loving? We should examine, then, the quality of the love that Jesus promises to bring to humans. It is not only Jehovah who is jealous. Jesus tells us his mission is to make family members hate one another, so that they shall love him more than their kin (Matt. 10:35–37). He promises salvation to those who abandon their wives and children for him (Matt. 19:29, Mark 10:29–30, Luke 18:29–30). Disciples must hate their parents, siblings, wives, and children (Luke 14:26). The rod is not enough for children who curse their parents; they must be killed (Matt. 15:4–7, Mark 7:9–10, following Lev. 20:9). These are Jesus's "family values." Peter and Paul add to these family values the despotic rule of husbands over their silenced wives, who must obey their husbands as gods (1 Cor. 11:3, 14:34–5; Eph. 5:22–24; Col. 3:18; 1 Tim. 2:11–12; I Pet. 3:1).

To be sure, genocide, God-sent plagues, and torture do not occur in the times chronicled by the New Testament. But they are prophesied there, as they are repeatedly in the Old Testament (for instance, in Isaiah, Jeremiah, Ezekiel, Micah, and Zephaniah). At the second coming, any city that does not accept Jesus will be destroyed, and the people will suffer even more than they did when God destroyed Sodom and Gomorrah (Matt. 10:14–15, Luke 10:12). God will flood the Earth as in Noah's time (Matt. 24:37). Or perhaps He will set the Earth on fire instead, to destroy the unbelievers (2 Pet. 3:7, 10). But not before God sends Death and Hell to kill one quarter of the Earth "by sword, famine and plague, and by the wild beasts" (Rev. 6:8). Apparently, it is not enough to kill people once; they have to be killed more than once to satisfy the genocidal mathematics of the New Testament. For we are also told that an angel will burn up one third of the Earth (8:7), another will poison a third of its water (8:10–11), four angels will kill another third of humanity by plagues of fire, smoke, and sulfur (9:13, 17–18), two of God's witnesses will visit plagues on the Earth as much as they like (11:6), and there will be assorted deaths by earthquakes (11:13, 16:18–19) and hailstones (16:21). Death is not bad enough for unbelievers, however; they must be tortured first. Locusts will sting them like scorpions until they want to die, but they will be denied the relief of death (9:3–6). Seven angels will pour seven bowls of God's wrath, delivering plagues of painful sores, seas and rivers of blood, burns from solar flares, darkness and tongue-biting (16:2–10).

That's just what's in store for people while they inhabit the Earth. Eternal damnation awaits most people upon their deaths (Matt. 7:13–14). They will be cast into a fiery furnace (Matt. 13:42, 25:41), an unquenchable fire (Luke 3:17). For what reason? The New Testament is not consistent on this point. Paul preaches the doctrine of predestination, according to which salvation is granted as an arbitrary gift from God, wholly unaffected by any choice humans may make (Eph. 1: 4–9). This implies that the rest are cast into the eternal torments of hell on God's whim. Sometimes salvation is promised to those who abandon their families to follow Christ (Matt. 19:27–30, Mark 10:28–30, Luke 9:59–62). This conditions salvation on a shocking indifference to family members. More often, the Synoptic Gospels promise salvation on the basis of good works, especially righteousness and helping the poor (for example, Matt. 16:27, 19:16–17; Mark 10:17–25; Luke 18:18–22, 19:8–9). This at least has the form of justice, since it is based on considerations of desert. But it metes out rewards and punishments grossly disproportional to the deeds people commit in their lifetimes. Finite sins cannot justify eternal punishment. Since the Reformation, Christian thought has tended to favor either predestination or justification by faith. In the latter view, the saved are all and only those who believe that Jesus is their savior. Everyone else is damned. This is the view of the Gospel of John (John 3:15–16, 18, 36; 6:47; 11:25–26). It follows that infants and anyone who never had the opportunity to hear about Christ are damned, through no fault of their own. Moreover, it is not clear that even those who hear about Christ have a fair chance to assess the merits of the tales about him. God not only thwarts our free will so as to visit harsher punishments upon us than we would have received had we been free to choose. He also messes with our heads. He sends people "powerful delusions" so they will not believe what is needed for salvation, to make sure that they are condemned (2 Thess. 2:11–12). Faith itself may be a gift of God rather than a product of rational assessment under our control and for which we could be held responsible. If so, then justification by faith reduces to God's arbitrary whim, as Paul held (Eph. 2:8–9). This at least has the merit of acknowledging that the evidence offered in favor of Christianity is far from sufficient to rationally justify belief in it. Granting this fact, those who do not believe are blameless and cannot be justly punished, even if Jesus really did die for our sins.

And what are we to make of the thought that Jesus died for our sins (Rom. 5:8–9, 15–18; 1 John 2:2; Rev. 1:5)? This core religious teaching of Christianity takes Jesus to be a scapegoat for humanity. The practice of scapegoating contradicts the whole moral principle of personal responsibility. It also contradicts any moral idea of God. If God is merciful and loving, why doesn't He forgive humanity for its sins straightaway, rather than demanding His 150 pounds of flesh, in the form of His own son? How could any loving father do that to his son?

I find it hard to resist the conclusion that the God of the Bible is cruel and unjust and commands and permits us to be cruel and unjust to others. Here are religious doctrines that on their face claim that it is all right to mercilessly punish people for the wrongs of others and for blameless error, that license or even command murder, plunder, rape, torture, slavery, ethnic cleansing, and genocide. We know such actions are wrong. So we should reject the doctrines that represent them as right.

Of course, thoughtful Christians and Jews have struggled with this difficulty for centuries. Nothing I have said would come as a surprise to any reflective person of faith. Nor are theists without options for dealing with these moral embarrassments. Let us consider them.

One option is to bite the bullet. This is the only option open to hard-core fundamentalists, who accept the inerrancy of the Bible. In this view, the fact that God performed, commanded, or permitted these actions demonstrates that they are morally right. This view concedes my objection to theism, that it promotes terrible acts of genocide, slavery, and so forth. But it denies the moral force of this objection. We know where this option has led: to holy war, the systematic extirpation of heretics, the Crusades, the Inquisition, the Thirty Years War, the English Civil War, witch-hunts, the cultural genocide of Mayan civilization, the brutal conquest of the Aztecs and the Inca, religious support for ethnic cleansing of Native Americans, slavery of Africans in the Americas, colonialist tyranny across the globe, confinement of the Jews to ghettos, and periodic pogroms against them, ultimately preparing the way for the Holocaust. In other words, it has led to centuries steeped in bloodshed, cruelty, and hatred without limit across continents.

Since this is clearly reprehensible, one might try a stopgap measure. One could deny that the dangerous principles in the Bible have any application after biblical times. For example, one might hold that, while it is in principle perfectly all right to slaughter whoever God tells us to, in fact, God has stopped speaking to us. This argument runs into the difficulty that many people even today claim that God has spoken to them. It is hard to identify any reason to be comprehensively skeptical about current claims to have heard divine revelation that does not apply equally to the past. But to apply such skepticism to the past is to toss out revelation and hence the core evidence for God.

Another option is to try to soften the moral implications of embarrassing biblical episodes by filling in unmentioned details that make them seem less bad. There is a tradition of thinking about "hard sayings" that tries to do this. It imagines some elaborate context in which, for instance, it would be all right for God to command Abraham to sacrifice his son, or for God to inflict unspeakable suffering on His blameless servant Job, and then insists that that was the context in which God actually acted. I have found such excuses for God's depravity to be invariably lame. To take a typical example, it is said of David's seemingly innocent census of his army that he sinned by counting what was not his, but God's. Even if we were to grant this, it still does not excuse God for slaughtering seventy thousand of David's men, rather than focusing His wrath on David alone. I also find such casuistic exercises to be morally dangerous. To devote one's moral reflections to constructing elaborate rationales for past genocides, human sacrifices, and the like is to invite applications of similar reasoning to future actions.

I conclude that there is no way to cabin off or soft-pedal the reprehensible moral implications of these biblical passages. They must be categorically rejected as false and depraved moral teachings. Morally decent theists have always done so in practice. Nevertheless, they insist that there is much worthy moral teaching that can be salvaged from the Bible. They would complain that the sample of biblical moral lessons I cited above is biased. I hasten to agree. There are many admirable moral teachings in the Bible, even beyond the obvious moral rules—against murder, stealing, lying, and the like—that are acknowledged by all societies. "Love your neighbor as yourself" (Lev. 19:18, Matt. 22:39, Mark 12:31, Luke 10:27, James 2:8) concisely encapsulates the moral point of view. The Bible courageously extends this teaching to the downtrodden, demanding not just decency and charity to the poor and disabled (Ex. 23:6, 23:11; Lev. 19:10, 23:22; Deut. 15:7–8, 24:14 15; Prov. 22:22; Eph. 4:28; James 2:15–16), but provisions in the structure of property rights to liberate people from landlessness and oppressive debts (Deut. 15, Lev. 25:10–28). Although the details of these provisions make little economic sense (for instance, canceling debts every seven years prevents people from taking out loans for a longer term), their general idea, that property rights should be structured so as to enable everyone to avoid oppression, is sound. Such teachings were not only morally advanced for their day but would dramatically improve the world if practiced today.

So, the Bible contains both good and evil teachings. This fact bears upon the standing of Scripture, both as a source of evidence for moral claims, and as a source of evidence for theism. Consider first the use of Scripture as a source of evidence for moral claims. We have seen that the Bible is morally inconsistent. If we try to draw moral lessons from a contradictory source, we must pick and choose which ones to accept. This requires that we use our own independent moral judgment, founded on some source other than revelation or the supposed authority of God, to decide which biblical passages to accept. In fact, once we recognize the moral inconsistencies in the Bible, it's clear that the hardcore fundamentalists who today preach hatred toward gay people and the subordination of women, and who at other times and places have, with biblical support, claimed God's authority for slavery, apartheid, and ethnic cleansing, have been picking and choosing all along. What distinguishes them from other believers is precisely their attraction to the cruel and despotic passages in the Bible. Far from being a truly independent guide to moral conduct, the Bible is more like a Rorschach test: which passages people choose to emphasize reflects as much as it shapes their moral character and interests.

Moral considerations, then, should draw theists inexorably away from fundamentalism and toward liberal theology—that is, toward forms of theism that deny the literal truth of the Bible and that attribute much of its content to ancient confusion, credulity, and cruelty. Only by moving toward liberal theology can theists avoid refutation at the hands of the moralistic argument that is thought to undermine atheism. Only in this way can theists affirm that the heinous acts supposedly committed or commanded by God and reported in the Bible are just plain morally wrong.

The great Enlightenment philosopher Immanuel Kant took this line of reasoning to its logical conclusion for morality. He considered the case of an inquisitor who claims divine authority for executing unbelievers. That the Bible commends such acts is undeniable (see Ex. 22:20, 2 Chron. 15:13, Luke 19:27, Acts 3:23). But how do we know that the Bible accurately records God's revealed word? Kant said:

> That it is wrong to deprive a man of his life because of his religious faith is certain, unless . . . a Divine Will, made known in extraordinary fashion, has ordered it otherwise. But that God has ever ordered this terrible injunction can be asserted only on the basis of historical documents and is never apodictically certain. After all, the revelation has reached the inquisitor only through men and has been interpreted by men, and even did it appear to have come from God Himself (like the command delivered to Abraham to slaughter his own son like a sheep) it is at least possible that in this instance a mistake has prevailed. But if this is so, the inquisitor would risk the danger of doing what would be wrong in the highest degree; and in this very act he is behaving unconscientiously.

Kant advances a moral criterion for judging the authenticity of any supposed revelation. If you hear a voice or some testimony purportedly revealing God's word and it tells you to do something you know is wrong, don't believe that it's really *God* telling you to do these things.

I believe that Kant correctly identified the maximum permissible moral limits of belief in extraordinary evidence concerning God. These limits require that we reject the literal truth of the Bible. My colleague Jamie Tappenden argues in this volume that such a liberal approach to faith is theologically incoherent. Perhaps it is. Still, given a choice between grave moral error and theological muddle, I recommend theological muddle every time.

But these are not our only alternatives. We must further ask whether we should accept *any* part of the Bible as offering evidence about the existence and nature of God. Once we have mustered enough doubt in the Bible to reject its inerrancy, is there any stable position short of rejecting altogether its claims to extraordinary evidence about God? And once we reject its claims, would this not undermine all the extra-biblical extraordinary evidence for God that is of the same kind alleged by believers in the Bible? Here we have a body of purported evidence for theism, consisting of what seem to be experiences of divine presence, revelation, and miracles, testimonies of the same, and prophecies. We have seen that such experiences, testimonies, and prophecies are at least as likely to assert grave moral errors as they are to assert moral truths. This shows that these sources of extraordinary evidence are deeply unreliable. *They can't be trusted.* So not only should we think that they offer no independent support for *moral* claims, but we should not think they offer independent support for *theological* claims.

Against this, defenders of liberal theology need to argue that the claims derived from these extraordinary sources fall into two radically distinct groups. In one group, there are the purported revelations that assert moral error, which should not be accepted as having come from God and offer no independent support for any claim about God. In the other group there are the genuine revelations that assert moral truths or some morally neutral proposition (for example, claims about historical events and prophecies of the future), as well as testimonies of miracles and experiences of divine presence, which should be accepted as having come from God and do provide evidence for the existence and nature of God.

I think this fallback position should be rejected for two reasons. First, it does not explain why these extraordinary types of evidence should be thought to fall into two radically distinct groups. Why should they *ever* have generated grave moral errors? Second, it does not explain why all religions, whether monotheistic, polytheistic, or non theistic, appear to have access to the same sources of evidence. Believers in any one religion can offer no independent criteria for accepting their own revelations, miracles, and religious experiences while rejecting the revelations, miracles, and religious experiences that appear to support contradictory religious claims. I believe that the best explanation for both of these phenomena—that the extraordinary sources of evidence generate grave moral error as well as moral truth and that they offer equal support for contradictory religious claims—undermines the credibility of these extraordinary sources of evidence altogether.

So first, why were the ancient biblical peoples as ready to ascribe evil as good deeds to God? Why did they think God was so angry that He chronically unleashed tides of brutal destruction on humanity? The answer is that they took it for granted that *all* events bearing on human well-being are willed by some agent for the purpose of affecting humans for good or ill. If no human was observed to have caused the event, or if the event was of a kind (e.g., a plague, drought, or good weather) that no human would have the power to cause, then they assumed that some unseen, more-powerful agent had to have willed it, precisely for its good or bad effects on humans. So, if the event was good for people, they assumed that God willed it out of love for them; if it was bad, they assumed that God willed it out of anger at them. This mode of explanation is universally observed among people who lack scientific understanding of natural events. It appears to be a deeply rooted cognitive bias of humans to reject the thought of meaningless suffering. If we are suffering, someone *must* be responsible for it!

Why did these representations of God as cruel and unjust not make God repugnant to the authors of Scripture and their followers? They were too busy trembling in their sandals to question what they took to be God's will. The seventeenth-century philosopher Thomas Hobbes observed that people honor raw power irrespective of its moral justification:

> Nor does it alter the case of honour, whether an action (so it be great and difficult, and consequently a sign of much power) be just or unjust: for honour consisteth only in the opinion of power. Therefore the ancient heathen did not think they dishonoured, but greatly honoured the Gods, when they introduced them in their poems, committing rapes, thefts, and other great, but unjust, or unclean acts: insomuch as nothing is so much celebrated in Jupiter, as his adulteries; nor in Mercury, as his frauds, and thefts: of whose praises, in a hymn of Homer, the greatest is this, that being born in the morning, he had invented music at noon, and before night, stolen away the cattle of Apollo, from his herdsmen.

Hobbes's psychological explanation applies even more emphatically to the authors of Scripture, the ancient Hebrews and the early Christians, whose God commits deeds several orders of magnitude more terrible than anything the Greek gods did.

Ancient social conditions also made God's injustice less obvious to the early Jews and Christians. Norms of honor and revenge deeply structure the social order of tribal societies. These norms treat whole clans and tribes, rather than individuals, as the basic units of responsibility. A wrong committed by a member of a tribe could therefore be avenged by an injury inflicted on any other member of that tribe, including descendents of the wrongdoer. Given that people in these societies habitually visited the iniquities of the fathers on the sons, it did not strike the early Hebrews and Christians as strange that God would do so as well, although on a far grander scale.

So the tendency, in the absence of scientific knowledge, to ascribe events having good *and bad* consequences for human beings to corresponding benevolent *and malevolent* intentions of unseen spirits, whether these be gods, angels, ancestors, demons, or human beings who deploy magical powers borrowed from some spirit world, explains the belief in a divine spirit as well as its (im)moral character. This explanatory tendency is pan-cultural. The spiritual world everywhere reflects the hopes and fears, loves and hatreds, aspirations and depravities of those who believe in it. This is just as we would expect if beliefs in the supernatural are, like Rorschach tests, projections of the mental states of believers, rather than based on independent evidence. The same cognitive bias that leads pagans to believe in witches and multiple gods leads theists to believe in God. Indeed, once the explanatory principle—to ascribe worldly events that bear on human well-being to the intentions and powers of unseen spirits, when no actual person is observed to have caused them—is admitted, it is hard to deny that the evidence for polytheism and spiritualism of all heretical varieties is *exactly on a par* with the evidence for theism. Every year in my town, Ann Arbor, Michigan, there is a summer art fair. Not just artists, but political and religious groups, set up booths to promote their wares, be these artworks or ideas. Along one street one finds booths of Catholics, Baptists, Calvinists, Christian Orthodox, other denominational and nondenominational Christians of all sons, Muslims, Hindus, Buddhists, Baha'i, Mormons, Christian Scientists, Jehovah's Witnesses, Jews for Jesus, Wiccans, Scientologists, New Age believers—representatives of nearly every religion that has a significant presence in the United States. The believers in each booth offer evidence of exactly the same kind to advance their religion. Every faith points to its own holy texts and oral traditions, its spiritual experiences, miracles and prophets, its testimonies of wayward lives turned around by conversion, rebirth of faith, or return to the church.

Each religion takes these experiences and reports them as conclusive evidence for *its* peculiar set of beliefs. Here we have purported sources of evidence for higher, unseen spirits or divinity, which systematically point to *contradictory* beliefs. Is there one God, or many? Was Jesus God, the son of God, God's prophet, or just a man? Was the last prophet Jesus, Muhammad, Joseph Smith, or the Rev. Sun Myung Moon?

Consider how this scene looks to someone like me, who was raised outside of any faith. My father is nominally Lutheran, in practice religiously indifferent. My mother is culturally Jewish but not practicing. Having been rejected by both the local Lutheran minister and the local rabbi (in both cases, for being in a mixed marriage), but thinking that some kind of religious education would be good for their children, my parents helped found the local Unitarian church in the town where I grew up. Unitarianism is a church without a creed; there are no doctrinal requirements of membership. (Although Bertrand Russell once quipped that Unitarianism stands for the proposition that there is *at most* one God, these days pagans are as welcome as all others.) It was a pretty good fit for us, until New Age spiritualists started to take over the church. That was too loopy for my father's rationalistic outlook, so we left. Thus, religious doctrines never had a chance to insinuate themselves into my head as a child. So I have none by default or habit.

Surveying the religious booths every year at the Ann Arbor art fair, I am always struck by the fact that they are staffed by people who are convinced of their own revelations and miracles, while most so readily disparage the revelations and miracles of other faiths. To a mainstream Christian, Jew, or Muslim, nothing is more obvious than that founders and prophets of other religions, such as Joseph Smith, the Rev. Moon, Mary Baker Eddy, and L. Ron Hubbard, are either frauds or delusional, their purported miracles or cures are tricks played upon a credulous audience (or worse, exercises of black magic), their prophecies false, their metaphysics absurd. To me, nothing is more obvious than that the evidence cited on behalf of Christianity, Judaism, and Islam is of exactly the same type and qualify as that cited on behalf of such despised religions. Indeed, it is on a par with the evidence for Zeus, Baal, Thor, and other long-abandoned gods, who are now considered ridiculous by nearly everyone.

The perfect symmetry of evidence for all faiths persuades me that the *types* of extraordinary evidence to which they appeal are not credible. The sources of evidence for theism—revelations, miracles, religious experiences, and prophecies, nearly all known only by testimony transmitted through uncertain chains of long-lost original sources—systematically generate contradictory beliefs, many of which are known to be morally abhorrent or otherwise false. Of course, ordinary sources of evidence, such as eyewitness testimony of ordinary events, also often lead to conflicting beliefs. But in the latter case, we have independent ways to test the credibility of the evidence—for instance, by looking for corroborating physical evidence. In the former cases, the tests advanced by believers tend to be circular: don't believe that other religion's testimonies of miracles or revelations, since they come from those who teach a false religion (Deut. 13:1–5). It is equally useless to appeal to the certainty in one's heart of some experience of divine presence. For exactly the same certainty has been felt by those who think they've seen ghosts, been kidnapped by aliens, or been possessed by Dionysus or Apollo. Furthermore, where independent tests exist, they either disconfirm or fail to confirm the extraordinary evidence. There is no geological evidence of a worldwide flood, no archaeological evidence that Pharaoh's army drowned in the Red Sea after Moses parted it to enable the Israelites to escape. Jesus' central prophecy, that oppressive regimes would be destroyed in an apocalypse, and the Kingdom of God established *on Earth, within the lifetime of those witnessing his preaching* (Mark 8:38–9:1, 13:24–27, 30), did not come to pass. If any instance of these extraordinary sources of evidence is what it purports to be, it is like the proverbial needle in the haystack—except that there is no way to tell the difference between it and the hay. I conclude that none of the evidence for theism—that is, for the God of Scripture—is credible. Since exactly the same types of evidence are the basis for belief in pagan Gods, I reject pagan religions too.

It follows that we cannot appeal to God to underwrite the authority of morality. How, then, can I answer the moralistic challenge to atheism, that without God moral rules lack any authority? I say: the authority of moral rules lies not with God, but with each of us. We each have moral authority with respect to one another. This authority is, of course, not absolute. No one has the authority to order anyone else to blind obedience. Rather, each of us has the authority to make claims on others, to call upon people to heed our interests and concerns. Whenever we lodge a complaint, or otherwise lay a claim on others' attention and conduct, we *presuppose* our own authority to give others reasons for action that are not dependent on appealing to the desires and preferences they already have. But whatever grounds we have for assuming our own authority to make claims is equally well possessed by anyone who we expect to heed our own claims. For, in addressing others as people to whom our claims are justified, we acknowledge *them* as judges of claims, and hence as moral authorities. Moral rules spring from our practices of reciprocal claim making, in which we work out together the kinds of considerations that count as reasons that all of us must heed, and thereby devise rules for living together peacefully and cooperatively, on a basis of mutual accountability.

What of someone who refuses to accept such accountability? Doesn't this possibility vindicate Craig's worry, that without some kind of higher authority external to humans, moral claims amount to nothing more than assertions of personal preference, backed up by power? No. We deal with people who refuse accountability by restraining and deterring their objectionable behavior. Such people have no proper complaint against this treatment. For, in the very act of lodging a complaint, they address others as judges of their claims, and thereby step into the very system of moral adjudication that demands their accountability.

I am arguing that morality, understood as a system of reciprocal claim making, in which everyone is accountable to everyone else, does not need its authority underwritten by some higher, external authority. It is underwritten by the authority we all have to make claims on one another. Far from bolstering the authority of morality, appeals to divine authority can undermine it. For divine command theories of morality may make believers feel entitled to look only to their idea of God to determine what they are justified in doing. It is all too easy under such a system to ignore the complaints of those injured by one's actions, since they are not acknowledged as moral authorities in their own right. But to ignore the complaints of others is to deprive oneself of the main source of information one needs to improve one's conduct. Appealing to God rather than those affected by one's actions amounts to an attempt to escape accountability to one's fellow human beings.

This is not an indictment of the conduct of theists in general. Theistic moralities, like secular ones, have historically inspired both highly moral and highly immoral action. For every bloodthirsty holy warrior we can find an equally violent communist or fascist, enthusiastically butchering and enslaving others in the name of some dogmatically held ideal. Such observations are irrelevant to my argument. For my argument has not been about the *causal consequences* of belief for action. It has been about the *logical implications* of accepting or rejecting the core evidence for theism.

I have argued that if we take with utmost seriousness the core evidence for theism, which is the testimonies of revelations, miracles, religious experiences, and prophecies found in Scripture, then we are committed to the view that the most heinous acts are morally right, because Scripture tells us that God performs or commands them. Since we know that such acts are morally wrong, we cannot take at face value the extraordinary evidence for theism recorded in Scripture. We must at least reject that part of the evidence that supports morally repugnant actions. Once we have stepped this far toward

liberal theological approaches to the evidence for God, however, we open ourselves up to two further challenges to this evidence. First, the best explanation
of extraordinary evidence—the only explanation that accounts for its tendency
to commend heinous acts as well as good acts—shows it to reflect either our
own hopes and feelings, whether these be loving or hateful, just or merciless,
or else the stubborn and systematically erroneous cognitive bias of representing all events of consequence to our welfare as *intended* by some agent who
cares about us, for good or for ill. Extraordinary evidence, in other words, is a
projection of our own wishes, fears, and fantasies onto an imaginary deity.
Second, all religions claim the same sorts of extraordinary evidence on their
behalf. The perfect symmetry of this type of evidence for completely contradictory theological systems, and the absence of any independent ordinary evidence that corroborates one system more than another, strongly supports the
view that such types of evidence are not credible at all. And once we reject such
evidence altogether, there is nothing left that supports theism (or polytheism,
either). The moralistic argument, far from threatening atheism, is a critical
wedge that should open morally sensitive theists to the evidence against the
existence of God.

40

There Is No God

PENN JILLETTE

Together with his sidekick Teller and his comrade James Randi, Penn Jillette can discredit any levitating or spoon bending guru, re-stage any "miracle," expose any cruel exploitation by any "faith-healer," and shame any water-diviner, astrologer, card-reader, or spiritualist. In the grand tradition of Harry Houdini, Penn puts his own powers at the service of the rational and the humane.

I believe that there is no God. I'm beyond atheism. Atheism is not believing in God. Not believing in God is easy—you can't prove a negative, so there's no work to do. You can't prove that there isn't an elephant inside the trunk of my car. You sure? How about now? Maybe he was just hiding before. Check again. Did I mention that my personal heartfelt definition of the word "elephant" includes mystery, order, goodness, love, and a spare tire?

So, anyone with a love for truth outside of herself has to start with no belief in God and then look for evidence of God. She needs to search for some objective evidence of a supernatural power. All the people I write e-mails to often are still stuck at this searching stage. The atheism part is easy.

But, this "This I Believe" thing seems to demand something more personal, some leap of faith that helps one see life's big picture, some rules to live by. So, I'm saying, "This I believe: I believe there is no God."

Having taken that step, it informs every moment of my life. I'm not greedy. I have love, blue skies, rainbows, and Hallmark cards, and that has to be enough. It has to be enough, but it's everything in the world, and everything in the world is plenty for me. It seems just rude to beg the invisible for more. Just the love of my family that raised me and the family I'm raising now is enough that I don't need heaven. I won the huge genetic lottery and I get joy every day.

Believing there's no God means I can't really be forgiven except by kindness and faulty memories. That's good; it makes me want to be more thoughtful. I have to try to treat people right the first time around.

Believing there's no God stops me from being solipsistic. I can read ideas from all different people from all different cultures. Without God, we can agree on reality, and I can keep learning where I'm wrong. We can all keep adjusting, so we can really communicate. I don't travel in circles where people say, "I have faith, I believe this in my heart and nothing you can say or do can shake my faith." That's just a long-winded religious way to say, "shut up," or another two words that the FCC likes less. But all obscenity is less insulting than, "How I was brought up and my imaginary friend means more to me than anything you can ever say or do." So, believing there is no God lets me be proven wrong and that's always fun. It means I'm learning something.

Believing there is no God means the suffering I've seen in my family, and indeed all the suffering in the world, isn't caused by an omniscient, omnipresent, omnipotent force that isn't bothered to help or is just testing us, but rather something we all may be able to help others with in the future. No God means the possibility of less suffering in the future.

Believing there is no God gives me more room for belief in family, people, love, truth, beauty, sex, Jell-O, and all the other things I can prove and that make this life the best life I will ever have.

41

End of the World Blues

IAN MCEWAN

A novelist who has worked luminously on the frontier that sepa-
rates the ordinary from the mystical, Ian McEwan has even less patience than Joseph Conrad with the silly invocation of the
supernatural. Here is what happens when a cool and lucid intelligence confronts the hysteria and mystification of the apocalyptic:
the wretched death-wish that lurks horribly beneath all sub-
servience to faith. Mr. McEwan delivered these thoughts in a lecture
at Stanford University in 2007; they appear here in print for the first
time.

Since 1839, the world inventory of photographs has been accumulating at an
accelerating pace, multiplying into a near infinitude of images, into a resemblance of a Borgesian library. This haunting technology has been with us long
enough now that we are able to look at a crowd scene, a busy street, say, in the
late nineteenth century and know for certain that every single figure is dead.
Not only the young couple pausing by a park railing, but the child with a hoop
and stick, the starchy nurse, the solemn baby upright in its carriage—their lives
have run their course, and they are all gone. And yet, frozen in sepia, they appear
curiously, busily, oblivious of the fact that they must die—as Susan Sontag put
it, "photographs state the innocence, the vulnerability of lives heading towards
their own destruction. . . ." "Photography," she said, "is the inventory of mortality. A touch of the finger now suffices to invest a moment with posthumous
irony. Photographs show people being so irrefutably *there* and at a specific age
in their lives; [they] group together people and things which a moment later
have already disbanded, changed, continued along the course of their independent destinies."

So, one day, it could be the case with a photograph of us all assembled here
today in this hall. Imagine us scrutinized in an old photograph two hundred
years hence, idly considered by a future beholder as quaintly old-fashioned, possessed by the self-evident importance of our concerns, ignorant of the date and
manner of our certain fate, and long gone. And long gone, en masse.

We are well used to reflections on individual mortality—it is the shaping force in the narrative of our existence. It emerges in childhood as a baffling fact, re-emerges possibly in adolescence as a tragic reality which all around us appear to be denying, then perhaps fades in busy middle life, to return, say, in a sudden premonitory bout of insomnia. One of the supreme secular meditations on death is Larkin's *Aubade*:

> . . . The sure extinction that we travel to
> And shall be lost in always. Not to be here,
> Not to be anywhere,
> And soon; nothing more terrible, nothing more true.

We confront our mortality in private conversations, in the familiar consolations of religion—"That vast moth-eaten musical brocade," thought Larkin, "Created to pretend we never die." And we experience it as a creative tension, an enabling paradox in our literature and art: what is depicted, loved, or celebrated cannot last, and the work must try to outlive its creator. Larkin, after all, is now dead. Unless we are a determined, well-organized suicide, we cannot know the date of our demise, but we know the date must fall within a certain window of biological possibility which, as we age, must progressively narrow to its closing point.

Estimating the nature and timing of our *collective* demise, not a lecture-roomful, but the end of civilization, of the entire human project, is even less certain— it might happen in the next hundred years, or not happen in two thousand, or happen with imperceptible slowness, a whimper, not a bang. But in the face of that unknowability, there has often flourished powerful certainty about the approaching end. Throughout recorded history people have mesmerized themselves with stories which predict the date and manner of our whole-scale destruction, often rendered meaningful by ideas of divine punishment and ultimate redemption; the end of life on earth, the end or last days, end time, the apocalypse.

Many of these stories are highly specific accounts of the future and are devoutly believed. Contemporary apocalyptic movements, Christian or Islamic, some violent, some not, all appear to share fantasies of a violent end, and they affect our politics profoundly. The apocalyptic mind can be demonizing—that is to say there are other groups, other faiths, that it despises for worshipping false gods, and these believers of course will not be saved from the fires of hell. And the apocalyptic mind tends to be totalitarian—which is to say that these are intact, all-encompassing ideas founded in longing and supernatural belief, immune to evidence or its lack, and well-protected against the implications of fresh data. Consequently, moments of unintentional pathos, even comedy, arise—and perhaps something in our nature is revealed—as the future is constantly having to be rewritten, new anti-Christs, new Beasts, new Babylons, new Whores located, and the old appointments with doom and redemption quickly replaced by the next.

Not even a superficial student of the Christian apocalypse could afford to ignore the work of Norman Cohn. His magisterial *The Pursuit of the Millennium* was published fifty years ago and has been in print ever since. This is a study of a variety of end-time movements that swept through northern Europe between the eleventh and sixteenth centuries. These sects, generally inspired by the symbolism in the Book of Revelation, typically led by a charismatic prophet who emerged from among the artisan class or from the dispossessed, were seized by the notion of an impending end, to be followed by the establishing of the Kingdom of God on earth. In preparation for this, it was believed necessary to slaughter Jews, priests, and property owners. Fanatical rabbles, tens of thousands strong, oppressed and often starving and homeless, roamed from town to town, full of wild hope and murderous intent. The authorities, church and lay, would put down these bands with overwhelming violence. A few years, or a generation later, with a new leader, and a faintly different emphasis, a new group would rise up. It is worth remembering that the impoverished mob that trailed behind the knights of the first Crusades started their journey by killing Jews in the thousands in the Upper Rhine area. These days, when Muslims of radical tendency pronounce their formulaic imprecations against "Jews and Crusaders," they would do well to remember that both Jewry and Islam were victims of the Crusades.

Now, the slaughter has abated, but what strikes the reader of Cohn's book are the common threads that run between medieval and contemporary apocalyptic thought. First, and in general, the resilience of the end-time forecasts—time and again, for five hundred years, the date is proclaimed, nothing happens, and no one feels discouraged from setting another date. Second, the Book of Revelation spawned a literary tradition that kept alive in medieval Europe the fantasy, derived from the Judaic tradition, of divine election. Christians, too, could now be the Chosen People, the saved or the Elect, and no amount of official repression could smother the appeal of this notion to the unprivileged as well as the unbalanced. Third, there looms the figure of a mere man, apparently virtuous, risen to eminence, but in reality seductive and Satanic—he is the anti-Christ, and in the five centuries that Cohn surveys, the role is fulfilled by the Pope, just as it frequently is now.

Finally, there is the boundless adaptability, the undying appeal and fascination of the Book of Revelation itself, the central text of apocalyptic belief. When Christopher Columbus arrived in the Americas, making landfall in the Bahaman islands, he believed he had found, and was fated to find, the Terrestrial Paradise promised in the Book of Revelation. He believed himself to be implicated in God's planning for the millennial kingdom on earth. The scholar Daniel Wocjik (in his brilliant account of apocalyptic thought in America, "The end of the world as we know it") quotes from Columbus's record of his first journey: "God made me the messenger of the new heaven and the new earth of which he spoke in the Apocalypse of St John . . . and he showed me the spot where to find it."

Five centuries later, the United States, responsible for more than four-fifths of the world's scientific research and still a land of plenty, can show the world an abundance of opinion polls concerning its religious convictions. The litany will be familiar. Ninety percent of Americans say they have never doubted the existence of God and are certain they will be called to answer for their sins. Fifty-three percent are creationists who believe that the cosmos is six thousand years old, 44 percent are sure that Jesus will return to judge the living and the dead within the next fifty years. Only 12 percent believe that life on earth has evolved through natural selection without the intervention of supernatural agency.

In general, belief in end-time biblical prophecy, in a world purified by catastrophe and then redeemed and made entirely Christian and free of conflict by the return of Jesus in our lifetime, is stronger in the United States than anywhere on the planet and extends from marginal, ill-educated, economically deprived groups, to college-educated people in the millions, through to governing elites, to the very summits of power. The social scientist J. W. Nelson notes that apocalyptic ideas "are as American as the hot dog." Wojcik reminds us of the ripple of anxiety that ran round the world in April 1984 when President Reagan expressed that he was greatly interested in the biblical prophecy of imminent Armageddon.

To the secular mind, the polling figures have a pleasantly shocking, titillating quality—one might think of them as a form of atheist's pornography. But perhaps we should enter a caveat before proceeding. It might be worth retaining a degree of skepticism about these polling figures. For a start, they vary enormously—one poll's 90 percent is another's 53 percent. From the respondent's point of view, what is to be gained by categorically denying the existence of God to a complete stranger with a clipboard? And those who tell pollsters they believe that the Bible is the literal word of God from which derive all proper moral precepts, are more likely to be thinking in general terms of love, compassion, and forgiveness rather than of the slave-owning, ethnic cleansing, infanticide, and genocide urged at various times by the jealous God of the Old Testament.

Furthermore, the mind is capable of artful compartmentalizations; in one moment, a man might confidently believe in predictions of Armageddon in his lifetime, and in the next, he might pick up the phone to enquire about a savings fund for his grandchildren's college education or approve of long-term measures to slow global warming. Or he might even vote Democrat, as do many Hispanic biblical literalists. In Pennsylvania, Kansas, and Ohio, the courts have issued ringing rejections of Intelligent Design, and voters have ejected creationists from school boards. In the Dover case, Judge John Jones the third, a Bush appointee, handed down a judgment that was not only a scathing dismissal of the prospect of supernatural ideas imported into science classes, but it was an elegant, stirring summary of the project of science in general, and of natural selection in particular, and a sturdy endorsement of the rationalist, Enlightenment values that underlie the Constitution.

Still the Book of Revelation, the final book of the Bible, and perhaps its most bizarre, certainly one of its most lurid, remains important in the United States, just as it once was in medieval Europe. The book is also known as the Apocalypse—and we should be clear about the meaning of this word, which is derived from the Greek word for revelation. Apocalypse, which has become synonymous with "catastrophe," actually refers to the literary form in which an individual describes what has been revealed to him by a supernatural being. There was a long Jewish tradition of prophecy, and there were hundreds, if not thousands of seers like John of Patmos between the second century B.C. and the first century A.D. Many other Christian apocalypses were deprived of canonical authority in the second century A.D. Revelation most likely survived because its author was confused with John, the Beloved Disciple. It is interesting to speculate how different medieval European history, and indeed the history of religion in Europe and the United States would have been if the Book of Revelation had also failed, as it nearly did, to be retained in the Bible we now know.

.   .   .

The scholarly consensus dates Revelation to 95 or 96 A.D. Little is known of its author beyond the fact that he is certainly not the apostle John. The occasion of writing appears to be the persecution of Christians under the Roman emperor Domitian. Only a generation before, the Romans had sacked the Second Temple in Jerusalem and are, therefore, identified with the Babylonians who had destroyed the First Temple centuries earlier. The general purpose quite likely was to give hope and consolation to the faithful in the certainty that their tribulations would end, that the Kingdom of God would prevail. Ever since the influential twelfth-century historian, Joachim of Fiore, Revelation has been seen, within various traditions of gathering complexity and divergence, as an overview of human history whose last stage we are now in; alternatively, and this is especially relevant to postwar United States, as an account purely of those last days. For centuries, within the Protestant tradition, the anti-Christ was identified with the Pope, or with the Catholic Church in general. In recent decades, the honor has been bestowed on the Soviet Union, the European Union, or secularism and atheists. For many millennial dispensationalists, international peacemakers, who risk delaying the final struggle by sowing concord among nations—the United Nations, along with the World Council of Churches—have been seen as Satanic forces.

The cast or contents of Revelation in its contemporary representations has all the colorful gaudiness of a children's computer fantasy game—earthquakes and fires, thundering horses and their riders, angels blasting away on trumpets, magic vials, Jezebel, a red dragon and other mythical beasts, and a scarlet woman. Another familiar aspect is the potency of numbers—seven each of seals, heads of beasts, candlesticks, stars, lamps, trumpets, angels, and vials; then four riders, four beasts with seven heads, ten horns, ten crowns, four and twenty elders, twelve tribes with twelve thousand members . . . and finally, most resonantly, spawning nineteen centuries of dark tomfoolery, "Here is wisdom. Let him that hath understanding count the number of the beast; for it is the number of a man; and his number is six hundred, three score and six." To many minds, 666 bristles with significance. The Internet is stuffed with tremulous speculation about supermarket barcodes, implanted chips, numerical codes for the names of world leaders. However, the oldest known record of this famous verse, from the Oxyrhynchus site, gives the number as 616, as does the Zurich bible. I have the impression that any number would do. One senses in the arithmetic of prophecy the yearnings of a systematizing mind, bereft of the experimental scientific underpinnings that were to give such human tendencies their rich expression many centuries later. Astrology gives a similar impression of numerical obsession operating within a senseless void.

But Revelation has endured in an age of technology and skepticism. Not many works of literature, not even the *Odyssey* of Homer, can boast such wide appeal over such an expanse of time. One celebrated case of this rugged durability is that of William Miller, the nineteenth-century farmer who became a prophet and made a set of intricate calculations, based on a line in verse 14 of the Book of Daniel: "unto two thousand and three hundred days; then shall the sanctuary be cleansed." Counting for various reasons this utterance to date from 457 B.C., and understanding one prophetic day to be the equivalent of a year, Miller came to the conclusion that the last of days would occur in 1843. Some of Miller's followers refined the calculations further to October 22. After nothing happened on that day, the year was quickly revised to 1844, to take into account the year zero. The faithful Millerites gathered in their thousands to wait. One may not share the beliefs, but it is quite possible to understand the mortifying disenchantment. One eyewitness wrote,

> [We] confidently expected to see Jesus Christ and all the holy angels with
> him . . . and that our trials and sufferings with our earthly pilgrimage would
> close and we should be caught up to meet our coming Lord . . . and thus we
> looked for our coming Lord until the bell tolled twelve at midnight. The day
> had then passed and our disappointment became a certainty. Our fondest
> hopes and expectations were blasted, and such a spirit of weeping came over
> us as I never experienced before. It seemed that the loss of all our earthly friends
> could have been no comparison. We wept, and wept, till the day dawned.

One means of dealing with the disillusionment was to give it a title—the Great Disappointment—duly capitalized. More importantly, according to Kenneth Newport's impressive new account of the Waco siege, the very next day after the Disappointment, one Millerite leader in Port Gibson, New York, by the name of Hiram Edson had a vision as he walked along, a sudden revelation that "the cleansing of the sanctuary" referred to events not on earth, but in heaven. Jesus had taken his place in the heavenly holy of holies. The date had been right all along, it was simply the *place* they had got wrong. This "masterstroke," as Newport calls it, this "theological lifeline" removed the whole affair into a realm immune to disproof. The Great Disappointment was explained, and many Millerites were drawn, with hope still strong in their hearts, into the beginnings of the Seventh Day Adventist movement—which was to become one of the most successful churches in the United States.

In passing, I note the connections between this church and the medieval sects that Cohn describes—the strong emphasis on the Book of Revelation, the looming proximity of the end, the strict division between the faithful remnant who keep the Sabbath, and those who join the ranks of the "fallen," of the antiChrist, identified with the Pope whose title, Vicarius Filii Dei (vicar of the son of God) apparently has a numerical value of 666.

I mention Hiram Edson's morning-after masterstroke to illustrate the adaptability and resilience of end-time thought. For centuries now, it has regarded the end as "soon" —if not next week, then within a year or two. The end has not come, and yet no one is discomfited for long. New prophets, and soon, a new generation, set about the calculations, and always manage to find the end looming within their own lifetime. The million sellers like Hal Lindsey predicted the end of the world all through the seventies, eighties, and nineties— and today, business has never been better. There is a hunger for this news, and perhaps we glimpse here something in our nature, something of our deeply held notions of time, and our own insignificance against the intimidating vastness of eternity, or the age of the universe—on the human scale there is little difference. We have need of a plot, a narrative to shore up our irrelevance in the flow of things.

In *The Sense of an Ending*, Frank Kermode proposes that the enduring quality, the vitality of the Book of Revelation suggests a "consonance with our more naïve requirements of fiction." We are born, as we will die, in the middle of things, in the "middest." To make sense of our span, we need what he calls "fictive concords with origins and ends. 'The End,' in the grand sense, as we imagine it, will reflect our irreducibly intermediary expectations." What could grant us more meaning against the abyss of time than to identify our own personal demise with the purifying annihilation of all that is. Kermode quotes with approval from Wallace Stevens—"the imagination is always at the end of an era." Even our notions of decadence contain the hopes of renewal; the religious minded as well as the most secular, looked on the transition to the year two thousand as inescapably significant, even if all the atheists did was to party a little harder. It was inevitably a transition, the passing of an old age into the new—and who is to say now that Osama bin Laden did not disappoint, whether we mourned at the dawn of the new millennium with the bereaved among the ruins of lower Manhattan, or danced for joy, as some did, in the Gaza Strip.

Islamic eschatology from its very beginnings embraced the necessity of violently conquering the world and gathering up souls to the faith before the expected hour of judgment—a notion that has risen and fallen over the centuries, but in past decades has received new impetus from Islamist revivalist movements. It is partly a mirror image of the Protestant Christian tradition (a world made entirely Islamic, with Jesus as Mohammed's lieutenant), partly a fantasy of the inevitable return of "sacred space," the Caliphate, that includes most of Spain, parts of France, the entire Middle East, right up to the borders of China. As with the Christian scheme, Islam foretells of the destruction or conversion of the Jews.

Prophecy belief in Judaism, the original source for both the Islamic and Christian eschatologies, is surprisingly weaker—perhaps a certain irony in the relationship between Jews and their god is unfriendly to end-time belief, but it lives on vigorously enough in the Lubavitch movement and various Israeli settler groups, and of course is centrally concerned with divine entitlement to disputed lands.

.   .   .

We should add to the mix more recent secular apocalyptic beliefs—the certainty that the world is inevitably doomed through nuclear exchange, viral epidemics, meteorites, population growth, or environmental degradation. Where these calamities are posed as mere possibilities in an open-ended future that might be headed off by wise human agency, we cannot consider them as apocalyptic. They are minatory, they are calls to action. But when they are presented as unavoidable outcomes driven by ineluctable forces of history or innate human failings, they share much with their religious counterparts—though they lack the demonizing, cleansing, redemptive aspects, and are without the kind of supervision of a supernatural entity that might give benign meaning and purpose to a mass extinction. Clearly, fatalism is common to both camps, and both, reasonably enough, are much concerned with a nuclear holocaust, which to the prophetic believers illuminates in retrospect biblical passages that once seemed obscure. Hal Lindsey, preeminent among the popularizers of American apocalyptic thought, writes,

Zacheriah 14:12 predicts that "their flesh will be consumed from their bones, their eyes burned out of their sockets, and their tongues consumed out of their mouths while they stand on their feet." For hundreds of years students of Bible prophecy have wondered what kind of plague could produce such instant ravaging of humans while still on their feet. Until the event of the atomic bomb such a thing was not humanly possible. But now everything Zacheriah predicted could come true in a thermonuclear exchange!

Two other movements, now mercifully defeated or collapsed, provide a further connection between religious and secular apocalypse—so concluded Norman Cohn in the closing pages of *The Pursuit of the Millennium*. The genocidal tendency among the apocalyptic medieval movements faded somewhat after fifteen hundred. Vigorous end-time belief continued, of course, in the Puritan and Calvinist movements, the Millerites, as we have seen, and in the American Great Awakening, Mormonism, Jehovah's Witnesses, and the Adventist movement. The murderous tradition, however, did not die away completely. It survived the passing of centuries in various sects, various outrages, to emerge in the European twentieth century transformed, revitalized, secularized, but still recognizable in what Cohn depicts as the essence of apocalyptic thinking—"the tense expectation of a final, decisive struggle in which a world tyranny will be overthrown by a 'chosen people' and through which the world will be renewed and history brought to its consummation." The will of god was transformed in the twentieth century into the will of history, but the essential demand remained, as it still does today—"to purify the world by destroying the agents of corruption." The dark reveries of Nazism about the Jews shared much with the murderous anti-Semitic demonology of medieval times. An important additional element, imported from Russia, was *The Protocols of the Elders of Zion*, the 1905 Tsarist police forgery, elevated by Hitler and others into a racist ideology. (It's interesting to note how the *Protocols* has re-emerged as a central text for Islamists, frequently quoted on Web sites, and sold in street book stalls across the Middle East.) The Third Reich and its dream of a thousand-year rule was derived, in a form of secular millennial usurpation, directly from Revelation. Cohn draws our attention to the apocalyptic language of *Mein Kampf.* "If our people . . . fall victims to these Jewish tyrants of the nations with their lust for blood and gold, the whole earth will sink down . . . if Germany frees itself from this embrace, this greatest of dangers for the peoples can be regarded as vanquished for all the earth."

In Marxism in its Soviet form, Cohn also found a continuation of the old millenarian tradition of prophecy, of the final violent struggle to eliminate the agents of corruption—this time it is the bourgeoisie who will be vanquished by the proletariat in order to enable the withering away of the state and usher in the peaceable kingdom. "The kulak . . . is prepared to strangle and massacre hundreds of thousands of workers . . . Ruthless war must be waged on the kulaks! Death to them!" Thus spoke Lenin, and his word, like Hitler's, became deed.

Thirty years ago, we might have been able to convince ourselves that contemporary religious apocalyptic thought was a harmless remnant of a more credulous, superstitious, pre-scientific age, now safely behind us. But today prophecy belief, particularly within the Christian and Islamic traditions, is a force in our contemporary history, a medieval engine driving our modern moral, geo-political, and military concerns. The various jealous sky-gods—and they are certainly not one and the same god—who in the past directly addressed Abraham, Paul, or Mohammed, among others, now indirectly address us through the daily television news. These different gods have wound themselves inextricably around our politics and our political differences.

Our secular and scientific culture has not replaced or even challenged these mutually incompatible, supernatural thought systems. Scientific method, skepticism, or rationality in general, has yet to find an overarching narrative of sufficient power, simplicity, and wide appeal to compete with the old stories that give meaning to people's lives. Natural selection is a powerful, elegant, and economic explicator of life on earth in all its diversity, and perhaps it contains the seeds of a rival creation myth that would have the added power of being true—but it awaits its inspired synthesizer, its poet, its Milton. The great American biologist E. O. Wilson has suggested an ethics divorced from religion, and derived instead from what he calls biophilia, our innate and profound connection to our natural environment—but one man alone cannot make a moral system. Science may speak of probable rising sea levels and global temperatures, with figures that it constantly refines in line with new data, but on the human future it cannot compete with the luridness and, above all, with the meaningfulness of the prophecies in the Book of Daniel, or Revelation. Reason and myth remain uneasy bedfellows.

Rather than presenting a challenge, science has in obvious ways strengthened apocalyptic thinking. It has provided us with the means to destroy ourselves and our civilization completely in less than a couple of hours, or to spread a fatal virus around the globe in a couple of days. And our spiraling technologies of destruction and their ever-greater availability have raised the possibility that true believers, with all their unworldly passion, their prayerful longing for the end times to begin, could help nudge the ancient prophecies towards fulfillment. Wojcik quotes a letter by the singer Pat Boone addressed to fellow Christians. All out nuclear war is what he appears to have had in mind. "My guess is that there isn't a thoughtful Christian alive who doesn't believe we are living at the end of history. I don't know how that makes you feel, but it gets me pretty excited. Just think about actually seeing, as the apostle Paul wrote it, the Lord Himself descending from heaven with a shout! Wow! And the signs that it's about to happen are everywhere."

If this possibility of a willed nuclear catastrophe appears too pessimistic or extravagant, or hilarious, consider the case of another individual, remote from

Pat Boone—President Ahmadinejad of Iran. His much reported remark about wiping Israel off the face of the earth may have been mere bluster of the kind you could hear any Friday in a thousand mosques around the world. But this posturing, coupled with his nuclear ambitions, becomes more worrying when set in the context of his end-time beliefs. In Jamkaran, a village not far from the holy city of Qum, a small mosque is undergoing a 20 million dollar expansion, driven forward by Ahmadinejad's office. Within the Shi'ite apocalyptic tradition, the Twelfth Imam, the Mahdi, who disappeared in the ninth century, is expected to reappear in a well behind the mosque. His re-emergence will signify the beginning of the end days. He will lead the battle against the Dajjal, the Islamic version of the anti-Christ, and with Jesus as his follower, will establish the global Dar el Salaam, the dominion of peace, under Islam. Ahmadinejad is extending the mosque to receive the Mahdi, and already pilgrims by the thousands are visiting the shrine, for the president has reportedly told his cabinet that he expects the visitation within two years.

Or again, consider the celebrated case of the red heifer, or calf. On the Temple Mount in Jerusalem, the end-time stories of Judaism, Christianity, and Islam converge in both interlocking and mutually exclusive ways that are potentially explosive—they form incidentally the material for the American novelist Bob Stone's fine novel, *Damascus Gate*. What is bitterly contested is not only the past and present, it is the future. It is hardly possible to do justice in summary to the complex eschatologies that jostle on this thirty-five acre patch of land. The stories themselves are familiar. For the Jews, the Mount—the biblical Mount Moriah—is the site of the First Temple, destroyed by Nebuchadnezzar in 586 B.C., and of the Second Temple destroyed by the Romans in 70 A.D. According to tradition, and of particular interest to various controversial groups, including the Temple Institute, the Messiah, when he comes at last, will occupy the Third Temple. But that cannot be built, and therefore the Messiah will not come, without the sacrifice of a perfectly unblemished red calf.

For Muslims of course, the Mount is the site of the Dome of the Rock, built over the location of the two temples and enclosing the very spot from which Mohammed departed on his Night Journey to heaven—leaving as his horse stepped upwards a revered hoofprint in the rock. In the prophetic tradition, the Dajjal will be a Jew who leads a devastating war against Islam. Any attempt to bless a foundation stone of a new temple is seen as highly provocative for it implies the destruction of the mosque. The symbolism surrounding Ariel Sharon's visit to the Mount in September 2000 remains a matter of profoundly different interpretation by Muslims and Jews. And if lives were not at stake, the Christian fundamentalist contribution to this volatile mix would seem amusingly cynical. These prophetic believers are certain that Jesus will return at the height of the battle of Armageddon, but his thousand-year reign, which will ensure the conversion of Jews and Muslims to Christianity, or their extinction, cannot begin until the Third Temple is built.

And so it came about that a cattle-breeding operation emerges in Israel with the help of Texan Christian fundamentalist ranchers to promote the birth of the perfect, unspotted red calf, and thereby, we have to assume, bring the end days a little closer. In 1997 there was great excitement, as well as press mockery, when one promising candidate appeared. Months later, this cherished young cow nicked its rump on a barbed wire fence, causing white hairs to grow at the site of the wound and earning instant disqualification. Another red calf appeared in 2002 to general acclaim, and then again, later disappointment. In the tight squeeze of history, religion, and politics that coverage on the Temple Mount, the calf is a minor item indeed. But the search for it, and the hope and longing that surround it, illustrates the dangerous tendency among prophetic believers to bring on the cataclysm that they think will lead to a form of paradise on earth. The reluctance of the current U.S. administration to pursue in these past six years a vigorous policy towards a peace settlement in the Israel-Palestine dispute may owe less to the pressures of Jewish groups than to the eschatology of the Christian Right.

Periods of uncertainty in human history, of rapid, bewildering change, and of social unrest appear to give these old stories greater weight. It does not need a novelist to tell you that where a narrative has a beginning, it needs an end. Where there is a creation myth, there must be a final chapter. Where a god makes the world, it remains in his power to unmake it. When human weakness or wickedness is apparent, there will be guilty fantasies of supernatural retribution. When people are profoundly frustrated, either materially or spiritually, there will be dreams of the perfect society where all conflicts are resolved, and all needs are met.

That much we can understand or politely pretend to understand. But the problem of fatalism remains. In a nuclear age, and in an age of serious environmental degradation, apocalyptic belief creates a serious second order danger. The precarious logic of self-interest that saw us through the Cold War would collapse if the leaders of one nuclear state came to welcome, or ceased to fear, mass death. The words of Ayatollah Khomeini are quoted approvingly in an Iranian eleventh grade textbook: "Either we shake one another's hands in joy at the victory of Islam in the world, or all of us will turn to eternal life and martyrdom. In both cases, victory and success are ours."

And if we let global temperatures continue to rise because we give room to the faction that believes it is God's will, then we are truly—and literally—sunk.

.   .   .

If I were a believer, I think I would prefer to be in Jesus's camp—he is reported by Matthew to have said, "No one knows about that day or hour, not even the angels in heaven, nor the Son, but only the Father."

But even a skeptic can find in the historical accumulation of religious expression joy, fear, love, and above all, seriousness. I return to Philip Larkin—

an atheist who also knew the moment and the nature of transcendence. He once wrote a famous description of a church:

> A serious house on serious earth it is,
> In whose blent air all our compulsions meet,
> Are recognised, and robed as destinies.
> And that much never can be obsolete,
> Since someone will forever be surprising
> A hunger in himself to be more serious . . .

And how could one be more serious than the writer of this prayer for the interment of the dead, from *The Book of Common Prayer*, an incantation of bleak, existential beauty, even more so in its beautiful setting by Henry Purcell: "Man that is born of a woman hath but a short time to live, and is full of misery. He cometh up, and is cut down, like a flower; he fleeth as it were a shadow, and never continueth in one stay."

Ultimately, apocalyptic belief is a function of faith—that luminous inner conviction that needs no recourse to evidence. It is customary to pose against immoveable faith the engines of reason, but in this instance I would prefer that delightful human impulse—curiosity, the hallmark of mental freedom. Organized religion has always had—and I put this mildly—a troubled relationship with curiosity. Islam's distrust, at least in the past two hundred years, is best expressed by its attitude to those whose faith falls away, to apostates who are drawn to other religions or to none at all. In recent times, in 1975, the mufti of Saudi Arabia, Bin Baz, in a fatwa, quoted by Shmuel Bar, ruled as followed: "Those who claim that the earth is round and moving around the sun are apostates and their blood can be shed and their property can be taken in the name of god." Bin Baz rescinded this judgment ten years later. Mainstream Islam routinely prescribes punishment for apostates that ranges from ostracism to beatings to death. To enter one of the many Web sites where Muslim apostates anonymously exchange views is to encounter a world of brave and terrified men and women who have succumbed to their disaffection and intellectual curiosity. And Christians should not feel smug. The first commandment—on pain of death if we were to take the matter literally—is Thou shalt have no other gods before me. In the fourth century, St. Augustine put the matter well for Christianity, and his view prevailed for a long time:"There is another form of temptation, even more fraught with danger. This is the disease of curiosity. It is this which drives us to try and discover the secrets of nature which are beyond our understanding, which can avail us nothing, and which man should not wish to learn."

And yet it is curiosity, scientific curiosity, that has delivered us genuine, testable knowledge of the world and contributed to our understanding of our place within it and of our nature and condition. This knowledge has a beauty of its own, and it can be terrifying. We are barely beginning to grasp the implications of what we have relatively recently learned. And what exactly have we learned? I draw here from a Stephen Pinker essay on his ideal of a university: Among other things we have learned that our planet is a minute speck in an inconceivably vast cosmos; that our species has existed for a tiny fraction of the history of the earth; that humans are primates; that the mind is the activity of an organ that runs by physiological processes; that there are methods for ascertaining the truth that can force us to conclusions which violate common sense, sometimes radically so at scales very large and very small; that precious and widely held beliefs, when subjected to empirical tests, are often cruelly falsified; that we cannot create energy or use it without loss.

As things stand, after more than a century of research in a number of fields, we have no evidence at all that the future can be predicted. Better to look directly to the past, to its junkyard of unrealized futures, for it is curiosity about history that should give end-time believers reasonable pause when they reflect that they stand on a continuum, a long and unvarying thousand-year tradition that has fantasized imminent salvation for themselves and perdition for the rest. On one of the countless end-time/rapture sites that litter the Web, there is a section devoted to Frequently Asked Questions. One is: when the Lord comes, what will happen to the children of other faiths? The answer is staunch: "Ungodly parents only bring judgment to their children." In the light of this, one might conclude that end-time faith is probably as immune to the lessons of history as it is to fundamental human decency.

If we do destroy ourselves, we can assume that the general reaction will be terror, and grief at the pointlessness of it all, rather than rapture. Within living memory we have come very close to extinguishing our civilization when, in October 1962, Soviet ships carrying nuclear warheads to installations in Cuba confronted a blockade by the U.S. Navy, and the world waited to discover whether Nikita Khrushchev would order his convoy home. It is remarkable how little of that terrifying event survives in public memory, in modern folklore. In the vast literature the Cuban Missile Crisis has spawned—military, political, diplomatic—there is very little on its effect at the time on ordinary lives, in homes, school, and the workplace, on the fear and widespread numb incomprehension in the population at large. That fear has not passed into the national narrative, here, or anywhere else as vividly as you might expect. As Spencer Weart put it, "When the crisis ended, most people turned their attention away as swiftly as a child who lifts up a rock, sees something slimy underneath, and drops the rock back." Perhaps the assassination of President Kennedy the following year helped obscure the folk memory of the missile crisis. His murder in Dallas became a marker in the history of instantaneous globalized news transmission—a huge proportion of the world's population seemed to be able to recall where they were when they heard the news. Conflating these two events, Christopher Hitchens opened an essay on the Cuban Missile Crisis with the words—"Like everyone else of my generation, I can remember exactly where I was standing and what I was doing on the day that President John Fitzgerald Kennedy nearly killed me." Heaven did not beckon during those tense hours of the crisis. Instead, as Hitchens observes, "It brought the world to the best view it has had yet of the gates of hell."

I began with the idea of photography as the inventory of mortality, and I will end with a photograph of a group death. It shows fierce flames and smoke rising from a building in Waco, Texas, at the end of a fifty-one-day siege in 1993. The group inside was the Branch Davidians, an offshoot of the Seventh Day Adventists. Its leader, David Koresh, was a man steeped in biblical, end-time theology, convinced that America was Babylon, the agent of Satan, come in the form of the Bureau of Alcohol, Tobacco, and Firearms and the FBI to destroy the Sabbath-keeping remnant, who would emerge from the cleansing, suicidal fire to witness the dawn of a new Kingdom. Here is Susan Sontag's "posthumous irony" indeed, as medieval Europe recreated itself in the form of a charismatic man, a messiah, a messenger of God, the bearer of the perfect truth, who exercised sexual power over his female followers and persuaded them to bear his children in order to begin a "Davidian" line. In that grim inferno, children, their mothers, and other followers died. Even more died two years later when Timothy McVeigh, exacting revenge against the government for its attack on Waco, committed his slaughter in Oklahoma City. It is not for nothing that one of the symptoms in a developing psychosis, noted and described by psychiatrists, is "religiosity."

Have we really reached a stage in public affairs when it really is no longer too obvious to say that all the evidence of the past and all the promptings of our precious rationality suggest that our future is not fixed? We have no reason to believe that there are dates inscribed in heaven or hell. We may yet destroy ourselves; we might scrape through. Confronting that uncertainty is the obligation of our maturity and our only spur to wise action. The believers should know in their hearts by now that, even if they are right and there actually is a benign and watchful personal God, he is, as all the daily tragedies, all the dead children attest, a reluctant intervener. The rest of us, in the absence of any evidence to the contrary, know that it is highly improbable that there is anyone up there at all. Either way, in this case it hardly matters who is wrong—there will be no one to save us but ourselves.

42

What About God?

From *Dreams of a Final Theory*

STEVEN WEINBERG

Physics, biology, genetics, paleontology, anthropology—how much more punishment can religion take from the world of science and free inquiry? Professor Weinberg earned a Nobel Prize for his work, elucidated the big bang in his wonderful book *The First Three Minutes*, and has vastly expanded our knowledge of subatomic particles. He poses the inescapable question and proceeds to offer some equally inescapable answers.

> *"You know," said Port, and his voice sounded unreal, as voices are likely to do after a long pause in an utterly silent spot, "the sky here's very strange. I often have the sensation when I look at it that it's a solid thing up there, protecting us from what's behind."*
>
> *Kit shuddered slightly as she said: "From what's behind?"*
> *"Yes."*
> *"But what is behind?" Her voice was very small.*
> *"Nothing, I suppose. Just darkness. Absolute night."*
>
> —PAUL BOWLES, *THE SHELTERING SKY*

"The heavens declare the glory of God; and the firmament showeth his handiwork." To King David or whoever else wrote this psalm, the stars must have seemed visible evidence of a more perfect order of existence, quite different from our dull sublunary world of rocks and stones and trees. Since David's day the sun and other stars have lost their special status; we understand that they are spheres of glowing gas, held together by gravitation, and supported against collapse by pressure that is maintained by the heat rising up from thermonuclear reactions in the stars' cores. The stars tell us nothing more or less about the glory of God than do the stones on the ground around us.

If there were anything we could discover in nature that *would* give us some special insight into the handiwork of God, it would have to be the final laws of nature. Knowing these laws, we would have in our possession the book of rules that governs stars and stones and everything else. So it is natural that Stephen Hawking should refer to the laws of nature as "the mind of God." Another physicist, Charles Misner, used similar language in comparing the perspectives of physics and chemistry: "The organic chemist, in answer to the question, 'Why are there ninety-two elements, and when were they produced?' may say 'The man in the next office knows that.' But the physicist, being asked, 'Why is the universe built to follow certain physical laws and not others?' may well reply, 'God knows.'" Einstein once remarked to his assistant Ernst Straus that "What really interests me is whether God had any choice in the creation of the world." On another occasion he described the aim of the enterprise of physics as "not only to know how nature is and how her transactions are carried through, but also to reach as far as possible the Utopian and seemingly arrogant aim of knowing why *nature is thus and not otherwise.* . . . Thereby one experiences, so to speak, that God Himself could not have arranged these connections in any other way than that which factually exists. . . . This is the Promethean element of the scientific experience. . . . Here has always been for me the particular magic of scientific effort." Einstein's religion was so vague that I suspect that he meant this metaphorically, as suggested by his "so to speak." It is doubtless because physics is so fundamental that this metaphor is natural to physicists. The theologian Paul Tillich once observed that among scientists only physicists seem capable of using the word "God" without embarrassment. Whatever one's religion or lack of it, it is an irresistible metaphor to speak of the final laws of nature in terms of the mind of God.

I encountered this connection once in an odd place, in the Rayburn House Office Building in Washington. When I testified there in 1987 in favor of the Superconducting Super Collider (SSC) project before the House Committee on Science, Space, and Technology, I described how in our study of elementary particles we are discovering laws that are becoming increasingly coherent and universal, and how we are beginning to suspect that this is not merely an accident, that there is a beauty in these laws that mirrors something that is built into the structure of the universe at a very deep level. After I made these remarks there were remarks by other witnesses and questions from members of the committee. There then ensued a dialogue between two committee members. Representative Harris W. Fawell, Republican of Illinois, who had generally been favorable to the Super Collider project, and Representative Don Ritter, Republican of Pennsylvania, a former metallurgical engineer who is one of the most formidable opponents of the project in Congress:

MR. FAWELL: . . . Thank you very much. I appreciate the testimony of all of you. I think it was excellent. If ever I would want to explain to one and all the reasons why the SSC is needed I am sure I can go to your testimony. It would be very helpful. I wish sometimes that we have some one word that could say it all and that is kind of impossible. I guess perhaps Dr. Weinberg you came a little close to it and I'm not sure but I took this down. You said you suspect that it isn't all an accident, that there are rules which govern matter and I jotted down, will this make us find God? I'm sure you didn't make that claim, but it certainly will enable us to understand so much more about the universe.

MR. RITTER: Will the gentleman yield on that? If the gentleman would yield for a moment I would say . . .

MR. FAWELL: I'm not sure I want to.

MR. RITTER: If this machine does that I am going to come around and support it.

I had enough sense to stay out of this exchange, because I did not think that the congressmen wanted to know what I thought about finding God at the SSC and also because it did not seem to me that letting them know what I thought about this would be helpful to the project.

Some people have views of God that are so broad and flexible that it is inevitable that they will find God wherever they look for Him. One hears it said that "God is the ultimate" or "God is our better nature" or "God is the universe." Of course, like any other word, the word "God" can be given any meaning we like. If you want to say that "God is energy," then you can find God in a lump of coal. But if words are to have any value to us, we ought to respect the way that they have been used historically, and we ought especially to preserve distinctions that prevent the meanings of words from merging with the meanings of other words.

In this spirit, it seems to me that if the word "God" is to be of any use, it should be taken to mean an interested God, a creator and lawgiver who has established not only the laws of nature and the universe but also standards of good and evil, some personality that is concerned with our actions, something in short that it is appropriate for us to worship.[1] This is the God that has mattered to men and women throughout history. Scientists and others sometimes use the word "God" to mean something so abstract and unengaged that He is hardly to be distinguished from the laws of nature. Einstein once said that he believed in "Spinoza's God who reveals Himself in the orderly harmony of what exists, not in a God who concerns himself with fates and actions of human beings." But what possible difference does it make to anyone if we use the word

_____

1. It should be apparent that in discussing these things I am speaking only for myself and that in this chapter I leave behind me any claim to special expertise.

"God" in place of "order" or "harmony," except perhaps to avoid the accusation of having no God? Of course, anyone is free to use the word "God" in that way, but it seems to me that it makes the concept of God not so much wrong as unimportant.

Will we find an interested God in the final laws of nature? There seems something almost absurd in asking this question, not only because we do not yet know the final laws, but much more because it is difficult even to imagine being in the possession of ultimate principles that do not need any explanation in terms of deeper principles. But premature as the question may be, it is hardly possible not to wonder whether we will find any answer to our deepest questions, any sign of the workings of an interested God, in a final theory. I think that we will not.

All our experience throughout the history of science has tended in the opposite direction, toward a chilling impersonality in the laws of nature. The first great step along this path was the demystification of the heavens. Everyone knows the key figures: Copernicus, who proposed that the earth is not at the center of the universe; Galileo, who made it plausible that Copernicus was right; Bruno, who guessed that the sun is only one of a vast number of stars, and Newton, who showed that the same laws of motion and gravitation apply to the solar system and to bodies on the earth. The key moment I think was Newton's observation that the same law of gravitation governs the motion of the moon around the earth and a falling body on the surface of the earth. In our own century the demystification of the heavens was taken a step farther by the American astronomer Edwin Hubble. By measuring the distance to the Andromeda Nebula, Hubble showed that this, and by inference thousands of other similar nebulas, were not just outlying parts of our galaxy but galaxies in their own right, quite as impressive as our own. Modern cosmologists even speak of a Copernican principle: the rule that no cosmological theory can be taken seriously that puts our own galaxy at any distinctive place in the universe.

Life, too, has been demystified. Justus von Liebig and other organic chemists in the early nineteenth century demonstrated that there was no barrier to the laboratory synthesis of chemicals like uric acid that are associated with life. Most important of all were Charles Darwin and Alfred Russel Wallace, who showed how the wonderful capabilities of living things could evolve through natural selection with no outside plan or guidance. The process of demystification has accelerated in this century, in the continued success of biochemistry and molecular biology in explaining the workings of living things.

The demystification of life has had a far greater effect on religious sensibilities than has any discovery of physical science. It is not surprising that it is reductionism in biology and the theory of evolution rather than the discoveries of physics and astronomy that continue to evoke the most intransigent opposition.

Even from scientists one hears occasional hints of vitalism, the belief in biological processes that cannot be explained in terms of physics and chemistry. In this century biologists (including antireductionists like Ernst Mayr) have generally steered clear of vitalism, but as late as 1944 Erwin Schröndinger argued in his well-known book *What Is Life?* that "enough is known about the material structure of life to tell exactly why present-day physics cannot account for life." His reason was that the genetic information that governs living organisms is far too stable to fit into the world of continual fluctuations described by quantum mechanics and statistical mechanics. Schröndinger 's mistake was pointed out by Max Perutz, the molecular biologist who among other things worked out the structure of hemoglobin: Schröndinger had ignored the stability that can be produced by the chemical process known as enzymatic catalysis.

The most respectable academic critic of evolution may currently be Professor Phillip Johnson of the University of California School of Law. Johnson concedes that evolution has occurred and that it is sometimes due to natural selection, but he argues that there is no "incontrovertible experimental evidence" that evolution is not guided by some divine plan. Of course, one could never hope to prove that no supernatural agency ever tips the scales in favor of some mutations and against others. But much the same could be said of any scientific theory. There is nothing in the successful application of Newton's or Einstein's laws of motion to the solar system that prevents us from supposing that every once in a while some comet gets a small shove from a divine agency. It seems pretty clear that Johnson raises this issue not as a matter of impartial open-mindedness but because for religious reasons he cares very much about life in a way that he does not care about comets. But the only way that any sort of science can proceed is to assume that there is no divine intervention and to see how far one can get with this assumption.

Johnson argues that naturalistic evolution, "evolution that involves no intervention or guidance by a creator outside the world of nature," in fact does not provide a very good explanation for the origin of species. I think he goes wrong here because he has no feeling for the problems that any scientific theory always has in accounting for what we observe. Even apart from outright errors, our calculations and observations are always based on assumptions that go beyond the validity of the theory we are trying to test. There never was a time when the calculations based on Newton's theory of gravitation or any other theory were in perfect agreement with all observations. In the writings of today's paleontologists and evolutionary biologists we can recognize the same state of affairs that is so familiar to us in physics; in using the naturalistic theory of evolution biologists are working with an overwhelmingly successful theory, but one that is not yet finished with its work of explication. It seems to me to be a profoundly important discovery that we can get very far in explaining the world without invoking divine intervention, and in biology as well as in the physical sciences.

In another respect I think that Johnson is right. He argues that there is an incompatibility between the naturalistic theory of evolution and religion as generally understood, and he takes to task the scientists and educators who deny it.

He goes on to complain that "naturalistic evolution is consistent with the existence of 'God' only if by that term we mean no more than a first cause which retires from further activity after establishing the laws of nature and setting the natural mechanism in motion."

The inconsistency between the modern theory of evolution and belief in an interested God does not seem to me one of logic—one can imagine that God established the laws of nature and set the mechanism of evolution in motion with the intention that through natural selection you and I would someday appear—but there is a real inconsistency in temperament. After all, religion did not arise in the minds of men and women who speculated about infinitely prescient first causes but in the hearts of those who longed for the continual intervention of an interested God.

The religious conservatives understand, as their liberal opponents seem often not to, how high the stakes are in the debate over teaching evolution in the public schools. In 1983, shortly after coming to Texas, I was invited to testify before a committee of the Texas Senate on a regulation that forbade the teaching of the theory of evolution in state-purchased high-school textbooks unless equal emphasis was given to creationism. One of the members of the committee asked me how the state could support the teaching of a scientific theory like evolution that was so corrosive of religious belief. I replied that just as it would be wrong for those who are emotionally committed to atheism to give evolution more emphasis than would be otherwise appropriate in teaching biology, so it would be inconsistent with the First Amendment to give evolution less emphasis as a means of protecting religious belief. It is simply not the business of the public schools to concern themselves one way or the other with the religious implications of scientific theories. My answer did not satisfy the senator because he knew as I did what would be the effect of a course in biology that gives an appropriate emphasis to the theory of evolution. As I left the committee room, he muttered that "God is still in heaven anyway." Maybe so, but we won that battle; Texas high-school textbooks are now not only allowed but required to teach the modern theory of evolution, and with no nonsense about creationism. But there are many places (today especially in Islamic countries) where this battle is yet to be won and no assurance anywhere that it will stay won.

One often hears that there is no conflict between science and religion. For instance, in a review of Johnson's book, Stephen Gould remarks that science and religion do not come into conflict, because "science treats factual reality, while religion treats human morality." On most things I tend to agree with Gould, but here I think he goes too far; the meaning of religion is defined by what religious people actually believe, and the great majority of the world's religious people would be surprised to learn that religion has nothing to do with factual reality.

But Gould's view is widespread today among scientists and religious liberals. This seems to me to represent an important retreat of religion from positions it once occupied. Once nature seemed inexplicable without a nymph in every brook and a dryad in every tree. Even as late as the nineteenth century the design of plants and animals was regarded as visible evidence of a creator. There are still countless things in nature that we cannot explain, but we think we know the principles that govern the way they work. Today, for real mystery, one has to look to cosmology and elementary particle physics. For those who see no conflict between science and religion, the retreat of religion from the ground occupied by science is nearly complete.

Judging from this historical experience, I would guess that, though we shall find beauty in the final laws of nature, we will find no special status for life or intelligence. *A fortiori*, we will find no standards of value or morality. And so we will find no hint of any God who cares about such things. We may find these things elsewhere, but not in the laws of nature.

I have to admit that sometimes nature seems more beautiful than strictly necessary. Outside the window of my home office there is a hackberry tree, visited frequently by a convocation of politic birds: blue jays, yellow-throated vireos, and, loveliest of all, an occasional red cardinal. Although I understand pretty well how brightly colored feathers evolved out of a competition for mates, it is almost irresistible to imagine that all this beauty was somehow laid on for our benefit. But the God of birds and trees would have to be also the God of birth defects and cancer.

Religious people have grappled for millennia with the theodicy, the problem posed by the existence of suffering in a world that is supposed to be ruled by a good God. They have found ingenious solutions in terms of various supposed divine plans. I will not try to argue with these solutions, much less to add one more of my own. Remembrance of the Holocaust leaves me unsympathetic to attempts to justify the ways of God to man. If there is a God that has special plans for humans, then He has taken very great pains to hide His concern for us. To me it would seem impolite if not impious to bother such a God with our prayers.

Not all scientists would agree with my bleak view of the final laws. I do not know of anyone who maintains explicitly that there is scientific evidence for a divine being, but several scientists do argue for a special status in nature for intelligent life. Of course, everyone knows that as a practical matter biology and psychology have to be studied in their own terms, not in terms of elementary particle physics, but that is not a sign of any special status for life or intelligence; the same is true of chemistry and hydrodynamics. If, on the other hand, we found some special role for intelligent life in the final laws at the point of convergence of the arrows of explanation, we might well conclude that the creator who established these laws was in some way specially interested in us.

John Wheeler is impressed by the fact that, according to the standard Copenhagen interpretation of quantum mechanics, a physical system cannot be said to have any definite values for quantities like position or energy or momentum until these quantities are measured by some observer's apparatus. For Wheeler, some sort of intelligent life is required in order to give meaning to quantum mechanics. Recently Wheeler has gone further and proposed that intelligent life not only must appear but must go on to pervade every part of the universe in order that every bit of information about the physical state of the universe should eventually be observed. Wheeler's conclusions seem to me to provide a good example of the dangers of taking too seriously the doctrine of positivism, that science should concern itself only with things that can be observed. Other physicists including myself prefer another, realist, way of looking at quantum mechanics, in terms of a wave function that can describe laboratories and observers as well as atoms and molecules, governed by laws that do not materially depend on whether there are any observers or not.

Some scientists make much of the fact that some of the fundamental constants have values that seem remarkably well suited to the appearance of intelligent life in the universe. It is not yet clear whether there is anything to this observation, but even if there is, it does not necessarily imply the operation of a divine purpose. In several modern cosmological theories, the so-called constants of nature (such as the masses of the elementary particles) actually vary from place to place or from time to time or even from one term in the wave function of the universe to another. If that were true, then as we have seen, any scientists who study the laws of nature would have to be living in a part of the universe where the constants of nature take values favorable for the evolution of intelligent life.

For an analogy, suppose that there is a planet called Earthprime, in every respect identical to our own, except that on this planet mankind developed the science of physics without knowing anything about astronomy. (E.g., one might imagine that Earthprime's surface is perpetually covered by clouds.) Just as on earth, students on Earthprime would find tables of fundamental constants at the back of their physics textbooks. These tables would list the speed of light, the mass of the electron, and so on, and also another "fundamental" constant having the value 1.99 calories of energy per minute per square centimeter, which gives the energy reaching Earthprime's surface from some unknown source outside. On earth this is called the solar constant because we know that this energy comes from the sun, but no one on Earthprime would have any way of knowing where this energy comes from or why this constant takes this particular value. Some physicist on Earthprime might note that the observed value of this constant is remarkably well suited to the appearance of life. If Earthprime received much more or much less than two calories per minute per square centimeter the water of the oceans would instead be vapor or ice, leaving Earthprime with no liquid water or reasonable substitute in which life could have evolved. The physicist might conclude that this constant of 1.99 calories per minute per square centimeter had been fine-tuned by God for man's benefit. More skeptical physicists on Earthprime might argue that such constants are eventually going to be explained by the final laws of physics, and that it is just a lucky accident that they have values favorable for life. In fact, both would be wrong. When the inhabitants of Earthprime finally develop a knowledge of astronomy, they learn that their planet receives 1.99 calories per minute per square centimeter because, like earth, it happens to be about 93 million miles away from a sun that produces 5,600 million million million million calories per minute, but they also see that there are other planets closer to their sun that are too hot for life and more planets farther from their sun that are too cold for life and doubtless countless other planets orbiting other stars of which only a small proportion are suitable for life. When they learn something about astronomy, the arguing physicists on Earthprime finally understand that the reason why they live on a world that receives roughly two calories per minute per square centimeter is just that there is no other kind of world where they *could* live. We in our part of the universe may be like the inhabitants of Earthprime before they learn about astronomy, but with other parts of the universe instead of other planets hidden from our view.

I would go further. As we have discovered more and more fundamental physical principles, they seem to have less and less to do with us. To take one example, in the early 1920s it was thought that the only elementary particles were the electron and the proton, then considered to be the ingredients from which we and our world are made. When new particles like the neutron were discovered it was taken for granted at first that they had to be made up of electrons and protons. Matters are very different today. We are not so sure anymore what we mean by a particle being elementary, but we have learned the important lesson that the fact that particles are present in ordinary matter has nothing to do with how fundamental they are. Almost all the particles whose fields appear in the modern standard model of particles and interactions decay so rapidly that they are absent in ordinary matter and play no role at all in human life. Electrons are an essential part of our everyday world; the particles called muons and tauons hardly matter at all to our lives; yet, in the way that they appear in our theories, electrons do not seem in any way more fundamental than muons and tauons. More generally, no one has ever discovered any correlation between the importance of *anything* to us and its importance in the laws of nature.

Of course it is not from the discoveries of science that most people would have expected to learn about God anyway. John Polkinghorne has argued eloquently for a theology "placed within an area of human discourse where science also finds a home" that would be based on religious experience such as revelation, in much the way that science is based on experiment and observation. Those who think that they have had religious experiences of their own have to judge for themselves the quality of that experience. But the great majority of the adherents to the world's religions are relying not on religious experience of their own but on revelations that were supposedly experienced by others. It might be thought that this is not so different from the theoretical physicist relying on the experiments of others, but there is a very important distinction. The insights of thousands of individual physicists have converged to a satisfying (though incomplete) common understanding of physical reality. In contrast, the statements about God or anything else that have been derived from religious revelation point in radically different directions. After thousands of years of theological analysis, we are no closer now to a common understanding of the lessons of religious revelation.

There is another distinction between religious experience and scientific experiment. The lessons of religious experience can be deeply satisfying, in contrast to the abstract and impersonal worldview gained from scientific investigation. Unlike science, religious experience can suggest a meaning for our lives, a part for us to play in a great cosmic drama of sin and redemption, and it holds out to us a promise of some continuation after death. For just these reasons, the lessons of religious experience seem to me indelibly marked with the stamp of wishful thinking.

In my 1977 book, *The First Three Minutes,* I was rash enough to remark that "the more the universe seems comprehensible, the more it seems pointless." I did not mean that science teaches us that the universe is pointless, but rather that the universe itself suggests no point. I hastened to add that there were ways that we ourselves could invent a point for our lives, including trying to understand the universe. But the damage was done: that phrase has dogged me ever since. Recently Alan Lightman and Roberta Brawer published interviews with twenty-seven cosmologists and physicists, most of whom had been asked at the end of their interview what they thought of that remark. With various qualifications, ten of the interviewees agreed with me and thirteen did not, but of those thirteen, three disagreed because they did not see why anyone would *expect* the universe to have a point. The Harvard astronomer Margaret Geller asked, "Why should it have a point? What point? It's just a physical system, what point is there? I've always been puzzled by that statement." The Princeton astrophysicist Jim Peebles remarked, "I'm willing to believe that we are flotsam and jetsam." (Peebles also guessed that I had had a bad day.) Another Princeton astrophysicist, Edwin Turner, agreed with me but suspected that I had intended the remark to annoy the reader. My favorite response was that of my colleague at the University of Texas, the astronomer Gerard de Vaucouleurs. He said that he thought my remark was "nostalgic." Indeed it was—nostalgic for a world in which the heavens declared the glory of God.

About a century and a half ago Matthew Arnold found in the withdrawing ocean tide a metaphor for the retreat of religious faith, and heard in the water's sound "the note of sadness." It would be wonderful to find in the laws of nature a plan prepared by a concerned creator in which human beings played some special role. I find sadness in doubting that we will. There are some among my scientific colleagues who say that the contemplation of nature gives them all the spiritual satisfaction that others have traditionally found in a belief in an interested God. Some of them may even really feel that way. I do not. And it does not seem to me to be helpful to identify the laws of nature as Einstein did with some sort of remote and disinterested God. The more we refine our understanding of God to make the concept plausible, the more it seems pointless.

Among today's scientists I am probably somewhat atypical in caring about such things. On the rare occasions when conversations over lunch or tea touch on matters of religion, the strongest reaction expressed by most of my fellow physicists is a mild surprise and amusement that anyone still takes all that seriously. Many physicists maintain a nominal affiliation with the faith of their parents, as a form of ethnic identification and for use at weddings and funerals, but few of these physicists seem to pay any attention to their nominal religion's theology. I do know two general relativists who are devout Roman Catholics; several theoretical physicists who are observant Jews; an experimental physicist who is a born-again Christian; one theoretical physicist who is a dedicated Muslem; and one mathematical physicist who has taken holy orders in the Church of England. Doubtless there are other deeply religious physicists whom I don't know or who keep their opinions to themselves. But, as far as I can tell from my own observations, most physicists today are not sufficiently interested in religion even to qualify as practicing atheists.

Religious liberals are in one sense even farther in spirit from scientists than are fundamentalists and other religious conservatives. At least the conservatives, like the scientists, tell you that they believe in what they believe because it is true, rather than because it makes them good or happy. Many religious liberals today seem to think that different people can believe in different mutually exclusive things without any of them being wrong, as long as their beliefs "work for them." This one believes in reincarnation, that one in heaven and hell; a third believes in the extinction of the soul at death, but no one can be said to be wrong as long as everyone gets a satisfying spiritual rush from what they believe. To borrow a phrase from Susan Sontag, we are surrounded by "piety without content." It all reminds me of a story that is told about an experience of Bertrand Russell, when in 1918 he was committed to prison for his opposition to the war. Following prison routine, a jailer asked Russell his religion, and Russell said that he was an agnostic. The jailer looked puzzled for a moment, and then brightened, with the observation that "I guess it's all right. We all worship the same God, don't we?"

Wolfgang Pauli was once asked whether he thought that a particularly ill-conceived physics paper was wrong. He replied that such a description would be too kind—the paper was not even wrong. I happen to think that the religious conservatives are wrong in what they believe, but at least they have not forgotten what it means really to believe something. The religious liberals seem to me to be not even wrong.

One often hears that theology is not the important thing about religion—the important thing is how it helps us to live. Very strange, that the existence and nature of God and grace and sin and heaven and hell are not important! I would guess that people do not find the theology of their own supposed religion important because they cannot bring themselves to admit that they do not believe any of it. But throughout history and in many parts of the world today people have believed in one theology or another, and for them it has been very important. One may be put off by the intellectual muzziness of religious liberalism, but it is conservative dogmatic religion that does the harm. Of course it has also made great moral and artistic contributions. This is not the place to argue how we should strike a balance between these contributions of religion on one hand and the long cruel story of crusade and jihad and inquisition and pogrom on the other. But I do want to make the point that in striking this balance, it is not safe to assume that religious persecution and holy wars are perversions of true religion. To assume that they are seems to me a symptom of a widespread attitude toward religion, consisting of deep respect combined with a profound lack of interest. Many of the great world religions teach that God demands a particular faith and form of worship. It should not be surprising that *some* of the people who take these teachings seriously should sincerely regard these divine commands as incomparably more important than any merely secular virtues like tolerance or compassion or reason.

Across Asia and Africa the dark forces of religious enthusiasm are gathering strength, and reason and tolerance are not safe even in the secular states of the West. The historian Hugh Trevor-Roper has said that it was the spread of the spirit of science in the seventeenth and eighteenth centuries that finally ended the burning of witches in Europe. We may need to rely again on the influence of science to preserve a sane world. It is not the certainty of scientific knowledge that fits it for this role, but its *uncertainty*. Seeing scientists change their minds again and again about matters that can be studied directly in laboratory experiments, how can one take seriously the claims of religious tradition or sacred writings to certain knowledge about matters beyond human experience?

Of course, science has made its own contribution to the world's sorrows, but generally by giving us the means of killing each other, not the motive. Where the authority of science has been invoked to justify horrors, it really has been in terms of perversions of science, like Nazi racism and "eugenics." As Karl Popper has said, "It is only too obvious that it is irrationalism and not rationalism that has the responsibility for all national hostility and aggression, both before and after the Crusades, but I do not know of any war waged for a 'scientific' aim, and inspired by scientists."

Unfortunately I do not think that it is possible to make the case for scientific modes of reasoning by rational argument. David Hume saw long ago that in appealing to our past experience of successful science we are assuming the validity of the very mode of reasoning we are trying to justify. In the same way, all logical arguments can be defeated by the simple refusal to reason logically. So we cannot simply dismiss the question why, if we do not find the spiritual comfort we want in the laws of nature, we should *not* look for it elsewhere—in spiritual authority of one sort or another, or in an independent leap of faith?

The decision to believe or not is not entirely in our hands. I might be happier and have better manners if I thought I were descended from the emperors of China, but no effort of will on my part can make me believe it, any more than I can will my heart to stop beating. Yet it seems that many people are able to exert some control over what they believe and choose to believe in what they think makes them good or happy. The most interesting description I know of how this control can work appears in George Orwell's novel *1984*. The hero, Winston Smith, has written in his diary that "freedom is the freedom to say that two plus two is four." The inquisitor, O'Brien, takes this as a challenge, and sets out to force Smith to change his mind. Under torture Smith is perfectly willing to say that two plus two is five, but that is not what O'Brien is after. Finally, the pain becomes so unbearable that in order to escape it Smith manages to convince himself for an instant that two plus two *is* five. O'Brien is satisfied for the moment, and the torture is suspended. In much the same way, the pain of confronting the prospect of our own deaths and the deaths of those we love impels us to adopt beliefs that soften that pain. If we are able to manage to adjust our beliefs in this way, then why not do so?

I can see no scientific or logical reason not to seek consolation by adjustment of our beliefs—only a moral one, a point of honor. What do we think of someone who has managed to convince himself that he is bound to win a lottery because he desperately needs the money? Some might envy him his brief great expectations, but many others would think that he is failing in his proper role as an adult and rational human being, of looking at things as they are. In the same way that each of us has had to learn in growing up to resist the temptation of wishful thinking about ordinary things like lotteries, so our species has had to learn in growing up that we are not playing a starring role in any sort of grand cosmic drama.

Nevertheless, I do not for a minute think that science will ever provide the consolations that have been offered by religion in facing death. The finest statement of this existential challenge that I know is found in *The Ecclesiastical History of the English*, written by the Venerable Bede sometime around A.D. 700. Bede tells how King Edwin of Northumbria held a council in A.D. 627 to decide on the religion to be accepted in his kingdom, and gives the following speech to one of the king's chief men:

> Your majesty, when we compare the present life of man on earth with that
> time of which we have no knowledge, it seems to me like the swift flight of a
> single sparrow through the banqueting-hall where you are sitting at dinner on

a winter's day with your thanes and counsellors. In the midst there is a comforting fire to warm the hall; outside, the storms of winter rain or snow are raging. This sparrow flies swiftly in through one door of the hall, and out through another. While he is inside, he is safe from the winter storms; but after a few moments of comfort, he vanishes from sight into the wintry world from which he came. Even so, man appears on earth for a little while; but of what went before this life or of what follows, we know nothing.

It is an almost irresistible temptation to believe with Bede and Edwin that there must be something for us outside the banqueting hall. The honor of resisting this temptation is only a thin substitute for the consolations of religion, but it is not entirely without satisfactions of its own.

43

"Imagine There's No Heaven"

A Letter to the
Six Billionth World Citizen

SALMAN RUSHDIE

Born a Muslim in the year that his Indian homeland was fatally sundered by religious partition and war, Salman Rushdie has achieved global renown for his novels and for the way in which they illuminate cross-cultural migrations. In 1989, the Ayatollah Khomeini publicly offered money in his own name to suborn his murder, adding the inducement of a ticket to paradise for anyone willing to take the bribe. Ever since, Rushdie has come to symbolize the defense of free expression and unfettered literary activity (it was his novel *The Satanic Verses* that was also the object of Khomeini's mad rage) as well as the right of any person to apostatize from religion. In 1997, Rushdie contributed a letter to a UN-sponsored anthology, addressed to the six-billionth human child who was expected to be born that year. In consequence of Rushdie's contribution, the ever-courageous Kofi Annan, who was at the time Secretary-General, withdrew his own introduction to the volume. Mr. Rushdie very handsomely agreed to update and expand his letter for this collection.

Dear Little Six Billionth Living Person,

As the newest member of a notoriously inquisitive species, it probably won't be too long before you start asking the two sixty-four thousand dollar questions with which the other 5,999,999,999 of us have been wrestling for some time: How did we get here? And, now that we are here, how shall we live?

Oddly—as if six billion of us weren't enough to be going on with—it will almost certainly be suggested to you that the answer to the question of origins requires you to believe in the existence of a further, invisible, ineffable Being "somewhere up there," an omnipotent creator whom we poor limited creatures are unable even to perceive, much less to understand. That is, you will be strongly encouraged to imagine a heaven with at least one god in residence. This sky-god, it's said, made the universe by churning its matter in a giant pot. Or he danced. Or he vomited Creation out of himself. Or he simply called it into being, and lo, it Was. In some of the more interesting creation stories, the single mighty sky-god is subdivided into many lesser forces—junior deities, *avatars*, gigantic metamorphic "ancestors" whose adventures create the landscape, or the whimsical, wanton, meddling, cruel pantheons of the great polytheisms, whose wild doings will convince you that the real engine of creation was lust: for infinite power, for too-easily-broken human bodies, for clouds of glory. But it's only fair to add that there are also stories which offer the message that the primary creative impulse was, and is, love.

Many of these stories will strike you as extremely beautiful and, therefore, seductive. Unfortunately, however, you will not be required to make a purely literary response to them. Only the stories of "dead" religions can be appreciated for their beauty. Living religions require much more of you. So you will be told that belief in "your" stories and adherence to the rituals of worship that have grown up around them must become a vital part of your life in the crowded world. They will be called the heart of your culture, even of your individual identity. It is possible that they may, at some point, come to feel inescapable, not in the way that the truth is inescapable, but in the way that a jail is. They may at some point cease to feel like the texts in which human beings have tried to solve a great mystery, and feel, instead, like the pretexts for other properly anointed human beings to order you around. And it's true that human history is full of the public oppression wrought by the charioteers of the gods. In the opinion of religious people, however, the private comfort that religion brings more than compensates for the evil done in its name.

As human knowledge has grown, it has also become plain that every religious story ever told about how we got here is quite simply wrong. This, finally, is what all religions have in common. They didn't get it right. There was no celestial churning, no maker's dance, no vomiting of galaxies, no snake or kangaroo ancestors, no Valhalla, no Olympus, no six-day conjuring trick followed by a day of rest. Wrong, wrong, wrong. But here's something genuinely odd. The wrongness of the sacred tales hasn't lessened the zeal of the devout. If anything, the sheer out-of-step zaniness of religion leads the religious to insist ever more stridently on the importance of blind faith.

As a result of this faith, by the way, it has proved impossible in many parts of the world to prevent the human race's numbers from swelling alarmingly. Blame the overcrowded planet at least partly on the misguidedness of the race's spiritual guides. In your own lifetime, you may well witness the arrival of the nine billionth world citizen. If you're Indian (and there's a one-in-six chance that you are) you will be alive when, thanks to the failure of family planning schemes in that poor, God-ridden land, its population surges past China's. And if too many people are being born as a result, in part, of religious strictures against birth control, then too many people are also dying because religious culture, by refusing to face the facts of human sexuality, also refuses to fight against the spread of sexually transmitted diseases.

There are those who say that the great wars of the new century will once again be wars of religion, jihads, and crusades, as they were in the Middle Ages. Even though, for years now, the air has been full of the battle-cries of the faithful as they turn their bodies into God's bombs, and the screams of their victims too, I have not wanted to believe this theory, or not in the way most people mean it.

I have long argued that Samuel Huntington's "clash of civilizations" theory is an oversimplification: that most Muslims have no interest in taking part in religious wars, that the divisions in the Muslim world run as deep as the things it has in common (just take a look at the Sunni-Shia conflict in Iraq if you doubt the truth of this). There's very little resembling a common Islamic purpose to be found. Even after the non-Islamic Nato fought a war for the Muslim Kosovar Albanians, the Muslim world was slow in coming forward with much-needed humanitarian aid.

The real wars of religion, I have argued, are the wars religions unleash against ordinary citizens within their "sphere of influence." They are wars of the godly against the largely defenseless: American fundamentalists against pro-choice doctors, Iranian mullahs against their country's Jewish minority, the Taliban against the people of Afghanistan, Hindu fundamentalists in Bombay against that city's increasingly fearful Muslims.

And the real wars of religion are also the wars religions unleash against unbelievers, whose unbearable unbelief is re-characterized as an offense, as a sufficient reason for their eradication.

But as time has passed I have been obliged to recognize a harsh truth: that the mass of so-called ordinary Muslims seems to have bought into the paranoid fantasies of the extremists and seems to spend more of its energy in mobilizing against cartoonists, novelists, or the Pope than in condemning, disenfranchising, and expelling the fascistic murderers in their midst. If this silent majority allows a war to be waged in its name, then it does, finally, become complicit in that war.

So perhaps a war of religion is beginning, after all, because the worst of us are being allowed to dictate the agenda to the rest of us, and because the fanatics, who really mean business, are not being opposed strongly enough by "their own people."

And if that is so, then the victors in such a war must not be the closed-minded, marching into battle with, as ever, God on their side. To choose unbelief is to choose mind over dogma, to trust in our humanity instead of all these dangerous divinities. So, how did we get here? Don't look for the answer in "sacred" storybooks. Imperfect human knowledge maybe be a bumpy, pot-holed street, but it's the only road to wisdom worth taking. Virgil, who believed that the apiarist Aristaeus could spontaneously generate new bees from the rotting carcass of a cow, was closer to a truth about origins than all the revered old books.

The ancient wisdoms are modern nonsenses. Live in your own time, use what we know, and as you grow up, perhaps the human race will finally grow up with you and put aside childish things.

As the song says, *It's easy if you try.*

As for morality, the second great question—how to live? what is right action, and what wrong?—it comes down to your willingness to think for yourself. Only you can decide if you want to be handed down the law by priests and accept that good and evil are somehow external to ourselves. To my mind religion, even at its most sophisticated, essentially infantilizes our ethical selves by setting infallible moral Arbiters and irredeemably immoral Tempters above us; the eternal parents, good and bad, light and dark, of the supernatural realm.

How, then, are we to make ethical choices without a divine rulebook or judge? Is unbelief just the first step on the long slide into the brain-death of cultural relativism, according to which many unbearable things—female circumcision, to name just one—can be excused on culturally specific grounds, and the universality of human rights, too, can be ignored? (This last piece of moral unmaking finds supporters in some of the world's most authoritarian régimes, and also, unnervingly, on the op-ed pages of the *Daily Telegraph*.)

Well, no, it isn't, but the reasons for saying so aren't clear cut. Only hard-line ideology is clear cut. Freedom, which is the word I use for the secular-ethical position, is inevitably fuzzier. Yes, freedom is that space in which contradiction can reign; it is a never-ending debate. It is not in itself the answer to the question of morals but the conversation about that question.

And it is much more than mere relativism because it is not merely a never-ending talk-shop but a place in which choices are made, values defined and defended. Intellectual freedom, in European history, has mostly meant freedom from the restraints of the Church, not the state. This is the battle Voltaire was fighting, and it's also what all six billion of us could do for ourselves, the revolution in which each of us could play our small, six-billionth part: once and for all, we could refuse to allow priests, and the fictions on whose behalf they claim to speak, to be the policemen of our liberties and behavior. Once and for all, we could put the stories back into the books, put the books back on the shelves, and see the world undogmatized and plain.

Imagine there's no heaven, my dear Six Billionth, and at once the sky's the limit.

44

The Koran

From *Why I Am Not a Muslim*

IBN WARRAQ

One of those moved into action and response by Ayatollah Khomeini's assault on civilization was Ibn Warraq, the *nom de plume* of a scholarly ex-Muslim who is obliged to keep his true identity a secret. In this long extract from his outstanding book *Why I Am Not A Muslim*, he considers the fantastic claim that the Koran is the final and unalterable word of god, as delivered to an illiterate merchant in seventh-century Arabia.

> *Timeo hominem unius libri* (I fear that I am a man of one book).
> —ST. THOMAS AQUINAS

The Koran is written in Arabic and divided into chapters (suras or surahs) and verses (ayah; plural, ayat). There are said to be approximately 80,000 words, and between 6,200 and 6,240 verses, and 114 suras in the Koran. Each sura, except the ninth and the Fatihah (the first sura), begins with the words "In the name of the Merciful, the Compassionate." Whoever was responsible for the compilation of the Koran put the longer suras first, regardless of their chronology, that is to say, regardless of the order in which they were putatively revealed to Muhammad.

For the average, unphilosophical Muslim of today, the Koran remains the infallible word of God, the immediate word of God sent down, through the intermediary of a "spirit" or "holy spirit" or Gabriel, to Muhammad in perfect pure Arabic; and everything contained therein is eternal and uncreated. The original text is in heaven (the mother of the book, 43.3; a concealed book, 55.77; a well-guarded tablet, 85.22). The angel dictated the revelation to the Prophet who repeated it after him, and then revealed it to the world. Modern Muslims also claim that these revelations have been preserved exactly as revealed to Muhammad, without any change, addition, or loss whatsoever. The Koran is used as a charm on the occasions of birth, death, or marriage. In the words of Guillaume, "It is the holy of holies. It must never rest beneath other books but always on top of them; one must never drink or smoke when it is being read aloud, and it must be listened to in silence. It is a talisman against disease and disaster." Shaykh Nefzawi, in his erotic classic *The Perfumed Garden*, even recommends the Koran as an aphrodisiac: "It is said that reading the Koran also predisposes for copulation."

Both Hurgronje and Guillaume point to the mindless way children are forced to learn either parts of or the entire Koran (some 6,200 odd verses) by hearing at the expense of teaching children critical thought: "[The children] accomplish this prodigious feat at the expense of their reasoning faculty, for often their minds are so stretched by the effort of memory that they are little good for serious thought."

Hurgronje observed:

> This book, once a world reforming power, now serves but to be chanted by teachers and laymen according to definite rules. The rules are not difficult but not a thought is ever given to the meaning of the words; the Quran is chanted simply because its recital is believed to be a meritorious work. This disregard of the sense of the words rises to such a pitch that even pundits who have studied the commentaries—not to speak of laymen—fail to notice when the verses they recite condemn as sinful things which both they and the listeners do every day, nay even during the very common ceremony itself.
>
> The inspired code of the universal conquerors of thirteen centuries ago has grown to be no more than a mere textbook of sacred music, in the practice of which a valuable portion of the youth of well-educated Muslims is wasted.

The Word of God?

Suyuti, the great Muslim philologist and commentator on the Koran, was able to point to five passages whose attribution to God was disputable. Some of the words in these passages were obviously spoken by Muhammad himself and some by Gabriel. Ali Dashti also points to several passages where the speaker cannot have been God.

For example, the opening sura called the Fatihah:

> In the name of the Merciful and Compassionate God. Praise belongs to God, the Lord of the Worlds, the merciful, the compassionate, the ruler of the day of judgment! Thee we serve and Thee we ask for aid. Guide us in the right path, the path of those Thou art gracious to; not of those Thou art wroth with, nor of those who err.

These words are clearly addressed *to* God, in the form of a prayer. They are Muhammad's words of praise to God, asking God's help and guidance. As many have pointed out, one only needs to add the imperative "say" at the beginning of the sura to remove the difficulty. This imperative form of the word "say" occurs some 350 times in the Koran, and it is obvious that this word has, in fact, been inserted by later compilers of the Koran, to remove countless similarly embarrassing difficulties. Ibn Masud, one of the companions of the Prophet and an authority on the Koran, rejected the Fatihah and suras 113 and 114 that contain the words "I take refuge with the Lord," as not part of the Koran. Again at sura 6.104, the speaker of the line "I am not your keeper" is clearly Muhammad: "Now proofs from your Lord have come to you. He who recognises them will gain much, but he who is blind to them, the loss will be his. I am not your keeper." Dawood in his translation adds as a footnote that the "I" refers to Muhammad.

In the same sura at verse 114, Muhammad speaks the words, "Should I [Muhammad] seek other judge than God, when it is He who has sent down to you the distinguishing book [Koran]?" Yusuf Ali in his translation adds at the beginning of the sentence the word "say," which is not there in the original Arabic, and he does so without comment or footnote. Ali Dashti also considers sura 111 as the words of Muhammad on the grounds that these words are unworthy of God: "It ill becomes the Sustainer of the Universe to curse an ignorant Arab and call his wife a firewood carrier." The short sura refers to Abu Lahab, the Prophet's uncle, who was one of Muhammad's bitterest opponents: "The hands of Abu Lahab shall perish, and he shall perish. His riches shall not profit him, neither that which he has gained. He shall go down to be burned into flaming fire, and his wife also, bearing wood having on her neck a cord of twisted fibres of a palm tree." Either these are Muhammad's words or God is fond of rather feeble puns, since "Abu Lahab" means "father of flames." But surely these words are not worthy of a prophet either.

As Goldziher points out, "Devout Mu'tazilites voiced similar opinions [as the Kharijites who impugned the reliability of the text of the Quran] about those parts of the Quran in which the Prophet utters curses against his enemies (such as Abu Lahab). "God could not have called such passages 'a noble Quran on a well-guarded tablet.'" As we shall see, if we were to apply the same reasoning to all parts of the Koran, there would not be much left as the word of God, since very little of it is worthy of a Merciful and Compassionate, All-Wise God.

Ali Dashti also gives the example of sura 17.1 as an instance of confusion between two speakers. God and Muhammad: "Gloried be He Who carried His servant by night from the Inviolable Place of worship [mosque at Mecca] to the Far Distant Place of Worship [mosque at Jerusalem], the neighborhood whereof We have blessed, that We might show him of our tokens! Lo! He is the Hearer, the Seer."

Dashti comments:

The praise of Him who carried His servant from Mecca to Palestine cannot be God's utterance, because God does not praise Himself, and must be Mohammad's thanksgiving to God for this favor. The next part of the sentence, describing the Furthest Mosque [whose precincts "We have blessed"], is spoken by God, and so too is the following clause ["so that We might show him of our tokens"]. The closing words ["He is the Hearer, the Seer"] seem most likely to be Mohammad's.

Again, in the interest of dogma, translators are led to dishonesty when confronted by sura 27, 91, where the speaker is clearly Muhammad: "I have been commanded to serve the Lord of this city." Dawood and Pickthall both interpolate "say" at the beginning of the sentence, which is lacking in the Arabic. At sura 81.15–29, one presumes it is Muhammad who is swearing: "I swear by the turning planets, and by the stars that rise and set and the close of night, and the breath of morning." Muhammad, unable to disguise his pagan heritage, swears again at sura 84.16–19, "I swear by the afterglow of sunset, and by the night and all that it enshrouds, and by the moon when she is at the full." There are other instances where it is possible that it is Muhammad who is speaking, e.g., 112.14–21 and 111.1–10.

Even Bell and Watt, who can hardly be accused of being hostile to Islam, admit that

The assumption that God is himself the speaker in every passage, however leads to difficulties. Frequently God is referred to in the third person. It is no doubt allowable for a speaker to refer to himself in the third person occasionally, but the extent to which we find the Prophet apparently being addressed and told about God as a third person, is unusual. It has, in fact, been made a matter of ridicule that in the Quran God is made to swear by himself. That he uses oaths in some of the passages beginning, "I swear (not) . . ." can hardly be denied [e.g., 75.1, 2: 90.1]. . . . "By thy Lord," however, is difficult in the mouth of God. . . . Now there is one passage which everyone acknowledges to be spoken by angels, namely 19.64: "We come not down but by command of thy Lord; to him belongs what is before us and what is behind us and what is between that; nor is thy Lord forgetful. Lord of the heavens and the earth and what is between them; so serve him, and endure patiently in his service; knowest thou to him a namesake?"

In 37.161–166 it is almost equally clear that angels are the speakers. This, once admitted, may be extended to passages in which it is not so clear. In fact, difficulties in many passages are removed by interpreting the "we" of angels rather than of God himself speaking in the plural of majesty. It is not always easy to distinguish between the two, and nice questions sometimes arise in places where there is a sudden change from God being spoken of in the third person to "we" claiming to do things usually ascribed to God, e.g., 6.99; 25.45.

The Foreign Vocabulary of the Koran

Although many Muslim philologists recognized that there were numerous words of foreign origin in the Koran, orthodoxy silenced them for a while. One tradition tells us that "anyone who pretends that there is in the Koran anything other than the Arabic tongue has made a serious charge against God: 'Verily, we have made it an Arabic Koran'" (sura 12.1). Fortunately, philologists like al-Suyuti managed to come up with ingenious arguments to get around the orthodox objections. Al-Tha'alibi argued that there were foreign words in the Koran but "the Arabs made use of them and Arabicized them, so from this point of view they are Arabic." Although al-Suyuti enumerates 107 foreign words, Arthur Jeffery in his classic work finds about 275 words in the Koran that can be considered foreign: words from Aramaic, Hebrew, Syriac, Ethiopic, Persian, and Greek. The word "Koran" itself comes from the Syriac, and Muhammad evidently got it from Christian sources.

Variant Versions, Variant Readings

We need to retrace the history of the Koran text to understand the problem of variant versions and variant readings, whose very existence makes nonsense of Muslim dogma about the Koran. As we shall see, there is no such thing as *the* Koran; there never has been a definitive text of this holy book. When a Muslim dogmatically asserts that the Koran is the word of God, we need only ask "Which Koran?" to undermine his certainty.

After Muhammad's death in A.D. 632, there was no collection of his revelations. Consequently, many of his followers tried to gather all the known revelations and write them down in codex form. Soon we had the codices of several scholars such as Ibn Mas'ud, Ubai b. Kab, Ali', Abu Bakr, al-Ash'ari, al-Aswad, and others. As Islam spread, we eventually had what became known as the Metropolitan Codices in the centers of Mecca, Medina, Damascus, Kuta, and Basra. As we saw earlier, Uthman tried to bring order to this chaotic situation by canonizing the Medinan Codex, copies of which were sent to all the metropolitan centers, with orders to destroy all the other codices.

Uthman's codex was supposed to standardize the consonantal text; yet we find that many of the variant traditions of this consonantal text survived well into the fourth Islamic century. The problem was aggravated by the fact the consonantal text was unpointed, that is to say, the dots that distinguish, for example, a "b" from a "t" or a "th" were missing. Several other letters (f and q; j, h, and kh; s and d; r and z; s and sh; d and dh; t and z) were indistinguishable. As a result, a great many variant readings were possible according to the way the text was pointed (had dots added). The vowels presented an even worse problem. Originally, the Arabs had no signs for the short vowels—these were only introduced at a later date. The Arabic script is consonantal. Although the short vowels are sometimes omitted, they can be represented by orthographical signs placed above or below the letters—three signs in all, taking the form of a slightly slanting dash or a comma.

After having settled the consonants, Muslims still had to decide what vowels to employ: using different vowels, of course, rendered different readings.

This difficulty inevitably led to the growth of different centers with their own variant traditions of how the texts should be pointed and vowelized. Despite Uthman's order to destroy all texts other than his own, it is evident that the older codices survived. As Charles Adams says, "It must be emphasized that far from there being a single text passed down inviolate from the time of Uthman's commission, literally thousands of variant readings of particular verses were known. . . . These variants affected even the Uthmanic codex, making it difficult to know what its true original form may have been." Some Muslims preferred codices other than the Uthmanic, for example, those of Ibn Masud, Ubayy ibn Kab, and Abu Musa. Eventually under the influence of the great Koranic scholar Ibn Mujahid (d. A.D. 935), there was a definite canonization of one system of consonants and a limit placed on the variations of vowels used in the text that resulted in acceptance of the systems of the seven:

1. Nafi of Medina (d. A.D. 785)
2. Ibn Kathir of Mecca (d. A.D. 737)
3. Ibn Amir of Damascus (d. A.D. 736)
4. Abu Amr of Basra (d. A.D. 770)
5. Asim of Kufa (d. A.D 744)
6. Hamza of Kufa (d. AD. 772)
7. Al-Kisai of Kufa (d. A.D. 804)

But other scholars accepted ten readings, and still others accepted fourteen readings. Even Ibn Mujahid's seven provided fourteen possibilities, since each of the seven was traced through two different transmitters, viz.,

1. Nafi of Medina according to Warsh and Qalun
2. Ibn Kathir of Mecca according to al-Bazzi and Qunbul
3. Ibn Amir of Damascus according to Hisham and Ibn Dhakwan
4. Abu Amr of Basra according to al-Duri and al-Susi
5. Asim of Kufa according to Hafs and Abu Bakr
6. Hamza of Kufa according to Khalaf and Khallad
7. Al-Kisai of Kufa according to al-Duri and Abul Harith

In the end three systems prevailed, for some reason—to quote Jeffery—"which has not yet been fully elucidated," those of Warsh (d. A.D. 812) from Nafi of Medina, Hafs (d. 805) from Asim of Kufa, and al-Duri (d. A.D. 860) from Abu Amr of Basra. At present in modern Islam, two versions seem to be in use: that of Asim of Kufa through Hafs, which was given a kind of official seal of approval by being adopted in the Egyptian edition of the Koran in 1924; and that of Nafi through Warsh, which is used in parts of Africa other than Egypt.

To quote Charles Adams:

It is of some importance to call attention to a possible source of misunderstanding with regard to the variant readings of the Quran. The seven [versions] refer to actual differences in the written and oral text, to distinct versions of Quranic verses, whose differences, though they may not be great, are nonetheless real and substantial. Since the very existence of variant readings and versions of the Quran goes against the doctrinal position toward the holy Book held by many modern Muslims, it is not uncommon in an apologetic context to hear the seven [versions] explained as modes of recitation; in fact the manner and technique of recitation are an entirely different matter.

Guillaume also refers to the variants as "not always trifling in significance."

Any variant version or reading poses serious problems for orthodox Muslims. Thus it is not surprising that they should conceal any codices that seem to differ from the Uthman text. Arthur Jeffery describes just such an attempt at concealment:

[The late Professor Bergstrasser] was engaged in taking photographs for the Archive and had photographed a number of the early Kufic Codices in the Egyptian Library when I drew his attention to one in the Azhar Library that possessed certain curious features. He sought permission to photograph that also, but permission was refused and the Codex withdrawn from access, as it was not consistent with orthodoxy to allow a Westen scholar to have knowledge of such a text. . . . With regard to such variants as did survive there were definite efforts at suppression in the interests of orthodoxy.

Perfect Arabic?

The great scholar Noldeke pointed out the stylistic weaknesses of the Koran long ago:

On the whole, while many parts of the Koran undoubtedly have considerable rhetorical power, even over an unbelieving reader, the book aesthetically considered, is by no means a first rate performance. . . . Let us look at some of the more extended narratives. It has already been noticed how vehement and abrupt they are where they ought to be characterised by epic repose. Indispensable links, both in expression and in the sequence of events, are often omitted, so that to understand these histories is sometimes far easier for us than for those who heard them first, because we know most of them from better sources. Along with this, there is a good deal of superfluous verbiage; and nowhere do we find a steady advance in the narration. Contrast in these respects the history of Joseph (xii) and its glaring improprieties with the admirably conceived and admirably executed story in Genesis. Similar faults are found in the non narrative portions of the Koran. The connexion of ideas is extremely loose, and even the syntax betrays great awkwardness. Anacolutha [want of syntactical sequence; when the latter part of a sentence does not grammatically fit the earlier] are of frequent occurrence, and cannot be explained as conscious literary devices. Many sentences begin with a "when" or "on the day when" which seems to hover in the air, so that commentators are driven to supply a "think of this" or some such ellipsis. Again, there is no great literary skill evinced in the frequent and needless harping on the same words and phrases; in xviii, for example "till that" occurs no fewer than eight times. Mahomet in short, is not in any sense a master of style.

We have already quoted Ali Dashti's criticisms of the Prophet's style (chap. 1). Here, I shall quote some of Ali Dashti's examples of the grammatical errors contained in the Koran. In verse 162 of sura 4, which begins, "But those among them who are well-grounded in knowledge, the believers, . . . and the performers of the prayer, and the payers of the alms-tax," the word for "performers" is in the accusative case; whereas it ought to be in the nominative case, like the words for "well-grounded," "believers," and "payers."

In verse 9 of sura 49, "If two parties of believers have started to fight each other, make peace between them," the verb meaning "have started to fight" is in the plural, whereas it ought to be in the dual like its subject "two parties." (In Arabic, as in other languages, verbs can be conjugated not only in the singular and plural, but also in the dual, when the subject is numbered at two).

In verse 63 of sura 20, where Pharaoh's people say of Moses and his brother Aaron, "These two are magicians," the word for "these two" (*hadhane*) is in the nominative case; whereas it ought to be in the accusative case (*hadhayne*) because it comes after an introductory particle of emphasis.

Ali Dashti concludes this example by saying,

Othman and Aesha are reported to have read the word as hadhayne. The comment of a Moslem scholar illustrates the fanaticism and intellectual ossification of later times: "Since in the unanimous opinion of the Moslems the pages bound in this volume and called the Quran are God's word, and since there can be no error in God's word, the report that Othman and Aesha read hadhayne instead of hadhayne is wicked and false."

Ali Dashti estimates that there are more than one hundred Koranic aberrations from the normal rules and structure of Arabic.

Verses Missing, Verses Added

There is a tradition from Aisha, the Prophet's wife, that there once existed a "verse of stoning," where stoning was prescribed as punishment for fornication, a verse that formed a part of the Koran but that is now lost. The early caliphs carried out such a punishment for adulterers, despite the fact that the Koran, as we know it today, only prescribes a hundred lashes. It remains a puzzle—if the story is not true—why Islamic law to this day decrees stoning when the Koran only demands flogging. According to this tradition, over a hundred verses are missing. Shiites, of course, claim that Uthman left out a great many verses favorable to Ali for political reasons.

The Prophet himself may have forgotten some verses, the companions' memory may have equally failed them, and the copyists may also have mislaid some verses. We also have the case of *The Satanic Verses*, which clearly show that Muhammad himself suppressed some verses.

The authenticity of many verses has also been called into question not only by modern Western scholars, but even by Muslims themselves. Many Kharijites, who were followers of Ali in the early history of Islam, found the sura recounting the story of Joseph offensive, an erotic tale that did not belong in the Koran. Even before Wansbrough there were a number of Western scholars such as de Sacy, Weil, Hirschfeld, and Casanova who had doubted the authenticity of this or that sura or verse. It is fair to say that so far their arguments have not been generally accepted. Wansbrough's arguments, however, are finding support among a younger generation of scholars not inhibited in the way their older colleagues were, as described in Chapter 1 ("Trahison des Clercs").

On the other hand, most scholars do believe that there are interpolations in the Koran; these interpolations can be seen as interpretative glosses on certain rare words in need of explanation. More serious are the interpolations of a dogmatic or political character, such as 42.36–38, which seems to have been added to justify the elevation of Uthman as caliph to the detriment of Ali. Then there are other verses that have been added in the interest of rhyme, or to join together two short passages that on their own lack any connection.

Bell and Watt carefully go through many of the alterations and revisions and point to the unevenness of the Koranic style as evidence for great many alterations in the Koran:

> There are indeed many roughnesses of this kind, and these, it is here claimed, are fundamental evidence for revision. Besides the points already noticed—

hidden rhymes, and rhyme-phrases not woven into the texture of the passage—
there are the following: abrupt changes of rhyme; repetition of the same rhyme
word or rhyme phrase in adjoining verses; the intrusion of an extraneous subject into a passage otherwise homogeneous; a differing treatment of the same
subject in neighbouring verses, often with repetition of words and phrases;
breaks in grammatical construction which raise difficulties in exegesis; abrupt
changes in the length of verses; sudden changes of the dramatic situation,
with changes of pronoun from singular to plural, from second to third person, and so on; the juxtaposition of apparently contrary statements; the juxtaposition of passages of different date, with the intrusion of late phrases into
early verses.

In many cases a passage has alternative continuations which follow one
another in the present text. The second of the alternatives is marked by a
break in sense and by a break in grammatical construction, since the connection is not with what immediately precedes, but with what stands some distance back.

The Christian al-Kindi, writing around A.D. 830, criticized the Koran in similar terms: "The result of all this [process by which the Quran came into being] is
patent to you who have read the scriptures and see how, in your book, histories
are all jumbled together and intermingled; an evidence that many different
hands have been at work therein, and caused discrepancies, adding or cutting
out whatever they liked or disliked. Are such, now, the conditions of a revelation
sent down from heaven?"

Here, it might be appropriate to give some examples. Verse 15 of sura 20 is totally out of place; the rhyme is different from the rest of the sura. Verses 1–5 of
sura 78 have obviously been added on artificially, because both the rhyme and
the tone of the rest of the sura changes; in the same sura verses 33 and 34 have
been inserted between verses 32 and 35, thus breaking the obvious connection
between 32 and 35. In sura 74, verse 31 is again an obvious insertion since it is in
a totally different style and of a different length than the rest of the verses in the
sura. In sura 50, verses 24–32 have again been artificially fitted into a context in
which they do not belong.

To explain certain rare or unusual words or phrases, the formula "What has
let you know what . . . is?" (or "What will teach you what . . . is?") is added on to
a passage, after which a short explanatory description follows. It is clear that
these explanatory glosses—twelve in all—have been added on at a later time,
since in many instances the "definitions" do not correspond to the original
meaning of the word or phrase. Bell and Watt give the example of sura
101.9–11, which should read: "his mother shall be 'hawiya.' And what shall
teach you what it is? A blazing fire." "Hawiya" originally meant "childless" owing to the death or misfortune of her son, but the explanatory note defines it as
"Hell." Thus most translators now render the above sentence as, "shall plunge

in the womb of the Pit. And what shall teach you what is the Pit? A blazing fire!"
(see also 90.12–16.)

Of course any interpolation, however trivial, is fatal to the Muslim dogma
that the Koran is literally the word of God as given to Muhammad at Mecca or
Medina. As Regis Blachere in his classic *Introduction to the Koran* said, on this
point, there is no possible way of reconciling the findings of Western philologists and historians with the official dogma of Islam.

We also have the story of Abd Allah b. Sa'd Abi Sarh:

> The last named had for some time been one of the scribes employed at Medina
> to write down the revelations. On a number of occasions he had, with the
> Prophet's consent, changed the closing words of verses. When the Prophet had
> said "And God is mighty and wise," Abd Allah suggested writing down "know-
> ing and wise" and the Prophet answered that there was no objection. Having
> observed a succession of changes of this type, Abd Allah renounced Islam on
> the ground that the revelations, if from God, could not be changed at the
> prompting of a scribe such as himself. After his apostasy he went to Mecca
> and joined the Qorayshites.

Needless to say, the Prophet had no qualms about ordering his assassination
once Mecca was captured, but Uthman obtained Muhammad's pardon with
difficulty.

Abrogation of Passages in the Koran

William Henry Burr, the author of *Self-Contradictions of the Bible,* would have a
field day with the Koran, for the Koran abounds in contradictions. But Burr's
euphoria would be short-lived; for Muslim theologians have a rather convenient
doctrine, which, as Hughes puts it, "fell in with that law of expediency which appears to be the salient feature in Muhammad's prophetical career." According
to this doctrine, certain passages of the Koran are abrogated by verses with a different or contrary meaning revealed afterwards. This was taught by Muhammad at sura 2.105: "Whatever verses we [i.e., God] cancel or cause you to forget,
we bring a better or its like." According to al-Suyuti, the number of abrogated
verses has been estimated at from five to five hundred. As Margoliouth remarked,

> To do this, withdraw a revelation and substitute another for it, was, [Muham-
> mad] asserted, well within the power of God. Doubtless it was, but so obvi-
> ously within the power of man that it is to us astonishing how so
> compromising a procedure can have been permitted to be introduced
> into the system by friends and foes.

Al-Suyuti gives the example of sura 2.240 as a verse abrogated (superseded) by verse 234, which is the abrogating verse. How can an earlier verse abrogate a later verse? The answer lies in the fact that the traditional Muslim order of the suras and verses is not chronological, the compilers simply having placed the longer chapters at the beginning. The commentators have to decide the chronological order for doctrinal reasons; Western scholars have also worked out a chronological scheme. Though there are many differences of detail, there seems to be broad agreement about which suras belong to the Meccan (i.e., early) period of Muhammad's life and which belong to the Medinan (i.e., later) period. It is worth noting how time-bound the "eternal" word of God is.

Muslims have gotten themselves out of one jam only to find themselves in another. Is it fitting that an All-Powerful, Omniscient, and Omnipotent God should revise His commands so many times? Does He need to issue commands that need revising so often? Why can He not get it right the first time, after all, He is all-wise? Why does He not reveal the better verse first? In the words of Dashti,

> It seems that there were hecklers in those days too, and that they were persis-
> tent. A reply was given to them in verses 103 and 104 of sura 16: "When We
> have replaced a verse with another verse—and God knows well what He sends
> down—they say, 'You are a mere fabricator.' But most of them have no knowl-
> edge. Say (to them), 'The Holy Ghost brought it down from your Lord, truly
> so, in order to confirm the believers.'"
>
> On the assumption that the Quran is God's word, there ought to be no
> trace of human intellectual imperfection in anything that God says. Yet in
> these two verses the incongruity is obvious. Of course God knows what He
> sends down. For that very reason the replacement of one verse by another
> made the protesters suspicious. Evidently even the simple, uneducated Hejazi
> Arabs could understand that Almighty God, being aware of what is best for
> His servants, would prescribe the best in the first place and would not have
> changes of mind in the same way as His imperfect creatures.

The doctrine of abrogation also makes a mockery of the Muslim dogma that the Koran is a faithful and unalterable reproduction of the original scriptures that are preserved in heaven. If God's words are eternal, uncreated, and of universal significance, then how can we talk of God's words being superseded or becoming obsolete? Are some words of God to be preferred to other words of God? Apparently yes. According to Muir, some 200 verses have been canceled by later ones. Thus we have the strange situation where the entire Koran is recited as the word of God, and yet there are passages that can be considered not "true"; in other words, 3 percent of the Koran is acknowledged as falsehood.

Let us take an example. Everyone knows that Muslims are not allowed to drink wine in virtue of the prohibition found in the Koran sura 2.219; yet many would no doubt be surprised to read in the Koran at sura 16.67, "And among fruits you have the palm and the vine, from which you get wine and healthful nutriment: in this, truly, are signs for those who reflect" (Rodwell). Dawood has "intoxicants" and Pickthall, "strong drink," and Sale, with eighteenth-century charm, has "inebriating liquor" in place of "wine." Yusuf Ali pretends that the Arabic word concerned, "sakar," means "wholesome drink," and in a footnote insists that nonalcoholic drinks are being referred to; but then, at the last moment, he concedes that *if* "sakar must be taken in the sense of fermented wine, it refers to the time before intoxicants were prohibited: this is a Meccan sura and the prohibition came in Medina."

Now we can see how useful and convenient the doctrine of abrogation is in bailing scholars out of difficulties. Of course, it does pose problems for apologists of Islam, since all the passages preaching tolerance are found in Meccan, i.e., early suras, and all the passages recommending killing, decapitating, and maiming are Medinan, i.e., later: "tolerance" has been abrogated by "intolerance." For example, the famous verse at sura 9.5, "Slay the idolaters wherever you find them," is said to have canceled 124 verses that dictate toleration and patience.

The Doctrines of the Koran

There is no deity but God ("la ilaha illa llahu"). Islam is uncompromisingly monotheistic—it is one of the greatest sins to ascribe partners to God. Polytheism, idolatry, paganism, and ascribing plurality to the deity are all understood under the Arabic term "shirk." Theological apologists and perhaps nineteenth-century cultural evolutionists have all uncritically assumed that monotheism is somehow a "higher" form of belief than "polytheism." It seems to me that philosophers have paid little attention to polytheism until very recently. Is it so obvious that monotheism is philosophically or metaphysically "superior" to polytheism? In what way is it superior? If there is a natural evolution from polytheism to monotheism, then is there not a natural development from monotheism to atheism? Is monotheism doomed to be superseded by a higher form of belief, that is, atheism—via agnosticism, perhaps? In this section I wish to argue that:

1. Monotheism is not necessarily philosophically or metaphysically superior to polytheism, given that no proof for the existence of one and only one God is valid.
2. Historically speaking, monotheistic creeds often secretly harbor at the popular level a de facto polytheism, despite the official dogma.
3. Superstitions are not reduced in monotheism but concentrated into the one god or his apostle.
4. Historically speaking, monotheism has often shown itself to be ferociously intolerant, in contrast to polytheism on behalf of which

religious wars have never been waged. This intolerance follows logically from monotheistic ideology. Monotheism has a lot to answer for. As Gore Vidal says,

The great unmentionable evil at the centre of our culture is monotheism. From a barbaric Bronze Age text known as the Old Testament, three anti-human religions have evolved—Judaism, Christianity and Islam. These are sky-god religions. They are patriarchal—God is the omnipotent father—hence the loathing of women for 2,000 years in those countries afflicted by the sky-god and his male delegates. The sky-god is jealous. He requires total obedience. Those who would reject him must be convened or killed. Totalitarianism is the only politics that can truly serve the sky-god's purpose. Any movement of a liberal nature endangers his authority. One God, one King, one Pope, one master in the factory, one father-leader in the family.

5. Islam did not replace Arabian polytheism because it better met the spiritual needs of the Arabs, but because it offered them material rewards in the here and now. The unjustified assumption of the superiority of monotheism has colored the views of historians in regard to the causes of the adoption of Islam in Arabia.

6. Far from raising the moral standard of the Arabs, Islam seems to have sanctioned all sorts of immoral behavior.

Monotheism does seem to bring some kind of superficial intellectual order into the welter of "primitive" gods, apparently reducing superstition. But this is only apparent, not real. First, as Zwi Werblowsky observed, "When polytheism is superseded by monotheism, the host of deities is either abolished (theoretically) or bedevilled (i.e., turned into demons), or downgraded to the rank of angels and ministering spirits. This means that an officially monotheistic system can harbor a functional de facto polytheism."

Hume made the same observation:

It is remarkable, that the principles of religion have a kind of flux and reflux in the human mind, and that men have a natural tendency to rise from idolatry to theism and to sink from theism into idolatry. . . . But the same anxious concern for happiness, which engenders the idea of these invisible, intelligent powers, allows not mankind to remain long in the first simple conception of them; as powerful but limited beings; masters of human fate, but slaves to destiny and the course of nature. Men's exaggerated praises and compliments still swell their idea upon them; and elevating their deities to the utmost bounds of perfection, at last beget the attributes of unity and infinity, simplicity and spirituality. Such refined ideas, being somewhat disproportioned to vulgar comprehension, remain not long in their original purity; but require to be supported by the notion of inferior mediators or subordinate agents, which interpose betwixt mankind and their supreme deity. These demi-gods or middle beings, partaking more of human nature, and being more familiar to us, become the chief objects of devotion, and gradually recall that idolatry, which had been formerly banished by the ardent prayers and panegyrics of timorous and indigent mortals.

This is nowhere more real than in Islam where a belief in angels and Jinn is officially recognized by the Koran. Edward Lane divides this species of spiritual beings in Islam into five orders: Jann, Jinn, Shaitans, Ifrits, and Marids. "The last . . . are the most powerful, and the Jann are transformed Jinn, like as certain apes and swine were transformed men. . . . The terms Jinn and Jann are generally used indiscriminately as names of the whole species, whether good or bad. . . . Shaitan is commonly used to signify any evil genius. An Ifrit is a powerful evil genius; a Marid, an evil genius of the most powerful class." Many evil Jinn are killed by shooting stars, "hurled at them from heaven." Jinn can propagate their species in conjunction with human beings, in which case the offspring partakes of the nature of both parents. "Among the evil Jinn are distinguished the five sons of their chief, Iblis; namely Tir who brings about calamities, losses, and injuries; al-Awar, who encourages debauchery; Sut, who suggests lies; Dasim, who causes hatred between man and wife; and Zalambur, who presides over places of traffic. . . . The Jinn are of three kind: one have wings and fly; another are snakes and dogs; and the third move about from place to place like men."

Enough has been said to show that such a system is as rich and superstitious as any Greek, Roman, or Norse polytheistic mythology.

The veneration of saints in Islam serves the very purpose that Hume so perceptively ascribed to mediators between man and God. Here is how Goldziher puts the point:

Within Islam . . . the believers sought to create through the concept of saints, mediators between themselves and omnipotent Godhead in order to satisfy the need which was served by the gods and masters of their old traditions now defeated by Islam. Here too applies what Karl Hase says of the cult of saints in general: that it "satisfies within a monotheistic religion a polytheistic need to fill the enormous gap between men and their god, and that it originated on the soil of the old pantheon."

The Muslim doctrine of the Devil also comes close at times to ditheism, i.e., the positing of two powerful Beings. The Devil is said to have been named Azazil and was created of fire. When God created Adam from clay, the Devil refused to prostrate before Adam as commanded by God, whereupon he was expelled from Eden. Eventually he will be destroyed by God, since it is only God who is all-powerful. But given the prevalence of evil in the world—wars, famines, disease, the Holocaust—one wonders if the Devil is not more powerful. Why he has not been destroyed already is a puzzle. Also it seems rather inconsistent of God to ask Satan, before his fall, to *worship* Adam, when God forbids man to worship anyone but God Himself.

Nowhere does the Koran give a real philosophical argument for the existence of God; it merely assumes it. The closest one gets to an argument is perhaps in the Koranic notion of "signs," whereby various natural phenomena are seen as signs of God's power and bounty.

> The phenomena most frequently cited [in the Koran] are: the creation of the heavens and the earth, the creation or generation of man, the various uses and benefits man derives from the animals, the alternation of night and day, the shining of sun, moon and stars, the changing winds, the sending of rain from the sky, the revival of parched ground and the appearance of herbage, crops and fruits, the movement of the ship on the sea and the stability of the mountains. Less frequently cited are: shadows, thunder, lightning, iron, fire, hearing, sight, understanding, and wisdom.

In philosophy such an argument is known as the argument from design or the teleological argument, and like all arguments for the existence of God it is found wanting by most philosophers. All the phenomena adduced by Muhammad in the Koran can be explained without assuming the existence of a God or cosmic designer. But in any case, to return to monotheism, why should there be only one cosmic architect or planner? As Hume asks,

> And what shadow of an argument, continued Philo, can you produce, from your Hypothesis, to prove the Unity of the Deity? A great number of men join in building a house or ship, in rearing a city, in framing a Commonwealth: Why may not several deities combine in contriving and framing a world? This is only so much greater similarity to human affairs. By sharing the work among several, we may so much farther limit the attributes of each, and get rid of that extensive power and knowledge, which must be suppos'd in one deity, and which, according to you, can only serve to weaken the proof of his existence. And if such foolish, such vicious creatures as man can yet often unite in framing and executing one plan, how much more those deities or demons, whom we may suppose several degrees more perfect?
>
> To multiply causes without necessity is indeed contrary to true philosophy: but this principle applies not to the present case. Were one deity antecedently prov'd by your theory, who were possessed of every attribute, requisite to the production of the universe; it wou'd be needless, I own *(tho' not absurd)* [my emphasis] to suppose any other deity existent. But while it is still a question, whether all these attributes are united in one subject, or dispersed among

several independent beings: by what phenomena in nature can we pretend to decide the controversy? Where we see a body rais'd in a scale, we are sure that there is in the opposite scale, however, concealed from sight, some counter-poising weight equal to it: But it is still allow'd to doubt, whether that weight be an aggregate of several distinct bodies, or one uniform united Mass. And if the weight requisite very much exceeds any thing which we have ever seen con-join'd in any single body, the former supposition becomes still more probable and natural. An intelligent being of such vast power and capacity, as is neces-sary to produce the universe, or to speak in the language of ancient philoso-phy, so prodigious an animal, exceeds all analogy and even comprehension.

One of the great achievements of Muhammad, we are told, was ridding Ara-bia of polytheism. But this, I have tried to argue, is monotheistic arrogance. There are no compelling arguments in favor of monotheism, as opposed to polytheism. Indeed, as Hume showed, there is nothing inherently absurd in polytheism. And as to the Koranic hint at the argument from design, Hume showed that all hypotheses regarding the origins of the universe were equally absurd. There is no justification for believing any of the forms of the argument from design: "We have no data to establish any system of cosmogony. Our expe-rience, so imperfect in itself, and so limited both in extent and duration, can af-ford us no probable conjecture concerning the whole of things. But if we must needs fix on some hypothesis, by what rule, pray, ought we to determine our choice?"

Monotheism has also been recognized as inherently intolerant. We know from the Koran itself the hatred preached at all kinds of belief labeled "idolatry" or "polytheism." As the *Dictionary of Islam* says, Muslim writers are "unanimous in asserting that no religious toleration was extended to the idolaters of Arabia in the time of the Prophet. The only choice given them was death or the recep-tion of Islam." Implicit in all kinds of monotheism is the dogmatic certainty that it alone has access to the true God, it alone has access to truth. Everyone else is not only woefully misguided but doomed to perdition and everlasting hellfire. In the words of Lewis, "Traditional Christianity and Islam differed from Judaism and agreed with each other in that both claimed to possess not only universal but exclusive truths. Each claimed to be the sole custodian of God's final revelation to mankind. Neither admitted salvation outside its own creed."

Schopenhauer asks us to reflect on the "cruelties to which religions, espe-cially the Christian and Mohammedan, have given rise" and "the misery they have brought on the world." Think of the fanaticism, the endless persecutions, then the religious wars that bloody madness of which the ancients had no con-ception. Think of the Crusades which were a quite inexcusable butchery and lasted for two hundred years, their battle cry being: "It is the will of God."

Christianity is no more spared than Islam in Schopenhauer's indictment. The object of the Crusades was

> to capture the grave of him who preached love, tolerance, and indulgence. Think of the cruel expulsion and extermination of the Moors and Jews from Spain; of the blood baths, inquisitions, and other courts for heretics; and also of the bloody and terrible conquests of the Mohammedans in three continents. . . . In particular, let us not forget India . . . where first Mohammedans and then Christians furiously and most cruelly attacked the followers of mankind's sacred and original faith. The ever-deplorable, wanton, and ruthless destruction and disfigurement of ancient temples and images reveal to us even to this day traces of the *monotheistic fury* [my emphasis] of the Mohammedans which was pursued from Mahmud of Ghazni of accursed memory down to Aurangzeb the fratricide.

Schopenhauer contrasts the peaceable historical record of the Hindus and the Buddhists with the wickedness and cruelty of the monotheists, and then concludes:

> Indeed, intolerance is essential only to monotheism; an only God is by nature a jealous God who will not allow another to live. On the other hand, polytheistic gods are naturally tolerant; they live and let live. In the first place, they gladly tolerate their colleagues, the gods of the same religion, and this tolerance is afterwards extended even to foreign gods who are accordingly, hospitably received and later admitted, in some cases, even to an equality of rights. An instance of this is seen in the Romans who willingly admitted and respected Phrygian, Egyptian, and other foreign gods. Thus it is only the monotheistic religions that furnish us with the spectacle of religious wars, religious persecutions, courts for trying heretics, and also with that of iconoclasm, the destruction of the images of foreign gods, the demolition of Indian temples and Egyptian colossi that had looked at the sun for three thousand years; all this because their jealous God had said: "Thou shall make no graven image" and so on.

Nearly a hundred years earlier than Schopenhauer, Hume with his customary genius saw the same advantages of polytheism:

> Idolatry is attended with this evident advantage, that, by limiting the powers and functions of its deities, it naturally admits the gods of other sects and nations to a share of divinity, and renders all the various deities, as well as rites, ceremonies, or traditions, compatible with each other. . . . While one sole object of devotion is acknowledged [by monotheists], the worship of other deities is regarded as absurd and impious. Nay, this unity of object seems

naturally to require the unity of faith and ceremonies, and furnishes designing
men with a pretext for representing their adversaries as prophane [profane],
and the subjects of divine as well as human vengeance. For as each sect is positive that its own faith and worship are entirely acceptable to the deity, and as
no one can conceive that the same being should be pleased with different and
opposite rites and principles; the several sects fall naturally into animosity,
and mutually discharge on each other, that sacred zeal and rancor, the most
furious and implacable of all human passions.

The tolerating spirit of idolaters both in ancient and modern times, is very
obvious to any one, who is the least conversant in the writings of historians or
travelers. . . . The intolerance of almost all religions, which have maintained
the unity of god, is as remarkable as the contrary principle in polytheists. The
implacable, narrow spirit of the Jews is well known. Mahometanism set out
with still more bloody principles, and even to this day, deals out damnation,
tho' not fire and faggot, to all other sects.

Professor Watt, in his enormously influential and important two-volume biography of Muhammad, has presented an interpretation of the rise of Muhammad and his message that is still accepted by many despite skepticism of
scholars such as Bousquet and, more recently, Crone. Watt's entire account is
permeated, unsurprisingly, with the assumption that the monotheism preached
by Muhammad is superior to the polytheism prevalent in Central Arabia. Watt
contends that the very success of Muhammad's message lies in the fact that this
message responded to the deep spiritual needs of the people. Mecca, at the time,
argues Watt, was beset with a social malaise—nay, even a spiritual crisis—that
found no answers in the local cults and gods. The Meccans were sunk in moral
degradation and idolatry until Muhammad came along and lifted them up
onto a higher moral and spiritual level. Such is Watt's argument. But as Crone
and Bousquet pointed out, there is very little evidence for a social malaise in
Mecca. As Crone argues:

The fact is that the tradition knows of no malaise in Mecca, be it religious, social, political or moral. On the contrary, the Meccans are described as eminently successful; and Watt's impression that their success led to cynicism
arises from his otherwise commendable attempt to see Islamic history
through Muslim eyes. The reason why the Meccans come across as morally
bankrupt in the [Muslim] sources is not that their traditional way of life had
broken down, but that it functioned too well: the Meccans preferred their traditional way of life to Islam. It is for this reason that they are penalized in the
sources; and the more committed a man was to this way of life, the more cynical, amoral, or hypocritical he will sound to us: Abu Sufyan [a leader of the
aristocratic party in Mecca hostile to Muhammad] cannot swear by a pagan
deity without the reader feeling an instinctive aversion to him, because the

reader knows with his sources that somebody who swears by a false deity is somebody who believes in nothing at all.

As for the spiritual crisis, there does not appear to have been any such thing in sixth-century Arabia.

But how do we explain the mass conversion of Arabia to Islam? As we saw in Chapter 2, society was organized around the tribe, and each society had its principal deity, which was worshipped in the expectation that it would help the tribe in some practical way, especially with bringing rain, providing fertility, eliminating disease, generally protecting them from the elements. The tribal gods did not embody "ultimate truths regarding the nature and meaning of life," neither were they "deeply entrenched in everyday life." Hence it was easy to renounce one god for another since it did not require any change in outlook or behavior. Furthermore, the Muslim god "endorsed and ennobled such fundamental tribal characteristics as militance and ethnic pride." The Muslim God offered something more than their own idols: He offered "a program of Arab state formation and conquest: the creation of an umma [a people or a nation], the initiation of jihad [holy war against the unbelievers]." "Muhammad's success evidently had something to do with the fact that he preached both state formation and conquest: without conquest, first in Arabia and next in the Fertile Crescent, the unification of Arabia would not have been achieved." Of course, as Muhammad proved more and more successful in Medina, his followers increased, realizing that Allah is indeed great, and certainly greater than any of their own deities: the true God is the successful God, the false, the unsuccessful. Scholars such as Becker had argued that the Arabs had been impelled to their conquests by the gradual drying up of Arabia, but as Crone maintains:

> We do not need to postulate any deterioration in the material environment of Arabia to explain why they found a policy of conquest to their taste. Having begun to conquer in their tribal homeland, both they and their leaders were unlikely to stop on reaching the fertile lands: this was, after all, where they could find the resources which they needed to keep going and of which they had availed themselves before. Muhammad's God endorsed a policy of conquest, instructing his believers to fight against unbelievers wherever they might be found. . . . In short, Muhammad had to conquer, his followers liked to conquer, and his deity told him to conquer: do we need any more?
>
> But holy war was not a cover for material interests; on the contrary, it was an open proclamation of them. "God says . . . 'my righteous servants shall inherit the earth'; now this is your inheritance and what your Lord has promised you. . . ." Arab soldiers were told on the eve of the battle of Qadisiyya, with reference to Iraq: "if you hold out . . . then their property, their women, their children, and their country will be yours." God could scarcely have been more explicit. He told the Arabs that they had a right to despoil others of their

women, children, and land, or indeed that they had a duty to do so: holy war consisted of obeying. Muhammad's God thus elevated tribal militance and rapaciouness into supreme religious virtues.

To summarize, far from answering the spiritual doubts and questions of the tribes (there were no such doubts or spiritual crises), Muhammad created a people and offered the Arabs what they had been accustomed to: namely, military conquests with all the attendant material advantages, loot, women, and land. Allah was preferable to the old gods simply because He had not failed them. He had delivered the goods here and now. Allah was certainly not preferable to the gods for some deep metaphysical reason; the Arabs had not suddenly learned the use of Occam's Razor. "Indeed," as Crone points out, "in behavioral terms the better part of Arabia was still pagan in the nineteenth century."

As early as 1909, Dr. Margoliouth had anticipated Watt's thesis and had found it wanting. What is also important in Margoliouth's work is that he denies that Islam somehow lifted the newly converted to a higher moral level: "There is no evidence that the Moslems were either in personal or altruistic morality better than the pagans." In fact the contrary seems to have been the case:

> When [Muhammad] was at the head of a robber community it is probable that the demoralising influence began to be felt, it was then that men who had never broken an oath learned that they might evade their obligations, and that men to whom the blood of the clansmen had been as their own began to shed it with immunity in the cause of God; and that lying and treachery in the cause of Islam received divine approval, hesitation to perjure oneself in that cause being reprehended as a weakness. It was then, too, that Moslems became distinguished by the obscenity of their language. It was then, too, that the coveting of goods and wives (possessed by the Unbelievers) was avowed without discouragement from the Prophet.

This is not all. Monotheism has been criticized for suppressing human freedom. Many scholars have argued that it inevitably leads to totalitarianism; whereas more and more modern philosophers see polytheism as a possible source of pluralism, creativity, and human freedom. Feminists have also criticized the monotheistic God as a male chauvinist who is unwilling to change, and is insensitive to "femininity."

The Muslim Concept of God

The omnipotence of God is asserted everywhere in the Koran; man's will is totally subordinate to God's will to the extent that man cannot be said to have a will of his own. Even those who disbelieve in Him, disbelieve because it is God who wills them to disbelieve. This leads to the Muslim doctrine of predestination that prevails over the doctrine of man's free will, also to be found in the Koran. As Macdonald says, "The contradictory statements of the Koran on free will and predestination show that Muhammad was an opportunist preacher and politician and not a systematic theologian."

"Taqdir, or the absolute decree of good and evil, is the sixth article of the Muhammadan creed, and the orthodox believe that whatever has, or shall come to pass in this world, whether it be good or bad, proceeds entirely from the Divine Will, and has been irrevocably fixed and recorded on a preserved tablet by the pen of fate." Some quotes from the Koran illustrate this doctrine:

54.49. All things have been created after fixed decree.

3.139. No one can die except by God's permission according to the book that fixes the term of life.

87.2. The Lord has created and balanced all things and has fixed their destinies and guided them.

8.17. God killed them, and those shafts were God's, not yours.

9.51. By no means can anything befall us but what God has destined for us.

13.30. All sovereignty is in the hands of God.

14.4. God misleads whom He will and whom He will He guides.

18.101. The infidels whose eyes were veiled from my warning and had no power to hear.

32.32. If We had so willed, We could have given every soul its guidance, but now My Word is realized—"I shall fill Hell with Jinn and men together."

45.26. Say unto them, O Muhammad: Allah gives life to you, then causes you to die, then gathers you unto the day of resurrection.

57.22. No disaster occurs on earth or accident in yourselves which was not already recorded in the Book before we created them.

But there are inevitably some passages from the Koran that seem to give man some kind of free will:

41.16. As to Thamud, We vouchsafed them also guidance, but to guidance did they prefer blindness.

18.28. The truth is from your Lord: let him then who will, believe; and let him who will, be an unbeliever.

But as Wensinck, in his classic *The Muslim Creed,* said, in Islam it is predestination that ultimately predominates. There is not a single tradition that advocates free will, and we have the further evidence of John of Damascus, who "flourished in the middle of the eighth century A.D., and who was well acquainted with Islam. According to him the difference regarding predestination and free will is one of the chief points of divergence between Christianity and Islam."

It is evident that, toward the end of his life, Muhammad's predestinarian position hardened; and "the earliest conscious Muslim attitude on the subject seems to have been of an uncompromising fatalism."

Before commenting on the doctrine of predestination, I should like to consider the Koranic hell. Several words are used in the Koran to evoke the place of torment that God seems to take a particular delight in contemplating. The word "Jahannum" occurs at least thirty times and describes the purgatorial hell for all Muslims. According to the Koran, all Muslims will pass through hell: (sura 19.72) "There is not one of you who will not go down to it [hell], that is settled and decided by the Lord." The word "al-nar," meaning the fire, appears several times. Other terms for hell or hellfire are

LAZA (THE BLAZE): "For Laza dragging by the scalp, shall claim him who turned his back and went away, and amassed and hoarded" (sura 97.5).

AL-HUTAMAH (THE CRUSHER): "It is God's kindled fire, which shall mount above the hearts of the damned" (sura 104.4).

SAIR (THE BLAZE): "Those who devour the property of orphans unjustly, only devour into their bellies fire, and they broil in sair" (sura 4.11).

SAQAR: "The sinners are in error and excitement. On the day when they shall be dragged into the fire on their faces. Taste the touch of saqar" (sura 54.47).

Al-Jahim (the Hot Place) and Hawiyah also occur in sura 2 and 101, respectively. Muhammad really let his otherwise limited imagination go wild when describing, in revolting detail, the torments of hell: boiling water, running sores, peeling skin, burning flesh, dissolving bowels, and crushing of skulls with iron maces. And verse after verse, sura after sura, we are told about the fire, always the scorching fire, the everlasting fire. From sura 9.69 it is clear that unbelievers will roast forever.

What are we to make of such a system of values? As Mill said, there is something truly disgusting and wicked in the thought that God purposefully creates beings to fill hell with, beings who cannot in any way be held responsible for their actions since God Himself chooses to lead them astray: "The recognition, for example, of the object of highest worship in a being who could make a Hell; and who could create countless generations of human beings with the certain foreknowledge that he was creating them for this fate. . . . Any other of the outrages to the most ordinary justice and humanity involved in the common Christian conception of the moral character of God sinks into insignificance beside this dreadful idealization of wickedness." Of course, Mill's words apply, *mutatis mutandis*, to the Muslim conception also, or to any god of predestination.

We cannot properly call such a system an ethical system at all. Central to any valid system of ethics is the notion of moral responsibility, of a moral person who can legitimately be held responsible for his actions: a person who is capable of rational thought, who is capable of deliberation, who displays intentionality, who is capable of choosing and is, in some way, free to choose. Under the Koranic system of predestination, "men" are no more than automata created by a capricious deity who amuses himself by watching his creations burning in hell. We cannot properly assign blame or approbation in the Koranic system; man is not responsible for his acts, thus it seems doubly absurd to punish him in the sadistic manner described in the various suras quoted earlier.

Bousquet begins his classic work on Islamic views on sex with the blunt sentence: "There is no ethics in Islam." The Muslim is simply commanded to obey the inscrutable will of Allah; "good" and "bad" are defined as what the Koran, and later, Islamic law considers permissible or forbidden. The question posed by Socrates in the *Euthyphro*, "Whether the pious or holy is beloved by the gods because it is holy, or holy because it is beloved of the gods?" receives a very definitive answer from an orthodox Muslim: something is good if God wills it, and bad if God forbids it; there is nothing "rationally" or independently good or bad. But as Plato pointed out this is not a satisfactory answer. As Mackie puts it (n.d., p. 256): "If moral values were constituted wholly by divine commands, so that goodness consisted in conformity to God's will, we could make no sense of the theist's own claims that God is good and that he seeks the good of his creation." In an earlier work (1977, p. 230), Mackie observes that the Muslim view has the consequence:

> that the description of God himself as good would reduce to the rather trivial statement that God loves himself, or likes himself the way he is. It would also seem to entail that obedience to moral rules is merely prudent but slavish conformity to the arbitrary demands of a capricious tyrant. Realizing this, many religious thinkers have opted for the first alternative [i.e., "the pious or holy is beloved by the gods because it is holy"]. But this seems to have the almost equally surprising consequence that moral distinctions do not depend on God, . . . hence ethics is autonomous and can be studied and discussed without reference to religious beliefs, that we can simply close the theological frontier of ethics.

It is worth emphasizing the logical independence of moral values from any theistic system. Russell formulates this insight in this manner:

> If you are quite sure there is a difference between right and wrong, you are then in this situation: is that difference due to God's fiat or is it not? If it is due to God's fiat, then for God Himself there is no difference between right

and wrong, and it is no longer a significant statement to say that God is good. If you are going to say, as theologians do, that God is good, you must then say that right and wrong have some meaning which is independent of God's fiat, because God's fiats are good and not bad independently of the mere fact that He made them. If you are going to say that, you will then have to say that it is not only through God that right and wrong came into being but that they are in their essence logically anterior to God (n.d., p. 19).

We cannot escape our moral responsibility that our independent moral understanding gives us.

Nor can we regard the concept of hell as ethically admirable. All but two suras (i.e., the fatihah and sura 9) tell us that God is merciful and compassionate, but can a truly merciful God consign somebody to hell or everlasting torment for not believing in Him? As Russell put it, "I really do not think that a person with a proper degree of kindliness in his nature would have put fears and terrors of that sort into the world." As Antony Flew remarked, there is an inordinate disparity between finite offenses and infinite punishment. The Koranic doctrine of hell is simply cruelty and barbaric torture and divinely sanctioned sadism. More than that, it means Islam is based on fear, which corrupts true morality. ("There is no God but I, so fear Me" [sura 16.2]). As Gibb said, "Man must live in constant fear and awe of [God], and always be on his guard against Him—such is the idiomatic meaning of the term for 'fearing God' which runs through the Koran from cover to cover" (1953, p. 38). Instead of acting out of a sense of duty to our fellow human beings, or out of spontaneous generosity or sympathetic feelings, under Islam we act out of fear to avoid divine punishments and, selfishly, to gain rewards from God in this life and the life to come. Mackie (p. 256) argues correctly that

> This divine command view can also lead people to accept, as moral, requirements that have no discoverable connection—indeed, no connection at all— with human purposes or well-being, or with the well-being of any sentient creatures. That is, it can foster a tyrannical, irrational morality. Of course, if there were not only a benevolent god but also a reliable revelation of his will, then we might be able to get from it expert moral advice about difficult issues, where we could not discover what are the best policies. But there is no such reliable revelation. Even a theist must see that the purported revelations, such as the Bible and the Koran, condemn themselves by enshrining rules that we must reject as narrow, outdated, or barbarous. As Hans Kueng says, "We are responsible for our morality." More generally, tying morality to religious belief is liable to devalue it, not only by undermining it temporarily if the belief decays, but also by subordinating it to other concerns while the belief persists.

God's Weaknesses

We are told that God is omnipotent, omniscient, and benevolent; yet He behaves like a petulant tyrant, unable to control his recalcitrant subjects. He is angry, He is proud. He is jealous: all moral deficiencies surprising in a perfect Being. If He is self-sufficient, why does He need mankind? If He is all-powerful, why does He ask the help of humans? Above all, why does He pick an obscure Arabian merchant in some cultural backwater to be His last messenger on earth? Is it consistent with a supremely moral being that He should demand praise and absolute worship from creatures He Himself has created? What can we say of the rather curious psychology of a Being who creates humans—or rather automata—some of whom are preprogrammed to grovel in the dirt five times a day in homage to Himself? This obsessive desire for praise is hardly a moral virtue and is certainly not worthy of a morally supreme Being. Palgrave [p. 147] gave this vivid but just description of the Koranic God:

> Thus immeasurably and eternally exalted above, and dissimilar from, all creatures, which lie leveled before Him on one common plane of instrumentality and inertness. God is One in the totality of omnipotent and omnipresent action, which acknowledges no rule, standard, or limit, save His own sole and absolute will. He communicates nothing to His creatures, for their seeming power and act ever remain His alone, and in return He receives nothing from them; for whatever they may be, that they are in Him, by Him and from Him only [sura 8.17]. And secondly, no superiority, no distinction, no pre-eminence, can be lawfully claimed by one creature over its fellow, in the utter equalisation of their unexceptional servitude and abasement; all are alike tools of the one solitary Force which employs them to crush or to benefit, to truth or to error, to honour or shame, to happiness or misery, quite independently of their individual fitness, deserts, or advantage, and simply because "He wills it," and "as He wills it."
>
> One might at first sight think that this tremendous Autocrat, this uncontrolled and unsympathizing Power, would be far above anything like passions, desires, or inclinations. Yet such is not the case, for He has, with respect to His creatures, one main feeling and source of action, namely, jealousy of them, lest they should perchance attribute to themselves something of what is His alone and thus encroach on His all-engrossing kingdom. Hence He is ever more prone to punish than to reward, to inflict pain than to bestow pleasure, to ruin than to build. It is His singular satisfaction to let created beings continually feel that they are nothing else than His slaves. His tools—and contemptible tools too—that they may thus the better acknowledge His superiority, and know His power to be above their power. His cunning above their cunning. His will above their will. His pride above their pride; or rather,

that there is no power, cunning, will, or pride, save His own. (For pride, see sura 59; God as schemer, 3.47; 8.30.)

"But He Himself, sterile in His inaccessible height, neither loving nor enjoying aught save His own and self-measured decree, without son, companion, or counsellor, is no less barren of Himself than for His creatures, and His own barrenness and lone egoism in Himself is the cause and rule of His indifferent and unregarding despotism around." The first note is the key of the whole tune, and the primal idea of God runs through and modifies the whole system and creed that centers in Him.

That the notion here given of the Deity, monstrous and blasphemous as it may appear, is exactly and literally that which the Koran conveys or intends to convey, I at present take for granted. But that it indeed is so, no one who has attentively perused and thought over the Arabic text . . . can hesitate to allow. In fact, every phrase of the preceding sentences, every touch in this odious portrait, has been taken, to the best of my ability, word for word, or at least meaning for meaning, from the "Book," the truest mirror of the mind and scope of its writer.

And that such was in reality Mahomet's mind and idea, is fully confirmed by the witness-tongue of contemporary tradition. Of this we have many authentic samples. . . . 1 will subjoin a specimen . . . a repetition of which I have endured times out of number from admiring and approving Wahhabis in Nejd.

"Accordingly, when God . . . resolved to create the human race. He took into His hands a mass of earth, the same whence all mankind were to be formed, and in which they after a manner pre-existed; and having then divided the clod into two equal portions. He threw the one half into hell, saying, 'These to eternal fire, and I care not'; and projected the other half into heaven adding, 'and these to Paradise, I care not'" [Mishkatu 'l-Masabih Babu 'l-Qadr].

But in this we have before us the adequate idea of predestination, or, to give it a truer name, pre-damnation, held and taught in the school of the Koran. Paradise and hell are at once totally independent of love or hatred on the part of the Deity, and of merits or demerits, of good or evil conduct, on the part of the creature; and in the corresponding theory, rightly so, since the very actions which we call good or ill-deserving, right or wrong, wicked or virtuous, are in their essence all one and of one, and accordingly merit neither praise nor blame, punishment nor recompense, except and simply after the arbitrary value which the all-regulating will of the great despot may choose to assign or impute to them. In a word, He bums one individual through all eternity amid red-hot chains and seas of molten fire, and seats another in the plenary enjoyment of an everlasting brothel between forty celestial concubines, just and equally for His own good pleasure, and because He wills it.

Men are thus all on one common level, here and hereafter, in their physical, social, and moral light—the level of slaves to one sole Master, of tools to one universal Agent.

And Muhammad Is His Apostle

Every national church or religion has established itself by pretending some special mission from God, communicated to certain individuals. The Jews have their Moses; the Christians their Jesus Christ, their apostles and saints; and the Turks their Mahomet, as if the way to God was not open to every man alike. Each of those churches show certain books, which they call revelation, or the Word of God. The Jews say that their Word of God was given by God to Moses, face to face; the Christians that their Word of God came by divine inspiration; and the Turks say that their Word of God (the Koran) was brought by an angel from heaven. Each of those churches accuses the other of unbelief; and for my own part, I disbelieve them all.

—THOMAS PAINE, *THE AGE OF REASON*

Allah or God chose Muhammad to be a messenger to all mankind. Though Muslim and sympathetic Western commentators deny it, it is clear that Muhammad himself thought that he had seen God Himself in person, as in sura 53.2–18. At other times, Muhammad talked to the angel Gabriel, who periodically revealed God's message. How did Muhammad himself know that he had seen God or an angel? How did he know that the particular experiences he had were manifestations of God? Even if we grant Muhammad's sincerity, could he not have been sincerely mistaken? Most people claiming that they had direct access to God would now be seen as mentally ill. How do we know that in Muhammad's case it really was God or an angel that delivered God's message? As Paine said (n.d., p. 52),

But admitting for the sake of a case, that something has been revealed to a certain person, and not revealed to any other person, it is revelation to that person only. When he tells it to a second person, a second to a third, a third to a fourth, and so on, it ceases to be revelation to all those persons. It is revelation to the first person only, and *hearsay* to every other, and consequently they are not obliged to believe it.

It is a contradiction in terms and ideas, to call anything a revelation that comes to us at second-hand, either verbally or in writing. Revelation is necessarily limited to the first communication—after this it is only an account of something which that person says was a revelation made to him; and though he may find himself obliged to believe it, it cannot be incumbent on me to believe it in the same manner; for it was not a revelation made to *me,* and I have only his word for it that it was made to him. When Moses told the children of Israel that he received the two tables of the commandments from the hands of God, they were not obliged to believe him, because they had no other authority for it than his telling them so; and I have no other authority for it than some historian telling me so. The commandments carry no internal evidence of divinity with them; they contain some good moral precepts, such as any man qualified to be a lawgiver, or legislator, could produce himself, without having recourse to supernatural intervention.

When I am told that the Koran was written in heaven and brought to Mahomet by an angel, the account comes too near the same kind of hearsay evidence and second-hand authority as the former. I did not see the angel myself and, therefore, I have a right not to believe it.

Given the theory of Wansbrough, Crone, and Cook (that Islam emerged later than hitherto thought, under the influence of rabbinic Judaism, and taking Moses as an example of a prophet with a revelation, invented Muhammad as an Arabian prophet with a similar revelation), Paine's choice and juxtapositioning of the two examples of Moses and Muhammad is rather appropriate.

Moreover, as Paine says, very importantly, the revelations, as later recorded in the Bible or the Koran, do not carry any internal evidence of divinity with them. On the contrary, the Koran contains much—far too much—that is totally unworthy of a deity. In addition, the Bible and the Koran often contradict each other. On which basis should we decide between them? Both sides claim divine authority for their scriptures. In the end, we can only say that no specific revelation has reliable credentials.

It is very odd that when God decides to manifest Himself, He does so to only one individual. Why can He not reveal Himself to the masses in a football stadium during the final of the World Cup, when literally millions of people around the world are watching? But as Patricia Crone said, "It is a peculiar habit of God's that when he wishes to reveal himself to mankind, he will communicate only with a single person. The rest of mankind must learn the truth from that person and thus purchase their knowledge of the divine at the cost of subordination to another human being, who is eventually replaced by a human institution, so that the divine remains under other people's control." [TLS, January 21, 1994, p. 12]

Abraham, Ishmael, Moses, Noah, and Other Prophets

We are told that [Abraham] was born in Chaldea, and that he was the son of a poor potter who earned his living by making little clay idols. It is scarcely credible that the son of this potter went to Mecca, 300 leagues away in the tropics, by way of impassable deserts. If he was a conqueror he no doubt aimed at the fine country of Assyria; and if he was only a poor man, as he is depicted, he founded no kingdoms in foreign parts.

—VOLTAIRE

For the historian, the Arabs are no more the descendents of Ishmael, son of Abraham, than the French are of Francus, son of Hector.

—MAXIME RODINSON

It is virtually certain that Abraham never reached Mecca.

—MONTGOMERY WATT

The essential point . . . is that, where objective fact has been established by sound historical methods, it must be accepted.

—MONTGOMERY WATT

According to Muslim tradition, Abraham and Ishmael built the Kaaba, the cubelike structure in the Sacred Mosque in Mecca. But outside these traditions there is absolutely no evidence for this claim—whether epigraphic, archaeological, or documentary. Indeed Snouck Hurgronje has shown that Muhammad invented the story to give his religion an Arabian origin and setting; with this brilliant improvisation Muhammad established the independence of his religion, at the same time incorporating into Islam the Kaaba with all its historical and religious associations for the Arabs.

Given the quantity of material in the Koran that comes from the Pentateuch—Moses: 502 verses in 36 suras; Abraham: 245 verses in 25 suras; Noah: 131 verses in 28 suras—it is surprising that higher biblical criticism has had no impact on Koranic studies. The Muslims as much as the Jews and the Christians are committed to the Pentateuch being authored by Moses. In the Koran, the Pentateuch is referred to as the Taurat (word derived from the Hebrew Torah).

Scholars have been casting doubt on the historical veracity of one biblical story after another, and Islam cannot escape the consequences of their discoveries and conclusions. As long ago as the seventeenth century, La Peyrere, Spinoza, and Hobbes were arguing that the Pentateuch could not have been written by Moses: "From what has been said, it is thus clearer than the sun at noonday that the Pentateuch was not written by Moses, but by someone who lived long after Moses," concludes Spinoza in *A Theologico-Political Treatise*.

Then, in the nineteenth century, higher critics such as Graf and Wellhausen showed that the Pentateuch (that is, the books of Genesis, Exodus, Leviticus, Numbers, and Deuteronomy) was a composite work, in which one could discern the hand of four different "writers," usually referred to by the four letters J, E, D, and P.

Robin Lane Fox takes up our story:

In the Bible the four earlier sources were combined by a fifth person, an unknown author who must have worked on them at some point between c. 520

and 400 B.C., in my view, nearer to 400 B.C. As he interwove these sources, he tried to save their contents and have the best of several worlds (and Creations). He was a natural sub-editor . . . he was not, in my view, a historian, but I think he would be amazed if somebody told him that nothing in his amalgamated work was true. . . . Its chances of being historically true were minimal because none of those sources was written from primary evidence or within centuries, perhaps a millennium of what they tried to describe. How could an oral tradition have preserved true details across such a gap? . . . As for the "giants on earth," the Tower of Babel or the exploits of Jacob or Abraham, there is no good reason to believe any of them: the most detailed story in Genesis is the story of Joseph, a marvelous tale, woven from two separate sources, neither of which needs to rest on any historical truth.

The Torah was not written by, nor "given" to, Moses, and there is no good reason to believe any of the exploits of Abraham and others to be true. Certainly no historian would dream of going to the Muslim sources for the historical verification of any biblical material; the Muslim accounts of Abraham, Moses, and others are, as we saw earlier, taken from rabbinical Jewish scriptures or are nothing more than legends (the building of the Kaaba, etc.) invented several thousand years after the events they purport to describe.

Historians have gone even farther. There seems to be a distinct possibility that Abraham never existed: "The J tradition about the wandering of Abraham is largely unhistorical in character. By means of the theological leitmotif of the wandering obedient servant of Yahweh, it gives a structure to the many independent stories at J's disposal. It is an editorial device used to unite the many disparate Abraham and Lot traditions" (Thompson 1974). Thompson goes on to say (p. 328):

> Not only has "archaeology" not proven a single event of the patriarchal traditions to be historical, it has not shown any of the traditions to be likely. On the basis of what we know of Palestinian history of the Second Millennium B.C., and of what we understand about the formation of the literary traditions of Genesis, it must be concluded that any such historicity as is commonly spoken of in both scholarly and popular works about the patriarchs of Genesis is hardly possible and totally improbable.

Finally, "the quest for the historical Abraham is a basically fruitless occupation both for the historian and the student of the Bible."

And Lane Fox observes: "Historians no longer believe the stories of Abraham as if they are history: like Aeneas or Heracles, Abraham is a figure of legend."

Noah and the Flood

The building of the ark by Noah, the saving of all the animals, the universal deluge are all taken over into the Koran from Genesis. As the manifest absurdities of the tale were pointed out, Christians were no longer prone to take the fable literally; except, of course, the literal minded fundamentalists, many of whom still set out every year to look for the remnants of the lost ark. Muslims, on the other hand, seem immune to rational thought, and refuse to look the evidence in the face. I shall set out the arguments to show the absurdities in the legend, even though it may seem I am belaboring the obvious. I wish more people would belabor the obvious, and more often.

Noah was asked to take into the ark a pair from every species (sura 11.36–41). Some zoologists estimate that there are perhaps ten million living species of insects; would they all fit into the ark? It is true they do not take up much room, so let us concentrate on the larger animals: reptiles, 5,000 species; birds, 9,000 species; and 4,500 species of class Mammalia (p. 239). In all, in the phylum Chordata, there are 45,000 species (p. 236). What sized ark would hold nearly 45,000 species of animals? A pair from each species makes nearly 90,000 individual animals, from snakes to elephants, from birds to horses, from hippopotamuses to rhinoceroses. How did Noah get them all together so quickly? How long did he wait for the sloth to make his slothful way from the Amazon? How did the kangaroo get out of Australia, which is an island? How did the polar bear know where to find Noah? As Robert Ingersoll asks, "Can absurdities go farther than this?" Either we conclude that this fantastic tale is not to be taken literally, or we have recourse to some rather feeble answer, such as, for God all is possible. Why, in that case, did God go through all this rather complicated, time-consuming (at least for Noah) procedure? Why not save Noah and other righteous people with a rapid miracle rather than a protracted one?

No geological evidence indicates a universal flood. There is indeed evidence of local floods but not one that covered the entire world, not even the entire Middle East. We now know that the biblical accounts of the Flood, on which the Koranic account is based, are derived from Mesopotamian legends: "There is no reason to trace the Mesopotamia and Hebrew stories back to any one flood in particular; the Hebrew fiction is most likely to have developed from the Mesopotamians' legends. The stories are fictions, not history."

David and the Psalms

The Koran also commits Muslims to the belief that David "received" the Psalms in the way Moses received the Torah (sura 4.163–65). But once again biblical scholars doubt that David wrote many, if any, of them. David probably lived around 1000 B.C., but we know that the Psalms were put together much later in the post-exilic period, that is, after 539 B.C.:

> The Book of Psalms consists of five collections of hymns, mostly written for use in the second temple (the temple of Zerubbabel). Though very old poems may have been adapted in several instances, these collections appear to be wholly, or almost wholly, post-exilian. Probably none of the psalms should be ascribed to David. Several of them, praising some highly idealised monarch, would seem to have been written in honour of one or other of the Hasmonean kings [142–163 B.C.].

Adam and Evolution, Creation, and Modern Cosmology

> Many Muslims have not yet come to terms with the fact of evolution . . . the story of Adam and Eve . . . has no place in a scientific account of the origins of the human race.
>
> —MONTGOMERY WATT

The Koran gives a contradictory account of the creation, posing great problems for the commentators:

> Of old we created the heavens and the earth and all that is between them in six days, and no weariness touched us. (sura 50.37)
>   Do you indeed disbelieve in Him who in two days created the earth? Do you assign Him equals? The Lord of the World is He. And He has placed on the earth the firm mountains which tower above it, and He has blessed it and distributed its nourishments throughout it (for the craving of all alike) in four days. Then He applied Himself to the heaven which was but smoke; and to it and to the earth He said, "Do you come in obedience or against your will?" And they both said, "We come obedient." And He completed them as seven heavens in two days, and He assigned to each heaven its duty and command; and He furnished the lower heavens with lights and guardian angels. This is the disposition of the Almighty, the All-Knowing One." (sura 41.9)

Two days for the earth, four days for the nourishment, and two days for the seven heavens make eight days (sura 41), whereas in sura 50 we are told the creation took six days. It is not beyond the commentators to apply some kind of hocus-pocus to resolve this contradiction.
    The heavens and the earth and the living creatures that are in them are proof of God and His power (Levy 1957, p. 2, 4); they and man in particular were not

created frivolously (sura 21.16). Men and Jinn have been assigned the special duty of worshipping God, and though the privilege of obedience to God's law was first offered to the heavens and the earth and the mountains, it was man who received it after their refusal (sura 33.72) (Levy 1957, p. 2, 4).

What are we to make of this strange doctrine? The heavens, the earth, and the mountains are seen as persons, and furthermore as persons who had the temerity to disobey God! An omnipotent God creates the cosmos, and then asks it if it would accept the "trust" or the "faith," and His own creation declines to accept this burden.

> Creation was by the word of Allah, "Be," for all things are by His fiat. Before Creation His throne floated above the primeval waters and the heavens and the earth were of one mass (of water). Allah split it asunder, the heavens being built up and spread forth as a well-protected (supported) roof, without flaws, which He raised above the earth and holds there without pillars, whilst the earth was stretched out and the mountains were cast down upon its surface as firm anchors to prevent its moving with the living creatures upon it, for the world is composed of seven earths. Also the two seas were let loose alongside one another, the one sweet and the other salt, but with a barrier set between them so that they should not mingle. (Levy 1957, p. 2, 5)

Earth was created first, then the heavens. The moon was given its own light (sura 10.5), and for it, stations were "decreed so that it changes like an old and curved palm-branch, for man to know the number of the years and the reckoning" (Levy 1957, p. 2, 5).

As for Adam, "We have created man from an extract of clay; then we made him a clot in a sure depository; then we created the clot congealed blood, and we created the congealed blood a morsel; then we created the morsel bone, and we clothed the bone with flesh; then we produced it another creation; and blessed be God, the best of creators!" (sura 23.12).

Another account tells us that man was created from sperm (an unworthy fluid) (sura 77.22), and yet another version has it that all living things were created out of the same primeval water as the rest of the universe (sura 21.31, 25.56, 24.44). Animals have been created especially for the sake of mankind; men are the masters of these animals: "We have created for them the beasts of which they are masters. We have subjected these to them, that they may ride on some and eat the flesh of others; they drink their milk and put them to other uses" (sura 36.71).

The Jinn were created out of fire, before the creation of man out of clay. They live on earth with men.

While Muslim commentators have no problems in reconciling the apparent contradictions, a modern, scientifically literate reader will not even bother to look for scientific truths in the above vague and confused accounts of creation. Indeed, it is that very vagueness that enables one to find whatever one wants to find in these myths, legends, and superstitions. So, many Muslims believe that the whole of knowledge is contained in the Koran or the traditions. As Ibn Hazm said, "Any fact whatsoever which can be proved by reasoning is in the Koran or in the words of the Prophet, clearly set out." Every time there is a new scientific discovery in, say, physics, chemistry, or biology, the Muslim apologists rush to the Koran to prove that the discovery in question was anticipated there; everything from electricity to the theory of relativity (Ascha 1989, p. 14). These Muslims point to the Koranic notion of the aquatic origin of living things (sura 21.31), and the current idea in biology that life began, to quote Darwin, in "a warm little pond." Other putative scientific discoveries anticipated in the Koran include the fertilization of plants by wind (sura 15.22) and the mode of life of bees (sura 16.69). No doubt when they hear of the Glasgow chemist A. G. Cairns-Smith's suggestion that the answer to the riddle of the origins of life may lie in ordinary clay, these Muslim apologists will leap up and down with triumph and point to the Koranic doctrine that Adam was created from clay (Dawkins, pp. 148–165).

Since Muslims still take the Koranic account literally, I am duty bound to point out how it does not accord with modern scientific opinion on the origins of the universe and life on earth. Even on its own terms the Koranic account is inconsistent and full of absurdities. We have already noted the contradictions in the number of days for the creation. Allah merely has to say "Be," and His will is accomplished, and yet it takes the Almighty six days to create the heavens. Also, how could there have been "days" before the creation of the earth and the sun, since a "day" is merely the time the earth takes to make a revolution on its axis? We are also told that *before* the creation God's throne floated above the "waters." Where did this "water" come from before the creation? The whole notion of God having a throne is hopelessly anthropomorphic but is taken literally by the orthodox. Then we have several accounts of the creation of Adam. According to the Koran, Allah created the moon and its phases for man to know the number of the years (sura 10.5). Again, a rather primitive Arabian notion, since all the advanced civilizations of the Babylonians, Egyptians, Persians, Chinese, and Greeks used the solar year for the purpose of time reckoning.

Let us turn to the modern account of the origins of the universe.

In 1929, Edwin Hubble published his discovery that remote galaxies are rushing away from the earth with speeds proportional to their distances from the earth. The Hubble law states that the recessional velocity, v, of a galaxy is related to its distance, r, from the earth by the equation $v = H_0 r$, where H_0 is the Hubble constant. In other words, the Hubble law is telling us that the universe is expanding. As Kaufmann says: "The universe has been expanding for billions of years, so there must have been a time in the ancient past when all the matter in the universe was concentrated in a state of infinite density. Presumably, some sort of colossal explosion must have occurred to start the expansion of the universe. This explosion, commonly called the big bang, marks the creation of the universe." The age of the universe has been calculated to be between fifteen and twenty billion years.

Before what is called the Planck time (approximately ten seconds after the projected time of the big bang), the universe was so dense that the known laws of physics are inadequate to describe the behavior of space, time, and matter. During the first million years, matter and energy formed an opaque plasma (called the primordial fireball), consisting of high-energy photons colliding with protons and electrons. About one million years after the big bang, protons and electrons could combine to form hydrogen atoms. We had to wait ten billion years before our solar system came into existence. "Our solar system is formed of matter created in stars that disappeared billions of years ago. The Sun is a fairly young star, only five billion years old. All of the elements other than hydrogen and helium in our solar system were created and cast off by ancient stars during the first ten billion years of our galaxy's existence. We are literally made of star dust." (Kaufmann, p. 110) The solar system formed from a cloud of gas and dust, called the solar nebula, which can be described as a "rotating disk of snowflakes and ice-coated dust particles." The inner planets, Mercury, Venus, Earth, and Mars, formed through the accretion of dust particles into planetesimals and then into larger protoplanets. The outer planets, Jupiter, Saturn, Uranus, Neptune, and Pluto, formed through the break up of the outer nebula into rings of gas and ice-coated dust that coalesced into huge protoplanets. The Sun was formed by accretion at the center of the nebula. After about 100 million years, temperatures at the protosun's center were high enough to ignite thermonuclear reactions (Kaufmann, p. 116).

The preceding account is hopelessly at variance with the account given in the Koran. The earth was not, as the Koran claims (sura 41.12), created before the heavens; we have already noted that the sun and the solar system formed millions of years after the big bang, millions of other stars had already formed before our sun. Furthermore, the term "heavens" is hopelessly vague; does it mean our solar system? Our galaxy? The universe? No amount of juggling will make sense of the Koranic or biblical story of the creation of the "heavens" in six, eight, or two days. The light of the moon is, of course, not its own light (pace, sura 10.5) but the reflected light of the sun. The earth orbits the sun, not vice versa.

Those who are tempted to see in the Koran various anticipations of the big bang should realize that modern cosmology and physics in general is based on mathematics. Without the developments in mathematics, especially those in the seventeenth century (the calculus, for example), progress and understanding would not have been possible. In contrast to the vagueness of the Koran, the big bang in its modern cosmological formulation is stated with precision using advanced mathematics; indeed it is not possible to state these ideas in ordinary language without the loss of precision.

The Origins of Life and the Theory of Evolution

The earth was formed about 4.5 billion years ago, and perhaps less than one billion years later, life appeared on it for the first time after a period of chemical evolution. The Russian biochemist, Oparin, argued in *The Origin of Life* (1938) that the primitive earth contained chemical elements that reacted to the radiation from outer space as well as terrestrial sources of energy. "As a result of prolonged photochemical activity, these inorganic mixtures give rise to organic compounds [including amino acids that are the building blocks from which the protein molecules are constructed]. Through time and chemical selection, these . . . organic systems increased in complexity and stability, becoming the immediate precursors of living things" (Birx, n.d., pp. 417–418). Since Oparin's time, many scientists (Miller, Fox, Ponnamperuma) have succeeded in producing organic compounds from inorganic ones in the laboratory.

> Controversy still surrounds the biochemical explanation for the origin of life on earth, particularly as to whether something analogous to the DNA or RNA molecule arose first or, instead, basic amino acids necessary for protein synthesis. Living things emerged when organic systems became capable of metabolism and reproduction; the development of inorganic syntheses in chemical evolution paved the way for biological evolution and subsequently the adaptive radiation of more and more complex and diversified forms, (n.d., p. 419)

In 1859, Darwin published his *On the Origin of Species by Means of Natural Selection, or the Preservation of Favoured Races in the Struggle for Life*. In the Introduction of his great work, Darwin wrote:

> In considering the Origin of Species, it is quite conceivable that a naturalist, reflecting on the mutual affinities of organic beings, on their embryological relations, their geographical distribution, geological succession, and other such facts, might come to the conclusion that each species had not been independently created, but had descended, like varieties, from other species. Nevertheless, such a conclusion, even if well founded, would be unsatisfactory, until it could be shown how the innumerable species inhabiting this world have been modified, so as to acquire that perfection of structure and coadaptation which most justly excites our admiration.

Darwin's answer to his own question of "the How of Evolution" is, of course, natural selection. Species were a result of the long process of natural selection acting on "constantly appearing, random, heritable variations." Darwin put the matter himself in this way:

> As many more individuals of each species are born than can possibly survive; and as, consequently, there is a frequently recurring struggle for existence, it follows that any being, if it vary however slightly in any manner profitable to itself, under the complex and sometimes varying conditions of life, will have a better chance of surviving, and thus be naturally selected. From the strong principle of inheritance, any selected variety will tend to propagate its new and modified form.

The implications of the theory of evolution for man's place in nature were obvious. Darwin himself noted that "the conclusion that man is the co-descendant with other species of some ancient, lower, and extinct form is not in any degree new. Lamarck long ago came to this conclusion, which has lately been maintained by several eminent naturalists and philosophers; for instance, by Wallace, Huxley, Lyell, Vogt, Lubbock, Buchner, Rolle, &c., and especially Haeckel."

In the eighteenth century, de Lamettrie had classified man as an animal in *L 'Homme Machine* (1748). Linnaeus (1707–1778) had classified man with the manlike apes as Anthropomorpha. T. H. Huxley in his famous "Man's Relations to Lower Animals," begins his account by looking at the development of a dog's egg, and then concludes that

> The history of the development of any other vertebrate animal, Lizard, Snake, Frog, or Fish, tells the same story. There is always, to begin with, an egg having the same essential structure as that of the Dog:—the yolk of that egg always undergoes division, or "segmentation"; . . . the ultimate products of that segmentation constitute the building materials for the body of the young animal; and this is built up round a primitive groove, in the floor of which a notochord is developed. Furthermore, there is a period in which the young of all these animals resemble one another, not merely in outward form, but in all essentials of structure, so closely, that the differences between them are inconsiderable, while, in their subsequent course, they diverge more and more widely from one another.
>
> Thus the study of development affords a clear test of closeness of structural affinity, and one turns with impatience to inquire what results are yielded by the study of the development of Man. Is he something apart? Does he originate in a totally different way from Dog, Bird, Frog, and Fish, thus justifying those who assert him to have no place in nature and no real affinity with the lower world of animal life? Or does he originate in a similar germ, pass through the same slow and gradually progressive modifications—depend on the same contrivances for protection and nutrition, and finally enter the world by the help of the same mechanism? The reply is not doubtful for a moment, and has not

been doubtful any time these thirty years. Without question, the mode of origin and the early stages of the development of man are identical with those of the animals immediately below him in the scale:—without a doubt, in these respects, he is far nearer the Apes, than the Apes are to the Dog.

There is every reason to conclude that the changes [the human ovum] undergoes are identical with those exhibited by the ova of other vertebrated animals; for the formative materials of which the rudimentary human body is composed, in the earliest conditions in which it has been observed, are the same as those of other animals.

But, exactly in those respects in which the developing Man differs from the Dog, he resembles the ape, which, like man, has a spheroidal yolk-sac and a discoidal—sometimes partially lobed—placenta.

So that it is only quite in the later stages of development that the young human being presents marked differences from the young ape, while the latter departs as much from the dog in its development, as the man does.

Startling as the last assertion may appear to be, it is demonstrably true, and it alone appears to me sufficient to place beyond all doubt the structural unity of man with the rest of the animal world, and more particularly and closely with the apes.

The evidence for evolution comes from an impressive range of scientific disciplines: systematics, geopaleontology, biogeography, comparative studies in biochemistry, serology, immunology, genetics, embryology, parasitology, morphology (anatomy and physiology), psychology, and ethology.

This evidence points in the same direction, namely, that man, like all living things, is the result of evolution, and was descended from some apelike ancestor, and certainly was not the product of special creation. In this context, to talk of Adam and Eve as both the Bible and Koran do is meaningless. Man is, at present, classified under the order primates, along with tree shrews, lemurs, lorises, monkeys, and apes. Thus, not only apes and monkeys, but lemurs and tree shrews must be considered our distant cousins. As J. Z. Young states, "It is harder still to realize that our ancestry goes on back in a direct and continuous father-and-son line to a shrew, and from there to some sort of newt, to a fish, and perhaps to a kind of sea-lily."

God the Creator

Has the famous story that stands at the beginning of the Bible really been understood? the story of God's hellish fear of science? . . . Man himself had turned out to be [God's] greatest mistake; he had created a rival for himself; science makes godlike—it is all over with priests and gods when man becomes scientific. . . . Knowledge, the emancipation from the priest, continues to grow.

—NIETZSCHE, THE ANTICHRIST

Nowhere in the foregoing account of the origins of the universe and the origin of life and the theory of evolution did I have recourse to "divine intervention" as an explanation. Indeed, to explain everything in terms of God is precisely not to explain anything—it is to cut all inquiry dead, to stifle any intellectual curiosity, to kill any scientific progress. To explain the wonderful and awesome variety and complexity of living organisms as "miracles" is not to give a very helpful, least of all a scientific, explanation. To quote Dawkins, "To explain the origin of the DNA/protein machine by invoking a supernatural Designer is to explain precisely nothing, for it leaves unexplained the origin of the Designer. You have to say something like 'God was always there,' and if you allow yourself that kind of lazy way out, you might as well just say 'DNA was always there,' or 'Life was always there,' and be done with it."

Darwin made the same point about his own theory in a letter to Sir Charles Lyell, the famous geologist: "If I were convinced that I required such additions to the theory of natural selection, I would reject it as rubbish. . . . I would give nothing for the theory of natural selection, if it requires miraculous additions at any one stage of descent." Quoting the above letter, Dawkins comments: "This is no petty matter. In Darwin's view, the whole point of the theory of evolution by natural selection was that it provided a non-miraculous account of the existence of complex adaptations. For what it is worth, it is also the whole point of this book [*The Blind Watchmaker*]. For Darwin, any evolution that had to be helped over the jumps by God was not evolution at all. It made a nonsense of the central point of evolution."

As for the big bang and modern cosmology, Stephen Hawking makes the same point. Trying to make amends for their treatment of Galileo, the Vatican organized a conference to which eminent cosmologists were invited.

> At the end of the conference the participants were granted an audience with the pope. He told us that it was all right to study the evolution of the universe after the big bang, but we should not inquire into the big bang itself because that was the moment of Creation and therefore the work of God. I was glad then that he did not know the subject of the talk I had just given at the conference—the possibility that space-time was finite but had no boundary, which means that it had no beginning, no moment of Creation. (Hawking, p. 122)

Elsewhere in his best-selling book, *A Brief History of Time,* Hawking observes that

> The quantum theory of gravity has opened up a new possibility, in which there would be no boundary to space-time and so there would be no need to specify the behaviour at the boundary. There would be no singularities at which the laws of science broke down and no edge of space-time at which one would have to appeal to God or some new law to set the boundary conditions for

space-time. One could say: "The boundary condition of the universe is that it has no boundary." The universe would be completely self-contained and not affected by anything outside itself. It would neither be created nor destroyed. It would just *be*.

A little later. Hawking asks, "What place, then, for a creator?"

Einstein observed that "the man who is thoroughly convinced of the universal operation of the law of causation cannot for a moment entertain the idea of a being who interferes in the course of events. . . . He has no use for the religion of fear."

Similarly, more recently, Peter Atkins argues, "That the universe can come into existence without intervention, and that there is no need to invoke the idea of a Supreme Being in one of its numerous manifestations."

Theories that explain the big bang by reference to God answer no scientific questions. They push questions of ultimate origin back one step, prompting questions about God's origins. As Feuerbach said, "The world is nothing to religion; the world, which is in truth the sum of all reality, is revealed in its glory only by theory. The joys of theory are the sweetest intellectual pleasures of life; but religion knows nothing of the joys of the thinker, of the investigator of Nature, of the artist. The idea of the universe is wanting to it, the consciousness of the really infinite, the consciousness of the species."

It is only the scientist with a sense of wonder who feels that life's awesome complexity needs explaining, who will propose refutable and testable scientific hypotheses, who will try to unravel the so-called mysteries of the universe. The religious man will content himself with the uninteresting and untestable remark that "it" was all created by God.

Food, Famine, and Drought

It is rather unfortunate that the Koran gives the example of the elements as signs of God's munificence since they are as much a cause of misery as happiness. Rain, we are told in sura 7.56, is a harbinger of God's mercy. Yet floods claim the lives of thousands of people in, ironically, a Muslim country, namely, Bangladesh. The cyclone of 1991, with winds of 200 kilometers per hour, resulted in floods that left 100,000 dead and 10,000,000 without shelter. Despite the omnipresence of water, Bangladesh goes through a period of drought from October to April. Thus, the wretched population, among the poorest in the world, is submitted to both periodic floods and drought. All the work of God, as sura 57.22 tells us: "No disaster occurs on earth or accident in yourselves which was not already recorded in the Book before we created them."

Indeed, all natural catastrophes from earthquakes to tornadoes seem hard to reconcile with a benevolent God, especially as they seem to be visited on particularly poor, and often Muslim, countries. During the Lisbon earthquake of 1755 literally thousands of people died, many in churches as they prayed, and these deaths had a profound effect on the eighteenth century, particularly on writers like Voltaire. Why were so many innocent people killed? Why were the brothels spared, while pious churchgoers were punished?

Miracles

Eighteenth-century deists, as we saw earlier, exaggerated Islam's rationality, pointing to the fact that Muhammad did not perform any miracles. It is true: throughout the Koran Muhammad says he is a mere mortal unable to perform miracles, he is only God's messenger (suras 29.49, 13.27–30, 17.92–97). Despite these disclaimers, there are at least four places in the Koran that Muslims believe refer to miracles:

1. The clefting of the moon: "The hour has approached, and the moon has been cleft. But if the unbelievers see a sign, they turn aside and say, 'Magic! that shall pass away!'" (sura 54.1, 2).
2. The assistance given to the Muslims at the battle of Badr: "When you said to the faithful: 'Is it not enough for you that your Lord helps you with three thousand angels sent down from high?' No: if you are steadfast and fear God, and the enemy come upon you in hot pursuit, your Lord will help you with five thousand angels with their distinguishing marks" (sura 3.120, 121).
3. The night journey: "We declare the glory of Him who transports his servant by night from Masjidu 'l-Haram to the Masjidul-Aqsa [i.e., Mecca to Jerusalem]" (sura 17.1).
4. The Koran itself, for Muslims, remains the great miracle of Islam (sura 29.48).

The traditions are full of Muhammad's miracles, curing the ill, feeding a thousand people on one kid, etc.

As our knowledge of nature has increased, there has been a corresponding decline in the belief in miracles. We are no longer prone to think that God intervenes arbitrarily in human affairs by suspending or altering the normal workings of the laws of nature. As our confidence in our discoveries of the laws of nature has increased, our belief in miracles has receded.

David Hume argued in the following manner:

A miracle is a violation of the laws of nature; and as a firm and unalterable experience has established these laws, the proof against a miracle, from the very nature of the fact, is as entire as any argument from experience can possibly be imagined. Why is it more than probable, that all men must die; that lead cannot, of itself, remain suspended in the air; . . . unless it be, that these

events are found agreeable to the laws of nature, and there is required a violation of these laws, or in other words a miracle to prevent them? Nothing is esteemed a miracle, if it ever happens in the common course of nature. . . . But
it is a miracle, that a dead man should come to life; because that has never
been observed in any age or country. There must, therefore, be a uniform experience against every miraculous event, otherwise the event would not merit
that appellation. And as a uniform experience amounts to a proof, there is
here a direct and full proof, from the nature of the fact, against the existence
of any miracle. . . .

   The plain consequence is . . . "That no testimony is sufficient to establish a
miracle, unless the testimony be of such a kind, that its falsehood would be
more miraculous, than the fact, which it endeavours to establish."

And in every putative miracle, it is more reasonable and in accordance with
our experience to deny that the "miracle" ever happened. People are duped and
deluded, are apt to exaggerate, and have this strong need to believe; or as Feuerbach put it, a miracle is "the sorcery of the imagination, which satisfies without
contradiction all the wishes of the heart." Koranic miracles occurred a long time
ago, and we are no longer in a position to verify them.
   Perhaps one of the most important arguments against miracles, an argument
often overlooked, is that, to quote Hospers:

We believe that most of the alleged miracles are in some way unworthy of an
omnipotent being. If God wanted people to believe in him, why perform a few
miracles in a remote area where few people could witness them? . . . Instead of
healing a few people of their disease, why not all sufferers? Instead of performing a miracle in Fatima [a Portuguese village where three illiterate children saw
visions of "Our Lady of the Rosary"] in 1917, why not put an end to the enormous slaughter of World War 1, which was occurring at the same time, or
keep it from starting?

Jesus in the Koran
The Annunciation and the Virgin Birth

The Koran tells us that Jesus was miraculously born of the Virgin Mary. The
Annunciation of the Virgin is recounted at sura 19.16–21 and sura 3.45–48:

Behold! the angels said: "O Mary! God gives you glad tidings of a Word from
Him: his name will be Jesus Christ, the son of Mary, held in honour in this
world and the hereafter and of those nearest to God; he shall speak to the
people in childhood and in maturity. And he shall be of the righteous."

"How, O my Lord, shall I have a son, when no man has touched me?" asked Mary. He said, "Thus: God creates whatever He wants, when He decrees a thing He only has to say, 'Be,' and it is. And God will teach him the Book and Wisdom, the Torah and the Gospel."

Although it remains a tenet of orthodox Christian theology, liberal Christian theologians and many Christians now, and even the Bishop of Durham (England), no longer accept the story as literally true, preferring to interpret "virgin" as "pure" or morally without reproach, in other words, symbolically. Martin Luther (1483–1546), writing in the sixteenth century, conceded that "We Christians seem fools to the world for believing that Mary was the true mother of this child, and nevertheless a pure virgin. For this is not only against all reason, but also against the creation of God, who said to Adam and Eve, 'Be fruitful and multiply.'"

The treatment of the Virgin Birth by Christian biblical scholars is a good example of how Muslims cannot hide from their conclusions, for these conclusions have a direct bearing on the veracity or at least the literal truth of the Koran. Charles Guignebert (1867–1939) has made a detailed examination of the legend of the Virgin birth. Guignebert points out the striking parallels to the Virgin birth legend in the Greco-Roman world:

> It is here that we find the legend of Perseus, born of Danae, a virgin who was impregnated by a shower of gold, [and] the story of Attis whose mother Nana, became pregnant as a result of eating a pomegranate. It was here especially that the birth of notable men—Pythagoras, Plato, Augustus himself—tended to be explained by some kind of parthenogenesis, or by the mysterious intervention of a god. It is quite conceivable that, in a community in which so many stories of this kind were current, the Christians, desirous of adducing conclusive vindication of their faith in the divinity of Jesus, naturally turned to the sign by which men bearing the divine stamp were commonly identified. There was no question, of course, of a conscious imitation of any particular story, but simply of the influence of a certain atmosphere of belief.

Some scholars, such as Adolf Hamack (1851–1930), believe the Virgin birth legend arose from the interpretation of a prophetic passage in the Old Testament, namely, Isa. 7.14, according to the Greek text of the Septuagint, a translation made in 132 B.C. On this occasion, Ahaz, King of Judah, fears a new attack by the allied kings of Syria and Israel, who have just failed to take Jerusalem. The prophet reassures Ahaz and says:

> Therefore the Lord shall give a sign. Behold the Virgin shall conceive and give birth to a son, and thou shalt call him Emmanuel. Butter and honey shall he

eat, that he may know how to refuse the evil and choose the good. But before this child shall know how to recognize good and evil and choose the good, the land whose two kings thou abhorrest shall be forsaken.

The Christians, while searching for all the prophetic sayings concerning the Messiah, discovered this passage from Isaiah and, taking it out of context, gave it a messianic meaning. Most important of all, the Hebrew original does not contain the word "virgin" ("bethulah") but the word "young woman" ("haalmah"); in Greek, "parthenos" and "neanis," respectively. As Guignebert says,

The orthodox theologians have made every effort to prove that "haalmah" might mean virgin, but without success. The prophet had no thought of predicting a miracle, and the Jews, as soon as they began to attack the Christians, did not miss the opportunity of pointing out that the term to which their opponents appealed was nothing but a blunder.
    The Christians, convinced that Christ was born of the Spirit of God, as the accounts of the Baptism must testify must eagerly have seized upon the word parthenos as a means of effectuating this divine relationship.

Guignebert himself does not accept this theory of the origin of the Virgin birth legend put forward by Harnack. Instead, Guignebert offers his own hypothesis [p. 247]:

It will be observed that in Paul, John, and Mark, none of whom believes in the Virgin Birth, Jesus is characterised as the Son of God. This description of him is accordingly, prior to the establishment of the belief in the miracle related by Matthew and Luke, and does not arise out of it. As soon as they were convinced that, not only had Jesus been raised up by God, as a man full of the Holy Spirit, to accomplish his plans, but that his birth into this life for God had been divinely predestined, and glorified by the Holy Ghost, they must have attempted to signalise and to express this special relationship between Jesus and God. They said that he was his "son," because that was the only term in human language by which they could intelligibly, if not completely and adequately, express this relation. Since the idea of the direct generation of a man by God could only appear to the Jewish mind as a monstrous absurdity, the expression was, in reality, to the Palestinians, only a manner of speaking, only a metaphor.
    [It is clear] that Jesus never applied it to himself and that, moreover, it had not hitherto, in Israel, any Messianic significance. That is to say, the Jews did not beforehand bestow this title of Son of God upon the expected Messiah. The Messiah must have been for them not the Son, but the Servant, of God (Ebed Yahweh), for such was the designation of the "men of Yahweh." But on Greek soil the Christological belief found an environment very different from

that of Palestine. There, the idea of the procreation of a human being by a god was current, and the relation of real sonship between Christ and God the Father could shock no one. . . . On the contrary, the term Son of God was more likely to arouse sympathy in that quarter than the too peculiarly Jewish, too nationalistic, name of Messiah. Hence it was, in all probability, in the first Christian communities among the Gentiles, that the expression arose. Possibly it did so, at first, as a simple translation of the Palestinian Ebed Yahweh, for the Greek word *pais* means both servant and child, and it would be an easy transition from child to son. But it soon took on the colouring of an original Christological idea, the idea which met the needs of the environment which called it forth, the idea expressed in the Epistles of Paul. It found its Pauline and Johannine justification in the doctrine of divine preexistence and of the incarnation of the Lord. The legend of the Virgin Birth is another of its justifications, sprung from a quite different intellectual environment, but analogous to the one just cited, and finding its scriptural confirmation, when the need arose to defend it in controversy, in Isaiah 7:14. Matthew and Luke represent two concrete embodiments, different in form, but similar in spirit and meaning, of the belief: "He is the Son of God. He is born of the Holy Spirit "

The Birth of Jesus

The account of the birth of Jesus in sura 19.22–34 shows remarkable similarity not only to, as was pointed out by Sale, the story of Leto, but also to something which I have not seen remarked on anywhere, the birth of the historical Buddha. Let us look at the Koran first, sura 19.22f.:

And she conceived him, and retired with him to a far-off place. And the throes came upon her by the trunk of a palm tree. She said: "Oh, would that I had died before this! would that I had been a thing forgotten and out of sight!"

But a voice cried to her from beneath her, "Grieve not! for thy Lord has provided a rivulet at your feet; and shake the trunk of the palm tree towards you, it will drop fresh ripe dates upon you. Eat then and drink, and cheer your eye; and if you see anyone, say, "Verily, I have vowed abstinence to the God of mercy. I will not speak with anyone today."

Then she brought it to her people, carrying it. They said, "Oh Mary! you have done a strange thing! O sister of Aaron! your father was not a bad man, nor was your mother a whore!" And she made a sign to them, pointing towards the babe. They said, "How shall we speak with him who is in the cradle, an infant?" [The babe] said, "Verily, I am the servant of God, He has given me a book, and He has made me a prophet, and He has made me blessed wherever I be; and He has required of me prayer and almsgiving so long as I live, and piety towards my mother, and has not made me a miserable tyrant; and peace upon me the day I was bom, and the day I die, and the day I shall be raised up alive."

Leto—or in Latin, Latona—was a Titaness, a daughter of Coeus and Phoebe. According to the Homeric hymn to the Delian Apollo, Leto gave birth to Apollo while grasping the sacred palm tree. Apollo is also said to have spoken from Leto's womb. Callimachus (ca. 305–240 B.C.) in his "Hymn in Delum" recounts a similar story.

According to the legends of the birth of the Buddha, Queen Maya Devi dreamed that a white elephant entered her right side. Many Brahmins reassured the king and the queen that their child would one day be a great monarch or a Buddha. The miraculous pregnancy lasted ten months. On her way to her own parents towards the end of her pregnancy, Maya Devi entered the Lumbini garden where, as she grasped the branch of the Shala tree, the child emerged from her right side. As soon as he was born, the future Buddha stood up and took seven steps toward the north, and then toward the other cardinal points of the earth to announce his possession of the universe, and proclaimed that this was his last birth. We have already remarked on the probable direct source of the Koranic story of the birth of Jesus, viz., the apocryphal book called *The History of the Nativity of Mary and the Saviour's Infancy*.

Did Jesus Exist?

It may come as a surprise to Muslims that there were, and are still, scholars who doubt the historicity of Jesus, to whose existence Muslims are totally committed. Bruno Bauer (1809–1882), J. M. Robertson (1856–1933), Arthur Drews (1865–1935), van den Bergh van Eysinga, Albert Kalthoff, and in recent years, Guy Fau (*Le Fable dc Jesus Christ,* Paris, 1967), Prosper Alfaric (*Ongines Sociales du Christianisme*, Paris, 1959), W. B. Smith (*The Birth of the Gospel*, New York, 1957), and Professor G. A. Wells of Birkbeck College, University of London, have all developed the "Christ-Myth" theory. Professor Joseph Hoffmann sums up the situation in this manner:

> Scholarly opinion still holds (albeit not tenaciously) to the postulate of an historical figure whose life story was very soon displaced by the mythmaking activity of a cult. [Other scholars hold] the view that the postulation of an historical figure is unnecessary to explain the apparently "biographical" features of the Gospels. A candid appraisal of the evidence would seem to favour the latter view but we cannot easily dismiss the possibility that an historical figure lies behind the Jesus legend of the New Testament.

I intend to discuss the not-so-negligible evidence for the view that Jesus did not exist for several reasons:

1. First, very generally, the debates, discussions, and arguments on the Jesus myth are as much the concern of Muslims as Christians; or rather,

they should be. I suspect that no book written on Islam has ever discussed the views of Bauer or those of the Radical Dutch school on the historicity of Jesus. It should be the deep concern of all educated people who are interested in our intellectual and spiritual heritage and origins. The early history of Christianity is one of the most important chapters in the history of civilization. For Muslims, Jesus was one of God's prophets and a historical figure who performed various miracles, and who would come again at the last day and kill the Antichrist. If it can be shown that Jesus did not exist, it will have obvious consequences for all Muslims, for such a revelation will automatically throw the veracity of the Koran into question.

However, it is not simply a question of the historicity of Jesus, but what we do and can know about him. Again these questions should be of the utmost importance for all, including Muslims. Muslims believe Jesus existed, therefore, what nearly two hundred years of dedicated and selfless research by some of the greatest historians and intellectuals has revealed about this man should be of passionate interest. Muslims as much as Christians should be concerned with the truth of the matter. Even the Christian theologians who accept Jesus's existence concede a number of problems concerning his life have not been resolved. Most of the stories in the New Testament concerning his life are now accepted, even by conservative Christian theologians, to be legends with no basis in history. The New Testament scholar Ernst Kasemann concluded: "Over few subjects has there been such a bitter battle among the New Testament scholars of the last two centuries as over the miracle-stories of the Gospels. . . . We may say that today the battle is over, not perhaps as yet in the arena of church life, but certainly in the field of theological science. It has ended in the defeat of the concept of miracle which has been tradition in the church."

Where does this leave the Koran? None of the stories of Jesus in the Koran is accepted as true; most of them contain gross superstitions and "miracles" that only the most credulous would deem worthy of attention. It is worth remarking that if the Koran is absolutely true and the literal word of God, why is it that no Christian theologian adduces it as proof of Jesus's existence? No historian has ever looked at the Koran for historical enlightenment, for the simple reason that no historian will look at a document, which he will presume to be of human origin, written some six hundred years after the events it purports to describe when there are documents written some fifty or sixty years after the same events. We also know the source of the Koran stories, namely, heretical Gnostic gospels such as the Gospel of St. Thomas, which in turn have been dismissed as unhistorical.

Even if we do not accept the thesis that Jesus never existed, the conclusions of the New Testament historians throw a very illuminating light on the growth of religions and religious mythology; furthermore, they point to the striking similarities to the recent theories put forward by Islamicist scholars on the rise of Islam and the Muhammad legend of the Muslim traditions.

2. Many of the criticisms of Christianity to be found in the works to be discussed apply, *mutatis mutandis,* to all religions, including Islam.

3. The discussions of the historicity of Jesus have been conducted in Europe and the United States for over a hundred and fifty years now, without any of the scholars who denied Jesus's historicity being threatened by assassination. It is true Bauer was dismissed from his university post in theology at Bonn in 1842, but he continued to publish until the end of his life. Professor Wells is alive (1994) and well and taught at the University of London until 1971, while still vigorously denying that Jesus ever existed. In all this, there is surely a lesson for the Islamic world.

4. Blind dogmatism has shut Muslims off from the intellectually challenging and exhilarating research, debate, and discussion of the last century and a half. In the words of Joseph Hoffmann: "It is through such discussion, however, that we avoid the dogmatism of the past and learn to respect uncertainty as a mark of enlightenment."

5. There is also a deeper methodological moral to be learned from the following discussions. The virtue of disinterested historical inquiry is undermined if we bring into it the Muslim or Christian faith. Historical research only leads to an approximation of the objective truth, after a process of conjectures and refutations, critical thought, rational arguments, presentation of evidence, and so on. However, if we bring subjective religious faith, with its dogmatic certainties, into the "historical approximation process, it inevitably undermines what R. G. Collingwood argued was the fundamental attribute of the critical historian, skepticism regarding testimony about the past."

The Arguments

Strauss

In his *Life of Jesus Critically Examined* (1835), David Strauss pointed out that we could not take the gospels as historical biographies; that was not their primary function. The early Christians wanted to win converts to their cause "through the propagation of a synthetic religious myth."

Strauss's main thesis is that the stories in the New Testament were the result of the messianic expectations of the Jewish people.

The evangelists made Jesus say and do what they expected—from their knowledge of the Old Testament—that the Messiah would say and do; and many passages that in fact make no reference to the Messiah were nevertheless taken as messianic prophecies. Thus, "then shall the eyes of the blind be opened" (Isa. 35) expresses the joy of Jewish exiles in Babylon at the prospect of release from captivity, but was understood by the evangelists as prophesying that the Messiah would cure blindness, which they accordingly make Jesus do.

Bauer

Bauer went a step further and contended that the early Christians fashioned Jesus Christ from the portraits of the prophets found in the Old Testament. Jesus never existed, and Christianity arose in the middle of the first century from a fusion of Judaic and Greco-Roman ideas. Bauer argues, for example, that the Christian use of the Greek term "Logos" ultimately derives from Philo, the Stoics, and Heraclitus. For Philo, the Logos was the creative power that orders the world and the intermediary through whom men knew God. Of course, in St. John's Gospel, the Logos is equated with God, who becomes incarnate in Jesus Christ.

As for other classical influences on Christianity, as early as the fourth century, anti-Christian writers were pointing out the striking resemblances of the life of Jesus to the life of Apollonius of Tyana, a neo-Pythagorean teacher who was born just before the Christian era. He led a wandering and ascetic life, claimed miraculous powers, and was in constant danger of his life during the reigns of Roman emperors Nero and Domitian. His followers referred to him as the son of God; they also claimed he was resurrected before their very eyes and that he ascended into heaven.

The mystery cult of Mithras was first established in the Roman world in the first half of the first century B.C. This cult developed secret rites and rituals and stages of initiation through which the god's devotees had to pass. Mithraic mysteries also showed striking similarities to the Christian Baptism and the Eucharist.

The early Christians attribute words and sayings to Jesus that in reality only reflect the experience, convictions, and hopes of the Christian community. For example, Mark 1.14–15: "Now after that John was put in prison, Jesus came into Galilee, preaching the gospel of the kingdom of God. And saying, "The time is fulfilled, and the kingdom of God is at hand: repent ye, and believe the gospel." Christ never spoke these words,

> They were merely an expression of the earliest Christian community's conviction that the time was ripe for the appearance of Christianity and the diffusion of its beliefs about spiritual salvation. But in time, attempts were made to find historical indications—from the ancient days recorded in the Old Testa-

ment to imperial times—that progressive preparations for the age of salvation were apparent. Each new generation has regarded its own time as the time when the ancient promises will be fulfilled. The first Christians believed, from their knowledge of the Old Testament, that before the Savior came Elijah would return to earth. Once they had come to see the historical John the Baptist as Elijah returned, they would naturally believe that the Savior had followed soon after; and eventually a story would be constructed in which this "savior" is made to call John by the name "Elijah." (Mark 9.13)

Wrede

Acknowledging his debt to Bauer, Wilhelm Wrede, writing at the beginning of the twentieth century, showed that Mark's gospel "was saturated with the theological beliefs of the early Christian community. Rather than a biography, the gospel was a reading back into Jesus's life, the faith and hope of the early Church that Jesus was the Messiah and Son of God."

Kalthoff

Albert Kalthoff, also writing at the beginning of this century, argued that we could explain the origins of Christianity without having to posit a historical founder. Christianity arose by spontaneous combustion when "the inflammable materials, religious and social, that had collected together in the Roman empire, came into contact with Jewish messianic expectations." "From the socio-religious standpoint the figure of the Christ was the sublimated religious expression for the sum of the social and ethical forces that were at work in a certain period."

Non-Christian Evidence

Despite the fact that there were approximately sixty historians active during the first century in the Roman world, there is remarkably little corroboration of the Christian story of Jesus outside the Christian traditions. What there is, is very inconclusive and unhelpful—Josephus, Tacitus, Suetonius, the Younger Pliny.

The Gospels

It is now recognized that the Gospels (Matthew, Mark, Luke, and John) were not written by the disciples of Jesus. They are not eyewitness accounts, and they were written by unknown authors some forty to eighty years after the supposed crucifixion of Christ. Matthew, Mark, and Luke are usually called the synoptic Gospels because of the common subject matter and similarity of phrasing to be found in them. Mark is considered the earliest of the three and was probably used by the other two as their source. It now seems highly unlikely that any of the sayings attributed to Jesus in the Gospels were ever spoken by a historical figure. As Hoffmann concludes,

> It is difficult even to speak of an "historical" Jesus, given the proportions and immediacy of the myth-making process that characterises the earliest days of the Jesus cult. Whether or not there was an historical founder (and such is not needed, as the mystery religions testify, for the success of a cult and a coherent story about its "founder"), scholars now count it a certainty that the Gospels are compilations of "traditions" cherished by the early Christians rather than historical annals.

The Sanhedrin trial, the trial before Pilate, and the main factors in the Passion story all pose serious problems, and we cannot take them as historical events; rather they were "created" by the early Christians' own theological convictions. As Nineham says, much of what we find in Mark may well be "deduction from Old Testament prophecy about what 'must have' happened when the Messiah came."

The Epistles of Paul

The letters of Paul were written before Mark's Gospel, and yet rather surprisingly they do not mention many of the details of Jesus's life that we find in the Gospels: no allusions to Jesus's parents, or to the Virgin Birth, or to Jesus's place of birth; there is no mention of John the Baptist, Judas, nor of Peter's denial of his master. As G. A. Wells points out, "they give no indication of the time or place of Jesus's earthly existence. They never refer to his trial before a Roman official nor to Jerusalem as the place of his execution. They mention none of the miracles he is supposed to have worked." Even when certain doctrines attributed to Jesus in the Gospels would have been of obvious use to Paul in his doctrinal disputes, there is no mention of them.

The early post-Pauline letters, written before A.D. 90, also fail to give any convincing historical details. It is only with the later post-Pauline letters, written between A.D. 90 and 110, do we get those details from the Gospels with which we are familiar. Consequently, Wells concludes:

> Since, then, these later epistles do give biographical references to Jesus, it cannot be argued that epistles writers generally were disinterested in his biography, and it becomes necessary to explain why only the earlier ones (and not only Paul) give the historical Jesus such short shrift. The change in the manner of referring to him after A.D. 90 becomes intelligible if we accept that his

earthly life in first-century Palestine was invented late in the first century. But it remains very puzzling if we take his existence then for historical fact.

The Date of Mark's Gospel

When and why did the biography of Jesus with which we are familiar first develop? The details of Jesus's life first appear in Mark, which is considered the earliest gospel and most New Testament scholars date it ca. A.D. 70. But G. A. Wells insists that it was written ca. A.D. 90, when "Palestinian Christianity had been overwhelmed by the Jewish War with Rome, and the gentile Christians who then first linked Jesus with Pilate, and first gave his life altogether a real historical setting, could have had only very imperfect knowledge of what had really happened in Palestine c. A.D. 30." The Christian apologists invented the historical setting and details of the life of Jesus in order to meet the challenge of Docetism that denied the humanity of Jesus, to serve as an antidote to the proliferation of myths in Christian circles, to establish the reality of the resurrection, and generally to answer the questions raised by the early contacts of the Christians with a hostile, skeptical world.

The Rise of Islam and the Origins of Christianity

In Chapter 3 we saw the theories on the rise of Islam of a new generation of Islamic scholars. We are now in position to appreciate the resemblance of these theories to the theories presented above on the origins of Christianity. We noted earlier how Goldziher dismissed a vast amount of the hadith or traditions about the life of the Prophet as spurious. Goldziher considered by far the greater part of the hadith as the result of the religious, historical, and social development of Islam during the first two centuries. The hadith was useless as a basis for any scientific history and could only serve as a reflection of the tendencies of the early Muslim community. In the foregoing sections, we noted how the early Christians attributed words and sayings to Jesus that in reality only reflected the experience, convictions, and hopes of the Christian community.

Just as we find that the early Christians fabricated details of the life of Jesus in order to answer doctrinal points, so we find that Arab storytellers invented biographical material about Muhammad in order to explain difficult passages in the Koran.

Let us compare Schacht's comments on the traditions in the legal context and what we said of Wrede's judgment on Mark's Gospel. Traditions were formulated polemically in order to rebut a contrary doctrine or practice; doctrines in this polemical atmosphere were frequently projected back to higher authorities: "Traditions from Successors [to the Prophet] become traditions from Companions [of the Prophet], and Traditions from Companions become Traditions from the Prophet." Details from the life of the Prophet were invented to support legal doctrines.

As discussed earlier, Wrede showed that Mark's Gospel was full of the early Christian community's beliefs and hopes rather than being the actual story of Jesus.

Both religions in their early days, as they came into contact and conflict with a hostile community with a religious tradition of its own, developed and defended their doctrinal positions by inventing biographical details of their founders that they then projected back onto an invented Arabian or Palestinian point of origin. Where Christianity arose from a fusion of Judaic and Greco-Roman ideas, Islam arose from Talmudic Judaic, Syriac Christian, and indirectly, Greco-Roman ideas.

As Morton Smith put it "the first-century [Christian] churches had no fixed body of gospels, let alone a New Testament." Similarly, it is now clear that the definitive text of the Koran still had not been achieved as late as the ninth century.

Judgment Day

Central to the Islamic creed is the doctrine of the Last Day. Several terms are used in the Koran to indicate this most awesome of days: Day of Standing Up, Day of Separation, Day of Reckoning, Day of Awakening, Day of Judgment, the Encompassing Day, or simply and ominously the hour. The ultimate source of Muhammad's notions of the Last Day was Syriac Christianity. These accounts obviously gripped his imagination, for the Koran is full of graphic descriptions of this day: this event will be marked by the sounding of the trumpet, the splitting asunder of the heavens, the reduction of the mountains to dust, the darkening of the sky, the boiling over of the seas, the opening of the graves when men and Jinn will be called to account. These beings will then have their deeds weighed in the Balance, will be judged by God, and then either assigned to everlasting bliss in Paradise, or consigned to everlasting torment and torture in Hell. The terrors of the Last Day are emphasized over and over again, especially in the later Meccan passages. Men and women will be restored to life, that is, there will be an actual resurrection of the physical body.

We know that this notion of the resurrection of the body was alien to Arabian thought, for many Meccan pagans scoffed at this manifestly absurd idea. The pagan philosophers in their polemics against the Christians also asked pertinent questions: "How are the dead raised up? And with what body do they come? What was rotten cannot become fresh again, nor scattered limbs be reunited, nor what was consumed be restored. . . . Men swallowed by the sea, men torn and devoured by wild beasts, cannot be given back by the earth."

All doctrines of personal survival, personal immortality, and personal resurrection confront the obvious observation that all men and women die, are buried or cremated, and even if buried their bodies eventually decompose—what is rotten cannot become fresh again.

The Muslim doctrine is committed to the physical survival of the body: "That is their reward for that they disbelieved in our signs, and said, 'What! when we are bones and rubbish, shall we then be raised up a new creation?' Could they not see that God who created the heavens and the earth is able to create the like of them, and to set for them an appointed time; there is no doubt therein, yet the wrong-doers refuse to accept it, save ungratefully!" (sura 17.100).

But there is one objection to such an account that Antony Flew has formulated:

> Certainly Allah the omnipotent must have "power to create their like." But in making Allah talk in these precise terms of what He might indeed choose to do, the Prophet was speaking truer than he himself appreciated. For thus to produce even the most indistinguishably similar object after the first one has been totally destroyed and disappeared is to produce not the same object again, but a replica. To punish or to reward a replica, reconstituted on Judgment Day, for the sins or virtues of the old Antony Flew dead and cremated in 1984 is as inept and as unfair as it would be to reward or to punish one identical twin for what was in fact done by the other.

The Muslim account is further dogged by contradictions. We are told all mankind will have to face their Maker (and Remaker) on the Judgment Day, and yet sura 2.159 and sura 3.169 tell us that those holy warriors who died fighting in God's cause are alive and in His presence now. God has evidently raised them from the dead before the Last Day. Similarly, without waiting for the Last Day, God will send the enemies of Islam straight to hell. Interesting questions arise in this age of organ transplants. If a holy warrior dies fighting for the propagation of Islam, and at the very moment of his death has one of his organs, let us say his heart, transplanted into someone else lying in a hospital waiting for the surgical operation and the organ to save his life, how will the holy warrior be reconstituted? In this case, the same body will not have been re-fashioned; indeed, it will only be a replica with a different heart.

To answer "all is possible for God" is simply to admit the essential irrationality of the doctrine of reconstitution. In general, despite centuries of seances, table rapping, mediums, magicians, and all kinds of mumbo jumbo, no one has ever come up with a convincing proof of an afterlife. Apart from personal vanity, it is clearly fear of death that causes the persistent belief in a future life, despite all indications to the contrary.

Moral Objections to the
Doctrine of the Last Judgment

What was the one thing that Mohammed later borrowed from Christianity?
Paul's invention, his means to priestly tyranny, to herd formation: the faith in
immortality—that is, the doctrine of the "judgment."

—NIETZSCHE, *THE ANTI CHRIST*

Apart from the empirical and logical objections to the doctrine of resurrection
of the body, there are some powerful moral objections to the whole Islamic notion of the afterlife. Nietzsche has argued in the *Twilight of the Idols* and the *Anti-
christ* that to talk of an afterlife is to do dirt on, to denigrate and besmirch *this*
life. Far from making this life meaningful, the doctrine of an afterlife makes this
life meaningless.

> To invent fables about a world "other" than this one has no meaning at all,
> unless an instinct of slander, detraction, and suspicion against life has gained
> the upper hand in us: in that case, we avenge ourselves against life with a
> phantasmagoria of "another," a "better" life.

> The "Last judgment" is the sweet comfort of revenge. . . The "beyond"—why a
> beyond, if not as a means for besmirching this world?

Furthermore, the beyond is a way for the self-proclaimed prophets and
priests to retain control, to terrorize the people with the tortures of hell, and
equally to seduce them with the licentious pleasures of paradise. "The concepts
'beyond,' 'last judgment,' 'immortality of the soul' and 'soul' itself are instruments of torture, systems of cruelties by virtue of which the priest became master, remained master.

Muhammad was able to develop one of the worst legacies of the teachings of
the Koran, the notion of a Holy War (discussed in Chapter 10), with the help of
the idea of rewards in paradise for the holy martyrs who died fighting for Islam.
As Russell put it, "at a certain stage of development, as the Mohammedans first
proved, belief in Paradise has considerable military value as reinforcing natural
pugnacity."

Those prepared to die for the faith have been used frighteningly throughout
Islamic history, "martyrs" were used for political assassinations long before the
assassins of the eleventh and twelfth century. Modern Middle Eastern terrorists
or Mujahheddin are considered martyrs and have been manipulated for political reasons, with considerable effect. Most of them have been immunized
against fear, to quote Dawkins, "since many of them honestly believe that a

martyr's death will send them straight to heaven. What a weapon! Religious faith deserves a chapter to itself in the annals of war technology, on an even footing with the longbow, the warhorse, the tank, and the neutron bomb."

The contingency of this life should make man aware of its beauty and preciousness. The harsh truth that this is the only life we have should make us try and improve it for as many people as possible.

> When one places life's center of gravity not in life but in the "beyond"—in nothingness—one deprives life of its center of gravity altogether. The great lie of personal immortality destroys all reason, everything natural in the instincts—whatever in the instincts is beneficent and life-promoting or guarantees a future now arouses mistrust. To live so, that there is no longer any sense in living, *that* now becomes the "sense" of life. Why communal sense, why any further gratitude for descent and ancestors, why cooperate, trust, promote, and envisage any common welfare?

The Ethics of Fear

Religion is based, I think, primarily and mainly upon fear. It is partly the terror of the unknown, and partly . . . the wish to feel that you have a kind of elder brother who will stand by you in all your troubles and disputes. Fear is the basis of the whole thing—fear of the mysterious, fear of defeat, fear of death. Fear is the parent of cruelty, and therefore it is no wonder if cruelty and religion have gone hand-in-hand.

—BERTRAND RUSSELL, *WHY I AM NOT A CHRISTIAN*

We have already referred to the fact that the Koranic ethical system is based entirely on fear. Muhammad uses God's wrath-to-come as a weapon with which to threaten his opponents, and to terrorize his own followers into pious acts and total obedience to himself. As Sir Hamilton Gibb put it, "That God is the omnipotent master and man His creature who is ever in danger of incurring His wrath—this is the basis of all Muslim theology and ethics."

The notion of everlasting punishment is also incompatible with and unworthy of a benevolent, merciful God; and even more incomprehensible when we conjoin it with the Koranic doctrine of predestination. God especially creates creatures to consign to hell.

Finally, fear corrupts all true morality—under its yoke humans act out of prudent self-interest, to avoid the tortures of hell, which are no less real to the believers than the delights of the cosmic bordello that goes by the name of paradise.

Divine Punishment

The Koran decrees punishments that can only be described as barbaric. The relativist who defends the inhuman customs prescribed in the Koran by claiming that these were normal practices at the time finds himself stumped by the gruesome revival of most of them in the putatively more enlightened twentieth century. The Koran is the word of God—true for always.

Amputation

Sura 5.38 sets the tone: "As to the thief, male or female, cut off his or her hands: a punishment by way of example from God, for their crime: and God is exalted in power." According to Muslim law, "the right hand of the thief is to be cut off at the joint of the wrist and the stump afterwards cauterized, and for the second theft the left foot, and for any theft beyond that he must suffer imprisonment."

Crucifixion

The same sura tells us: "The punishment of those who wage war against God and His Apostle, and strive with might and main for mischief through the land is: execution, or crucifixion, or the cutting off of hands and feet from opposite sides, or exile from the land: that is their disgrace in this world, and a heavy punishment is theirs in the hereafter."

Women to be Immured

As for the offence of "zina," an Arabic term that includes both adultery and fornication, the Koran says nothing about lapidation as a punishment for adultery. Originally, women found guilty of adultery and fornication were punished by being literally immured: sura 4.15: "If any of your women are guilty of lewdness, take the evidence of four witnesses from amongst you, and if these bear witness, then keep the women in houses until death release them, or God shall make for them a way."

Flogging

However, sura 24.2-4 prescribes one hundred lashes for fornication: "The woman and man guilty of fornication, flog each of them with a hundred stripes; let not pity move you in their case."

　　　Lapidation was instituted at a later stage. As noted earlier a lapidation verse may have formed a part of the Koran, but this is disputed by some scholars.

Apologists of Islam often argue the compatibility of Islamic law and human rights. Article 5 of the 1948 Universal Declaration of Human Rights states, "no one shall be subjected to torture or to cruel, inhuman or degrading treatment or punishment." Are amputating a limb, flogging, and lapidation inhuman or not?

Historical Errors in the Koran

At sura 40.38, the Koran mistakenly identifies Haman, who in reality was the minister of the Persian King Ahasuerus (mentioned in the book of Esther), as the minister of the Pharoah at the time of Moses.

We have already noted the confusion of Mary, the mother of Jesus, with the Mary who was the sister of Moses and Aaron. At sura 2.249, 250 there is obviously a confusion between the story of Saul as told therein, and the account of Gideon in Judg. 7.5.

The account of Alexander the Great in the Koran (18.82) is hopelessly confused historically; we are certain it was based on the Romance of Alexander. At any rate, the Macedonian was not a Muslim and did not live to an old age, nor was he a contemporary of Abraham, as Muslims contend.

Regulations for the Muslim Community

The Koran contains a host of other rules and regulations for the proper functioning of the new community. We shall be looking at the position of women, marriage, and divorce in Chapter 14, the institution of slavery and the doctrine of the Holy War in Chapters 8 and 9, and the taboos concerning food and drink in Chapter 15. Other social prescriptions concern legal alms or the poor tax, usury, inheritance, prayers, pilgrimage, and fasts. Some of these are treated in a perfunctory and confused manner. The Koran also enjoins many moral precepts with which, though hardly original or profound, no one would disagree: kindness and respect toward elders and parents, generosity towards the poor, forgiveness instead of revenge. It also contains passages of beauty and grandeur. But on balance, the effects of the teachings of the Koran have been a disaster for human reason and social, intellectual, and moral progress. Far from being the word of God, it contains many barbaric principles unworthy of a merciful God. Enough evidence has been provided to show that the Koran bears the fingerprints of Muhammad, whose moral values were imbued with the seventh-century world view, a view that can no longer be accepted as valid.

Of Religion in General, and Islam in Particular

One is often told that it is a very wrong thing to attack religion because religion makes men virtuous. So I am told; I have not noticed it.

—BERTRAND RUSSELL, *WHY I AM NOT A CHRISTIAN*

There is not sufficient reason to believe that any religion is true. Indeed, most of them make claims that can be shown to be false or highly improbable. Nonetheless, some eminent philosophers argue that, though false, these religions are necessary for moral guidance, moral restraint, and social stability. The philosopher Quine said, "There remains a burning question of the social value of the restraints and ideals imposed by some religions, however false to facts those religions be. If this value is as great as I suspect it may be, it poses a melancholy dilemma between promoting scientific enlightenment and promoting wholesome delusion."

Such a view is both empirically false and morally repulsive. Let us look at the evidence, first, as Russell argued,

> You find this curious fact, that the more intense has been the religion of any period and more profound has been the dogmatic belief, the greater has been the cruelty and worse has been the state of affairs. In the so called ages of faith, when men really did believe the Christian religion in all its completeness, there was the Inquisition, with its tortures; there were millions of unfortunate women burnt as witches; and there was every kind of cruelty practiced upon all sorts of people in the name of religion.

We are all familiar with the wars perpetrated by Christianity, but less familiar are the ones waged by Muslims. I discuss the intolerance and cruelty of Islam in Chapter 9. I shall only point to some of the atrocities committed in the name of Allah in the twentieth century. For the past few years, the self-righteous and sanctimonious leaders of various Islamic groups in Afghanistan have been waging a bitter civil war to gain total power. In between their five prayers to the most compassionate and merciful God, they have managed to kill hundreds of innocent civilians. Many thousands of these civilians have fled to neighboring Pakistan, where they have expressed a distinct nostalgia for the halcyon days of the godless Communists. According to a report in the *International Herald Tribune* (26 April 1994), the civil war, now entering its third year, has claimed more than ten thousand lives. In Kabul alone, fifteen hundred people were killed between January and April 1994.

Sudan

At the moment of writing (June 1994), genocide is in progress in Sudan where Islamic law was imposed by the then-dictator General Numeiri in 1983, even though almost one-third of the population is not Muslim, but Christian or Animist. The Islamic North of Sudan has been waging a pitiless war on the Christians and Animists of the South. Since 1983, more than half a million people have been killed. An equal number of people have been forcibly displaced from the Sudanese capital, Khartoum, to campsites in the desert where the temperatures can reach 120 degrees F., and where there are no health facilities, water, food, or sanitation. As an article in the *Economist* (9 April 1994) pointedly titled "The Blessings of Religion" said, "Financed by Iran, the Government has equipped its troops with modern Chinese-made weapons. In recent months the war has taken on a still cruder air of jihad, as the ranks of the army have been swelled by large numbers of young Sudanese mujahideen, ready to die for Islam."

Indonesia

The details of the massacre of somewhere between 250,000 and 600,000 Indonesians in 1965 are only now beginning to emerge. After a failed *coup d'etat* in 1965, the Indonesian army (with at least tacit approval from the United States) took its revenge on the Communists. The army encouraged nationalist and Muslim youth to settle old scores; gangs of Muslim youths massacred Chinese peasants in the most horrific manner. "'No-one went out after 6 p.m.,' recalls a Chinese whose family fled East Java. 'They cut off women's breasts; they threw so many bodies in the sea that people were afraid to eat fish. My brother still had to serve in the shop. In the morning young Muslims would come in swaggering, with necklaces of human ears'" (*Guardian Weekly*, September 23, 1990). In Indonesia's 1975 invasion of East Timor, at least two hundred thousand civilians were killed.

I emphasize these atrocities as a counter to the sentimental nonsense about the "spiritual East," which, we are constantly told, is so much superior to the decadent and atheistic West; and as counterexamples to the belief that religion somehow makes men more virtuous. Europeans and Asians, Christians and Muslims have all been guilty of the most appalling cruelty; whereas there have been thousands of atheists who have not only led blameless lives but have worked selflessly for the good of their fellow humans.

.   .   .

The Totalitarian Nature of Islam

IBN WARRAQ

> *Bolshevism combines the characteristics of the French*
> *Revolution with those of the rise of Islam.*
> *Marx has taught that Communism is fatally predestined to*
> *come about; this produces a state of mind not unlike that of the*
> *early successors of Mahommet.*
> *Among religions, Bolshevism is to be reckoned with*
> *Mohammedanism rather than with Christianity and Buddhism.*
> *Christianity and Buddhism are primarily personal religions,*
> *with mystical doctrines and a love of contemplation.*
> *Mohammedanism and Bolshevism are practical, social,*
> *unspiritual, concerned to win the empire of this world.*
>
> —BERTRAND RUSSELL

Perhaps it was Charles Watson who, in 1937, first described Islam as totalitarian and proceeded to show how, "By a million roots, penetrating every phase of life, all of them with religious significance, it is able to maintain its hold upon the life of Moslem peoples." Bousquet, one of the foremost authorities on Islamic law, distinguishes two aspects of Islam that he considers totalitarian: Islamic law, and the Islamic notion of jihad that has for its ultimate aim the conquest of the entire world, in order to submit it to one single authority. We shall consider jihad in the next few chapters; here we shall confine ourselves to Islamic law.

Islamic law has certainly aimed at "controlling the religious, social, and political life of mankind in all its aspects, the life of its followers without qualification, and the life of those who follow tolerated religions to a degree that prevents their activities from hampering Islam in any way." The all-embracing nature of Islamic law can be seen from the fact that it does not distinguish among ritual, law (in the European sense of the word), ethics, and good manners. In principle this legislation controls the entire life of the believer and the Islamic community. It intrudes into every nook and cranny: everything—to give a random sample—from the pilgrim tax, agricultural contracts, the board and lodging of slaves, the invitation to a wedding, the use of toothpicks, the ritual fashion in which one's natural needs are to be accomplished, the prohibition for men to wear gold or silver rings, to the proper treatment of animals is covered.

Islamic law is a doctrine of duties—external duties—that is to say, those duties "which are susceptible to control by a human authority instituted by God. However, these duties are, without exception, duties toward God, and are founded

445

on the inscrutable will of God Himself. All duties that men can envisage being carried out are dealt with; we find treated therein all the duties of man in any circumstance whatsoever, and in their connections with anyone whatsoever."

Before looking at Islamic law in detail, we need to know why it developed the way it did.

No Separation of State and Church

Jesus Christ himself laid down a principle that was fundamental to later Christian thought: "Render unto Caesar the things which are Caesar's and unto God the things which are God's" (Matt. 22.17). These two authorities, God and Caesar, dealt with different matters and ruled different realms; each had its own laws and its own institutions. This separation of church and state is nonexistent in Islam—indeed, there are no words in classical Arabic for the distinctions between lay and ecclesiastical, sacred and profane, spiritual and temporal. Once again, we must look to the founder of Islam to understand why there was never any separation of state and church. Muhammad was not only a prophet but also a statesman; he founded not only a community but also a state and a society. He was a military leader, making war and peace, and a lawgiver, dispensing justice. Right from the beginning, the Muslims formed a community that was at once political and religious, with the Prophet himself as head of state. The spectacular victories of the early Muslims proved to them that God was on their side. Thus right from the start in Islam, there was no question of a separation between sacred history and secular history, between political power and faith, unlike Christianity, which had to undergo three centuries of persecution before being adopted by "Caesar."

Islamic Law

The sharia or Islamic law is based on four principles or roots (in Arabic, "usul," plural of "asl"): the Koran; the sunna of the Prophet, which is incorporated in the recognized traditions; the consensus ("ijma") of the scholars of the orthodox community; and the method of reasoning by analogy ("qiyas "or "kiyas").

The Koran

The Koran, as we saw earlier, is for Muslims the very word of God Himself. Though it contains rules and regulations for the early community on such matters as marriage, divorce, and inheritance, the Koran does not lay down general principles. Many matters are dealt with in a confusing and perfunctory manner, and a far greater number of vital questions are not treated at all.

The Sunna

The sunna (literally, a path or way; a manner of life) expresses the custom or manner of life of Muslims based on the deeds and words of the Prophet, and that which was done or said in his presence, and even that which was not forbidden by him. The sunna was recorded in the traditions, the hadith, but these, as we saw earlier, are largely later forgeries. Nonetheless, for Muslims the sunna complements the Koran and is essential for understanding it properly, for clarifying the Koranic vaguenesses and filling in the Koranic silences. Without the sunna Muslims would be at a loss for those details necessary in their daily lives.

The Koran and the sunna are the expressions of God's command, the definitive and inscrutable will of Allah that must be obeyed absolutely, without doubts, without questions, and without qualifications.

But with all their attendant obscurities, we still need some kind of interpretation of the sunna and the Koran, and this is the task of the science of sharia (fiqh). The specialists on law were called "faqih." They founded many "schools" of interpretation, four of which have survived to the present day and share among the whole population of orthodox (sunni) Islam. Oddly, all four are considered equally valid.

1. Malik ibn Abbas (d. 795) developed his ideas in Medina, where he is said to have known one of the last survivors of the companions of the Prophet. His doctrine is recorded in the work, Muwatta, which has been adopted by most Muslims in Africa with the exception of those in Lower Egypt, Zanzibar, and South Africa.
2. Abu Hanifa (d. 767), the founder of the Hanifi school, was born in Iraq. His school is said to have given more scope to reason and logic than the other schools. The Muslims of India and Turkey follow this school.
3. Al-Shafi'i (d. 820), who was considered a moderate in most of his positions, taught in Iraq and then in Egypt. The adherents of his school are to be found in Indonesia, Lower Egypt, Malaysia, and Yemen. He placed great stress on the sunna of the Prophet, as embodied in the hadith, as a source of the sharia.
4. Ahmad ibn Hanbal (d. 855) was born in Baghdad. He attended the lectures of al-Shafi'i, who also instucted him in the traditions. Despite persecution, ibn Hanbal stuck to the doctrine that the Koran was uncreated. The modern Wahhabis of Saudi Arabia are supposed to follow the teachings of ibn Hanbal.

When the various schools came under criticism for introducing innovations without justification for adapting religious law to suit worldly interests, and for tolerating abuses, the learned doctors of the law developed the doctrine of the infallibility of the consensus (ijma), which forms the third foundation of Islamic law or sharia.

IJMA

The saying "My community will never agree on an error" was ascribed to the Prophet and, in effect, was to make an infallible church of the recognized doctors of the community as a whole. As Hurgronje says, "This is the Muslim counterpart of the Christian Catholic doctrine of ecclesiastical tradition: 'quod semper, quod ubique, quod ab omnibus creditum est.'" The notion of consensus has nothing democratic about it; the masses are expressly excluded. It is the consensus of suitably qualified and learned authorities.

However, there were still disputes as to whose ijma was to be accepted: some only accepted the ijma of the companions of the Prophet, while others accepted only the ijma of the descendants of the Prophet, and so on.

The doctrine of the infallibility of the consensus of the scholars, far from allowing some liberty of reasoning as one might have expected, worked "in favor of a progressive narrowing and hardening of doctrine; and, a little later, the doctrine which denied the further possibility of 'independent reasoning' sanctioned officially a state of things which had come to prevail in fact."

By the beginning of A.D. 900, Islamic law became rigidly and inflexibly fixed because, to quote Schacht:

> The point had been reached when the scholars of all schools felt that all essential questions had been thoroughly discussed and finally settled, and a consensus gradually established itself to the effect that from that time onwards no one might be deemed to have the necessary qualifications for independent reasoning in law, and that all future activity would have to be confined to the explanation, application, and, at most, interpretation of the doctrine as it had been laid down once and for all.

This closing of the gate of independent reasoning, in effect, meant the unquestioning acceptance of the doctrines of established schools and authorities. Islamic law until then had been adaptable and growing, but henceforth, it

> became increasingly rigid and set in its final mould. This essential rigidity of Islamic law helped it to maintain its stability over the centuries which saw the decay of the political institutions of Islam. It was not altogether immutable, but the changes which did take place were concerned more with legal theory and the systematic superstructure than with positive law. Taken as a whole, Islamic law reflects and fits the social and economic conditions of the early

Abbasid period, but has grown more and more out of touch with later developments of state and society.

Kiyas

Kiyas or analogical reasoning is considered by many learned doctors to be
subordinate to, and hence less important than, the other three foundations of
Islamic law. Its inclusion may well have been a compromise between unrestricted liberty of opinion and the rejection of all human reasoning in religious law.

The Nature of Islamic Law

1. All human acts and relationships are assessed from the point of view of
   the concepts obligatory, recommended, indifferent, reprehensible, and
   forbidden. Islamic law is part of a system of religious duties, blended
   with nonlegal elements.
2. The irrational side of Islamic law comes from two of its official bases,
   the Koran and the sunna, which are expressions of God's commands. It
   follows from the irrational side of Islamic law that its rules are valid by
   virtue of their mere existence and not because of their rationality. The
   irrational side of Islamic law also calls for the observance of the letter
   rather than of the spirit: this fact has historically facilitated the vast
   development and acceptance of legal devices such as legal fictions. For
   example, the Koran explicitly prohibits the taking of interest, and, to
   quote Schacht:

   "This religious prohibition was strong enough to make popular
   opinion unwilling to transgress it openly and directly, while at the same
   time there was an imperative demand for the giving and taking of
   interest in commercial life. In order to satisfy this need, and at the same
   time to observe the letter of the religious prohibition, a number of
   devices were developed. One consisted of giving real property as a
   security for the debt and allowing the creditor to use it, so that its use
   represented the interest. . . . Another . . . device consisted of a double
   sale. . . . For instance, the (prospective) debtor sells to the (prospective)
   creditor a slave for cash, and immediately buys the slave back from him
   for a greater amount payable at a future date; this amounts to a loan
   with the slave as security, and the difference between the two prices
   represents the interest."

   How can we characterize the above practices? "Legal fictions" is too
   kind an expression. Moral evasiveness? Moral hypocrisy? Moral
   dishonesty?

3. Although Islamic law is a sacred law, it is by no means essentially
   irrational; it was created not by an irrational process of continuous
   revelation . . . but by a rational method of interpretation, in this way it
   acquired its intellectualist and scholastic exterior. But whereas Islamic
   law presents itself as a rational system on the basis of material
   considerations, its formal juridical character is little developed. Its aim
   is to provide concrete and material standards, and not to impose formal
   rules on the play of contending interests [which is the aim of secular
   laws]. This leads to the result that considerations of good faith, fairness,
   justice, truth, and so on play only a subordinate part in the system.
4. Unlike Roman law, Islamic law brings legal subject matter into a system
   by the analogical method, by parataxis and association. Closely linked
   to this method is the casuistical way of thinking, which is one of the
   striking aspects of traditional Islamic law. "Islamic law concentrates not
   so much on disengaging the legally relevant elements of each case and
   subsuming it under general rules—as on establishing graded series of
   cases." For example, on the question of succession, we find discussions
   of the case of an individual who leaves as sole inheritors his thirty-two
   great-great-grandparents; the rights of succession of hermaphrodites
   (since the two sexes do not have the same rights); the inheritance of an
   individual who has been changed into an animal; and, in particular, the
   inheritance of that same individual when only half has been
   transformed, either horizontally or vertically.

   Thus, a soul-destroying pedantry, a spirit of casuistry took over. As
Goldziher says:
   "The task of interpreting God's word and of regulating life in
conformity to God's word became lost in absurd sophistry and dreary
exegetical trifling: in thinking up contingencies that will never arise and
debating riddling questions in which extreme sophistry and hair-
splitting are joined with the boldest and most reckless flights of fancy.
People debate far-fetched legal cases, casuistic constructs quite
independent of the real world. . . . Popular superstition, too, furnishes
the jurists with material for such exercises. Since . . . demons frequently
assume human shape, the jurists assess the consequences of such
transformations for religious law; serious arguments and
counterarguments are urged, for example, whether such beings can be
numbered among the participants necessary for the Friday service.
Another problematic case that the divine law must clarify: how is one to
deal with progeny from a marriage between a human being and a
demon in human form. . . . What are the consequences in family law of
such marriages? Indeed, the problem of (marriages with the Jinn) is

treated in such circles with the same seriousness as any important point of the religious law."

5. In what we would call penal law, Islamic law distinguishes between the rights of God and the rights of humans.

Only the rights of God have the character of a penal law proper, of a law which imposes penal sanctions on the guilty. Even here, in the center of penal law, the idea of a claim on the part of God predominates, just as if it were a claim on the part of a human plaintiff. This real penal law is derived exclusively from the Koran and the traditions [hadith], the alleged reports of the acts and sayings of the Prophet and of his Companions. The second great division of what we should call penal law belongs to the category of "redress of torts," a category straddling civil and penal law which Islamic law has retained from the law of pre-Islamic Arabia where it was an archaic but by no means unique phenomenon. Whatever liability is incurred here, be it retaliation or blood-money or damages, is subject of a private claim, pertaining to the rights of humans. In this Held, the idea of criminal guilt is practically nonexistent, and where it exists it has been introduced by considerations of religious responsibility. So there is no fixed penalty for any infringement of the rights of a human to the inviolability of his person and property, only exact reparation of the damage caused. This leads to retaliation for homicide and wounds on one hand, and to the absence of fines on the other.

In sum, sharia is the total collection of theoretical laws that apply in an ideal Muslim community that has surrendered to the will of God. It is based on divine authority that must be accepted without criticism. Islamic law is thus not a product of human intelligence, and in no way reflects a constantly changing or evolving social reality (as does European law). It is immutable, and the fiqh or the science of the sharia constitutes the infallible and definitive interpretation of the Sacred Texts. It is infallible because the group of Doctors of law have been granted the power to deduce authoritative solutions from the Koran and the traditions; and definitive because after three centuries, all the solutions have been given. While European law is human and changing, the sharia is divine and immutable. It depends on the inscrutable will of Allah, which cannot be grasped by human intelligence—it must be accepted without doubts and questions. The work of the learned doctors of the sharia is but a simple application of the words of Allah or His Prophet: it is only in certain narrowly defined limits, fixed by God Himself, that one can use a kind of reasoning known as qiyas, reasoning by analogy. The decisions of the learned, having the force of law, rest on the infallibility of the community, an infallibility that God Himself conferred through Muhammed on his community [Bousquet, Hurgronje, Schacht].

Criticisms of Islamic Law

1. Two of the roots of Islam are the Koran and the sunna as recorded in the hadith. First, we have already given reasons why the Koran cannot be considered of divine origin—it was composed sometime between the seventh and the ninth centuries, full of borrowings from talmudic Judaism, apocryphal Christianity, the Samaritans, Zoroastrianism, and pre-Islamic Arabia. It contains historical anachronisms and errors, scientific mistakes, contradictions, grammatical errors, etc. Second, the doctrines contained therein are incoherent and contradictory and not worthy of a compassionate deity. Nowhere is there any proof for the existence of any deity. On the other hand, the Koran also contains praiseworthy, even if not particularly original moral principles—the need for generosity, respect for parents, and so on. But these are outweighed by unworthy principles: intolerance of pagans, the call to violence and murder, the lack of equality for women and non-Muslims, the acceptance of slavery, barbaric punishments, and the contempt for human reason.

2. Goldziher, Schacht, and others have convincingly shown that most— and perhaps all—of the traditions (hadith) were forgeries put into circulation in the first few Muslim centuries. If this fact is allowed, then the entire foundation of Islamic law is seen to be very shaky indeed. The whole of Islamic law is but a fantastic creation founded on forgeries and pious fictions. And since Islamic law is seen by many as "the epitome of Islamic thought, the most typical manifestation of the Islamic way of life, the core and kernel of Islam itself," the consequences of Goldziher's and Schacht's conclusions are, to say the least, shattering.

3. Priestly Power:
   That there is a will of God, once and for all, as to what man is to do and what he is not to do; that the value of a people, of an individual, is to be measured according to how much or how little the will of God is obeyed; that the will of God manifests itself in the destinies of a people, of an individual, as the ruling factor, that is to say, as punishing and rewarding according to the degree of obedience.... One step further: the "will of God" (that is, the conditions for the preservation of priestly power) must be known: to this end a "revelation" is required. In plain language: a great literary forgery becomes necessary, a "holy scripture" is discovered; it is made public with full hieratic pomp.... With severity and pedantry, the priest formulates once and for all, ... what he wants to have, "what the will of God is." From now on all things in life are so ordered that the priest is indispensable.

Muslim apologists and Muslims themselves have always claimed that there were no clergy in Islam; but in reality, there was something like a clerical class, which eventually acquired precisely the same kind of social and religious authority as the Christian clergy. This is the class I have been referring to throughout this chapter as "the learned doctors" or the "doctors of law," otherwise known as the "ulama." Given the importance attached to the Koran and the sunna (and hadith), there grew a need to have a professional class of people competent enough to interpret the Sacred texts. As their authority grew among the community, they grew more confident and claimed absolute authority in all matters relating to faith and law. The doctrine of "ijma" merely consolidated their absolute power. As Gibb says, "It was . . . only after the general recognition of ijma as a source of law and doctrine that a definite legal test of heresy was possible and applied. Any attempt to raise the question of the import of a text in such a way as to deny the validity of the solution already given and accepted by consensus became a 'bid'a,' an act of 'innovation,' that is to say, heresy."

The continuing influence of the ulama is the major factor why there has been so little intellectual progress in Muslim societies, why critical thought has not developed. Throughout Islamic history, but especially in recent times, the ulama have actively hindered attempts to introduce the idea of human rights, freedom, individualism, and liberal democracy. For example, the ulama reacted violently to Iran's 1906-1907 constitution, regarding it as "un-Islamic"; they were totally opposed to the idea of freedom contained within it. The ulama have been involved in the process of Islamization in modern times in three countries in particular, Iran, the Sudan, and Pakistan. In each of these countries, "Islamization has effectively meant the elimination of human rights or their restrictions by reference to Islamic criteria."

4. Is the sharia still valid?

We may well ask how a law whose elements were first laid down over a thousand years ago, and whose substance has not evolved with the times can possibly be relevant in the twentieth century. The sharia only reflects the social and economic conditions of the time of the early Abbasids and has simply grown out of touch with all the later developments—social, economic, and moral. It seems improbable but we have progressed morally: we no longer regard women as chattel that we can dispose of as we will: we no longer believe that those who do not share our religious beliefs are not worthy of equal respect; we even accord children and animals rights. But as long as we continue to regard the Koran as eternally true, with an answer for all the problems of the modern world we will have no progress. The principles enshrined in the Koran are inimical to moral progress.

45

In the Shadow of God

From *The End of Faith*

Sam Harris

The first decade of the twenty-first century has seen an extraordinary revival of courage and humor and intelligence in the face of dumb and sinister religiosity. One of the finest volunteers in this cause is the neuroscientist Sam Harris, whose book *The End of Faith* caused one reviewer, and millions of readers, to say that they felt they were being personally addressed.

Without warning you are seized and brought before a Judge. Did you create a thunderstorm and destroy the village harvest? Did you kill your neighbor with the evil eye? Do you doubt that Christ is bodily present in the Eucharist? You will soon learn that questions of this sort admit of no exculpatory reply.

You are not told the names of your accusers. But their identities are of little account, for even if, at this late hour, they were to recant their charges against you, they would merely be punished as false witnesses, while their original accusations would retain their full weight as evidence of your guilt. The machinery of justice has been so well oiled by faith that it can no longer be influenced.

But you have a choice, of sorts: you can concede your guilt and name your accomplices. Yes, you must have had accomplices. No confession will be accepted unless other men and women can be implicated in your crimes. Perhaps you and three acquaintances of your choosing *did* change into hares and consort with the devil himself. The sight of iron boots designed to crush your feet seems to refresh your memory. Yes, Friedrich, Arthur, and Otto are sorcerers too. Their wives? Witches all.

You now face punishment proportionate to the severity of your crimes: flogging, a pilgrimage on foot to the Holy Land, forfeiture of property, or, more likely, a period of long imprisonment, probably for life. Your "accomplices" will soon be rounded up for torture.

Or you can maintain your innocence, which is almost certainly the truth (after all, it is the rare person who can create a thunderstorm). In response, your jailers will be happy to lead you to the furthest reaches of human suffering,

454

before burning you at the stake. You may be imprisoned in total darkness for months or years at a time, repeatedly beaten and starved, or stretched upon the rack. Thumbscrews may be applied, or toe screws, or a pear-shaped vise may be inserted into your mouth, vagina, or anus, and forced open until your misery admits of no possible increase. You may be hoisted to the ceiling on a *strappado* (with your arms bound behind your back and attached to a pulley, and weights tied to your feet), dislocating your shoulders. To this torment *squassation* might be added, which, being often sufficient to cause your death, may yet spare you the agony of the stake. If you are unlucky enough to be in Spain, where judicial torture has achieved a transcendent level of cruelty, you may be placed in the "Spanish chair": a throne of iron, complete with iron stocks to secure your neck and limbs. In the interest of saving your soul, a coal brazier will be placed beneath your bare feet, slowly roasting them. Because the stain of heresy runs deep, your flesh will be continually larded with fat to keep it from burning too quickly. Or you may be bound to a bench, with a cauldron filled with mice placed upside-down upon your bare abdomen. With the requisite application of heat to the iron, the mice will begin to burrow into your belly in search of an exit.

Should you, while in extremis, admit to your torturers that you are indeed a heretic, a sorcerer, or a witch, you will be made to confirm your story before a judge—and any attempt to recant, to claim that your confession has been co-erced through torture, will deliver you either to your tormentors once again or directly to the stake. If, once condemned, you repent of your sins, these compassionate and learned men—whose concern for the fate of your eternal soul really knows no bounds—will do you the kindness of strangling you before lighting your pyre.

.   .   .

The medieval church was quick to observe that the Good Book was good enough to suggest a variety of means for eradicating heresy, ranging from a communal volley of stones to cremation while alive. A literal reading of the Old Testament not only permits but *requires* heretics to be put to death. As it turns out, it was never difficult to find a mob willing to perform this holy office, and to do so purely on the authority of the Church—since it was still a capital of-fense to possess a Bible in any of the vernacular languages of Europe. In fact, scripture was not to become generally accessible to the common man until the sixteenth century. As we noted earlier, Deuteronomy was the preeminent text in every inquisitor's canon, for it explicitly enjoins the faithful to murder anyone in their midst, even members of their own families, who profess a sympathy for foreign gods. Showing a genius for totalitarianism that few mortals have ever fully implemented, the author of this document demands that anyone too squeamish to take part in such religious killing must be killed as well

(Deuteronomy 17:12–13). Anyone who imagines that no justification for the Inquisition can be found in scripture need only consult the Bible to have his view of the matter clarified:

> If you hear that in one of the towns which Yahweh your God has given you for a home, there are men, scoundrels from your own stock, who have led their fellow-citizens astray, saying, "Let us go and serve other gods," hitherto unknown to you, it is your duty to look into the matter, examine it, and inquire most carefully. If it is proved and confirmed that such a hateful thing has taken place among you, you must put the inhabitants of that town to the sword; you must lay it under the curse or destruction—the town and everything in it. You must pile up all its loot in the public square and burn the town and all its loot, offering it all to Yahweh your God. It is to be a ruin for all time and never rebuilt. (Deuteronomy 13:12–16).

For obvious reasons, the church tended to ignore the final edict: the destruction of heretic property.

In addition to demanding that we fulfill every "jot" and "tittle" of Old Testament law, Jesus seems to have suggested, in John 15:6, further refinements to the practice of killing heretics and unbelievers: "If a man abide not in me, he is cast forth as a branch, and is withered; and men gather them, and cast them into the fire, and they are burned." Whether we want to interpret Jesus metaphorically is, of course, our business. The problem with scripture, however, is that many of its possible interpretations (including most of the literal ones) can be used to justify atrocities in defense of the faith.

The Holy Inquisition formally began in 1184 under Pope Lucius III, to crush the popular movement of Catharism. The Cathars (from the Greek *katharoi*, "the pure ones") had fashioned their own brand of Manicheanism (Mani himself was flayed alive at the behest of Zoroastrian priests in 276 CE), which held that the material world had been created by Satan and was therefore inherently evil. The Cathars were divided by a schism of their own and within each of their sects by the distinction between the renunciate *perfecti* and the lay *credentes* ("the believers") who revered them. The *perfecti* ate no meat, eggs, cheese, or fat, fasted for days at a time, maintained strict celibacy, and abjured all personal wealth. The life of the *perfecti* was so austere that most *credentes* only joined their ranks once they were safely on their deathbeds, so that, having lived as they pleased, they might yet go to God in holiness. Saint Bernard, who had tried in vain to combat this austere doctrine with that of the church, noted the reasons for his failure: "As to [the Cathars'] conversation, nothing can be less reprehensible . . . and what they speak, they prove by deeds. As for the morals of the heretic, he cheats no one, he oppresses no one, he strikes no one; his cheeks are pale with fasting, . . . his hands labor for his livelihood."

There seems, in fact, to have been nothing wrong with these people apart from their attachment to certain unorthodox beliefs about the creation of the world. But heresy is heresy. Any person who believes that the Bible contains the infallible word of God will understand why these people had to be put to death.

The Inquisition took rather genteel steps at first (the use of torture to extract confessions was not "officially" sanctioned until 1215, at the Fourth Lateran Council), but two developments conspired to lengthen its strides. The first came in 1199 when Pope Innocent III decreed that all property belonging to a convicted heretic would be forfeited to the church; the church then shared it both with local officials and with the victim's accusers, as a reward for their candor. The second was the rise of the Dominican order. Saint Dominic himself, displaying the conviction of every good Catholic of the day, announced to the Cathars, "For many years I have exhorted you in vain, with gentleness, preaching, praying, weeping. But according to the proverb of my country, 'where blessing can accomplish nothing, blows may avail.' We shall rouse against you princes and prelates, who, alas, will arm nations and kingdoms against this land. . . ." It would appear that sainthood comes in a variety of flavors. With the founding of Dominic's holy order of mendicant friars, the Inquisition was ready to begin its work in earnest. It is important to remember, lest the general barbarity of time inure us to the horror of these historical accounts, that the perpetrators of the Inquisition—the torturers, informers, and those who commanded their actions—were ecclesiastics of one rank or another. They were men of God— popes, bishops, friars, and priests. They were men who had devoted their lives, in word if not in deed, to Christ as we find him in the New Testament, healing the sick and challenging those without sin to cast the first stone:

> In 1234, the canonization of Saint Dominic was finally proclaimed in Toulouse, and Bishop Raymond du Fauga was washing his hands in preparation for dinner when he heard the rumor that a fever-ridden old woman in a nearby house was about to undergo the Cathar ritual. The bishop hurried to her bedside and managed to convince her that he was a friend, then interrogated her on her beliefs, then denounced her as a heretic. He called on her to recant. She refused. The bishop thereupon had her bed carried out into a field, and there she was burned. "And after the bishop and the friars and their companions had seen the business completed," Brother Guillaume wrote, "they returned to the refectory and, giving thanks to God and the Blessed Dominic, ate with rejoicing what had been prepared for them."

The question of how the church managed to transform Jesus' principal message of loving one's neighbor and turning the other cheek into a doctrine of murder and rapine seems to promise a harrowing mystery; but it is no mystery at all. Apart from the Bible's heterogeneity and outright self-contradiction, allowing it to justify diverse and irreconcilable aims, the culprit is clearly the doctrine of faith itself. Whenever a man imagines that he need only believe the truth of a proposition, without evidence—that unbelievers will go to hell, that Jews drink the blood of infants—he becomes capable of anything.

The practice for which the Inquisition is duly infamous, and the innovation that secured it a steady stream of both suspects and guilty verdicts, was its use of torture to extract confessions from the accused, to force witnesses to testify, and to persuade a confessing heretic to name those with whom he had collaborated in sin. The justification for this behavior came straight from Saint Augustine, who reasoned that if torture was appropriate for those who broke the laws of men, it was even more fitting for those who broke the laws of God. As practiced by medieval Christians, judicial torture was merely a final, mad inflection of their faith. That anyone imagined that *facts* were being elicited by such a lunatic procedure seems a miracle in itself. As Voltaire wrote in 1764, "There is something divine here, for it is incomprehensible that men should have patiently borne this yoke."

A contemporaneous account of the Spanish auto-da-fé (the public spectacle at which heretics were sentenced and often burned) will serve to complete our picture. The Spanish Inquisition did not cease its persecution of heretics until 1834 (the last auto-da-fé took place in Mexico in 1850), about the time Charles Darwin set sail on the *Beagle* and Michael Faraday discovered the relationship between electricity and magnetism.

> The condemned are then immediately carried to the Riberia, the place of execution, where there are as many stakes set up as there are prisoners to be burnt. The negative and relapsed being first strangled and then burnt; the professed mount their stakes by a ladder, and the Jesuits, after several repeated exhortations to be reconciled to the church, consign them to eternal destruction, and then leave them to the fiend, who they tell them stands at their elbow to carry them into torments. On this a great shout is raised, and the cry is, "Let the dogs' beards be made"; which is done by thrusting flaming bunches of furze, fastened to long poles, against their beards, till their faces are burnt black, the surrounding populace rending the air with the loudest acclamations of joy. At last fire is set to the furze at the bottom of the stake, over which the victims are chained, so high that the flame seldom reaches higher than the seat they sit on, and thus they are rather roasted than burnt. Although there cannot be a more lamentable spectacle and the sufferers continually cry out as long as they are able, "Pity for the love of God!" yet it is beheld by persons of all ages and both sexes with transports of joy and satisfaction.

And while Protestant reformers broke with Rome on a variety of counts, their treatment of their fellow human beings was no less disgraceful. Public executions were more popular than ever: heretics were still reduced to ash,

scholars were tortured and killed for impertinent displays of reason, and for-
nicators were murdered without a qualm. The basic lesson to be drawn from
all this was summed up nicely by Will Durant: "Intolerance is the natural con-
comitant of strong faith; tolerance grows only when faith loses certainty; certainty is murderous."

There really seems to be very little to perplex us here. Burning people who are
destined to burn for all time seems a small price to pay to protect the people you
love from the same fate. Clearly, the common law marriage between reason and
faith—wherein otherwise reasonable men and women can be motivated by the
content of unreasonable beliefs—places society upon a slippery slope, with confusion and hypocrisy at its heights, and the torments of the inquisitor waiting
below.

Witch and Jew

Historically, there have been two groups targeted by the church that deserve
special mention. Witches are of particular interest in this context because their
persecution required an extraordinary degree of credulity to get underway, for
the simple reason that a confederacy of witches in medieval Europe seems never
to have existed. There were no covens of pagan dissidents, meeting in secret, be-
trothed to Satan, abandoning themselves to the pleasures of group sex, cannibalism, and the casting of spells upon neighbors, crops, and cattle. It seems that
such notions were the product of folklore, vivid dreams, and sheer confabula-
tion—and confirmed by confessions elicited under the most gruesome torture.
Anti-Semitism is of interest here, both for the scale of the injustice that it has
wrought and for its explicitly theological roots. From the perspective of Christian teaching, Jews are even worse than run-of-the-mill heretics; they are heretics
who explicitly repudiate the divinity of Jesus Christ.

.   .   .

While the stigmas applied to witches and Jews throughout Christendom shared
curious similarities—both were often accused of the lively and improbable offense of murdering Christian infants and drinking their blood—their cases remain quite distinct. Witches, in all likelihood, did not even exist, and those
murdered in their stead numbered perhaps 40,000 to 50,000 over three hundred
years of persecution; Jews have lived side by side with Christians for nearly two
millennia, fathered their religion, and for reasons that are no more substantial
than those underlying the belief in the Resurrection, have been the objects of
murderous intolerance since the first centuries after Christ.

The accounts of witch hunts resemble, in most respects, the more widespread persecution of heretics throughout the Inquisition: imprisonment on
the basis of accusations alone, torture to extract confession, confessions

deemed unacceptable until accomplices were named, death by slow fire, and the rounding up of the freshly accused. The following anecdote is typical:

> In 1595, an old woman residing in a village near Constance, angry at not being invited to share the sports of the country people on a day of public rejoicing, was heard to mutter something to herself, and was afterwards seen to proceed through the fields towards a hill, where she was lost sight of. A violent thunderstorm arose about two hours afterwards, which wet the dancers to the skin, and did considerable damage to the plantations. This woman, suspected before of witchcraft, was seized and imprisoned, and accused of having raised the storm, by filling a hole with wine, and stirring it about with a stick. She was tortured till she confessed, and burned alive the next evening.

Though it is difficult to generalize about the many factors that conspired to make villagers rise up against their neighbors, it is obvious that belief in the existence of witches was the *sine qua non* of the phenomenon. But what was it, precisely, that people believed? They appear to have believed that their neighbors were having sex with the devil, enjoying nocturnal flights upon broomsticks, changing into cats and hares, and eating the flesh of other human beings. More important, they believed utterly in *maleficium*—that is, in the efficacy of harming others by occult means. Among the many disasters that could befall a person over the course of a short and difficult life, medieval Christians seemed especially concerned that a neighbor might cast a spell and thereby undermine their health or good fortune. Only the advent of science could successfully undercut such an idea, along with the fantastical displays of cruelty to which it gave rise. We must remember that it was not until the mid-nineteenth century that the germ theory of disease emerged, laying to rest much superstition about the causes of illness.

Occult beliefs of this sort are clearly an inheritance from our primitive, magic-minded ancestors. The Fore people of New Guinea, for instance, besides being enthusiastic cannibals, exacted a gruesome revenge upon suspected sorcerers:

> Besides attending public meetings, Fore men also hunted down men they believed to be sorcerers and killed them in reprisal. The hunters used a specialized attack called *tukabu* against sorcerers: they ruptured their kidneys, crushed their genitals and broke their thigh bones with stone axes, bit into their necks and tore out their tracheas, jammed bamboo splinters into their veins to bleed them.

No doubt each of these gestures held metaphysical significance. This behavior seems to have been commonplace among the Fore at least until the 1960s. The horrible comedy of human ignorance achieves a rare moment of transparency here: the Fore were merely responding to an epidemic of kuru—a fatal spongiform infection of the brain—brought on not by sorcerers in their midst but by their own religious observance of eating the bodies and brains of their dead. Throughout the Middle Ages and the Renaissance, it was perfectly apparent that disease could be inflicted by demons and black magic. There are accounts of frail, old women charged with killing able-bodied men and breaking the necks of their horses—actions which they were made to confess under torture—and few people, it seems, found such accusations implausible. Even the relentless torture of the accused was given a perverse rationale: the devil, it was believed, made his charges insensible to pain, despite their cries for mercy. And so it was that, for centuries, men and women who were guilty of little more than being ugly, old, widowed, or mentally ill were convicted of impossible crimes and then murdered for God's sake.

After nearly four hundred years some ecclesiastics began to appreciate how insane all this was. Consider the epiphany of Frederick Spee: "Torture fills our Germany with witches and unheard-of wickedness, and not only Germany but any nation that attempts it. . . . If all of us have not confessed ourselves witches, that is only because we have not all been tortured." But Spee was led to this reasonable surmise only after a skeptical friend, the duke of Brunswick, had a woman suspected of witchcraft artfully tortured and interrogated in his presence. This poor woman testified that she had seen Spee himself on the Brocken, shape-shifting into a wolf, a goat, and other beasts and fathering numerous children by the assembled witches born with the heads of toads and the legs of spiders. Spee, lucky indeed to be in the company of a friend, and certain of his own innocence, immediately set to work on his *Cautio Criminalis* (1631), which detailed the injustice of witch trials.

Bertrand Russell observed, however, that not all reasonable men were as fortunate as Spee:

> Some few bold rationalists ventured, even while the persecution was at its height, to doubt whether tempests, hail-storms, thunder and lightning were really caused by the machinations of women. Such men were shown no mercy. Thus towards the end of the sixteenth century Flade, Rector of the University of Treves, and Chief Judge of the Electoral Court, after condemning countless witches, began to think that perhaps their confessions were due to the desire to escape from the tortures of the rack, with the result that he showed unwillingness to convict. He was accused of having sold himself to Satan, and was subjected to the same tortures as he had inflicted upon others. Like them, he confessed his guilt, and in 1589 he was strangled and then burnt.

As late as 1718 (just as the inoculation against smallpox was being introduced to England and the English mathematician Brook Taylor was making refinements to the calculus), we find the madness of the witch hunt still a potent social force. Charles Mackay relates an incident in Caithness (northeast Scotland):

A silly fellow, named William Montgomery, a carpenter, had a mortal antipathy to cats; and somehow or other these animals generally chose his backyard as the scene of their catterwaulings. He puzzled his brains for a long time to know why he, above all his neighbors, should be so pestered. At last he came to the sage conclusion that his tormentors were no cats, but witches. In this opinion he was supported by his maid-servant, who swore a round oath that she had often heard the aforesaid cats talking together in human voices. The next time the unlucky tabbies assembled in his backyard, the valiant carpenter was on the alert. Arming himself with an axe, a dirk, and a broadsword, he rushed out among them. One of them he wounded in the back, a second in the hip, and the leg of a third he maimed with his axe; but he could not capture any of them. A few days afterwards, two old women of the parish died; and it was said, that when their bodies were laid out, there appeared upon the back of one the mark as of a recent wound, and a similar scar upon the hip of the other. The carpenter and his maid were convinced that they were the very cats, and the whole county repeated the same story. Every one was upon the look-out for proofs corroborative; a very remarkable one was soon discovered. Nancy Gilbert, a wretched old creature upwards of seventy years of age, was found in bed with her leg broken. As she was ugly enough for a witch, it was asserted that she also was one of the cats that had fared so ill at the hands of the carpenter. The latter, when informed of the popular suspicion, asserted that he distinctly remembered to have struck one of the cats a blow with the back of his broadsword, which ought to have broken her leg. Nancy was immediately dragged from her bed and thrown into prison. Before she was put to the torture, she explained in a very natural and intelligible manner how she had broken her limb; but this account did not give satisfaction. The professional persuasions of the torturer made her tell a different tale, and she confessed that she was indeed a witch, and had been wounded by Montgomery on the night stated; that the two old women recently deceased were witches also, besides about a score of others whom she named. The poor creature suffered so much by the removal from her own home, and the tortures inflicted upon her, that she died the next day in prison.

Apart from observing, yet again, the astonishing consequences of certain beliefs, we should take note of the reasonable way these witch-hunters attempted to confirm their suspicions. They looked for correlations that held apparent significance: not *any* old woman would do; they needed one who had suffered a wound similar to the one inflicted upon the cat. Once you accept the premise that old women can shape-shift into cats and back again, the rest is practically *science*.

The church did not officially condemn the use of torture until the bull of Pope Pius VII in 1816.

.   .   .

Anti-Semitism is as integral to church doctrine as the flying buttress is to a Gothic cathedral, and this terrible truth has been published in Jewish blood since the first centuries of the common era. Like that of the Inquisition, the history of anti-Semitism can scarcely be given sufficient treatment in the context of this book. I raise the subject, however briefly, because the irrational hatred of Jews has produced a spectrum of effects that have been most acutely felt in our own time. Anti-Semitism is intrinsic to both Christianity and Islam; both traditions consider the Jews to be bunglers of God's initial revelation. Christians generally also believe that the Jews murdered Christ, and their continued existence as Jews constitutes a perverse denial of his status as the Messiah. Whatever the context, the hatred of Jews remains a product of faith: Christian, Muslim, as well as Jewish.

Contemporary Muslim anti-Semitism is heavily indebted to its Christian counterpart. *The Protocols of the Elders of Zion,* a Russian anti-Semitic forgery that is the source of most conspiracy theories relating to the Jews, is now considered an authoritative text in the Arab-speaking world. A recent contribution to *Al-Akhbar,* one of Cairo's mainstream newspapers, suggests that the problem of Muslim anti-Semitism is now deeper than any handshake in the White House Rose Garden can remedy: "Thanks to Hitler, of blessed memory, who on behalf of the Palestinians took revenge in advance, against the most vile criminals on the face of the Earth. . . . Although we do have a complaint against him, for his revenge was not enough." This is from *moderate* Cairo, where Muslims drink alcohol, go to the movies, and watch belly dancing—and where the government actively represses fundamentalism. Clearly, hatred of the Jews is white-hot in the Muslim world.

The gravity of Jewish suffering over the ages, culminating in the Holocaust, makes it almost impossible to entertain any suggestion that Jews might have brought their troubles upon themselves. This is, however, in a rather narrow sense, the truth. Prior to the rise of the church, Jews became the objects of suspicion and occasional persecution for their refusal to assimilate, for the insularity and professed superiority of their religious culture—that is, for the content of their own unreasonable, sectarian beliefs. The dogma of a "chosen people," while at least implicit in most faiths, achieved a stridence in Judaism that was unknown in the ancient world. Among cultures that worshiped a plurality of Gods, the later monotheism of the Jews proved indigestible. And while their explicit demonization as a people required the mad work of the Christian church, the ideology of Judaism remains a lightning rod for intolerance to this day. As a system of beliefs, it appears among the least suited to survive in a theological state of nature. Christianity and Islam both acknowledge the sanctity of the Old Testament and offer easy conversion to their faiths. Islam honors Abraham, Moses, and Jesus as forerunners of Muhammad. Hinduism embraces almost anything in sight with its manifold arms (many Hindus, for instance, consider Jesus an avatar of Vishnu). Judaism alone finds itself surrounded by unmitigated errors. It seems little wonder, therefore, that it has drawn so much sectarian fire. Jews, insofar as they are religious, believe that they are bearers of a unique covenant with God. As a consequence, they have spent the last two thousand years collaborating with those who see them as different by seeing themselves as irretrievably so. Judaism is as intrinsically divisive, as ridiculous in its literalism, and as at odds with the civilizing insights of modernity as any other religion. Jewish settlers, by exercising their "freedom of belief" on contested land, are now one of the principal obstacles to peace in the Middle East. They will be a direct cause of war between Islam and the West should one ever erupt over the Israeli-Palestinian conflict.

.   .   .

The problem for first-century Christians was simple: they belonged to a sect of Jews that had recognized Jesus as the messiah (Greek *christos*), while the majority of their coreligionists had not. Jesus was a Jew, of course, and his mother a Jewess. His apostles, to the last man, were also Jews. There is no evidence whatsoever, apart from the tendentious writings of the later church, that Jesus ever conceived of himself as anything other than a Jew among Jews, seeking the fulfillment of Judaism—and, likely, the return of Jewish sovereignty in a Roman world. As many authors have observed, the numerous strands of Hebrew prophecy that were made to coincide with Jesus's ministry betray the apologetics, and often poor scholarship, of the gospel writers.

The writers of Luke and Matthew, for instance, in seeking to make the life of Jesus conform to Old Testament prophecy, insist that Mary conceived as a virgin (Greek *parthenos*), harking to the Greek rendering of Isaiah 7:14. Unfortunately for fanciers of Mary's virginity, the Hebrew word *alma* (for which *parthenos* is an erroneous translation) simply means "young woman," without any implication of virginity. It seems all but certain that the Christian dogma of the virgin birth, and much of the church's resulting anxiety about sex, was the result of a mistranslation from the Hebrew.

Another strike against the doctrine of the virgin birth is that the other evangelists, Mark and John, seem to know nothing about it— though both appear troubled by accusations of Jesus's illegitimacy. Paul apparently thinks that Jesus is the son of Joseph and Mary. He refers to Jesus as being "born of the seed of David according to the flesh" (Romans 1:3—meaning Joseph was his father), and "born of woman" (Galatians 4:4—meaning that Jesus was really human), with no reference to Mary's virginity.

Mary's virginity has always been suggestive of God's attitude toward sex: it is intrinsically sinful, being the mechanism through which original sin was bequeathed to the generations after Adam. It would appear that Western civilization has endured two millennia of consecrated sexual neurosis simply because the authors of Matthew and Luke could not read Hebrew. For the Jews, the true descendants of Jesus and the apostles, the dogma of the virgin birth has served as a perennial justification for their persecution, because it has been one of the principal pieces of "evidence" demonstrating the divinity of Jesus.

We should note that the emphasis on miracles in the New Testament, along with the attempts to make the life of Jesus conform to Old Testament prophecy, reveal the first Christians' commitment, however faltering, to making their faith seem *rational*. Given the obvious significance of any miracle, and the widespread acceptance of prophecy, it would have been only reasonable to have considered these purported events to be evidence for Christ's divinity. Augustine, for his part, came right out and said it: "I should not be a Christian but for the miracles." A millennium later, Blaise Pascal— mathematical prodigy, philosopher, and physicist—was so impressed by Christ's confirmation of prophecy that he devoted the last years of his short life to defending Christian doctrine in writing:

> Through Jesus we know God. All those who have claimed to know God and
> prove his existence without Jesus Christ have only had futile proofs to offer.
> But to prove Christ we have the prophecies which are solid and palpable
> proofs. By being fulfilled and proved true by the event, these prophecies show
> that these truths are certain and thus prove that Jesus is divine.

"Solid and palpable"? That so nimble a mind could be led to labor under such dogma was surely one of the great wonders of the age. Even today, the apparent confirmation of prophecy detailed in the New Testament is offered as the chief reason to accept Jesus as the messiah. The "leap of faith" is really a fiction. No Christians, not even those of the first century, have ever been content to rely upon it.

.   .   .

While God had made his covenant with Israel, and delivered his Son in the guise of a Jew, the earliest Christians were increasingly gentile, and as the doctrine spread, the newly baptized began to see the Jews' denial of Jesus's divinity as the consummate evil. This sectarian ethos is already well established by the time of Paul:

> For ye, brethren, became followers of the churches of God which in Judaea are
> in Christ Jesus: for ye also like things of your own countrymen, even as they

have of the Jews: Who both killed the Lord Jesus, and their own prophets, and have persecuted us; and they please not God, and are contrary to all men: Forbidding us to speak to the Gentiles that they might be saved, to fill up their sins alway: for the wrath is come upon them to the uttermost. (Thessalonians 2:14–16)

The explicit demonization of the Jews appears in the Gospel of John:

Jesus said unto them [the Jews], If God were your Father, ye would love me: for I proceeded forth and came from God; neither came I of myself, but he sent me. Why do ye not understand my speech? Even because ye cannot hear my word. Ye are of your father the devil, and the lusts of your father ye will do. He was a murderer from the beginning, and abode not in the truth, because there is no truth in him. When he speaketh a lie, he speaketh of his own: for he is a liar, and the father of it. And because I tell you the truth, ye believe me not. (John 8:41–45)

With the destruction of the Temple in 70 CE, Christians—gentile and Jew alike—felt that they were witnessing the fulfillment of prophecy, imagining that the Roman legions were meting out God's punishment to the betrayers of Christ. Anti-Semitism soon acquired a triumphal smugness, and with the ascension of Christianity as the state religion in 312 CE, with the conversion of Constantine, Christians began openly to relish and engineer the degradation of world Jewry. Laws were passed that revoked many of the civic privileges previously granted to Jews. Jews were excluded from the military and from holding high office and were forbidden to proselytize or to have sexual relations with Christian women (both under penalty of death). The Justinian Code, in the sixth century, essentially declared the legal status of the Jews null and void—outlawing the Mishnah (the codification of Jewish oral law) and making disbelief in the Resurrection and the Last Judgment a capital offense. Augustine, ever the ready sectarian, rejoiced at the subjugation of the Jews and took special pleasure in the knowledge that they were doomed to wander the earth bearing witness to the truth of scripture and the salvation of the gentiles. The suffering and servitude of the Jews was proof that Christ had been the messiah after all.

Like witches, the Jews of Europe were often accused of incredible crimes, the most prevalent of which has come to be known as the "blood libel"—born of the belief that Jews require the blood of Christians (generally newborn) for use in a variety of rituals. Throughout the Middle Ages, Jews were regularly accused of murdering Christian infants, a crime for which they were duly despised. It was well known that all Jews menstruated, male and female alike, and required the blood of a Christian to replenish their lost stores. They also suffered from terrible hemorrhoids and oozing sores as a punishment for the murder of Christ—and as a retort to their improbable boast before the "innocent" Pontius Pilate

(Matthew 27:25), "His blood be on us and on our children." It should come as no surprise that Jews were in the habit of applying Christian blood as a salve upon these indignities. Christian blood was also said to ease the labor pains of any Jewess fortunate enough to have it spread upon pieces of parchment and placed into her clenched fists. It was common knowledge, too, that all Jews were born blind and that, when smeared upon their eyes, Christian blood granted them the faculty of sight. Jewish boys were frequently born with their fingers attached to their foreheads, and only the blood of a Christian could allow this pensive gesture to be broken without risk to the child.

Once born, a Jew's desire for Christian blood could scarcely be slaked. During the rite of circumcision it took the place of consecrated oil (crissam, an exclusively Christian commodity); and later in life, Jewish children of both sexes had their genitalia smeared with the blood of some poor, pious man—waylaid upon the road and strangled in a ditch—to make them fertile. Medieval Christians believed that Jews used their blood for everything from a rouge to a love philter and as a prophylactic against leprosy. Given this state of affairs, who could doubt that Jews of all ages would be fond of sucking blood out of Christian children "with quills and small reeds," for later use by their elders during wedding feasts? Finally, with a mind to covering all their bases, Jews smeared their dying brethren with the blood of an innocent Christian babe (recently baptized and then suffocated), saying, "If the Messiah promised by the prophets has really come, and he be Jesus, may this innocent blood ensure for you eternal life!"

The blood libel totters on shoulders of other giant misconceptions, of course, especially the notion, widely accepted at the time, that the various constituents of the human body possess magical and medicinal power. This explains the acceptance of similar accusations leveled at witches, such as the belief that candles made from human fat could render a man invisible while lighting up his surroundings. One wonders just how many a thief was caught striding through his neighbor's foyer in search of plunder, bearing a malodorous candle confidently aloft, before these miraculous tools of subterfuge fell out of fashion.

But for sheer gothic absurdity nothing surpasses the medieval concern over *host desecration,* the punishment of which preoccupied pious Christians for centuries. The doctrine of transubstantiation was formally established in 1215 at the Fourth Lateran Council (the same one that sanctioned the use of torture by inquisitors and prohibited Jews from owning land or embarking upon civil or military careers), and thereafter became the centerpiece of the Christian (now Catholic) faith. (The relevant passage from *The Profession of Faith of the Roman Catholic* was cited in chapter 2.) Henceforth, it was an indisputable fact of this world that the communion host is actually transformed at the Mass into the living body of Jesus Christ. After this incredible dogma had been established, by mere reiteration, to the satisfaction of everyone, Christians began to worry that these living wafers might be subjected to all manner of mistreatment, and even physical torture, at the hands of heretics and Jews. (One might wonder why *eating* the body of Jesus would be any less of a torment to him.) Could there be any doubt that the Jews would seek to harm the Son of God again, knowing that his body was now readily accessible in the form of defenseless crackers? Historical accounts suggest that as many as three thousand Jews were murdered in response to a *single* allegation of this imaginary crime. The crime of host desecration was punished throughout Europe for centuries.

It is out of this history of theologically mandated persecution that secular anti-Semitism emerged. Even explicitly anti-Christian movements, as in the cases of German Nazism and Russian socialism, managed to inherit and enact the doctrinal intolerance of the church. Astonishingly, ideas as spurious as the blood libel are still very much with us, having found a large cult of believers in the Muslim world.

The Holocaust

The National Socialism of all of us is anchored in uncritical loyalty, in the surrender to the Führer that does not ask for the why in individual cases, in the silent execution of his orders. We believe that the Führer is obeying a higher call to fashion German history. There can be no criticism of this belief.

—RUDOLF HESS, IN A SPEECH, JUNE 1934

The rise of Nazism in Germany required much in the way of "uncritical loyalty." Beyond the abject (and *religious)* loyalty to Hitler, the Holocaust emerged out of people's acceptance of some very implausible ideas.

Heinrich Himmler thought the SS should have leeks and mineral water for breakfast. He thought people could be made to confess by telepathy. Following King Arthur and the round table, he would have only twelve people to dinner. He believed that Aryans had not evolved from monkeys and apes like other races, but had come down to earth from the heavens, where they had been preserved in ice from the beginning of time. He established a meteorology division which was given the task of proving this cosmic ice theory. He also thought he was a reincarnation of Heinrich the First. Himmler was an extreme case: the picture is perhaps one of someone quite mad. But one of his characteristics was much more widely shared—his mind had not been encouraged to grow. Filled with information and opinion, he had no critical powers.

At the heart of every totalitarian enterprise, one sees outlandish dogmas, poorly arranged, but working ineluctably like gears in some ludicrous instrument of death. Nazism evolved out of a variety of economic and political factors, of course, but it was held together by a belief in the racial purity and superiority of the German people. The obverse of this fascination with race was the certainty that all impure elements—homosexuals, invalids, Gypsies, and, above all, Jews—posed a threat to the fatherland. And while the hatred of Jews in Germany expressed itself in a predominately secular way, it was a direct inheritance from medieval Christianity. For centuries, religious Germans had viewed the Jews as the worst species of heretics and attributed every societal ill to their continued presence among the faithful. Daniel Goldhagen has traced the rise of the German conception of the Jews as a "race" and a "nation," which culminated in an explicitly nationalistic formulation of this ancient Christian animus. Of course, the *religious* demonization of the Jews was also a contemporary phenomenon. (Indeed, the Vatican itself perpetuated the blood libel in its newspapers as late as 1914.) Ironically, the very fact that Jews had been mistreated in Germany (and elsewhere) since time immemorial—by being confined to ghettos and deprived of civic status—gave rise to the modern, secular strand of anti-Semitism, for it was not until the emancipation efforts of the early nineteenth century that the hatred of the Jews acquired an explicitly racial inflection. Even the self-proclaimed "friends of the Jews" who sought the admission of Jews into German society with the full privileges of citizenship did so only on the assumption that the Jews could be reformed thereby and rendered pure by sustained association with the German race. Thus, the voices of liberal tolerance within Germany were often as anti-Semitic as their conservative opponents, for they differed only in the belief that the Jew was capable of moral regeneration. By the end of the nineteenth century, after the liberal experiment had failed to dissolve the Jews in the pristine solvent of German tolerance, the erstwhile "friends of the Jews" came to regard these strangers in their midst with the same loathing that their less idealistic contemporaries had nurtured all along. An analysis of prominent anti-Semitic writers and publications from 1861 to 1895 reveals just how murderous the German anti-Semites were inclined to be: fully two-thirds of those that purported to offer "solutions" to the "Jewish problem" openly advocated the physical extermination of the Jews—and this, as Goldhagen points out, was several decades before the rise of Hitler. Indeed, the possibility of exterminating a whole people was considered before "genocide" was even a proper concept, and long before killing on such a massive scale had been shown to be practically feasible in the First and Second World Wars.

While Goldhagen's controversial charge that the Germans were Hitler's "willing executioners" seems generally fair, it is true that the people of other nations were equally willing. Genocidal anti-Semitism had been in the air for some time, particularly in Eastern Europe. In the year 1919, for instance, sixty-thousand Jews were murdered in Ukraine alone. Once the Third Reich began its overt persecution of Jews, anti-Semitic pogroms erupted in Poland, Rumania, Hungary, Austria, Czechoslovakia, Croatia, and elsewhere.

With passage of the Nuremberg laws in 1935, the transformation of German anti-Semitism was complete. The Jews were to be considered a race, one that was inimical to a healthy Germany in principle. As such, they were fundamentally

irredeemable, for while one can cast away one's religious ideology, and even accept baptism into the church, one cannot cease to be what one is. And it is here
that we encounter the overt complicity of the church in the attempted murder
of an entire people. German Catholics showed themselves remarkably acquies-
cent to a racist creed that was at cross-purposes with at least one of their core
beliefs: for if baptism truly had the power to redeem, then Jewish converts
should have been considered saved without residue in the eyes of the church.
But, as we have seen, coherence in any system of beliefs is never perfect—and the
German churches, in order to maintain order during their services, were finally
obliged to print leaflets admonishing their flock not to attack Jewish converts
during times of worship. That a person's race could not be rescinded was under-
scored as early as 1880, in a Vatican-approved paper: "Oh how wrong and deluded are those who think Judaism is just a religion, like Catholicism,
Paganism, Protestantism, and not in fact a race, a people, and a nation! . . . For
the Jews are not only Jews because of their religion . . . they are Jews also and especially because of their race." The German Catholic episcopate issued its own
guidelines in 1936: "Race, soil, blood and people are precious natural values,
which God the Lord has created and the care of which he has entrusted to us
Germans."

But the truly sinister complicity of the church came in its willingness to open
its genealogical records to the Nazis and thereby enable them to trace the extent
of a person's Jewish ancestry. A historian of the Catholic Church, Guenther
Lewy, has written:

> The very question of whether the [Catholic] Church should lend its help to
> the Nazi state in sorting out people of Jewish descent was never debated. On
> the contrary. "We have always unselfishly worked for the people without re-
> gard to gratitude or ingratitude," a priest wrote in *Klerusblatt* in September
> 1934. "We shall also do our best to help in this service to the people." And the
> cooperation of the Church in this matter continued right through the war
> years, when the price of being Jewish was no longer dismissal from a govern-
> ment job and loss of livelihood, but deportation and outright physical
> destruction.

All of this, despite the fact that the Catholic Church was in very real opposition to much of the Nazi platform, which was bent upon curtailing its power.
Goldhagen also reminds us that not a single German Catholic was excommunicated before, during, or after the war, "after committing crimes as great as any
in human history." This is really an extraordinary fact. Throughout this period,
the church continued to excommunicate theologians and scholars in droves for
holding unorthodox views and to proscribe books by the hundreds, and yet not
a single perpetrator of genocide—of whom there were countless examples—
succeeded in furrowing Pope Pius XII's censorious brow.

This astonishing situation merits a slight digression. At the end of the nineteenth century, the Vatican attempted to combat the unorthodox conclusions of modern Bible commentators with its own rigorous scholarship. Catholic scholars were urged to adopt the techniques of modern criticism, to demonstrate that the results of a meticulous and dispassionate study of the Bible could be compatible with church doctrine. The movement was known as "modernism," and soon occasioned considerable embarrassment, as many of the finest Catholic scholars found that they, too, were becoming skeptical about the literal truth of scripture. In 1893 Pope Leo XIII announced,

> All those books . . . which the church regards as sacred and canonical were written with all their parts under the inspiration of the Holy Spirit. Now, far from admitting the coexistence of error, Divine inspiration by itself excludes all error, and that also of necessity, since God, the Supreme Truth, must be incapable of teaching error.

In 1907, Pope Pius X declared modernism a heresy, had its exponents within the church excommunicated, and put all critical studies of the Bible on the index of proscribed books. Authors similarly distinguished include Descartes (selected works), Montaigne *(Essais)*, Locke *(Essay on Human Understanding)*, Swift *(Tale of a Tub)*, Swedenborg *(Principia)*, Voltaire *(Lettres philosophiques)*, Diderot *(Encyclopedie)*, Rousseau *(Du contrat social)*, Gibbon *(The Decline and Fall of the Roman Empire)*, Paine *(The Rights of Man)*, Sterne *(A Sentimental Journey)*, Kant *(Critique of Pure Reason)*, Flaubert *(Madame Bovary)*, and Darwin *(On the Origin of Species)*. As a censorious afterthought, Descartes' *Meditations* was added to the index in 1948. With all that had occurred earlier in the decade, one might have thought that the Holy See could have found greater offenses with which to concern itself. Although not a single leader of the Third Reich—not even Hitler himself—was ever excommunicated, Galileo was not absolved of heresy until 1992.

In the words of the present pope, John Paul II, we can see how the matter now stands: "This Revelation is definitive; one can only accept it or reject it. One can accept it, professing belief in God, the Father Almighty, Creator of heaven and earth, and in Jesus Christ, the Son, of the same substance as the Father and the Holy Spirit, who is Lord and the Giver of life. Or one can reject all of this." While the rise and fall of modernism in the church can hardly be considered a victory for the forces of rationality, it illustrates an important point: wanting to know how the world is leaves one vulnerable to new evidence. It is no accident that religious doctrine and honest inquiry are so rarely juxtaposed in our world.

When we consider that so few generations had passed since the church left off disemboweling innocent men before the eyes of their families, burning old women alive in public squares, and torturing scholars to the point of madness for merely speculating about the nature of the stars, it is perhaps little wonder that it failed to think anything had gone terribly amiss in Germany during the war years. Indeed, it is also well known that certain Vatican officials (the most notorious of whom was Bishop Alois Hudal) helped members of the SS like Adolf Eichmann, Martin Bormann, Heinrich Mueller, Franz Stangi, and hundreds of others escape to South America and the Middle East in the aftermath of the war. In this context, one is often reminded that others in the Vatican helped Jews escape as well. This is true. It is also true, however, that Vatican aid was often contingent upon whether or not the Jews in question had been previously baptized.

> There were, no doubt, innumerable instances in which European Christians risked their lives to protect the Jews in their midst, and did so because of their Christianity. But they were not innumerable enough. The fact that people are sometimes inspired to heroic acts of kindness by the teaching of Christ says nothing about the wisdom or necessity of believing that he, exclusively, was the Son of God. Indeed, we will find that we need not believe anything on insufficient evidence to feel compassion for the suffering of others. Our common humanity is reason enough to protect our fellow human beings from coming to harm. Genocidal intolerance, on the other hand, must inevitably find its inspiration elsewhere. Whenever you hear that people have begun killing noncombatants intentionally and indiscriminately, ask yourself what dogma stands at their backs. What do these freshly minted killers *believe*? You will find that it is always—*always*—preposterous.

My purpose in this chapter has been to intimate, in as concise a manner as possible, some of the terrible consequences that have arisen, logically and inevitably, out of Christian faith. Unfortunately, this catalog of horrors could be elaborated upon indefinitely. Auschwitz, the Cathar heresy, the witch hunts— these phrases signify depths of human depravity and human suffering that would surely elude description were a writer to set himself no other task. As I have cast a very wide net in the present chapter, I can only urge readers who may feel they have just been driven past a roadside accident at full throttle to consult the literature on these subjects. Such extracurricular studies will reveal that the history of Christianity is principally a story of mankind's misery and ignorance rather than of its requited love of God.

While Christianity has few living inquisitors today, Islam has many. In the next chapter we will see that in our opposition to the worldview of Islam, we confront a civilization with an arrested history. It is as though a portal in time has opened, and fourteenth-century hordes are pouring into our world. Unfortunately, they are now armed with twenty-first-century weapons.

46

Can an Atheist
Be a Fundamentalist?

From *Against All Gods*

A. C. GRAYLING

As the faithful began to find themselves in a fight, they evolved
some low and foolish last-ditch tactics. One such was the stupid
argument that unbelievers, too, were "fundamentalists." In his
admirable book *Against All Gods,* the British moral philosopher
Anthony Grayling douses this unimportant little brushfire with a
shower of the coldest and purest water of reason, incidentally insisting that words must have some relationship to meaning and
thus dealing a double blow to religion.

It is also time to put to rest the mistakes and assumptions that lie behind a phrase
used by some religious people when talking of those who are plain-spoken about
their disbelief in any religious claims: the phrase "fundamentalist atheist." What
would a non-fundamentalist atheist be? Would he be someone who believed only
somewhat that there are no supernatural entities in the universe—perhaps that
there is only part of a god (a divine foot, say, or buttock)? Or that gods exist only
some of the time—say, Wednesdays and Saturdays? (That would not be so strange:
for many unthinking quasi-theists, a god exists only on Sundays.) Or might it be
that a non-fundamentalist atheist is one who does not mind that other people
hold profoundly false and primitive beliefs about the universe, on the basis of
which they have spent centuries mass-murdering other people who do not hold
exactly the same false and primitive beliefs as themselves—and still do?

Christians among other things mean by "fundamentalist atheists" those who
would deny people the comforts of faith (the old and lonely especially) and the
companionship of a benign invisible protector in the dark night of the soul—and
who (allegedly) fail to see the staggering beauty in art prompted by the inspirations
of belief. Yet in its concessive, modest, palliative modern form Christianity is a recent and highly modified version of what, for most of its history, has been an often
violent and always oppressive ideology—think Crusades, torture, burnings at the

stake, the enslavement of women to constantly repeated childbirth and undivorce-able husbands, the warping of human sexuality, the use of fear (of hell's torments) as an instrument of control, and the horrific results of its calumny against Judaism. Nowadays, by contrast, Christianity specialises in soft-focus mood music; its threats of hell, its demand for poverty and chastity, its doctrine that only the few will be saved and the many damned, have been shed, replaced by strummed guitars and saccharine smiles. It has reinvented itself so often, and with such breath-taking hypocrisy, in the interests of retaining its hold on the gullible, that a medieval monk who woke today, like Woody Allen in *Sleeper,* would not be able to recognise the faith that bears the same name as his own.

For example: vast Nigerian congregations are told that believing will ensure a high income—indeed they are told by Reverend X that they will be luckier and richer if they join his congregation than if they join that of Reverend Y. What happened to the eye of the needle? Oh—but that tiny loophole was closed long ago. What then of "my kingdom is not of this world"? What of the blessedness of poverty and humility? The Church of England officially abolished Hell by an Act of Synod in the 1920s, and St. Paul's strictures on the place of women in church (which was that they are to sit at the back in silence, with heads covered) are so far ignored that there are now women vicars, and there will soon be women bishops.

One does not have to venture as far as Nigeria to see the hypocrisies of rein-vention at work. Rome will do, where the latest eternal verity to be abandoned is the doctrine of limbo—the place for the souls of unbaptised babies—and where some cardinals are floating the idea that condoms are acceptable, within marital relationships only of course, in countries with high incidences of HIV infection. This latter, which to anyone but an observant Catholic is not merely a plain piece of common sense but a humanitarian imperative, is an amazing development in its context. Sensible Catholics have for generations been ignoring the views on contraception held by reactionary old men in the Vatican, but alas, since it is the business of all religious doctrines to keep their votaries in a scare of intellectual infancy (how else do they keep absurdities seeming credible?), insufficient numbers of Catholics have been able to be sensible. Look at Ireland until very recent times for an example of the misery Catholicism inflicts when it can.

"Intellectual infancy": the phrase reminds one that religions survive mainly because they brainwash the young. Three-quarters of Church of England schools are primary schools; all the faiths currently jostling for our tax money to run their "faith-based" schools know that if they do not proselytise intellectually defenceless three- and four-year-olds, their grip will eventually loosen. Inculcating the various competing—competing, note—falsehoods of the major faiths into small children is a form of child abuse, and a scandal. Let us challenge religion to leave children alone until they are adults, whereupon they can be presented with the essentials of religion for mature consideration. For example: tell an averagely intelligent adult hitherto free of religious brainwashing

that somewhere, invisibly, there is a being somewhat like us, with desires, interests, purposes, memories, and emotions of anger, love, vengefulness, and jealousy, yet with the negation of such other of our failings as mortality, weakness,
corporeality, visibility, limited knowledge and insight; and that this god magi-
cally impregnates a mortal woman, who then gives birth to a special being who
performs various prodigious feats before departing for heaven. Take your pick
of which version of this story to tell: let a King of Heaven impregnate—let's see—
Danaë or Io or Leda or the Virgin Mary (etc., etc.) and let there be resulting
heaven-destined progeny (Heracles, Castor and Pollux, Jesus, etc., etc.)—or any
of the other forms of exactly such tales in Babylonian, Egyptian, and other
mythologies—then ask which of them he wishes to believe. One can guarantee
that such a person would say: none of them.

So: in order not to be a "fundamentalist" atheist, which of the absurdities
connoted in the foregoing should an atheist temporise over? Should a "moderate atheist" be one who does not mind how many hundreds of millions of
people have been deeply harmed by religion throughout history? Should he or
she be one who chuckles indulgently at the antipathy of Sunni for Shi'ite, Christian for Jew, Muslim for Hindu, and all of them for anyone who does not think
the universe is controlled by invisible powers? Is an acceptable (to the faithful)
atheist one who thinks it is reasonable for people to believe that the gods suspend the laws of nature occasionally in answer to personal prayers, or that to
save someone's soul from further sin (especially the sin of heresy) it is in his own
interests to be murdered?

As it happens, no atheist should call himself or herself one. The term already
sells a pass to theists, because it invites debate on their ground. A more appropriate term is "naturalist," denoting one who takes it that the universe is a natural realm, governed by nature's laws. This properly implies that there is
nothing supernatural in the universe—no fairies or goblins, angels, demons,
gods or goddesses. Such might as well call themselves "a-fairyists" or "a-goblin-
ists" as "atheists"; it would be every bit as meaningful or meaningless to do so.
(Most people, though, forget that belief in fairies was widespread until the beginning of the twentieth century; the Church fought a long hard battle against
this competitor superstition, and won, largely because—you guessed it—of the
infant and primary church schools founded in the second half of the nineteenth
century.)

By the same token, therefore, people with theistic beliefs should be called supernaturalists, and it can be left to them to attempt to refute the findings of
physics, chemistry, and the biological sciences in an effort to justify their alternative claim that the universe was created, and is run, by supernatural beings.
Supernaturalists are fond of claiming that some irreligious people turn to
prayer when in mortal danger, but naturalists can reply that supernaturalists
typically repose great faith in science when they find themselves in (say) a hospital or an aeroplane—and with far greater frequency. But of course, as votaries of

the view that everything is consistent with their beliefs—even apparent refutations of them—supernaturalists can claim that science itself is a gift of god, and thus justify doing so. But they should then remember Popper: "a theory that explains everything explains nothing."

In conclusion, it is worth pointing out an allied and characteristic bit of jesuitry employed by folk of faith. This is their attempt to describe naturalism (atheism) as itself a "religion." But by definition a religion is something centred upon belief in the existence of supernatural agencies or entities in the universe; and not merely in their existence, but in their interest in human beings on this planet; and not merely their interest, but their particularly detailed interest in what humans wear, what they eat, when they eat it, what they read or see, what they treat as clean and unclean, who they have sex with and how and when; and so for a multitude of other things, like making women invisible beneath enveloping clothing, or strapping little boxes to their foreheads, or iterating formulae by rote five times a day, and so endlessly forth; with threats of punishment for getting any of it wrong.

But naturalism (atheism) by definition does not premise such belief. Any view of the world which does not premise the existence of something supernatural is a philosophy, or a theory, or at worst an ideology. If it is either of the two first, at its best it proportions what it accepts to the evidence for accepting it, knows what would refute it, and stands ready to revise itself in the light of new evidence. This is the essence of science. It comes as no surprise that no wars have been fought, pogroms carried out, or burnings conducted at the stake, over rival theories in biology or astrophysics.

And one can grant that the word "fundamental" does after all apply to this: in the phrase "fundamentally sensible."

47

How (and Why)
I Became an Infidel

AYAAN HIRSI ALI

In her memoir *Infidel*, Ayaan Hirsi Ali states calmly that she believes herself to be the only survivor of the maternity ward in Somalia in which she was born. The overwhelming probability is that her surmise is correct, and when one reads her account of genital mutilation, clerical cruelty, and ethno-religious barbarism, it is not difficult to understand why. Having escaped Islamism in her native land and moved to the same Holland that once sheltered discrepant religious dissidents, she saw her colleague Theo Van Gogh butchered in an Amsterdam street for satirizing the Muslim tyranny over women and was very vividly informed that she herself was to be the next victim of theocratic fascism. Initially attracted to the false hope that Islam could be open to a reformation, she soon came to see that faith itself was the problem and emancipated herself (and helped to emancipate many others) by declaring a courageous independence from the whole dictatorship of piety. Now living in exile and anonymity, like so many enemies of the foul ideology of *jihad*, she honors this volume by contributing a specially written essay on her decision to say farewell to all gods.

When I finally admitted to myself that I was an unbeliever, it was because I simply couldn't pretend any longer that I believed. Leaving Allah was a long and painful process for me, and I tried to resist it for as long as I could. All my life I had wanted to be a good daughter of my clan, and that meant above all that I should be a good Muslim woman, who had learned to submit to God—which in practice meant the rule of my brother, my father, and later my husband.

When I was a child, I had a child's revulsion against injustice. I could not understand why Allah, if he were truly merciful and all-powerful, would tolerate and indeed require that I stand behind my brother at prayer and obey his whims, or that the courts should consider my statements to be inherently less valid than his. But shame and obedience had been drilled into me from my earliest years. I obeyed my parents, my clan, and my religious teachers, and I felt ashamed that by my questioning I seemed to be betraying them.

As I became a teenager, my rebellion grew. It was not yet a revolt against Islam. Who was I to contest Allah? But I did feel constricted by my family and our Somali clan, where family honor was the overriding value, and seemed principally to reside in the control, sale, and transfer of girls' virginity. Reading Western books—even trashy romance novels—gave me a vision of an astounding alternative universe where girls had choices.

Still, I struggled to conform. I voluntarily robed in a black *hijab* that covered my body from head to toe. I tried to pray five times a day and to obey the countless strictures of the Koran and the Hidith. I did so mostly because I was afraid of Hell. The Koran lists Hell's torments in vivid detail: sores, boiling water, peeling skin, burning flesh, dissolving bowels. An everlasting fire burns you forever for as your flesh chars and your juices boil, you form a new skin. Every preacher I encountered hammered more mesmerizing details onto his nightmarish tableau. It was genuinely terrifying.

Ultimately, I think, it was books, and boys, that saved me. No matter how hard I tried to submit to Allah's will, I still felt desire—sexual desire, urgent and real, which even the vision of Hellfire could not suppress. It made me ashamed to feel that way, but when my father told me he was marrying me off to a stranger, I realized that I could not accept being locked forever into the bed of a man who left me cold.

I escaped. I ended up in Holland. With the help of many benevolent Dutch people, I managed to gain confidence that I had a future outside my clan. I decided to study political science, to discover why Muslim societies—Allah's societies—were poor and violent, while the countries of the despised infidels were wealthy and peaceful. I was still a Muslim in those days. I had no intention of criticizing Allah's will, only to discover what had gone so very wrong.

It was at university that I gradually lost my faith. The ideas and the facts that I encountered there were thrilling and powerful, but they also clashed horribly with the vision of the world with which I had grown up. At first, when the cognitive dissonance became too strong, I would try to shove these issues to the back of my mind. The ideas of Spinoza and Freud, Darwin and Locke and Mill, were indisputably true, but so was the Koran; and I vowed to one day resolve these differences. In the meantime, I could not make myself stop reading. I knew the argument was a weak one, but I told myself that Allah is in favor of knowledge.

The pleasures and anonymity of life in the clan-less West were almost as beguiling as the ideas of Enlightenment philosophers. Quite soon after I arrived in Holland, I replaced my Muslim dress with jeans. I avoided socializing with other Somalis first, and then with other Muslims—they preached to me about fear of the Hereafter and warned that I was damned. Years later, I drank my first glass of wine and had a boyfriend. No bolt of Hellfire burned me; chaos did not ensue. To pacify my mind, I adopted an attitude of "negotiating" with Allah: I told myself these were small sins, which hurt no one; surely God would not mind too much.

Then the Twin Towers were toppled in the name of Allah and his prophet, and I felt that I must choose sides. Osama bin Laden's justification of the attacks was more consistent with the content of the Koran and the Sunna than the chorus of Muslim officials and Western wishful thinkers who denied every link between the bloodshed and Islam. Did I, as a Muslim, support bin Laden's act of "worship"? Did I feel it was what God commanded? And if not, was I a Muslim?

I picked up a book—*The Atheist Manifesto* by Herman Philipse, who later became a great friend. I began reading it, marveling at the clarity and naughtiness of its author. But I really didn't have to. Just looking at it, just wanting to read it—that already meant I doubted. Before I'd read four pages, I realized that I had left Allah behind years ago. I was an atheist. An apostate. An infidel. I looked in a mirror and said out loud, in Somali, "I don't believe in God."

I felt relief. There was no pain but a real clarity. The long process of seeing the flaws in my belief structure, and carefully tip-toeing around the frayed edges as parts of it were torn out piece by piece—all that was over. The ever-present prospect of Hellfire lifted, and my horizon seemed broader. God, Satan, angels: these were all figments of human imagination, mechanisms to impose the will of the powerful on the weak. From now on I could step firmly on the ground that was under my feet and navigate based on my own reason and self-respect. My moral compass was within myself, not in the pages of a sacred book.

In the next few months, I began going to museums. I needed to see ruins and mummies and old dead people, to look at the reality of the bones and to absorb the realization that, when I die, I will become just a bunch of bones. Some of them were five hundred million years old, I noted; if it took Allah longer than that to raise the dead, the prospect of his retribution for my lifetime of enjoyment seemed distinctly less plausible.

I was on a psychological mission to accept living without a God, which means accepting that I give my life its own meaning. I was looking for a deeper sense of morality. In Islam you are Allah's slave; you submit, which means that ideally you are devoid of personal will. You are not a free individual. You behave well because you fear Hell, which is really a form of blackmail—you have no personal ethic.

Now I told myself that we, as human individuals, are our own guides to good and evil. We must think for ourselves; we are responsible for our own morality. I arrived at the conclusion that I couldn't be honest with others unless I was honest with myself. I wanted to comply with the goals of religion—which are to be a better and more generous person—without suppressing my will and forcing it to obey an intricate and inhumanly detailed web of rules. I had lied many times in my life, but now, I told myself, that was over: I had had enough of lying.

After I wrote my memoir, *Infidel* (published in the United States in 2007), I did a book tour in the United States. I found that interviewers from the Heartland often asked if I had considered adopting the message of Jesus Christ. The idea seems to be that I should shop for a better, more humane religion than Islam, rather than taking refuge in unbelief. A religion of talking serpents and heavenly gardens? I usually respond that I suffer from hayfever. The Christian take on Hellfire seems less dramatic than the Muslim vision, which I grew up with, but Christian magical thinking appeals to me no more than my grandmother's angels and djinns.

The only position that leaves me with no cognitive dissonance is atheism. It is not a creed. Death is certain, replacing both the siren-song of Paradise and the dread of Hell. Life on this earth, with all its mystery and beauty and pain, is then to be lived far more intensely: we stumble and get up, we are sad, confident, insecure, feel loneliness and joy and love. There is nothing more; but I want nothing more.

Credits and Permissions

Index